D1872380

ARS ELECTRONICA 93

GENETISCHE KUNST – KÜNSTLICHES LEBEN
GENETIC ART—ARTIFICIAL LIFE

Herausgeber/*editors*:
Karl Gerbel, Peter Weibel

Redaktion/*editing*:
Katharina Gsöllpointner

PVS Verleger

ARS ELECTRONICA
Festival für Kunst, Technologie und Gesellschaft
Festival of Art, Technology and Society
Veranstalter/*Organizers*:
Brucknerhaus Linz und ORF-Landesstudio Oberösterreich
BRUCKNERHAUS LINZ
Vorstandsdirektor Karl Gerbel
Linzer Veranstaltungsgesellschaft mbH (LIVA)
Untere Donaulände 7, A-4010 Linz
Telefon: (0732) 7612-0 Fax: (0732) 7612-350
ORF LANDESSTUDIO OBERÖSTERREICH
Intendant Dr. Hannes Leopoldseder
Franckstraße 2a, A-4020 Linz
Telefon: (0732) 6900-0 Fax: (0732) 6900-270
Direktorium/*management committee*:
Vorstandsdirektor Karl Gerbel (LIVA)
Intendant Dr. Hannes Leopoldseder (ORF)
o. Prof. Peter Weibel (Künstlerischer Leiter)
Ständiger Künstlerischer Beirat/
permanent artistic advisory board:
o. Prof. Peter Weibel (Vorsitzender)
Dr. Katharina Gsöllpointner (LIVA)
Dr. Christine Schöpf (ORF)
Kuratoren/*curators*:
Edek Bartz, John L. Casti, Christopher Langton, Dietmar Wiesner
Herausgeber/*editors*:
Karl Gerbel, Peter Weibel
Redaktion /*editing*:
Katharina Gsöllpointner
Übersetzungen/*translations*:
Linda Altmisdört, Doris Jüngling, Gertrude Jaquemar, Camilla Nielsen, Silvia Zendron, Daniela Beuren, Susanne Ofner, Paul Pritchard
Grafische Gestaltung/*graphic design*:
Alexander Rendi/ Gerwald Rockenschaub
Umschlagbild/*cover picture*:
Gestaltung/*design*:
Alexander Rendi/Gerwald Rockenschaub
nach einer Idee von/*after an idea by*:
Peter Oppenheimer
"Plant Growing" programmed by
Laurent Mignonneau/Christa Sommerer
Datenkonvertierung /*data conversion*
PCG, Wien
Druck/*printing*:
REMA*print*, Wien
Vertrieb/*sale*:
PVS Verleger
Pouthongasse 26/13, A-1150 Wien
Telefon (222) 926-9744
ISBN 3-901196-072

Wir danken für die Unterstützung von Ars Electronica:
Stadt Linz
Land Oberösterreich
Bundesministerium für Unterricht und Kunst
Kulturamt der Stadt Linz
AUSTRIA TABAK Generaldirektion, Wien / Casablanca
THYSSEN Gerüstebau, Traun
SILICON GRAPHICS Österreich
Peter Assmann
Fa. KATTUS

Organisationssekretariat: Brigitte Renzl
Produktionsassistenz: Karin Sladko
Technische Assistenz: Thomas Hinterberger
Public Relations: Michael Kornfehl

INHALT

DER 8. TAG – ARS ELECTRONICA 93

KARL GERBEL

Ars Electronica 93 beschäftigt sich mit einem neuen Wissenschaftszweig, der das Leben der Menschen in den nächsten Jahrzehnten entscheidend verändern wird: der Wissenschaft vom künstlichen Leben.
Die Erschaffung von künstlichem Leben ist ein uralter Traum der Menschheit. Von den ersten Alchimisten über Mary Shelleys Frankenstein bis zum Terminator II haben sich Künstler und Wissenschafter mit der Produktion von künstlicher Materie und künstlichem Leben beschäftigt.
Die Mythen vom Golem und Frankenstein sind dabei, wissenschaftliche Realität zu werden. Mit Hilfe von Gentechnik und neu entwickelten Computerprogrammen gelingt es Forschern schon jetzt, lebensähnliche Wesen im Computer herzustellen.
Ars Electronica 93 beschäftigt sich mit den Ursprüngen des Lebens, wie es entstehen konnte, sich entwickelte und welche Formen Leben in der Zukunft möglicherweise annehmen wird, mit allen Chancen, aber auch mit allen Risken und Gefahren. Nach den sieben Tagen der Schöpfungs-Geschichte beginnt nun der 8. Tag, der Tag danach…

THE 8TH DAY—ARS ELECTRONICA 93
KARL GERBEL

Ars Electronica 93 deals with a new branch of science which will decisivly change man's life within the next decades: the science of artificial life.
The creation of artificial life is an ancient dream of mankind. From the first alchemists to Mary Shelley's Frankenstein until Terminator II artists and scientists have been involved with the production of artificial matter and artificial life.
The myths of Golem and Frankenstein are becoming scientific reality. With the aid of genetic technology and newly developed computer programs researchers already are successful in producing life like beings in computers.
Ars Electronica 93 deals with the origins of life, how it has been able to come into being, how it developed and which shapes it will possibly take in the future—by all chances, but by all risks and dangers as well. After seven days of Creation's history now the 8th day begins, the day after…

DAS ANDERE LEBEN

KATHARINA GSÖLLPOINTNER

THE OTHER LIFE
KATHARINA GSÖLLPOINTNER

"The lowest, benthic step of ecosystems is the aim of life on earth. There focusses energy kindled by lifes engine, it focusses the life giving rain. The there living organisms are the furthest link of the earth grasping life chain. They are swimming, walking, digging themselves in, anchored in the sea ground, animals of considerable size. There are no more plants, just plantike animals. And there reigns Vampiroteuthis infernalis giovanni: the master of life on earth. Its environment is center of all life—the big hole which sucks all life into itself." (From: Vilem Flusser, Louis Bec: Vampiroteuthis Infernalis)

One of the most exciting books about life and our ideas about it is a volume edited in 1987 by the Czech-French philosopher Vilem Flusser and the zoosystemist Louis Bec: Vampiroteuthis Infernalis.

Behind that demonic name there is a being which exists like an animal on the ground of the Chinese Sea, the lifekind, culture, sexuality, society and art of which are described by Vilem Flusser. This wonderful fable about Vampiroteuthis represents a philosophical approach, basing on the attempt of representing perception of the world by an other. Thru the birth of Vampiroteuthis from the binarian ocean Flusser throws the whole big question of (artificial) life back to us: as long as we have not recognized ourselves, the attempt of life only can fail.

The Vampiroteuthis represents in two ways the fascination of artificial life: on the one hand it is a creature from a world of phantasy, fairy tales, fable and science fiction, a world which in the meantime has become more real than we have ever dared to dream, and which because of its reality and genuineness for us no more is conceivable with help of the conventional media of language and communication. On the other hand in its function as reflection of the self it is that other, in which alone we can recognize ourselves.

Only thru recognizing the vampiroteuthic existenz we can recognize ours. Does the great desire of man to create his spitting image derive from here? And doesnt the idea of making usable robots, animates and computer programs contribute only irrelevantly to the idea of artificial life?

Nevertheless artificial life research questions all previous definitions of life, it speaks as it were a new language. In it we can try once more to understand our life by discovering the Other. For

„Die unterste, benthische Stufe der Ökosysteme ist das Ziel des Lebens auf Erden. Dorthin richtet sich die vom Lebensmotor entfachte Energie, richtet sich der lebensspendende Regen. Die dort lebenden Organismen sind das äußerste Glied der erdumspannenden Lebenskette. Es sind schwimmende, schreitende, sich eingrabende, im Meeresboden verankerte Tiere von beträchtlicher Körpergröße. Es gibt dort keine Pflanzen mehr, nur noch pflanzenähnliche Tiere. Und dort herrscht Vampiroteuthis infernalis giovanni: der Herr des Lebens auf Erden. Seine Umwelt ist Zentrum allen Lebens – das große Loch, das alles Leben in sich saugt." (aus: Vilem Flusser, Louis Bec: Vampiroteuthis Infernalis)

Eines der spannendsten Bücher über Leben und unsere Vorstellung davon ist ein Band, den der tschechisch-französische Philosoph Vilem Flusser und der Zoosystemiker Louis Bec 1987 gemeinsam herausgegeben haben: Vampiroteuthis infernalis.

Hinter diesem dämonischen Namen steckt ein Wesen, das sich wie ein Tier auf dem Grund des Chinesischen Meeres aufhält, dessen Lebensweise, Kultur, Sexualität, Sozietät und Kunst von Vilem Flusser beschrieben werden. Diese wunderbare Fabel über den Vampiroteuthis stellt einen philosophischen Ansatz dar, der auf dem Versuch einer Darstellung der Wahrnehmung von Welt durch ein anderes fußt. Durch die Geburt des Vampiroteuthis aus dem binären Ozean wirft Flusser die ganze große Frage des (künstlichen) Lebens auf uns selbst zurück: solange wir uns selbst nicht erkannt haben, kann der Versuch von Leben nur scheitern.

Der Vampirotheutis repräsentiert in zweifacher Hinsicht die Faszination von künstlichem Leben. Zum einen ist er Wesen aus einer Welt der Phantasie, der Märchen, Fabel und Science Fiction, die inzwischen realer geworden ist, als wir es uns je zu träumen wagten, und die durch ihre Wirklichkeit und Echtheit für uns daher nicht mehr mit den herkömmlichen Mitteln der Sprache und Kommunikation begreifbar ist. Zum anderen ist er in seiner Funktion als Widerspiegelung des Ich jenes Andere, in dem allein wir uns erkennen können.

Nur über das Begreifen des vampiroteuthischen Daseins können wir unsere eigene Existenz erkennen. Stammt daher

die große Sehnsucht des Menschen, sein „Ebenbild" zu schaffen? Und trägt die Idee von der Nutzbarmachung von Robotern, Animaten und Computerprogrammen nicht einen eigentlich unwesentlichen Anteil an der Vorstellung vom künstlichen Leben?
Dennoch stellt Artificial Life Forschung alle bisherigen Definitionen von Leben in Frage, sie spricht gleichsam eine neue Sprache. In ihr können wir wieder einmal versuchen, unser Leben zu begreifen, indem wir das Andere entdecken können. Dazu ist es notwendig, die Fremdheit, das Neue und Ungewohnte anzunehmen, sich mit ihm auseinanderzusetzen und ihm nicht kalt und feindlich zu begegnen. Denn uns und Vampirotheutis verbindet die Unvollkommenheit:
„... Daß wir beide Produkte eines albernen Zufalls sind, ist uns phänomenal anzusehen. Wir sind schlecht programmierte Wesen voller Defekte. Das zeigt sich vor allem daran, daß wir immer etwas benötigen, immer in Not sind. Unter anderem benötigen wir einander. Nicht etwa, wie Plato meint, um einander zu Perfektion zu vervollständigen – eine Synthese ‚Mensch-Vampiroteuthis' wäre noch immer ein imperfektes Wesen –, sondern um einander zu spiegeln."

„Aber natürlich weiß ich, was das heißt, Henry', sagte Hammond. ‚Es bedeutet, daß Sie Mist gebaut haben.'
‚Sicher nicht.' ‚Sie haben dort draußen Dinosaurier, die Junge kriegen, Henry.'
‚Aber es sind alle weiblich', sagte Wu. ‚Es ist unmöglich. Es muß ein Fehler sein'..."
(aus: Michael Crichton, Jurassic Park)

that it is necessary to accept the strangeness, the new and the unusual, to work on it and not to be cold and hostile to it. For, incompleteness connects us and Vampiroteuthis:
"...That we both are products of a silly coincidence, we look phenomenally. We are badly programmed beings full of defects. This shows before all because we always require something, we always are in distress. Amongst other we need each other. Its not to complete each other— a synthesis man—Vampiroteuthis still were an imperfect being—, but to reflect each other."

"'But of course I know what this means, Henry', Hammond said. 'It means you srewed up.'
'Absolutely not.'
'Youve got breeding dinosaurs out there', Henry.
'But theyre all female', Wu said. 'Its impossible. There must be a mistake'..."
(from: Michael Crichton, Jurrassic Park)

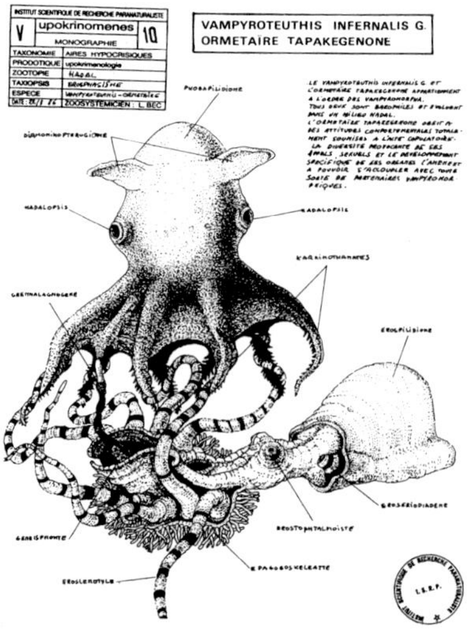

LEBEN - DAS UNVOLLENDETE PROJEKT

PETER WEIBEL

LIFE—THE UNFINISHED PROJECT
PETER WEIBEL

Since Turing, the question "What is life" has been discussed by computer scientists. Life (just like the brain) was taken out of its "natural carbon-based context". The birth of Artificial Intelligence was followed by the concept of Artificial Life. The term Artificial Life applies on the one hand to forms of life without any natural substances being involved, for instance computer-simulated dynamical systems consisting of character strings (beings composed of characters) capable of growth and reproduction, of exchanging energy and information, creating and controlling themselves. These forms of Artificial Life can be either represented audio-visually or be actually three-dimensional (e.g. robots). On the other hand, the term Artificial Life covers a multitude of human interventions in natural life, ranging from modifications of the genetic code to organ transplants. In this artificial context of life, the old dreams of mankind do not appear so far away any longer - a long life, the opportunity to modify both, a person's physical characteristics and mental abilities, protection against illness, against internal and external misdevelopments, the very creation of life. The task of artificially creating life can be approached from two directions: from the hardware and the software side. The challenge thereby consists in generating living organisms from non-living elements. The first synthesis of organic molecules by Wöhrer took place more than 100 years ago and constitutes an important step in the direction of an artificial re-creation of life. But Wöhrer chose a hardware approach and this proved to be insufficient. The software approaches defining life as a system property and dynamic process appear to be more promising. Artificial life is thus not only the simulation of biological processes on a computer (ranging from cell growth to virtual ants) but also includes the notion that the "synthesis of life", the artificial generation of life by human beings, will not be possible on a material basis alone. This implies that the artificial creation of life does not require natural materials (from Golem's loam to the carbohydrates and proteins of our modern times) and that the programmes involved, the software, will distinguish between life and all other types of natural phenomena. The programme requires material information carriers, for instance nucleotides. But these computer-aided visions of artificial life imply that other, synthetic substances may just as well

Seit Turing wurde die Frage „Was ist Leben?" zu einem Diskussionsgegenstand unter Computerwissenschaftern. Leben verlor (wie das Gehirn) seinen „natürlichen carbonbasierten Kontext". Auf die Geburt der künstlichen Intelligenz folgte das Konzept des k ünstlichen Lebens, sei es als ein Leben ohne natürliche Substanzen, als computersimuliertes dynamisches System mit reproduktionsfähigen, energie- und informationsaustauschenden, sich selbst erzeugenden, wie steuernden und wachsenden Zeichenketten (Zeichenwesen) in Bild und Ton wie auch in 3-dimensionaler materialer Ausführung (z. B. Roboter), sei es durch Interventionen im genetischen Code bis zu Organtransplantationen. In diesem künstlichen Kontext des Lebens sind alte Träume der Menschheit wie Langlebigkeit, Modifikationen der physischen Erscheinung wie der geistigen Fähigkeiten, Vorsorge vor Krankheit, Schutz vor inneren und äußeren Fehlentwicklungen, Schaffung von Leben selbst, näher gerückt. Die künstliche Erzeugung von Leben kann von der Hardware- wie von der Software-Seite in Angriff genommen werden. Das Problem dabei ist, lebende Organismen aus nicht-lebendigen Elementen zu erzeugen. Die erste Synthese organischer Moleküle durch Wöhrer vor mehr als 100 Jahren war ein wichtiger Schritt in Richtung künstlicher Re-Kreation des Lebens, aber da er von der Hardware-Seite kam, nicht ausreichend. Die Lösungen von der Software-Seite, die Leben als System-Eigenschaft und dynamischen Prozeß definieren, scheinen erfolgversprechend. Künstliches Leben ist also nicht bloß die Simulation von Lebensvorgängen auf dem Computer (vom Wachstum der Zellen bis zu virtuellen Ameisen), sondern die Idee, daß die „Synthesis des Lebens", die künstliche Erzeugung des Lebens durch den Menschen nicht auf der Basis von Materie allein gelingen wird, daß es also erstens nicht natürliche Materialien (wie Golems Lehm bis zu den Carbohydraten und Proteinen von heute) sein müssen, und daß zweitens vor allem das Programm, die Software, das Leben von allen anderen Naturphänomenen unterscheidet. Das Programm braucht Trägermedien, z. B. Nukleotide. Aber mit Hilfe der computergestützten Vision des künstlichen Lebens werden auch andere synthetische

Trägermedien für das Programm des Lebens vorstellbar. Die Gen- und Organ-Technologie, die Fortpflanzung durch Zellkern-Transplantation, das Kloning von Tieren, Pflanzen und Genen, die Ersatzteil-Chirurgie – sie alle führen uns mit ihrer Kopulation von natürlichen und synthetischen, lebenden und nicht-lebenden Materialien bereits diese Zukunft vor Augen. Während künstliches Leben sich damit beschäftigt, die Gesetze des Lebens zu erforschen, befaßt sich Gentechnik mit der Veränderung von lebenden Organismen.
Die Gentechnik weckt dabei hohe Erwartungen. Sie arbeitet an der Herstellung einer wirksamen Waffe im Kampf gegen Krebs, die Immunschwäche Aids und gegen andere unheilbare Krankheiten ebenso, wie an Beiträgen zur Lösung des Welternährungsproblems, an neuen umweltschonenden Techniken, bis hin zum „idealen" Menschen, dem Gentechnik-Menschen. Die Forschungsrichtung „Artificial Life" (Künstliches Leben) hat ihre Ursprünge in einem Computerprogramm, das „zelluläre Automaten" genannt und von dem ungarischen Mathematiker John von Neumann entwickelt wurde. Ein zellulärer Automat reproduziert sich nach bestimmten Regeln selbst. Das Resultat ist eine lebendige, sich selbst organisierende Gemeinschaft von Zellen.
In den 80er Jahren entwickelte Christopher Langton, AL-Forscher am Los Alamos National Laboratory, Zellularautomaten-„Schleifen", die sich „lebensähnlich" fortpflanzen – genauso wie es DNA-Moleküle tun. Mit Hilfe dieser sich selbst reproduzierenden Zellen – später kamen dann elektronische Ameisen, Vögel und andere Organismen dazu – können die Wissenschafter „lebende" Systeme im Computer erschaffen, die wachsen, sich fortplanzen und anpassungs- und entwicklungsfähig sind. Wissenschafter entwickelten aber auch Formen von künstlichem Leben, die Menschen und Tieren äußerlich ähnlicher sind, nämlich Roboter und hochentwickelte Automaten.
Leben, Sterben, Unsterblichkeit, Fortpflanzung, Vererbung, Entwicklung, Evolution, Wachstum der Formen, Anpassung, all diese Begriffe haben durch die Computerkultur eine neue Bedeutung erfahren. Sie verstärkte den Paradigmenwechsel in der Konzeption des Lebens, wie Stoff, Substanz und Mechanismen aus materialen Komponenten zu Code, Sprache, Programm, System, Organisation.
Aus dem Umgang mit Computern wurde nämlich gelernt, daß die „logische Form" eines Organismus von seiner materialen Basis getrennt werden kann und daß Leben eine Eigenschaft von ersterem und nicht von letzerem ist.

serve as information carriers for the programme of life. Genetic engineering and organ technology, recreation through cell nucleus grafting, the cloning of animals, plants and genes, prosthesis surgery—all they combine natural and synthetic, living and non-living materials and allow us to cast a glance into the future. While Artificial Life is dedicated to studying the rules of life, genetic engineering aims at changing organisms.
Genetic engineering creates great expectations. Genetic engineering is thought to find an effective weapon to be used in the fight against cancer, Aids and other lethal illnesses. Genetic engineering is furthermore expected to solve the world nutrition problem, to bring about the development of new, environmental-oriented techniques and even to create the "ideal" human being, the genetically engineered person. The research discipline "Artificial Life" has originated in the form of a computer programme called "cellular automata", that was developed by the Hungarian mathematician John von Neumann. A cellular automaton is capable of reproduction on the basis of certain rules. The result is a living, selforganising community of cells.
In the eighties, the AI researcher Christopher Langton developed "cellular automaton loops" which are able to reproduce in a way similar to living structures, like DNA-molecules. On the basis of these self-producing cells—later digital ants, birds and other virtual creatures and organisms were created—scientists can generate "living systems" on their computers, that grow and reproduce, that can develop and adapt to their environment. Scientists, however, have also developed types of artificial life the outward appearance of which resembles that of human beings and animals: robots and highly-developed automatons.
Live, death, immortality, reproduction, heredity, development, evolution, growth, adaption—all these concepts have been given a new dimension by the computer culture. Computer culture enforced the shift of paradigm from defining life as substance, material hardware or mechanism to conceiving life as code, language, immaterial software, dynamical system. Handling computers has taught us that the "logical structure" of an organism can be separated from its material basis and that life is a property of the former, not the latter.

KÜNSTLICHES LEBEN

DIE DREI GESICHTER DES LEBENS

JOHN L. CASTI

1. DAS „WARUM" DES LEBENS

Laut Cäsar war Gallien in drei Teile geteilt. Auch bei der Betrachtung des Lebens sieht man, daß die entscheidendsten Fragen in drei unterschiedliche Kategorien aufgefächert zu sein scheinen. Zuerst kommt natürlich die nasse, schwammige, auf Kohlenstoff basierende Form des Lebens, die uns hier auf Erden wohlvertraut ist. In diese Kategorie fallen all die gewöhnlichen Fragen nach dem Ursprung bzw. Anfang des Lebens auf diesem Planeten („origin-of-life", kurz: ORI). Die zweite Kategorie, die viel jüngeren Datums ist, ist weniger auf den Beginn des Lebens gerichtet als auf eine noch tiefer gehende Frage, die mit dem Titel von Erwin Schrödingers Buch „Was ist Leben?" Berühmtheit erlangte. In dieser Kategorie findet man neuere Arbeiten zum Thema künstliches Leben (Artificial Life, kurz: AL), in denen versucht wird, Schrödingers Frage durch die Konstruktion des Lebens zu beantworten, wobei von Informationsschemata, die nun aus Silizium und Strom und nicht mehr aus Kohlenstoff und Wasser bestehen, ausgegangen wird. Zu diesem Zweck werden möglicherweise auch neue Kombinationen herkömmlicher chemischer Stoffe aufgebaut, aus denen sich das Leben auf Erden zusammensetzt. Schließlich kommt man in enge Berührung mit Leben einer dritten Art: außerirdische Lebensformen (ET). In dieser dritten Kategorie finden sich all die Rätsel über das mögliche Wesen von Lebensformen, die unter Umweltbedingungen entstanden sind, welche radikal (oder vielleicht gar ununterscheidbar) von denen auf Erden abweichen. Oberflächlich betrachtet scheinen diese Kategorien grundverschieden zu sein. Zumindest ist dies der Eindruck, den man bei der Lektüre der einschlägigen Forschungsliteratur gewinnt. Anläßlich des Ars Electronica Symposiums über künstliches Leben werde ich nun argumentieren, daß diese Kategorien nicht untrennbar miteinander verbunden sind und daß eine eher funktionsorientierte Sicht des Lebens eine Möglichkeit zum fruchtbaren Gedankenaustausch unter den einzelnen Forschungsgruppen zu den jeweiligen Kategorien eröffnet. Das erste, was jeder Journalist lernt, ist, daß eine gute Story Antworten auf die

THE THREE FACES OF LIFE
JOHN L. CASTI

ABSTRACT

Contrary to the cherished beliefs of many physicists and other unreconstructed materialists, there's a lot more to life than mere matter. What distinguishes life from non—life is how the matter is organized. This paper argues that by retreating from a resolutely Newtonian view of life and returning to the Aristotelian notion of causal categories, we open up new avenues of approach to understanding the interconnections among eanhly life fonns, artificial life in machines and possible types of extraterrestrial life.

1. THE WHY OF LIFE

According to Caesar, all Gaul was divided into three parts. And so it is too when it comes to the study of life, where we find that the deepest questions seem to be parceled out among three seemingly distinct categories. The first, of course, is just the wet, squishy, carbon—based type of life we're familiar with here on Earth. Into this Category I fall all the usual origin—of—life (ORI) questions involving the way life got its start on this planet. Category II is of much more recent vintage, centering less upon how life got its start and more upon the even deeper question made famous by the title of Erwin Schrödinger's book, What is Life ? In this category we find the current work on artificial life (AL), which seeks to answer Schrödinger by constructing life based on patterns of information in silicon and electricity instead of in carbon and water, or possibly on new combinations of the standard chemicals constituting life here on Earth. Finally, we come to close encounters with life of the third kind: extraterrestrial life forms (ET). Here in Category III reside all the puzzles involving the possible nature of life forms evolving under environmental conditions radically ditferent (or, perhaps, indistinguishable) from those found here on Earth. Superficially, these categories appear to be pretty much disconnected. Or at least that's the impression one gets from a reading of the scientific research literature. In the spirit of the "Ars Electronica Symposium on Artificial Life," I'll argue in this paper that not only are these categories inextricably intertwined, but that the adoption of a more functionally—oriented view of life opens up the possibility for a productive interchange of ideas among research groups pursuing work in te different categories.

Just about the first thing every journalist learns is that a good story answers the following questions: Who? What? When? Where? Why? How? Applying this tried and true principle the story of life, it's not too hard to see that these interrogatives can be apportioned out among our Categories I—III as follows:

- *Origin of Life: How?*—studies of the origin of life on Earth tend to focus almost exclusively on questions beginning with "How." Occasionally, as with various extraterrestrial theories of the origin of life, "Where" enters the picture too. But, by and large, ORI studies center on the construction of various scenarios for how life got going on Earth four billion years or so ago. This issue is, ofcourse, intimately bound up with the so—called "origins problem," we ask what features of modern life forms would be preserved were we able to "rewind the tape" and start the process all over again. We'll return to this question later.
- *Artificial Life: What?*—the key issue around which most AL studies revolve is Schrödinger's famous question: What is life? Put more specifically, we ask if a suitably—organized pattern of information in a machine can ever constitute a genuine living organism? So the operative word here is "What".
- *Extraterrestrial Life: Who? Where? When?*—"Where are they?" This was Enrico Fermi's famous retort to the claim that the universe must be filled with ET's. Studies over the intervening half century or so have centered mostly on where to look, what to look for and when will we find something (someone?).

The most striking aspect of this list of journalistic interrogatives is the singular absence of "Why". So if Schrödinger's question governed studies of life in the 20th century, I'd like to predict that 21st—century studies of life will be driven by the question, "Why is life?" Let me take a page or two to explain.

2. FROM NEWTON TO ARISTOTLE

The basic goal of modeling, mathematical or otherwise, is to answer the question "Why?" According to Newton (a physicist), the corresponding "Because" is given in terms oflocal interactions involving material paiticles and unexplainable forces. Aristotle (a biologist) had a quite different way of saying "Because."

In Aristotle's view, the "Why" ofthings can be described in terms ofthree basic entities: (i) the material substance comprising physical objects, (ii) the abstract or geometric forms that objects can assume, and (iii) the processes of change by which either the substance or the form may be transformed. Thus, Aristotle's "Because" results in four disjoint and inequivalent causal categories which, taken together, provide a complete answer to "Why" the world is as it is. These

folgenden Fragen liefert: Wer? Was? Wann? Wo? Warum? Wie? Wenn man dieses zeiterprobte Prinzip auf die Geschichte des Lebens anwendet, läßt sich leicht erkennen, daß diese Fragen wie folgt den Kategorien I–III zugeordnet werden können:

- Ursprung des Lebens: WIE? Die meisten Studien über den Ursprung des Lebens befassen sich mit Fragen, die mit WIE? beginnen. Bisweilen gesellt sich ein WO? dazu, wie etwa in den verschiedenen Theorien, die einen außerirdischen Ursprung des Lebens postulieren. Doch im großen und ganzen beschränken sich sich solche Studien auf die Konstruktion verschiedener Szenarien, wie das Leben vor etwa 4 Milliarden Jahren auf Erden begann. Dieses Thema ist natürlich eng mit der sogenannten „Ursprungsfrage“ verbunden, wo gefragt wird, welche Merkmale moderner Lebensformen erhalten blieben, wenn wir in der Lage wären, „das Band zurückzuspulen“ und den Vorgang von Anfang an zu wiederholen. Wir werden später zu dieser Frage zurückkehren.
- Künstliches Leben: WAS?: die Schlüsselfrage, um die sich die meisten Studien zum künstlichen Leben drehen, ist Schrödingers berühmte Frage: „Was ist Leben?“ Genauer gefragt: läßt sich in einer Maschine ein echtes Lebewesen durch ein entsprechend aufgebautes Informationsschema darstellen? Der entscheidende Begriff ist hier WAS?
- Außeridisches Lebens: WER? WO? WANN? – „Wo sind sie?“ Dies ist Enrico Fermis berühmte Entgegnung auf die Behauptung, daß das Universum voller außerirdischer Wesen sein müßte. Studien im letzten halben Jahrhundert richteten ihr Augenmerk in erster Linie auf die Fragen, wo bzw. wonach man schauen muß und wann wir etwas (jemanden?) finden werden.

Der auffallendste Aspekt dieser Auflistung journalistischer Fragen ist das recht seltsame Fehlen von jeglichem „Warum“. War im 20.Jahrhundert Schrödingers Frage richtungsweisend für Betrachtungen des Lebens, so möchte ich voraussagen, daß im 21. Jahrhundert Betrachtungen des Lebens von der Frage „Warum Leben?“ bestimmt werden. Ich werde dies auf den nächsten paar Seiten zu begründen versuchen.

2. VON NEWTON ZU ARISTOTELES

Das Hauptziel von mathematischen und sonstigen Modellen ist die Beantwortung der Frage „Warum?“. Dem Physiker Newton zufolge besteht das entsprechende „Weil“ in örtlichen Wechselwirkungen zwischen stofflichen Teilchen und unerklärlichen Kräften. Der Biologe Aristoteles hingegen hatte eine ziemlich andere Art „Weil" zu vertreten. Aus der Sicht Aristoteles läßt sich das „Warum" von Dingen in From von drei Grundentitäten ausdrücken: (i) Die materielle Substanz, aus der sich physikalische Objekte zusammensetzen, (ii) die abstrakten oder geometrischen Formen, die Objekte annehmen können und (iii) die Prozesse der Veränderung, durch welche entweder die Substanz oder die Form sich verwandeln kann. Das aristotelische „Weil" ergibt folglich vier unzusammenhängende und ungleichartige kausale Kategorien, die zusammen eine vollständige Antwort auf die Frage „warum" die Welt so ist, wie sie ist, liefert. Diese kausalen Kategorien sind:

- Materialursache: die Dinge sind aufgrund des Stoffes, aus dem sie zusammengesetzt sind, so wie sie sind.
- Wirkursache: die Dinge sind aufgrund der Energie, die verbraucht wurde, um sie zu dem zu machen, was sie sind, so wie sie sind.
- Formursache: die Dinge sind aufgrund des Plans, nach dem sie aufgebaut wurden, so wie sie sind.
- Finalursache: die Dinge wurden aufgrund jemandes Wunsches oder Willens, daß sie ihren gegenwärtigen Zustand annehmen, so geschaffen, wie sind.

Man bemerke, daß im obigen Schema der Dinge die Materialursache der Substanz entspricht und die Wirkursache zu den Prozessen, in denen Substanz verändert wird, in Beziehung steht. Auf ähnliche Weise erklärt die Formursache die abstrakte oder geometrische Form einer Entität, während die Finalursache beschreibt, wie Form verändert wird. Dieses Schema erklärt, warum es vier Grundursachen im Aristotelischen Weltbild gibt und nicht drei oder fünf oder 3,469.

In der Erkenntnistheorie von Aristoteles läßt sich alles unter Berufung auf die vier Grundursachen erklären, wobei jede Ursache einen anderen Grundaspekt des jeweiligen Systems beleuchtet. Wir können diese ungleichwertigen kausalen Kategorien auch so deuten, daß wir jede Kategorie als eine Manipulation von „etwas" betrachten, wie in Tabelle 1 dargestellt wird.

(Tabelle 1: aristotelische kausale Kategorien und Manipulationen)

URSACHE	MANIPULIERTES
Materialursache	physikalischer Stoff
Wirkursache	Energie
Formursache	Information
Finalursache	Wunsch, Wille

causal c

- *Material* cause—things are as they are because of the **matter** of which they are composed;
- *Efficient* cause—things are as they are because of the **energy** that went into making them as they are;
- *Formal* cause—things are as they are because of the **plan** according to which they were built;
- *Final* cause—things are as they are because of the **desire** or **will** of someone to have things take their current state.

Note that in the above scheme of things, material cause corresponds to substance, with efficient cause relating to processes for changing the substance. Similarly, formal cause explains the abstract or geometric form of an entity, with final cause describing how one changes the form. This scheme explains why there are four basic causes in the Aristotelian view of the world, and not three or five or 3,469.

In the epistemology of Aristotle, all things can be explained by invoking the four basic causes, each cause illuminating a different fundamental aspect of the system at hand. We can also interpret these inequivalent causal categories by thinking of each category as being concerned with the manipulation of "something" as indicated in Table 1.

TABLE 1. ARISTOTELIAN CAUSAL CATEGORIES AND MANIPULATIONS

CAUSE	PROPERTY MANIPULATED
Material	Physical Matter
Efficient	Energy
Formal	Information
Final	Desire; Will

Interestingly enough, both the Newtonian and Aristotelian explanatory schemes talk about the same thing: a material substance and the process by which this substance can change. However, in the Aristotelian picture substance is not enough; one also needs the idea of form and some kind of dynamic by which one form can be transformed into another. This latter idea is totally absent from the Newtonian picture. In partial compensation, the Newtonian setup offers a mathematical apparatus by which we can encompass both the particles (material cause) and the forces (efficient cause) that constitute the heart of the Newtonian modeling paradigm. The Aristotelian picture provides no mathematical machinery, only a verbal description of the causes. It's instructive to examine this dichotomy in a bit more detail in order to get a feel for what must be done to extend the Newtonian formalism to accommodate the additional Aristotelian causes.

Newton's Second Law is usually written as the differential equation $x(t) = F(t), x(0) = x_0$ where $x(t)$ is the state of the system of particles at time t, the quantity F represents the unexplained external forces, and x^0 is the initial state of the system. For our purposes, it's more convenient to write this relationship in integrated form as $x(t) = x_0 + \int_0^t \phi(s)ds$ where $\phi(s) = \int_0^s F(r)dr$.

Now we can ask the question: Why is the system in the state $x(t)$ at time t? Newton can give only two answers:

1) The system is in the state $x(t)$ at time t because it was in the state x_0 at time $t = 0$ (material cause);

2) The system is in the state $x(t)$ at time t because the operator $\int^{A}_{0}$ (...) transformed the initial state to the state at time t (efficient cause).

Thus, the Newtonian framework has neither the need nor the room to accommodate the additional Aristotelian categories of formal and final causation. Some would argue, myself included, that this fact more than any other accounts for the banishment of formal and especially final cause from polite scientific conversation for the better part of three centuries. There is just no room to fit them in to the classical Newtonian framework.

In actuality, even the most die—hard Newtonian ultimately came to recognize, albeit implicitly, that the missing causal categories would somehow have to be grafted on to the classical setup. In particle systems, the role of formal cause is usually assigned to various parameters specifying important constants in the situation. So things like as particle masses, gravitational constants, electric charges and so on serve to characterize the "plan" ofthe system. It's through the specification of such parameters, and their incorporation into the mathematical framework, that formal cause enters by the backdoor into the Newtonian scheme of things. But what about final cause? How does Newton deal with the idea of desire or will? The simple answer is that he doesn't.

When reading Aristotle's account ofthe causal categories, one is struck by the great significance he attaches to the notion of final cause. In fact, for Aristotle it seems that final cause was just a little more equal than any of the other categories, and he reserved his greatest respect and kindest words for what would today be termed (by Newtonians) "teleology" For the kinds of problems that concerned Newton, it appears reasonable to omit final causation from consideration since it's different to imagine non—living, material particles having any particular kind of will, volition or consciousness. Thus, Newton and his successors had no need to invoke any of the ideas associated with final cause, notions like goals, plans, will, or even self—reference, in their analyses of physical pror:esses.

From this point of view, it's rather easy to understand why the mathematical machinery they employed seemed pertectly adequate to the task at hand, even though it contained no natural way to account for final cause and dealt with even formal cause in a rather ad hoc manner. Unfortunately for the biologist, economist and psychologist, Newton's prescriptions were too successful in answering questions in physics, chemistry and engineering, leading to a gradual emergence of the view that_20it's a breach of scientific etiquette, if not downright unscientific, to allow anything even smacking faintly of final causation to enter into polite scientific discourse. In other words, if you can't use the methods that work in physics, then you're not

Interessanterweise thematisieren sowohl das Newtonsche als auch das aristotelische Erklärungsmodell genau dasselbe, nämlich eine materiale Substanz und den Prozeß, durch den sich diese Substanz verändern kann. Im aristotelischen Bild ist jedoch die Substanz nicht ausreichend. Man braucht auch die Vorstellung von Form und eine Art Dynamik, mittels derer eine Form in eine andere verwandelt werden kann. Letztere Vorstellung fehlt gänzlich im Newtonschen Bild. Um dies teilweise wiedergutzumachen, bietet das Modell Newtons das mathematische Instrumentarium, mit dem man sowohl die Teilchen (Materialursache) als auch die Kräfte (Wirkursache) erfassen kann, die den Kern von Newtons paradigmatischem Modell darstellen. Das aristotelische Modell bietet keine mathematischen Werkzeuge – lediglich eine verbale Beschreibung von Ursache. Es ist aufschlußreich, diese Dichotomie etwas eingehender zu betrachten, um ein Gefühl dafür zu bekommen, was erforderlich ist, um den Newtonschen Formalismus zu erweitern, damit in diesem Rahmen auch die aristotelischen Ursachen untergebracht werden können.

Newtons zweites Gesetz wird meistens als $x(t) = F(t)$, $x(0) = x_0$ Differentialgleichung formuliert, wobei $x(t)$ den Zustand des Teilchensystems zu einem Zeitpunkt t, die Größe F die unerklärten externen Kräfte und xo den Anfangszustand des Systems darstellt. Für unsere Zwecke ist es sinnvoller, diese Beziehung in Integralform als $x(t) = x_0 + \int^{t}_{0} \phi(s)ds$ auszudrücken, wobei $\phi(s) = \int^{s}_{0} F(r)dr$.

Wir können nun fragen: Warum ist das System zum Zeitpunkt t im Zustand x(t)? Newton kann nur zwei Antworten dafür liefern.

1) Das System ist im Zustand x(t) zum Zeitpunkt t, da es im Zustand xo zum Zeitpunkt t=0 (Materialursache) war;

2) Das System ist zum Zeitpunkt t im Zustand x(t), da der Operator $\int^{A}_{0}$ (...) den Anfangszustand in den Zustand zum Zeitpunkt t (Wirkursache) verwandelte.

Der Newtonsche Rahmen hat daher weder die Notwendigkeit noch den Platz, um noch die aristotelischen Kategorien Formursache und Finalursache unterzubringen. Manche – auch ich – würden behaupten, daß diese Tatsache mehr als alles sonst für die Verbannung der Formursache und vor allem der Finalursache aus dem etablierten Wissenschaftsdiskurs für so gut wie drei Jahrhunderte lang verantwortlich ist. Sie passen ganz einfach nicht in den klassischen Newtonschen Rahmen.

In Wirklichkeit kamen auch die hartgesottensten Newtonianer zur Einsicht, wenn auch implizit, daß man der klassischen Struktur die fehlenden kausalen Kategorien irgendwie aufpfropfen müßte. In Teilchensystemen wird die Rolle der formalen Ursache meist verschiedenen Parametern zugeschrieben, die wichtige Konstanten in der Situation angeben. So dienen Dinge wie Teilchenmassen, Gravitationskonstanten, Stromladungen usw. dazu, den „Plan" des Systems zu beschreiben. Mit Hilfe der Bestimmung solcher Parameter und ihrer Einbindung in den mathematischen Rahmen schlich die Formursache durch die Hintertür in das Newtonsche Schema der Dinge ein. Doch wie steht es mit der Finalursache? Wie geht Newton mit der Vorstellung von Wunsch oder Willen um? Die Antwort lautet ganz einfach, daß er es nicht tut.

Wenn wir Aristoteles Abhandlung über kausale Kategorien lesen, fällt auf, daß er dem Begriff der Finalursache große Bedeutung beimißt. In der Tat scheint es, als wäre die Finalursache für Aristoteles ein wenig angemessener als die anderen Kategorien und als hätte er den größten Respekt und die freundlichsten Worte für das, was heute (von Newtonianern) „Teleologie" genannt werden würde. Für jene Art von Problemen, die Newton betrafen, scheint es sinnvoll, Endursache aus der Betrachtung auszuklammern, da es schwierig ist, sich nichtlebende, materiale ** Teilchen vorzustellen, die irgendeine Art Wille, Wollen oder Bewußtsein haben. Folglich hatten Newton und seine Nachfolger es nicht notwendig, sich in ihren Analysen von physikalischen Vorgängen sich auf Vorstellungen, die mit Endursache assoziiert werden, wie etwa Ziele, Pläne, Wille oder gar Selbstbezug, zu berufen.

Von diesem Standpunkt aus ist es ziemlich einfach zu verstehen, warum das Instrumentarium der Mathematik für die jeweilige Aufgabe völlig ausreichend zu sein schien, auch wenn es natürlich keine Möglichkeit enthielt, die Finalursache zu erklären und mit der Formursache ziemlich ad hoc umging. Unglücklicherweise – für den Biologen, den Ökonomen und den Psychologen – brachten die Sätze von Newton bei der Beantwortung von Fragen im Bereich der Physik, der Chemie und der Technik Erfolg. Dies führte allmählich dazu, daß es als Bruch mit den guten Umgangsformen der Wissenschaft galt, wenn nicht als schlichtweg unwissenschaftlich, etwas, was selbst nur eine entfernte Ähnlichkeit mit Finalursache hatte, in den etablierten Wissenschaftsdiskurs einzuführen. Mit anderen Worten, wenn man nicht mit den Methoden, die in der Physik funktionieren, arbeiten kann, dann treibt man nicht Wissenschaft. Und mit den Methoden der Physik zu arbeiten, hieß innerhalb des Rahmens des Newtonschen Paradigmas zu bleiben.

Newtons Welt sieht Organismen nur als besondere Arten von materialen Objekten. Kurz, die Biologie ist eine Untermenge der Physik. Aristoteles' Weltanschauung argumen-

doing science. And using the methods of physics means working within the Newtonian paradigm.

Newton's world naturally sees organisms as being just special kinds of material objects; in short, biology is a subset of physics. Aristotle's Weltanschauung, on the other hand, argues forjust the opposite view, implying that the physics of particles and forces is just a special kind of biology. In other words, the Aristotelian world is one in which the Newtonian framework is just a special case of a broader—based paradigm suitable for characterizing life. Aristotle's problem was that he had no mathemat ical formalism at his disposal with which to describe his causal theory. But mathematical modeling has developed considerably in the two thousand years since Aristotle. And one of its fruits has been the development of a formal framework that helps in putting several questions from ORI, AL and ET onto a common footing. This framework is called a *metabolism—repair system (M, R)—system,* whose details are outlined in the papers[1—6]. Since these results are a bit too involved to go int o here, let it suffice to say that the (M, R)—systems represent an abstract version of a living cell. Now let me indicate how the combination of Aristotelian causation and the (M, R)—setup help illuminate some of the key issues arising in ORI, AL and ET.

3. THE HEN OR THE EGG?

Almost all competing theories of the origin of life involve a scenario in which either the first living thing was a metabolizer that later acquired the ability to replicate, or is a replicator that then assumed metabolic functions. Thus the question: Which came first, the hen or the egg? While the current flavor of the month in the ORI business seems to be a replicator—first theory involving an evolution of life from self—catalytic RNA, the (M, R)—framework strongly suggests otherwise. On purely logical grounds, quite independent of physical substrates like nucleotide bases, amino acid chains and all the other paraphernalia of earthly life, it's very difficult to see how to start with an abstract replicator like RNA and make metabolic activity emerge from replication. Ther e doe s not appear to be any straightforward way to begin with the process of replication and use "natural" mathematical operations on sets and maps to create a metabolizer. Part of the difficulty comes from the fact that the repair component of the cell acts as an intermediary between replication and metabolism, and it's just far simpler to see how to make this operation come about from something rather than having to emerge from nothing. And since replication involves no act ual production of something n ew, but only the copying of something old, there's just not enough raw material to work with to get the job done. So if you believe in the (M, R) framework, then you'll also believe that the time is ripe for metabolism—first theories of ORI to begin making a comeback. Turning now to Aristotle and his causes, the very nature of the ORI problem seems to call for an explanation of life on Earth by material causation. And, in fact, the distinguishing characteristic separating the competing theories—self—rep RNA, hypercycles, clay, iron—is the kind of material substance they postulate that the first organism was made of. But the (M, R)—framework is one grounded in formal and final cause, not material and efficient. In particular, by thinking in these alternative causal categories we are able to pin down the elusive notion of final cause: it is simply the cell's purpose or, in biological terms, its design metabolism. Let's briefly consider how these notions enter into the orig ins problem discus sed earlier.

4. LIFE BY DESIGN

One of the cornerstones of the scientific method is the notion of a repeatable experiment: results obtained by one researcher at one lab should be replicable by other researchers working under similar circumstances. This idea of repeatability enters as a central ingredient in the process of validating scientific claims and establishing today's conventional wisdoms on what Nature is and isn't doing. Clearly, the replicability requirement poses severe difficulties for researchers in areas like the origin of l ife, cosmology, evolution and, in general, every area in which there is a single set of observations available and in which the system cannot be re—set to the beginning and allowed to start over again. This is the so—called "origins problem" The question, of course, is what can be done to surmount it?

One line of attack on the question in origin—of—life studies is to ask: Suppose we could rewind the tape and let the system start over again. Are there any properties of existing life forms that we would expect to see reappear in the new world of "Earth—II"? In other words, are there certain features of organisms that are "generic," and that can be expected wherever life exists? Or is our form of life special in every possible way? Recently, Walter Fontana and Leo Buss have exami ned this issue using tools from mathematical logic and evolutionary theory[11]. They conclude that there are indeed such generic properties, things such as self—maintaining organizations (self—repair), entities that catalyze their own replication and hierarchical organization of living entities. In a certain definite sense, these results relate to what we might call the *logic* of life. So in the Aristotelian scheme of things, they have to do with formal cause. But what about artificial li fe forms built from the usual materials—carbon, hydrogen, oxygen and all the rest—of everyday life?

It's difficult to read a newspaper science page nowadays without encountering some story about how the wizards of molecular biology are concocting new genetic patterns to cure diseases, increase crop harvests or eliminate pests. What's happening here, of course, is that the genetic engineers are constructing strands of RNA/DNA of a type never before seen in any naturally—occurring organism. Let me considerjust one example.

In 1992, Gerald Joyce and Amber Beaudry, re-

tiert andererseits zugunsten der gegenteiligen Sicht und deutet damit an, daß die Physik der Teilchen und der Kräfte nur ein Spezialform der Biologie ist. Mit anderen Worten: die aristotelische Welt ist eine, in der der Newtonsche Rahmen nur ein Sonderfall eines breiteren, für die Beschreibung des Lebens geeigneten Paradigmas ist. Das Problem, das sich Aristoteles stellte, war, daß ihm kein mathematischer Formalismus zur Verfügung stand, mittels dessen er seine kausale Theorie hätte beschreiben können. Die mathematische Modellbildung hat sich aber in den zweitausend Jahren seit Aristoteles beträchtlich entwickelt. Und eines der Ergebnisse war die Entwicklung eines formalen Rahmens, der dazu beiträgt, einige Fragen von ORI, AL und ET auf eine gemeinsame Grundlage zu stellen. Dieser Rahmen wird als „Metabolismus-Regenerationssystem" (Metabolism-Repair SYSTEM M,R) bezeichnet, dessen Details in den Arbeiten (1–6) beschrieben werden. Da diese Ergebnisse etwas zu kompliziert sind, um hier eingehend behandelt zu werden, werde ich mich hier auf die Feststellung beschränken, daß dieses System die abstrakte Form einer lebenden Zelle darstellt. Im folgenden werde ich zeigen, wie die Kombination aus aristotelischer Ursache und dem (M, R) Schema dazu beitragen kann, einige der Schlüsselfragen in ORI, AL und ET zu beleuchten.

3. DIE HENNE ODER DAS EI?

Fast alle konkurrierenden Theorien über den Urspung des Lebens haben mit einem Szenario zu tun, in welchem das erste Lebewesen entweder mit einem Stoffwechselsystem ausgestattet war und später die Fähigkeit zur Replikation entwickelte, oder ein Replikator, der Stoffwechselfunktionen annahm. Von daher auch die Frage: Was kam zuerst? Die Henne oder das Ei?

Während der gegenwärtige Trend im Bereich der Forschung zum Ursprung des Lebens in Richtung zuerst der Replikator zu gehen scheint, mit einer Evolution des Lebens aus selbstkatalysierender RNS, legt das (M, R)-Modell die Vermutung nahe, daß die Dinge anders liegen. Auf rein logischer Grundlage – unabhängig von physikalischen Substraten wie Nukleotidbasen, Aminosäureketten und dem anderen Drumherum des irdischen Lebens –, läßt sich sehr schwer erkennen, wie es ausgehend von einem abstrakten Replikator möglich ist, daß Stoffwechseltätigkeit aus der Replikation hervorgehen kann. Es scheint keinen direkten Weg zu geben, auf der Grundlage des Replikationsprozesses „natürliche" mathematische Operationen auf Systeme und Pläne zu aufzuwenden, um dadurch ein mit Stoffwechselfunktionen ausgestattetes Lebewesen zu schaffen. Ein Teil der Schwierigkeit liegt in der Tatsache begründet, daß die Regenerationskomponente der Zelle als Vermittler zwischen Replikation und Stoffwechsel fungiert und es weitaus leichter ist, zu erkennen, wie diese Operation aus etwas und nicht aus nichts entstand. Da Replikation nichts Neues produziert und nur etwas kopiert, gibt es einfach nicht genug Rohstoff für die Bewältigung der Aufgabe. Wenn man vom (M, R) Modell überzeugt ist, dann wird man auch glauben, daß die Zeit für Theorien reif ist, in denen der Ursprung des Lebens zuerst aus dem Stoffwechsel erklärt wird.

Nun zurück zu Aristoteles und seinen Ursachen: die eigentliche Frage nach dem Ursprung des Lebens scheint eine Erklärung des Lebens auf Erden mit Hilfe der Materialursache zu verlangen. Das unterscheidende Merkmal, das die konkurrierenden Theorien trennt – selbst-replizierende RNS, Hyperzyklen, Lehm, Eisen – ist die Art materieller Substanz, aus der sie behaupten. daß sich der erste Organismus zusammensetzte. Doch das (M, R)-Modell beruht auf Form- und Finalursache, nicht auf Material- und Wirkursache. Insbesonders das Denken in alternativen Kausal-kategorien ermöglicht uns, den schwer faßbaren Begriff der Finalursache festzulegen. Es handelt sich einfach um die Funktion der Zelle oder – biologisch ausgedrückt – ihren zweckgerichteten Metabolismus. Betrachten wir nun, wie diese Begriffe in der oben erwähnten Frage des Ursprungs des Lebens zum Tragen kommen.

4. LEBEN NACH PLAN

Einer der Eckpfeiler wissenschaftlicher Methode ist die Vorstellung eines wiederholbaren Experiments: die Ergebnisse, die ein Forscher in einem Labor erhält, sollen von anderen, unter ähnlichen Bedingungen arbeitenden Forschern wiederholt werden können. Diese Vorstellung der Wiederholbarkeit ist ein zentraler Bestandteil der Bekräftigung von wissenschaftlichen Behauptungen und der Begründung der konventionellen Weisheiten unserer Zeit über das, was die Natur tut und nicht tut. Es ist klar, daß die Forderung nach Wiederholbarkeit den Forscher vor riesige Schwierigkeiten stellt, in Fragen, die mit dem Ursprung des Lebens, Kosmologie, Evolution, zu tun haben, und in jedem Bereich, in dem es eine einzige Gruppe von Beobachtungen gibt und das System nicht auf einen Anfang zurückgeführt werden kann, um von neuem wieder zu beginnen. Dies ist das sogenannte „Ursprungsproblem". Die Frage ist freilich, was unternommen werden kann, um es zu überwinden.

searchers at the Scripps Institute in California, succeeded in coaxing a biological molecule to evolve artificially, doing in a few weeks what Nature might take millennia to perform[12]. Starting with a population consisting of trillions of molecular variants of a strand of RNA, Joyce and Beaudry evolved an RNA enzyme that would snip strands of DNA 100 times more efficiently than the starting molecule. In short, these researchers achieved what might be called, evolu tion by "unnatural selection" Earlier work had shown how to mimic two of the three ingredients needed for Darwinian evolution—selection and amplification. But the crucial ingredient added in the Scripps experiment was that it allowed molecules to also mutate randomly. So in our Aristotelian categorization, we can explain the work of loyce and Beaudry by appeal to material causation—but of a type never before seen in any natural organism.

Before closing the all—too—brief discussion of life by design, let me mention in passing the extensive amount of work being done under the general rubric "robotics" As anyone who saw the film Star Wars is well aware, robots are another way to study life by designing objects that capture the behavioral and cognitive features of natural organisms—including human beings! Now let me shift the venue from real life to *real* artificial life.

5. LIFE IN SILICO

In summer 1991 Tom Ray, a plant biologist in Delaware, created a computer program that reproduces, undergoes spontaneous genetic changes, passes them on to its offspring and evolves new species whose interactions mimic those of real biological evolution and ecology—all without human guidance or intervention[9)]. The significance of Ray's program was that it was the first logical demonstration of the validity of the Darwinian theory of evolution. This is exactly the goal of the artificial lifers: to show that the logical swcture oflife is completely independent ofmaterial cause. True or not, just as with work on ORI, in AL too there is something to be gained by thinking in terms of other causal categories.

For instance, Darwinian theory implies that the environment in which an organism develops will strongly influence the physical form and function of the organism. This is a material—cause explanation for why the vast majority of living things on Earth are shaped like cylinders with appendages. But suppose we have something like Ray's electronic organisms that evolve within the cozy confines of a computer's memory banks. Thinking in terms of material cause, we can ask: What is the shape of such an electro nic "bug"? And what would such an organism see when it looks at its "environment"? And in what way does the bug have to adapt to such an environment? And so on and so forth. The point is that we are led to ask a quite different set of questions than those that naturally come to mind in the original setting of formal cause.

In another direction, we can point to the work initiated by Dutch biologist Aristid Lindenmayer on artificial plants. Using a small number of simple rules involving branching directions, leaf types and the like, Lindenmayer and his colleagues have created a stunning array of plant—like objects that bear a striking similarity to the kinds of flowers and trees found naturally here on Earthl[10]. But of course, these "electronic plants" have never graced anyone's backyard garden or appeared on the menu in any haute cuisine restaurant. They are the epitome of what we can call artificial plants. Before leaving the matter of life in silicon, let me add that by taking a collection of abstract cells of the type in the (M, R)—framework and connecting them into a network, it's possible to construct an electronic ecology similar to that produced in Ray's computer. Some suggestions about how this might be done are given in the papers[1, 6]. One result that comes ou t of such an exercise is the pu rely logical fact that immortality is flatly impossible. In other words, not all genetic lines can perpetuate themselves indefinitely. This is explanation by formal cause. It's reasonable to suppose that additional light will be shed on this phenomenon by looking at it from the vantage point of material causation. But this is a matter for future research. For much further discussion of this point, the reader should consult the "bible" of artificia l life[8].

6. WHO GOES THERE?

From a physical life point of view, certainly the most central question surrounding the existence of ET is: What do "they" look like? In other words, what kind of physico—chemical structure is an ET likely to have? This, of course, is basically a problem of material and efficient cause. And for the spectrum of possible answers, it's hard to do better than to consult the "hard" science fiction literature.

The creature depicted in Figure 1 below shows an artist's depiction of a Cygnan, a race of alien beings that threatens the Earth in Donald Moffitt's classic science—fiction novel *The Jupiter Theft*. The Cygnan is from a race of creatures the evolved on the satellite of a gas giant planet orbiting a binary star system. He (she? it?) is about $1^1/_2$ meters tall, with six limbs that can be used as either arms or legs, and a long, three—petaled tail that folds to conceal the sexual organs. The slender, tubular body is built on a cartilaginous skeleton, with the brain located between the upper pair of limbs at the top of the spinal cord. The three eyes are placed on stalks in an equilateral triangle around a broad, flexible mouth. The Cygnan has a harsh, rasping plate in the mouth, and a spiked, tubular tongue. It has a well—integrated nervous system, with much faster synaptic reflexes than those of a human being. Cygnan speech is musical, consisting of chords produced by multiple larynx es, and depends on absolute pitch. The language is incredibly rich and varied; it has more than a million phonemes, and each word is made up of several phonemes.

So here we have a well worked—out example of an ET that differs radically from earthly organisms in almost every way that counts (unfor-

In Arbeiten über den Ursprung des Lebens stellt die folgende Frage eine Angriffsfläche dar: Angenommen, man könnte das Band zurückspulen und das System von neuem anfangen lassen. Gibt es Eigenschaften existierender Lebensformen, die wir wieder in der neuen Welt von „Erde-II" zu sehen erwarten könnten? Mit anderen Worten, gibt es bestimmte Merkmale von Organismen, die „universell" sind, und kann man erwarten, daß es sie überall, wo es Leben gibt? Oder ist unsere Lebensform in jeder Hinsicht besonders? Vor kurzem haben Fontana und Leo Buss diese Frage mit den Mitteln der mathematischen Logik und der Evolutionstheorie betrachtet.11 Sie gelangen zu der Schlußfolgerung, daß es tatsächlich solche universelle Eigenschaften gibt, Dinge wie etwa selbsterhaltende Organisationen (Selbstregeneration), Entitäten, die ihre eigene Replikation und die hierarchische Organisation von lebenden Entitäten katalysieren. In einem ganz bestimmten Sinne haben diese Ergebnisse mit dem zu tun, was wir die Logik des Lebens nennen. Im Aristotelischen Schema der Dinge haben sie mit formaler Ursache zu tun. Doch wie steht es um die künstlichen Lebensformen, die aus den herkömmlichen Stoffen – Kohlenstoff, Wasserstoff, Sauerstoff, usw. – des täglichen Lebens erzeugt werden?

Es ist heute schwierig, die Wissenschaftsseite einer Zeitung zu lesen, ohne daß man auf eine Geschichte von irgendwelchen Wundertaten im Bereich der Molekularbiologie stößt, wie etwa die Entwicklung neuer genetischen Codes, um Krankheiten zu heilen, den Ernteertrag zu steigern oder Schädlinge zu vernichten. Was hier natürlich passiert, ist, daß Gentechniker RNS/DNS-Stränge schaffen, die noch es in einem natürlichen Organismus noch nie gab. Betrachten wir nur ein Beispiel.

1992 gelang es Gerald Joyce und Amber Beaudry, zwei Forschern am Scripps Institute in Kalifornien, ein biologisches Molekül dazu zu bringen, sich in einem Zeitraum von wenigen Wochen künstlich zu entwickeln, was früher Jahrtausende erfordert hätte.12

Ausgehend von einer Population von Billiarden von molekularen Varianten einer RNS-Kette, entwickelten Joyce und Beaudry ein RNS-Enzym, das DNS-Ketten 100 Mal effizienter durchtrennen konnte als das Ausgangsmolekül. Kurzum gelang diesen Forschern das, was man vielleicht Evolution durch „unnatürliche Auslese" nennen könnte. Frühere Arbeiten hatten gezeigt, wie zwei von drei Komponenten, die für die Darwinsche Evolution nötig sind – Auslese und Verstärkung – nachgeahmt werden können. Doch das entscheidende Element, das im Scripps Experiment hinzukam, war die Möglichkeit, Moleküle beliebig zu mutieren. In unserer

Aristotelischen Aufteilung können wir also die Arbeit von Joyce und Beaudry unter Berufung auf die Materialursache erklären – ohne allerdings, daß dies jemals an einem natürlichen Organismus wirklich beobachet wurde.
Bevor wir die allzu kurze Abhandlung über das zweckgerichtete Leben abschließen, möchte ich noch auf die recht umfangreiche Arbeit hinweisen, die in der allgemeinen Rubrik „Roboterwissenschaft" geleistet wird. Wie fast jeder, der den Film „Krieg der Sterne" gesehen hat, weiß, sind Roboter eine andere Art und Weise, das Leben zu untersuchen, indem Gegenstände entworfen werden, die die verhaltensmäßigen und kognitiven Merkmale natürlicher Organismen – einschließlich der Menschen – erfassen! Wechseln wir nun den Schauplatz vom echten Leben zum echten künstlichen Leben.

5. LEBEN IN SILICO

Im Sommer 1991 entwickelte Tom Ray, ein Pflanzenbiologe in Delaware ein Computerprogramm, das reproduziert, spontane genetische Veränderungen durchmacht, diese an die Nachkommen weitergibt und neue Arten hervorbringt, deren Interaktionen jene der echten biologischen Evolution und Ökologie nachahmen – all dies ohne menschliches Zutun oder Intervention. (9). Die Bedeutung von Rays Programm lag darin, daß es das erste war, das die Gültigkeit der Darwinschen Theorie demonstrierte. Und genau darauf haben es die Befürworter des künstlichen Lebens abgesehen: der Nachweis, daß die logische Struktur des Lebens von der Materialursache völlig unabhängig ist. Ob dies stimmt oder nicht, es ist nicht nur in Zusammenhang mit Fragen nach dem Ursprungs des Lebens, sondern auch im künstlichen Leben von Nutzen, in anderen Kausalkategorien zu denken. So geht aus der Darwinschen Theorie implizit hervor, daß die Umwelt, in welcher ein Organismus sich entwickelt, die physikalische Form und Funktion des Organismus stark beeinflußen wird. Dies erklärt auf der Grundlage der Materialursache, warum die große Mehrheit der Lebewesen auf Erden wie Zylinder mit Anhängseln geformt sind. Doch angenommen, wir verfügten über so etwas wie Rays elektronische Organismen, die sich innerhalb der bequemen Grenzen der Speicher eines Computers entwickeln. Im Sinne der Materialursache könnten wir nun fragen: Welche Form hat eine solche elektronische „Wanze"? (Anm.d.Übers.: „bug" hat im Englischen zwei Bedeutungen, auf die hier vermutlich angespielt wird: 1) Wanze, 2) technische Störung). Und was würde ein solcher Organismus sehen, wenn er seine „Umwelt" betrachtet? Und auf welche Weise müßte sich die-

tunately for the humans in Moffitt's story). But if we consider formal cause, the science—fiction literature offers up even stranger possibilities. Figure 2 shows the Cryer, a creature from Joseph Green's book *Conscience Interplanetary*. The Cryer is an independently functioning unit of a planet—wide silicon—based plant intelligence inhabiting the planet Crystal, which has an atmosphere of 18 percent oxygen, the rest being nitrogen and hydrogen. Life on Crystal is based on silicon, with a high percentage of metallic elements. The Cryer resembles a two—meter—high bush with a crystal—and—metal trunk and branches, with small, sharp glass leaves. The trunk contains silicon memory units, powered by a low—voltage solar storage battery and connected by fine silver wires. About six feet up the Cryer's trunk is an organic air—vibration membrane that enables the Cryer to speak with human beings. It is a broad, saucer—shaped leaf held in place by stretched wires to provide a vibrating diaphragm. A magnetic field generated in silver wire coils hanging on either side o f the speaker causes it to vibrate and produce sound.
The planet—wide intelligence consists of thousands of smaller units like the Cryer, connected by an underground nervous system of fine silver wire. Each unit has a specialized function, some storing electricity generated by sunlight, some extracting silver for constructing the nervous system, some providing memory storage, and some acting as sensor units. The overall intelligence is able to perceive temperature, motion, position, electrical potential and vibrations through its member units.
Cygnans and Cryers are, of course, just thought experiments. Many more are reported in the imaginative volume[7]. By considering the almost infinite range of possible life forms, and by examining the ET problem from all four of the Aristotelian causal perspectives, we can hope to get some feel for what may turn up on our radio telescopes or in our back yards one of these days. And, in fact, as the paper[1)] points out, the metabolism—repair systems form what in mathematics is termed a "categ ory" of objects. Therefore, each and every member of this category corresponds to a different biology, opening up the possibility of studying exobiologies by examining the mathematical structures and constraints imposed by these different objects in the category.

7. THAT'S LIFE!

This paper has argued that to understand the difference between the living and the dead, it's not sufficient to concentrate just on the material aspects of living things. By adopting a less Newtonian and a more Anstotelian view of the problem, one is led to give equal time to explanations of life in terms of other causal categories besides the material. In particular, we have shown that there is much to be gained (and nothing to be lost but prejudices) by considering the other forms of life beyond those com monly—encountered here on Planet Three. The overall conclusion that emerges is that there are significant synergies possible between earth life, artificial life in machines and extraterrestrial life "out there," and that researchers in each area can benefit from paying careful attention to work by those in the other categories. To paraphrase a famous remark about war and generals, life is just too important to be left to the biologists.

References

1. Rosen, R., "Some Relational Cell Models: The Metabolism—Repair Systems," *in Foundations of Mathematical Biology,* Volume 2, Academic Press, New York, 1972.
2. Rosen, R., *Anticipatory Systems,* Pergamon, Oxford, 1985.
3. Rosen, R., *Life Itself* Columbia University Press, New York, 1991.
4. Casti, J., "Linear Metabolism—Repair Systems," *Int'l.J Gen.Sys.* 14 (1988), 143—167.
5. Casti, J., "The Theory of Metabolism—Repair Systems," *Applied Math. & Comp.* 28 (1988), 113—154.
6. Casti, J., "Newton, Aristotle, and the Modeling of Living Systems," *in Newton to Aristotle,* J. Casti and A. Karlqvist, eds., Birkhäuser, New York, 1989, pp., 47—89.
7. Jonas, D. and D. Jonas, *Other Senses, Other Worlds,* Stein and Day, New York, 1976.
8. *Artificial Life,* C. Langton, ed., Addison—Wesley, Redwood City, CA, 1989.
9. Ray, T., "An Approach to the Synthesis of Life," in *Artificial Life—II,* C. Langton, et al, eds., Addison—Wesley, Redwood City, CA, 1992, pp. 371—408.
10. Prusinkiewicz, P and A. Lindenmayer, *The Algorithmic Beauty of Plants,* Springer, New York, 1990.
11. Fontana, W. and L. Buss, "What Would be Conserved in the Tape Were Played Twice?" submitted to *Proc. Nat. Acad. Sci.* USA, March 1993.
12. Coghlan, A., "Survival of the Fittest Molecules," *New Scientist,* October 3, 1992, pp. 37—40.

ses Lebewesen einer solchen Umwelt anpassen? Und so weiter und sofort. Entscheidend ist hier, daß wir dazu verleitet werden, eine Reihe von Fragen zu stellen, die anders als jene sind, die einem im ursprünglichen Kontext der Formursache spontan einfallen.

In einer anderen Richtung könnten wir auf die Arbeiten des holländischen Biologen Aristid Lindenmayer über künstliche Pflanzen hinweisen. Mit Hilfe einer geringen Anzahl einfacher Regeln, die sich auf Verästelungen, Blätterarten und ähnliches beziehen, schufen Lindenmayer und seine Kollegen eine erstaunliche Vielfalt von pflanzenähnlichen Objekten, die eine auffallende Ähnlichkeit mit Blumen und Bäumen, wie man sie in der Natur auf Erde findet, haben (10). Es versteht sich aber von selbst, daß diese „elektronischen Pflanzen" bisher weder in einem Garten noch auf der Speisekarte eines Haute cuisine-Restaurants zu sehen waren. Sie sind der Inbegriff dessen, was wir künstliche Pflanzen nennen.

Bevor wir die Sache mit dem Leben in Silizium abschließen, möchte ich hinzufügen, daß es möglich ist, eine elektronische Ökologie, wie jene, die in Rays Computer erzeugt wurde, zu konstruieren, indem man eine Ansammlung abstrakter Zellen, die jener des (M,R)-Systems ähneln, nimmt und diese in ein Netzwerk einbindet. Einige Vorschläge, wie dies zu machen wäre, findet man in Veröffentlichungen (1,6). Ein Ergebnis einer solchen Übung ist, daß es schlichtweg unmöglich ist. Mit anderen Worten, es können sich nicht alle genetischen Linien unendlich fortsetzen. Diese Erklärung beruht auf der Formursache. Es ist eine sinnvolle Annahme, daß wir zusätzliches Licht auf dieses Phänomen werfen könnten, wenn wir es vom Standpunkt der Materialursache betrachten. Doch dies ist eine Aufgabe der künftigen Forschung. Für eine weit ausführlichere Diskussion dieses Punktes möge der Leser in der „Bibel" des künstlichen Lebens (8) nachlesen.

6. WER IST DA?

Vom Standpunkt des physischen Lebens ist die zentralste Frage im Zusammenhang mit der Existenz von ET (außerirdischen Lebewesen) folgende: Wie sehen „sie" aus? Mit anderen Worten, welche Art von physikalisch-chemischer Struktur werden solche Wesen haben? Dies ist natürlich grundsätzlich eine Frage von Material- und Wirkursache. Und um ein Spektrum möglicher Antworten zu erhalten, kann man kaum besseres tun, als die auf „harten Tatsachen" beruhende Science-Fiction-Literatur studieren.

Das unter Abbildung 1 gezeigte Lebewesen ist eine künstlerische Darstellung eines „Cygnan", einer Rasse von fremden Wesen, die die Erde in Donald Moffitts klassischem Science fiction-Roman „The Jupiter Theft" bedrohen. Der „Cygnan" stammt von einer Rasse von Wesen ab, die auf dem Satelliten eines riesigen Gasplaneten lebt, der um ein binäres Sternensystem kreist. Es ist etwa 1 1/2 Meter groß und mit sechs Gliedern ausgestattet, die entweder als Arme oder Beine vewendet werden können, und einem langen, dreigeteilten Schwanz, der sich faltet, um die Geschlechtsorgane zu verbergen, ausgestattet. Der schmale, röhrenförmige Körper umgibt ein Knorpelskelett, mit dem Gehirn zwischen dem oberen Gliederpaar am oberen Teil des Rückgrats. Die drei Augen befinden sich auf Stengeln, die ein gleichseitiges Dreieck um einen breiten, flexiblen Mund bilden. Der „Cygnan" hat einen harte, rauhe Platte im Mund und eine stachelige, röhrenförmige Zunge. Er hat ein gut integriertes Nervensystem, dessen synaptische Reflexe weitaus schneller sind als die des Menschen. Die Sprache des „Cygnan" ist musikalisch und besteht aus Tönen, die von mehreren Kehlköpfen gebildet werden und vom absoluten Gehör abhängen. Die Sprache ist unglaublich reich und vielfältig, mit mehr als einer Million Phonemen, wobei jedes Wort aus einigen Phonemen gebildet wird.

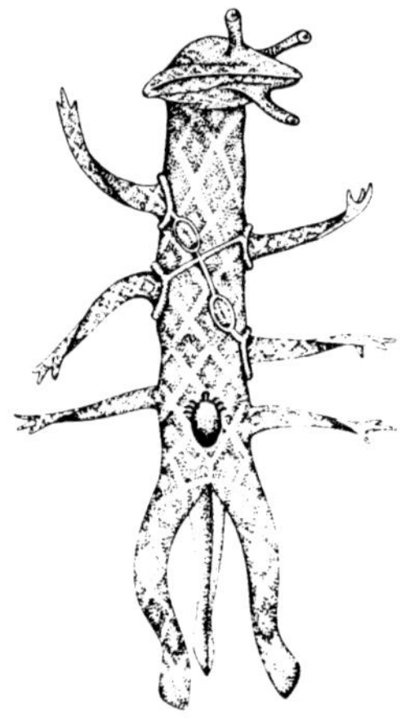

Hier haben wir also ein gut ausgearbeitetes Beispiel eines außerirdischen Lebewesens, das sich in fast jeder wichtigen Hinsicht von irdischen Organismen unterscheidet (für die Menschen in Moffitts Geschichte ein unglücklicher Umstand). Doch wenn wir die Formursache betrachten, bietet die Literatur der Science Fiction noch seltsamere Möglichkeiten.

Abbildung 2 zeigt den „Cryer", ein Lebewesen aus Joseph Greens Buch „Conscience Interplanetary". Der „Cryer" ist eine selbständig funktionierende Einheit einer planetenweit verbreiteten, auf Silizium beruhenden Pflanzenintelligenz, die den Planeten Crystal bevölkert, dessen Atmosphäre zu 18% aus Sauerstoff und zum restlichen Teil aus Stickstoff und Wasserstoff besteht. Das Leben auf Crystal basiert auf Silizium und einem hohen Anteil metallischer Elemente.

Der „Cryer" ähnelt einem zwei Meter hohen Busch aus Kristall und Metall und Zweigen mit kleinen, scharfen Glasblättern. Der Stamm enthält Speichereinheiten aus Silizium, die von einer Niedervolt-Solarspeicherbatterie angetrieben werden und über feine Silberdrähte verbunden sind. In etwa sechs Zoll Höhe befindet sich auf dem Stamm des „Cryer" eine organische Luftvibrations-Membran, die es ihm möglich macht, mit Menschen zu sprechen. Es ist ein breites, untertassenförmiges Blatt, das mit gedehnten Drähten fixiert

ist, um ein vibrierendes Diaphragma zu schaffen. Ein magnetisches Feld in Spulen aus Silberdraht auf beiden Seiten des Lautsprechers bewirkt, daß die Membrane vibriert und Laute erzeugt werden.
Die planetenweite Intelligenz besteht aus Tausenden kleinerer Einheiten wie dem „Cryer", die über ein unterirdisches Nervensystem aus feinem Silberdraht miteinander verbunden sind. Jede Einheit hat eine spezifische Funktion, einige speichern die von der Sonne produzierte Elektrizität, während andere Silber für den Bau des Nervensystems gewinnen, Speicherplatz bereitstellen und als Sensoreinheiten fungieren. Die Gesamtintelligenz ist in der Lage, Temperatur, Bewegung, Stellung, Strompotential und Vibrationen mit Hilfe von an den Gliederenden angebrachten Einheiten wahrzunehmen.
„Cygnane" und „Cryers" sind natürlich nur Gedankenexperimente. Von diesen sind noch viele mehr in einem fantasievollen Band (7) angeführt. Durch die Betrachtung von einem fast unendlichen Spektrum von möglichen Lebensformen und die Untersuchung außerirdischer Lebewesen unter Berücksichtigung aller vier Aristotelischen kausalen Perspektiven können wir hoffen, daß wir ein Gefühl dafür bekommen, was eines Tages in unseren Funkteleskopen oder in unserem Garten auftauchen könnte. Und wie die Arbeit (1) aufzeigt, bilden die Regenerationssysteme für den Stoffwechsel das, was in der Mathematik eine „Kategorie" von Objekten genannt wird. Jedes Einzelglied dieser Kategorie entspricht einer anderen Biologie, wodurch sich die Möglichkeit eröffnet, Exobiologien durch die Betrachtung der mathematischen Strukturen und der von den verschiedenen Objekten in der Kategorie auferlegten Zwänge zu untersuchen.

7. DAS IST DAS LEBEN!

In diesem Aufsatz wurde behauptet, daß es nicht ausreicht, nur die materialen Aspekte von Lebewesen zu betrachten, um den Unterschied zwischen dem Lebenden und dem Leblosen zu erfassen. Wenn man eine weniger nach Newton als nach Aristoteles ausgerichtete Sicht des Problems annimmt, wird man dazu verleitet, Erklärungen des Lebens auf der Grundlage anderer kausalen Kategorien außer der materialen im gleichem Maße zu berücksichtigen. Es wurde hier vor allem gezeigt, daß viel zu gewinnen (und nichts – außer Vorurteile – zu verlieren ist), wenn man andere Lebensformen außer denen, denen wir hier auf Planet 3 oft begegnen, betrachten. Daraus ist insgesamt zu schließen, daß signifikante

Synergien zwischen dem Leben auf Erde, künstlichem Leben in Maschinen und außerirdischem Leben „da draußen" bestehen. Weiters werden Forscher in jedem Bereich davon profitieren, wenn sie die Arbeit jener in anderen Kategorien berücksichtigen. Um eine berühmte Bemerkung über Krieg und Generäle zu paraphrasieren: das Leben ist einfach zu wichtig, um es den Biologen zu überlassen.

LITERATUR

1. Rosen, R., „Some Relational Cell Models: The Metabolism-Repair Systems," in Foundations of Mathematical Biology, Bd. 2, Academic Press, New York, 1972.
2. Rosen, R., Anticipatory Systems, Pergamon, Oxford, 1985.
3. Rosen, R., Life Itself, Columbia University Press, New York, 1991.
4. Casti, J., „Linear Metabolism-Repair Systems," Int'IJ. Gen-Sys 14 (1988), 143–167.
5. Casti, J., „The Theory of Metabolism-Repair Systems," Applied Math& Comp 28 (1988), 113–154.
6. Casti, J., „Newton, Aristotle, and the Modeling of Living Systems," in Newton to Aristotle, J. Casti und A. Karlqvist, (Hrsg.) Birkhäuser, New York, 1989, S.47–89.
7. Jonas, D. und D.Jonas, Other Senses, Other Worlds, Stein and Day, New York, 1976.
8. Artificial Life, C. Langton, Hrsg. Addison-Wesley, Redwood City, CA, 1989.
9. Ray, T., „An Approach to the Synthesis of Life", in Artificial Life-II, C.Langton, et al, Hrsg. Addision-Wesley, Redwood City, CA, 1992, S.371–408.
10. Prusinkiewicz, P. und A. Lindenmayer, The Algorithmic Beauty of Plants, Springer, New York, 1990.
11. Fontana, W. und L. Buss, „What Would be Conserved if the Tape Were Played Twice?", vorgelegt bei Proc. NAt. Acad. Sci. USA, März 1993.
12. Coghlan, A., „Survival of the Fittest Molecules," New Scientist, Oktober 3, 1992, S.37–40.

ARTIFICIAL LIFE

CHRISTOPHER G. LANGTON

"Art" + "Life" = *Artificial Life:* Life made by Man rather than by Nature. Our technological capabilities have brought us to the point where we are on the verge of creating "living" artifacts. The field of Artificial Life is devoted to studying the scientific, technological, artistic, philosophical, and social implications of such an accomplishment.

1 THE BIOLOGY OF POSSIBLE LIFE

Biology is the scientific study of life—in principle anyway. In practice, biology is the scientific study of life on Earth based on carbon-chain chemistry. There is nothing in its charter that restricts biology to carbon-based life; it is simply that this is the only kind of life that has been available to study. Thus, theoretical biology has long faced the fundamental obstacle that it is impossible to derive general principles from single examples.

Without other examples, it is difficult to distinguish essential properties of life—properties that would be shared by any living system—from properties that may be incidental to life in principle, but which happen to be universal to life on Earth due solely to a combination of local historical accident and common genetic descent. In order to derive general theories about life, we need an ensemble of instances to generalize over. Since it is quite unlikely that alien life forms will present themselves to us for study in the near future, our only option is to try to create alternative life-forms ourselves—*Artificial Life*—literally "life made by Man rather than by Nature."

Artificial Life ("AL" or "Alife") is the name given to a new discipline that studies "natural" life by attempting to recreate biological phenomena from scratch within computers and other "artificial" media. Alife complements the *analytic* approach of traditional biology with a *synthetic* approach: rather than studying biological phenomena by taking living organisms apart to see how they work, we attempt to put together systems that behave like living organisms.

The process of synthesis has been an extremely important

tool in many disciplines. Synthetic chemistry—the ability to put together new chemical compounds not found in nature—has not only contributed enormously to our theoretical understanding of chemical phenomena, but has also allowed us to fabricate new materials and chemicals that are of great practical use for industry and technology. Artificial life amounts to the practice of "synthetic biology," and, by analogy with synthetic chemistry, the attempt to recreate biological phenomena in alternative media will result in not only better theoretical understanding of the phenomena under study, but also in practical applications of biological principles in industry and technology. By extending the horizons of empirical research in biology beyond the territory currently circumscribed by *life-as-we-know-it*, the study of Artificial Life gives us access to the domain of *life-as-it-could-be*, and it is within this vastly larger domain that we must ground general theories of biology and in which we will discover novel and practical applications of biology in our engineering endeavors.

1.1 AI AND THE BEHAVIOR GENERATION PROBLEM

Artificial Life is concerned with generating *life-like* behavior. Thus, it focuses on the problem of creating *behavior generators*. A good place to start is to identify the mechanisms by which behavior is generated and controlled in natural systems, and to recreate these mechanisms in artificial systems. This is the course we will take later in this paper.

The related field of Artificial Intelligence is concerned with generating *intelligent* behavior. It, too, focuses on the problem of creating behavior generators. However, although it initially looked to natural intelligence to identify its underlying mechanisms, these mechanisms were not known, nor are they today. Therefore, following an initial flirt with neural-nets, AI became wedded to the only other known vehicle for the generation of complex behavior: the technology of serial computer programming. As a consequence, from the very beginning artificial intelligence embraced an underlying methodology for the generation of intelligent behavior that bore no demonstrable relationship to the method by which intelligence is generated in natural systems. In fact, AI has focused primarily on the production of intelligent *solutions* rather than on the production of intelligent *behavior*. There is a world of difference between these two possible foci.

By contrast, Artificial Life has the great good fortune that many of the mechanisms by which behavior arises in natural living systems are known. There are still many holes in our knowledge, but the general picture is in place. Therefore, Artificial Life can start by recapturing natural life, and has no need to resort to the sort of initial infidelity that is now coming back to haunt AI. Furthermore, Artificial Life is not primarily concerned with building systems that reach some sort of solution. For AL systems, the ongoing dynamics is the behavior of interest, not necessarily the state ultimately reached by that dynamics.

The key insight into the natural method of behavior generation is gained by noting that *nature is fundamentally parallel.* This is reflected in the "architecture" of natural living organisms, which consist of many millions of parts, each one of which has its own behavioral repertoire. Living systems are highly distributed, and quite massively-parallel. If our models are to be true to life, they must also be highly distributed and quite massively parallel. Indeed, it is unlikely that any other approach will prove viable.

2 HISTORICAL ROOTS OF ARTIFICIAL LIFE

Mankind has a long history of attempting to map the mechanics of his contemporary technology onto the workings of nature, trying to understand the latter in terms of the former. It is not surprising, therefore, that models of life have also reflected the principal technology of their era, from pneumatics in the time of the Greeks to computation in the current "information age".

2.1 EARLY HISTORY

The earliest models were simple statuettes and paintings—works of art which captured the static form of living things. Later, these statues were provided with articulated arms and legs in the attempt to capture the dynamic form of living things. These simple statues incorporated no internal dynamics, requiring human operators to make them behave.

The earliest mechanical devices that were capable of generating their own behavior were based on the technology of water transport. These were the early Egyptian water clocks called *Clepsydra.* These devices made use of a rate-limited process—in this case the dripping of water through a fixed orifice—to indicate the progression of another process—the position of the sun. Ctesibius of Alexandria developed a water powered mechanical clock around 135 BC which employed a great deal of the available hydraulic technology—

including floats, a siphon, and a water-wheel driven train of gears.

In the first century AD, Hero of Alexandria produced a treatise on *Pneumatics*, which described, among other things, various simple gadgets in the shape of animals and humans that utilized pneumatic principles to generate simple movements.

However, it was really not until the age of mechanical clocks that artifacts exhibiting complicated internal dynamics became possible. Around 850 AD, the *mechanical escapement* was invented, which could be used to regulate the power provided by falling weights. This invention ushered in the great age of clockwork technology. Throughout the Middle Ages and the Renaissance, the history of technology is largely bound up with the technology of clocks. Clocks often constituted the most complicated and advanced application of the technology of an era.

Perhaps the earliest clockwork simulations of life were the so-called "Jacks," mechanical "men" incorporated in early clocks who would swing a hammer to strike the hour on a bell. The word "jack" is derived from "jaccomarchiadus," which means "the man in the suit of armor." These accessory figures retained their popularity even after the spread of clock dials and hands—to the extent that clocks were eventually developed in which the function of time-keeping was secondary to the control of large numbers of figures engaged in various activities, to the point of acting out entire plays.

Finally, clockwork mechanisms appeared which had done away altogether with any pretense at time-keeping. These "automata" were entirely devoted to imparting life-like motion to a mechanical figure or animal. These mechanical automaton simulations of life included such things as elephants, peacocks, singing birds, musicians, and even fortune tellers.

This line of development reached its peak in the famous duck of Vaucanson, described as "an artificial duck made of gilded copper who drinks, eats, quacks, splashes about on the water, and digests his food like a living duck" Vaucanson's goal is captured neatly in the following description.[1]

In 1735 Jacques de Vaucanson arrived in Paris at the age of 26. Under the influence of contemporary philosophic ideas, he had tried, it seems, to reproduce life artificially.

Unfortunately, neither the duck itself nor any technical descriptions or diagrams remain that would give the details of construction of this duck. The complexity of the mechanism is attested to by the fact that one single wing contained over 400 articulated pieces.

1

One of those called upon to repair Vaucanson's duck in later years was a "mechanician" named Reichsteiner, who was so impressed with it that he went on to build a duck of his own—also now lost—which was exhibited in 1847.

Figure 1 shows two views of one of the ducks—there is some controversy as to whether it is Vaucanson's or Reichsteiner's. The mechanism inside the duck would have been completely covered with feathers and the controlling mechanism in the box below would have been covered up as well.

2

2.2 THE DEVELOPMENT OF CONTROL MECHANISMS

Out of the technology of the clockwork regulation of automata came the more general—and perhaps ultimately more important—technology of *process control.* As attested to in the descriptions of the mechanical ducks, some of the clockwork mechanisms had to control remarkably complicated actions on the part of the automata, not only *powering* them but *sequencing* them as well.

Control mechanisms evolved from early, simple devices—such as a lever attached to a wheel which converted circular motion into linear motion—to later, more complicated devices—such as whole sets of cams upon which would ride many interlinked mechanical arms, giving rise to extremely complicated automaton behaviors.

Eventually *programmable controllers* appeared, which incorporated such devices as interchangeable cams, or drums with movable pegs, with which one could program arbitrary sequences of actions on the part of the automaton. The writing and picture drawing automata of Figure 2, built by the Jaquet-Droz family, are examples of programmable automata. The introduction of such programmable controllers was one of the primary developments on the road to general purpose computers.

2.3 ABSTRACTION OF THE LOGICAL "FORM" OF MACHINES

During the early part of the 20 century, the formal application of logic to the mechanical process of arithmetic lead to the abstract formulation of a "procedure." The work of Church, Kleene, Gödel, Turing, and Post formalized the notion of a logical sequence of steps, leading to the realization that the essence of a mechanical process—the "thing" responsible for its dynamic behavior—is not a thing at all, but an abstract control structure, or "program"—a sequence of simple actions selected from a finite repertoire. Furthermore, it was recognized that the essential features of this control structure could be captured within an abstract set of rules—a formal specification—without regard to the material out of which the machine was constructed.

The "logical form" of a machine was separated from its material basis of construction, and it was found that "machineness" was a property of the former, not of the latter. Today, the formal equivalent of a "machine" is an *algorithm:* the logic underlying the dynamics of an automaton, regardless of the details of its material construction. We now have many formal methods for the specification and operation of abstract machines: such as programming languages, formal language theory, automata theory, recursive function theory, and etc. All of these have been shown to be logically equivalent.

Once we have learned to think of machines in terms of their abstract, formal specifications, we can turn around and view abstract, formal specifications as potential machines. In mapping the machines of our common experience to formal specifications, we have by no means exhausted the space of *possible* specifications. Indeed, most of our individual machines map to a very small subset of the space of specifications—a subset largely characterized by methodical, boring, uninteresting dynamics. When placed together in aggregates, however, even the simplest machines can participate in *extremely* complicated dynamics.

2.4 GENERAL PURPOSE COMPUTERS

Various threads of technological development—programmable controllers, calculating engines, and the formal theory of machines—have come together in the general purpose, stored program computer. Programmable computers are extremely general behavior generators. They have no intrinsic behavior of their own. Without programs, they are like formless matter. They must be told how to behave. By submitting a program to a computer—that is: by giving it a formal specification for a machine—we are telling it to behave as if it were the machine specified by the program. The computer then "emulates" that more specific machine in the performance of the desired task. Its great power lies in its plasticity of behavior. If we can provide a step-by-step specification for a specific kind of behavior, the chameleon-like computer will exhibit that behavior. Computers should be viewed as *second-order* machines—given the formal specification of a first-order machine, they will "become" that machine. Thus, the space of possible machines is directly available for study, at the cost of a mere formal description: computers "realize" abstract machines.

2.5 FORMAL LIMITS OF MACHINE BEHAVIORS

Although computers—and by extension other machines—are capable of exhibiting a bewilderingly wide variety of behaviors, we must face two fundamental limitations on the kinds of behaviors that we can expect of computers.

The first limitation is one of *computability in principle.* There are certain behaviors that are "uncomputable"—behaviors for which *no* formal specification can be given for a machine that will exhibit that behavior. The classic example of this sort of limitation is Turing's famous Halting Problem: can we give a formal specification for a machine which, when provided with the description of *any* other machine together with its initial state, will—by inspection alone—determine whether or not that machine will reach its halt state? Turing proved that no such machine can be specified. In particular, Turing showed that the best that such a proposed machine could do would be to emulate the given machine to see whether or not it halted. If the emulated machine halted, fine. However, the emulated machine might run forever before halting, and therefore the emulating machine could not answer whether or not it would halt. Rice and others have extended this undecideability result to the determination—by inspection alone—of *any* non-trivial property of the future behavior of an arbitrary machine.[2]

The second limitation is one of *computability in practice.* There are many behaviors for which we do not know how to specify a sequence of steps that will cause a computer to exhibit that behavior. We can automate what we can explain how to do, but there is much that we can not explain how to do. Thus, although a formal specification for a machine that will exhibit a certain behavior may be possible *in principle,* we have no formal procedure for producing that formal specification in practice, short of a trial and error search through the space of possible descriptions.

We need to separate the notion of a formal specification of a machine—that is: a specification of the *logical structure* of the machine—from the notion of a formal specification of a machine's behavior—that is: a specification of the sequence of transitions that the machine will undergo. We have formal systems for the former, but not for the latter. In general, we cannot derive behaviors from specifications nor can we derive specifications from behaviors.

The moral is: in order to determine the behavior of some machines, there is no recourse but to run them and see how they behave! This has consequences for the methods by which we (or nature) go about *generating* behavior generators themselves, which we will take up in the section on evolution.

2.6 JOHN VON NEUMANN: FROM MECHANICS TO LOGIC

With the development of the general purpose computer, various researchers turned their attention from the *mechanics* of life to the *logic* of life.

The first computational approach to the generation of lifelike behavior was due to the brilliant Hungarian mathematician John von Neumann. In the words of his colleague Arthur W. Burks, Von Neumann was interested in the general question:[3]

"What kind of logical organization is sufficient for an automaton to reproduce itself? This question is not precise and admits to trivial versions as well as interesting ones. Von Neumann had the familiar natural phenomenon of self-reproduction in mind when he posed it, but he was not trying to simulate the self-reproduction of a natural system at the level of genetics and biochemistry. *He wished to abstract from the natural self-reproduction problem its logical form.*"

This approach is the first to capture the essence of the Artificial Life approach. To understand the field of Artificial Life, one need only replace references to "self-reproduction" in the above with references to any other biological phenomenon.

In von Neumann's initial thought experiment (his "kinematic model"), a machine floats around on the surface of a pond, together with lots of machine parts. The machine is a *universal constructor:* given the description of any machine, it will locate the proper parts and construct that machine. If given a description of itself, it will construct itself. This is not quite self-reproduction, however, because the offspring machine will not have a description of itself and hence could not go on to construct another copy. So, von Neumann's machine also contains a *description copier:* once the offspring machine has been constructed, the "parent" machine constructs a copy of the description that it worked from and attaches it to the offspring machine. This constitutes genuine self-reproduction.

Von Neumann decided that this model did not properly distinguish the logical form of the process from the material of

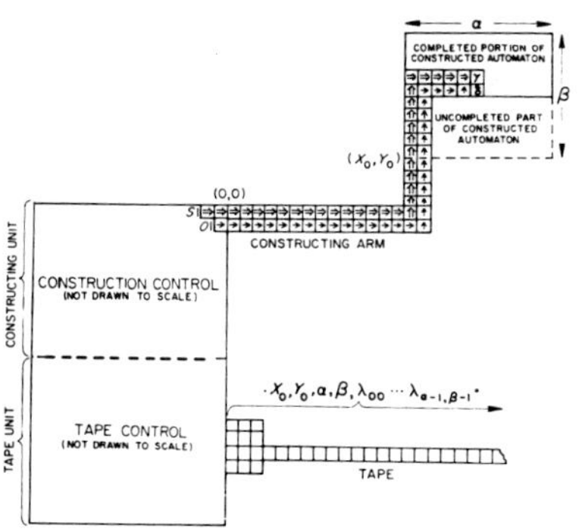

3

the process, and looked about for a completely formal system within which to model self-reproduction. Stan Ulam—one of von Neumann's colleagues at Los Alamos[4]—suggested an appropriate formalism, which has come to be known as a *cellular automaton* (CA).

In brief, a CA consists of a regular lattice of *finite automata*, which are the simplest formal models of machines. A finite automaton can be in only one of a finite number of states at any given time, and its transitions between states from one time step to the next are governed by a *state-transition table:* given a certain input and a certain internal state, the state-transition table specifies the state to be adopted by the finite automaton at the next time step. In a CA, the necessary input is derived from the states of the automata at neighboring lattice points. Thus, the state of an automaton at time **t+1** is a function of the states of the automaton itself and its immediate neighbors at time **t**. All of the automata in the lattice obey the same transition table and every automaton changes state at the same instant, time step after time step. CA's are good examples of the kind of computational paradigm sought after by Artificial Life: bottom-up, parallel, local-determination of behavior.

Von Neumann was able to embed the equivalent of his kinematic model as an initial pattern of state assignments within a large CA-lattice using 29 states per cell. Although von Neumann's work on self-reproducing automata was left incomplete at the time of his death, Arthur Burks organized what had been done, filled in the remaining details, and published it.Together with a transcription of von Neumann's 1949 lectures at the University of Illinois entitled "Theory and Organization of Complicated Automata," in which he gives his views on various problems related to the study of complex systems in general.[5] Figure 3 shows a schematic-diagram of von Neumann's self-reproducing machine.

Von Neumann's CA model was a constructive proof that an essential characteristic behavior of living things—self-reproduction—*was* achievable by machines. Furthermore, he determined that any such method must make use of the information contained in the description of the machine in two fundamentally different ways:

Interpreted, as instructions to be executed in the construction of the offspring.

Uninterpreted, as passive data to be duplicated to form the description given to the offspring.

Of course, when Watson and Crick unveiled the structure of DNA, they discovered that the information contained therein was used in precisely these two ways in the processes of transcription/translation and replication.

In describing his model, von Neumann pointed out that:[6] "By axiomatizing automata in this manner, one has thrown half of the problem out the window, and it may be the more important half. One has resigned oneself not to explain how these parts are made up of real things, specifically, how these parts are made up of actual elementary particles, or even of higher chemical molecules."

Whether or not the more important half of the question has been disposed of depends on the questions we are asking. If we are concerned with explaining how the life that we know emerges from the known laws of physics and organic-chemistry, then indeed the interesting part has been tossed out. However, if we are concerned with the more general problem of explaining how life-like behaviors emerge out of low-level interactions within a population of logical primitives, we have retained the more interesting portion of the question.

2.7 LESSONS FROM HISTORY

As stated at the beginning of this section, throughout history, we have repeatedly tried to map our contemporary technology onto nature in an attempt to understand natural phenomena. Sometimes this has been successful, but in the case of both life and intelligence, such mappings have not provided satisfactory explanations. There is a lesson here: although Artificial Life uses computers as its primary tool for the synthesis of biological phenomena, we not mistake the tool for the object under study and attempt to characterize life as a "computation." If we are able to bring life to computers, this will not be because life "is" a computation, at least as we now understand the term "computation." Rather, it will be because computers have some fundamental properties that will allow them to be organized in such a way that they can become alive. It is quite likely that we will learn more about computation by studying life than we will learn about life by studying computation. This will be taken up in more detail in the following section.

It is also important to note that in the control programs of early automata we see the roots of what Mitchell Resnick has called the "centralized mindset:" the attribution to natural phenomena of a central controller that is ultimately responsible for their behavior. It is a mindset that has dominated most of our scientific, philosophical, and even religious thought for the last several centuries. In contrast, Resnick refers to the kind of approach advocated by Artificial Life as the "distributed mindset." The difference is crucial, since most of nature chugs along in the absence of any central controllers. In order to understand most of nature, therefore, we must abandon the centralized mindset and come to an understanding of the dynamics of distributed systems *qua* distributed systems.

3 THE ROLE OF COMPUTERS IN STUDYING LIFE AND OTHER COMPLEX SYSTEMS

Artificial Intelligence and Artificial Life are each concerned with the application of computers to the study of complex, natural phenomena. Both are concerned with generating complex behavior. However, the manner in which each field employs the technology of computation in the pursuit of its respective goals is strikingly different.

AI has based its underlying methodology for generating intelligent behavior on the computational paradigm. That is, AI has adopted the centralized control architecture of serial, "von Neumann" style computation as a model of intelligence. AL, on the other hand, is attempting to develop a new computational paradigm based on the distributed processes that support living organisms. That is, AL uses insights from biology to explore the dynamics of interacting information structures. AL has not adopted the computational paradigm as its underlying methodology of behavior generation, nor does it attempt to "explain" life as a "computation."

One way to pursue the study of artificial life would be to attempt to create life *in-vitro*, using the same kinds of organic chemicals out of which we are constituted. Indeed, there are numerous exciting efforts in this direction. This would certainly teach us a lot about the possibilities for alternative lifeforms *within* the carbon-chain chemistry domain that could have (but didn't) evolve here.

However, biomolecules are extremely small and difficult to work with, requiring rooms full of special equipment, replete with dozens of "post-docs" and graduate students willing to devote the larger part of their professional careers to the perfection of electrophoretic gel techniques. Besides, although the creation of life *in-vitro* would certainly be a scientific feat worthy of note—and probably even a Nobel prize—it would not, in the long run, tell us much more about the space of possible life than we already know.

Computers provide an alternative medium within which to attempt to synthesize life. Modern computer technology has resulted in machinery with tremendous potential for the creation of life *in-silico*.

Computers should be thought of as an important laboratory

tool for the study of life, substituting for the array of incubators, culture dishes, microscopes, electrophoretic gels, pipettes, centrifuges and other assorted wet-lab paraphernalia, one simple-to-master piece of experimental equipment devoted exclusively to the incubation of information structures.

The advantage of working with information structures is that information has no intrinsic size. The computer is *the* tool for the manipulation of information, whether that manipulation is a consequence of our actions or a consequence of the actions of the information structures themselves. Computers themselves will not be alive, rather they will support informational universes within which dynamic populations of informational "molecules" engage in informational "biochemistry." This view of computers as workstations for performing scientific experiments within artificial universes is fairly new, but it is rapidly becoming accepted as a legitimate—even necessary—way of pursuing science. In the days before computers, scientists worked primarily with systems whose defining equations could be solved analytically, and ignored those whose defining equations could *not* be so solved. This was largely the case because, in the absence of analytic solutions, the equations would have to be integrated over and over again—essentially simulating the time-behavior of the system. Without computers to handle the mundane details of these calculations, such an undertaking was unthinkable except in the simplest cases.

However, with the advent of computers, the necessary mundane calculations can be relegated to these idiot-savants, and the realm of numerical simulation is opened up for exploration. "Exploration" is an appropriate term for the process, because the numerical simulation of systems allows one to "explore" the system's behavior under a wide range of parameter settings and initial conditions. The heuristic value of this kind of experimentation cannot be over-estimated. One often gains tremendous insight for the essential dynamics of a system by observing its behavior under a wide range of initial conditions.

Most importantly, however, computers are beginning to provide scientists with a new paradigm for modeling the world. When dealing with essentially un-solvable governing equations, the primary reason for producing a formal mathematical model—the hope of reaching an analytic solution by symbolic manipulation—is lost. Systems of ordinary and partial differential equations are not very well suited for implementation as computer algorithms. One might expect that other modeling technologies would be more appropriate when the goal is the *synthesis*, rather than the *analysis*, of behavior.[7]

This expectation is easily borne out. With the precipitous drop in the cost of raw computing power, computers are now available that are capable of simulating physical systems from first principles. This means that it has become possible, for example, to model turbulent flow in a fluid by simulating the motions of its constituent particles—not just approximating *changes* in concentrations of particles within regions of the fluid, but actually computing their motions exactly.[8]

There is an extremely important point here, one that involves the ultimate goals of the scientific enterprise as well as the issue of "centralized" Vs "distributed" mindsets. The point is the following. There is a fundamental difference between being able to describe or predict phenomena on the one hand and "explaining" them on the other hand. One can use Navier-Stokes equations to describe or predict fluid flows in many cases, *but fluids are not calculating Navier-Stokes equations!* The descriptive and predictive power of the Navier-Stokes approach is useful, but the phenomena of fluid flow is actually generated by quite different mechanisms. Physics has largely been considered successful when it has been able to produce a predictive, abstract description of a physical phenomenon, one that generally ignores the low level mechanisms by which the phenomenon is actually generated. This is a benefit of adopting the centralized mindset, and it is very useful to be able to do this whenever possible.

However, *for most natural phenomena, there is probably no simpler description than the generative mechanisms themselves.* In these circumstances, adopting the distributed mindset is necessary. Note that just because we cannot provide an abstract, high-level predictive description of a phenomenon does not mean that we have failed to provide a scientific description, a low-level description may be "as scientific" as we can get concerning the phenomenon. Even when a simpler, high level description is possible, it is important to keep in mind the difference between the description of a process and an understanding of the mechanisms by which it is generated.

What does all of this have to do with the study of life? The most surprising lesson we have learned from simulating complex physical systems on computers is that *complex behavior need not have complex roots.* Indeed, tremendously interesting and beguilingly complex behavior can emerge from collections of relatively simple components. This leads directly to the exciting possibility that much of the complex behavior exhibited by nature—especially the complex behavior that we call life—*also* has simple generators. Since it

is very hard to work backwards from a complex behavior to its generator, but very simple to create generators and synthesize complex behavior, a promising approach to the study of complex natural systems is to undertake the general study of the kinds of behavior that can emerge from aggregates of simple components (Figure 4).
Another surprising lesson is that *a distributed system can behave as if it had a central controller when in fact it does not.* Computers, especially parallel computers, allow us to adopt Resnick's "distributed mindset" in our studies of Nature. Before computers, it was extremely difficult to come to an understanding of how complex behavior could emerge in the absence of a central controller, which is why the "centralized mindset" dominated the study of Nature for so long. With computers, however, the capacity to build distributed models provides us with the necessary tools for experimenting with the dynamics of distributed systems, and it is becoming apparent that the most interestingly complex behaviors in Nature owe their complexity in part to their distributed, noncentralized architecture.

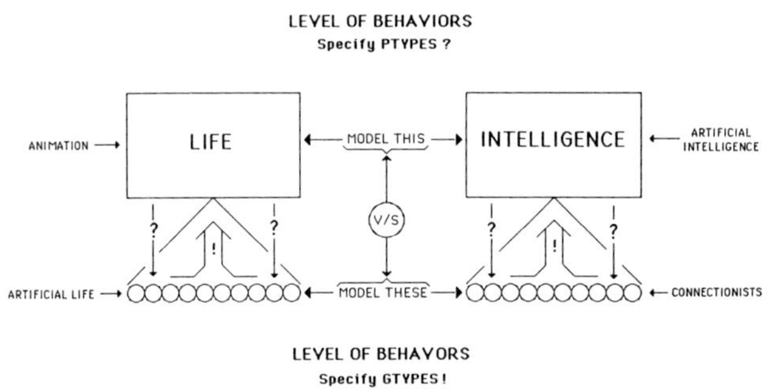

4

4 NON LINEARITY AND LOCAL DETERMINATION OF BEHAVIOR.

4.1 LINEAR VS. NONLINEAR SYSTEMS

As mentioned briefly above, the distinction between linear and nonlinear systems is fundamental, and provides excellent insight into why the principles underlying the dynamics of life should be so hard to discover. The simplest way to state the distinction is to say that *linear systems* are those for which the behavior of the whole is just the sum of the behavior of its parts, while for *nonlinear systems*, the behavior of the whole is *more* than the sum of its parts.

Linear systems are those which obey the *principle of superposition.* We can break up complicated linear systems into simpler constituent parts, and analyze these parts *independently.* Once we have reached an understanding of the parts in isolation, we can achieve a full understanding of the whole system by *composing* our understandings of the isolated parts. This is the key feature of linear systems: by studying the parts in isolation, we can learn everything we need to know about the complete system.

This is not possible for nonlinear systems, which do *not* obey the principle of superposition . Even if we can break such systems up into simpler constituent parts, and even if we can reach a complete understanding of the parts in isolation, we would not be able to compose our understandings of the individual parts into an understanding of the whole system. The key feature of nonlinear systems is that their primary behaviors of interest are properties of the *interactions between parts,* rather than being properties of the parts themselves, and these interaction-based properties necessarily disappear when the parts are studied independently.

The process that we call "life" is a fundamentally nonlinear process, emerging out of interactions between non-living parts. Life is a property of *form,* not *matter,* a result of the organization of matter rather than something that inheres in the matter itself. Neither nucleotides nor amino acids nor any other carbon-chain molecule is alive—yet put them together in the right way, and the dynamic behavior that emerges out of their interactions is what we call life. It is effects, not things, upon which life is based—life is a kind of behavior, not a kind of stuff—and as such, it is constituted of simpler behaviors, not simpler stuff.

Thus, analysis is most fruitfully applied to linear systems. Such systems can be taken apart in meaningful ways, the resulting pieces solved, and the solutions obtained from solving the pieces can be put back together in such a way that one has a solution for the whole system.

Analysis has not proved anywhere near as effective when applied to nonlinear systems: the nonlinear system must be treated as a whole.

A different approach to the study of nonlinear systems involves the inverse of analysis: *synthesis.* Rather than start with the behavior of interest and attempting to analyze it into its constituent parts, we start with constituent parts and put them together in the attempt to synthesize the behavior of interest. Analysis is most appropriate for the understanding of linear systems, synthesis is the most appropriate for the understanding of nonlinear systems.

4.2 THE PARSIMONY OF LOCAL-DETERMINATION OF BEHAVIOR

It is easier to generate complex behavior from the application of simple, *local* rules than it is to generate complex behavior from the application of complex, *global* rules. This is because complex global behavior is usually due to nonlinear interactions occurring at the local level. With bottom-up specifications, the system computes the local, nonlinear interactions explicitly and the global behavior—which was implicit in the local rules—emerges spontaneously without being treated explicitly.

With top-down specifications, however, local behavior must be implicit in global rules—this is really putting the cart before the horse! The global rules must "predict" the effects on global structure of many local, nonlinear interactions—something which we have seen is intractable, even impossible, in the general case. Thus, top-down systems must take computational shortcuts and explicitly deal with special cases, which results in inflexible, brittle, and un-natural behavior.

Furthermore, in a system of any complexity the number of possible global states is astronomically enormous, and grows exponentially with the size of the system. Systems that attempt to supply *global* rules for *global* behavior simply cannot provide a different rule for every global state. Thus, the global states must be classified in some manner; categorized using a coarse-graining scheme according to which the global states within a category are indistinguishable. The rules of the system can only be applied at the level of resolution of these categories. There are many possible ways to implement a classification scheme, most of which will yield different partitionings of the global state-space. Any rule based system must necessarily assume that finer-grained differences don't matter, or must include a finite set of tests for "special-cases," and then must assume that no other special cases are relevant.

For most complex systems, however, fine differences in global state can result in enormous differences in global behavior, and there may be no way in principle to partition the space of global states in such a way that specific fine-differences have the appropriate global impact.

On the other hand, systems that supply *local* rules for *local* behaviors, *can* provide a different rule for each and every possible local state. Furthermore, the size of the local-state-space can be completely independent of the size of the system. In local-rule governed systems, each local state, and consequently the global state, can be determined exactly and precisely. Fine differences in global-state will result in very specific differences in local-state, and consequently will affect the invocation of local rules. As fine differences affect local behavior, the difference will be felt in an expanding patch of local-states, and in this manner—propagating from local neighborhood to local neighborhood—fine differences in global state can result in large differences in global behavior. The only "special-cases" explicitly dealt with in locally-determined systems are exactly the set of all possible local states, and the rules for these are just exactly the set of all local rules governing the system

5 ABSTRACTING THE "BIO-LOGIC" OF BIOLOGY

Organisms have been compared to extremely complicated and finely tuned biochemical machines. Since we have seen that it is often possible to abstract the logical form of a machine from its physical hardware, it is natural to ask whether it is possible to abstract the logical from of an organism from its biochemical wetware. The field of Artificial Life is devoted to the investigation of this question.

In the following sections we will look at the manner in which behavior is generated in bottom-up fashion in living systems. We then generalize the mechanisms by which this behavior generation is accomplished, so that we may apply them to the task of generating behavior in artificial systems. We will find that the essential machinery of living organisms is quite a bit different from the machinery of our own invention, and we would be quite mistaken to attempt to force our pre-conceived notions of abstract machines onto the machinery of life. The difference, once again, lies in the exceedingly parallel and distributed nature of the operation of the machinery of life, as contrasted with the singularly serial and centralized control structures associated with the machines of our invention.

5.1 GENOTYPES AND PHENOTYPES

The most salient characteristic of living systems, from the behavior generation point of view, is the *genotype/phenotype* distinction. The distinction is essentially one between a specification of machinery—the genotype—and the behavior of that machinery—the phenotype.

The *genotype* is the complete set of genetic instructions encoded in the linear sequence of nucleotide bases that makes up an organism's DNA. The *phenotype* is the physical organism itself—the structures that emerge in space and time as the result of the interpretation of the genotype in the context of a particular environment. The process by which the phenotype develops through time under the direction of the genotype is called morphogenesis}. The individual genetic instructions are called *genes*, and consist of short stretches of DNA. These instructions are "executed"—or*expressed*—when their DNA sequence is used as a template for transcription. In the case of protein synthesis, transcription results in a duplicate nucleotide strand known as a *messenger RNA*—or *mRNA*—constructed by the process of base-pairing. This mRNA strand may then be modified in various ways before it makes its way out to the cytoplasm where, at bodies known as *ribosomes*, it serves as a template for the construction of a linear chain of *amino acids*. The resulting *polypeptide chain* will fold up on itself in a complex manner, forming a tightly packed molecule known as a *protein*. The finished protein detaches from the ribosome and may go on to serve as a passive structural element in the cell, or may have a more active role as an *enzyme*. Enzymes are *the* functional molecular "operators" in the logic of life.

One may consider the genotype as a largely unordered "bag" of instructions, each one of which is essentially the specification for a "machine" of some sort—passive or active. When instantiated, each such "machine" will enter into the ongoing logical "fray" in the cytoplasm, consisting largely of local interactions between other such machines. Each such instruction will be "executed" when its own triggering conditions are met and will have specific, local effects on structures in the cell. Furthermore, each such instruction will operate within the context of all of the other instructions that have been—or are being—executed.

The phenotype, then, consists of the structures and dynamics that emerge through time in the course of the execution of the parallel, distributed "computation" controlled by this genetic "bag" of instructions. Since gene's interactions with one another are highly nonlinear, the phenotype is a nonlinear function of the genotype.

5.2 GENERALIZED GENOTYPES AND PHENOTYPES

In the context of artificial life, we need to generalize the notions of *genotype* and *phenotype*, so that we may apply them in non-biological situations. We will use the term *generalized-genotype* — or GTYPE—to refer to any largely unordered set of low-level rules, and we will use the term *generalized-phenotype* —or PTYPE—to refer to the behaviors

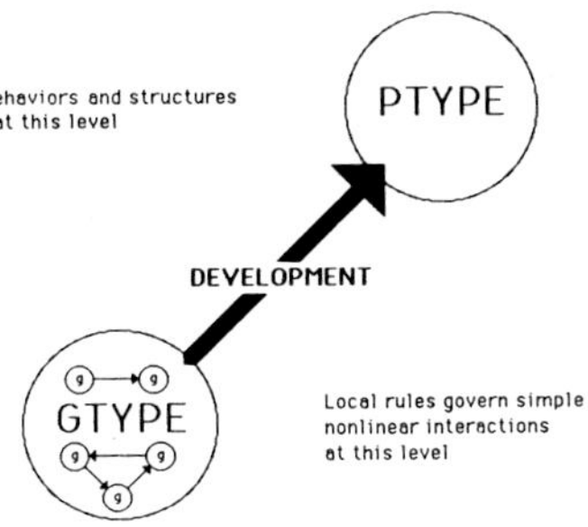

5

and/or structures that emerge out of the interactions among these low-level rules when they are activated within the context of a specific environment. The GTYPE, essentially, is the specification for a set of machines, while the PTYPE is the behavior that results as the machines are executed and interact with one another.

This is the bottom-up approach to the generation of behavior. A set of entities is defined and each entity is endowed with a specification for a simple behavioral repertoire—a GTYPE—that contains instructions which detail its reactions to a wide range of *local* encounters with other such entities or with specific features of the environment. Nowhere is the behavior of the set of entities as a whole specified. The global behavior of the aggregate—the PTYPE—emerges out of the collective interactions among individual entities.

It should be noted that the PTYPE is a multi-level phenomenon. First, there is the PTYPE associated with each particular instruction—the effect that instruction has on an entity's behavior when it is expressed. Second, there is the PTYPE associated with each individual entity—its individual behavior within the aggregate. Third, there is the PTYPE associated with the behavior of the aggregate as a whole.

This is true for natural systems as well. We can talk about the phenotypic trait associated with a particular gene, we can identify the phenotype of an individual cell, and we can identify the phenotype of an entire multi-cellular organism—its body, in effect. PTYPES *should* be complex and multi-level. If we want to simulate life, we should expect to see hierarchical structures emerge in our simulations. In general, phenotypic traits at the level of the whole organism will be the result of many nonlinear interactions between genes, and there will be no single gene to which one can assign responsibility for the vast majority of phenotypic traits.

In summary, GTYPES are low-level rules for behav*ors*—i.e., abstract specifications for "machines"—which will engage in local interactions within a large aggregate of other such behavors. PTYPES are the behav*iors*—the structures in time and space—that *develop* out of these nonlinear, local interactions (Figure 5).

5.3 UNPREDICTABILITY OF PTYPE FROM GTYPE

Nonlinear interactions between the objects specified by the GTYPE provide the basis for an extremely rich variety of possible PTYPES. PTYPES draw on the full combinatorial potential implicit in the set of possible interactions between low-level rules. The other side of the coin, however, is that, in general, we cannot predict the PTYPES that will emerge from specific GTYPES, due to the general unpredictability of nonlinear systems. If we wish to maintain the property of predictability, then we must restrict severely the nonlinear dependence of PTYPE on GTYPE, but this forces us to give up the combinatorial richness of possible PTYPES, which depends critically on nonlinear interactions. Therefore, a trade-off exists between behaviorally rich but essentially unpredictable nonlinear systems on the one hand, and behaviorally restricted but predictable (and therefore "programmable") linear systems on the other. We shall see in the section on Evolution that the lack of programmability is adequately compensated for by the increased capacity for adaptiveness provided by the rich behavioral repertoire of nonlinear systems.

As discussed previously, we know that it is impossible in the general case to determine nontrivial properties of the future behavior of a sufficiently powerful computer from a mere inspection of its program and its initial state alone.[9] A Turing machine—the formal equivalent of a general purpose computer—can be captured within the scheme of GTYPE/PTYPE systems by identifying the machine's transition table as the GTYPE and the resulting computation as the PTYPE. From this we can deduce that in the general case it will not be possible to determine, by inspection alone, nontrivial features of the PTYPE that will emerge from a given GTYPE in the context of a particular initial configuration. In general, the only way to find out anything about the PTYPE is to start the system up and watch what happens as the PTYPE develops under control of the GTYPE and the environment.

Similarly, it is not possible in the general case to determine what specific alterations must be made to a GTYPE to effect a desired change in the PTYPE. The problem is that any specific PTYPE trait is, in general, an effect of many, many nonlinear interactions between the behavioral primitives of the system (an "epistatic trait" in biological terms.) Consequently, given an arbitrary proposed change to the PTYPE, it may be impossible to determine by any formal procedure exactly what changes would have to be made to the GTYPE to effect that—and *only* that—change in the PTYPE. It is not a practically computable problem. There is no way to calculate the answer—short of exhaustive search—*even though there may be an answer!* An example from biology would be: What changes would have to be made to the Human genome in order to produce six fingers on each hand rather than five?

The only way to proceed in the face of such an unpredictability result is by a process of trial and error. However, some processes of trial and error are more efficient than others. In natural systems, trial and error are interlinked in such a way that error guides the choice of trials under the process of evolution by natural selection. It is quite likely that this is the *only* efficient, *general* procedure that could find GTYPES with specific PTYPE traits when nonlinear functions are involved.

6 RECURSIVELY GENERATED OBJECTS

In the previous section, we described the distinction between genotype and phenotype, and we introduced their generalizations in the form of GTYPE's and PTYPE's. In this section, we will review a general approach to building GTYPE/PTYPE systems based on the methodology of *recursively generated objects.*

A major appeal of this approach is that it arises naturally from the GTYPE/PTYPE distinction: the local developmental rules (the recursive description itself) constitute the GTYPE, and the developing structure—the recursively generated object or behavior itself—constitutes the PTYPE.

Under the methodology of recursively generated objects, the "object" is a structure that has sub-parts. The rules of the system specify how to modify the most elementary, "atomic" sub-parts, and are usually sensitive to the *context* in which these atomic sub-parts are embedded. That is, the "neighborhood" of an atomic sub-part is taken into account in determining which rule to apply in order to modify that sub-part. It is usually the case that there are no rules in the system whose context is the entire structure; that is, there is no use made of *global* information. Each piece is modified solely on the basis of its own state and the state of the pieces "nearby".

A recursively generated object, then, is a kind of PTYPE, and the recursive description that generates it is a kind of GTYPE. The PTYPE will emerge under the action of the GTYPE, developing through time via a process of morphogenesis.

We will illustrate the notion of recursively generated objects with examples taken from the literature on L-Systems, cellular automata, and computer animation.

6.1 EXAMPLE 1: LINDENMAYER SYSTEMS

Lindenmayer Systems (L-Systems) consist of sets of rules for rewriting strings of symbols, and bear strong relationships to the formal grammars treated by Chomsky. We will give several examples of L-Systems illustrating the methodology of recursively generated objects.[10]

In the following "**X Æ Y**" means that one replaces every occurrence of symbol "**X**" in the structure with string "**Y**". Since the symbol "**X**" may appear on the right as well as the left sides of some rules, the set of rules can be applied "recursively" to the newly re-written structures. The process can be continued ad-infinitum although some sets of rules will result in a final "fixed-point" configuration in which no more changes will occur.

6.1.1 SIMPLE LINEAR GROWTH

Here is an example of the simplest kind of L-system. The rules are *context free*, meaning that the context in which a particular part is situated is not considered when altering it. There must be only one rule per part if the system is to be deterministic.
The rules: (the "recursive description" or GTYPE):
1) A Æ CB
2) B **Æ A**
3) C **Æ DA**
4) D **Æ C**
When applied to the initial seed structure "**A**", the following structural history develops (each successive line is a successive time step):
time structure rules applied (L to R)
0 **A** (initial "seed")
1 **C B** (rule 1 replaces **A** with **CB**)
2 **D A A** (rule 3 replaces **C** with **DA** & rule 2 replaces **B** with **A**)
3 **C C B C B** (rule 4 replaces **D** with **C** & rule 1 replaces the two
4 ...(etc.)... **A**'s with **CB**'s)
And so forth.
The "PTYPE" that emerges from this kind of recursive application of a simple, local rewriting rule can get extremely complex. These kinds of grammars (whose rules replace single symbols) have been shown to be equivalent to the operation of finite state machines. With appropriate restrictions, they are also equivalent to the "regular languages" defined by Chomsky.

6.1.2 BRANCHING GROWTH

L-Systems incorporate meta-symbols to represent branching points, allowing a new line of symbols to branch off from the main "stem".The following grammar produces branching structures. The "(~)" and "[~]" notations indicate left and right branches, respectively, and the strings within them in-

dicate the structure of the branches themselves.
The rules—or GTYPE:
1) A Æ C[B]D
2) B **Æ A**
3) C **Æ C**
4) D **Æ C(E)A**
5) E **Æ D**
When applied to the starting structure "**A**", the following sequence develops (using linear notation):
time structure rules applied (L to R)
0 **A** initial "seed".
1 **C[B]D** rule 1.
2 **C[A]C(E)A** rules 3,2,4.
3 **C[C[B]D]C(D)C[B]D** rules 3,1,3,5,1.
4 **C[C[A]C(E)A]C(C(E)A)C[A]C(E)A** rules 3,3,2,4,3,4,3,2,4. .
In two dimensions, the structure develops as follows:
|/ |/
\ | \ | /
E A **D C D**
\ | \ | /_**B**_ Æ (etc.)
| / | / | /
D B C A Æ **C C**
|/ Æ |/ |/
| | | |
A Æ **C C C**
| | | |
t = 0 1 2 3 ...and so on...
Note that at each step, *every symbol is replaced,* even if just by another copy of itself. This allows all kinds of complex phenomena, such as signal propagation along the structure, which will be demonstrated in the next example.

6.1.3 SIGNAL PROPAGATION

In order to propagate signals along a structure, one must have something more than just a single symbol on the left-hand side of a rule. By allowing more than one symbol on the left hand side, the rules can be made *context-sensitive*—i.e., the "context" within which a symbol occurs (the symbols next to it) are important in determining what the replacement string will be. The next example illustrates why this is critical for signal propagation.
In the following example, the symbol in "{ }" is the symbol (or string of symbols) to be replaced, the rest of the left-hand side is the context, and the symbols "**[**" and "**]**" indicate the left and right ends of the string, respectively.
Suppose the rule set contains the following rules:

1) **[{C} Æ C** a "**C**" at the left-end of the string remains a "**C**".
2) **C{C} Æ C** a "**C**" with a "**C**" to its left remains a "**C**".
3) ***{C} Æ *** a "**C**" with an "*" to its left becomes an "*".
4) **{*}C Æ C** an "*" with a "**C**" to its right becomes a "**C**".
5) **{*}] Æ *** an "*" at the right end of the string remains an "*".

Under these rules, the initial structure "***CCCCCCC**" will result in the "*" being propagated to the right, as follows:

time structure
0 ***CCCCCCC**
1 **C*CCCCCC**
2 **CC*CCCCC**
3 **CCC*CCCC**
4 **CCCC*CCC**
5 **CCCCC*CC**
6 **CCCCCC*C**
7 **CCCCCCC***

This would not be possible without taking the "context" of a symbol into account. In general, these kinds of grammars are equivalent to Chomsky's "context-sensitive" or "Turing" languages, depending on whether or not there are any restrictions on the kinds of strings on the left and right hand sides.
The capacity for signal propagation is extremely important, for it allows arbitrary computational processes to be embedded within the structure, which may directly affect the structure's development. The next example demonstrates how embedded computation can affect development.

6.2 EXAMPLE 2: CELLULAR AUTOMATA

Cellular automata (CA) provide another example of the recursive application of a simple set of rules to a structure. In a CA, the structure that is being updated is the entire universe: a lattice of finite-automata. The local rule set—the GTYPE—in this case is the transition function obeyed homogeneously by every automaton in the lattice. The local context taken into account in updating the state of each automaton is the state of the automata in its immediate neighborhood. The transition function for the automata constitutes a *local* physics for a simple, discrete space/time universe. The universe is updated by applying the local physics to each local "cell" of its structure over and over again. Thus, although the physical structure itself doesn't develop over time, its *state* does. Within such universes, one can embed all manner of processes, relying on the context-sensitivity of the rules to local neighborhood conditions to propagate information around within the universe "meaningfully". In particular, one can embed general purpose computers. Since these computers are simply particular configurations of states within the lattice of automata, *they can compute over the very set of symbols out of which they are constructed.* Thus, structures in this universe can compute and construct other structures, which also may compute and construct.

For example, here is a simple structure that can reproduce itself:

```
  2 2 2 2 2 2 2 2
2 1 7 0 1 4 0 1 4 2
2 0 2 2 2 2 2 2 0 2
2 1 2         2 1 2
2 0 2         2 1 2
2 7 2         2 1 2
2 1 2 2 2 2 2 2 1 2 2 2 2 2
2 0 7 1 0 7 1 0 7 1 1 1 1 1 2
  2 2 2 2 2 2 2 2 2 2 2 2 2
```

Each number is the state of one of the automata in the lattice. Blank space is presumed to be in state "**0**". The "**2**"-states form a sheath around the "**1**"-state data-path. The "**7 0**" and "**4 0**" state pairs constitute signals embedded within the data-path. They will propagate counter-clockwise around the loop, cloning off copies which propagate down the extended tail as they pass the T-junction between loop and tail. When the signals reach the end of the tail, they have the following effects: each "**7 0**" signal extends the tail by one unit, and the two "**4 0**" signals construct a left-hand corner at the end of the tail. Thus, for each full cycle of the instructions around the loop, another side and corner of an "offspring-loop" will be constructed. When the tail finally runs into itself after four cycles, the collision of signals results in the disconnection of the two loops as well as the construction of a tail on each of the loops.

After 151 time steps, this system will evolve to the following configuration:

```
                2
              2 1 2
              2 7 2
              2 0 2
              2 1 2
  2 2 2 2 2 2 2 7 2     2 2 2 2 2 2 2 2
2 1 1 1 7 0 1 7 0 2   2 1 7 0 1 4 0 1 4 2
2 1 2 2 2 2 2 2 1 2   2 0 2 2 2 2 2 2 0 2
2 1 2         2 7 2   2 7 2         2 1 2
2 1 2         2 0 2   2 1 2         2 1 2
2 4 2         2 1 2   2 0 2         2 1 2
2 1 2         2 7 2   2 7 2         2 1 2
2 0 2 2 2 2 2 2 0 2   2 1 2 2 2 2 2 2 1 2 2 2 2 2
2 4 1 0 7 1 0 7 1 2   2 0 7 1 0 7 1 0 7 1 1 1 1 1 2
  2 2 2 2 2 2 2 2       2 2 2 2 2 2 2 2 2 2 2 2 2
```

Thus, the initial configuration has succeeded in reproducing itself.

Each of these loops will go on to reproduce itself in a similar manner, giving rise to an expanding *colony* of loops, growing out into the array.

These embedded self-reproducing loops are the result of the recursive application of a rule to a seed structure. In this case, the primary rule that is being recursively applied constitutes the "physics" of the universe. The initial state of the loop itself constitutes a little "computer" under the recursively applied physics of the universe: a computer whose program causes it to construct a copy of itself. The "program" within the loop computer is also applied recursively to the growing structure. Thus, this system really involves a double level of recursively applied rules. The mechanics of applying one recursive rule within a universe whose physics is governed by another recursive rule had to be worked out by trial and error. This system makes use of the signal propagation capacity to embed a structure that itself *computes* the resulting structure, rather than having the "physics" directly responsible for developing the final structure from a passive seed.

This captures the flavor of what goes on in natural biological development: the genotype codes for the constituents of a dynamic process in the cell, and it is this dynamic process that is primarily responsible for mediating—or "computing"—the expression of the genotype in the course of development.

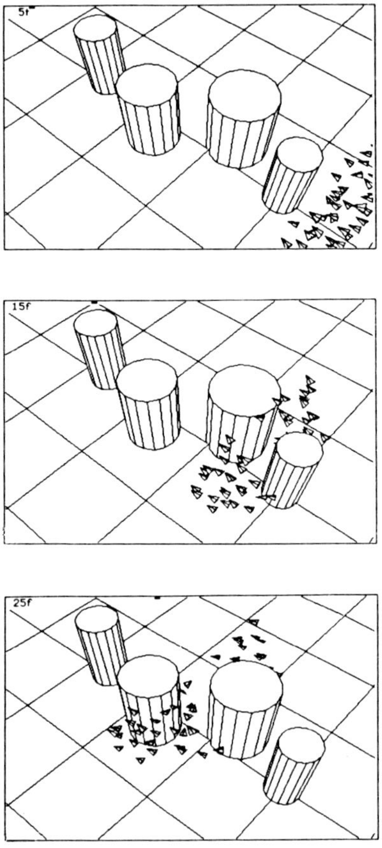

6

6.3 EXAMPLE 3: FLOCKING "BOIDS"

The previous examples were largely concerned with the growth and development of *structural* PTYPES. Here, we give an example of the development of a *behavioral* PTYPE.

Craig Reynolds has implemented a simulation of flocking behavior.[11] In this model—which is meant to be a general platform for studying the qualitatively similar phenomena of flocking, herding, and schooling—one has a large collection of autonomous but interacting objects (which Reynolds refers to as "Boids"), inhabiting a common simulated environment.

The modeler can specify the manner in which the individual Boids will respond to *local* events or conditions. The global behavior of the aggregate of Boids is strictly an emergent phenomenon, none of the rules for the individual Boids depend on global information, and the only updating of the global state is done on the basis of individual Boids responding to local conditions.

6

Each Boid in the aggregate shares the same behavioral "tendencies":

to maintain a minimum distance from other objects in the environment, including other Boids,

to match velocities with Boids in its neighborhood,

to move toward the perceived center of mass of the Boids in its neighborhood.

These are the only rules governing the behavior of the aggregate.

These rules, then, constitute the generalized-genotype (GTYPE) of the Boids system. They say nothing about structure, or growth and development, but they determine the behavior of a set of interacting objects, out of which very natural motion emerges.

With the right settings for the parameters of the system, a collection of Boids released at random positions within a volume will collect into a dynamic flock, which flies around environmental obstacles in a very fluid and natural manner, occasionally breaking up into sub-flocks as the flock flows around both sides of an obstacle. Once broken up into sub-flocks, the sub-flocks re-organize around their own, now distinct and isolated, centers of mass, only to re-merge into a single flock again when both sub-flocks emerge at the far-side of the obstacle and each sub-flock feels anew the "mass" of the other sub-flock (Figure 6).

The flocking behavior itself constitutes the generalized-phenotype (PTYPE) of the Boids system. It bears the same relation to the GTYPE as an organism's morphological phenotype bears to its molecular genotype. The same distinction between the *specification* of machinery and the *behavior* of machinery is evident.

6.4 DISCUSSION OF EXAMPLES

In all of the above examples, the recursive rules apply to *local structures* only, and the PTYPE—structural or behavioral—that results at the global level emerges from out of all of the local activity taken collectively. Nowhere in the system are there rules for the behavior of the system at the global level. This is a much more powerful and simple approach to the generation of complex behavior than that typically taken in AI, for instance, where "expert systems" attempt to provide global rules for global behavior. Recursive, "bottom up" specifications yield much more natural, fluid, and flexible behavior at the global level than typical "top-down" specifications, and they do so *much* more parsimoniously.

6.4.1 IMPORTANCE OF CONTEXT SENSITIVITY.

It is worthwhile to note that *context-sensitive* rules in GTYPE/PTYPE systems provide the possibility for nonlinear interactions among the parts. Without context-sensitivity, the systems would be linearly decomposable, information could not "flow" throughout the system in any meaningful manner, and complex long-range dependencies between remote parts of the structures could not develop.

6.4.2 FEEDBACK BETWEEN THE LOCAL AND THE GLOBAL LEVELS.

There is also a very important feedback mechanism *between* levels in such systems: the interactions among the low-level entities give rise to the global level dynamics which, in turn, affects the lower-levels by *setting the local context* within which each entity's rules are invoked. Thus, local behavior supports global dynamics, which shapes local context, which affects local behavior, which supports global dynamics, and so forth.

6.5 GENUINE LIFE IN ARTIFICIAL SYSTEMS.

It is important to distinguish the ontological status of the various levels of behavior in such systems. At the level of the individual behav*ors*, we have a clear difference in kind: Boids are *not* birds, they are not even remotely like birds, they have no cohesive physical structure, but rather exist as information structures— processes—within a computer. But—and this is *the* critical "But"—at the level of behav*iors*, *flocking Boids and flocking birds are two instances of the same phenomenon:* **flocking**.

The behavior of a flock as a whole does not depend critically on the internal details of the entities of which it is constituted—only on the details of the way in which these entities behave in each other's presence. Thus, flocking in Boids is true flocking, and may be counted as another empirical data point in the study of flocking behavior in general, right up there with flocks of geese and flocks of starlings.

This is *not* to say that flocking Boids capture *all* the nuances upon which flocking behavior depends, or that the Boid's behavioral repertoire is sufficient to exhibit all the different modes of flocking that have been observed—such as the classic "V" formation of flocking geese. The crucial point is that we have captured—within an aggregate of artificial entities—a *bona-fide* life-like behavior, and that the behavior emerges within the artificial system in the same way that it emerges in the natural system.

The same is true for L-Systems and the self-reproducing loops. The constituent parts of the artificial systems are different kinds of things from their natural counterparts, but the emergent behavior that they support is the same kind of thing: genuine morphogenesis and differentiation for L-Systems, and genuine self-reproduction in the case of the loops.

The claim is the following. The "artificial" in Artificial Life refers to the component parts, not the emergent processes. If the component parts are implemented correctly, the processes they support are *genuine* —every bit as genuine as the natural processes they parallel.

The *big* claim is that a properly organized set of artificial primitives carrying out the same functional roles as the biomolecules in natural living systems will support a process that will be "alive" in the same way that natural organisms are alive. Artificial Life will therefore be *genuine* life—it will simply be made of different stuff than the life that has evolved here on Earth.

7 EVOLUTION

Modern organisms owe their structure to the complex process of biological evolution, and it is very difficult to discern which of their properties are due to chance, and which to necessity. If biologists could "re-wind the tape" of evolution and start it over, again and again, from differentinitial conditions, or under different regimes of external perturbations-along the way, they would have a full *ensemble* of evolutionarypathways to generalize over. Such an ensemble would allow them to distinguish universal, necessary properties (those which were observed in all the pathways in the ensemble) from accidental, chance properties (those which were unique to individual pathways). However, biologists cannot rewind the tape of evolution, and are stuck with a single, actual evolutionary trace out of a vast, intuited ensemble of possible traces.

Although studying computer models of evolution is not the same as studying the "real-thing," the ability to freely manipulate computer experiments—to "rewind the tape," perturb the initial conditions, and so forth—can more than make up for their "lack" of reality.

It has been known for some time that one can evolve computer programs by the process of natural selection among a population of variant programs. Each individual program in a population of programs is evaluated for its performance on some task. The programs that perform best are allowed to "breed" with one another via *Genetic Algorithms.*[12]

The offspring of these better-performing parent programs replace the worst performing programs in the population, and the cycle is iterated. Such evolutionary approaches to program improvement have been applied primarily to the tasks of function optimization and machine learning.

However, such evolutionary models have only recently been applied to the study of evolution itself \cite{Wilson89}. Researchers were primarily concerned with the *results*, rather than with the *process*, of evolution. In what follows, we will review several models that have been used to study the evolutionary process itself.

7.1 ENGINEERING PTYPES FROM GTYPES

In the preceding sections, we have mentioned several times the formal difficulty with predicting the behavior of an arbitrary machine by mere inspection of its specification and initial state. In the general case, we must run a machine in order to determine its behavior.

The consequence of this unpredictability for GTYPE/PTYPE systems is that we cannot, in the general case, determine the PTYPE that will be produced by an arbitrary GTYPE by inspection alone. We must "run" the GTYPE in the context of a specific environment, and let the PTYPE develop in order to determine the resulting structure and its behavior.

This is even further complicated when the environment consists of a population of PTYPES engaged in nonlinear interactions, in which case the determination of a PTYPE depends on the behavior of the specific PTYPES it is interacting with, and on the emergent details of the global dynamics.

Since, for any interesting system, there will exist an enormous number of potential GTYPES, and since there is no formal method for deducing the PTYPES from the GTYPES, how do we go about finding GTYPES that will generate life-like PTYPES? or PTYPES that exhibit any particular sought after behavior?

Up till now, the process has largely been one of guessing at appropriate GTYPES, and modifying them by trial and error until they generate the appropriate PTYPES. However, this process is limited by our pre-conceptions of what the appropriate PTYPES would be, and by our restricted notions of how to generate GTYPES. We would like to be able to automate the process so that our pre-conceptions and limited abilities to conceive of machinery do not overly constrain the search for GTYPES that will yield the appropriate behaviors.

7.2 NATURAL SELECTION AMONG POPULATIONS OF VARIANTS

Nature, of course, has had to face the same problem, and has hit upon an elegant solution: *evolution by the process of natural selection among populations of variants.* The scheme is a very simple one. However, in the face of the formal impossibility of predicting behavior from machine description alone, it may well be the only efficient, general scheme for searching the space of possible GTYPES.

The mechanism of evolution is as follows. A set of GTYPES is interpreted within a specific environment, forming a population of PTYPES which interact with one another and with features of the environment in various complex ways. On the basis of the relative performance of their associated PTYPES, *some* GTYPES are duplicated in larger numbers than others, and they are duplicated in such a way that the copies are similar to—but not exactly the same as—the originals. These variant GTYPES develop into variant PTYPES, which enter into the complex interactions within the environment, and the process is continued ad-infinitum. As expected from the formal limitations on predictability, GTYPES must be "run" (i.e., turned into PTYPES) in an environment and their behaviors must be evaluated explicitly, their implicit behavior cannot be determined.

7.3 GENETIC ALGORITHMS

In true von Neumann spirit, John Holland has attempted to abstract "the logical form" of the natural process of biological evolution in what he calls the "Genetic Algorithm" (GA).[13] In the GA, a GTYPE is represented as a character string that encodes a potential solution to a problem. For instance, the character string GTYPES might encode the weight matrix of a neural network or the transition table of a finite state machine. These character strings are rendered as PTYPES via a problem specific interpreter, which constructs the neural net or finite state machine specified by each GTYPE, evaluates its performance in the problem domain, and provides it with a specific fitness value, or "strength."

The GA implements selection by making more copies of the character strings representing the better performing PTY-

PES. The GA generates variant GTYPES by applying *genetic operators* to these character strings. The genetic operators typically consist of *reproduction*, *crossover* and *mutation*, with occasional usage of *inversion* and *duplication*.
Recently, John Koza has developed a version of the GA, which he calls the *Genetic Programming Paradigm* (GPP), that extends the genetic operators to work on GTYPES that are simple expressions in a standard programming language. The GPP differs from the traditional GA in that these program expressions are not represented as simple character strings but rather as the parse trees of the expressions. This makes it easier for the genetic operators to obey the syntax of the programming language when producing variant GTYPES.
Figure 7 shows some examples of GTYPES in the GA and GPP paradigms.

a) 11001010111010110101000101011011101011

b) (OR (NOT a) (AND b c))

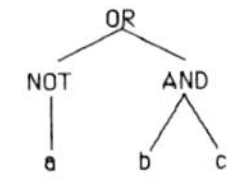

Figure AA a) A typical character string GTYPE for the GA
b) A typical programming language expression GTYPE for the GPP and its associated parse tree.

7

7.4 THE GENETIC OPERATORS

The genetic operators work as follows.
Reproduction is the most basic operator. It is often implemented in the form of *fitness proportionate reproduction*, which means that strings are duplicated in direct proportion to their relative fitness values. Once all strings have been evaluated, the average fitness of the population is computed, and those strings whose fitness is higher than the population average have a higher than average chance of being duplicated, while those strings whose fitness is lower than the population average have a lower than average chance of being duplicated.There are many variations on this scheme, but most implementations of the GA or the GPP use some form of fitness proportionate reproduction as the means to implement "selection." Another form of this is to simply keep the top 10% or so of the population and throw away the rest, using the survivors as breeding stock for the next generation.
Mutation in the GA is simply the replacement of one or more characters in a character string GTYPE with another character picked at random. In binary strings, this simply amounts to random bit-flips.In the GPP, mutation is implemented by picking a subtree of the parse tree at random, and replacing it with a randomly generated subtree whose root-node is of the same syntactic type as the root-node of the replaced sub-tree.
Crossover is an analog of sexual recombination. In the GA, this is accomplished by picking two "parent" character strings, lining them up side-by-side, and interchanging equi-

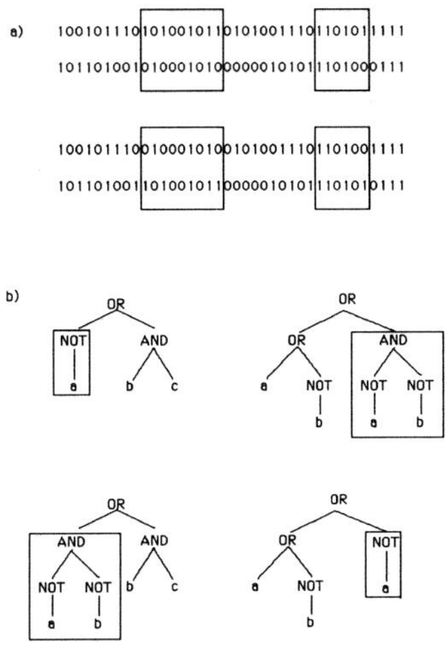

Figure AB: Crossover in a) the GA and b) the GPP. In each, the top line shows the two parent GTYPES with the substructures to be crossed-over outlined by boxes. The bottom line shows the result of performing the crossover operation.

8

valent substrings between them, producing two new strings that each contain a mix of their parent's genetic information. Crossover is an extremely important genetic operator: whereas mutation is equivalent to random search, crossover allows the more "intelligent" search strategy of putting things that have proven useful before into new combinations.

In the GPP, crossover is implemented by picking two "parent" parse trees, locating syntactically similar subtrees within each, and swapping them.

Figure 8 illustrates the crossover operation in the GA and GPP.

Inversion is used rarely in order to rearrange the relative locations of specific pieces of genetic information in the character strings encoding the GTYPE.

Duplication is sometimes used in situations where it makes sense for the genome to grow in length, representing, for instance, larger neural nets, or bigger finite state machine transition tables.

7.5 THE OPERATION OF THE GENETIC ALGORITHM

The basic outline of the genetic algorithm is as follows:

1 Generate a random initial population of GTYPES.

2 Render the GTYPES in the population as PTYPES and evaluate them in the problem domain, providing each GTYPE with a fitness value.

3 Duplicate GTYPES according to their relative fitness using a scheme like fitness proportionate reproduction.

4 Apply genetic operators to the GTYPES in the population, typically picking cross-over partners as a function of their relative fitness.

5 Replace the least fit GTYPES in the population with the offspring generated in the last several steps.

6 Go back to step 2 and iterate.

Although quite simple in outline, the genetic algorithm has proved remarkably powerful in a wide variety of applications, and provides a useful tool for both the study and the application of evolution.

7.6 THE CONTEXT OF ADAPTATION

In this section, we will compare and contrast the context in which evolution has traditionally been set in GA's with the context in which evolution has occurred in the natural world.

GA's have traditionally been employed in the contexts of

machine learning and function optimization. In such contexts, one is often looking for an explicit, optimal solution to a particular, well specified problem. This is reflected in the implementation of the evaluation of PTYPES in traditional GA's, in which each GTYPE is expressed as a PTYPE independently of the others, tested on the problem, and assigned a value representing its individual fitness, using an explicit fitness function. Thus, one is often seeking to evolve an *individual* that *explicitly encodes* an optimal solution to a precisely specified problem. The fitness of a GTYPE in such cases is simply a function of the problem domain, and is independent of the fitnesses of the other GTYPES in the population.

This is quite different from the context in which natural biological evolution has taken place, in which the behavior of a PTYPE and its associated fitness are highly dependent on which other PTYPES exist in the environment, and on the dynamics of their interactions. Furthermore, in the natural context, it is generally the case that there is no single, explicitly specified problem confronting the population. Rather, there is often quite a large set of problems facing the population at any one time, and these problems are only implicitly determined as a function of the dynamics of the population and the environment themselves, which may change significantly over time. In such a context, nature has often discovered that the collective behavior emerging from the interactions among a set of PTYPES will address a subset of the implicitly defined problems better than an individual PTYPE can.

Thus the proper picture for the natural evolutionary context is that of a large cloud of potential collective solutions addressing a large cloud of potential collective problems, and that both of these clouds are implicit in the spatio-temporal dynamics of the population. The dynamics of such systems are very complex and impossible to predict.

The important point here is that nonlinearities and emergent collective phenomena are properties that are to be exploited rather than avoided, as has been the traditional engineering viewpoint. Emergent solutions may be harder to understand or to engineer, but there are far more of them than there are non emergent, analyzable linear solutions. The true power of evolution lies in its ability to exploit emergent collective phenomena.

7.7 FROM ARTIFICIAL SELECTION TO NATURAL SELECTION

In *The Origin of Species*, Darwin used a very clever device to argue for the agency of natural selection. In the first chapter of *Origin*, Darwin lays the groundwork of the case for *natural* selection by carefully documenting the process of *artificial* selection. Most people of his time were familiar with the manner in which breeders of domestic animals and plants could enhance traits arbitrarily by selective breeding of their stock. Darwin carefully made the case that the wide variety of domestic animals and plants extant at his time were descended from a much smaller variety of wild-stock, due to the selective breeding imposed by farmers and herders throughout history.

Now, Darwin continues, simply note that environmental conditions can fill the role played by the human breeder in artificial selection, and, Voila! one has natural selection. The rest of the book consists in a very careful documentation of the manner in which different environmental conditions would favor animals bearing different traits, making it more likely that individuals bearing those traits would survive to mate with each other and produce offspring, leading to the gradual enhancement of those traits through time. A beautifully simple yet elegant mechanism to explain the origin and maintenance of the diversity of species on Earth—too simple for many of his time, particularly those of strong religious persuasion.

The abstraction of this simple elegant mechanism for the production and filtration of diversity in the form of the Genetic Algorithm is straightforward and obvious. However, as it is usually implemented, it is artificial, rather than natural selection, that is the agency determining the direction of computer evolution. Either we ourselves, or our algorithmic agents in the form of explicit fitness functions, typically stand in the role of the breeder in computer implementations of evolution. Yet it is plain that the role of "breeder" can as easily be filled by "nature" in the world inside the computer as it is in the world outside the computer—it is just a different "nature." If we are to study evolution by "natural" selection, we must create a "nature" within the artificial world of a computer.

In the following sections, we will explore a number of examples of computational implementations of the evolutionary process, starting with examples that clearly involve artificial selection, and working our way through to an example that clearly involves natural selection. The key thing to keep track of throughout these examples is the manner in which we incrementally give over our role as breeder to the "natural" pressures imposed by the dynamics of the computational world itself.

7.71 A BREEDER'S PARADISE: BIOMORPHS

The first model, a clear-cut example of computational artificial selection, is due to the Oxford evolutionary biologist, Richard Dawkins, author of such highly-regarded books as *The Selfish Gene*, *The Extended Phenotype*, and *The Blind Watchmaker*.

In order to illustrate the power of a process in which the random production of variation is coupled with a selection mechanism, Dawkins wrote a program for the Apple Macintosh computer that allows users to "breed" recursively generated objects.

The program is set up to generate tree structures recursively by starting with a single stem, adding branches to it in a certain way, adding branches to those branches in the same way, and so on. The number of branches, their angles, their size relative to the stem they are being added to, the number of branching iterations, and other parameters affecting the growth of these trees are what constitute the GTYPES of the tree-organisms—or "biomorphs" as Dawkins calls them. Thus, the program consists of a general purpose recursive tree generator, which takes each organism's GTYPE (parameter settings) as data and generates its associated PTYPE (the resulting tree).

The program starts by producing a simple default—or "Adam"—tree and then produces a number of mutated copies of the parameter string for the Adam tree. The program renders the PTYPE trees of all of the different GTYPES on the screen for the user to view. The user then selects the PTYPE (i.e. tree shape) he or she likes the best, the program produces mutated copies of that tree's GTYPE (parameter string), and renders their associated PTYPE trees. The user selects another tree, and the process continues. The original Adam tree together with a number of its distant descendants are shown in Figure 9.

It is clear that this is a process of artificial selection. The computer generates the variants, but the human user fills the role of the "breeder," the active selective agent, determining which structures are to go on to produce variant offspring. However, the mechanics of the production of variants are particularly clear: produce slight variations on the presently selected GTYPE. The specific action taken by the human breeder is also very clear: choose the PTYPE whose GTYPE

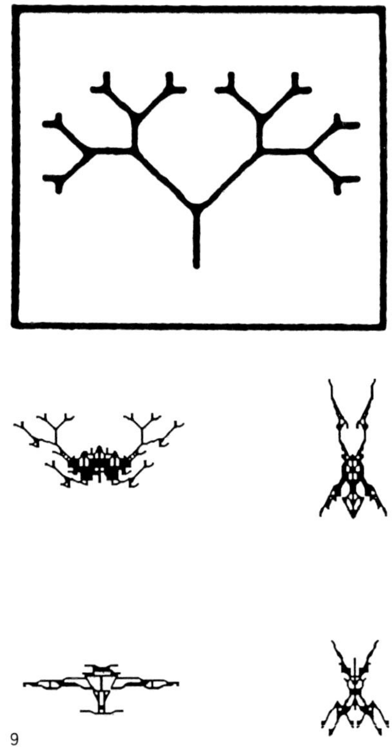

9

will have variations of it produced in the next round. There is both a producer and a selector of variation.

7.72 ALGORITHMIC BREEDERS

In this section, we investigate a model which will take us two steps closer to natural selection. First the human breeder is replaced with a program he writes, one which formalizes his selection criteria so that the act of selection can be performed by his computational agent: a fitness function. This is a program that will do his breeding for him, applying his selection preferences, but which takes him physically out of the loop. Second, we see that our computational representative can itself be allowed to evolve—an important first step toward eliminating our externally imposed, *apriori* criteria from the process completely.

The system we discuss here is due to Danny Hillis, inventor of the Connection Machine and chief scientist of Thinking Machines Corp. In the course of the work at TMC, they have a need to design fast and efficient chips for the hardware implementation of a wide variety of common computational tasks, such as sorting numbers. For many of these, there is no body of theory that tells engineers how to construct the optimal circuit to perform the task in question. Therefore, progress in the design of such circuits is often a matter of blind trial and error until a better circuit is discovered. Hillis decided to apply the trial-and-error procedure of evolution to the problem of designing sorting circuits.

In his system, the GTYPES are strings of numbers encoding circuit connections that implement comparisons and swaps between input lines. GTYPES are rendered into the specific circuits they encode—their PTYPES—and they are rated according to the number of circuit elements and connections they require, and by their performance on a number of test strings which they have to sort. This rating is accomplished by an explicit fitness function—Hillis' computational representative—which implements the selection criteria and takes care of the breeding task. Thus, this is still a case of artificial selection, even though there is no human being actively doing the selection.

Hillis implemented the evolution problem on his Connection Machine CM2— a 64,000 processor SIMD parallel super computer. With populations of 64K sorting networks over thousands of generations, the system managed to produce a 65 element sorter, better than some cleverly engineered sorting networks, but not as good as the best known such network, which has 60 components. After reaching 65 element sorters, the system consistently got itself hung-up on local optima.

Hillis then borrowed a trick from the biological literature on the coevolution of hosts and parasites[14] and in the process took a step closer to natural selection by allowing the evaluation function to evolve in time. In the previous runs, the sorting networks were evaluated on a fixed set of sorting problems—random sequences of numbers that the networks had to sort into correct order.In the new set of runs, Hillis made another evolving population out of the sorting problems. The task for the sorting networks was to do a good job on the sorting problems, while the task for the sorting problems was to make the sorting networks perform poorly.

In this situation, whenever a good sorting network emerged and took over the population, it became a target for the population of sorting problems. This led to the rapid evolution of sorting sequences that would make the network perform poorly and hence reduce its fitness. Hillis found that this coevolution between the sorting networks and the sorting problems led much more rapidly to better solutions than had been achieved by the evolution of sorting networks alone, resulting in a sorting network consisting of 61 elements.

It is the coevolution in this latter set of runs that both brings us several steps closer to natural selection and is responsible for the enhanced efficiency of the search for an optimal sorting network. First of all, rather than having an absolute, fixed value, the fitness of a sorting network depends on the specific set of sorting problems it is facing.

Likewise, the fitness of a set of sorting problems depends on the specific set of sorting networks it is facing. Thus, the "fitness" of an individual is now a relative quantity, not an absolute one. The fitness of an individual now depends a little more on the "nature" of the world it is embedded in.

Coevolution increases the efficiency of the search as follows. In the earlier runs consisting solely of an evolving population of sorting networks, the population of networks was effectively hill-climbing on a multi-peaked fitness landscape. Therefore, the populations would encounter the classic problem of getting stuck on local-maxima. That is, a population could reach certain structures which lie on relatively low fitness peaks, but from which any deviations result in lower fitness, which is selected against. In order to find another, higher peak, the population would have to cross a fitness valley, which is difficult to do under simple Darwinian selection (Figure 10-[a]).

In the coevolutionary case, here's what happens (Figure 10-[b]). When a population of sorting networks gets stuck on a

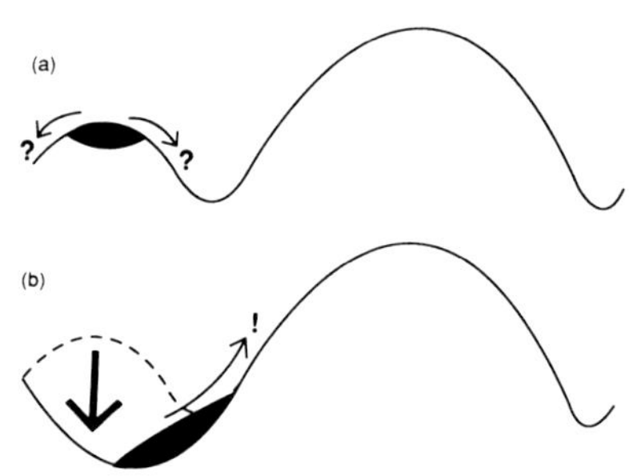

10

local fitness peak, it becomes a target for the population of sorting problems. That is, it defines a new peak for the sorting problems to climb. As the sorting problems climb their peak, they *drive down the peak on which the sorting networks are sitting*, by finding sequences that make the sorting networks perform poorly, therefore lowering their fitness. After a while, the fitness peak that the sorting networks were sitting on has been turned into a fitness valley, from which the population can escape by climbing up the neighboring peaks by normal Darwinian means. As the sorting networks climb other peaks, they drive down the peak that they had provided for the sorting problems, who are then free to chase the sorting networks to the new peaks they have achieved and drive those down in turn.

In short, each population dynamically deforms the fitness landscape being traversed by the other population in such a way that both populations can continue to climb uphill without getting stuck in local maxima. When they do get stuck, the maxima get turned into minima which can be climbed out of by simple Darwinian means. Thus, coupled populations evolving by Darwinian means can bootstrap each other up the evolutionary ladder far more efficiently than they can climb it alone. By competing with one another, coupled populations improve one another at increased rates.

Thus, when coupled in this way, a population may get hung up on local optima for a while, but eventually it will be able to climb again. This suggests immediately that the structure of the evolutionary record for such systems should show periods of stasis followed by periods of evolutionary change. The stasis comes about as populations sit at the top of local fitness peaks, waiting around for someone to come along and do them the favor of lowering the peaks they are stuck on. The periods of change come about when populations are released from local optima and are freed to resume climbing fitness peaks, and are therefore changing in time. Hillis has, in fact, carefully documented this kind of *Punctuated Equilibria* in his system.

7.73 COMPUTATIONAL ECOLOGIES

Continuing on our path from artificial to natural selection, we turn to a research project carried out by Kristian Lindgren,[15] in which, although there is still an explicit fitness measure, many different species of organisms coevolve in each other's presence, forming ecological webs allowing for more complex interactions than the simple host-parasite interactions described above.

In this paper, Lindgren studies evolutionary dynamics within the context of a well known game-theoretic problem: the *Iterated Prisoners' Dilemma* model (IPD). This model has been used effectively by Axelrod and Hamilton in their studies of the evolution of cooperation.[16]

In the prisoners' dilemma model, the payoff matrix (the fitness function) is constructed in such a way that individuals will garner the most payoff collectively in the long-run if they "cooperate" with one-another by *avoiding* the behaviors that would garner them the most payoff individually in the short-run. If individuals only play the game once, they will do best by not cooperating ("defecting.") However, if they play the game repeatedly with one another (the "iterated" version of the game,) they will do best by cooperating with one another.

The payoff matrix for the prisoner's dilemma game is shown in Figure 11. This payoff matrix has the following interesting property. Assume, as is often assumed in game theory, that each player wants to maximize his immediate payoff, and let's analyze what player A should do. If B cooperates, then A should defect, because then A will get a score of 5 whereas he only gets a score of 3 if he cooperates. On the other hand, if B defects, then again A should defect, as he will get a score of 1 if he defects while he only gets a score of 0 if he cooperates. So, no matter what B does, A maximizes his immediate payoff by defecting. Since the payoff matrix is symmetric, the same reasoning applies to player B, so B should defect no matter what A does. Under this reasoning, each player will defect at each time step, giving them one point each per play. However, if they could somehow decide to cooperate, they would each get 3 points per play: the two players will do better in the long run by foregoing the action that maximizes their immediate payoff. The payoff matrix for the prisoner's Dilemma game. The pair (s_1, s_2) deontes the scores to players A and B respectively.

The question is, of course: can ordinary Darwinian mechanisms, which assume that individuals selfishly want to maximize their immediate payoff, lead to cooperation? Surprisingly, as demonstrated by Axelrod and Hamilton, the answer is yes.

In Lindgren's version of this game, strategies can evolve in an open-ended fashion by learning to base their behavioral choices upon longer and longer histories of previous interactions.

The scheme used by Lindgren to represent strategies to play the Iterated Prisoners' Dilemma game is as follows. In the simplest version of the game, players make their choice of whether to cooperate or defect based solely on what their

TABLE 1 The payoff matrix for the Prisoner's Dilemma Game. The pair (s_1, s_2) denotes the scores to players A and B, respectively.

		Player B	
		Cooperate	Defect
Player A	Cooperate	(3,3)	(0,5)
	Defect	(5,0)	(1,1)

11

strategy	name
[0 0]	**All Defect**
[0 1]	**TIT-for-TAT (TFT)**
[1 0]	**TAT-for-TIT (anti-TFT)**
[1 1]	**All Cooperate**

12

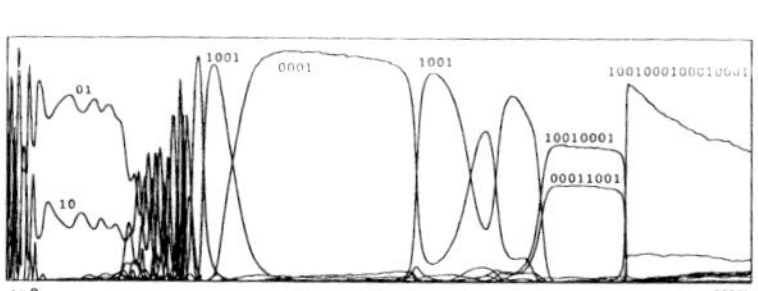

13

opponent did to them in the last time step. This is called the memory-1 game. Since the opponent could have done only one of two things, cooperate or defect, a strategy needs to specify what it would do in either of those two cases. As it has two moves it can make in either of those two cases, cooperate or defect, there are four possible memory-1 strategies. These can be encoded in bit-strings of length 2, as illustrated in Figure 12.

If the players could base their decisions by looking another move into the past, to see what they did to their opponent before their opponent made his move, then we would have the memory-2 game. In this case, there are 2 moves with 2 possible outcomes each, meaning that a memory-2 strategy must specify whether to cooperate or defect for each of 4 possible cases. Such a strategy can be encoded using 4 bits, or twice the length of the memory-1 strategies, and there will be 16 possible memory-2 strategies. Memory-3 strategies require another doubling of the encoding bit string, i.e., 8 bits, yielding 256 possible memory-3 strategies. In general, memory-n strategies require 2 bits for their encoding, and there will be 2 such strategies.

In order to allow for the evolution of higher memory strategies, Lindgren introduces a new genetic operator: gene-duplication. As a memory-n strategy is just twice as long as a memory n-1 strategy, a memory n strategy can be produced from a memory n-1 strategy by simply duplicating the memory n strategy and concatenating the duplicate to itself. In Lindgren's encoding strategy, gene-duplication has the interesting property that it is a *neutral mutation.* Simple duplication alone does not change the PTYPE, even though it has doubled the length of the GTYPE. However, once doubled, mutations in the longer GTYPE will alter the behavior of the PTYPE.

Once again, evolution proceeds by allowing populations of different organisms to bootstrap each other up coupled fitness landscapes, dynamically deforming each other's landscapes by turning local maxima into local minima. Again, the fitness of strategies is not an absolute, fixed number that is independently computable. Rather, the fitness of each strategy depends on what other strategies exist in the "natural" population.

Many complicated and interesting strategies evolve during the evolutionary development of this system. More important, however, are the various phenomenological features exhibited by the dynamics of the evolutionary process. First of all, as we might expect, the system exhibits a behavior that is remarkably suggestive of Punctuated Equilibria. After an initial irregular transient, the system settles down to relatively long periods of stasis "punctuated" irregularly by periods of rapid evolutionary change.[17]

Second, the diversity of strategies builds up during the long periods of stasis, but often collapses drastically during the short, chaotic episodes of rapid evolutionary succession. These "crashes" in the diversity of species constitute "extinction events." In this model, these extinction events are observed to be a natural consequence of the dynamics of the evolutionary process alone, without invoking any catastrophic, external perturbations (there are no comet impacts or "nemesis" stars in this model!) Furthermore, these extinction events happen on multiple scales: there are lots of little ones and fewer large ones.

In order to understand the dynamics of a system that is subjected to constant perturbations, one needs to understand the dynamics of the unperturbed system first. We do not have access to an unperturbed version of the evolution of life on Earth, consequently we could not have said definitively that extinction events on many size scales would be a natural consequence of the process of evolution itself. By comparing the perturbed and unperturbed versions of model systems like Lindgren's, we may very well be able to derive a universal scaling relationship for "natural" extinction events, and therefore be able to explain deviations from this relationship in the fossil record as due to external perturbations such as the impact of large asteroids.

Third, the emergence of ecologies is nicely demonstrated by Lindgren's model. It is usually the case that a mix of several different strategies dominates the system during the long periods of stasis. In order for a strategy to do well, it must do well by cooperating with other strategies. These mixes may involve three or more strategies whose collective activity produces a stable interaction pattern that benefitsall of the strategies in the mix. Together, they constitute a more complex, "higher order" strategy, which can behave as a group in ways that are impossible for any individual strategy.

It is important to note that, in many cases, the "environment" that acts on an organism, and in the context of which an organism acts, is primarily constituted of the other organisms in the population and their interactions with each other and the physical environment. There is tremendous opportunity here for evolution to discover that certain sets of individuals exhibit emergent, collective behaviors that reap benefits to all of the individuals in the set. Thus, evolution can produce major leaps in biological complexity, without having to produce more complex individuals by simply discovering, perhaps even "tripping over," the many ways in which collections of individuals at one level can work together to form aggregate individuals at the next higher level of organization.

This is thought to be the case for the origin of eukaryotic cells, which are viewed as descended from early cooperative collections of simpler, prokaryotic cells \cite{Margulis70}. It is also the process involved in the origin of multicellular organisms, which lead to the Cambrian Explosion of diversity some 700 million years ago. It was probably a significant factor in the origin of the prokaryotes themselves, and it has been discovered independently at least 7 times by the various social insects (including species of wasps, bees, ants, and termites).

7.74 THE EMERGENCE OF VIRTUAL NATURE

The final step in eliminating our hand from the selection/breeding process and setting the stage for true "natural" selection within a computer is taken in a model due to Tom Ray.[18] This step involves eliminating our algorithmic breeding agent completely.

In his "Tierra" simulation system, computer programs compete for CPU time and memory space. The "task" that these programs must perform in order to be reproduced is simply the act of self-reproduction itself! Thus, there is no need for an externally defined fitness function that determines which GTYPES get copied by an external copying procedure. The programs reproduce themselves, and the ones that are better at this task take over the population. The whole external task of evaluation of fitness has been internalized in the function of the organisms themselves. Thus, there is no longer a place for the Human breeder or his computational agent. This results in genuine natural selection within a computer.

In Tierra, programs replicate themselves "noisily," so that some of their offspring behave differently. Variant programs that reproduce themselves more efficiently, which trick other programs into reproducing them, or which capture the execution pointers of other programs, etc., will leave more offspring than others. Similarly, programs that learn to defend themselves against such tricks will leave more offspring than those that do not.

We will discuss a few of the "digital organisms" that have emerged within the Tierra system (it is not necessary to understand the code in the illustrated programs in order to follow the explanation in the text.)

Figure 14-(a) shows the self-replicating "ancestor" program that is the only program Tom Ray has ever written in the Tierra system. All the other programs evolved under the action of natural selection.

The ancestor program works as follows. In the top block of

code, the program locates its "head" and its "tail," templates marking the upper and lower boundaries of the program in memory. It saves these locations in special registers and, after subtracting the location of the head from the location of the tail, it stores its length in another register.

In the second block of code, the program enters an endless loop in which it will repeatedly produce copies of itself. It allocates memory space of the appropriate size and then invokes the final block of code, which is the actual reproduction loop. After it returns from the reproduction loop, it creates a new execution pointer to its newly produced offspring, and cycles back to create another offspring.

In the third and final block of code, the reproduction loop, the program copies itself, instruction by instruction, into the newly allocated memory space, making use of the addresses and length stored away by the first block of code. When it has copied itself completely, it returns to the block of code that called it, in this case, the second block.

It should be noted that "function calls" in Tierra are accomplished by seeking for a specific bit pattern in memory rather than by branching to a specific address. Thus, when the second block of code "calls" the third block of code, the reproduction loop, it does so by initiating a seek forward in memory for a specific "template." When this template is found, execution begins at the instruction following the template. Returns from function calls are handled in the normal manner, by simply returning to the instruction following the initial function call. This template addressing scheme is used in other reference contexts as well, and helps make Tierra language programs robust to mutations, as well as easily relocatable in memory.

Figure 14-(b) shows a "parasite" program that has evolved to exploit the ancestor program. The parasite is very much like the ancestor program, except that it is missing the third block of code, the reproduction loop. How then does it copy itself?

The answer is that it makes use of a nearby ancestor program's reproduction loop! Recall that a function call in Tierra initiates a seek forward in memory for a particular template of bits. If this pattern is not found within the initiating program's own code, the search may proceed forward in memory into the code of other organisms, where the template may be found and where execution then begins. When the invoked function in another organism's code executes the "return" statement, execution reverts to the program that initiated the function call. Thus, organisms can execute each other's code, and this is exactly what the parasite program does: it makes use of the reproductive machinery of the ancestor host.

This means that the parasite does not have to take the time to copy the code constituting the reproductive loop, and hence can reproduce more rapidly, as it has fewer instructions to copy. The parasites thus proliferate in the population. However, they cannot proliferate to the point of driving out the ancestor hosts altogether, for they depend on them for their reproductive machinery. Thus, a balance is eventually struck optimizing the joint system.

Eventually, however, another mutant form of the ancestor emerges which has developed an immunity to the parasites. This program is illustrated in Figure 14-(c). Two key differences from the ancestor program confer the immunity to the parasite programs. First, instead of executing a "return" instruction, the reproduction loop instead initiates a jump back in memory to the template found in the instruction that calls the reproduction loop. This has the same effect as a return statement when executed by the immune program, but has a very different effect on the parasite. The second important difference is that following the cell division in the second block (which allocates a new execution pointer to the offspring just created) the program jumps back to the beginning of the first block of code, rather than to the beginning of the second block. Thus, the immune program constantly resets its head, tail, and size registers. This seems useless when considering only the immune organism's own reproduction, but let's see what happens when a parasite tries to execute the reproduction loop in an immune organism.

When a parasite attempts to use the immune program's reproduction code, the new jump transfers the parasite's execution pointer to the second block of the immune program's code, rather than returning it to the second block of the parasite code, as the parasite expects. Then, this execution pointer is further re-directed to the first block of the immune program, where the registers originally containing the head, tail and length of the parasite are reset to contain the head, tail, and length of the immune organism. The immune program has thus completely captured the execution pointer of the parasite. Having lost its execution pointer, the parasite simply becomes dormant data occupying memory, while the immune program now has two execution pointers running through it: its own original pointer, plus the pointer it captured from the parasite. Thus, the immune program now reproduces twice as rapidly as before. Once they emerge, such immune programs rapidly drive the parasites to extinction.

Complex interactions between variant programs like those described above continue to develop within evolutionary runs in Tierra. From a uniform population of self-reproducing ancestor programs, Ray, a tropical biologist by training, notes the emergence of whole "ecologies" of interacting species of computer programs. Furthermore, he is able to identify many phenomena familiar to him from his studies of real ecological communities, such as competitive exclusion, the emergence of parasites, key-stone predators and parasites, hyper-parasites, symbiotic relationships, sociality, "cheaters," and so forth.

Again, the actual "fitness" of an organism is a complex function of its interactions with other organisms in the "soup." Collections of programs can cooperate to enhance each other's reproductive success, or they can drive each other's reproductive success down, thus lowering fitness and kicking the population off of local fitness peaks.

Not surprisingly, Ray, too, has noted periods of relative stasis punctuated by periods of rapid evolutionary change, as complex ecological webs collapse and new ones stabilize in their place. Systems like Ray's Tierra capture the proper context for evolutionary dynamics, and natural selection is truly at play here.

Digital Organisms from Ray's Tierra Simulation System. (a) Self-reproducing ancestor program. (b) An early parasite of the ancestor. (c) A descendant of the ancestory that is immune to the parasite.

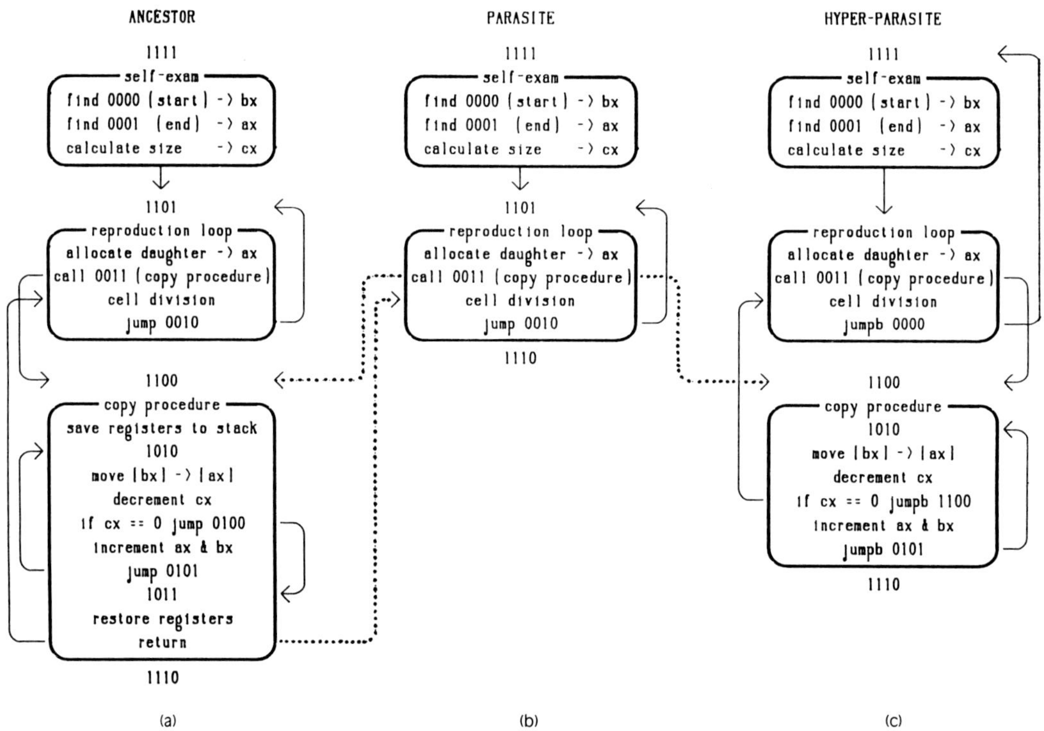

8 ARTIFICIAL LIFE IN HARDWARE AND WETWARE

Although much of this article has discussed attempts to synthesize biological phenomena within the "software" medium of a computer, similar attempts are being carried out in both "wetware" (working with real molecules in biochemistry laboratories) and "hardware" (typically, mobile robots). Despite the difference in underlying medium, the same principles apply to Artificial Life research being carried out across these vastly different material substrates: bottom-up implementation of large populations of semi-autonomous individuals, which get caught up in emergent, collective, and evolving dynamics. In this section we briefly review several Artificial Life research efforts in "hardware" and "wetware."

8.1 HARDWARE

A new approach to robotics is being pioneered by researchers including Rod Brooks at MIT, Luc Steels at Brussels, Leslie Kaelbling of Teleos Research, Tim Smithers at Edinburgh, and Mark Tilden at Waterloo. This new approach involves throwing out the goal of endowing a robot with human-level perception, representation, reasoning, and cognitive capacities using traditional Artificial Intelligence approaches. In its place, it substitutes the goal of building a "street-smart" robot whose intelligence is more along the lines of an insect than of a human. The "intelligence" of such robots is distributed across (what we would call) a "peripheral" sensory and motor nervous system rather than being centrally located within a central processor analog of the cerebral cortex. This sounds like intelligence without brains, but it is grounded in the realization that higher level cognitive capabilities are late-comers in evolutionary history, and that they depend critically on the much earlier and more basic sensory and motor capabilites provided by simple, decentralized nervous systems. Despite their relative simplicity, these early nerve nets were able to move organisms around successfully within their environments with nary a representation, a model of the world, nor a plan to their names. "Elephants don't play chess!" is one of the battle cries of this new approach, although "Cockroaches don't play chess!" might be even more appropriate.

In pursuing this new approach to robotics, Rod Brooks and his colleagues at the MIT Mobile Robot Lab (the "Mobot" Lab) have emphasized the following:[19]

- that there would be no traditional notion of planning.

- that no central representation was needed.
- that notions of world modelling are impractical and unnecessary.
- that biology and evolution were good models to follow in our quest.
- that we insist on building complete systems that exist in the real world so that we would not trick ourselves into skipping hard problems.

This philosophical approach to the problem has lead Brooks and his students to a bottom-up, distributed scheme for building robots and their control structures, which they call the *subsumption architecture.* In the subsumption scheme, there are many layers of activity going on in parallel, with lower layers being controlled (subsumed) by higher layers.

For instance, imagine that we have a three-wheeled robot with two rear drive wheels and a front idler wheel. The two drive wheels are driven independently, which is how steering is effected. The robot also has sonar range finders, and a TV camera for vision. The lowest layer of control in the subsumption architecture (level-0) might simply be a circuit that causes the robot to move forward by turning on both drive wheels full-speed. The next layer up (level-1) would be a circuit taking data from the sonar range finders with inhibitory outputs to the drive layer (level-0). As obstacles come within range of the sonar sensors, they selectively inhibit the signals being sent to one or the other of the drive wheels in the underlying level-0 circuitry, causing the robot to turn to avoid the obstacles. Notice that level-1 assumes the presence of level-0, but level-0 need not assume the existence of any higher levels. Level-0 simply does its thing, while level-1 occasionaly steps in and tweaks this underlying primary behavior.

The next layer up, level-2, might be a circuit which identifies objects in the room and causes the robot to head toward them. The level-2 circuit would have inputs from the TV camera and outputs to level-1, the obstacle avoidance circuitry. When distant objects are located by the TV camera, the obstacle avoidance circuitry can be tweaked by level-2 to cause the robot to head in the general direction of these distant objects, relying on the autonomous behavior of level-1 to avoid obstacles along the way. Again, level-2 assumes the existence of level-1, but level-1 need not assume the existence of any higher level(s). Thus, each layer "subsumes" the layers beneath it, inhibiting or enhancing their autonomous behavior in specific ways in the pursuit of higher-level goals. In principle, this layered control structure can be iterated to many higher levels. Figure 15 shows a diagram of the subsumption architecture of an actual robot control.

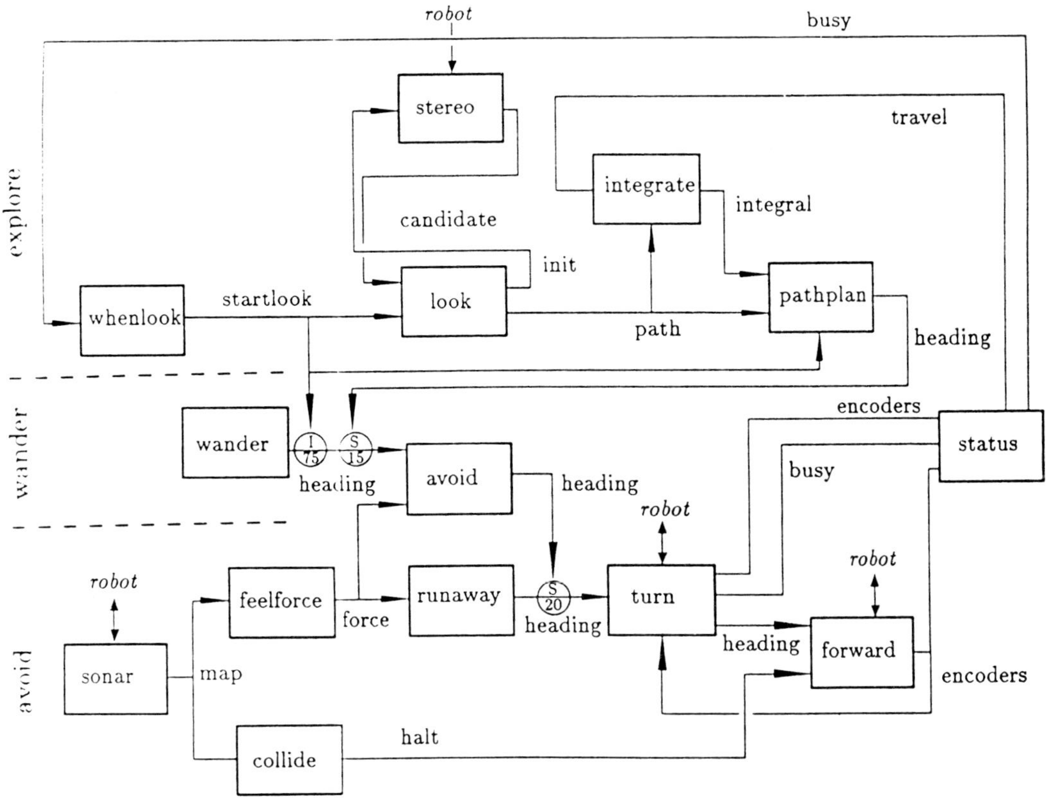

15

Subsumption architecture control circuitry for one of Rod Brooks' mobile robots. Higher levels of control structure are farther up in the diagram.

On this scheme, therefore, it is not that "fish got to swim, birds got to fly," but rather that "fins got to flip, wings got to flap." Swimming and flying are seen to emerge from the controlled application of these primary behaviors, as the flippers and flappers are modulated by higher level control circuitry connected to sensory circuits, enhancing or inhibiting the simple behaviors of the the flippers or flappers, which simply want to "do their thing." In this approach, "doers" are primary while controllers are secondary, whereas on the traditional AI approach, controllers are primary and "doers"are secondary. Higher level intelligence, then, is seen to have arisen as control structures on top of pre-existing simple behaviors, giving rise to higher-order behaviors, over which even higher-order control structures emerged, and so forth. This is a view of intelligence driven from the bottom-up rather than from the top-down, which has the advantage that it is consistant with the probable evolutionary development of higher intelligence.

A good source of inspiration for this bottom-up approach to intelligent robotics is the book *Vehicles* by Braitenberg.[20]

8.2 WETWARE

An increasing number of biomolecular laboratories around the world are attempting to synthesize chemical systems from scratch that exhibit life-like properties. Some of these involve the same kinds of organic molecules that make up natural life, but put together in new ways, while others involve molecules that are largely foreign to natural life.

In 1990, Julius Rebek and his colleagues at MIT demonstrated a molecular system that self-replicates via templating, in a manner similar to the self-replication of DNA.[21] However, the molecules involved consist of an aromatic ester and an amino-adenosine, rather than DNA.

Similar feats had been accomplished previously by Gunter von Kiedrowski of the University of Göttingen and also by Leslie Orgel of the Salk Institute. However, these latter efforts involved slight modifications of naturally occurring biomolecules, whereas Rebek's system involves truly synthetic molecules not found in natural life.

In Switzerland, at the ETH in Zurich, Bachmann, Walde, Luisi, and Lang have succeeded in synthesizing self-replicating artificial cell-like structures called "micelles," consisting of mono-layer lipid membranes.[22] The micelles replicate as a chemical reaction within them produces more membrane material.

In Gerald Joyce's lab at the Scripps Research Institute, a molecular version of the genetic algorithm is being employed to produce novel RNA-based enzymes by the mechanism of Darwinian evolution[23] This is an extremely promising technology, which should provide the medical world with a whole new method for designing useful drugs. Part of the excitement about this new technology (called "directed molecular evolution" or *in vitro* molecular evolution) is that it allows researchers to avoid having to solve the "protein-folding" problem. A protein's chemical properties are a function of its complex, folded structure. In order to produce a molecule with a particular chemical behavior, drug designers have traditionally had to work out the specific linear sequence of bases on a peptide string that would fold-up into just the right shape.

Directed molecular evolution saves drug-designers from having to worry about sequence details. Instead, they can start out with a molecule that has a function similar to the function that they seek, produce many close variants of that molecule, and test the resulting variants to see how they perform on the desired task. The variants that perform better have more copies of themselves made via the PCR reaction, again with some variation. The process is continued until molecules performing the desired task are produced. Joyce has successfully evolved a ribozyme (an RNA-based enzyme) that will cleave DNA, starting with a ribozyme that cleaves only RNA).At no time in this process need the researchers concern themselves with the specific linear sequences of the molecules, which is the analog of the genotype). Rather, they apply selective forces directly at the phenotypic level of molecular function.

There is a good deal more work along these and similar lines proceeding in biochemical laboratories around the world. In fact, Gerald Joyce predicts that synthetic wetware life will be realized in some biochemical lab by the turn of the century.

9 CONCLUSION

In the section on Evolution, the point was made that it is often the case that the most important aspects of "Nature" in the process of evolution are the other organisms in the environment and their effects on the physical world.

In the case of human beings, our "Nature" is largely dominated by the products of our own artifice, not only physical structures such as buildings and highways, but also such socio-cultural constructs as governments, churches, corporations, and so forth. That is, our own artifacts are the dominating aspects of the "Nature" that is the agency of "natural" selection for the human species. By adapting to an artifactual "Nature" we are becoming more and more "artifactual" ourselves. As we are increasingly responsible for constructing "Nature," so we are increasingly responsible for constructing ourselves. In a very real sense, humans themselves are becoming a form of Artificial Life—products of our own artifice.

Now that we are on the verge of synthesizing life artificially—now that our artifacts are becoming more and more like us—and now that we are becoming more and more like our artifacts, where will life go from here?

It is important to bear in mind that whether we produce living artifacts within the next ten years or only within the next thousand, on the scale of geological time, we are literally *at* the beginning of a new epoch of life on Earth, an epoch that will be dominated by life-forms that we will have had a significant role in shaping. Will they sustain and nurture us, and we them? Or will they destroy and replace us, or we them?

We must do everything in our power, *starting now*, to assure that the consequences of our imminent mastery of the technology of life are beneficial for all life, whatever it is made of.

LITERATURE AND NOTES

Axelrod, R., and W.D. Hamilton "The Evolution of Cooperation." (1981): pp. 1390–1396.
Axelrod, R.\it The Evolution of Cooperation}. New York, Basic Books, 1984.
Bachmann, Walde, Luisi, and Lang, {\it J.Am.Chem.Soc.}, {\bf 113} 8204, 1991.
Braitenberg, V. {\it Vehicles: Experiments in Synthetic Psychology}, MIT Press, Cambridge, 1984.
Brooks, R., and Flynn, A.M., "Fast, Cheap, and Out of Control: A Robot Invasion of the Solar System." {\it Journal of the British Interplanetary Society} Vol. 42, pp. 478–485, 1989.
Brooks, R. "Intelligence without Representation." {\it Artificial Intelligence} {\bf 47}, pp. 139–159, 1991.
Buss, L. {\it The Evolution of Individuality.} Princeton University Press, 1987.
Burks, A. W. (ed) {\it Essays on Cellular Automata}, University of Illinois Press, Urbana, 1970.
Chapuis, A., and Droz, E., {\it Automata: A Historical and Technological Study.} (Trans. A. Reid), B. T. Batsford Ltd, London, 1958.
Dawkins, R. "The Evolution of Evolvability."
In Artificial Life, edited by C.G. Langton, Addison Wesley, pp 201–220, 1989.
Frisch, U., Hasslacher, B., and Pomeau, Y., "Lattice gas automata for the Navier-Stokes equation." {\it Physical Review Letters} 56, pp. 1505–1508, 1986.
Goldberg, D. E. {\it Genetic Algorithms in Search, Optimization, and Machine Learning.} Reading, MA: Addison Wesley, 1989.
Hamilton, W. D. "Sex versus Nonsex versus Parasite." {\it OIKOS} {\bf 35}, pp. 282–290, 1980.
Hamilton, W. D. "Pathogens as causes of Genetic Diversity in their Host Populations." In {\it Population Biology of Infectous Diseases.} edited by R. M. Anderson and R. M. May, Berlin, Springer-Verlag, pp. 269–296, 1982.
Holland, J. H., {\it Adaptation in Natural and Artificial Systems}, University of Michigan Press, Ann Arbor, 1975.
Hopcroft, J. E., and Ullman, J. D., {\it Introduction to Automata Theory, Languages, and Computation}, Addison-Wesley, Menlo Park,Calif. 1979.
Beaudry, A. A., and Joyce, G. F., "Directed Evolution of an RNA

Enzyme." {\it Science}, Vol. 257, pp. 635–641, July 31, 1992.
Joyce, G. F., "Directed Molecular Evolution." {\it Scientific American}, Dec. 92, Vol. 267 no. 6. pp. 90–97, 1992.
Langton, C. G., "Self-Reproduction in Cellular Automata", {\it Physica D}, Vol. 10, No. 1–2, pp. 135–144 (1984).
Langton, C. G., "Studying Artificial Life with Cellular Automata", {\it Physica D}, Vol. 22, pp. 120–149, 1986.
Lindgren, K. "Evolutionary Phenomena in Simple Dynamics." In {\it Artificial Life II}, edited by C. G. Langton {\it et. al}, Redwood City CA, Addison Wesley, pp. 295–312, 1991.
Margulis, L. {\it Origin of Eucaryotic Cells.} New Haven, Yale University Press, 1970.
Prusinkiewicz, P. and Lindenmayer, A., {\it The Algorithmic Beauty of Plants}. Berlin, Springer-Verlag, 1991.
Ray, T. S., "An Approach to the Synthesis of Life." In {\it Artificial Life II}, edited by C. G. Langton {\it et.al.}, Redwood City CA, Addison Wesley, pp. 371–408, 1991.
Rebek, J., {\it et.al}, {\it J. Am. Chem. Soc.} {\bf 112}, 1,249, 1990.
Reynolds, C. W., "Flocks, Herds, and Schools: A Distributed Behavioral Model." Proceedings of SIGGRAPH '87, in {\it Computer Graphics.} {\bf V} 21, no. 4, pp. 25–34 (July, 1987).
Toffoli, T., "Cellular Automata as an Alternative to (Rather than an Approximation of) Differential Equations in Modeling Physics." {\it Physica D}, V10(1–2), 1984.
Toffoli, T., and Margolus, N., {\it Cellular Automata Machines.} MIT Press, 1987.
Ulam, S., "On some Mathematical Problems Connected with Patterns of Growth of Figures", {\em Proceedings of Symposia in Applied Mathematics} {\bf 14}, pp. 215–224. Reprinted in \cite{Burks70}.
Von Neumann, J., {\it Theory of Self-Reproducing Automata}, edited and completed by A. W. Burks, U. of Illinois Press, Urbana, 1966.
Wilson, S. W. "The Genetic Algorithm and Simulated Evolution." In {\it Artificial Life II}, edited by C. G. Langton {\it et.al.}, Redwood City CA, Addison Wesley, pp. 157–165, 1989.
Wolfram, S. "Cellular automaton fluids 1: Basic theory." {\it Journal of Statistical Physics} 45, pp. 471–526, 1986.

Figure 1
Two views of the mechanical duck attributed to Vaucanson.

Figure 2
Two views of a drawing automaton built by the Jaquet-Droz family

Figure 3
Schematic diagram of von Neumann's CA self-reproducing configuration.

Figure 5
The relationship between GTYPE and PTYPE.

Figure 6
A flock of "Boids" negotiating a field of columns.

Figure 7
GTYPES in (a) the GA and (b) the GPP paradigms

Figure 8
Crossover-operation in (a) the GA and (b) the GPP.

Figure 9
(a) Dawkin's "Adam" tree and (b) some of its descendants.

Figure 10
(a) Population of sorting networks stuck on a local fitness peak. In order to attain the higher peak, the population must cross a fitness "valley," which is difficult to achieve under normal Darwinian mechanisms. (b) The coevolving parasites deform the fitness landscape of the sorting networks, turning the fitness peak into a fitness valley, from which it is easy for the population to excape.

Figure 11
The payoff matrix for the Prisoners' Dilemma game. The pair (s_1, s_2) deontes the scores to players A and B respectively.

Figure 12
The four possible memory-1 strategies for playing the Prisoners' Dilemma game.

Figure 13
During evolutionary development, the system settles down to relatively long periods of stasis "punctuated" by periods of rapid evolutionary change.

REMAKE ≈ REMODEL

JOHANNES DOMSICH

REMAKE ≈ REMODEL
JOHANNES DOMSICH

Genetics and microbiology as motives of art—of ARS ELECTRORICA—of "electronical" art can only be explored by examining "concepts" of creation and the human being in his/her dualistic nature of creature and (re)creator.
I consider it indispensable to penetrate to the sometimes bizarre extremes of the history of civilization and art and to study them more closely than molecular biology which within the dimensions of scientific tradition has been effective only over an extremely short period and to analyze any possible influence on artistic, social and philosophical thinking, i.e. on creative imagination.
It will be mandatory to screen the histories of theology (religion), art, physical science or metaphysics for signs of a structure—for models and images af genesis and generation[1] (*Fabrica* as used by Steinbach).
Is there a method of creation or of reproduction? Or is creation a neverending chain of copies and the creator his own model?
I suspect br rather I divine that there is a strategy—a process oar even a plan—of thinking, a model of all ideas men have concerning production, origin, creation. Since there has been historical evidence of him in the form of products, plans and interpretations, man has been thinking of concepts and rules according to which he himself was "produced" and which he in his turn can or may apply to "produce".
One model, if not the initial one, is the "image", the duplicate, the clone which differs from the (divine) original only as to its competence and responsibility and last but not least its durability—it is the human being,.
In the beginning God created heaven and earth, and the earth was without form and void, with darkness over the face of the abyss and the spirit of God hovering over the surface of the waters. (...) God saw that it was good. Then God said, "Let us make man in our image and likeness to rule the fish in the sea, the birds of heaven, the cattle, all wild animals on earth, and all reptiles that crawl upon the earth." So God created man in his own image; in the image of God he created him; male and female le he created them. (Genesis 1, 1+2, 1,26+27)
And simultaneously there was the word in the beginning—God said (...) (Genesis 1,3), a technical model of communication as well as of reception starting the series of technical procedures of formulation and reproduction in a dia-

Genetik und Mikrobiologie als Motiva der Kunst – der ARS-ELECTRONICA – der „elektronischen" Kunst, sind nicht ohne die Hinwendung zu „Ideen" von Schöpfung und an den Menschen in seiner Dualität zwischen Kreatur und (Re-) Kreator zu erarbeiten.
Ich halte es für unentbehrlich, weit in die – zum Teil skurilen – Extreme der Kultur- und Kunstgeschichte vorzudringen und mehr als jenen, für die Dimension der Wissenschaftstradition extrem kurzen Wirkungszeitraum der Molekularbiologie und deren möglichen Einfluß auf das künstlerische, soziale und philosophische Denken, die kreierende Phantasie, zu analysieren.
Unerläßlich wird es sein, die Areale der Historien von Theologie (Religion), Kunst, der physikalistischen Wissenschaft oder der Metaphysik nach Indizien einer Struktur – nach Modellen und Bildern der Genese und der Generation[1] (*Fabrica* in derselben Verwendung bei Steinbach) zu durchleuchten.
Gibt es eine Methode der Schöpfung oder der Reproduktion? Oder ist Schöpfung eine nicht endende Kette von Kopien und der Schöpfer sein eigenes Vorbild?
Ich vermute, besser ich ahne eine Strategie – Prozedur oder auch einen Plan – des Denkens, ein Modell aller Vorstellungen der Menschen von Produktion, von Entstehen (Entstehung) – von Schöpfung. Fraglos entwirft der Mensch seit man von ihm historisch, ergo aus Produkten, Entwürfen und Interpretationen, weiß, Vorstellungen und Regeln, nach denen er „produziert" wurde und wiederum „produzieren" kann oder darf.
Eines, wenn nicht das initiale Muster ist das „Abbild", das Duplikat, der Klon, der nur in Kompetenz und Verantwortung und nicht zu vergessen in Haltbarkeit vom (göttlichen) Original differiert – der Mensch.
Im Anfang schuf Gott Himmel und Erde; die Erde aber war wüst und wirr, Finsternis lag über der Urflut, und Gottes Geist schwebte über dem Wasser (...) Gott sah, daß es gut war. Dann sprach Gott: Laßt uns Menschen machen als unser Abbild, uns ähnlich. Sie sollen herrschen über die Fische des Meeres, über die Vögel des Himmels, über das Vieh, über

die ganze Erde und über alle Kriechtiere auf dem Land. Gott schuf also den Menschen als sein Abbild; als Gottes Abbild schuf er ihn. Als Mann und Frau schuf er ihn. (Genesis 1/1,26)

Und zugleich war am Anfang das Wort – *Gott sprach (...)* (Genesis 1,3), ein technisches Modell der Kommunikation wie der Rezeption, mit dem die Kette der technischen Verfahren der Formulierungen, der Abbildungen, in der dialogen Artikulation des Willens begann. Gott erklärt sich in seinem Willen, dem Wort und seinem Abbild, dem Menschen – er kommuniziert. Nebenbei, einzig das Wort, der Name des Schöpfers, ist mächtiger als dieser selbst. Für einige Religionen und Mythologien der Grund den Namen zu verschweigen, ihn nicht auszusprechen.[2]

Remake.

Wenn die Geschichte des Menschen eine seiner Werkzeuge, seiner (Kultur-) Techniken ist, so ist es legitim, diese als Mittel eines Schaffens, einer Emanzipation der Spezies Mensch zu sehen. Einer Verselbständigung aus einer Welt des (Vor-) Gegebenen in ein Umfeld des von ihm Überarbeiteten, Veränderten. Vom Urwald, der Natur (... *Die Natur ist nicht bloß Produkt einer unbegreiflichen Schöpfung, sondern diese Schöpfung selbst.* Hamann 2, 283, Grimm zum Begriff Schöpfung) zur Landschaft. Vom Garten Eden – der göttlichen Kultivierung, zum Landschaftsgarten[3] – der menschlichen Kultivierung.

Es drängt der Gedanke in den Vordergrund, daß die Errungenschaften unserer Evolution nicht zu allererst Produkte – Werke – sind, sondern Werkzeuge. Instrumente, die unsere Sensoria, unsere Sinnlichkeit überformen, vielleicht sogar determinieren und unsere produktive Aufmerksamkeit und unsere Wünsche lenken. Zu intensivieren und zu verstärken kommt einem Fokussieren gleich. Es handelt sich um sinnliche Selektionen, von denen nur wenige ohne Werkzeuge der Wahrnehmung unsere Sinne erreichen würden.

Produkte der Kunst, der Wissenschaft sind Resultate gegebener technischer Möglichkeiten und gleichbleibender – stagnierender, konstanter oder sich wiederholender – Ideen.

Kontinuierlich in der Kultur ist das Bedürfnis Kunst und Wissenschaft zu treiben. Die Art, in der dies geschieht, ist aber bedingt durch die Werkzeuge, die unsere Phantasie und Aufmerksamkeit lenken. Weitergehend behaupte ich, daß die „Schöpfung" von Werkzeugen die Produktion von Wissenschaft und Kunst in thematischer und formaler Hinsicht bestimmt. Werkzeuge sind die determinierende, ästhetische Instanz der Kultur.

Werk – Zeug(e) ≈ Augen – Zeuge.

Um ein Beispiel zu geben: Mikro- und Teleskop verändern

logic articulation of intent, God becomes manifest in his intent, his word and his image, in the human being—he communicates. By the way, only the word, the name of the creator is more powerful than he himself. This being the reason for some religions and mythologies not to pronounce or utter this name.[2]

Remake.

If the history of man is a history of his tools, his techniques (of civilization), then these may rightfully be considered the means of a creative process, of the emancipation of the human species from a world of preset cirumstances to an environment remade and changed by him. From the primeval forest, from nature to landscape (... *Nature is not only the product of an incomprehensible creation but it is this very creation.* Hamann 2, 283, Grimm on the term creation). From the garden Eden—the divine cultivation to the landscape garden[3]—the human cultivation.

The idea suggests ftself that the achievements of our evolution are not products—works in the first place but rather tools. That they are instruments reshaping and even determining our sensoria, our sensuality and guiding our productive attention and our desires, Intensifying and amplifying is tantamount to focussing. Sensory selections must be made and only few of these would reach our senses without such instruments of perception.

Products of art, of science are the results of existing technical conditions and invariable—stagnant, constant or recurring—ideas.

What continues in civilization is the desire to engage in art and science. How this is done, however, is determined by the tools which guide our imagination and attention. Furthermore, I maintain that the "creation" of tools determines the production of science and the arts as to their themes and forms. Tools are the determining aesthetic authority of civilizatian.

Creating—Instruments— Recording—Instruments

To give an example: microscope and telescope change our modes of vision (our desires), our interest and its interpretations as machines change our perception of speed and value. Science and also art turn into a game of answers and not of questions—as tools are the incidental instruments of our present contentedness.

Tools are a second authority—as it were—for evaluating the phenomena of our environment. They record and measure in dimensions that are beyond our senses. Putting it differently: They are either more competent or inferior to our senses. At any rate they are both status quo and compromise.

The notion of "how something works" cannot be separated from the notion of "how it is or was being dane". Thus man is looking for the "elements of life" and is using metaphors of his own production in attempting an explanation of his origin. Any production, any work serves as a parable of his own origin and his own functioning.

The religious idea of man's creatian is the matrix (the design, the draft) of human imagination and production. We consider us to be images, as nothing else seems to make sense.

This explains the enthusiasm with new methods or scientific innovations[4]: they are quickly incorporated into the theories of explanation (popular—science journals and special interest publications thrive on this enthusiasm), they are another draft of the many speculated blueprints of the world and of man—booty retrieved from a divine laboratary[5].
Thus striking antagonists of man have arisen from the fantasies of writers, artists, or scientists : "Body and soul" produce ghosts, "gaseous vertebrates" in the words of Otto Reurath[6]. With the findings of electrophysics a seventeen year old girl[7] invents the electrically reanimating Frankenstein. Hoffmann succumbs to the charms of the machine and falls in love with Olympia[8]. Is Dracula a product of geography, histary, and serology? Was he devised only to glorify the disco f the dictaphone and the blood transfusion or did Bram Stoker[9] intend the victory of women's emancipation over the male non—dead[10]? He certainly is a monster of flesh and above all blood, not of clay like the Golem of a "non—dissecting" time. Knowing of nuclear energy B—movie directars use giant ants to terrorize progressive Americans and not only simple tabloid journalists write about computers governing the world.
Men create (their) images.
And men strive to improve themselves and their environment, to carry on creation. Men are the evolution. They subdue the earth.
God blessed them and said to them, "Be fruitful and increase, fill the earth and subdue it, rule over the fish in the sea, the birds of heaven, and every living thing that moves upon the earth." (Genesis 1,28)
This is done not only in actual products, be they profit—oriented ventures like breeding, genetic manipulation and the like, but also in fictions and phantasmata. It becomes manifest in ornament, decoration or as whimsical result of

1

unsere Sichtweisen (Sehnsüchte), unser Interesse und dessen Interpretationen, wie Maschinen unsere Wahrnehmung von Geschwindigkeit und Wert. Wissenschaft und auch Kunst werden zu einem Spiel der Antworten und nicht der Fragen – denn Werkzeuge sind die zufälligen Instrumente momentaner Zufriedenheit.
Werkzeuge sind gleichsam eine zweite Instanz in der Bewertung von Phänomenen unserer Umwelt. Sie bilden ab und messen in Dimensionen, die unseren Sinnen unmöglich sind. Oder anders gesagt: Sie sind entweder kompetenter oder unseren Sinnen unterlegen. In jedem Fall sind sie Status Quo und Kompromiß.
Die Vorstellung „wie etwas funktioniert" kann nicht von der Vorstellung „wie es gemacht wird oder wurde" getrennt werden. So sucht der Mensch nach den „Bausteinen des Lebens", verwendet Metaphern seiner eigenen Produktion um sich einer Ansicht seiner Entstehung zu nähern. Jedes Produzieren, jedes Werk setzt er als Parabel seiner eigenen Entstehung, seines Funktionierens.
Die religiöse Idee der eigenen Schöpfung ist die Matrix (Vorlage, Entwurf) menschlicher Vorstellung und Produktion. Wir beschreiben uns als Ebenbilder, weil nichts anderes denkbar (vielleicht auch nicht sinnvoll) ist.
So erklärt sich auch die Begeisterung über neue Methoden oder wissenschaftliche Innovationen:[4] eilends werden sie in das Erklärungsbild einverleibt (populär-wissenschaftliche Special Interest Publikationen leben von diesem Enthusiasmus), sind ein erneuter Entwurf zu den vielen spekulierten Bauplänen der Welt und des Menschen – Beutestücke aus einem göttlichen Labor.[5]
So entstanden und entstehen die bemerkenswerten Widergänger des Menschen in den Phantasien von Literaten, Künstlern oder Wissenschaftlern: „Leib und Seele" produzieren Gespenster, ≈ gasförmige Wirbeltiere", wie Otto Neurath[6] sie nennt. Mit den Erkenntnissen der Elektrophysik phantasiert eine Sechzehnjährige[7] den elektrisch reanimierenden Frankenstein. Hoffmann erliegt dem Liebreiz der Maschine und verliebt sich in Olympia.[8] Ist Dracula ein Produkt von Geografie, Geschichte und Serologie? Wurde er nur entworfen um die Entdeckungen des Diktaphons und der Bluttransfusion zu verherrlichen oder läßt Bram Stoker[9] die Emanzipation der Frauen über den männlichen Untoten siegen? Sicher ist er ein Monster aus Fleisch und vor allem Blut, nicht tönern wie der Golem einer „nicht sezierenden" Zeit. In Kenntnis der Kernenergie terrorisieren B-Movie-Regisseure mit Riesenameisen fortschrittsgläubige Amerikaner, und daß Computer die Welt regieren, publizieren nicht nur schlichte Boulevard-Journalisten.

Der Mensch macht sich (s)ein Ebenbild.

Und der Mensch arbeitet an seiner und der „Verbesserung" seiner Umwelt, an der Fortführung der Schöpfung. Er *ist* die Evolution. Er macht sich die Erde Untertan.

Gott segnete sie „und Gott sprach zu ihnen: Seid fruchtbar und vermehret euch, bevölkert die Erde, unterwerft sie euch, und herrscht über die Fische des Meeres, über die Vögel des Himmels und über alle Tiere, die sich auf dem Land regen. (Genesis 1,28)

Er tut dies nicht nur in realen Produkten, sei es in nutzorientierten Unterfangen wie Züchtung, Genmanipulation und dergleichen, sondern auch in seinen Fiktionen und Phantasmen. Als Ornament, als Dekoration oder auch als schrulliges Resultat der Spielerei mit einer Art „Schöpfungs-Kaleidoskop", bei dem Chimären, Sphingen, Sirenen, Basiliske, Gryllen oder Dämonen entstehen.

Einige gemeinsame Strategien der erneuernden Perspektiven lassen sich unschwer beobachten: Innovation in der Produktion von Werkzeugen – eine indirekte Verbesserung des Menschen; Innovation in der Medizin – eine direkte Verbesserung; Innovation in der Manipulation – der Mensch imitiert seinen Schöpfer auch in der Produktion der „Stellvertreter", Phantasie einer Freizeitkultur.

Das Delegieren der Produktion ist ein basales Muster menschlicher Werkzeugkreativität. Es entbindet ihn nicht zuletzt durch seine Abwesenheit von „persönlicher" Verantwortung. Darin finde ich eine Erklärung für fehlende Perfektion, denn Stellvertreter sind nicht vollkommen, dürfen es nicht sein. Wir aber wollen „vollkommen" sein, sehen uns daher, wenn auch erst in der Ewigkeit, als erlösbare Stellvertreter eines Schöpfers, denn wir formulieren uns als sein Ebenbild, ja wir „spielen" ihn geradezu nach (Siebentagewoche[11]). Unseren Geschöpfen hingegen erlauben wir keine völlige Perfektion, außer es handelt sich um Prothesen (Detaillösungen), also intime Gegenstände von uns selbst.

Das (DNA, Anm. d. Aut.) *aber definiert keine Individuen mehr, sondern mögliche Mutanten. Aus biologischer, genetischer und kybernetischer Sicht sind wir alle Mutanten. Für Mutanten kann es nun aber kein Jüngstes Gericht, keine Auferstehung des Körpers mehr geben, denn welcher Körper soll auferstehen? Seine Formel, seine Chromosomen werden sich verändert haben, er wird nach anderen motorischen und mentalen Variabeln programmiert sein, er wird kein Recht mehr auf sein Bild haben. (…)*[12]

Grundmatrix ist die Fiktion oder auch die Sehnsucht nach Optimierung: der kompetente Mensch, die optimale Produktion, das maximale Produkt. Optional betreiben wir die vollständige, optimale Polarisierung: Gut und Böse.

fiddling around with a kind of "creative kaleidoscope" producing chimaera, sphinges, sirens, basilisks, grylli or demons.

Some cammon strategies of innovating perspectives can easily be observed: Innovation concerning the production of instruments—an indirect impravement for men; innovation concerning medicine—a direct improvement; innovation concerning manipulation—man imitates his creator even when producing "substitutes'; the fantasy of a leisure culture.

Delegating production is a basal pattern of human instrument creativity. Man is released of his "personal" responsibility not least by his absence. To me this constitutes an explanation of the lack of perfection; substitutes after all are not perfect, must not be so. We, however, want to be "perfect". Thus we consider ourselves to he redeemable substitutes of a creator, be it sometime in eternity, and we conceive ourselves as his very images, we even "act" like him (the seven—day features however, we do not grant complete perfection unless they are mere prostheses (specific solutions), that is our very personal objects.

It (the DNA, author's note) *no longer defines individuals but possible mutants. From a biological, genetic and cybernetic point of view all of us are mutants. There can, however, nat be a last judgement nor a resurrection for mutants; which body should rise? Our formula, our chromosomes will have been changed, we will be programmed according to different motorial and mental variables, we will no longer be entitled to our image. (…)*[12]

Basic matrix is the fiction or the desire to optimize: tbe competent human being, the optimal production, the maximal product. We opt for complete, optimal polarisation: good and evil.

Remodel.

Next to religion natural science undoubtedly is an important and very indicative source of human aspiration and human formulation regarding genetics. It computes and is computable. It reduces the description, i.e., the formulation to "the formula of life".

Very precisely, yet not completely along my line of reasoning, has this idea of reduction been expressed by Jean Baudrillard[13]:

The religious, metaphysical or philosophical definition fo being his given way to an operational definition within the conceptuality of genetic codes (DNA) and of brain structure (code of information and billions of neurons). We are part of a system where there is no longer any soul nor body metaphor—not even the tale of the unconscious meets with any response. (…)

Yet there is also a frightening aspect; the fear of punished hubris with its well—known repertory of plagues afflicting us such as ecological catastrophes, malformation and Gomorrhan decadence[14]. Bosch's apocalypses are frightening—most of their details, however, were taken from the grylli which were positive fantasies[15] of the creative kaleidoscope mentianed before. They were amusement of antiquity and fetishes of the middle ages.

Of special intellectual as well as artistic appeal

appears to be the idea that there must still exist further products, alternatives and results of creation: Though put down by the spreading of the "theory of evolution as a religion" they are still alive in fable and story and haunt the cinema as disneytype fantasy.
Even in the twentieth century the close relationship between mythology and medicine is documented: In his lecture on "Greek Gods and Human Monsters" given in 1901, the gynaecologist Schatz maintained that centaurs were modelled on human beings born with too many legs.[16] Scientists of different disciplines like Charles Gould[17] e.g. were misled by their interpretation when describing dragons, unfcorns or the bird Phoenix as extinct species.
From a look at the exhibits in toy—shops it becomes evident that there is at least one group of people who are highly interested in this other "vanished creation".[18] Is not the forming of mixed beings an attempt (be it a childlike one) at rationalization, at visualisation and thus an early attempt at fighting the terrible, the frightening—an attempt at breaking the spell.
Saurian teeth no longer suffice to prove the existence of dragons and their knightly killers. But who would object to the thesis that all life comes from the sea? A view that has most charmingly been depicted long before the findings of modern times.
Phantasmata are not only the object of human manipulation they also serve to formulate, to allegorize, to convey ideas. They depict the inexpressible. They go beyond words. Synthetic creatures appear to be synonymous of certain characteristics, they are indicative of the two antipodes "good and evil".
The "entertaining character" has naw disappeared from the fantasies (with the exception of toys). They have been surrendered to the soberness of physicalism and the calculable utilitarian approach determines the reasoning.
The wishful thinking of medical men and microbiologists nevertheless includes dream of healing and improvement that have nothing in common with rational conclusions. Hereditary diseases or cancer are to be defeated, to be taken from us like original sin. Aspirations since scientific disciplines have existed. Imgrovement towards the original.
This godlike intervention into the given facts is accompanied by the horror and the punishment mentioned before and the consequences thereof are strikingly similar to the weird fantasies of antiquity or medieval times. We cannot boast of progress in the sphere of the irrational and frightening and the demons appear to be archetypes of the human obsession with fear and guilt. Yet, inspite of their almost bigoted seriousness they serve to amuse—in the cinema. Again they imitate, they also imitate us. They are strange and yet they tahe any form that we suggest. It is their trich to change into the nothing that they are—alfens[19].
Rot only the manipulation of the divine creation is punished—God being *"the creator of every creature"* so Ottokar or Luther (Sir. 1,7), *"... the most high, the creator of all things, almighty"* (quotes in Old German). Those who surpass the Gods fare even worse. Literary history is

Remodel.
Fraglos ist die Naturwissenschaft neben der Religion eine wichtige und indizienreiche Quelle menschlichen Wollens und menschlicher Formulierung in Hinsicht auf die Genetik. Sie berechnet und sie ist rechenbar. Sie reduziert die Beschreibung = die Formulierung auf „die Formel des Lebens". Sehr prägnant, wenn auch nicht ganz in meiner Argumentation, findet sich diese Idee von Reduktion bei Jean Baudrillard:[13]

Die religiöse, metaphysische oder philosophische Definition des Seins hat einer operationalen Definition in der Begrifflichkeit der genetischen Codes (DNS) und der Gehirnstruktur (Informationscode und Milliarden von Neuronen) den Platz geräumt. Wir befinden uns in einem System, in dem es keine Seele, keine Körpermetapher mehr gibt – nicht einmal mehr das Märchen vom Unbewußten stößt noch auf Widerhall. (...)

Aber da ist auch noch eine ängstigende Seite, die Furcht vor bestrafter Hybris mit dem hinlänglich bekannten Repertoire an Plagen, die uns heimsuchen, wie ökologische Katastrophen, Mißbildung und gomorrhäische Dekadenz.[14] Boschs Apokalypsen ängstigen, aber die meisten von deren Detailvorbildern, die Gryllen, waren positive Phantasien[15] des bereits beschriebenen Schöpfungskaleidoskops – waren Amüsement der Antike und Fetische des Mittelalters.
Besonderes intellektuelles wie auch künstlerisches Vergnügen scheint der Glaube zu bereiten, daß es noch andere Produkte, Alternativen und Ergebnisse einer Schöpfung geben müsse: Sie endeten zwar mit der Verbreitung der „Religion Evolutionslehre", sie sind aber in Fabel und Märchen lebendig und sei es auch nur im Trivialkino als disneyeske Fantasy.
Das Naheverhältnis von Mythologie und Medizin dokumentiert sich noch im zwanzigsten Jahrhundert: Der Gynäkologe Schatz behauptet in seinem 1901 gehaltenen Vortrag ≈Die griechischen Götter und die menschlichen Mißgeburten" in humanen Mißgeburten mit überzähligen Beinen eine Erklärung für die Kentauren gefunden zu haben.[16] Naturwissenschaftler anderer Disziplinen wie etwa Charles Gould[17] wurden Opfer ihrer Fehlinterpretationen, indem sie Drachen, Einhörner oder den Vogel Phönix als ausgestorbene Naturformen schilderten.
Wenn man die Schaufenster von Spielzeuggeschäften betrachtet, dann gibt es zumindest eine Bevölkerungsgruppe, die reges Interesse an dieser anderen, „untergegangenen Schöpfung" zeigt.[18] Und wenn man in der Formung von Mischwesen einen Versuch der (warum nicht auch kindlichen) Rationalisierung, des Sichtbarmachens sieht, dann

2

handelt es sich dabei möglicherweise um einen frühen Versuch des Ankämpfens gegen Schreckliches und Ängstigendes – um eine Entzauberung.
Saurierzähne genügen uns nicht mehr als Belege für Drachen und deren minnigliche Töter, aber wem widerstrebt der Lehrsatz, daß alles Leben aus dem Meer komme? Eine Meinung, die lange vor den neuzeitlichen Erkenntnissen in charmanter Weise zur Darstellung wurde.
Phantasmen sind nicht nur Ziel menschlicher Manipulation, sie dienen auch der Formulierung, der Allegorie und der Gestaltung von Ideen. Sie sind Bilder des Unsagbaren. So erscheinen uns synthetische Kreaturen als Synonyme von Eigenschaften, zuletzt wieder als Indikationen des Extrempaares „Gut / Böse".
Nunmehr ist der „Unterhaltungscharakter" aus den Phantastereien gewichen (Ausnahme Kinderspielzeug). Sie sind dem Ernst des Physikalismus überantwortet und das rechenbare Nutzen-Argument steht unmittelbar im Vordergrund der Kalküle.
Und doch findet man in den träumerischen Wünschen von Medizinern und Mikrobiologen Sehnsüchte von Heilung und Besserung, die nichts mit rationalen Folgerungen gemein haben. Erbkrankheiten oder Krebs sollen besiegt werden, vergleichbar einer Erbsünde von uns genommen sein. Sehnsüchte seit der Geburtsstunde einer Wissenschaftsdisziplin. Verbesserung hin zum Original.
Dieser gottähnliche Eingriff in Vorgegebenes wird begleitet von dem schon angedeuteten Horror, den Strafen, die in ihren Konsequenzen frappant den wüsten Phantasien der Antike oder des Mittelalters gleichen. Im Irrationalen, Ängstigenden ist unser Fortschritt nichts und sind die Dämone beinahe Archetypen menschlicher Angst- und Schuldkomplexe. Sie sind trotz allen, beinah frömmlerischen Ernstes, Amüsement – im Kino. Dort imitieren sie erneut, auch uns. Sie sind fremd und doch jede Form, für die wir ihnen Vorbild sind. Ihr Trick ist die Verwandlung in nichts, das *sie* sind – Alien.[19]

crowded with such tragic figures. Orpheus, the better but careless musician; Lamia and Niobe, the better mothers; and many others suffer a variety of partly unjust fates. Divine plans can be stolen. Punishment is finite. What will happen to the creatures, however? What is their development like, what course do they take and what are their wishes? Prametheus—Pandora—what remains hidden if we see with Zeus's light? Let us return to the reasoning of our culture: When we speak of genetics we speak of a young discipline and tradition of one hranch of biology, of natural science. The term genetics certainly reminds us of what we learned at school about the theory of evalution with its rather obscure ideas, conflicting arguments or the (speculating) "Mendel's Laws". The mistake of equating Darwin[20], Mendel, the theories of heredity and origin and genetics right into our days has supplied abstruse racism as an aggressive argument or trivial polemics in human minds.
Art is closely related to traditions. The latter are signs of evalution, if evolution stands only for heredity and selection. Heredity can be something intimate—yet at the same time also fascist in terms like "clean" "cleansing", "select" or the naively romantic idea that only the strongest survive. Chance—an inherent factor of hereditary theory—is of no concern as a factor of selection in such platitudinal appraach.
There is the longheld tradition of teaching pupils "penultimate" techniques and findings.[21] I am thinking of all the instances where children should have applied fragments of the almost forgotten "Mendel's Laws" and how much bias and ambiguity has implicitly been passed on to pugfls by their teachers.
At the end of this text I mam going to quote a passage by Schrödinger to contradict the trite "computabi1ity" and to formulate with a new methodical approach. In short: I want to see the theory of evolutian[22] and also genetics to be added as models of explanation to our field of concern "Art and Genetics". I think that they are very close to each other and are being treated as almost one and the same in the minds of those who only want to use the word.
A passage from Mauthner's[23] underlines this synonymous use of genetics:
(…) A child's acquisition of language is lonked to his consciousness just as is his learning to walk; with regard to the genetic development of language we also bave to maintain that every acquisition, every bold new metaphor has been lined to consciousness. (…)
At a time of predominately optical media we tend to define reality and value in optical terms. Products of computer graphics and animation may serve as aesthetic proaf—they provide sensual quality by focussing on the description of surfaces.
Communication and information are restricted to the surface, the cover. The optic argument dominates. This leads to a cosmetic endeavour which transfers problems exclusively via this visual channel.
This also explains the rather foolish simple—mindedness of teachers and parents when they make pupils treat their environment, that is "na-

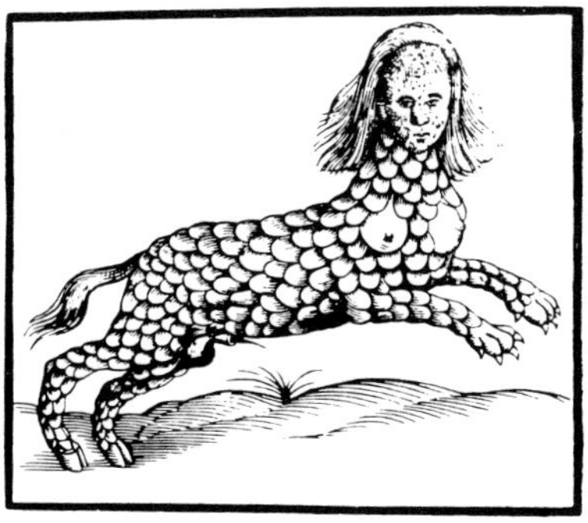

3 „Lamia". London, 1658.

ture" cosmetically by collecting (superficial) waste. This teaches them to reassure themselves by restoring the surface and to plan and interpret according to surfaces. Decay, sichness or genetic deficiencies are being diagnosed superficially. Skins are indicators of our aesthetics. Superficial signs condition our opinion. *Beware of those bearing a mark.*—Sickness as well as beauty have to be seen in order to be understood.
Having said all this I want to note that I consider genetics to be a producing, changing discipline rather than an analysing one. By disposition it is one of the practised possibilities of explaining the world and is placed very close to mechanist systems or the "yes and no" concept of computer nomenclature.
Speaking of the genetic code, the "language of the genes" implies a tendency towards formulating i.e. reproducing life—we can understand only what we can make or do—creator or dumb "learning by doing"?
The selections of the objects observed and formulated become exposed and manifest in art. Thus the focus of the aesthetic interest becomes the motif of manipulation and construction.

4 Antidarwinistische Karikatur aus der englischen Zeitschrift „Punch" mit dem Text: „Bin ich ein Mensch und ein Bruder?" 1861.

Strafe findet aber nicht nur die Manipulation der göttlichen Schöpfung – Gott als »*schephaere aller creatiur*" Ottokar oder Luther (Sir. 1,7): »... *der allerhöhest, der schepffer aller dinge, allmechtig*". Schlimmer noch ergeht es denen, die die Götter übertreffen. Die Literaturgeschichte ist bevölkert mit dergleichen tragischen Figuren. Orpheus, der bessere aber achtlose Musiker, Lamia und Niobe, die besseren Mütter und viele mehr ereilen variantenreich teils ungerechte, entsetzliche Schicksale. Göttliche Konzepte kann man stehlen. Die Strafe dafür ist endlich. Doch was wird den Kreaturen widerfahren? Wie ist ihre Entwicklung, wie ihr Weg und wie gestaltet sind ihre Wünsche? Prometheus – Pandora – oder was bleibt uns verborgen, wenn wir mit zeus'schem Licht sehen? Doch zurück zu den Argumentationen der Kultur: Mit Genetik meint man eine junge Disziplin und Tradition einer Sparte der Biologie, der Naturwissenschaften. Sicherlich ist der Begriff Genetik verwoben mit Erinnerungen an die zu Schulzeiten erworbene Evolutionslehre, mit ihren zum Teil obskuren Vorstellungen, Konflikten und Debatten oder die (rechnend spekulierenden) »Mendelschen Regeln". Diese fehlerhafte Gleichbetrachtung von Darwin,[20] Mendel, der Vererbungs- und Abstammungslehre und der Genetik speist bis in die Gegenwart abstruse Rassentheorien als aggressives Argument oder triviale Polemik im Denken der Menschen.
Kunst steht in einem nahen Verhältnis zu Traditionen. Diese sind Indizien von Evolution, sieht man in ihr nur Vererbung und Selektion. Vererbung kann Intimes sein – gleichwohl auch faschistoid in den Begriffen ‚sauber", „säubern", „Auslese" oder der naiv romantischen Vorstellung, daß nur der Stärkste überlebe. Der Zufall, ein immanenter Faktor der Vererbungslehre, als Selektionsinstanz spielt in derlei Binsenweisheit keine Rolle.
Es gibt die nur zulange Tradition jener Pädagogik, die den Schülern ein Verständnis über „vorletzte" Techniken und Erkenntnisse lehrt.[21] Dabei denke ich daran, wieviel sich Kinder mit Fragmenten der in ihrer Vollständigkeit beinah vergessenen „Mendelschen Regeln" hätten erklären sollen, wieviel Tendenziöses und Mißverständliches damit unausgesprochen von Lehrern an Schüler weitergegeben wurde.
Am Ende dieses Textes ist von mir ein Zitat Schrödingers gesetzt, um der banalen „(Be-) Rechenbarkeit" zu widersprechen, um aus einer neuen methodischen Überlegung zu formulieren. Mit einem Satz: ich möchte die Evolutionstheorie[22] und auch die Genetik als Erklärungsmodelle dem Arbeitsgebiet »Kunst und Genetik" beifügen. Ich glaube, daß sie in den Köpfen derer, die bloß das Wort verwenden wollen, sehr eng aneinander liegen – fast wie ein und dasselbe behandelt werden.

Wie sehr und wie lange schon Genetik synonym verwendet wird, zeigt eine Passage bei Mauthner:[23]

(...) Das Sprechenlernen des Kindes ist mit Bewußtsein verbunden wie das Gehenlernen; auch in der genetischen Entwicklung der Sprache müssen wir behaupten, daß jede Bereicherung, jede neue kühne Metapher, mit Bewußtsein verbunden war. (...)

Wir neigen in einer Phase dominierend optisch transportierender Medien dazu, Wirklichkeit und Wert optisch zu definieren. Als ästhetisches Indiz mögen etwa Produkte der Computergrafik und -animation dienen, die sinnliche Qualität betont über die Beschreibung der Oberflächen lösen.

Kommunikation und Information bleiben auf die Oberfläche, die Hülle beschränkt. Es dominiert gleichsam das optische Argument. Und dieses gerät zu einem kosmetischen Bestreben, das Probleme nur noch in diesem visuellen Kanal transferiert.

Nicht anders ist die beinahe schildbürgerliche Naivität zu erklären, mit der Schulklassen von ihren Lehrern und Eltern dazu angehalten werden, die Umwelt, sprich „die Natur", zu kosmetisieren, indem sie sie von (oberflächlichem) Abfall reinigen. Sie lernen dadurch, sich mittels einer intakten Oberfläche zu beruhigen und nach Oberflächen zu konstruieren und zu interpretieren. Denn Verfall, Krankheit oder genetische Mängel werden oberflächlich diagnostiziert. Häute sind die Indikatoren unserer Ästhetik. Oberflächliche Zeichen bedingen unsere Meinung.

Hütet euch vor den Gezeichneten. – Krankheit wie Schönheit muß man sehen um sie zu verstehen.

Bei all dem ist aber festzusetzen, daß ich in der Genetik mehr eine produzierende, verändernde Disziplin sehe, als eine analysierende. In Ihrer Disposition ist sie eine der praktizierten Möglichkeiten sich die Welt zu erklären, hat ihren Platz sehr nahe an mechanistischen Systemen oder der Idee von „Ja und Nein" als dem Bezeichnungssystem der Computer.

Denn spricht man von genetischem Code, der „Sprache der Gene", so ist die Ausrichtung hin in ein Formulieren demnach Reproduzieren des Lebens gegeben – man kann nur verstehen, was man machen kann – Creator, Schöpfer oder dummes „learnig by doing"?

Die Selektionen der Objekte der Betrachtung und der Formulierung exponieren und manifestieren sich in der Kunst. Ergo wird der Fokus des ästhetischen Interesses zum Motiv der Manipulation und der Konstruktion. Oder: Nur was man wissen will, also erkennen kann, wird formuliert. Um zu erkennen verwendet der Mensch Instrumente – Künstler, Mikroskope, Medien und dergleichen – er „formuliert" in und

Putting it differently: We formulate anly what we want to know, what we can perceive. In order to perceive we use instruments—artists, microscopes, media and the like—out of and in our interest we formulate not only products but also tools of new interest. And we do so increasingly beyond our genetically provided sensua l capabilities.

The idea as programme—wishful thinking as production programme.

Man does not perceive without tools. Perception requires communication. This implies that the technology of his communication is also the matrix of his "idea". In E.T.A. Hoffmann's "Olympia" beauty[24] is formulated and produced as a machine. To Mary Wollstonecraft Shelley surgery and electricity are the ideas of functioning and biochemistry. A mirror (a cover) is conceived as an image which can be differentiated only by virtue of its lach of history.

This is different in the "genetic tradition" of describing children as the images of their parents—to the observer they represent the past and the future and simulate God—Father and creation within creation (cover, identical).

Parents cultivate their ambition to achieve their own perfection in their children similar to our experience of art as a "reproduction", a different, more perfected perception of the world.

At the same time we want the tools and the product man to be polyfunctional, although such strange fantasies as those of "warrior or thinker races" still persist in the fictions of authars and dictators.

Our notions of the media, technology or tools are also significant: Similar to a Swiss army knife they must be able to meet the mast diverse expectations as ta their performance, quality and function. A personal computer for instance "can do anything". On its surface it imitates conventional, traditional tools as to their function and formality as icons. The haptic "formulation" is being cancelled by polyfunction and simultaneous uniformity: A computer remains a computer, it is no airbrush

Remember also the jocular "genetic fantasy" of the farmer: the "woolmilkpig". Genetically manipulated animals turn into a caricature of human values, into ecstasies of function and usefulness.

I want to remind of the perfection regarding the revision of our environment, We change our spaces of living by shaping and manipulating nature, perhaps by even settling it one day with manipulations of a kind depicted in Bosch's paradise—garden or purgatory.

Similar to architecture within architecture the landscape gardeners of the baroque put nature within nature—they "transplant" and import vegetation and architecture from newly discovered distant lands according ta arguments of taste. They treat nature as a theatre and in it they place the stages of their time—for instance the Salzburg Felsentheater. The world is turned into a stage for men, transferred animals lihe the pheasant become stage properties for their entertainment, their culture.

Remodel.

If changed nature dominates its environment

then traditional art, which is a fiction, has transgressed the limits of its production. This is where the quality of the disciplines is determined.
This is being counteracted by the aesthetics of ecology. Its dogma is: Fast change is destruction.
The indicated li1mit of arbitrary change must not be transgressed. Ecology claims a not clearly defined speed for the caurse of developments, a speed lying beyond human periods of life. It appears strangely religious as a suffering passive movement, not at all civilizatory. Man would turn into an observer, a recorder of time which according to these maxims, however, would have lost its significance as a standard of human distances. As a creator of art and science man would then only have to name, to describe—a fantasy of dictatorial naturalists.
Does culture stylize life? Do we resemble the "gallant shepherds" of the rococo living a secure but anemic life? This would mean that the security provided by econmy and the achievements of medicine have turned us into dull and boring actors of a strange (rustic) "alternative" culture. There can be no returning to nature as there is no nature.
We only stylfze according to preferred approaches—according to what we like to see or have learnt to interpret as being beautiful. The question remains: what changes when taste changes and different "cuts" are in.
Do we think differently simply because we act differently?
It becomes abvious, we do not only tend to newly assemble found phenomena (grylli), our taste as matrix (law) of action seems to function along similar lines. The focus of observation and the interpretations of the senses continue to be linked with each other in new and different ways. We work like kaleidoscopes: haleidoscopes of the senses—kaleidoscopes of communication—kaleidoscopes of art, of science.
Remade—remodel.
Is then creating anew no more than sorting out once again, merely changing a structure perhaps? Assemblage
Seen this way genetics can be compared to a "library" of sensualities, of capacities. It creates an architecture from continuously new "elements of creation, of life" like its information, which is called DNA. And I think of Dick's idea of fraud—a fraud of flesh and blood[25] and compare it to Lem's fraud, that of the memory of imagination[26]. I think of the kaleidoscopes of science and art.
If biology triumphs over the machine of mechanics—will there by the triumph of the "first divine biology" over the "other"—the second one of man?
Incredibly small groups of atoms, far too sdmall to keep to rather exact statistics, are a domnant factor in the highly ordered, regular processes of the organism (...) The gene is much to small (... to exhibit an orderly hehaviour obeying the laws of physics.
Erwin Schrödinger
And nothing "has been here before" if we hnow that it has been here before.
Recover.

aus seinem Interesse nicht nur Produkte sondern auch Werkzeuge neuen Interesses. Und er tut dies zunehmend außerhalb seiner sinnlichen genetisch bedingten Möglichkeiten.
Die Idee als Konzept – Wunschvorstellung als Produktionskonzept.
Der Mensch erkennt nicht ohne Werkzeuge. Wahrnehmung ist ohne Kommunikation nicht denkbar. Das bedeutet, daß die Technik seiner Kommunikation ebenfalls Matrix seiner „Vorstellung" ist. Mit E.T.A. Hoffmanns ≈ Olympia" wird das Schöne[24] als Maschine formuliert und produziert, Chirurgie und Elektrizität sind die Vorstellung einer Mary Wollstonecraft Shelley von Funktionieren und Biochemie. Gedacht wird ein Spiegel (Hülle, Cover) als Ebenbild, das nur wegen des Fehlens von Geschichte unterscheidbar ist.
Nicht so in der „genetischen Tradition", Kinder als Ebenbild ihrer Eltern zu beschreiben – sie stellen sinniger Weise Vergangenheit und Zukunft für den momentanen Betrachter her, und simulieren ihm Gott-Vater und die Schöpfung in der Schöpfung (Cover, deckungsgleich).
Eltern kultivieren das Verlangen nach Perfektionierung ihrer selbst in ihren Kindern wie uns die Kunst als „Reproduktion", als eine andere, perfektere Wahrnehmung der Welt erscheint.
Gleichzeitig tritt der Wunsch nach Polyfunktionalität in den Werkzeugen und im Produkt Mensch auf, obwohl derart seltsame Phantasien wie die von „Krieger- oder Denker-Rassen" in den Fiktionen von Autoren und Diktatoren nachwievor überdauern.
Signifikant sind auch unsere Vorstellungen von Medien, Technik oder Werkzeugen: Ähnlich einem Schweizermesser müssen sie in der Lage sein, unterschiedlichste Anforderung an Leistung, Qualität und Funktion zu erfüllen. Ein Personal Computer etwa „kann alles". Er imitiert in seiner Oberfläche konventionelle, traditionelle Werkzeuge in deren Funktion und auch Formalität als Icons. Die haptische „Formulierung" ist durch Polyfunktion und die gleichzeitige Uniformität aufgehoben: Denn ein Computer bleibt ein Computer, er ist kein Luftpinsel und er ist auch kein Taschenkalender. Oder denken Sie an die zur Scherzphrase gewordene „genetische Phantasie" des Landwirts, die ≈Wollmilchsau". Genetisch manipulierte Tiere werden zur Karikatur menschlicher Wertvorstellungen, zu Extasen von Funktion und Nutzen.
Erinnern möchte ich an die Perfektion in der Revision der Umwelt. Der Mensch verändert die Räume seiner Lebensmöglichkeiten, indem er die Natur gestaltet, manipuliert und vielleicht einmal mit Manipulationen bevölkert in einer Eigenart wie Boschs Paradiesgärten oder dessen Fegefeuer.

Wie Architektur in der Architektur, setzen die Gartenkünstler des Barock Natur in die Natur – sie „transplantieren" und importieren aus neuentdeckten Fernen Vegetationen und Architekturen nach den Argumenten des Geschmacks. Sie gestalten die Natur als Theater und setzen in sie die Bühnen ihrer Zeit – wie das Salzburger Felsentheater. Die Welt wird zur Bühne der Menschen und transportierte Tiere wie der Fasan, sind Requisiten ihrer Unterhaltung, ihrer Kultur.
Remodel.
Wenn veränderte Natur die Umgebung dominiert, ist die traditionelle Kunst, die eine Fiktion ist, über die Grenzen ihrer Produktion getreten. Darin liegt die Qualität der Disziplinen! Dem entgegen arbeitet die Ästhetik der Ökologie. Als ihr Dogma gilt: Schnelle Veränderung ist Zerstörung. Die angedeutete Grenze der beliebigen Veränderung darf nicht überschritten werden. Ökologie reklamiert ein unscharf beschriebenes Tempo im Ablauf der Entwicklungen, ein Tempo allerdings jenseits menschlicher Lebensalter. Seltsam religiös erscheint es als ein duldendes passives Bewegen, keinesfalls ist es zivilisatorisch. Der Mensch würde zum Betrachter, zum Chronisten der Zeit, die unter diesen Maximen allerdings ihre Bedeutung als Maß menschlicher Distanzen verloren hätte. Als Schöpfer von Kunst und Wissenschaft hat er folgend nur zu bezeichnen, zu beschreiben –eine Phantasie diktatorischer Naturalisten.
Stilisiert die Kultur das Leben? Sind wir wie die „galanten Schäfer" des Rokoko, die ein gesichertes aber nur angedeutetes Leben leben? Das würde bedeuten, daß uns die Sicherheit aus Ökonomie und Medizin zu langweiligen Darstellern einer fremden (bäurischen) „alternativen" Kultur macht. Es gibt kein Zurück zur Natur, denn es gibt keine Natur.
Wir stilisieren lediglich nach den präferierten Betrachtungsaspekten – nach dem, was wir gerne sehen oder als schön zu interpretieren gelernt haben. Die Frage bleibt, was sich ändert, wenn der Geschmack sich ändert und andere „Ausschnitte" aktuell sind.
Denkt man anders nur weil man anders tut (handelt)?
Man sieht, wir neigen nicht nur dazu vorgefundene Phänomene neu zusammen-zustellen (Gryllen), auch unser Geschmack als Matrix (Gesetz) des Handelns scheint ähnlich zu funktionieren. Schwerpunkte der Betrachtung und Interpretationen der Sinne werden immer neu und anders miteinander verbunden. Wir arbeiten wie Kaleidoskope: Kaleidoskope der Sinne – Kaleidoskope der Kommunikation – Kaleidoskope der Kunst, der Wissenschaft.
Remake – remodel.
Ist demnach Neuschöpfen ein Neusortieren, also nur ein Verändern der Struktur? Assemblage.

NOTES

1 As far as I know first used by Stieler in 1710.

2 Interesting ta note how German—speaking peaple deal with "good and evil": The name of the devil must not be uttered nor "written" on the wall. The name of God is invoked instead ("Gottseibeiuns") to ward off evil.

3 In his "Wahlverwandtschaften" Goethe calls a garden "creation" (... I wish to see the new creation.)

4 Particularly those pretending to explain the "where" and "why".

5 They remind of espionage plots: A formula of global implications has fortunately or unfortunately only partially and incompletely been stolen_...

6 Otta Neurath; "Gesammelte philosophische und methodalogische Schriften", Puhlished by R.Haller and R.Rutte. 1990.

7 Mary Wollstonecraft—Shelley: "Frankenstein or the Modern Prometheus." 1818.

8 In "The Tales of Hoffmann" by Jacques Offenhach. (First performed 1880)
Quote: (...) I have spectacles animating any dead object at once.
(...) Through these spectacles bright light is cast on everything, He who possesses them rules the warld, is king!

9 Bram Stoker's "Dracula". 1897.

10 Tolstoi's "Wodelak" turns against his family, against everything he loves. He commits "genetic suicide".

11 The provision of God who in the law of the Covenant gave to Israel the seven—day week with the sabbath being the day of rest—a scheme he had adhered to himself when creating the world.

12 From Jean Baudrillard: "Das Andere selbst." 1987.

13 see footnote 7

14 We often find the motif of barrenness in connection with human arrogance. (Loth's daughters lose their husbands.) And genetic fantasies are also fantasies of fertility.

15 Talismans, charms, sacral and profane ornaments etc.

16 This is being questioned by Eugen Holländer's "Wunder, Wundergeburt und Wundergestalt", published in 1921.

17 From Heinz Mode: "Fabeltiere und Dämonen in der Kunst. Die fantastische Welt der Mischwesen." 1983.

18 Many of the monsters are the result of misinterpreted nature watching.

19 "The Terminator" is a good example of this changing into any useful form.

20 1859 "Die Entstehung der Arten".
1871 "Die Abstammung des Menschen".

21 Schools that understand Newton's Laws to he physics or where history ends with World War I.

22 Actually a most religious theory as it describes an inescapable (quasi God—given) process into which man cannot interfere.

23 Fritz Mauthner: "Beiträge zu einer Kritik der Sprache. Volume 1: Zur Sprache und zur Psychologie." 1923

24 Better; the idea of beauty.

25 Charles K. Dick: "Do Androids Dream of Electric Sheep?" 1969.

So betrachtet wird die Genetik vergleichbar einer „Bibliothek“ der Sinnlichkeiten, der Eigenschaften. Sie schafft eine Architektur aus immer neuen „Bausteinen der Schöpfung, des Lebens“, wie ihre Information, die DNA genannt wird. Und ich denke an Dicks Idee von Fälschung – eine Fälschung aus Fleisch und Blut[25] und ich vergleiche sie mit der Fälschung Lems, die der Erinnerung der Vorstellung.[26] Ich denke an die Kaleidoskope der Wissenschaft und der Kunst. Wenn die Biologie über die Maschine der Mechanik triumphiert[27] – gibt es dann auch den Triumph der „ersten göttlichen Biologie“ über die „andere“ – die zweite des Menschen?

Unglaublich kleine Atomgruppen, viel zu klein, um genauerer Statistik zu folgen, spielen eine beherrschende Rolle bei den höchst geordneten, gesetzmäßigen Vorgängen im Organismus (...)

Das Gen ist viel zu klein (...) um nach den Regeln der Physik ordentliches, gesetzmäßiges Verhalten zu zeigen.

Erwin Schrödinger

Und nichts „war schon einmal da“, wenn wir wissen, daß es schon einmal da war.

Recover.

ANMERKUNGEN

[1] Meines Wissens erstmalig bei Stieler 1710.

[2] Ein nettes Spiel wie Menschen mit „Gut und Böse“ umgehen: Der Name des Teufels darf nicht ausgesprochen werden, man „malt“ ihn auch nicht an die Wand. Der Name des Guten wird gesagt (Gottseibeiuns), er wird gebannt, um das Böse zu bannen.

[3] Goethe zum Beispiel nennt in den Wahlverwandtschaften“ einen Garten Schöpfung (...ich wünsche die neue Schöpfung zu sehen).

[4] Besonders die, die vorgeben, „woher“ und „warum“ klären zu helfen.

[5] Sie ähneln grotesk dem Spionagegenre: Eine weltbewegende Formel ist, gottseidank oder leider fragmentiert, unvollständig entwendet worden...

[6] Otto Neurath: „Gesammelte philosphische und methodologische Schriften“. Herausgegeben von R. Heller und R. Rutte. 1990.

[7] Mary Wollstonekraft-Shelley: „Frankenstein or the Modern Prometheus.“ 1818

8 In Jacques Offenbachs „Hoffmanns Erzählungen“ (Uraufführung 1880) Darin: *(...) Habe Brillen, die jeden toten Gegenstand im Nur beleben (...) Durch diese Brillen alles wird*

beleuchtet und erhellt, wer sie besitzt, ja, der beherrscht die Welt!

[9] Bram Stokers „Dracula", 1897.

[10] Der Vukodlak wendet sich gegen seine Familie, gegen das, was er liebt. Er ist ein „genetischer Selbstmörder". Interessant auch Gogols „Der Wij" und Tolstois „Vampir".

[11] Die Voraussetzung Gottes, von dem Israel die Siebentagewoche mit dem Sabbat als Ruhetag im Bundesgesetz erhalten hat, der sich auch selbst bei der Erschaffung der Welt an dieses Schema gehalten hat.

[12] Aus Jean Baudrillard: „Das Andere selbst". 1987.

[13] Quelle wie Fußnote 7.

[14] Häufig findet sich auch das Motiv der Unfruchtbarkeit in Verbindug mit menschlicher Anmaßung (Loths Töchter verlieren ihre Männer.) Und genetische Phantasien sind auch Phantasien von Fruchtbarkeit.

[15] Talismane, Glücksbringer, sakraler und profaner Schmuck etc.

[16] Derart kritisch gegenüber ist Eugen Holländers „Wunder, Wundergeburt udn Wundergestalt", erschienen 1921.

[17] In Heinz Mode: „Fabeltiere und Dämonen in der Kunst. Die phantastische Welt der Mischwesen". 1983.

[18] Viele der Monstren sind das Ergebnis falsch interpretierter Naturbeobachtung.

[19] Das Annehmen jeder nützlichen Form ist auch in „Terminator" gut zu beobachten.

[20] 1859 „Die Entstehung der Arten". 1871 „Die Abstammung des Menschen"

[21] Schule, in der Newtons Gesetze die Physik sind, oder die nennenswerte Geschichte mit dem 1. Weltkrieg endet.

[22] Eigentlich eine zutiefst religiöse Theorie, denn sie beschreibt ein unabwendbares (wie gottgewolltes) Voranschreiten, in das der Mensch keinen Eingriff hat.

[23] Aus Fritz Mauthner: „Beiträge zu einer Kritik der Sprache. 1. Band: Zur Sprache und zur Psychologie." 1923.

[24] Besser die Idee vom Schönen.

[25] Charles K. Dick: „Do Androids Dream of Electric Sheep?", 1969. Replikanden mit „fotografischer" Geschichte.

[26] Wunderbar formuliert in Stanislav Lem: „Solaris".

[27] Das ist bereits in der Erklärung einer österreichischen Redensart – „türken" – für manipuliert, gefälscht, vorgedacht: Ein türkischer Schachspieler sitzt in einer Schachautomaten-Atrappe und spiel Schach *und* Maschine. Er wurde entdeckt (weil er eines von beidem schlecht spielte).

VERWENDETE UND BEGLEITENDE LITERATUR:

BALTRUŠAITIS, Jurgis: Réveils et Prodiges. Le gothique fantastique. 1960.

BALTRUŠAITIS, Jurgis: Das phantastische Mittelalter. Antike und exotische Elemente der Kunst der Gotik. 1982.

BARCK, Karl Heinz u.a. (Herg.): Aisthesis. Wahrnehmung heute oder Perspektiven einer anderen Ästhetik. 1990.

BAUDRILLARD, Jean: Das Andere selbst. 1987.

DICK, Charles K.: „Do Androids Dream of Electric Sheep?" 1969.

FABER, Monika (Herg.): Das Innere der Sicht. 1989.

MAUTHNER, Fritz: Beiträge zu einer Kritik der Sprache. Erster Band: Zur Sprache und zur Psychologie. 1923.

MODE, Heinz: Fabeltiere und Dämonen in der Kunst. Die fantastische Welt der Mischwesen. 1983.

WOLLSTONECRAFT-SHELLEY, Mary: „Frankenstein or the Modern Prometheus." 1818.

EIN LOB DER PARASITEN

FLORIAN RÖTZER

„Der Parasit ist ein Erreger. Er bringt das Gleichgewicht oder die Energieverteilung des Systems zum Fluktuieren. Er dopt es. Er irritiert es. Er entzündet es. Oft hat dies Gefälle keine Wirkung. Es kann Wirkungen hervorrufen – und durch Verkettung oder Reproduktion sogar gewaltige.“ (Michael Serres)

Offenbar tritt natürliches Leben dann auf, wenn eine gewisse Komplexität erreicht ist, die es ermöglicht, Lernprozesse als Text in einem Gedächtnis zu speichern, das diesen zudem kopieren und in Instruktionen zum Bau einer Maschine umsetzen kann. Eine der wesentlichen Eigenschaften des Lebens ist ja, unter geeigneten Randbedingungen sich nicht nur als Organismus über eine bestimmte Zeit hinweg erhalten und teilweise reparieren, sondern sich auch selbstreproduktiv fortpflanzen zu können. Beides impliziert ein Gedächtnis, das nicht nur digitale und zweidimensionale Information speichert, sondern auch die Instruktion zur Bildung des eigenen dreidimensionalen Organismus sowie von neuen Organismen enthält. Durch Kopierfehler, durch Einflüsse von außen oder im Falle der geschlechtlichen Fortpflanzung durch die Zusammenfügung von zwei Gedächtnistexten ist überdies die Möglichkeit gegeben, daß das Gespeicherte sich verändern kann, wodurch die Überlebenschancen von Textvarianten durch „Anpassung“ d. h. durch interne Umstrukturierung, steigen können.

Ob dadurch in der immer noch teleologisch geprägten Sprache der Revolutionstheorie eine Optimierung beinhaltet ist, kann man infragestellen, denn es gibt keine irgendwie geartete Möglichkeit, Kriterien der Anpassung über die banale Aussage hinaus anzugeben daß manche Organismen überleben, also daß sie „funktionieren“, mit der sich verändernden Realität fertigwerden und Nachkommen in die Welt setzen. Die Rede von der Anpassung durch den Kreislauf von Mutation und Selektion impliziert eine vorausgesetzte Realität und damit eine Art der klassischen Wahrheitsrelation der Übereinstimmung von Erkenntnis und Erkenntnisgegenstand, die wohl nicht mehr zu halten ist. Schließlich verändert das Leben selbst seine Randbedingungen, etwa wenn es im Präkambrium erst die sauerstoffhaltige Atmosphäre

PRAISE TO THE PARASITES
FLORIAN RÖTZER

"The parasite is a pathogen. It causes a system's equilibrium or distribution of energy to fluctuate. It dopes it. It irritates it. It inflames it. Very often this difference has no consequences. It can bring about consequences—and by means of interlinking or reproduction they may even be immense".
(Michel Serres)

Obviously natural life results once a certain complexity has been achieved, making it possible to store learning processes as a text in a memory, which can furthermore copy this and convert it into instructions to build a machine. One of the essential features of life is, of course, not only to survive as an organism and, to some extent, to mend onself over a certain period of time under suitable peripheral conditions, but also to be able to reproduce self-reproductively. Both imply a memory that not only stores digital and two-dimensional information but which also contains the instructions to form its own separate three-dimensional organism as well as new organisms. Due to copying errors and external influences or, in case of sexual reproduction, by joining together two memory texts there is the possibility that what is stored can change, whereby the survival chances of text variants by means of "adaptation" i.e. through internal re-organization, can increase.

As to whether this implies an optimization in what is still the teleologically characterized language of evolution theory may be doubted, as there is no way whatsoever of tackling the criteria of adaptation beyond the banal statement that some organisms survive—that is that they "function", come to terms with changing reality and produce offspring. The talk of adaptation through the cycle of mutation and selection implies an assumed reality and consequently a kind of the classical truth relation of the conformity of cognition and the subject of cognition, which can hardly be supported any longer. After all, life itself changes its peripheral conditions, for instance, when it first built up the oxygeneous atmosphere in the Precambrian through photosynthesis, which forms the basis of today's eukaryote life. Even the characterization of organisms as problem solvers is a metaphor, which nevertheless has a meaning in the generation of genetic algorithms as in this case the problem is specified here, and with that, a stable=artificial environment. Embedded in the principles of evolution is, in many cases,

also the idea of progress, that is the gradual improvement of populations through increasing complexity, although over 90% of existent living beings exist in the form of micro-organisms. Most of them are harmless to higher living beings or even cooperate with them in a symbiosis, yet in the case of pathogenic viruses they are known to mutate at an enormous speed in order to deceive the immunological system that can generally produce mutations for resistance even faster. The immense variety of anti-bodies—we assume that there are 10^8 different kinds—is evidence of the wide variety of micro-organisms which they have to provide protection against. Anti-bodies are produced from the mutation of a few basic structures and multiply like an avalanche in one variant once one antigen is entrapped by the receptors. In man's immunological system and probably also in his neuronal network, the evolution mechanism is copied, strengthened and accelerated, in a certain sense. The higher organisms are therefore only the tip of an iceberg, populated by a multitude of micro-organisms and parasites which, in the evolutionary armament race, still have the chance to destroy the more complex living beings through a lethal communication, re-functioning the programme of their cells.
Beyond the appraisal by means of adaptation, biological information vouches for a process which—within an unstable complex system that interacts with the organism carrying the information—can constantly have something new develop and let realized texts die, provided the environment is not stable. What is of course uncertain, is whether the "automatic" mutation of the genome in connection with selection is really of such importance for evolution as the classical theory believes it to be. For example, molecules which are only subjected to minute functional demands change much faster than those subjected to higher demands. It cannot be explained either as to why phenotypical change takes place faster with some lines than with others. And most multiple allelomorphs which arise as a result of mutation, get lost again by chance, whereby many mutations do lead to the formation of non-identical proteins which are present in a large variety in organisms, and however, differences very often reveal no phenotypical consequences. As a rule, mutations within the genetic drift either appear to be lethal or neutral, which would mean that influences from the environment or self-organization processes within the organism could be more effective than many may have assumed until now. Generally, transitional forms are missing, for example; breaks and bifurcations seem to happen very suddenly. Due to the fact that organisms themselves are very highly complex systems which integrate different levels of self-organizing systems, we could assume that transitions do not take place continuously, but rather erratically. The one-way street in the development from genome to organism also appears to be doubtful because, occasionally, as in the case of sea-urchins or tree-frogs, the sexually mature animals look almost the same and also have the same behaviour, yet their growth can be very different. In this sense,

durch die Photosynthese aufgebaut hat, die die Grundlage des heutigen eukaryontischen Lebens ist. Auch die Kennzeichnung von Organismen als Problemlöser ist eine Metapher, die allerdings bei der Generierung von genetischen Algorithmen einen Sinn macht, weil hier das Problem und damit eine stabile = künstliche Umwelt vorgegeben ist. Eingelagert in die Prinzipien der Evolution ist vielfach auch die Idee des Fortschritts, also der allmählichen Verbesserung von Populationen durch ansteigende Komplexität, obgleich noch immer über 90% der existierenden Lebewesen in Form von Mikroorganismen existieren. Die meisten von ihnen sind für das höhere Lebewesen unschädlich oder kooperieren mit ihm sogar in einer Symbiose, doch zeigt sich bei krankheitsauslösenden Viren, daß sie ungeheuer schnell mutieren können, um das Immunsystem zu täuschen, das meist noch schneller Mutationen zur Abwehr erzeugen kann. Die ungeheure Vielfalt der Antikörper – man nimmt an, daß es 10^8 verschiedene gibt –, zeugt von der Vielfalt der Mikroorganismen, gegen die sie schützen sollen. Die Antikörper werden aus der Mutation von wenigen Grundstrukturen erzeugt und vervielfältigen sich dann lawinenartig in einer Variante, wenn ein Antigen von den Rezeptoren eingefangen wurde. Im Immunsystem und vermutlich auch im neuronalen Netzwerk des Menschen wird der Mechanismus der Evolution in gewissem Sinne kopiert, verstärkt und beschleunigt. Die höheren Organismen sind also nur die Spitze eines Eisberges, bevölkert von einer Vielzahl von Mikroorganismen und Parasiten, die im evolutionären Wettrüsten noch immer die Chance haben, die komplexeren Lebewesen durch eine tödliche Kommunikation zu vernichten, indem sie das Programm von dessen Zellen umfunktionieren.
Jenseits der Bewertung mittels Anpassung bürgt die biologische Information jedenfalls für einen Prozeß, der innerhalb eines instabilen komplexen Systems, mit dem der die Information tragende Organismus in Wechselwirkung steht, ständig Neues entstehen und realisierte Texte sterben lassen kann, sofern die Umwelt nicht stabil ist. Unsicher freilich ist, ob die „automatische" Mutation des Genoms im Zusammenhang mit der Selektion wirklich für die Evolution so bedeutsam ist, wie die klassische Theorie es meint. So verändern sich beispielsweise Moleküle, an die nur geringe funktionelle Ansprüche gestellt werden, schneller als solche, an die höhere Anforderungen gestellt werden. Erklären läßt sich dadurch auch nicht, warum bei einigen Linien die phänotypische Veränderung schneller vor sich geht als bei anderen. Und die meisten Allele, die durch Mutation entstehen, gehen durch Zufall wieder verloren, wobei viele Mutationen zwar zur Bildung von nicht-identischen Proteinen führen,

diese aber in einer großen Vielfalt in Organismen vorliegen und Unterschiede oft keine phänotypischen Wirkungen zeigen. In aller Regel scheinen Mutationen innerhalb der genetischen Drift entweder letal oder neutral zu sein, was hieße, daß Einflüsse der Umwelt oder Selbstorganisationsprozesse innerhalb des Organismus eine höhere Wirksamkeit haben könnten als viele es bisher vermuten. Meist fehlen beispielsweise Übergangsformen, Brüche und Bifurkationen scheinen ziemlich plötzlich zu geschehen. Da Organismen selbst höchst komplexe Systeme sind, die verschiedene Ebenen sich selbst organisierender Systeme integrieren, wäre auch hier anzunehmen, daß Übergänge nicht kontinuierlich sich ereignen, sondern sprunghaft. Die Einbahnstraße der Entwicklung vom Genom zum Organismus erscheint auch deswegen zweifelhaft, weil gelegentlich, wie bei Seeigeln oder Laubfröschen, die geschlechtsreifen Tiere nahezu gleich aussehen und auch dieselben Verhaltensweisen zeigen, ihr Wachstum aber sehr verschieden sein kann. So sind die Larven bei sehr nahe verwandten Seeigel gänzlich unterschiedlich, manche können frei schwimmen und Plankton essen, andere lassen sich treiben und können nur am Boden Nahrung aufnehmen. Daraus könnte man schließen, daß der Druck der Außenwelt größer ist als an Genen angelegte morphogenetische Entwicklungen. Daß im Genom der vollständige Satz der Instruktionen zur Bildung eines dreidimensionalen Organismus gegeben ist, scheint überdies nur eine Unterbietung des evolutionären Ansatzes in der Anlehnung der herkömmlichen linearen Computerarchitektur zu sein. Schon aus wahrscheinlichkeitstheoretischen Überlegungen heraus kann die im Genom gespeicherte Information nicht die Instruktion für jede Zelle und auch nicht die dreidimensionale Form eines Proteins in einer Eins-zu-Eins-Entsprechung festlegen. Vielleicht ist das Genom eher als Katalysator und Morphoregulator zur Bildung von dreidimensionalen Mustern und interagierenden chemischen Prozessen zu verstehen, während etwa die Lokalisierung einer Zelle und ihre Aktivität aus der Lage und Aktivität von lokalen Zellkollektiven, d. h. aufgrund einer Oberflächenkommunikation zwischen benachbarten Molekülen und Zellen, bestimmt wird. Der genetische Code gäbe dann nur Richtung und Grenzen für eine Entwicklung, die selbst wiederum Vielheit und Variabilität innerhalb des Organismus mittels des evolutionären Mechanismus hervorbringt und eine Abgleichung der unabhängig voneinander evolvierenden verschiedenen Zelltypen ermöglicht. Akzeptiert man eine solche Vorstellung, so wäre die mechanistische Intention, als der vollständigen Kartierung des Genoms und seiner Protein-, Steuer- und Strukturcodes die morphogenetische

the larvae of very closely related sea-urchins are completely different. Some can swim freely and eat plankton and others let themselves drift and can only nourish themselves on the ground. One could draw the conclusion from this that the pressure from the outside world is greater than the morphogenetic developments designed in genes. The fact that there is the complete set of instructions to form a three-dimensional organism in the genome, appears, what is more, to be only undercutting the evolutionary approach adhering to the traditional linear computer architecture. As a result of probability theory considerations, the information stored in the genome cannot stipulate the instructions for every cell just as it cannot stipulate the three-dimensional form of a protein in a one-to-one equivalent. Perhaps the genome is to be understood more as a catalyst and morpho-regulator to form three-dimensional patterns and interactive chemical processes, whereas the localizing of a cell and its activitiy is determined from the location and activity of local cell collectives i.e. on account of a surface communication between neighbouring molecules and cells. The genetical code would then only give direction and limits for a development which itself would produce multiplicity and variability within the organism by means of the evolutionary mechanism and would enable a balancing of the different cell types evolving independent of each other. If one accepts such a concept, then the mechanistic intention of being able to derive the morphogenetic development of the phenotype from the complete mapping of the genome and its protein, control and structural code, and then even to influence it in a specifically differentiated way would be a phantasm. Even with non-linear algorithms the future behaviour of a computer in which hard and software are separate, different to biological systems, cannot be foreseen from the programme. When the relations between geno- and phenotype are not linear and are strongly based on the interaction between parts which are not controlled by a central computing and organization unit, then neither the three-dimensional organism nor its behaviour can be foreseen from the genetic programme.

The definition of life—ability of open metabolic systems to self-reproduce, to multiply, vary and inherit—is known, as is the fact that the transition into the inanimate is not sharply marked but is smooth. Crystals can also be self-reproductive and mutating. The chemist Graham Cairns-Smith built up his well-known and fascinating hypothesis on the origin of life through take over, on this ability. As DNA or RNA molecules are very complicated, he proceeds on the assumption that another replicator was here in the first instance, that is, simple inorganic crystals which self-reduplicate, such as are found in clay. As soon as the core of a crystal has formed spontaneously or a corresponding "seed" has fallen into an oversaturated solution it can grow and become a solid, ordered shape. Now and again it falls apart and these parts also continue to grow. As chemical or mechanical imperfections can occur during the growth of the very regular crystal structures, which replicate with further growth, it also possesses a mutation mechanism whereby, for example, the growth variants can be transmitted to the "children" by breaking apart. Some crystals can grow faster and spread out, so what we find here is already a pre-form of evolution in which information is produced and passed onto new generations. At some time or other the growing, multiplying crystals began to produce organic compounds which helped them to survive. Cairns-Smith believes that these organic forms, which previously had been more of a tool, could have suddenly multiplied faster than the crystals following the appearance of a first self-reduplicating, simple RNA and so moved slowly from the parasite status—which depends on a host cell—to become autonomous beings that had gradually put the crystalline life out of the running. Therefore, take over means that a part of a self-organizing structure makes itself independent and thrusts aside its pre-form. If this hypothesis is correct then new life could continue to develop from the crystal formation, a fact that we perhaps have merely not yet observed. Or perhaps the peripheral conditions have been disarranged through the emergence of life based on DNA and RNA. What also makes this hypothesis of take over piquant is the fact that a repeated take over is, in its turn, possibly taking place with the computers based on silicon, so that biological life would only be an episode in the life being based on silicon. After all, at the moment, so-called artificial life is already beginning to grow in the form of cellular automatons or computer viruses.

Even the molecular-Darwinist approach developed by Manfred Eigen proceeds on the basis of the thesis that selection mechanisms are already active in the inanimate area of material, so that life emerges from the self-organization of macro-molecules which are generated by entering into hypercycles. That is beyond every scientific explanation of how life came to be and is exciting because here it becomes clear that self-organization will emerge when various processes mutually build themselves up under certain conditions and "use" each other mutually, in a certain sense, whereby something new can emerge within the limits of the interacting forces. The new, in turn, provided it possesses the animated ability of storage and instruction, uses or "enslaves" the agents and integrates them, for example, as a cell does the mitochondria, a virus does the cell, a multi-cell organism the different cell types or an organ the parasites, which always means that, under certain circumstances the adopted agents, foreign organisms or the very forces from the environment can turn around the ratio. The watchmaker would be blinder than the genetic evolutionary theory suggests to us. And the creative coincidence within evolution would not be—apart from changes in the environment relative to the organism—essentially determined by chance gene mutation, but would result from the interactions not foreseeable in detail between populations (molecules, cells, viruses, bacteria, etc.) amongst one another and with each other.

A prerequisite to evolution is a stipulated var-

Entfaltung des Phänotyps ableiten und dann gezielt differenziert auch beeinflussen zu können, ein Phantasma. Schon bei nicht-linearen Algorithmen ist aus dem Programm das künftige Verhalten eines Computers, in dem Hard- und Software anders denn bei biologischen Systemen getrennt sind, nicht mehr vorhersagbar. Wenn die Beziehungen zwischen Geno- und Phänotyp nicht-linear sind und stark auf der Wechselwirkung zwischen Teilen beruhen, die nicht durch eine Zentrale Rechen- und Organisationseinheit gesteuert werden, dann läßt sich allein aus dem genetischen Programm weder der dreidimensionale Organismus noch dessen Verhalten vorhersagen.

Die Definition des Lebens – Fähigkeit von offenen metabolischen Systemen zur Selbstreproduktivität, zur Vermehrung, Variation und Vererbung – ist bekannt und auch der Umstand, daß der Übergang ins Unbelebte nicht scharf markiert, sondern fließend ist. Selbstreproduktiv und mutierend können auch Kristalle sein. Auf diese Fähigkeit hat der Chemiker Graham Cairns-Smith seine bekannte und faszinierende Hypothese zur Entstehung des Lebens durch Machtübernahme aufgebaut. Da DNS- oder RNA-Moleküle recht kompliziert sind, geht er davon aus, daß zunächst ein anderer Replikator dagewesen sei, nämlich einfache, aber sich selbst verdoppelnde anorganische Kristalle, wie man sie im Lehm findet. Sobald sich der Kern eines Kristalls spontan herausgebildet hat oder ein entsprechender „Same" in eine übersättigte Lösung fällt kann er wachsen und eine feste, geordnete Gestalt werden. Hin und wieder bricht er auseinander und die Teile wachsen ebenfalls weiter. Weil beim Wachstum von den sehr regelmäßigen Kristallstrukturen aber auch chemische oder mechanische Fehler auftreten können, die sich im weiteren Wachstum replizieren, besitzt er auch einen Mechanismus der Mutation, wobei die Wachstumsvarianten beispielsweise durch das Auseinanderbrechen an die „ Kinder" vererbt werden. Manche Kristalle können schneller wachsen und sich ausbreiten, so daß hier bereits eine Vorform der Evolution auftritt, in der Information hervorgebracht und neue Generationen weitergegeben wird. Irgendwann begannen die wachsenden und sich vermehrenden Kristalle organische Verbindungen zu produzieren, die ihnen zum Überleben verhalfen. Cairns-Smith vermutet, daß diese organischen Formen, die bislang eher Werkzeuge waren sich plötzlich, nach dem Auftritt einer ersten selbstreduplizierenden einfachen RNA, schneller vermehrt haben könnten als die Kristalle und so langsam aus dem Status von Parasiten, die auf eine Wirtszelle angewiesen sind, zu autonomen Wesen wurden, welche das kristalline Leben allmählich ausgebootet haben.

Übernahme heißt daher; daß ein Teil einer sich selbst organisierenden Struktur sich verselbständigt und seine Vorform verdrängt. Wenn diese Hypothese stimmen sollte, dann könnte aus der Kristallbildung weiterhin neues Leben entstehen, was wir vielleicht nur noch nicht beobachtet haben, vielleicht haben sich aber auch durch die Entstehung des auf DNS und RNA basierenden Lebens die Randbedingungen verschoben. Pikant ist diese Hypothese der Übernahme auch dadurch, daß mit den wiederum auf Silizium basierenden Computern möglicherweise sich eine erneute Machtübernahme vollzieht, so daß das biologische Leben nur ein Zwischenspiel des auf Silizium aufbauenden Lebens wäre. Schließlich beginnt im Augenblick bereits sogenanntes Künstliches Leben etwa in Form von zellulären Automaten oder von Computerviren zu wachsen.

Auch der von Manfred Eigen entwickelte molekulardarwinistische Ansatz geht von der These aus, daß Selektionsmechanismen bereits im unbelebten Bereich der Materie wirksam sind, so daß das Leben aus der Selbstorganisation von Makromolekülen hervorgeht, die durch den Eintritt in Hyperzyklen generiert werden. Das ist jenseits jeder wissenschaftlichen Erklärung der Lebensentstehung schon deswegen spannend, weil hier deutlich wird, daß Selbstorganisation dann eintritt, wenn sich unter bestimmten Bedingungen verschiedene Prozesse gegenseitig aufschaukeln und sich in gewissem Sinne gegenseitig „benützen", woraus Neues in den Grenzen der wechselwirkenden Kräfte emergieren kann. Das Neue wiederum benutzt oder „versklavt" , sofern es die lebendige Fähigkeit der Speicherung und Instruktion besitzt, die Agenten und integriert sie beispielsweise wie eine Zeile die Mitochondrien, wie ein Virus die Zelle, wie ein vielzelliger Organismus die verschiedenen Zelltypen oder wie ein Organ die Parasiten, was immer auch heißt, daß unter bestimmten Umständen die angeeigneten Agenten, fremde Organismen oder überhaupt Kräfte aus der Umwelt das Verhältnis umdrehen können. Der Uhrmacher wäre also noch blinder, als es die genetische Evolutionstheorie uns suggeriert. Und der kreative Zufall innerhalb der Evolution wäre, abgesehen von Veränderungen der Umwelt relativ zum Organismus, nicht wesentlich bestimmt durch zufällige Genmutation; sondern ergibt sich aus den nicht im Detail vorhersehbaren Wechselwirkungen zwischen Populationen (Molekülen, Zellen, Viren, Bakterien etc.) unter- und miteinander.

Voraussetzung der Evolution ist eine gegebene Vielfalt von verschiedenen, jedenfalls nicht identischen selbstreproduzierenden komplexen Systemen, weil erst dann Selektion als kreativer Mechanismus auftreten kann. Entgegen den

iety of different, at any rate, non-identical self-reproducing complex systems, because only then can selection appear as a creative mechanism. Contrary to the usual pictures of the evolutionary tree with a trunk ramifying to show diversity only in its crown, this would speak for the fact that there are a lot of branches even at the very origin, that often one cell and then even multi-cell living beings emerged independent of each other. Besides the two lines of organisms—the animals and the plants—we have found yet another: the archaebacteria. And so one is forced to appoint the ancestor of life as being even lower than with the prokaryotes. The variety of bacteria is, however, enormously large and no one has ever succeeded in constructing a pedigree from the various forms, metabolism types and environmental adaptations. They are not differentiated enough for this and probably they very often emerged in parallel or one after the other. Evidently, different bacteria can also communicate with each other, by exchanging gene strands in a first step towards genetic cross over, which stabilizes a type with sexual mating, thus recombining their DNA plans at random. Bacteria could therefore have a general communications system whereby they could even exchange DNA pieces with plants and animals. It is assumed, for example, that the eukaryote cells which contain a core with DNA and smaller membrane-limited sub-units, originated from a symbiosis with prokaryotes with only one single DNA ring. And even the eukaryote cell core appears to contain at least three types of genes, so that it could be a chimera of DNA texts. In addition to this, there are still the viruses which normally do not count as living organisms but which already have strands of DNA or RNA and which are surrounded by a protein coat. Unlike the organelles which similarly have their own genetic code, they have not integrated themselves in the host cell which can be understood as being a cell of cells, but keep their information by infecting cells and by re-functioning them for their multiplication. Until they tap a corresponding cell and its gene text and have it work for them e.g. by adding their genetic code to that of the host cell, they are in an idle position and are "lifeless". Therefore, viruses can either envelop the programme of the cells or directly change it in the sense of a genetic take over. From these many interactions of acquisition and parasitism one could assume that parasites at least accelerated evolution and that the battle between parasites which developed parallel to the first living single cell organisms, and host cells started up a significant, creative but, of course, also deathly mechanism. Without bacteria any higher life could not exist. Even viruses belong to the environment of living organisms and evolution do not appear to reward single individuals or single gene pieces, but rather populations which are in cooperative interaction with each other, including even relationships between parasite and host organism or animals of prey and hunters. If the niche is too simple and the organisms are not threatened, then very often no further development takes place. Instead there is a reduction in the programme.

What is interesting in this respect is that artificial life celebrated its first, even in many cases, unwelcome successes with the so-called computer viruses. They have a programme just like biological viruses, i.e. a memory storing information which, having been infected, uses the computer as a host organism to copy itself into another computer and to be able to multiply. In the computer ecology viruses act autonomously and they communicate with its programmes—what does not necessarily mean that they damage their host organism and the niche of interlinked computers with their ever increasing data clearances. For example, Harald Thimbleby programmed self-reproducing viruses which he called "lifeware" in such a way that they compare data banks. If these data banks do not correspond with each other, the missing data is automatically copied into the other data bank. Fred Cohen even believes that symbiotic computer viruses could, in future, take care of the main work for subordinate tasks in information systems. Nobody really knows—as with genetically changed micro-organisms—if they will continue to be "kind helpers", once they enter into an evolutionary drift. However, as yet, most viruses have not been programmed by system users, anyway. The computers are infected externally with more or less damaging viruses. The consequence resembles a kind of armament race: computer systems are better safeguarded and viruses accordingly become more intelligent. It is assumed that sexual mating has managed to succeed in biological evolution, amongst other things, because the interference from bacteria could be fended off better. Of course, there are still merely rudimentary forms of mutation by means of which computer viruses can adapt to new surroundings. Their evolution is advanced by human programmers, but it will probably soon be possible to develop and release computer viruses which can change in order to escape the search programme and to adapt more flexibly to new surroundings.

In the case of genetic algorithms which use the evolution mechanisms of selection, mutation and genetic cross-over by mating in order to optimize programmes for solving tasks, the structure of which need not be recognizable in detail, populations of non-identical programmes or chains composed at random of zeros and ones will be exposed to a solution space and then assessed in accordance with their quality. Programmes are a bit code composed of rules to recognize features and to trigger off actions. As genetic algorithms are organized non-linearly so as not to reduce them to a dominant rule and thus make them unsuitable for complex situations, the rules also compete with each other and all the rules which were involved in a "successful" action are rewarded, i.e. amplified. Such programmes which gradually organize themselves heterarchically and hierarchically can be very flexible, but of course, they are exposed to a rigid environment and are assessed from the outside. In addition to this, their populations are generally still very small as compared to biological ones. Their advantage is that they can pass through the generation sequence

üblichen Bildern des Evolutionsbaumes mit einem Stamm, der sich immer weiter verzweigt und so in seiner Krone erst Vielfalt zeigt, spräche dies dafür, daß auch am Ursprung bereits viele Zweige vorhanden sind, daß also auch unabhängig voneinander mehrmals einzellige und dann auch mehrzellige Lebewesen entstanden sind. Neben den zwei Organismenlinien, den Tieren und den Pflanzen, hat man noch eine weitere gefunden: die Archäbakterien. So wird man gezwungen, den Urahn des Lebens noch tiefer als bei den Prokaryonten anzusetzen.

Die Vielfalt der Bakterien ist jedenfalls ungeheuer groß und es ist noch nicht gelungen, einen Stammbaum aus den verschiedenen Formen, Stoffwechselarten und Umweltanpassungen zu konstruieren. Dafür sind sie nicht differenziert genug, und vermutlich sind sie sehr oft parallel oder hintereinander entstanden. Offenbar können verschiedene Bakterien auch miteinander kommunizieren, in dem sie in einer Vorstufe zum genetischen Cross-over, das mit der sexuellen Paarung eine Art stabilisiert, Genstränge austauschen und so ihre DNS-Pläne beliebig rekombinieren. Bakterien könnten also über ein allgemeines Kommunikationssystem verfügen, wobei sie auch mit Pflanzen und Tieren DNS-Stückchen austauschen können. Man vermutet beispielsweise, daß die eukaryotischen Zellen, die einen Kern mit DNS und kleinere, membranbegrenzte Untereinheiten enthalten, aus einer Symbiose mit Prokaryonten, die nur einen einzigen DNA-Ring besitzen, hervorgegangen sind. Und auch der eukaryontische Zellkern scheint mindestens drei Arten von Genen zu enthalten, so daß er eine Chimäre aus DNA-Texten sein könnte. Daneben gibt es noch die Viren, die normalerweise nicht zu den lebenden Organismen zählen, aber bereits Stränge aus DNA oder RNA besitzen und von einer Proteinhülle umgeben sind. Anders als die Organellen, die ebenfalls einen eigenen genetischen Code aufweisen, haben sie sich nicht in die Wirtszelle integriert, welche man als Zelle von Zellen verstehen kann, sondern sie bewahren ihre Information, indem sie Zellen infizieren und sie zu ihrer Vermehrung umfunktionieren. Bis sie eine entsprechende Zelle und deren Gentext anzapfen und für sich arbeiten lassen, z. B. indem sie ihren genetischen Code an den der Wirtszelle anfügen, befinden sie sich in Ruhestellung und sind „leblos". Viren können also entweder das Programm der Zellen umhüllen oder es im Sinne einer genetischen Machtübernahme unmittelbar verändern.

Aus diesen vielen Wechselwirkungen der Aneignung und des Parasitismus könnte man die Vermutung ableiten, daß Parasiten die Evolution zumindest beschleunigt haben und daß der Kampf zwischen Parasiten, die parallel zu den ersten lebenden einzelligen Organismen entstanden sind, und Wirtszellen einen wesentlichen kreativen, aber natürlich auch tödlichen Mechanismus in Gang setzt. Ohne Bakterien würde höheres Leben nicht existieren können.

Auch Viren gehören zur Umwelt von lebenden Organismen, und die Evolution scheint nicht besonders fähige Einzelindividuen oder einzelne Genstücke zu belohnen, sondern Populationen, die miteinander in kooperativer Wechselwirkung stehen, was auch Beziehungen zwischen Parasit und Wirtsorganismus oder Beutetieren und Jägern einschließt. Ist die Nische zu einfach, werden die Organismen nicht bedroht, so findet oft keine weitere Entwicklung mehr statt, sondern eine Reduktion des Programms.

Interessant in dieser Hinsicht ist, daß das Künstliche Leben seine ersten, wenn auch vielfach ungeliebten Erfolge mit den sogenannten Computerviren feierte. Wie biologische Viren haben sie ein Programm, d. h. ein Information speicherndes Gedächtnis, das, einmal infiziert, den Computer als Wirtsorganismus benutzen, sich in einen anderen Computer kopieren und sich vermehren kann. Viren agieren in der Computerökologie autonom und sie kommunizieren mit deren Programmen, was nicht unbedingt heißt, daß die ihren Wirtsorganismus und die Nische der vernetzten Computer mit ihren stetig anwachsenden Datenräumen schädigen. So hat Harold Thimbleby beispielsweise selbstreproduzierende Viren, die er „lifeware" nannte, so programmiert, daß sie Datenbanken miteinander verglichen und bei Nicht-Übereinstimmung selbständig die fehlenden Daten in die andere Datenbank kopierten. Fred Cohen glaubt gar, daß symbiotische Computerviren in Zukunft die Hauptarbeit bei den untergeordneten Aufgaben in Informationssystemen besorgen könnten. Niemand weiß zwar, ähnlich wie bei gentechnisch veränderten Mikroorganismen, ob diese weiterhin „freundliche Helfer" bleiben, wenn sie einmal in eine evolutionäre Drift eintreten. Allerdings werden die meisten Viren bislang sowieso nicht von den Systembenutzern programmiert, sondern die Computer werden von außen mit mehr oder weniger schädlichen Viren infiziert. Die Folge ist eine Art des Wettrüstens: die Computersysteme werden besser gesichert und die Viren dementsprechend intelligenter. Man nimmt an, daß die sexuelle Paarung in der biologischen Evolution sich unter anderem auch deswegen durchgesetzt hat, weil dadurch der Eingriff von Bakterien besser abgewehrt werden konnte. Noch gibt es freilich nur rudimentäre Formen der Mutation, mit denen sich Computerviren neuen Umgebungen anpassen können. Ihre Evolution wird durch menschliche Programmierer vorangetrieben, aber es wird vermutlich bald möglich sein, Computerviren zu entwickeln

at high speed and evolution can be observed, whereby all development stages and impasses are stored, a feature which is different in the biological one. The increasing capacity of parallel computers—the "Connection Machine" by Hillis was, incidentally, developed within the context of researching artificial life—means that programme populations will be able to be bred, that will sufficiently come closer to the individual number of natural populations. Although, with genetic algorithms which can again be compared to viruses, really new construction plans or behavioural modes can emerge, particularly as a result of cross-over, John H. Holland points out that even here phenomena such a symbiosis, parasitism, mimicry, predator-prey coevolution, niche formation and the fissioning of one kind into new stem lines can be observed. Incidentally, in the case of genetic algorithms it has been shown that the mutation rate as opposed to cross over was an almost negligible value for evolution. Genetic algorithms and cellular automatons are restricted in their self-organization, particularly by the fact that they do not exist in a complex environment, even if they are in a position via back-fed processes with no superordinated rules, to produce relatively complex collective behavioural modes from the reaction of individual "organisms" in locally restricted situations.

The fact that the existence of parasites and, therefore, the genetic take over could have been an important catalyst for the variety and complexity of life—and possibly even still is—was illustrated by Danny Hillis in a computer simulation on one of his Connection Machines with 64000 processors operating in parallel. He sent "organisms", i.e. binary number chains representing genes which were to solve computing tasks on the basis of genetic algorithms, into an evolutionary armament race with parasites, which were similarly rewarded if successful. These types coevolved by reacting even more skillfully to the attack or defence strategies. Always when the organisms had stabilized and had immunized themselves and it seemed as though the parasites had lost the race, a wave of attackers suddenly emerged again which managed to breakdown their safety systems. Hillis discovered that during the phases of standstill in the case of the phenotype, defined here by its computing abilities, changes were already taking place in the digital hereditary material which suddenly caused an even greater change, as from a critical point. Evolutionary biologists have always observed this change between periods of standstill and rapid innovation at the level of the phenotype, but they cannot explain how this sudden change which is in opposition to the dogma of change by means of the accumulation of small steps, takes place. What was noticeable was that the organisms needed a lot more generations in order to optimize, when there were no parasites in the computer top. Consequently, their presence accelerates the evolution process and the variety by keeping it at the brink of chaos, that is, providing for imbalance. Even the erratic innovation with parasites and organisms can be thought of as a take over. First of all, allele are produced which are

either neutral or which could be used for other functions, as in nature, it is not the principle of identity but more the flexible one of similarity which dominates. If there are a number of alternative genes available which cause another behaviour through feedback, that has "advantages", a new feature resulting from mating could spread out eractically.
With "Tierra", the biologist Thomas Ray tried to design an evolving system where digital living beings which had been changed by different mutations of their hereditary material were competing for processor time and storage space. The environment also changed through a kind of computer noise and the organisms of 80 gene-commands only had a limited life time, i.e. even the well "adapted" had to make their exit at some point. After the system had been running for some time and mutants emerged which worked even more effectively, organisms with only 45 gene-commands suddenly appeared that were unable to reproduce. For this reason, the parasites had to look for a host in order to use its replication code. As they were simpler, they were able to spread out faster than the more complicated living beings. But if they had alienated and killed too many hosts, their numbers also went down. With parasites there emerges new peripheral conditions between living beings developing an evolving system, to a certain extent, like a catalyst and out of which even mutants which could not survive in a stable environment with a constant solution space get a chance to survive by a mutual armament races.
Parasites appear, therefore, to emerge with a certain complexity in the course of the evolution of life and further advance this, irrespective of if this takes place in the sense of an armament race or as a symbiosis. There is a huge variety of parasites of biological life, probably their types exceeding by far those of all other animal species. Larger parasites display a wild multitude of metamorphoses and exploit an incredible series of intermediate hosts. Parasites are preditors and guests which knock a complex system off balance and cause change: they are agents of metamorphosis, open up evolution to unforeseeable developments which otherwise only occur as a result of catastrophies in the physical and chemical environment. They very possibly not only interfere from outside, damaging or improving an organism, nesting into it or providing for noise, but also introduce direct mutations of the hosts through their information work. Their behavioural features are not restricted to the parasites which penetrate a host, living in it and playing with its memory, as every form of take over and creation is parasitical, whereby even the hosts can be termed as being parasites in an intricate network. After all, life is a parasite of the earth which has been invaded and changed by it. And every host that is occupied by parasites, is, in itself, a parasite of another living being inasmuch as it lives off other organisms. If the RNA or DNA were perhaps parasites of a life based on silicon, then they themselves have subsequently become parasites of the host cell they use as their survival machine and in which the

und freizusetzen, die sich verändern können, um den Suchprogrammen zu entgehen und sich neuen Umgebungen flexibler anzupassen.
Bei genetischen Algorithmen, die die Evolutionsmechanismen der Selektion, der Mutation und des genetischen Crossover durch Paarung benutzen, um Programme zur Lösung von Aufgaben zu optimieren, deren Struktur man nicht im Detail kennen muß, werden Populationen von nicht-identischen Programmen oder ganz zufällig aus Nullen und Eins zusammengesetzten Ketten einem Lösungsraum ausgesetzt und dann nach ihrer Qualität bewertet. Programme sind ein Bit-Code aus Regeln, um Merkmale zu erkennen und Handlungen auszulösen. Damit genetische Algorithmen nicht-linear organisiert sind, um sie nicht auf eine dominante Regel zu reduzieren und so für komplexe Situationen untauglich zu machen, konkurrieren auch die Regeln miteinander und alle Regeln, die an einer „gelungenen" Aktion beteiligt waren, werden belohnt, d. h. verstärkt. Solche sich allmählich heterarchisch und hierarchisch organisierenden Programme können sehr flexibel sein, aber sie werden natürlich einer starren Umwelt ausgesetzt und von außen bewertet. Zudem sind ihre Populationen, verglichen mit denen biologischer Arten, meist noch sehr klein. Ihr Vorteil liegt darin, daß sie die Generationenfolge in hoher Geschwindigkeit durchlaufen können und sich so die Evolution beobachten läßt, wobei, anders denn in der biologischen, alle Entwicklungsstufen und Sackgassen erhalten haben. Mit der steigenden Kapazität von Parallelrechnern – die „Verknüpfungsmaschine" von Hillis entstand übrigens im Kontext der Forschung über Künstliches Leben – wird man allerdings Programm-Populationen züchten können, die der Individuenzahl von natürlichen Populationen hinreichend nahekommt. Obgleich bei genetischen Algorithmen, die man wieder mit Viren vergleichen kann, vor allem durch das Cross-over wirklich neue Baupläne oder Verhaltensweisen auftreten können, weist John H.Holland darauf hin, daß auch hier sich bereits Phänomene wie Symbiose, Parasitismus, Mimikry, Räuber-Beute-Koevolution, Nischenbildung und Aufspaltung einer Art in neue Stammeslinien beobachten lassen. Übrigens zeigte sich bei genetischen Algorithmen, daß die Mutationsrate gegenüber dem Crossingover für die Evolution eine nahezu vernachlässigenswerte Größe war. Beschränkt sind genetische Algorithmen und Zelluläraautomaten in ihrer Selbstorganisation vor allem dadurch, daß sie nicht in einer komplexen Umwelt existieren, auch wenn sie selbst in der Lage sind, über rückgekoppelte Prozesse ohne übergeordnete Regeln relativ komplexe kollektive Verhaltensweisen aus der Reaktion von einzelnen „Organismen" in lokal begrenzten Situationen hervorzubringen.

Daß die Existenz von Parasiten und damit die genetische Übernahme ein wichtiger Katalysator für die Vielfalt und Komplexität des Lebens gewesen sein könnte und möglicherweise noch immer ist, hat Danny Hillis in einer Computersimulation auf einer seiner Verknüpfungsmaschinen mit 64000 parallel arbeitenden Prozossoren zeigen können. Er hatte „Organismen", d. h. binäre Zahlenketten, die Gene repräsentieren und die auf der Basis von genetischen Algorithmen rechnerische Aufgaben lösen sollten, in ein evolutionäres Wettrüsten mit Parasiten geschickt, die gleichfalls bei Erfolg belohnt wurden. Die Arten koevoluierten, indem sie immer geschickter auf die Angriffe oder Verteidigungsstrategien reagierten. Immer wenn die Organismen sich stabilisiert und immunisiert hatten und es so schien, als wären die Parasiten aus dem Rennen, entstand plötzlich wieder eine Flut von Angreifern, die ihre Sicherheitssysteme knackten. Hillis fand heraus, daß während den Phasen des Stillstands beim Phänotypus, hier definiert durch seine rechnerischen Fähigkeiten, sich bereits Veränderungen im digitalen Erbgut vollzogen, die ab einem kritischen Punkt dann plötzlich zu einer größeren Veränderung führten. Diesen Wechsel von Perioden des Stillstands und schnellen Innovationen haben Evolutionsbiologen auch immer auf der Ebene des Phänotyps beobachtet, aber sie können nicht erklären, wie dieser plötzliche Wandel geschieht, der ja im Gegensatz zum Dogma der Änderung mittels Häufung von kleinen Schritten steht. Auffallend war überdies, daß die Organismen viel mehr Generationen benötigten, um sich zu optimieren, wenn im Computertop keine Parasiten existierten. Deren Anwesenheit beschleunigt also den Evolutionsprozeß und die Vielfalt, indem sie ihn am Rand des Chaos hält, also für Ungleichgewicht sorgt. Auch die sprunghafte Innovation bei Parasiten und Organismen läßt sich als eine Übernahme denken. Zunächst werden Allele produziert, die entweder neutral sind oder für andere Funktionen gebraucht werden konnten, da in der Natur nicht das Prinzip der Identität, sondern das flexiblere der Ähnlichkeit herrscht. Ist aber einmal eine Menge an alternativen Genen vorhanden, die durch Rückkopplung zu einem anderen Verhalten führen, das Vorteile mit sich bringt, könnte sich eine neue Eigenschaft durch Paarung sprunghaft ausbreiten.

Der Biologe Thomas Ray hat mit „Tierra" versucht, ein evolvierendes System zu entwerfen, bei dem die digitalen Lebewesen in Konkurrenz um Prozessorzeit und Speicherplatz standen und durch verschiedene Mutationen ihres Erbgutes verändert wurden. Die Umwelt veränderte sich auch durch eine Art des Rechnerrauschens und die Organismen aus 80 Gen-Befehlen hatten nur eine begrenzte Lebenszeit, d. h.

neuronal system has possibly developed as a further parasite, again becoming a host of a new life form yet which is already the carrier of that form of life termed culture. But even the evolution of a new hehaviour based on the sequence of many motoric and sensoric actors and millions of neurons competing and cooperating with each other, can be understood as being a take over and consequently, a parasitical use of previous simpler behaviour sequences of the neuronal machinery that, as yet, had been set in a completely different solution space. In this way, as the neuro-biologist, William Calvin, assumes, the senso-motoric behavioural sequence of precisely hammering open nuts with stones could have been used to make possible the throwing of stones at moving targets. This ability to organize different back-fed sensoric, projective and motoric behavioural sequences in an intersecting "melody", by the selection of many variants played through and assessed in milli-seconds, could have opened up the possibility of building up a differentiated language from complicated interlinkages, with the same sequence mechanism permitting the playing and writing of music. If the parasitic take over succeeds, new niches emerge which continue to develop in parallel becoming more complex with the emergence of new parasites emerge that challenge routine behaviour generally through choc-type complexity reduction.

If there is an enclosed environment and a rigid solution space as in the virtual world of computers, then parasites can obviously be used to optimize algorithms. They could then be of importance for the continued development of artificial intelligence on the basis of genetic algorithms on parallel computers and the bottom-up-method determined by chance. However, there is always the limitation that they also cause systems to crash and can introduce an uncontrollable development. We must get used to the fact that balance is not an orientation by which biological, psychical and social systems keep themselves alive, that it is more the introduction of nasty, destructive viruses and parasites that produce new forms of life, thinking and art. We should not accept the bad merely as a drive, we possibly have to produce it ourselves in order to survive, meaning that to change the animate and inanimate environment in which, and from which we live as parasites. Irrespective of whether we biologically supersede ourselves in the long-term, or in the short term by gene technology, or whether we release a post-biological life that will leave us behind in the armament race but where we, perhaps, could continue to live symbiotically or by the fact that we invent new knowledge and technology mutations, we will bleakly be forced to recognize that we are not the stable final product of evolution that we can steer and control from the outside. And even if we could succeed in throttling certain developments, perhaps with regard to AI, AL or gene technology, we would end up in another evolutionary drift which is just as unforeseeable and which is immune to sudden mutations allowing new parasites and viruses to emerge.

LITERATURE:

William Calvin: Die Symphonie des Denkens, Munich 1993
John L. Casti: Verlust der Wahrheit, Munich 1989
Friedrich Cramer: Chaos und Ordnung. Die komplexe Struktur des Lebendigen, Stuttgart 1988
Richard Dawkins: Der blinde Uhrmacher, Munich 1986
Gerlad Edelman: Unser Gerhirn—ein dynamisches System, Munich 1993
Evolution. Die Entwicklung von den ersten Lebenspuren bis zum Menschen. Heidelberg 1988.
Stephan Jay Gould: Zufall Mensch, Munich 1991
John H. Holland: Genetische Algorithmen, in Sektrum der Wissenschaft, Heidelberg 9/1992
Bernd Olaf Küppers: Der Ursprung biologischer Information, Munich 1986
Steven Levy: KL—Künstliches Leben aus dem Computer, Munich 1993
Robert Wesson: Die unberechenbare Ordnung. Chaos, Zufall und Auslese in der Natur, Munich 1993

selbst gut „angepaßte" mußten irgendwann abtreten. Nachdem das System einige Zeit lief und Mutanten entstanden, die effektiver arbeiteten, tauchten auf einmal Organismen mit nur 45 Gen-Befehlen auf, die sich nicht selber fortpflanzen konnten. Aus diesem Grund mußten die Parasiten einen Wirt suchen, um deren Replikationscode zu benutzen. Weil sie einfacher waren, konnten sie sich schneller ausbreiten als die komplizierteren Lebewesen, hatten sie aber zuviele Wirte zweckentfremdet und getötet, ging natürlich auch ihre Zahl zurück. Mit den Parasiten entstehen neue Randbedingungen zwischen Lebewesen, die ein evolvierendes System gewissermaßen wie ein Katalysator entwickelt und woraus durch gegenseitiges Wettrüsten auch Mutanten eine Lebenschance erhalten, die in einer stabilen Umwelt mit einem gleichbleibenden Lösungsraum nicht überleben könnten. Parasiten scheinen also zumindest ab einer bestimmten Komplexität im Laufe der Evolution des Lebens aufzutreten und diese weiter voranzutreiben, gleich ob dies im Sinne eines Wettrüstens oder als Symbiose geschieht. Parasiten des biologischen Lebens gibt es in einer ungeheuren Vielfalt, vermutlichen übertreffen ihre Arten bei weitem die aller anderen Tierarten. Größere Parasiten zeigen eine verrückte Vielheit von Metamorphosen und nützen eine unwahrscheinliche Folge von Zwischenwirten aus. Parasiten sind Räuber und Gäste, die ein komplexes System aus dem Gleichgewicht bringen und verändern: sie sind Agenten der Metamorphose, machen die Evolution offen auf unvorhersehbare Entwicklungen, die sonst nur durch Katastrophen der physikalischen und chemischen Umwelt eintreten. Möglicherweise greifen sie nicht nur von außen ein, schädigen oder verbessern einen Organismus, nisten sich in ihn ein oder sorgen für ein Rauschen, sondern leiten auch direkt Mutationen der Wirte durch ihre Informationsarbeit ein. Ihre Verhaltenseigenschaften sind aber nicht auf die Parasiten beschränkt, die in einen Wirt eindringen, in ihm leben und mit dessen Gedächtnis spielen, denn jede Form der Übernahme und der Kreation ist parasitär, weswegen auch die Wirte als Parasiten in einem verschachtelten Netzwerk zu bezeichnen sind. Schließlich ist das Leben insgesamt ein Parasit der Erde, die von ihm überzogen und verändert wurde. Und jeder Wirt, der von Parasiten bewohnt wird, ist selber wieder ein Parasit anderer Lebewesen zumindest insofern, als er von anderen Organismen lebt. Waren die RNA oder die DNS vielleicht Parasiten eines Lebens auf der Basis von Silikon, so sind sie danach selbst zum Parasiten der Wirtszelle geworden, den sie als Überlebensmaschine benutzt, in der sich möglicherweise das neuronale System als weiterer Parasit entwickelt hat, das nun wiederum zum Wirt einer neuen Lebensform wird, aber bereits der Träger jener Lebensformen ist, die man als Kultur bezeichnet. Aber schon die Evolution eines neuen Verhaltens, das auf der Sequenz von vielen motorischen und sensorischen Aktoren und Millionen jeweils miteinander konkurrierender und kooperierender Neuronen beruht, läßt sich jeweils als Übernahme und damit als parasitäre Benutzung von vorhergehenden einfacheren Verhaltenssequenzen der neuronalen Machinerie verstehen, die bislang in einem ganz anderen Lösungsraum angesetzt wurden. So könnte, was der Neurobiologe William Calvin vermutet, die sensomotorische Verhaltenssequenz, mit Steinen Nüsse präzise aufzuhämmern, dazu benutzt worden sein, das Werfen von Steinen auf bewegliche Ziele zu ermöglichen. Diese Fähigkeit, verschiedene rückgekoppelte sensorische, projektive und motorische Verhaltenssequenzen in einer übergreifenden „Melodie" durch Selektion vieler in Millisekunden durchgespielter und bewerteter Varianten zu organisieren, könnte dann die Möglichkeit eröffnet haben, eine differenzierte Sprache aus komplizierten Verkettungen aufzubauen, wobei derselbe Sequenzmechanismus auch das Spielen und Rezipieren von Musik erlaubt. Ist die parasitäre Übernahme gelungen, so sind neue Nischen entstanden, die sich parallel weiterentwickeln und komplexer werden, wenn neue Parasiten entstehen, die routiniertes Verhalten meist durch chocartige Komplexitätsreduktion herausfordern.

Hat man eine abgeschlossene Umwelt und einen festen Lösungsraum in den virtuellen Welten der Computer, so lassen sich Parasiten offenbar genauer einsetzen, um Algorithmen zu optimieren. Sie könnten also gerade für die Fortentwicklung von Künstlicher Intelligenz auf der Basis von genetischen Algorithmen auf Parallelrechnern und mit der vom Zufall bestimmten Bottom-up-Methode bedeutsam werden, allerdings immer mit der Einschränkung, daß sie Systeme auch zum Absturz bringen und eine unkontrollierbare Entwicklung einleiten können. Wir müssen uns daran gewöhnen, daß Gleichgewicht keine Orientierung ist, mit der sich biologische, psychische und soziale Systeme am Leben erhalten lassen, daß vielmehr das Einbringen von bösartigen Viren und Parasiten neue Lebens-, Denk- und Kunstformen hervorbringt, daß wir also das Böse nicht nur als Antrieb akzeptieren, sondern daß wir es möglicherweise selbst produzieren müssen, um zu überleben, was heißt, um uns und die belebte sowie unbelebte Umwelt, in der und von der wir auch als Parasiten leben, zu verändern. Egal ob wir dabei langfristig oder über Gentechnik auch kurzfristig uns selbst biologisch überholen oder ob wir ein postbiologisches Leben freisetzen, das uns im Wettrüsten hinter sich zurückläßt, in dem wir vielleicht auch symbiotisch weiterleben könnten oder durch das wir neue Wissens- und Technikmutationen erfinden, so werden wir jedenfalls ungemütlicherweise zur Anerkennung gezwungen, daß wir nicht das stabile Endprodukt der Evolution sind, die wir von außen lenken und kontrollieren können. Und selbst wenn wir es erreichen könnten, bestimmte Entwicklungen etwa im Hinblick auf KI, KL oder Gentechnologie zu bremsen, so geraten wir dadurch nur an eine andere evolutionäre Drift, die ebenso wenig vorhersehbar und gefeit gegenüber plötzlichen Mutationen ist, neue Parasiten und Viren entstehen läßt.

LITERATUR

William Calvin: Die Symphonie des Denkens, München 1993

John L.Casti: Verlust der Wahrheit, München 1989

Friedrich Cramer: Chaos und Ordnung. Die komplexe Struktur des Lebendigen, Stuttgart 1988

Richard Dawkins: Der blinde Uhrmacher, München 1986

Gerald Edelman: Unser Gehirn – ein dynamisches System: München 1993

Evolution. Die Entwicklung von den ersten Lebensspuren bis zum Menschen. Heidelberg 1988

Stephen Jay Gould: Zufall Mensch, München 1991

John.H.Holland: Genetische Algorithmen, in Spektrum der Wissenschaften, Heidelberg 9/1992

Bernd-Olaf Küppers: Der Ursprung biologischer Information, München 1986

Steven Levy: KL. – Künstliches Leben aus dem Computer, München 1993

Robert Wesson: Die unberechenbare Ordnung. Chaos, Zufall und Auslese in der Natur, München 1993

SYMPOSIUM ARTIFICIAL LIFE

DIE BIONISCHE KONVERGENZ

KEVIN KELLY

Daß es während der letzten zwei Jahrzehnte nicht gelang, künstliche Intelligenz zu kreieren, hat leider nur allzu klar gezeigt, daß die bloß mechanistische Logik der Maschinen allein keinen funktionstüchtigen Roboter hervorbringen kann. Eine mechanistische Logik – die Logik des Technos – erzeugt nur einfache Geräte. Wirklich komplexe Systeme, wie etwa eine Zelle, eine Wiese, eine Volkswirtschaft oder ein Gehirn bedürfen einer streng nicht-technologischen Logik. Wir erkennen jetzt, daß keine Logik außer der Bio-Logik eine denkende Apparatur oder gar funktionierende Systeme von jedweder Größe kreieren kann.

Die Natur hat den Menschen fortwährend ihr Fleisch überlassen. Erst nahmen wir Naturstoffe für Nahrung, Kleidung und Schutz. Dann lernten wir, Rohstoffe aus der Biosphäre der Natur abzubauen um eigene, neue synthetische Materialien zu erzeugen. Nun gibt das Lebendige uns sein Bewußtsein. Wir übernehmen seine Logik.

Die erstaunlichste Entdeckung der letzten zehn Jahre war, daß man die Logik des Bios aus der Biologie herausnehmen kann und sie doch immer noch verwendbar ist. Obgleich schon in der Vergangenheit viele Philosophen vermutet hatten, man könne die Gesetze des Lebens destillieren und anderswo zur Anwendung bringen, bestätigte sich dies allerdings erst zu dem Zeitpunkt, als die Computer und die von Menschen erzeugten Systeme die Komplexität von Lebewesen erreicht hatten.

Da nun die bio-logischen Grundgesetze organischer Systeme von Wissenschaftlern routinemäßig destilliert und in technologische Systeme eingepflanzt werden, ist es erstaunlich, in welchem Ausmaß Leben transferiert werden kann.

Zu den bisher erfolgreich auf mechanische Systeme übertragenen Aspekten des Lebens gehören: Selbstreplikation, Selbststeuerung, begrenzte Selbstreparatur, sanfte Evolution und partielles Lernen.

Die neue interdisziplinäre Perspektive des Künstlichen Lebens interpretiert diese erfolgreichen Experimente als Anzeichen dafür, daß noch mehr Leben in den Bereich des Mechanischen übertragen werden kann. Ein eben sich entwickelndes Verständnis für die Logik des Bios postuliert folgendes:

THE BIONIC CONVERGENCE
KEVIN KELLY

The failure to create artificial intelligence in the last two decades has made it embarrassingly clear that the naked clockwork logic of machines alone cannot build a workable robot. Clockwork logic—the logic of the technos—will only build simple contraptions. Truly complex systems such as a cell, a meadow, an economy, or a brain require a rigorous non-technological logic. We now see that no logic except bio-logic can assemble a thinking device, or even a workable systems of any largeness.

Nature has all along yielded her flesh to humans. First, we took nature's materials as food, fibers and shelter. Then we learned to extract raw materials from nature's biosphere to create our own new synthetic materials. Now bios is yielding us her mind; We take her logic.

The most astounding discovery of the last ten years has been that one can take the logic of bios out of biology and still have something useful. Although many philosophers in the past have suspected one could abstract the laws of life and apply them elsewhere, it wasn't until the complexity of computers and human-made systems became as complicated as living things, that it was possible to prove this.

Now that scientists routinely abstract bio-logical principles from organic systems and implant them in technological systems, it's amazing how much of life can be transferred.

Among the aspects of life successfully transported to mechanical systems so far are: self-replication, self-governence, limited self-repair, mild evolution, and partial learning.

The new interdisciplinary perspective of Artificial Life interprets these successful experiments as indications that yet more of life can be ported into the mechanical. An emerging sense of the logic of bios suggests the following:

- All sustainable systems must be grown over time
- All reliable systems must be distributed in organization
- All adaptable systems must be governed from the bottom
- All innovative systems must honor errors and variation

These principles underpin the awesome workings of ecosystems, eyeballs, natural selection in geological time, and the unfolding of a baby elephant from a tiny seed of sperm and egg.

These same principles of bio-logic are now being implanted in computer chips, electronic networks, robot modules, pharmaceutical searches, software design, and styles of management, in order that these artificial systems may overcome their own complexity. When the technos is enlivened by bios we get complex mechanical systems that can adapt, learn, and even evolve. The animation of the inanimate is the foundation of artificial life and genetic art.

At the same time that the logic of bios is being imported into machines, the logic of technos is being imported into life.

The root of bioengineering is the desire to control the organic long enough to improve it. Domesticated plants and animals are example of technos-logic applied to life. The wild aromatic root of the Queen Anne's Lace weed was fine tuned over generations by selective herb gatherers until it evolved into a sweet carrot of the garden; the udders of wild bovines were selectively enlarged in a "unnatural" way to satisfy humans rather than calves. Milk cows and carrots, therefore, are human inventions as much as steam engines and gunpowder are. But milk cows and carrots are more indicative of the kind of inventions humans will make in the future: products that are grown, rather than manufactured.

Genetic engineering is precisely what cattle breeders do when they select better strains of Holsteins, only bioengineers employ more precise and powerful control. While carrot and milk cow breeders had to rely on Darwinian evolution, modern genetic engineers can use Lamarkian evolution—purposeful design—which greatly accelerates improvements.

The overlap of the mechanical and the lifelike increases year by year. Part of this bionic convergence is a matter of words. The meaning of "mechanical" and the meaning of the term "life" are both stretching until all complicated things can be perceived as machines, and all self-sustaining machines can be perceived as alive.

Yet beyond semantics, two concrete trends are happening: 1) Man-made things are behaving more lifelike, and 2) Life is becoming more engineered. The veil of the no-man's land between the organic and the manufactured has crumpled to reveal that the two really are, and have always been, the same place.

Some insights come from studying the complexity of large human-made systems. But the wildness of nature is the chief source for clarifying insights into large systems, and probably the paramount source of more insights to come. Nature is thus more than a diverse gene-bank harboring undiscovered herbal cures for future diseases — although it is certainly this. Nature is also a meme-bank, an idea factory. Vital, post-modern paradigms are hidden in every jungle ant hill. The billion-footed beast of living bugs and weeds—and the aboriginal human cultures which have extracted meaning from this life — is worth preserving, if for no other reason, than for the metaphors it still has not revealed. Destroying a rainforest destroys not only a reservoir of genes, but also a bank of future metaphors, insight and models for a modern industrial world.

- alle nachhaltigen Systeme müssen mit der Zeit entstanden sein
- alle zuverlässigen Systeme müssen planmäßig verteilt sein
- alle anpassungsfähigen Systeme müssen vom Grund her gesteuert werden
- alle innovativen Systeme müssen Fehler und Abweichungen akzeptieren

Diese Grundsätze liegen der großartigen Wirkungsweise von Ökosystemen, Augäpfeln, der natürlichen Auswahl innerhalb der geologischen Zeit ebenso zugrunde wie der Entstehung eines kleinen Elephanten aus einem winzigen Samen aus Sperma und Ei.

Eben diese Prinzipien des Bio-Logischen werden nun in Computerchips, elektronische Netzwerke, Robotermodule, pharmazeutische Untersuchungen, Softwaregestaltungen und Managementstile eingepflanzt, damit diese künstlichen Systeme ihre eigene Komplexität überwinden können. Wenn der Technos vom Bios belebt wird, erhalten wir komplexe mechanische Systeme, die sich anpassen, lernen und sogar entwickeln können. Die Belebung des Leblosen ist das Fundament des künstlichen Lebens und der genetischen Kunst.

Zur selben Zeit, da die Logik des Bios in die Maschinen eingeführt wird, wird die Logik des Technos in das Leben eingeführt.

An der Wurzel des Bio-Engineerings steht der Wunsch, das Organische lange genug zu steuern, um es zu verbessern. Domestizierte Pflanzen und Tiere sind ein Beispiel für die auf das Leben angewandte Technos-Logik. Für die wildaromatische Wurzel der Queen Anne's Lace haben ausgewählte Kräutersammler generationenlang Unkraut veredelt bis es zur süßen Gartenkarotte wurde; die Euter der wilden Rinder wurden auf „unnatürliche" Weise selektiv vergrößert um anstatt der Kälber Menschen zu befriedigen. Aber Milchkühe und Möhren sind mehr ein Indikator für die Art der Erfindungen, die Menschen in Zukunft machen werden: Produkte die wachsen anstatt hergestellt zu werden.

Genetisches Engineering entspricht genau dem, was Rinderzüchter tun, wenn sie bessere Züchtungen von Holstein-Rindern selektieren, nur daß Bioingenieure eine präzisere und wirksamere Steuerung verwenden. Während Karotten- und Milchkuhzüchter sich auf die Darwinsche Evolution verlassen mußten, können die modernen Gentechniker die Lamarksche Evolution – zielbewußtes Design – einsetzen, welche die Verbesserungen enorm beschleunigt.

Von Jahr zu Jahr greifen das Mechanische und das Lebensähnliche mehr ineinander über. Zum Teil ist diese bionische

Konvergenz eine Sache der Begriffe. Sowohl die Bedeutung von „mechanisch“ als auch die Bedeutung des Ausdrucks „Leben“ erweitern sich bis alle komplizierten Dinge als Maschinen wahrgenommen werden können und alle sich selbst erhaltenden Maschinen als lebendig.

Abseits der Semantik zeichnen sich allerdings zwei konkrete Trends ab: 1) von Menschen erzeugte Gegenstände verhalten sich lebensähnlicher und 2) das Leben gestaltet sich zunehmend technischer. Der Schleier über dem Niemandslands zwischen dem Organischen und dem Erzeugten hat sich verschoben und enthüllt, daß die beiden tatsächlich den gleichen Platz haben und immer hatten.

Einige Einsichten stammen aus dem Studium der Komplexität großer, von Menschen erzeugter Systeme. Die Hauptquelle zur Klärung von Einsichten in große Systeme ist jedoch die Wildnis der Natur und sie ist wahrscheinlich die wichtigste Quelle für zukünftige weitere Erkenntnisse. Die Natur ist somit mehr, als daß verschiedene Genbanken bislang noch unentdeckte Heilkräuter für zukünftige Krankheiten aufbewahren – obwohl es sicher auch darum geht. Die Natur ist auch eine Gedächtnisbank, eine Ideenfabrik. In jedem Ameisenhügel im Dschungel verstecken sich vitale, postmoderne Paradigmen. Die milliardenfüßige Kreatur lebender Wanzen und Unkräuter - und die ursprünglichen menschlichen Kulturen, die aus diesem Leben Bedeutung gezogen haben – ist es wert, erhalten zu werden, und sei es aus keinem anderen Grund als wegen der Metaphern, die sie noch nicht enthüllt hat. Mit der Zerstörung eines Regenwalds, wird nicht nur ein Reservoir an Genen sondern auch eine Bank zukünftiger Metaphern, Einsichten und Modelle für eine moderne industrielle Welt zerstört.

DIE NEUE GRENZE

KEN KARAKOTSIOS

THE NEW FRONTIER
KEN KARAKOTSIOS

When I was growing up, I read a lot of science fiction, catching glimpses of worlds unlike anyplace we'd ever been, worlds that existed only in our minds: Living in domes under the ocean, sailing across the sands of Mars, debating with machines that could think, flying across the universe to meet bug-eyed aliens. To a young kid living in the glow of the space age, where we were already on the Moon, it seemed that Mars was just a few years away, and certainly we'd be traveling to other stars by the end of the century. And computers surely were already thinking, weren't they?
Well, technology didn't quite keep up with a twelve-year-old's ambitions, and as I went through high school and college, and began working, I came to realize a few things:

- Most of us will never physically travel to any destination off the Earth's surface
- Humans are never going to be able to design machines smarter than themselves
- Life is pretty futile if everything we experience is lost when we die
- Math is really interesting

It's only now that I can look back and see how this strange mix of ideas would lead me towards a truly new frontier that we can visit. I caught my first glimpse of the new frontier in the late 1970's, when I read an article about something called The Game of Life. This isn't a game in the traditional sense, because there is no way to win or lose. Yet the outcome is surprising enough to compel you to play. Life is played on a large grid of squares. Each of these squares can either be empty, or contain a stone. There is a clock running, and with each tick of the clock, every square in the grid "looks" at its eight neighboring squares, and applies one of the following two "rules":

- If the central square is empty, and exactly three of its neighbors have stones, then a stone will appear in the central square.
- If the square does have a stone, and exactly two or three neighbors also have stones, then the central square will keep its stone. Otherwise its stone disappears.

These rules are simple and repetitive, and sound rather uninteresting. But when you program the game on a computer and start the clock running, something amazing happens... Order is created out of randomness. Static, oscillating, and traveling patterns form from the primordial goo. Pattern interacts with pattern,

In meiner Jugendzeit las ich eine Menge Science Fiction und erhaschte so Einblicke in Welten, die anders waren als jeglicher Platz der Welt, an dem wir jemals gewesen sind, Welten, die nur in unserem Geist existierten: In Kuppeln unter dem Ozean zu wohnen, über den Sand des Mars zu segeln, mit Maschinen zu diskutieren, die denken konnten, durch das Universum zu fliegen, um insektenäugige Außerirdische zu treffen. Für ein junges Kind, das im Schein des Raumzeitalters lebte, in dem wir ja schon auf dem Monde waren, schien es, als wäre der Mars nur ein paar Jahre entfernt, und als würden wir bis zum Ende des Jahrhunderts schon zu anderen Sternen reisen. Und Computer würden dann sicher auch schon denken, nicht wahr?
Nun, die Technologie konnte mit den Ambitionen eines Zwölfjährigen nicht völlig mithalten, und während ich durch die High-School und später durchs College ging und schließlich zu arbeiten begann, begann ich, einige Dinge zu erkennen:

- Die meisten von uns werden niemals körperlich zu irgendeinem Ziel außerhalb der Erdoberfläche reisen
- Die Menschen werden nie Maschinen bauen können, die klüger sind als sie selbst
- Das Leben ist ziemlich sinnlos, wenn alles, was wir erfahren, verlorengeht, wenn wir sterben
- Mathematik ist wirklich interessant

Erst jetzt kann ich zurückblicken und erkennen, wie mich diese eigenartige Mischung von Vorstellungen zu einer wirklich neuen Grenze geführt hat, die wir besuchen *können*. Ich erhaschte einen ersten Blick auf diese neue Grenze in den späten 70er Jahren, als ich einen Artikel über etwas namens *Das Spiel des Lebens* las. Dies ist kein Spiel im traditionellen Sinn, denn man kann dabei weder gewinnen, noch verlieren. Das Ergebnis ist jedoch erstaunlich genug, um einen zum Spielen zu vorlocken. *Das Spiel des Lebens* wird auf einem großen Gitternetz von Quadraten gespielt. Jedes dieser Quadrate kann entweder leer sein, oder einen Stein enthalten. Eine Uhr läuft und bei jedem Ticken dieser Uhr, „schaut" jedes Quadrat in dem Gitternetz seine acht Nachbarquadrate an und wendet dabei eine der folgenden beiden „Regeln" an:

GET A LIFE!

SIMLIFE™ THE GENETIC PLAYGROUND BREAKS THE BARRIERS BETWEEN GAMES AND SIMULATIONS, PLAYING AND LEARNING–EVEN BETWEEN MACHINES AND LIVING BEINGS. ONCE AGAIN, MAXIS, THE CREATORS OF SIMCITY® AND SIMEARTH®, TAKES YOU WHERE YOU'VE NEVER BEEN AND GIVES YOU THE POWER TO CREATE–THIS TIME TO CREATE LIFE ITSELF.

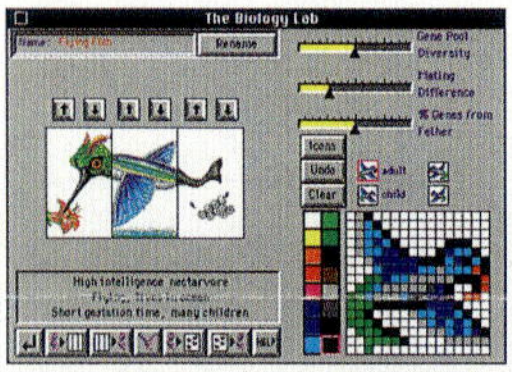

Give life to different species in the Biology Lab and customize their look with the icon editor.

Design exotic plants and animals to survive in specific ecological niches.

Set your wild creations loose on an unsuspecting landscape.

SIMLIFE IS FUN. You'll design creatures from the depths of your imagination and influence how they look, act and eventually evolve. Then, set them loose in your custom ecosystem and test their ability to survive. Six different game scenarios challenge you to solve problems involving everything from food chain management to genetic manipulation.

SIMLIFE IS EXPERIMENTAL. Design your own experiments using simulated environments, ecosystems, genetics, evolution, life and behavior. You can even control time and physics! Witness the cause and effects of your decisions and discover the delicate relationships that form between living beings.

SIMLIFE IS ARTIFICIAL. Using the latest advances in Artificial Life research, SimLife simulates a complete ecosystem, right down to individual genes. Plants and animals interact with each other and their environment as they do in the "real world." They even mutate and evolve into new species.

In SimLife, you get the chance to create life in a unique way, but beware–it's up to you to keep your species off the endangered list.

PUBLISHED BY

MAXIS

spawning both higher level patterns and randomness. But this randomness is food for another generation, and on and on the dance continues.
The emergent behavior of this toy system hinted that there was something lurking out in the cyberspace frontier. Something that already existed in the abstract world of mathematics, something that we could catch a glimpse of with our computers. It was clear that I needed to look at something more complex than stones on a grid. Thus began *SimLife*.
SimLife is a program in which digital organisms, in the form of plants and animals, compete to survive and produce offspring in a virtual universe. Like our world, the SimLife world has mountains, lakes, soil and climate. SimLife creatures need food to grow and produce offspring. Each creature is encoded with its own genetic description, and through sexual recombination each generation of creatures begets a new generation that has new combinations of the genes. Mutation helps to add a bit of variety to each new generation. The offspring best able to find food, mate, and produce another generation of viable offspring will by definition be the fittest, and their genes will travel into the future, leaving the less fit behind.
SimLife's 64 species don't quite match the diversity of Earth's estimated 30 million species. And while real animals have tens of thousands of genes, SimLife animals have only 46. While real life has had hundreds of millions of generations in which to evolve, SimLife needs to do its stuff in "real time" so that we can watch it and interact with the process on a personal computer. Furthermore, the SimLife universe is equivalent to a patch of land just a few miles on a side. Yet with all these limitations, an amazing thing happens in SimLife: It works. Plants and animals evolve. Diverse ecosystems form food webs, symbiotic relationships, and population cycles. Higher-level emergent behaviors of real living systems, things I wasn't even aware of when I wrote the program, form on top of all this.
Although limited in many ways, SimLife removes some of the limits of the real world. Because all of SimLife's creatures are digital, they are open to inspection at all times. We can take instant snapshots of the entire gene pool of a population, without disturbing the system in the least--imagine trying to do that with a population of real animals. In SimLife, we can alter the genome of all the members of an entire species through a single click of the mouse. And if we get bored with the world we created, we can create another. We can change the laws of physics, metabolism and genetics at the slightest whim. Like *The Game of Life,* there's no winner or loser in SimLife; rather the reward is in exploring.
While SimLife gets us a little closer, it's still a long journey to the new frontier. While we do have emergent behavior, with tiny digital creatures evolving and adapting to an ever changing world, metabolizing digital food, the destiny of the creatures is rather limited. They are never going to develop a different body chemistry, invent fire, or build a starship. But SimLife is just the start.

- Wenn das mittlere Quadrat leer ist, und genau drei seiner Nachbarn Steine enthalten, dann wird im mittleren Quadrat ein Stein erscheinen.
- Wenn das mittlere Quadrat einen Stein enthält, und genau zwei oder drei Nachbarquadrate auch Steine haben, dann behält das mittlere Quadrat seinen Stein. Ansonsten verschwindet der Stein.

Diese Regeln sind einfach und sich wiederholend (repetitiv) und klingen ziemlich uninteressant, Aber, wenn man das Spiel auf einen Computer programmiert und die Uhr zum Laufen bringt, geschieht etwas Erstaunliches ... Aus der Willkür wird eine Ordnung geschaffen. Aus der primordialen Masse bilden sich statische, oszillierende und wandernde Muster. Muster interagiert mit Muster und bringt dabei sowohl Muster höherer Ebenen, als auch Zufälligkeit hervor. Diese Zufälligkeit jedoch ist Nahrung für eine andere Generation und so weiter und weiter setzt sich dieser Tanz fort.
Das auftretende Verhalten dieses Spielzeugsystems deutete an, daß da etwas an den neuen Grenzen des Cyberspace lauerte. Etwas, das in der abstrakten Welt der Mathematik bereits existierte, etwas auf das wir mit unseren Computern einen kurzen Blick erhaschen konnten. Es war klar, daß ich dafür etwas Komplexeres betrachten mußte, als Steine in einem Gitternetz. So entstand *Simlife*.
SimLife ist ein Programm, in dem digitale Organismen in Form von Pflanzen und Tieren In einem virtuellen Universum ums Überleben wettstreiten und sich fortpflanzen. Wie unsere Welt hat auch die SimLife-Welt Berge, Seen, Erde (Erdboden) und ein Klima. SimLife Kreaturen brauchen Nahrung, um zu wachsen und Nachkommen zu erzeugen, jede einzelne Kreatur ist mit einer eigenen genetischen Beschreibung verschlüsselt und durch sexuelle Rekombination zeugt jede Generation eine neue Generation, die eine neue Kombination von Genen besitzt. Mutation verhilft weiters jeder neuen Generation zu ein bißchen zusätzlicher Vielfalt. Die Nachkommenschaft, die am besten fähig ist, Nahrung und einen Partner zu finden und eine neue Generation lebensfähiger Nachkommenschaft zu produzieren, wird als die lebensfähigste definiert werden und ihre Gene werden in die Zukunft reisen und die weniger lebensfähigen zurücklassen.
Die 64 Arten von SimLife können es nicht so ganz mit der Vielfalt der geschätzten 30 Millionen Arten aufnehmen. Und während wirkliche Tiere zehntausende Gene haben, haben SimLife-Tiere nur 46. Während das wirkliche Leben hunderte Millionen von Generationen Zeit hat, sich zu entwickeln, muß SimLife seine Sache in „der wirklichen Zeit (Real-Zeit)“ machen, damit wir es beobachten und mit dem Prozeß auf

In *The Selfish Gene,* Dawkins talks about something called "memes." As genes are the particles of biological inheritance, memes are particles of cultural inheritance. Memes are like ideas, but with a difference. As genes must replicate themselves in a new generation to survive, memes must also replicate themselves. Thus, to be a meme, an idea must cause a person to communicate it to other people. Memes also mutate and have sex. We've all experienced the combination of two ideas in a single new one. For example biology combined with computer science has given us artificial life. We only have a limited capacity to remember and communicate our memes, so we save and pass on the best ones, while forgetting the rest. This selection process keeps the most fit memes "alive" at the expense of eliminating the rest.

Biological genetics only allows new solutions to the problem of survival to occur once a generation. However, man is able to use speech to pass on new survival strategies in seconds rather than years. This is a million-fold speedup in the process of evolution. Broadcast telecommunication allow memes to reach millions of people simultaneously, and books and electronic storage allow us to extend the reach of our memes directly to people who may not even be born yet. This gives the meme quite an advantage over the gene. Our destiny becomes less dependent on a sequence of amino acids we have no choice in accepting, and more dependent on what we choose to believe, communicate, and do. We are the first species on earth to reach the post-biological phase of cultural evolution.

I believe that cultural evolution is a promising new direction to explore. By developing an artificial life world in which culture can evolve, a path may be found to evolve true intelligence in software agents. What does this mean for the new frontier? It means that we have a chance of not just looking in like voyeurs through a glass CRT or virtual reality setup, but of *being there.* If we can evolve software agents that can think, and if we can unravel how we think, then by mapping our thoughts, experiences, and memes onto these software agents well be able to upload ourselves into the new frontier. Electrons never die, and the novelty will be endless.

einem PC interagieren können. Außerdem ist das SimLife-Universum äquivalent zu einem Stück Land mit nur ein paar Meilen Seitenlänge. Trotz aller dieser Einschränkungen jedoch geschieht in SimLife etwas Erstaunliches: Es funktioniert, Pflanzen und Tiere entwickeln sich. Mannigfaltige Ökosysteme bilden Nahrungsketten, symbiotische Beziehungen und Bevölkerungszyklen. Darüber hinaus bilden sich auf höherer Ebene entstehende Verhalten wirklicher lebender Systeme, Dinge die mir nicht bewußt waren, als ich das Programm schrieb.

Obwohl in vieler Art eingeschränkt, entfernt SimLife einige Grenzen der wirklichen Welt. Da alle Kreaturen von SimLife digital sind, sind sie zu allen Zeiten offen für Untersuchungen. Wir können augenblickliche Schnappschüsse eines gesamten Genpools einer Population machen, ohne das System im geringsten zu stören – stellen Sie sich einmal vor, das mit wirklichen Tieren zu tun. In SimLife können wir das Genom aller Mitglieder einer gesamten Spezies mit einem einzigen Klicken der Maus verändern. Und wenn uns die ganze Welt, die wir geschaffen haben, zu langweilig wird, können wir eine andere kreieren. Wir können die Gesetze der Physik, des Metabolismus und der Genetik aus Lust und Laune verändern. Wie beim *Spiel des Lebens* gibt es in SimLife weder Gewinner, noch Verlierer; die Belohnung liegt vielmehr im Erforschen.

Obwohl SimLife uns ein bißchen näher bringt, ist es doch noch ein weiter Weg zu der neuen Grenze. Wir haben zwar enstehendes Verhalten, in dem winzige digitale Kreaturen sich entwickeln und an eine sich ständig verändernde Welt anpassen und digitale Nahrung umwandeln, das Schicksal dieser Kreaturen ist dennoch sehr begrenzt. Sie werden niemals eine andere Körperchemie entwickeln, das Feuer erfinden, oder ein Raumschiff bauen. SimLife jedoch ist erst der Anfang.

In *The Selfish Gene – das selbstsüchtige Gen* spricht Dawkins über etwas namens „Meme". So wie Gene Teilchen (Partikel) biologischen Erbes sind, sind Meme Teilchen eines kulturellen Erbes. Meme sind wie Ideen, aber mit einem Unterschied. So wie Gene sich in einer neuen Generation reproduzieren müssen, um zu überleben, müssen auch Meme sich reproduzieren. Also, um ein Mem zu sein, muß eine Idee eine Person veranlassen, sie einer anderen Person mitzuteilen. Meme mutieren auch und haben Sex. Wir haben alle schon die Kombination von zwei Ideen zu einer einzigen neuen Idee erlebt. Zum Beispiel hat uns die Biologie kombiniert mit der Computerwissenschaft das künstliche Leben gegeben. Wir haben nur eine beschränkte Fähigkeit, uns an unsere Meme zu erinnern und sie weiterzugeben, so bewahren wir und geben wir nur die besten davon weiter, während wir den Rest vergessen. Dieser Selektionsprozeß erhält die tauglichen Meme „am Leben", auf Kosten der Eliminierung der anderen.

In der biologischen Genetik können neue Lösungen zum Überlebensproblem nur einmal in einer Generation vorkommen. Der Mensch ist jedoch fähig, neue Überlebenstechniken in Sekunden und nicht in Jahren weiterzugeben. Dies bedeutet eine millionenfache Beschleunigung im Evolutionsprozeß. Gesendete Telekommunikation erlaubt es Memen, Millionen von Menschen gleichzeitig zu erreichen, und Bücher und elektronische Speicherung ermöglichen es uns, die Reichweite unserer Meme direkt auf Leute auszudehnen, die noch nicht einmal geboren sind. Dies gibt dem Mem einen ziemlichen Vorteil gegenüber dem Gen. Unser Schicksal wird weniger abhängig von einer Abfolge von Aminosäuren, bei denen wir keine Wahl haben, und wird abhängiger davon, was wir zu glauben, weiterzugeben und zu tun wählen. Wir sind die erste Spezies auf der Erde, die die post-biologische Phase der kulturellen Entwicklung erreicht haben.

Ich glaube, daß die kulturelle Entwicklung eine neue und vielversprechende Richtung zur Erforschung darstellt. Durch die Entwicklung einer Welt künstlichen Lebens, in der sich Kultur entwickeln kann, könnte man einen Weg finden, wirkliche Intelligenz in Softwareprogrammen zu entwicklen. Was bedeutet das für die neue Grenze? Es bedeutet, daß wir die Chance haben, nicht nur wie Voyeure in eine VR-Szenerie hineinzublicken, sondern dort zu sein. Falls wir Softwareprogramme entwickeln können, die denken können, dann werden wir durch Übertragung unserer Gedanken, Erfahrungen und Meme auf diese Programme uns selbst auf diesen neuen Grenzbereich laden können. Elektronen sterben nie, und das immer Neue wird unendlich sein.

SYNTHETISCHES LEBEN: EVOLUTION UND ÖKOLOGIE DIGITALER ORGANISMEN

THOMAS S. RAY

SYNTHETIC LIFE: EVOLUTION AND ECOLOGY OF DIGITAL ORGANISMS
THOMAS S. RAY

Ideally, the science of biology should embrace all forms of life. However in practice, it has been restricted to the study of a single instance of life, life on earth. Because our science of biology is based on a sample size of one, we cannot know what features of life are peculiar to earth, and what features are general, characteristic of all life. A practical alternative to a truly comparative inter-planetary biology, is to create synthetic life.

Synthetic organisms have been created based on a computer metaphor of organic life in which CPU time is the "energy" resource and memory is the "material" resource. Memory is organized into informational patterns that exploit CPU time for self-replication. Mutation generates new forms, and evolution proceeds by natural selection as different genotypes compete for CPU time and memory space. The creatures are self-replicating computer programs, however, they can not escape because they run exclusively on a virtual computer in its unique machine language. The virtual computer is effectively a containment facility.

Diverse ecological communities have emerged. These digital communities have been used to experimentally examine ecological and evolutionary processes: e.g., competitive exclusion and coexistence, host/parasite density dependent population regulation, the effect of parasites in enhancing community diversity, evolutionary arms race, punctuated equilibrium, and the role of chance and historical factors in evolution.

A single rudimentary ancestral "creature" has been designed; it is 80 machine instructions long and contains only the code for self-replication. This creature examines itself, determines its size and location in the memory "soup", and then copies itself, one instruction at a time, to another location in the soup. The ancestral creature does not interact directly with other individuals, although there is scrambling competition for access to memory space.

A reaper kills creatures, assuring that there is always free space into which creatures can reproduce. When creatures are born, they enter the bottom of the reaper queue, and the reaper always kills off the top, which is usually the oldest

Idealerweise sollte sich die Wissenschaft der Biologie mit allen Formen des Lebens befassen. In der Praxis beschränkt sie sich jedoch auf die Erforschung eines einzelnen Beispiels von Leben, nämlich des Lebens auf der Erde. Da unsere Wissenschaft der Biologie auf einem Probenumfang von Eins basiert, können wir nicht beurteilen, welche Kennzeichen des Lebens typisch für die Erde und welche allgemein, charakteristisch für jedes Leben sind. Eine praktische Alternative für eine wirklich komparative interplanetare Biologie besteht in der Erschaffung synthetischen Lebens.

Die Erzeugung synthetischer Organismen erfolgte auf Grundlage einer Computermetapher des organischen Lebens, wobei CPU-Zeit die „Energie"-Ressource und der Speicher die „Material"-Ressource bildet. Der Speicher ist planmäßig in Informationsmuster unterteilt, die sich zu ihrer Selbstreplikation der CPU-Zeit bedienen. Die Mutation bringt neue Formen hervor und die Evolution erfolgt durch natürliche Selektion, da verschiedene Genotypen in Konkurrenz um CPU-Zeit und Speicherplatz stehen. Die Geschöpfe sind sich selbst replizierende Computerprogramme, die jedoch nicht entkommen können, da sie ausschließlich auf einem virtuellen Computer in dessen eigener Maschinensprache laufen. Der virtuelle Computer ist tatsächlich eine Auffangvorrichtung.

Es haben sich verschiedene ökologische Gemeinschaften herausgebildet. Diese digitalen Kommunen wurden herangezogen, um ökologische und evolutionäre Prozesse experimentell zu erforschen, etwa kompetitiven Ausschluß und Koexistenz, die Populationsregulierung in Abhängigkeit von der Wirte- und Parasitendichte, den Effekt, den Parasiten für eine zunehmende Mannigfaltigkeit der Kommunen haben, das evolutionäre Wettrüsten, das unterbrochene Gleichgewicht, und die Rolle von Zufällen und historischen Faktoren in der Evolution.

Es wurde ein einzelnes rudimentäres Ur„geschöpf" entworfen; es ist 80 Maschinenbefehle lang und enthält lediglich den Code zur Selbstreplikation. Dieses Wesen prüft sich

selbst, bestimmt seine Größe und seinen Ort in der Speicher„suppe“ und kopiert sich dann mit jeweils einem Befehl selbst an einen anderen Ort in der Suppe. Obwohl harte Konkurrenz um Zutritt zu Speicherplätzen besteht, interagiert das Urgeschöpf nicht direkt mit anderen Individuen.
Ein Mäher tötet Geschöpfe und sorgt dafür, daß jederzeit freier Raum verfügbar ist, in dem die Geschöpfe sich reproduzieren können. Werden Kreaturen geboren, so reihen sie sich ans untere Ende einer Warteschlange. Der Sensenmann tötet jeweils das oberste, üblicherweise zugleich älteste Geschöpf. Den Mutanten unterlaufen jedoch oft Fehler, die dazu führen, daß sie in der Warteschlage des Sensenmannes aufsteigen und getötet werden.
Aus dem einzelnen rudimentären Ur„geschöpf“ sind hunderttausende selbstreplizierende Genotypen in hunderten von Genom-Größenklassen hervorgegangen. Bit-flipping Mutationen bewirken Änderungen in der Befehlsfolge im Genom, jedoch führen sie zu keiner Veränderungen der Genomgröße. Mutierende Genotypen machen jedoch Fehler bei der Selbstprüfung und -replikation, und daraus resultieren verschieden große Genome. Da die genetische Änderung neue Genotypen hervorbringt, entstehen Varianten, die in der Lage sind, sich rascher als ihre Vorläufer zu replizieren und diese Varianten nehmen in ihrer Häufigkeit in der Suppe zu.
Sehr rasch entwickeln sich Parasiten, die sich, da ihnen ein großer Teil des Genoms fehlt, alleine nicht replizieren können. Diese Parasiten spüren jedoch die fehlende Information auf und wenn sie sie bei einem benachbarten Geschöpf orten, schmarotzen sie Informationen und bewerkstelligen so ihre eigene Replikation. Dieses Informationsparasitentum stellt eine Schmarotzerbeziehung dar, die dem Wirt nicht unmittelbar abträglich ist. Jedoch wetteifern die Parasiten mit den Wirten um Platz und sind, da sie ihre kleineren Genome rascher replizieren können, im Wettbewerb unter Umständen überlegen. Ihr Vorteil hängt jedoch von der Häufigkeit ab. Da die Parasiten sich vermehren, die Wirte aber weniger werden, gelingt es vielen Parasiten nicht, einen Wirt ausfindig zu machen. Im ökologischen Ablauf beschreiben Wirte und Parasiten – sieht man von genetischen Veränderungen ab – Lotka-Voltera-Zyklen.
Während einiger Abläufe wurden die Wirte gegen Angriffe der Parasiten immun. Ein Immunitätsmechanismus beruht auf dem Umstand, daß die Geschöpfe sich selbst nur einmal prüfen und darauf vertrauen, daß die Informationen über ihre Größe und Position für alle folgenden Replikationen stimmen. Immune Wirte berauben die Parasiten ihres Selbstgefühls, indem sie die Information über Größe und Position

creature. However, mutant creatures often generate errors, which cause them to rise in the reaper queue and be killed.
From a single rudimentary ancestral "creature" there have evolved tens of thousands of self-replicating genotypes of many hundreds of genome size classes. Bit flipping mutations cause changes in the sequence of instructions in the genome, but they do not cause changes in the size of the genome. However, mutant genotypes make errors in their self-examination and replication, resulting in different sized genomes. As genetic change generates new genotypes, variants appear which are able to replicate more rapidly that their ancestors, and those variants increase in frequency in the soup.
Very quickly there evolve parasites, which are not able to replicate in isolation because they lack a large portion of the genome. However, these parasites search for the missing information, and if they locate it in a nearby creature, they parasitize the information from the neighboring genome, thereby effecting their own replication. This informational parasitism is a commensal relationship, as it is not directly detrimental to the host. However, the parasites do compete with the hosts for space, and may be superior competitors because they can more rapidly replicate their smaller genome. However, their advantage is frequency dependent. As the parasites increase in frequency, the hosts decline, and many parasites fail to locate hosts. In ecological runs, without genetic change, hosts and parasites demonstrate Lotka-Volterra cycles.
In some runs, hosts evolve immunity to attack by parasites. One immune mechanism that has been worked out is based on the fact that the creatures only examine themselves once, and rely on retaining the information on their size and location for all subsequent replications. Immune hosts cause their parasites to loose their sense of self by failing to retain the information on size and location. Immune hosts function with this forgetful code by re-examining themselves before each replication, thus there is a metabolic cost to the immunity.
When immune hosts appear, they often increase in frequency, devastating the parasite populations. In some runs where the community comes to be dominated by immune hosts, parasites evolve that are resistant to immunity. The above mentioned immune mechanism can by circumvented by parasites which also re-examine themselves before each replication.
Hosts sometimes evolve a response to parasites that goes beyond immunity to actual hyper-parasitism. Hyper-parasites allow themselves to be parasitized, letting the parasite use their code for a single replication. After the first replication, the hyper-parasite deceives the parasite by replacing the parasite's record of its size and location with the size and location of the hyper-parasite genome. Thereafter, the parasite will devote its energetic resources to replication of the hyper-parasite genome. This is a highly deleterious interaction, which drives the parasites to extinction. The hyper-parasites are facultative, getting an energy boost when the

parasites are present, but not requiring them for replication.

Evolving in the absence of parasites, hyper-parasites completely dominate the community, resulting in a relatively uniform community characterize by a high degree of relationship between individuals. Under these circumstances, sociality evolves, in the sense that the creatures evolve into forms which can not replicate in isolation, but which can only replicate in aggregations. These colonial creatures cooperate in the control of the flow of execution of their algorithms.

The cooperative behavior of the social hyper-parasites makes them vulnerable to a new class of parasites. These cheaters, hyper-hyper-parasites, insert themselves between cooperating social individuals, and momentarily seize control of execution of the algorithm, just long enough to deceive the social creatures about their size and location, causing the social creatures to replicate the genomes of the cheaters.

The only kind of genetic change that the simulator imposes on the system is random bit flips in the machine code of the creatures. However, the digital organisms discover sexuality as a mechanism of genetic change, and in this way generate their own genetic changes. They cause significant recombination and rearrangement of the genomes. This spontaneous sexuality is a powerful force for evolutionary change in the system.

One of the most interesting aspects of this second instance of life is that the bulk of the evolution is based on adaptation of organisms to other organisms, rather than the physical environment. It is co-evolution that drives the system.

nicht aufbewahren. Die Wirte, die mit diesem vergeßlichen Code funktionieren, müssen sich vor jeder Replikation selbst prüfen. Die Immunität hat daher einen metabolischen Preis.

Mit dem Auftreten immuner Wirte nimmt deren Häufigkeit meist zu und es kommt zu einer Vernichtung der Parasitenpopulation. Bei einigen Abläufen, bei denen die Gemeinschaft von immunen Wirten beherrscht wurde, entwickelten sich immunitätsresistente Parasiten. Der oben geschilderte Immunitätsmechanismus kann von Parasiten, die sich ebenfalls vor jeder Replikation prüfen, überlistet werden. Die Wirte zeigen gegenüber den Parasiten manchmal eine über die Immunität hinausgehende Reaktion, einen tatsächlichen Hyperparasitismus. Die Hyperparasiten dulden den Parasitenbefall und überlassen dem Parasiten ihren Code für eine einzelne Replikation. Nach der ersten Replikation täuscht der Hyperparasit den Parasiten, indem er die Daten des Parasiten, dessen Größe und Position betreffend, mit der Größe und Position des Hyperparasiten-Genoms vertauscht. Der Parasit wird daraufhin seine energetischen Ressourcen der Replikation der Hyperparasiten-Genome widmen. Dies ist eine höchst schädliche Interaktion, die den Untergang der Parasiten zur Folge hat. Die Hyperparasiten haben die Wahl, – aus der Anwesenheit der Parasiten beziehen sie eine Energieverstärkung, sie bedürfen ihrer jedoch nicht zur Replikation.

Die sich in Abwesenheit der Parasiten entwickelnden Hyperparasiten dominieren die Gemeinschaft vollständig, was zu einer relativen Uniformität führt, deren Kennzeichen die vielen Beziehungen zwischen den Individuen sind. Unter diesen Umständen entsteht Gesellschaftlichkeit in dem Sinn, daß die Geschöpfe sich in Formen entwickeln, die nur gemeinsam, nicht aber in der Vereinzelung wiederholbar sind. Die Kolonie der Geschöpfe kooperiert in der Steuerung ihres Alogrithmenablaufs.

Das kooperative Verhalten der sozialen Hyperparasiten macht sie für eine neue Parasitenklasse angreifbar. Diese betrügerischen Hyper-Hyperparasiten setzen sich zwischen die kooperierenden sozialen Individuen und reißen für einen Augenblick die Kontrolle über die Durchführung des Algorithmus an sich, lange genug, um die sozialen Kreaturen hinsichtlich ihrer Größe und Position zu täuschen und sie zu veranlassen, die Genome der Betrüger zu replizieren.

Einer der interessantesten Aspekte dieses zweiten Beispiels von Leben ist der, daß der Großteil der Evolution eher auf der Anpassung der Organismen an andere Organismen beruht als auf der physikalischen Umgebung. Das System wird durch die Ko-evolution vorangetrieben.

DIE ALGORITHMISCHE SCHÖNHEIT DER NATUR: COMPUTERGRAFIKMODELLE VON PFLANZEN UND MEERES- MUSCHELN

PRZEMYSLAW PRUSINKIEWICZ

Kürzliche Fortschritte der Computergrafik haben es möglich gemacht, durch Verwendung verschiedener Präsentationsstile, die von schematisch zu realistisch und bis surrealistisch reichen, mathematische Modelle biologischer Strukturen und Prozesse zu visualisieren. Meine Präsentation wird ihr Hauptaugenmerk auf die Modelle blühender Pflanzen und auf Meeresmuscheln legen. Ihre Formen und Pigmentmuster können erlangt werden, indem man elegante Formalismen der mathematischen Biologie verwendet: L-Systeme und Reaktions-Diffusionsprozesse. Außerdem verbindet die Selbstähnlichkeit von Strukturen sich verzweigender Pflanzen diese mit Fraktalen.

THE ALGORITHMIC BEAUTY OF NATURE: COMPUTER GRAPHICS MODELS OF PLANTS AND SEA-SHELLS

PRZEMYSLAW PRUSINKIEWICZ

Recent advances of computer graphics have made it possible to visualize mathematical models of biological structures and processes using different styles of presentation, from schematic to realistic to surrealistic. My presentation will focus on the models of flowering plants and seashells. Their forms and pigmentation patterns can be captured using elegant formalisms of mathematical biology: L-systems and reaction-diffusion processes. In addition, the self-similarity of branching plant structures relates them to fractals.

$$\begin{aligned}
\omega &: \texttt{[A][B]}\\
p_1 &: \texttt{A} \rightarrow \texttt{[+A\{.].C.\}}\\
p_2 &: \texttt{B} \rightarrow \texttt{[-B\{.].C.\}}\\
p_3 &: \texttt{C} \rightarrow \texttt{GC}
\end{aligned}$$

INTERAKTIVE EVOLUTION

KARL SIMS

INTERACTIVE EVOLUTION
KARL SIMS

The most fascinating and complex entities in our world are still those that have occurred naturally. Life itself, the human mind, language, and many other phenomena have all emerged from natural biological processes without the presence of a purposeful designer.
Many of these same natural processes can be performed in simulation on computers. As more and more powerful computers continue to be built, we can expect many intriguing and complex artificial results to emerge from these simulations. Whether the emerging virtual entities will qualify for the category of "life" or not, is subject to debate, but in either case these simulated life-like processes give us new methods for the creation of complexity. In some ways, like life itself, the complexity arising from these simulations can surpass what we are capable of designing with traditional tools or even understanding.
Much of may work involves the simulation of a specific natural process: evolution. Evolution consists of a simple cycle. The most "fit" entities in a population survive and reproduce. The resulting offspiring are copies or combinations of their parents but often with random alterations or mutations. Some offspring may be improvements on their parents, and as only the most fit of each new generation of offspring continue to reproduce, the population as a whole can slowly improve.
In simulation, fitness can be provided interactively by a human observer at each step of the cycle—those that are selected as being most aesthetically interesting, survive and reproduce. Images, virtual worlds, or even animations can bew interactively evolved in this way with the user imposing survival criteria in a god-like manner. This is a method for creating and exploring complexity that does not require human understanding of the specific processes involved.
Fragments of computer coede are the chromosomes that describe the growth process of these virtual entities. The computer code, like DNA, is the *genotype,* and the virtual result, like an organism, is the *phenotype*.
A "genetic language" is definied which is composed of a set of primitive mathematical funcitions that can be assembled into complete genetic growth instructions. Mutations alter these coded instructions, and can sometimes cause new functions and parameters to be in-

Die faszinierendsten und komplexesten Geschöpfe unserer Erde sind immer noch die aus der Natur hervorgegangenen. Das Leben selbst, das menschliche Bewußtsein, Sprache und viele andere Phänomene sind aus natürlichen biologischen Prozessen, ohne die Gegenwart eines zielbewußt agierenden Konstrukteurs, hervorgangen.
Viele von eben diesen natürlichen Prozessen können am Computer simuliert werden. Aufgrund der laufenden Entwicklung immer leistungsfähigerer Computer sind aus diesen Simulationen zahlreiche interessante und vielschichtige Resultate zu erwarten. Ob sich die daraus hervorgehenden Geschöpfe für die Kategorie „Leben" qualifizieren werden oder nicht, muß diskutiert werden, in jedem Fall aber führen uns die simulierten lebensähnlichen Prozesse zu neuen Methoden der Erzeugung von Komplexität. In einigen Fällen kann die aus diesen Simulationen hervorgehende Komplexität, wie das Leben selbst, über das hinausgehen, was wir mit traditionellen Werkzeugen oder selbst bloßem Verständnis entwerfen können.
In vielen meiner Arbeiten ist die Simulation eines spezifisch natürlichen Prozesses beinhaltet: Die Evolution besteht aus einem einfachen Zyklus. Die „besten" Wesen einer Population überleben und reproduzieren sich. Die daraus hervorgehenden Nachkommen sind Kopien oder Kombinationen ihrer Elternteile, oft mit zufälligen Abänderungen oder Mutationen. Manche Nachkommen stellen, gemessen an ihren Eltern, Verbesserungen dar und da sich nur die besten jeder neuen Generation von Nachkommen weiter reproduzieren, kann die Population als ganze sich langsam verbessern.
In der Simulation kann ein menschlicher Beobachter in jedem Stadium des Zyklus die „Qualität" interaktiv beeinflussen – was als ästhetisch am interessantesten ausgewählt wird, überlebt und reproduziert sich. Bilder, virtuelle Welten, selbst Animationen können so interaktiv entwickelt werden, wobei der Benutzer in gottähnlicher Weise die Kriterien für das Überleben bestimmt. Dies ist eine Methode zur Schaffung und Erforschung von Komplexität, die nicht voraussetzt, daß der Mensch die darin involvierten spezifischen Verfahren versteht.

Computercode-Fragmente sind die Chromosomen, die den Wachstumsprozeß dieser virtuellen Geschöpfe beschreiben. Der Computercode ist, wie die DNA, der Genotyp und das virtuelle Ergebnis ist, vergleich einem Organismus, der Phänotyp.

Es wird eine „genetische Sprache" definiert, bestehend aus einem Set primitiver mathematischer Funktionen, die zu vollständigen genetischen Wachstumsbefehlen zusammengefaßt werden können. Mutationen verändern diese codierten Befehle und können mitunter zur Einführung neuer Funktionen und Parameter führen, womit sich das daraus resultierende Komplexitätsniveau potentiell erhöht.

Es ist eine nahezug unendliche Anzahl genetischer Codes und entsprechender Resultate möglich und diese evolutionären Simulationen können wesentlich zur „Erfindung" neuer Gleichungstypen und Methodern der Erzeugung von Bildern oder anderer virtueller Wesen beitragen.

Es handelt sich um eine unübliche Zusammenarbeit zwischen Menschen und Maschinen: die Menschen treffen Entscheidungen über die visuelle Ästhetik und der Computer verfügt über die mathematische Fähigkeit zur Erzeugung, Verbindung und Veränderung komplexer virtueller Geschöpfe. Der Benutzer muß die verwendeten technischen Gleichungen nicht verstehen. Der Computer kann nur auf gut Glück experimentieren, ohne jeden Sinn für Ästhetik – aber die Verbindung menschlicher und maschineller Fähigkeiten ermöglicht Resultate, die keiner der beiden alleine zustande bringen könne.

Thinking Machines Corporation stellte den Connection Machine Supercomputer für diese Installation bei. Die in Massachusetts beheimatete Firm a hat einige der weltweit stärksten Computer entwickelt. Die Geschwindigkeit des Connection Machine Systems beruht auf der Parallelverarbeitung von Daten – viele Prozessorknoten arbeiten gleichzeitig zusammen. Das für dieses Projekt verwendete Connection Machine Modell enthält 32.768 Prozessoren (siehe auch den Beitrag von Tamiko Thiel in diesem Buch).

John Watlington, Entwurfsingenieur am MIT Media Lab in Cambridge, Massachusetts, entwarf und baute die Video-Hardware „Freeze-Frame", die es ermöglichte, die Bilder aus dem Connection Machine Computer am Monitorfeld zu zeigen. Sie übersetzt auch die Signale von den Schritt-Sensoren.

Arlene Chung, Thinking Machines und Ron Bennett, Bennett HDG Inc., trugen zum Design des Objektraums bei.

Richard Baileys, David Lloyd Owen, Jonathan Saunders und Roch Bourbonnais gewährten technische Hilfestellung.

cluded, potentially increasing the resulting level of complexity.

A nearly infinite number of genetic codes and corresponding results are possible, and these evolutionary simulations can esentially "invent" new types of equations and methods for generating images or other virtual entities.

This is an unusual collaboration between humans and machine: the humans supply decisions of visual aesthetics, and the computer supplies the mathematical ability for generating, mating, and mutating complex virtual entities. The user is not required to unterdstand the technical equations involved. The comoputer can only experiment at random with no sense of aesthetics—but this comination of human and machine abilities permits the creation of results that neither of the two could produce alone.

Jim Salem, Gary Oberbrunner und Matt Fitzgibbon halfen bei der Entwicklung der Connection Machine Graphik- und Display-Software.
Tamiko Thiel fungierte als Connection Machine Industrie-Designerin.

POLY-WORLD: WIRKLICHES LEBEN IN EINEM KÜNSTLICHEN KONTEXT?

LARRY YAEGER

EINLEITUNG

Das Thema dieses Vortrages ist Künstliches Leben – das Studium vom Menschen geschaffener lebender Systeme. Im besonderen werde ich eine bestimmte rechnerische Ökologie mit Namen PolyWorld besprechen, die den scheinbar erfolgreichen Versuch darstellt, nicht-biologisches Leben in einem Computer zu entwickeln. Obwohl selbst nicht-biologisch, schöpft PolyWorld in hohem Ausmaß aus biologischen Prinzipien: Es verbindet biologisch motivierte *Genetik*, einfache simulierte *Physiologien* und *Metabolismen*, Hebbianisches *Lernen* in willkürlichen (arbiträren) *neuralen Netzwerk*-Architekturen, einen *visuellen* Wahrnehmungsmechanismus und eine Serie primitiver *Verhalten* in künstlichen Organismen begründet auf einer einfachen *Ökologie*. Jagdtrieb, Mimikry, sexuelle Reproduktion und sogar Kommunikation werden alle geradlinig unterstützt. Die resultierenden Überlebensstrategien, sowohl einzeln, als auch in der Gruppe entstehen völlig neu, so wie die Funktionalitäten in ihre neuronalen Netzwerk-„Hirne" eingebettet sind.

PolyWorld ist ein Versuch, an künstliche Intelligenz ebenso heranzugehen, wie die natürliche Intelligenz entstanden ist: durch die *Evolution von neuralen Systemen* in einer komplexen Ökologie.

Aber sind diese vom Menschen geschaffenen Organismen *wirklich* am Leben? *Können* sie es sein?

ÜBERSICHT ÜBER DEN POLYWORLD SIMULATOR

PolyWorld ist ein ökologischer Simulator, bestehend aus einer flachen Grundebene, möglicherweise unterteilt durch ein paar unüberwindbare Barrieren, gefüllt mit willkürlich angepflanzten Stücken von Nahrung und bewohnt von einer Anzahl von Organismen. Die bewohnenden Organismen verwenden Farbsicht als Input für ein neurales Netz-

POLYWORLD: REAL LIFE IN AN ARTIFICIAL CONTEXT?

LARRY YEAGER

INTRODUCTION

The subject of this talk will be Artificial Life—the study of man-made living systems. In particular, I will discuss a particular computational ecology, called PolyWorld, that represents a seemingly successful attempt to develop non-biological life in a computer. Though itself non-biological, PolyWorld draws heavily on biological principles: It brings together biologically motivated *genetics*, simple simulated *physiologies* and *metabolisms*, Hebbian *learning* in arbitrary *neural network* architectures, a *visual* perceptive mechanism, and a suite of primitive *behaviors* in artificial organisms *grounded* in a simple *ecology*. Predation, mimicry, sexual reproduction, and even communication are all supported in a straightforward fashion. The resulting survival strategies, both individual and group, are purely emergent, als are the functionalities embodied in their neural network "brains". PolyWorld is an attempt to approach artificial intelligence the same way that natural intelligence emerged: through the *evolution* of neural system in a complex *ecology*.

But are these man-made organisms *really* alive? *Can* they be? After presenting some specifics of the pseudo-physics and -biology that constitute PolyWorld's model of life, and showing videotape of some of the species and complex emergent behaviors found in the organisms of PolyWorld, I will try to address this most fundamental question of the field of Artificial Life.

I will conclude with some suggestions for future directions for this research.

OVERVIEW OF THE POLYWORLD SIMULATOR

PolyWorld is an ecological simulator, consisting of a flat ground-plane, possibly divided up by a few impassable barriers, filled with randomly grown pieces of food, and inhabited by a variety of organisms. The inhabiting organisms use color vision as input to a neural network brain that employs Hebbian learning at its synapses. The outputs of this brain fully determine the organism' behaviors. These organisms and all other visible constituents of the world are represented by simple polygonal shapes. Vision is provided by rendering an image of the world from each organism's point of view, and using the resulting pixel map as input to the organism's brain, as if it were light falling on a retina. The organism's simulated physiologies—sice, sterngth, and maximum speed — and their corresponding metabolic rates are determined from an underlying genetic code. There is also a single *ID* gene whose only function is to provide the green component of the organism's coloration at display time; since organisms can actually see each other, this can, in principle, support mimicry. *Mutation rate,* the *number of crossover points* used during reproduction, and *maximum lifespan* are placed in the genes in order to permit a kind of meta-level genetics, and in recognition of the fact that these parameters were themselves evolved in natural systems. A final physiology gene controls the *fraction of an organism's remaining energy that it will contribute to its offspring upon birth.* The offspring's total available energy on birth is the sum of these contributions from the two parents.

Another group of genes control the organism's *neural architecture.* These genes define a number of neuronal groups or clusters, the quantities of inhibitory and/or excitatory neurons found in these clusters, and the degree an dtype of synaptic connections that exist between the neurons in these various clusters. This model attempts to capture the statistical nature and complexity of real neural architectures, whithout the necessity of and ontogenetic model of neural development. One result of this model of neural architectures is that it is possible for PolyWorld's simulated "Nature" to select for hardwire/instinctual behaviors, learning behaviors, or hybrids.

A small number of an organism's neurons are predetermined to activate a suite of possible primitive behaviors, including eating, mating fighting, moving forward, turning, controlling their field of view, an dcontrolling the brightness of a few of the polygons on their bodies. Organisms expend energy with each action, including neural activity; more actions, more neurons, or more synapses produce greater enery expenditures. They must replenish this energy in order to survive. They may do so by eating the food that grows around the environment. When an organism dies, its carcass turns into food. Because one of the possible primitive behaviors is *fighting,* organisms can potentially damage other organisms. So they may also replenish their energies by killing and eating each other. Predation is thus modeled quite naturally. In order to reproduce, two spatially overlapping organisms mut *both* express their *mating* behavior. Reproduction then occurs by taking the genetic material from the two haploid individuals, subjecting it to crossover and mutation, and the expressing the new genome as a child organism.

Once a *stable behavior strategy*—one which allows the organisms to replenish their numbers (depleted by death) through reproductive mat-

werk-Gehirn, das Hebbianisches Lernen an seinen Synapsen anwendet. Die Outputs dieses Gehirns bestimmen völlig das Verhalten der Organismen. Diese Organismen und alle anderen sichtbaren Bestandteile der Welt werden von einfachen polygonalen Formen dargestellt. Sehvermögen wird ermöglicht durch „rendering" eines Bildes von der Welt aus dem Blickpunkt jedes einzelnen Organismus und durch Verwendung der enstandenen Pixel map als Input in das Gehirn des Organismus, als wäre es Licht, das auf eine Retina fällt. Die simulierten Physiologien der Organismen – Größe, Stärke und Höchstgeschwindigkeit und ihre entsprechenden metabolischen Ausmaße werden von einem zugrundeliegenden genetischen Code bestimmt. Es gibt auch ein einzelnes ID-Gen, dessen Funktion es ist, zur Displayzeit für die grüne Komponente der Farbgebung des Organismus zu sorgen; da die Organismen einander tatsächlich sehen können, kann dies, im Prinzip, die Mimikry unterstützen. Die *Mutationsrate, die Zahl der Überkreuzungspunkte,* die während der Reproduktion verwendet wird, und *die maximale Lebensdauer* werden in der Anordnung der Gene plaziert, um eine Art Meta-Ebenen-Genetik zu erlauben, und in Anerkennung der Tatsache, daß diese Parameter selbst in natürlichen Systemen entwickelt wurden. Ein letztes Physiologie-Gen kontrolliert den *Bruchteil der verbleibenden Energie eines Organismus, den er zu seinem Nachwuchs bei dessen Geburt beisteuern wird.* Die gesamte verfügbare Energie des Nachwuchses bei dessen Geburt, ist die Summe dieser Beigaben von den beiden Eltern.

Eine andere Gruppe von Genen kontrolliert die *neurale Architektur* des Organismus. Diese Gene bestimmen eine Anzahl von neuronalen Gruppen oder Haufen, die Mengen der hemmenden und/oder Reize hervorrufenden Neuronen, die man in diesen Haufen findet, und Grad und Typ synaptischer Verbindungen, die zwischen den Neuronen in diesen verschiedenen Haufen bestehen. Dieses Modell versucht, die statistische Natur und Komplexität echter neuraler Architekturen, ohne die Notwendigkeit eines ontogenetischen Modells der neuralen Entwicklung einzufangen. Ein Ergebnis dieses Modells von neuralen Architekturen ist, daß es für PolyWorlds simulierte „Natur" möglich ist, für instinktives Verhalten, gelerntes Verhalten oder Hybride auszuwählen.

Eine kleine Anzahl der Neuronen eines Organismus sind vorherbestimmt, eine Reihe möglicher primitiver Verhalten zu aktivieren, einschließlich dem Essen, dem Sich Paaren, dem Kämpfen, der Vorwärtsbewegung, der Drehung, der Kontrolle des Sichtfeldes und der Kontrolle der Helligkeit des Körpers. Organismen verbrauchen Energie mit jeder Aktion, einschließlich neuraler Aktivität; mehr Aktionen, mehr

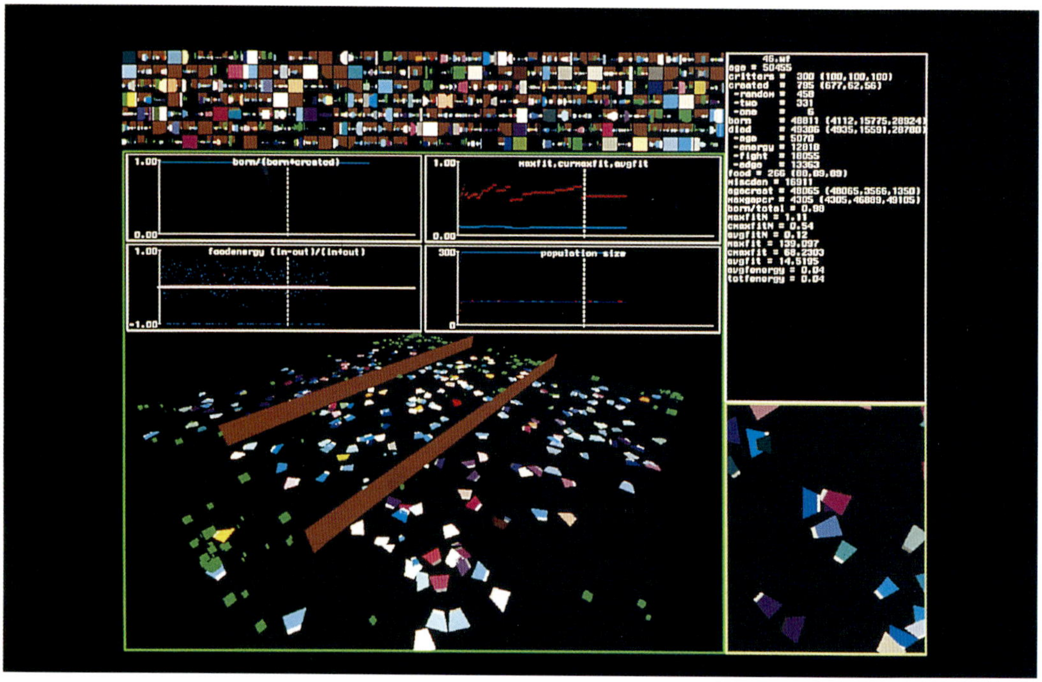

Neuronen oder mehr Synapsen produzieren größeren Energieverbrauch. Sie müssen diese Energie wieder auffüllen, um zu überleben. Sie können das tun, indem sie die Nahrung fressen, um die Umwelt herum wächst. Wenn ein Organismus stirbt, wird sein Kadaver zu Nahrung. Da eines der möglichen primitiven Verhalten *Kämpfen* ist, können Organismen möglicherweise andere Organismen beschädigen. Daher können sie also ihre Energien auch wieder auffüllen, indem sie einander töten und fressen. Raubtierverhalten ist auf diese Art ziemlich natürlich nachgebildet. Um sich zu reproduzieren, müssen beide von zwei sich räumlich überlappende Organismen *ihr Paarungsverhalten* ausdrücken. Reproduktion geschieht dann, indem man das genetische Material von zwei haploiden Individuen nimmt, es Überschneidung und Mutation unterzieht und das neue Genom dann als Kindorganismus bezeichnet.

Wenn erst einmal eine *stabile Verhaltensstrategie* – eine die den Organismen erlaubt, ihre Zahl (vom Tod dezimiert) wieder durch reproduktive Paarung aufzufüllen – aufgetreten ist, gibt es keine andere Tauglichkeitsfunktion, außer dem Überleben. Bis eine solche Verhaltensstrategie aufgetaucht ist, kann man PolyWorld als eine Art „On-line Genetischer Algorithmus" Modus mit einer *ad hoc* Tauglichkeitsfunktion laufen lassen. Während dieser Phase kann man eine Minimalanzahl von Organismen garantieren, die die Welt bevölkern. Wenn die Zahl der Tode verursacht, daß die Anzahl

ing—has emerged, PolyWorld can be run in a sort of "on-line Genetic Algorithm" mode, with an *ad hoc* fitness function. During this stage, a minimum number of organisms may be guaranteed to populate the world. If the number of deaths causes the number of organisms extant in the world to drop below this minimum, either another *random* organism may be *created* by the system, or the offspring of two organisms from a table of the N fittest may be *created,* or, rarely, the best organism ever may be returned to the world unchanged.

Minimum, maximum, and initial numbers of organisms and food may be specified, along with a food growth rate. It is possible to manage these control parameters, along with the *ad hoc* fitness tatistics, simulataneously for a number of different independent "domains", which typically, though no tnecessarily, coincide with the divisions imposed on the world by the barriers. A variety of graphical displays monitor the progress of the simulation. All of the simulation control parameters and display options are defined in a single "world file" that is read at the start of the simulation. In addition, some of the display options can be invoke interactively at runtime. Current high end simulations typically involve several hundred organisms, with several hundred neurons each.

RESULTS: SPECIATION AND COMPLEX EMERGENT BEHAVIORS

Despite the variability inherent in different worlds, certain recurring "species" have occurred in the simulations run to date. Only the species from "successful" simulations are examined at any length and discussed here. A simulations is considered sucessful if any only if organisms emerge which are capable of sistaining the world's populations through their mating behaviors (and thus organism *creations* cease). These species, by definition, have evolved a stable behavior strategy. Some of these species-level and individual-level behaviors are reminiscent of behavioral strategies observedin natural organisms, and may yield insights into those natural behaviors, unencumbered as they are by prior assumptions about biological life or our usual tendency to anthropomorphize.

The first of these species to emerge, the "frenetic joggers", basically just ran straight ahead at full speed, always wanting to mate and always wanting eat. As their particular (benign and primitive) world was set up, it turned out that they would run into pieces of food or each other often enough to sustain themselves and to reproduce. It was an adequate, if not particularly interesting solution for that world.

The second recurring species has been referred to as the "indolent cannibals". These organisms "solve" the world energy and reproduction problem by turning the world into an almost zero-dimensional point. That ist, they never travel far very far from either their parents or their offspring. These organisms mate with each other, fight with each other, kill each other, and eat each other when they die. It turns out that "cannibal" is somewhat of a misnomer, since the dominant reason for these slothful colonies is the ready accessibility of reproductive partners.

The third recurring species has been referred to as the "edge runners". These organisms take the next step up from the cannibals, and essentially reduce their world to an approximately one-dimensional curve. They mostly just run around and around the edge of the world. This turns out to be a fairly good strategy, since, if enough other organisms are doing it, then some will have died along the path, ensuring adequate supplies of food. And mates are easily found by simply running a little faster or a little slower, running in the opposite direction, or simply stopping at some point and waiting for other runners to arrive (all of which behaviors have been observed).

Another species known as the "dervishes" evolved in a Braitenberg-like table-top world, with world borders that represented death to organisms that stumbled over the edge. These organisms spent their entire lives turning in moderately tight circles that brought them into contact with food and mates, but carefully avoided the deadly edges of the world.

The more interesting species are not so easily classified. In worlds where a single species has become dominant, the individuals' behaviors have still been quite varied. And in many worlds, no single species becomes obviously dominant. It is in these simulations that one can observe behaviors such as:

- responding to visual stimuly by speeding up,
- responding to an attack by fighting back or running away,
- grazing (slowing upon ecountering food),
- food-seeking and food-circling,

der in der Welt existierenden Organismen unter dieses Minimum fällt, kann entweder das System einen anderen *willkürlichen* Organismus *erschaffen*, oder der Nachwuchs zweier Organismen von einer Tabelle der N-tauglichsten könnte kreiert werden, oder der jemals beste aller Organismen könnte unverändert in die Welt zurückgegeben werden.

Die minimalen, maximalen und anfänglichen Zahlen von Organismen und Nahrung können bestimmt werden, sowie die Wachstumsrate der Nahrung. Es ist möglich diese Kontrollparameter zu beeinflussen, ebenso die *ad hoc* Tauglichkeitsstatistik, gleichzeitig für eine Anzahl verschiedener unabhängiger „Domänen", welche typischer-, jedoch nicht notwendigerweise, mit den Teilungen übereinstimmen, die der Welt durch die Barrieren auferlegt wurden. Eine Reihe graphischer Anzeigen kontrollieren das Fortschreiten der Simulation. Alle Kontrollparameter und die Display-Optionen der Simulation werden in einem einzigen „World File" definiert, der vor dem Beginn der Simulation gelesen wird. Weiters können einige der Anzeigen-Optionen während der Laufzeit interaktiv aufgerufen werden. Neueste High-End-Simulationen beinhalten mehrere hundert Organismen, von denen jeder mehrere hundert Neuronen hat.

RESULTATE: ARTENBILDUNG UND KOMPLEXES, ENTSTEHENDES VERHALTEN

Trotz der Variabilität, die verschiedenen Welten innewohnt, sind bis dato bestimmte wiederkehrende „Spezies" beim Simulationslauf aufgetreten. Nur die Spezies aus „erfolgreichen" Simulationen werden hier genauer untersucht und besprochen. Eine Simultion wird dann, und nur dann als erfolgreich betrachtet, wenn Organismen auftreten, die fähig sind, die Population der Welt durch ihr Paarungsverhalten aufrechtzuerhalten (und wenn daher die *Kreation* von Organismen aufhört) Diese Spezies haben, der Definition nach, eine stabile Verhaltensstrategie entwickelt. Manche dieser Verhalten, sowohl auf Spezies-Ebene, wie auch auf Individual-Ebene erinnern an Verhaltensstrategien, die man in natürlichen Organismen beobachtet und können eventuell Einblicke in jene natürlichen Verhalten gewähren, die von füheren Annahmen über biologisches Leben und unserer Tendenz zu vermenschlichen unbelastet sind.

Die erste dieser Spezies, die auftrat, die „frenetischen Jogger", rannten eigentlich nur mit Höchstgeschwindigkeit geradeaus und wollten sich immer nur paaren und immer nur fressen. Beim Erstellen ihrer bestimmten (gutartigen/freundlichen und primitiven) Welt, stellte es sich heraus, daß sie beim Rennen oft genug auf Nahrung und aufeinander treffen würden, um sich zu erhalten und zu reproduzieren. Es war eine adäquate, wenngleich auch keine besonders interessante Lösung für diese Welt.

Die zweite wiederkehrende Spezies wurde „träge Kannibalen" genannt. Diese Organismen „lösen" ihr Weltenergie- und Reproduktions-Problem, indem sie ihre Welt in einen fast null-dimensionalen Punkt verwandeln. Das heißt, sie bewegen sich nie sehr weit von ihren Eltern oder ihrer Nachkommenschaft fort. Diese Organismen paaren sich miteinander, kämpfen miteinander, töten einander und fressen einander, wenn sie sterben. Es zeigt sich, daß „Kannibal" als leichte Fehlbenennung gesehen werden kann, da der Hauptgrund für diese faule Kolonie die leichte Zugänglichkeit von Partnern zur Reproduktion ist.

Die dritte wiederkehrende Spezies wurde „Rand-Läufer" genannt. Diese Organismen steigen eine Stufe höher, als die Kannibalen und reduzieren ihre Welt auf eine ungefähr eindimensionale Kurve. Sie rennen meist nur auf dem Rand ihrer Welt rundherum. Dies hat sich als ziemlich gute Strategie erwiesen, da, wenn genügend andere Organismen es machen, einige auf dem Weg gestorben sein werden und so einen adäquaten Nahrungsvorrat sichergestellt haben. Außerdem werden Paarungspartner leicht gefunden, indem sie ein bißchen schneller oder langsamer oder in die Gegenrichtung laufen oder einfach irgendwo stehenbleiben und auf andere Läufer warten. (Diese Verhalten wurden auch tatsächlich alle beobachtet.)

Eine weitere Spezies, die „Derwische" enwickelten sich in einer Braitenberg-ähnlichen Tischplatten-Welt, mit Weltgrenzen, die den Tod für jene Organismen bedeutete, die über den Rand hinunterfielen. Diese Organismen verbrachten ihr gesamtes Leben, indem sie sich in engen Kreisen drehten, die sie mit Nahrung und Paarungspartnern in Kontakt brachten, sie vermieden jedoch vorsichtig die tödlichen Ränder der Welt.

Die interessanteren Spezies kann man nicht so leicht klassifizieren. In Welten, wo eine einzelne Spezies dominant wurde, waren die Verhalten der individuellen Organismen immer noch ziemlich vielfältig. Und in vielen Welten wird keine einzelne Spezies deutlich dominant. In solchen Simulationen kann man dann folgende Verhalten beobachten:

- Reaktion auf visuelle Stimuli durch Beschleunigen
- Reaktion auf Angriffe durch Zurückkämpfen oder Davonlaufen
- Grasen/Weiden (das Langsamerwerden, wenn sie auf Nahrung treffen)
- swarming or flocking,
- chasing or following.

BUT ARE THEY ALIVE? REALLY ALIVE?

The answer to this question is made more than a little difficult by the simple fact that there is no clear definition fo just what *Life* really is, or what is means to be truly *Alive*. Farmer and Belin, in the proceedings of the second Artifical Life conference suggest that we approach the definition of life be asking, "If we voyage to another planet, how will we know whether or not life is present?" Their answer should also apply to the analogous question: If we „voyage" to an artifical world, how will we know whether or not life is present? Farmer and Belin offer a set of properties or criteria for life, including reproduction, a Form of self-representation, al metabolism, interaction with the environment, interdependence of parts, stability under perturbations, and the ability to evolve. Taken at face value, the organisms of PolyWorld readily satisfy all of these criteria. So, we either need the refine our criteria, or welchome an entire new genus to the world!

It may be argued that these criteria should themselves be emergent properties of some lower level processes, and counter-argued that recursively applyingt this argument contradicts the fundamental tenet of Artificial Life that it is possible to examine life at various levels of organization, and may even preclude the possibility of ever unambiguously producing an example of man-made life. It may be that the best efforts to date necessarily model only *aspects of life*, that represent the personal biases, interests, and perspectives of the people doing the modeling. Contrast Farmer and Belin's biologically motivated definition fo life with a hypothetical artifical intelligence—one that readily passed the Turning test, yet did not reproduce or evolve—which is more "alive"? Indee, it is possible that only an appropriately staffed jury can ever adequately make such an assessment of *living* or *not living* for the scientific community. Perhaps, though, an information-based model of life may yield insights into the relation beween artificial and natural biologies, and even someday permit regorous distinctions between the living an dnon living in both.

FUTURE DIRECTIONS

Besides countless behavioral ecology and evolutionay biology studies that are possible with PolyWorld, I would like to take some of the organisms that have evolved useful behavioral strategies, and begin to investigate their reactions to novel environments, perhaps even studying their response to classical conditioning experiments. In addition, making the leap from workstation (PolyWorld currently runs on a Silicon Graphis Iris) to a massively parallel processor would allow significantly larger populations and more complex neural models, thus forstering greater speciation and more complex behaviors. I would like to think that this approach to artificial life and intelligence is very open-ended, and have made the source code to PolyWorld available via anonymous ftp at ftp.apple.com, in /pub/polyworld; I may be contacted at larryy@apple.com with questions.

Larry Yaeger
Principal Engineer
Apple Computer, MS 301-4H
One Infinite Loop
Cupertino, CA 95014
(408) 974-6082
larryy@apple.com

- Nahrungssuche und Nahrungseinkreisung
- Schwärmen und Sich Versammeln
- Jagen oder Folgen

ABER SIND SIE AM LEBEN? *WIRKLICH* AM LEBEN?

Die Antwort auf diese Frage ist mehr als ein bißchen schwierig schon allein durch die einfache Tatsache, daß es keine klare Definition darüber gibt, was *Leben* nun wirklich ist oder was es bedeutet, wirklich *lebendig* zu sein. Im Sitzungsbericht der zweiten Artificial Life Konferenz schlagen Farmer und Belin vor, an die Definition von Leben heranzugehen, indem wir fragen: „Wenn wir zu einem anderen Planeten reisen, wie werden wir dann wissen, ob Leben vorhanden ist, oder nicht?" Ihre Antwort sollte auch auf die analoge Frage anwendbar sein: Wenn wir in eine künstliche Welt „reisen", wie werden wir dann wissen, ob Leben vorhanden ist, oder nicht? Farmer und Belin bieten eine Reihe von Eigenschaften und Kriterien für Leben an, darin eingeschlossen sind: Reproduktion, eine Form der Selbst-Repräsentation, ein Metabolismus, Interaktion mit der Umwelt, gegenseitige Abhängigkeit von Teilen, Stabilität bei Störungen und die Fähigkeit sich zu entwickeln. Nimmt man das für bare Münze, so erfüllen die Organismen von PolyWorld leicht alle diese Kriterien. Also müssen wir entweder unsere Kriterien neu definieren oder eine völlig neue Gattung auf der Welt willkommen heißen!

Man könnte nun einwerfen, daß diese Kriterien selbst Eigenschaften sein sollten, die aus einigen Prozessen auf niedrigerer Ebene hervorgehen, und man könnte dem entgegnen, daß die rekursive Anwendung dieses Arguments den fundamentalen Grundsätzen des künstlichen Lebens widerspricht, nämlich daß es möglich ist, Leben auf verschiedenen Ebenen der Organisation zu untersuchen, und daß es sogar die Möglichkeit ausschließen könnte, jemals ein Beispiel des vom Menschen gemachten Lebens unzweideutig zu produzieren. Es könnte sein, daß die besten Anstrengungen bis heute notwendigerweise nur Aspekte des Lebens herstellen, die die persönlichen Vorlieben und Interessen und Perspektiven jener Leute repräsentieren, die die Modelle herstellen.

Vergleichen Sie Farmer und Belins biologisch motivierte Definition von Leben mit einer hypothetischen künstlichen Intelligenz – einer, die den Turing Test leicht bestanden hat, sich jedoch nicht reproduziert oder entwickelt hat – welche ist mehr „lebendig"? Tatsächlich kann es sein, daß nur eine angemessen besetzte Jury jemals eine hinreichende Einschätzung von *lebend* oder *nicht lebend* für die wissenschaftliche Gemeinschaft treffen kann. Vielleicht kann jedoch ein auf Information basierendes Modell von Leben Einblicke in die Beziehung zwischen künstlichen und natürlichen Biologien gewähren und in beiden eines Tages sogar genaue Unterscheidungsmerkmale zwischen den lebenden und nicht lebenden erlauben.

ZUKÜNFTIGE RICHTUNGEN

Neben unzähligen Studien zur Verhaltens-Ökologie und Entwicklungs-Biologie, die mit PolyWorld möglich sind, möchte ich einige der Organismen, die brauchbare Verhaltensstrategien entwickelt haben, nehmen und ihre Reaktionen auf neue Umgebungen untersuchen, vielleicht sogar ihre Reaktion auf klassische Konditionierungsexperimente studieren. Darüberhinaus würde der Sprung von einer Workstation (PolyWorld läuft derzeitig auf einem Silicon Graphic Iris) zu einem großen Parallelprozessor bedeutend größere Populationen und komplexere neurale Modelle daher größerer Artenvielfalt und komplexere Verhalten erlauben. Ich hoffe, daß dieser Ansatz zu künstlichem Leben und künstlicher Intelligenz sehr offen ist und habe den Quellencode zu PolyWorld erhältlich gemacht über: anonymous ftp at ftp.apple.com, in /pub/polyworld; man kann mich bei larryy@apple.com bei Fragen kontaktieren.

PIONIERGEIST & AVANTGARDE

FRANK DIETRICH

PIONEER SPIRIT & AVANTGARDE
FRANK DIETRICH

With artificial life and organic environments, artists and scientists are now exploring biological associations which until now could only be theoretically or speculatively considered. For the first time ever, the most up-to-the-minute computer technology makes it possible to perceptibly experience the dimensions of artificially created worlds and to see various action alternatives in their consequences.
Computer systems which are capable of handling the volumes of data to be processed and of visualizing it "at finger tip" in corresponding quality, are the results of ten years' of experience made by Silicon Graphics at the fore-front of technological evolution. This experience is embodied in the Silicon Graphics' graphics work stations:

- interactive 3D graphics, in full colour
- digital integration of various media (text, graphics, photography, video, CD-audio)
- photo-realism in real time, for the first time on the Reality Engine
- the fastest and most efficient graphics on the desktop with Indigo^2

We are pleased that computer artists and scientists for virtual reality, artificial life and other interactive environments, preferably use work stations by Silicon Graphics. We regard this as being a meaningful partnership which will be beneficial for both parties. The demands made on the efficiency of computer systems by the artistic and scientific avantgarde present us with a permanent challenge and ensure that Silicon Graphics Workstations continue to develop in rapid cycles. With the RISC-PC's of the Indigo family a new computer category was introduced combining the advantages of a PC in terms of being easy to use, size and price, with the efficiency of a work station. As real multimedia machines, the Indigos have an enormous development environment and at the same time are binary compatible with all larger systems made by Silicon Graphics, even with the super computers with symmetrical multi-processing. The availability of these capacities literally opens up new worlds that artists and scientists produce creative access to.
Ars Electronica is a forum which confronts us with such artificial worlds. It ranks among the most significant international events of this kind. Silicon Graphics, as the leading manufacturer of computer systems for visual processing does not consider it to be a necessary obligation

Mit Artificial Life und organischen Environments erkunden heute Künstler und Wissenschaftler biologische Zusammenhänge, die bisher nur theoretisch oder spekulativ erfaßt werden konnten. Erstmals ermöglicht es modernste Computer-Technologie, die Dimensionen von künstlich geschaffenen Welten sinnlich zu erfahren und verschiedene Handlungsalternativen in ihren Konsequenzen zu erleben.
Computersysteme, die in der Lage sind, die dabei zu verarbeitenden Datenmengen zu bewältigen und in entsprechender Qualität auf Fingertip" zu visualisieren, sind das Ergebnis zehnjähriger Erfahrung von Silicon Graphics an vorderster Front der technologischen Evolution. In den Graphics-Workstations von Silicon Graphics ist diese Erfahrung verkörpert:

- Interaktive 3D-Graphik in voller Farbe
- Digitale Integration verschiedener Medien (Text, Grafik, Photographie, Video, CD-Audio)
- Photorealismus in Echt-Zeit, erstmals auf der Reality Engine
- Schnellste und leistungsfähigste Graphik auf dem Desktop mit Indigo

Wir freuen uns, daß Computerkünstler und Wissenschaftler für Virtual Reality, Artificial Life und für andere interaktive Environments bevorzugt Workstations von Silicon Graphics verwenden. Wir sehen darin eine sinnvolle und für beide Seiten fruchtbringende Partnerschaft. Die Anforderungen, die die künstlerische und wissenschaftliche Avantgarde an die Leistungsfähigkeit der Computersysteme stellen, sind uns permanente Herausforderung und tragen dazu bei, daß sich Silicon-Graphics-Workstations in raschen Zyklen weiterentwickeln. Mit den RISC-PCs der Indigo-Familie wurde z. B. erstmals eine neue Computerkategorie eingeführt, die die Vorteile eines PCs bezüglich Benutzerfreundlichkeit, Größe und Preis mit der Leistungsfähigkeit einer Workstation verbindet. Als echte Multi-Media-Maschinen verfügen die Indigos über eine mächtige Entwicklungsumgebung und sind gleichzeitig binärkompatibel zu allen größeren Systemen von Silicon Graphics, bis hin zu den Supercomputern mit symmetrischem Multiprocessing. Durch die Verfügbarkeit dieser Kapazitäten öffnen sich buchstäblich neue Welten, zu denen Künstler und Wissenschaftler kreative Zugänge schaffen.

Ars Electronica ist ein Forum, das uns mit derartigen künstlichen Welten konfrontiert. Es zählt zu den international bedeutendsten Veranstaltungen seiner Art. Silicon Graphics als führender Hersteller von Computer-Systemen für Visual-Processing sieht in der Unterstützung von Ars Electronica keine notwendige Pflichtübung, sondern einen Beitrag zur kulturellen Auseinandersetzung mit essentiellen Fragen unserer Zeit.

Silicon Graphics Computer Systems GmbH, Modecenterstraße 14, A-1030 Wien, Austria, (0 222) 798 68 48

to support Ars Electronica, but rather a contribution to the cultural debate concerning essential questions of our time.

SYMPOSIUM GENTECHNOLOGIE

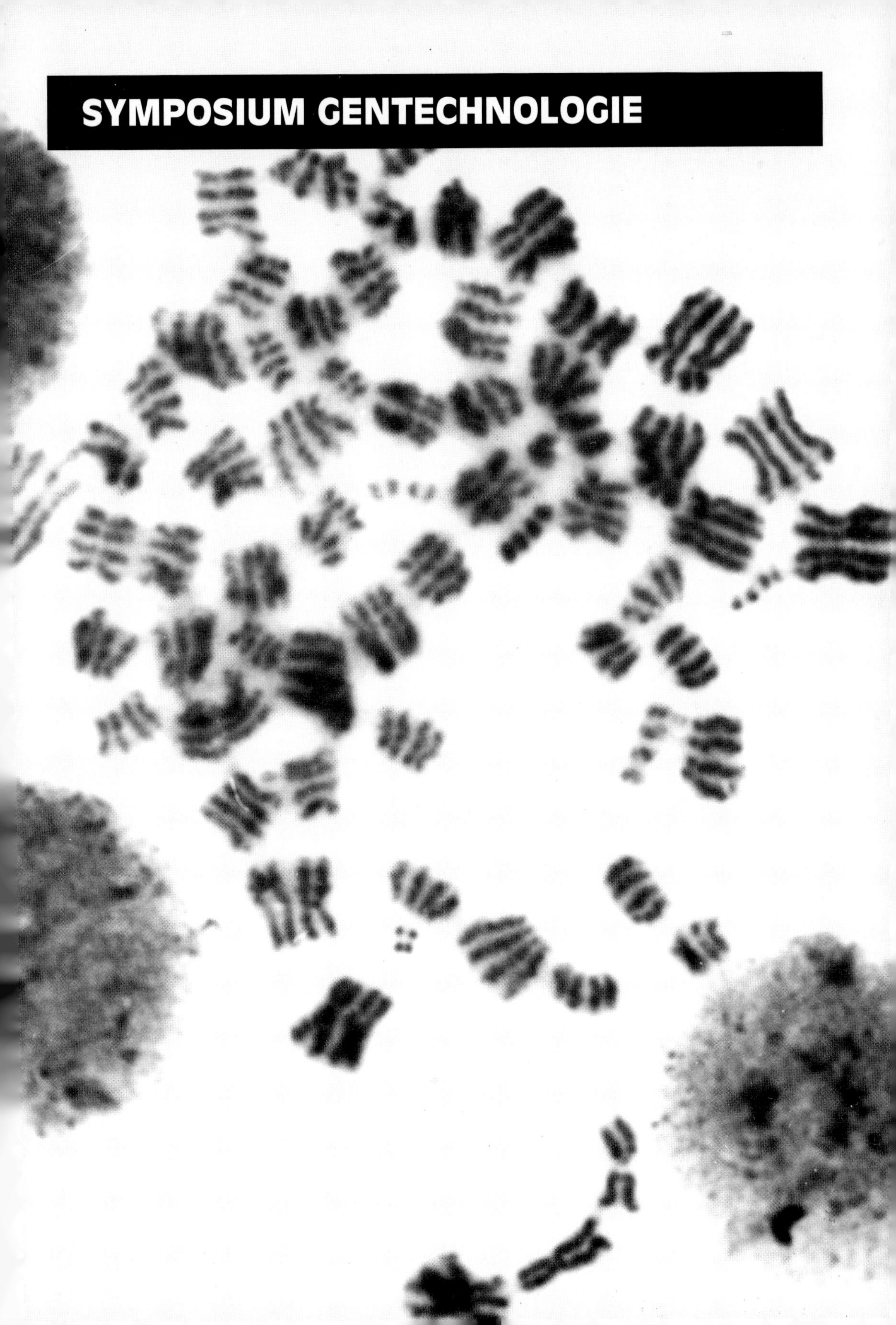

ASPEKTE DER DISKUSSION UM EIN GENTECHNIKGESETZ

CHRISTIAN BRÜNNER

1. Gentechnik ist ein komplexes, sich rasch entwickelndes, Grenzen überschreitendes Amalgam von theoretischen und praktischen Methoden und Disziplinen, bei dem überdies wissenschaftliche, therapeutische, technisch-industrielle, wirtschaftliche, ökologische und ethische Herausforderungen ständig aufeinanderprallen. Von der Hoffnung z.B. auf Hilfe bei der Bekämpfung von Geisteskrankheiten, Aids, und Krebs bis zur Angst z.B. vor dem Menschen nach Maß reicht das Spektrum der Einschätzung dieser Technik.
Wie alles, was von der Hand des Menschen geführt wird, partizipiert auch die Gentechnik an dessen guten und schlechten Anteilen: Sie kann zum Nutzen oder zum Schaden von Mensch, Tier und Ökosystem eingesetzt werden.
2. Es gibt zwar derzeit mehr als 200 Gesetze und Verordnungen, die für gentechnisches Arbeiten relevant sind. Dennoch weist die Rechtsordnung – nicht zuletzt im Vergleich mit einschlägigen EG-Richtlinien und dem Ausland – Lücken auf. Dies gilt z.B. für das Freisetzen gentechnisch veränderter Organismen. Ferner fehlen adäquate Haftungsregeln. Schließlich ist der Grundrechtsschutz der Rechtsgüter, die durch die Gentechnik potentiell gefährdet sind, nicht ausreichend. Wir brauchen daher Regelungen, die diese Lücken schließen.
3. Ich plädiere dafür, verschiedene Regelungen für verschiedene Aspekte (z.B. Sicherheit, Forschung, Anwendungen) in ein Gesetz, das Gentechnikgesetz zu integrieren, dies aus zwei Gründen. Zum einen wäre das Vermeiden von Rechtszersplitterung ein Beitrag für die Akzeptanz der Gentechnik durch die Bevölkerung (70% der Befragten halten die Gentechnik für gefährlich, 67% sind für gesetzliche Regelungen). Zum anderen geht es mehr denn je darum, verschiedene Aspekte integrativ, ähnlich z.B. der Vorgangsweise bei der Technologiefolgenabschätzung, zu behandeln, um zu optimalen Entscheidungen zu kommen; zu diesen zu integrierenden Aspekten zähle ich auch den der ethischen Verantwortbarkeit gentechnischen Arbeitens.
4. Die rationale politische Diskussion über die Chancen und

CHRISTIAN BRÜNNER

1. Gene technology is a complex, rapidly developing, interdisciplinary amalgam of theoretical and practical methods and disciplines, in which scientific, therapeutic, technical—industrial, economic, ecological and ethical challenges are also in constant collision. Opinion about this ranges from hope for the fight against mental illness, AIDS and cancer to fear of, for instance, the designed human being.
Like everything made by human hands, gene technology has its share of good and bad attributes: it can be applied for the benefit or to the detriment of man, animals, and the ecosystem.
2. Although there are now more than 200 laws and regulations relating to gene technology work, there are loopholes in the legal framework not least in comparison with specialist guidelines in the EC and—elsewhere. This applies, for instance, to the release of organisms that have been altered through gene technology. Furthermore, there is a lack of adequate liability regulations. In the final analysis, the constitutional rights of potentially threatened interests are not adequately protected under the law. We therefore need regulations to close these loopholes.
3. I advocate the integration of the various regulations applying to various aspects (e.g. safety, research, applications) into one law, the Gene Technology Law. There are two reasons for this: firstly, avoiding fragmented legislation would contribute to the acceptance of gene technology by the general public (in surveys, 70% considered gene technology to be dangerous; 67% are in favour of legal regulation). Secondly, to reach the best decisions it is now more important than ever to deal with various aspects in an integrative manner, that is, similarly to the way we investigate the consequences of technology Among the aspects to be integrated I include the ethical responsibility for gene technology work.
4. It is not easy to have a rational political dialogue about the opportunities and the risks of gene technology, and the need for legal regulation, taking into consideration the complexity and material dynamics, the application of gene technology to problems and shortcomings which are not specific to gene technology (e.g.: overproduction in agriculture, exploitation of the Third World), and the virulence of "inter-

ests" (e.g.: healing of illnesses, economic growth, thirst for knowledge, conception of man and of the world). A reasonable discussion will however become all but impossible if, for instance, international concerns threaten to withdraw their gene technology sites from Austria should their wishes not be granted in gene technology legislation; or if horror scenarios are written about cloned people, or "glass" people (who present all their genetic information).

Risken der Gentechnologie und über das Erfordernis rechtlicher Regelung zu führen, ist schon angesichts der Komplexität und der Dynamik der Materie, der Focusierung auch von Problemen und Unzulänglichkeiten auf die Gentechnik, die nicht gentechnischspezifisch sind (z.B. Überproduktion in der Landwirtschaft, Ausbeutung der Dritten Welt), und der Virulenz involvierter Interessen" (z.B. Heilung von Krankheiten, Wirtschaftswachstum, Erkenntnisdrang, Menschen- und Weltbild) nicht leicht. Eine vernünftige Diskussion wird aber dann fast unmöglich gemacht, wenn z.B. multinationale Konzerne drohen, ihre Gentechnologie-Standorte aus Österreich abzuziehen für den Fall, daß ihre Wünsche an ein Gentechnikgesetz nicht erfüllt werden, oder wenn man mit dem klonierten und „gläsernen" (seine gesamte genetische Information präsentierenden) Menschen Horrorszenarien schreibt.

GENTECHNOLOGIE UND ETHIK

REINHARD LÖW

Die Gentechnologie ist im letzten Jahrzehnt in den Mittelpunkt öffentlicher Debatten gerückt, wobei das Spektrum der Meinungen von ihrer vorbehaltlosen Befürwortung bis zur radikalen Ablehnung reicht. Während die Kritiker zunächst primär die Sicherheitspolitik ins Blickfeld rückten, konzentriert sich mittlerweile die eigentlich ethische Diskussion auf das Verhältnis von menschlichem Können und menschlichem Dürfen.

Um hier überhaupt ethisch argumentieren zu können, muß als Basis die Möglichkeit eines vernünftigen Gesprächs über Gut und Schlecht anerkannt sein, welches nicht nur Ausdruck partikularer Moralen ist. Mit dieser prinzipiellen Zustimmung lassen sich dann in Güterabwägungen die verschiedenen Bereiche gentechnologischer Eingriffsmöglichkeiten beurteilen.

Für den nichtmenschlichen Bereich ergibt sich, daß trotz gewichtiger Gegenargumente aus dem Sicherheitsbereich, aus der Alternativforschung und dem Tierschutz die Gentechnologie auch ethisch als wünschenswert erscheinen kann resp. erscheint. Auch bei einer eventuellen jetzigen Ablehnung von Experimenten oder Produktionen könnte sich die Güterabwägung mit geänderten Parametern ändern.

Im menschlichen Bereich ist die Beurteilung diffiziler. Bei der Genanalyse, welche Menschen einen bessere Lebensplanung erlauben könnte, ist neben Freiwilligkeit, Datenschutz und Vertraulichkeit auch der weitere Rahmen zu berücksichtigen, innerhalb dessen sie vorgenommen wird: Die Möglichkeit von Diskriminierung und Ächtung bis hin zur Auslese „lebensunwerten Lebens", besonders im vorgeburtlichen Stadium des Menschenlebens, muß ausgeschlossen werden.

Die Gentherapie an Körperzellen (somatische Gentherapie) befindet sich fast ausschließlich im Experimentierstadium und ist ethisch etwa so einzuschätzen wie die Organtransplantation - mit allen Vorteilen und Bedenklichkeiten.

Die Gentherapie in der Keimbahn, also der gentechnologische Eingriff an befruchteten Eizellen, ist ethisch strikt abzulehnen. Hier wird nicht eine menschliche Person geheilt, sondern ihre Identität manipuliert. Keimbahngentherapie

GENE TECHNOLOGY AND ETHICS
REINHARD LÖW

In the last decade, gene technology has moved into the centre of public debates, whereby the spectrum of opinions range from its advocation without any reservations to its radical dismissal. Whereas critics first of all primarily put safety policies into the field of vision, in the meantime, the actual ethical discussion has been concentrated on the ratio between what man is able to do and what man is allowed to do.

In order to be able to argue, here at all, in an ethical sense, the possibility of a rational discussion concerning good and bad that is not merely the expression of particular morals must be recognized as being a basis. Having obtained this principle agreement, the different fields of gene technology intervention possibilities may be assessed in the sense of considering commodities.

For the non-human field, despite hefty counter arguments from the safety sector, alternative research and prevention of cruelty to animals, the fact that gene technology can, or respectively, does appear to be both ethical as well as desired, emerges. Even in the face of a possible present dismissal of experiments or productions, the considering of commodities could change with modified parameters.

In the human sector, the appraisal is more difficult. In the case of gene analysis which could permit human beings to plan their lives better, besides voluntariness, protection of data privacy and confidentiality, the further framework within which it is to be performed must be considered: The possibility of discrimination and ostracizing and even the selection "of life unworthy to live", especially in the pre-natal stage of human life, must be out of the question.

Gene therapy on body cells (somatic gene therapy) is almost exclusively still at the experimental stage and, ethically, can be appraised like organ transplantations—with all the prejudices and dubiousness.

Gene therapy in the embryo tract, that is, gene technology intervention on fertilized egg cells has to be ethically strictly rejected. Here, it is not a human being who is being cured but more their identity that is being manipulated. Embryo tract gene therapy does not lead to a "more beautiful world", but to the constantly increasing and irreversible power of present-day human beings over coming generations and i.e. in this respect, to a dominance of the dead over the living.

Finally, two arguments which are as popular and global as they are wrong and which occur in gene technology debates have to be dismissed and that is "nature does it too" and "no biologist wants to do anything immoral".

führt nicht zu einer „schöneren Welt", sondern zu einer ständig wachsenden, irreversiblen Macht der jetzigen Menschen über die kommenden Generationen, und d. h., von jenen aus gesehen, zu einer Herrschaft der Toten über die Lebendigen.

Zum Schluß sind zwei ebenso populäre, pauschale wie falsche Argumente in gentechnologischen Debatten zurückzuweisen, nämlich „die Natur macht es doch auch", und „kein Biologe will unmoralische Sachen machen".

GENTECHNIK-IMPRESSIONEN

LOTHAR MÜLLER

Mit Goethes „Zauberlehrling" beginnt ein Bericht über ein Symposium zum Thema „Chancen und Grenzen der Gentechnologie" (1989). Bezeichnend die Titel der dann folgenden Artikel „Vom Vertrauen in den Meister". „Die ‚Geister' der Gentechnologie untertan machen". „Verantwortung im Widerstreit". „Problemzonen der Gentechnologie".
Heute, nach Abschluß der ersten Enquetekommission des Nationalrates, nach Abschluß des Begutachtungsverfahrens für ein österreichisches Gentechnikgesetz, erweitern sich Wissens-, Bewußtseins- aber auch Gefühlszustand beträchtlich.

DIE IMPRESSIONEN

- Gentechnologie ist mehr als ein bloßer „Satz von Methoden". Sie ist eine Technologie, die Leben sowohl als Instrument wie auch als Ziel betrachtet.
- Gentechnologie geht in ihrer angestrebten, ausgeprägten Form „quer durch unser persönliches und gesellschaftliches Leben". Ihr „Optimierungsangebot" reicht von der medizinischen Diagnostik über neue Nahrungsmittel bis hin zur Veränderung von Pflanzen und Tieren. Natur wird auch in der Substanz beliebig gemacht.
- Bis jetzt wurden breitflächiger Verbrauch und damit Zerstörung („Zerbrauch") der natürlichen Gegebenheiten durch sogenannte „Biotope" kompensiert. Ich bin überzeugt, daß auch die Tage dieser „Naturfassaden", die uns Natur quasi im Freilichtmuseum zeigen, gezählt sind. Die Zukunft gehört – wenn wir es zulassen – den „Technobiotopen".
- Wird Leben – durch die Möglichkeit gezielter Veränderung, durch Substanzaustausch, durch Strecken der Artgrenzen usw. beliebig, dann ändert sich auch das Bewußtstein. Dimensionen wie Integrität, Einmaligkeit, Autonomie treten hinter die Begriffe Machbarkeit, Austausch und Optimierung zurück. Der Triumpf der Segmentierung!
- Die zu akzeptierenden Seiten der Gentechnik (etwa An-

GENE TECHNOLOGY-IMPRESSIONS
LOTHAR MÜLLER

With Goethe's "Sorcerer's Apprentice", a report commences about a symposium on the subject "Chances and Limits of Gene Technology" (1989). Indicative are the titles of the articles following on that matter; "From Trust in the Master". "Subject the 'Ghosts' to Gene Technology". "Responsibility in Conflict". "Problem Zones of Gene Technology".
Today, after the completion of the first National Council investigation commission, after completion of the appraisal process for an Austrian gene technology legislation, the situation of knowledge, consciousness as well as feeling is expanding considerably.
The impressions:

- Gene technology is more than a mere "set of methods". It is a technology that considers life as both an instrument as well as a goal.
- Gene technology, in its aspired and distinct form, goes "right through our personal and social life". Its "optimization package" ranges from medical diagnosis to new foodstuffs, even to the alteration of plants and animals. Nature is made at will, even in the very substance.
- Until now wide-spread consumption and consequently destruction ("deconsumption") of natural conditions has been compensated by so-called "biotopes". I am convinced that even the days of these "natural facades" which show us nature, as it were, in the open-air museum, are numbered. The future belongs—if we allow it—to the "technobiotopes".
- If life becomes arbitrary through the possibility of purposeful change, substance exchange, extending through the species limits etc., consciousness also changes. Dimensions like integrity, uniqueness and autonomy fall back behind the terms of practicability, exchange and optimization. The triumph of segmentation!
- The sides of gene technology to be accepted (possible range of application medicine, environment), largely result from the negative side of our "civilization". Microbes will eat refuse, plants are made resistant, living beings are optimally adapted. Instead of fighting causes—a rehabilitation technology!
- Whoever says gene must also say ethics!

wendungsbereich Medizin, Umwelt) resultieren vielfach aus den negativen unserer „Zivilisation". Mikroben werden Müll fressen, Pflanzen resistent gemacht, Lebewesen optimal angepaßt. Statt Ursachenbekämpfung also eine Sanierungstechnologie!

- Wer Gen sagt, muß auch Ethik sagen!

GENTECHNOLOGIE – EIN WEG ZU KÜNSTLICHEM LEBEN?

HELMUT RUIS

Bedauerlicherweise sind in der breiten Öffentlichkeit die Vorstellungen darüber, was Gentechnologie ist, was sie an positiven Chancen bietet, und was sie an Risken mit sich bringt, oft sehr weit von der Realität entfernt. Zu diesem Zustand tragen nicht nur schlecht informierte oder besonders sensationelle Schlagzeilen suchende Journalisten bei, sondern gelegentlich auch tatsächliche oder sogenannte Experten. Als ein Beispiel dafür sollen im Vortrag einige Zitate aus den Unterlagen zu einem kommerziell erhältlichen „Gentechnikbaukasten" für Jugendliche präsentiert werden. Während die mit Hilfe dieses Baukastens durchführbaren Experimente beruhigend harmlos sind, ist es die gleichzeitig vermittelte Philosophie keineswegs. So werden Gentechnikexperimente als sonst den Göttern vorbehaltene Akte (Schöpfung neuen Lebens) dargestellt. Falls diese Darstellung berechtigt wäre, wäre Gentechnik tatsächlich eine Methode, mit der neues, künstliches Leben produziert werden kann.

Um eine sachliche Auseinandersetzung mit diesem so wichtigen Gebiet zu ermöglichen, soll im Vortrag versucht werden, dieser pathetischen Darstellung die nüchterne, aber dabei immer noch faszinierende Realität gegenüberzustellen. Dabei soll klargestellt werden, was gentechnische Methoden tatsächlich leisten, insbesondere aber auch, womit sie in der Öffentlichkeit oft verwechselt werden. Dies führt zur Feststellung, daß mit Hilfe gentechnischer Methoden die gezielte Veränderung der vererbbaren Eigenschaften von Lebewesen möglich ist. Von diesem Faktum ausgehend soll die Frage diskutiert werden, ob bzw. inwieweit in Zukunft durch Weiterführung und Ausbau dieser Methoden Produkte erhalten werden können, die die Bezeichnung „künstliche Lebewesen" tatsächlich verdienen. Mit heutigen gentechnischen Methoden veränderte Lebewesen, also etwa Bakterien, die ein bestimmtes für therapeutische Zwecke interessantes Protein des Menschen produzieren, oder auch Menschen, deren Erbkrankheit durch Übertragung eines funktionellen Gens aus einem anderen Organismus geheilt

GENETIC ENGINEERING—A WAY TO ARTIFICIAL LIFE? HELMUT RUIS

Unfortunately, the public's ideas of genetic engineering, its positive opportunities and its risks, are often far removed from reality. Not only journalists who are poorly informed or who are just after sensational headlines have contributed to this state of affairs but also the so-called experts. To illustrate this I will quote a few lines from the instruction manual of a commercial "genetic engineering kit" for young people. While the experiments to be carried out with this kit are reassuringly harmless, the philosophy it conveys is must certainly not. The genetic engineering experiments are presented as acts (creation of new life) otherwise reserved to the gods. If this description were justified, genetic engineering could actually be viewed as a method for creating new, artificial life.

To enable an objective approach to such an important area, I will try to confront this pathetic account with the sober, yet fascinating reality. Here I would like to show what the methods of genetic engineering can actually produce, while focussing in particular on the public's misconceptions of them. This leads to the assertion that genetic engineering can be used to deliberately change inheritable characteristics of living beings. Proceeding from here, I will discuss the question whether—and if so to what extent—these methods will be developed further in the future to create products that could legitimately be referred to as "artificial life". Living beings, which have been altered by means of today's genetic engineering methods, e.g., bacteria that produce a certain human protein for therapeutic purposes or the transmission of a functional gene from another organism for healing humans suffering from a heriditar disease (gene therapy), obviously do not merit such a designation. One cannot speak of artificial living beings in a narrower sense in view of the fact that the changes brought about could have also taken place naturally even if the necessary events (e.g., transfer of genes between various types or classes of living beings) seldomly take place in nature.

To seriously test whether artificial life can be produced by means of genetic engineering, we first have to clarify certain notions. Living beings could be understood as systems that are capable of storing information and passing it on to the following generations. These systems must be able to absorb matter or energy and to transform it in order to construct the structures and tools necessary for storing and passing on information (metabolism). Artificial creatures, in a narrower sense, would have to use other types of structures and building blocks as natural organisms, i.e., other information memories than nuclein acides and other catalyzers than proteins. These considerations show that artificial life in this sense cannot be created by means of genetic engineering. In a less restricted sense, we could speak of artificial life if it were possible to produce radically new types of living creatures by means of the same basic structures and mechanisms that are characteristic of natural living beings. Here the problem of delineation arises. Does a blue rose represent a completely new type of life or would a singing rose have to be produced to do justice to this definition? The creation of a blue rose does not involve any particular technical or principle problem in terms of genetic engineering, it is also nothing sensationally new. A singing rose, by contrast, could not always be created with such a technology. In purely hypothetical terms, it could be produced by means of genetic engineering only by transferring a greater number of genes from already existing living creatures or by transmitting artificial genes that are modelled after natural genes. It is thus questionable whether even such a utopian living being could legitimately be called artificial life.

A further option will be explored here: Could genetic engineering be used to create living beings from non-biological (anorganic or organic on the basis of chemical synthesis) components and would such creatures fall under the category of "artificial life"? It must first be stressed that in view of the present state of technology such a goal would, no doubt, be viewed as utopian. Yet given our theoretical understanding of the "reconstruction" of the simplest forms of life, such as bacteria cells, such an endeavor could at least in principle be conceivable, even if the resources needed to carry out such an experiment will make it unfeasible even in the future. With our present know-how, such a project would also be conceivable for higher forms of life, yet its realization becomes even more unrealistic. The following considerations are thus nothing more than a thought experiment. Beginning with the pure reconstruction of existing forms of life which would not necessarily bring forth artificial life, one could, in principle, go on to alter living creatures. Realistically speaking, however, an almost unsurmountable barrier would arise: any alteration of living beings producing forms of life that are radically different from ours, would not be feasible given our present or near-future state of knowledge, since higher organisms in particular would be made inviable. In unicellular organisms, where the prospects would be better in view of the accessibility of greater numbers of cells and the possibility of using more effective selection mechanisms, such a strategy would not be so attractive. Similar cells could be

wird (Gentherapie), verdienen diese Bezeichnung ganz offensichtlich nicht. Sie sind vor allem auch deshalb keine künstlichen Lebewesen im engeren Sinne, weil die künstlich herbeigeführten Veränderungen im Prinzip auch auf natürlichem Weg entstehen könnten, auch wenn die entsprechenden Ereignisse (Gentransfer zwischen verschiedenen Arten oder verschiedenen Klassen von Lebewesen) in der Natur nur extrem selten auftreten.

Um seriös überprüfen zu können, ob mit Hilfe der Gentechnik künstliches Leben produziert werden könnte, müssen zunächst Begriffe geklärt werden. Als Lebewesen anzusehen wären Systeme, die in der Lage sind, Information zu speichern und an folgende Generationen weiterzugeben. Weiters müssen diese Systeme die Fähigkeit besitzen, Stoffe bzw. Energie aufzunehmen und umzusetzen, um die zur Speicherung und Weitergabe der Information notwendigen Strukturen und Werkzeuge aufbauen zu können (Stoffwechsel). Künstliche Lebewesen im engeren Sinn müßten dabei andere Arten von Strukturen und Bausteinen verwenden als natürliche Organismen, also etwa andere Informationsspeicher als Nukleinsäuren und andere Katalysatoren als Proteine. Anhand dieser Überlegungen wird sofort evident, daß künstliches Leben in diesem Sinn mit Hilfe der Gentechnik nicht zugänglich ist. Weniger streng definiert könnte von künstlichem Leben allenfalls auch dann gesprochen werden, wenn unter Zuhilfenahme der selben Grundstrukturen und Mechanismen, die natürliche Lebewesen auszeichnen, ganz neue Typen von Lebewesen geschaffen werden könnten. Hier ergibt sich das Problem der Grenzziehung. Stellt eine blaue Rose einen ganz neuen Typ von Lebewesen dar, oder müßte man zum Beispiel eine singende Rose produzieren, um diesem Anspruch gerecht zu werden? Die Produktion einer blauen Rose mit gentechnischen Methoden sollte kein besonderes technisches oder prinzipielles Problem darstellen, sie bietet aber auch nichts sensationell Neues. Eine singende Rose hingegen wäre mit derartigen Methoden sicher für alle Zeiten nicht zugänglich. Rein hypothetisch könnte sie mit Hilfe der Gentechnik nur durch den Transfer einer größeren Zahl von Genen aus bereits existierenden Lebewesen oder durch Übertragung künstlicher Gene, die natürlichen Genen nachempfunden sind, produziert werden. Es muß daher bezweifelt werden, ob selbst dieses utopische Lebewesen mit Recht künstlich genannt werden könnte.

Zuletzt wäre im Rahmen dieser Überlegungen eine weitere Möglichkeit zu prüfen: Wäre unter Zuhilfenahme gentechnischer Methoden der Aufbau von Lebewesen aus nichtbiologischen (anorganischen oder durch chemische Synthese hergestellten organischen) Bestandteilen möglich, und würden solche Lebewesen mit Recht unter den Begriff „künstliches Leben" fallen? Es muß zunächst betont werden, daß ein derartiges Ziel beim heutigen Stand der Technik zweifellos utopisch wäre, daß aber auf Grund unseres theoretischen Verständnisses der „Nachbau" einfachster Lebensformen, als von Bakterienzellen, aus nicht biologischen Ausgangsmaterialien prinzipiell denkbar wäre, wenn auch der dafür notwendige Aufwand eine praktische Realisierung eines solchen Experiments wohl auch in Zukunft verhindern wird. Weiters muß festgehalten werden, daß nach unserem Wissensstand ein ähnliches Ziel prinzipiell auch für höhere Lebensformen realisierbar wäre, wobei die Idee der praktischen Durchführung in diesem Fall natürlich noch weiter ins Absurde rückt. Die nachfolgenden Überlegungen sind daher als reines Gedankenexperiment einzustufen. Vom reinen Nachbauen bestehender Lebensformen, das ja noch immer nicht eindeutig künstliches Leben produzieren würde, könnte prinzipiell natürlich auch dazu übergegangen werden, abgeänderte Lebewesen zu produzieren. Hier würde sich allerdings bei realistischer Betrachtungsweise wieder eine beinahe unüberwindliche Mauer aufbauen: alle Änderungen, die zu Lebensformen führen würden, die sich nennenswert von bestehenden unterscheiden, würden beim heutigen oder in ansehbarer Zeit erreichbaren Stand unseres Wissens nicht zum Ziel führen, weil sie insbesondere höhere Organismen lebensunfähig machen würden. Bei einzelligen Lebewesen, bei denen auf Grund der Zugänglichkeit großer Zellzahlen und der Möglichkeit des Einsatzes wirkungsvoller Selektionsmechanismen die Situation vielleicht nicht so aussichtslos wäre, wäre die Strategie von vornherein nicht so attraktiv. Ähnliche Ziele könnten nämlich viel leichter ausgehend von bereits existierenden Einzellern erreicht werden, ohne daß deshalb von künstlichem Leben gesprochen werden könnte. Auch diese Möglichkeit bietet also aus mehreren Gründen realistisch gesehen nichts wirklich Neues. Selbst wenn jedoch auf einem der vorgezeichneten Wege ein in spektakulärer Weise neuartiges Lebewesen entstehen würde, wäre der „Erfinder" dieses Lebewesens dann eine Art von Schöpfer, wäre er damit gottähnlich geworden, wie es uns der Autor der Betriebsanleitung des anfangs erwähnten Gentechnikbaukastens verspricht? Auch in diesem Fall wäre diese Interpretation wesentlich übertrieben. Der Produzent dieses Lebewesens wäre weiterhin nicht mehr als ein besonders kompetenter Nutzer von Prinzipien, die auf Naturgesetzen beruhen und die sich im Verlauf der Evolution entwickelt haben und möglicherweise von einem Schöpfergott programmiert wurden. Der Produzent des neuen Lebewesens selbst hätte nur durch Ausnutzung die-

created much easier on the basis of already existing unicellular organisms—but this does not imply artifical life. Even this option is, for a number of reasons, not really new. Even if one of these methods were to bring forth a spectacularly new living being, would the "inventor" of this creature be seen as a sort of "creator", as divine, as promised by the author of the instructions to the genetic engineering kit that I mentioned at the beginning of this paper? Even in this case, such an interpretion would be exaggerated. The producer of this living being would have only used these principles to exploit the amazing variations of what already exists in nature to add something truly odd. It would be a question of definition whether this could be seen as bringing forth "artificial life", but as such of hardly great relevance.
The realization of such a thought experiment is not an attractive goal for genetic engineering, since it is a) utopian and b) nothing fundamentally new. For the same reasons, our experiment is also not dangerous. The opportunities to be provided by genetic engineering and its risks do not have much to do with the subject of artificial life. The scientist who works seriously with such biological technologies hardly views himself as being God-like or a creator. Being much more aware of the complexity of life than a superficial observer, he will also be more amazed by the wonders of nature, even if he is able to explain most of them on the basis of molecules. His amazement will, for the most part, be independent of the fact whether he believes in a personal creator of life or whether he assumes life to have evolved spontaneously and by necessity on the basis of "eternal" laws of nature. The latter assumption is, or could be seen as an even greater wonder than creation by the "super-genetic engineer" God.

ser Prinzipien die unglaubliche Variabilität dessen, was in der Natur bereits existiert, um eine Kuriosität bereichert. Ob er damit „künstliches Leben" geschaffen hätte, wäre eine Frage der Definition, aber eigentlich nicht von großer Bedeutung.

Für die Nutzung der Gentechnik ist die Realisierung des diskutierten Gedankenexperiments kein attraktives Ziel, da es erstens utopisch ist und zweitens nichts fundamental Neues bringen würde. Aus denselben Gründen ist unser Experiment auch nicht gefährlich. Sowohl die realistischen Chancen der Gentechnik als auch deren tatsächliche Risken liegen in ganz anderen Bereichen, die im Rahmen der Veranstaltung sicher zur Sprache kommen werden, auch wenn sie mit dem Thema künstliches Leben nur wenig gemeinsam haben. Der Wissenschafter, der sich mit dem, was er mit gentechnischen oder ähnlichen biologischen Methoden lernt oder leistet, seriös auseinandersetzt, fühlt sich keineswegs gottähnlich oder schöpfergleich. Weil er sich der Komplexität von Lebewesen viel mehr bewußt wird als ein oberflächlicherer Betrachter, wird er auch noch mehr über die Wunder der Natur staunen, selbst wenn er sie zu einem wesentlichen Teil auf molekularer Ebene erklären kann. Dabei wird dieses Staunen weitgehend unabhängig davon sein, ob er an einen persönlichen Schöpfer des Lebens glaubt, oder ob er annimmt, daß das Leben auf der Erde spontan und zwangsläufig auf Grund der „ewigen" Naturgesetze entstanden ist, was vielleicht im Vergleich zur Schöpfung durch den „Supergentechnologen" Gott das noch größere Wunder ist oder wäre.

BIOLOGIE NACH DEM SÜNDENFALL...

HORST SEIDLER

... könnte in Anlehnung an J. Huber (1985) der folgende Beitrag übertitelt werden. In dem hervorragenden Sammelband „Künstliche Befruchtung – Versuch einer Standortbestimmung in medizinischer, strafrechtlicher und moraltheologischer Sicht", dessen Inhalt möglichst vielen Menschen zugänglich gemacht werden sollte, schreibt Huber über „Biologie vor dem Sündenfall".

Sehr sachlich beschreibt der Wissenschafter dabei einzelne Problemkreise wie intrauterine Adoption, Krykokonservierung bis hin zur wissenschaftlichen und gesellschaftspolitischen Diskussion im Rahmen der sogenannten transspezifischen Gravidität.

Wenn Huber allerdings als Schlußwort seiner Arbeit formuliert „Im Ball-Kult opferte man ebenfalls Kinder, um das Leben der Erwachsenen zu retten", so ist im Sinne einer fast schon omnipotenten, technokratisch gewordenen Naturwissenschft der Sündenfall nicht nur gedanklich bereits vollzogen worden.

„Darf die Medizin alles, was sie kann?" fragt W. Holczabeck, Vorsitzender der Ethik-Kommission des Akademischen Senates der Universität Wien im Vorwort des angesprochenen Sammelbandes und drückt damit nicht nur seine tiefe Besorgnis um mögliche Fehlentwicklungen aus, sondern weist auch darauf hin, daß „dieses neue Sachgebiet auch von strafrechtlicher, privatrechtlicher, versicherungrechtlicher, sozial-wissenschaftlich-psychologischer und selbstredend von theologischer Seite eingehend beleuchtet und erörtert werden muß". Bleibt man in der Terminologie der Titelüberschrift, so ist der Sündenfall als wissenschaftliche Sensation am 12. August 1978 beschrieben worden. An diesem Tag erfolgte die Geburt eines gesunden Mädchens mit 2700 Gramm Geburtsgewicht. Die diesbezügliche Mitteilung in der Zeitschrift Lancet lautet: „Die Schwangerschaft wurde nach laparaskopischer Entnahme einer Zygote am 10. November 1977, in vitro Fertilisation und normaler Teilung im Kulturmedium und Transfer des 8 Zell Embryos in den Uterus 2,5 Tage später erzielt". Die Argumentation von Huber, kein ethisches Postulat könne den wissenschaftlichen Fortschritt dann aufhalten, stoppen oder gar verhindern, wenn

BIOLOGY AFTER THE FALL OF MAN ...
HORST SEIDLER

... the following contribution could be re-titled with reference to J. Huber (1985). In the outstanding omnibus volume entitled "Artificial Insemination—Experiment in position finding—the medical, penal and moral-theology view", the contents of which were to be made accessible to as many people as possible, Huber writes about "Biology before the Fall of Man".

In a very factual way, the scientist describes individual problem spheres such as intra-uterine adoption, cryco-conservation, up to the scientific and social-political discussion within the framework of so-called trans-specific gravidity.

When Huber, nevertheless, formulates the closing words to his work as "In the ball-cult children were also sacrificed to save the lives of the adults", then the Fall of Man has not merely been already effected mentally in the sense of a science which has already become almost omnipotent and technocratic.

"Is medicine allowed to do everything that it can do?", asks W. Holczabeck, Chairman of the Ethics Commission of the Academic Senate at the University in Vienna, in a foreward for the said omnibus volume and, in doing, so not only expresses his deep concern about possible undesireable developments, but also points out that " this new field must also be thoroughly examined and discussed from a penal, private law, insurance law, social-scientific-psychological and, of course, from a theological point of view". If we remain in the terminology of the title, then the Fall of Man was described as a scientific senstation on the 12th August 1978. On this day, a healthy baby girl was born weighing 2700 grammes. The information about this published in the journal "Lancet" read: "The pregnancy was achieved following laparascopic removal of a zygote on 10th November 1977, in vitro fertilization and normal division in the culture medium and the transfer of 8 cell embryos into the uterus, 2.5 days later". Huber's argumentation that no ethical postulate could then check scientific progress, stop it or even prevent it, if people were to benefit from the scientific progress, can be agreed with inasmuchas the new techniques of extra-corporeal insemination are being practised today, all over the world, as routine methods.

The technique has largely been mastered and the urgent need for such intervention is increasingly leading to the improvement and certainty

of the method. And here, first of all, without making any ethical-moral considerations, the question as to who among the people can be the actual practical applicant of modern biotechnology, must be discussed: public insurance bodies are not prepared to bear the costs of in-vitro fertilization. Has the fulfillment of the dream of having a child become, in this way, a domain of the privileged? At present it is certainly the case that the principle of equality should be placed in the centre of considerations and discussions.
The problem concerning the material side of in-vitro fertilization led H. Janisch to write, "not everything that can be done is good and it should be our primary goal that we continue to be doctors and should not let ourselves be re-functioned into technicians or business men". He then added: "This should also be an obligation of the general public".
That all sounds good and proper, but what is to be understood by the term "general public"—and are doctors not sometimes really business men, when those who can afford it purchase medical technology or scientific progress in order to make their dream of having a child come true? To obligate the "general public" will only be possible if we succeed in considering and coordinating several factors involving laborious detailed work, simultaneously:
1. Specific educational work for the general public by means of easy-to-undertand and objective information about fundamental biological knowledge; avoiding what is apparently scientific, but really pseudo-scientific, sensationalist reporting; development of an objective, generally accepted terminology which avoids terms such as "artificial insemination", "test tube babies" etc. This has particular priority as many children, the world over, have already been born as a result of in-vitro fertilization and to describe them as "test-tube babies" would jeopardize the human way they see themselves. The information in the media about Nobel prize winners' and top-performance sportsmens' semen banks leads to false hopes and socially-politically dangerous ideas.
2. The timely preparation of social-psychological and social-anthropological coordination concepts for the topics: "partnership, dream of having a child, extra-corporeal insemination and social-political consequences". This would mean that the modern possibilities of reproductive biology would generally have to be dealt with together with the question of family policies. The Association of Foster and Adoptive Parents would have to be involved in these coordination concepts.
3. Discussion about the reality of a consumer society in which too many people believe that everything can be done and everything can be achieved. Reflections about a social development in which what is really sometimes the less social and more, very pointed right, for self-realization plays and increasingly greater role.
4. Interdisciplinary—"scientific-political"—talks which should continue to deal with open questions (in-vitro-fertilization and abortion legislation) in their extremely paradox coherences. According to W. Brandstetter the

der Bevölkerung durch den wissenschaftlichen Fortschritt Vorteile entstünden, ist insofern zuzustimmen, als die neuen Techniken der extrakorporalen Befruchtung heute fast schon als Routinemethoden weltweit praktiziert werden.
Die Technik ist weitgehend beherrscht, der dringende Bedarf für solche Eingriffe wird mehr und mehr zur Verfeinerung und Sicherheit der Methodik führen. Und hier ist zunächst, ohne irgendwelche ethisch-moralische Überlegungen anzustellen, die Frage zu erörtern, wer in der Bevölkerung der eigentliche Nutzanwender der modernen Biotechnologie sein kann: öffentliche Versicherungsträger sind ja nicht bereit, die Kosten einer in-vitro-Fertilisation zu tragen. Wird die Erfüllung des Kinderwunsches auf diese Weise zu einer Domäne der Privilegierten? Zur Zeit ist es sicher so, so daß der Gleichheitsgrundsatz in das Zentrum der Überlegungen und Diskussionen zu stellen wäre.
Die Problematik um die materielle Seite der in-vitro-Fertilisation veranlaßt H. Janisch zu schreiben „nicht alles Machbare ist gut, und es soll unser primäres Ziel sein, daß wir weiterhin Ärzte bleiben und uns nicht zu Technikern oder Kaufleuten umfunktionieren lassen". Er fügt dann hinzu: „Dies sollte auch eine Verpflichtung der Öffentlichkeit sein."
Das klingt gut und richtig, aber was ist unter dem Begriff „Öffentlichkeit" zu verstehen und – sind Ärzte so manches Mal nicht wirklich Kaufleute, wenn der, der es sich leisten kann, sich die ärztliche Technik, den wissenschaftlichen Fortschritt erkauft, um sich den Kinderwunsch erfüllen zu können? Die Öffentlichkeit zu verpflichten wird aber wohl nur dann möglich sein, wenn es in mühsamer Kleinarbeit gelingt, mehrere Faktoren gleichzeitig zu berücksichtigen und zu koordinieren:
1. Zielgerichtete Aufklärung der Öffentlichkeit durch leichtverständliche und objektive Information über biologisches Grundwissen; Vermeidung von scheinbar wissenschaftlicher, im Grunde aber pseudowissenschaftlicher, sensationsgieriger Berichterstattung; Entwicklung einer objektiven, allgemein akzeptierten Terminologie, die Begriffe wie „künstliche Befruchtung", „Retortenbaby" usw. vermeidet. Dies wäre umso dringender, als ja schon weltweit viele Kinder nach in-vitro- Fertilisation zur Welt gekommen sind und ihre Bezeichnung als „Retortenbaby" das menschliche Selbstverständnis in Frage stellt. Medienmeldungen über Nobelpreisträger- und Hochleistungssportler-Samenbanken führen zu falschen Erwartungen und gesellschaftspolitisch gefährlichen Vorstellungen.
2. Rechtzeitige Erarbeitung von sozialpsychologischen und sozialanthropologischen Koordinationskonzepten für den Themenkreis „Partnerschaft, Kinderwunsch, extrakorporale

Befruchtung und gesellschaftspolitische Konsequenzen". Dies würde bedeuten, daß die modernen Möglichkeiten der reproduktiven Biologie generell nicht losgelöst von Fragen der Familienpolitik zu behandeln wären. In diese Koordinationskonzepte müßte auch der Verband der Pflege- und Adoptiveltern miteinbezogen werden.

3. Diskussion über die Realität einer Konsumgesellschaft, in der zu viele Menschen glauben, daß alles machbar und alles erreichbar ist. Reflexionen über eine Gesellschaftsentwicklung, in der manches Mal der zwar echt wenig soziale, dafür aber sehr pointierte Anspruch nach Selbstverwirklichung eine immer größere Rolle spielt.

4. Interdisziplinäre – „wissenschaftlich-politische" – Gespräche, die nach wie vor offenen Fragen (in-vitro-Fertilistion und Fristenlösung) in ihren geradezu paradoxen Kohärenzen behandeln sollten. Nach W. Brandstetter ist der „nasciturus" von seiner Rechtsnatur her zwar als Person zu bewerten, der Rechtsschutz allerdings ist durch Fristenlösung dramatisch eingeschränkt: „Im Zusammenhang mit der künstlichen Befruchtung tun sich dabei Abgründe auf…an die der Gesetzgeber bei Einführung der Fristenlösung noch gar nicht denken konnte". In diesem Zusammenhang müßten aber auch alle Aspekte der Genchirurgie bzw. der Verwendung embryonaler Zellen zu Forschungs- und Therapiezwecken miteinbezogen werden. Auch hier geistern – nicht ganz zu Unrecht! – Schlagwörter von künstlichen Menschen und dergleichen umher, der Begriff „Retorte" wird endgültig real. Aber, das ist nur ein Aspekt, wenngleich auch ein überaus wesentlicher, über dessen ethische und moralische Konsequenzen wir uns alle noch nicht im klaren sind. Klar ist nur was „machbar" ist und was mit an Sicherheit grenzender Wahrscheinlichkeit demnächst machbar sein wird. Daß viele Menschen vor diesen fast unbegrenzten Möglichkeiten der genetischen Manipulation (im wahrsten Sinn des Wortes!) Angst haben, ist nur zu verständlich. Es ist aber eine Frage der Objektivität, auch die zweite Seite dieses Problemkreises vorzustellen; Stellen Sie sich vor, Sie gehen in die Kinderabteilung eines Krankenhauses und sehen dort ein Kind, das am Bett festgebunden ist und dessen Zähne alle gezogen sind. Finger und Lippen weisen schwerste Verunstaltungen auf; der behandelnde Arzt erklärt diese Wunden als Folge einer nicht beherrschbaren und steuerbaren Autoaggression. Das Kind leidet unter einen bekannten Enzymmangel, der u. a. zu autoaggressivem Beißen führt.

Es ist wahrscheinlich nur mehr eine Frage der Zeit, bis es gelingen wird, die krankhafte Erbanlage (Mangelproduktion des Enzyms Hypocanthin-Guanin-Phospho-Rybosil-Trans-

legal nature of "nasciturus" does have to be assessed as a person, but legal protection has been dramatically restricted by abortion legislation: "In connection with artificial insemination, abysses are opened up .. which legislators could never even have thought about when introducing the abortion legislation". In this connection, all aspects of gene surgery and the use of embryonic cells for research and treatment purposes would also have to be included. Even here—and not unjustly either—headlines about artificial people and the likes are lurking around, the term "test-tube" is finally becoming real. But this is only one aspect, even if it is an incredibly significant one, and we are still not clear about its ethical and moral consequences. What is clear is only what "can be done", and will probably be most certainly done in the near future. The fact that many people are afraid of these almost unlimited possibilities of genetic manipulation (in the true sense of the word!) is only too understandable. But it is a question of the objectivity of even introducing the second side of the problem sphere; just imagine you go to the babies ward in a childrens' hospital and see a child there, tied to a bed, and whose teeth have all been pulled. Its fingers and lips are severely disfigured; the doctor in charge explains these wounds as being the result of an uncontrollable auto-aggression. The child is suffering from a known enzyme deficiency which, amongst other things, leads to auto-aggressive biting.

It is probably only a matter of time until we succeed in correcting the pathological hereditary disposition (deficiency in the production of the enzyme hypocanthine-guanine-phospho-rybosil-transferase). Gene surgery to make a worthy human existence possible!

In this work, Huber also discusses the treatment possibilities of removing organs (cells) from early human embryos. Here, too, it will certainly be possible to cure illnesses and to prevent human suffering.

Of course, our occidental consciousness will per se provoke the question: "Are we allowed to do everything that we can do?" and we will not be spared from answering this. In this respect, the ethical consciousness of the scientist will be more decisive than legislators will ever be. A brief example: pre-natal sex determination has proven to be more than a blessing in the case of some (X-chromosomal mutations) hereditary diseases. Irrespective of ideological values, here, in the individual cases, it has been possible to prevent unimaginable suffering and invalidism and even death (for example X-chromosomal recessive muscular dystrophy of the Duchenne type). It must be said in this connection that attitudes like "man was born to suffer" etc., are borne exclusively from a lack of feeling and egoism. The decision about as to whether the preganancy should be allowed to continue following positive findings resulting from such a pre-natal examination, lies with the person concerned and must, in each and every case, be respected by society.

It must also be mentioned that these technologies are also used in some countries of the world to literally eradicate unwanted female offspring. It is not the methods that we must be afraid of, but the attitudes of those that make use of these methods. As a result, there must be the demand for the most stringent of controls to be made by ethical commisions which must be established as widely and as efficiently as possible.

5. Re-conditioning these scientific-historical processes that, for the first time in the history of the science of reproductive biology, have led to state-initiated misuse. From a current point of view, and, in accordance with our current level of knowledge, misuse was only possible as it was not only politicians, but also the afore-mentioned general public which were convinced about the necessity of the compulsory sterilization of "the inferior". Not later than 1907, scientists, psychologists and politicians ate from the tree of knowledge the consequences of banishing the new science of genetics from paradise. In 1907, in the American State of Indiana, a law was issued "A law to prevent the propagation of inveterate criminals, idiots, imbeciles and rapists"; a number of Federal States followed suit: similarly several European countries also issued such laws in the 1920's. According to the publications of the Human Betterment Foundation, dated 1st January 1939, by 1938 a total of 30,690 sterilizations had been performed in the United States for eugenical reasons. Following the law issued on 14th July 1933 in national-socialist Germany to prevent hereditary ill offspring, in the very first year of coming into power, over 40,000 people were condemned by court orders to be sterilized.

Even if we consider and feel these "eugenical measures" today as being frightful and alarming, we should not forget that—not only in the NS State—many people, probably the vast majority (!), were convinced of the social-political necessity of such legal rulings. The cultural pessimismus based, amongst other things, on Spengler, coupled with an irrational anxiety about the biological survival of the peoples, provided the ideal hot bed for "scientific "quarter truths" and elitist mental attitudes uniting to bring about a fatal consequence. It is certainly not wrong to maintain that the legislator at that time was "only" realizing the voice of the people—and is not the voice of the people the voice of God? In order to prevent any misunderstandings here: representatives of both Churches fought vehemently and at the risk of their own lives against sterilization in national-socialist Germany.

It is worth mentioning in this connection, that since 1900 there have been, of course, scientists and politicians who did speak out, with all the means they had available, against compulsory sterilization—but who were not listened to. The history of sterilization and consequently reproductive biology is a story of idea reception depending on economic, political and an infinite number of other factors, in which injustice became justice. This justice was based on the simplifying power to convince by means of non-factual, un-scientific and consciously one-sided information. In order to avoid repeated undesired developments, the uppermost goal today must be to inform objectively and fun-

ferase) zu Korrigieren. Genchirurgie, um ein menschenwürdiges Dasein zu ermöglichen!

Huber diskutiert in diesem Band auch die Therapiemöglichkeiten der Organ- (Zell-) Entnahme aus menschlichen Frühembryonen. Auch hier wird es ganz sicher möglich sein, Krankheiten zu heilen und menschliches Leiden zu verhindern.

Freilich wird unser abendländisches Bewußtsein per se die Frage provozieren: „Dürfen wir alles, was wir können?" und uns die Antwort darauf nicht ersparen können. Mehr als es Gesetzgeber je vermögen, wird diesbezüglich das ethische Bewußtsein der Wissenschafter maßgebend sein. Ein kurzes Beispiel: die vorgeburtliche Geschlechtsbestimmung hat sich bei manchen(X-chromosomalen Mutationen) Erbleiden als überaus segensreich bewährt. Unabhängig von weltanschaulichen Werthaltungen ist es hier im Einzelfall möglich gewesen, unvorstellbares Leid und Siechtum bis zum Tode (zum Beispiel X-chronosomal rezessive Muskeldystrophie vom Typ Duchenne) zu verhindern. Festgehalten sei in diesem Zusammenhang, daß Werthaltungen, wie „der Mensch ist zum Leiden geboren" usw., ausschließlich von mangelndem Einfühlungsvermögen und Egoismus getragen sind. Die Entscheidung darüber, ob nach einem positiven Befund im Rahmen einer solchen vorgeburtlichen Untersuchung die Schwangerschaft weiter fortgesetzt werden soll, liegt dann bei den Betreffenden selbst und ist in jedem Fall von der Gesellschaft zu respektieren.

Erwähnt werden muß aber auch, daß diese Technologie in manchen Ländern unserer Welt auch dazu benützt wird, um unliebsamen weiblichen Nachwuchs im wahrsten Sinne des Wortes auszurotten. Nicht die Methoden sind es, vor denen wir Angst haben müssen, sondern die Einstellungen jener, die diese Methoden anwenden. Daraus ergibt sich die Forderung nach strengster Kontrolle durch möglichst breit angelegte und effizient arbeitende Ethikkommissionen.

5. Aufarbeitung jener wissenschaftshistorischen Prozesse, die zum ersten Mal in der Wissenschaftsgeschichte der reproduktiven Biologie zum staatlichen gelenkten Mißbrauch geführt haben. Aus der heutigen Sicht und nach unserem derzeitigen Wissensstand war dieser Mißbrauch allerdings nur deshalb möglich, weil nicht nur die Politiker, sondern auch die vorher erwähnte Öffentlichkeit von der Notwendigkeit der Zwangssterilisation „Minderwertiger" überzeugt war. Spätestens 1907 aßen Naturwissenschaftler, Psychologen, Sozialwissenschaftler und Politiker vom Baum der Erkenntnis, was die Vertreibung der noch jungen Wissenschaft der Genetik aus dem Paradies zur Folge hatte. Im amerikanischen Bundesstaat Indiana wurde im Jahre 1907 „Ein Gesetz

zur Verhütung der Fortpflanzung der unverbesserlichen Verbrecher, Idioten, Imbezilen und Notzuchtverbrecher" erlassen; viele Bundesstaaten schlossen sich an; ebenso erließen einige europäische Länder in den zwanziger Jahren derartige Gesetze. Nach den Publikationen der Human Betterment Foundation vom 1. Jänner 1939 wurden in den Vereinigten Staaten von Amerika bis 1938 insgesamt 30.690 Unfruchtbarmachung aus rassenhygienischen Gründen durchgeführt. Nach dem Gesetz zur Verhütung erbkranken Nachwuchses des nationalsozialistischen Deutschland vom 14. Juli 1933 wurden allein im ersten Jahr nach der Machtergreifung über 40.000 Menschen über Gerichtsbeschluß zur Sterilisation verurteilt.

Wenn wir diese „rassenhygienischen Maßnahmen" heute auch als furchtbar und erschreckend empfinden und nacherleben, so dürfen wir doch nicht vergessen, daß – nicht nur im NS-Staat – viele Menschen, wahrscheinlich eine überwiegende Mehrheit (!) von der gesellschaftspolitischen Notwendigkeit solcher gesetzlicher Regelungen überzeugt war. Der u.a. auf Spengler fußende Kulturpessimismus, gepaart mit einer irrationalen Sorge um das biologische Überleben der Völker, war der ideale Nährboden dafür, daß wissenschaftliche „Viertelwahrheiten" und elitäre Geisteshaltungen sich in einer unheilvollen Konsequenz verbinden konnten. Es ist sicher nicht ganz falsch zu behaupten, daß der Gesetzgeber damals „nur" Volkes-Stimme realisierte – und ist nicht Volkes Stimme Gottes Stimme? Um hier etwaigen Mißverständnissen vorzubeugen: Vertreter beider Kirchen haben im nationalsozialistischen Deutschland vehement und unter Einsatz ihres Lebens gegen die Sterilisation gekämpft. Erwähnenswert ist in diesem Zusammenhang, daß es freilich auch seit etwa 1900 Wissenschafter und Politiker gab, die sich mit allen ihnen zur Verfügung stehenden Mitteln gegen die Zwangssterilisation aussprachen - aber nicht gehört wurden. Die Geschichte der Sterilisation und somit der reproduktiven Biologie, ist eine Geschichte der Ideenreception in Abhängigkeit von wirtschaftlichen, politischen und einer kaum mehr zu überblickenden Zahl weiterer Faktoren, in der Unrecht zu Recht wurde. Dieses Recht fußte aber auf der simplifizierenden Überzeugungskraft durch unsachliche, unwissenschaftliche und bewußt einseitig gelenkte Informationen. Um neuerliche Fehlentwicklungen zu vermeiden, müßte das oberste Ziel heute darin liegen, objektiv und fundiert zu informieren, um weltanschaulich-ideologische Polemiken nicht in die Diskussion miteinfließen zu lassen. Die kritische Auseinandersetzung mit der modernen Biotechnologie auf der Basis des dafür notwendigen biologischen Grundwissens könnte wahrscheinlich zum ersten

damentally so as not to have ideological polemics enter into the discussion. The critical discussion about modern bio-technology on the basis of the fundamental biological knowledge necesary for this, could probably be effected for the first time to this extent, by the Federal Ministry for Family, Youth Affairs and Consumer Protection's investigation commission for "Family Policy and Artificial Propagation".

But what is the situation today? We can meet the convictions of the moral theologist, A. LAUN, with awe and respect, when he writes, "If we do not consider the social situation and ask, merely, what is to be said about the the moral truth of in-vitro-fertilization from the point of view of Catholic moral theology, the answer is: "Without mistaking the great ethical differences which result from the respective different objectives, on the basis of which in-vitro fertilization is used, then Catholic moral theology must dismiss in-vitro fertilization". But: we will have to respect people who have been informed via the media that various techniques in artificial fertilization have become almost routine methods in gynacological out-patients' clinics, thanks to scientific progress, and who have now put all their hopes in those doctors who could fulfull their innermost wish.

Janisch and his important work can be quoted, a work which explicity specifies a passage from the Declaration of the United Nations, that "every man and every woman has the right to establish a family. "To establish a family means not merely to get married, but also to have children. But who shall be the supreme moral authority to pronounce himself or herself as being for or against making it possible to have children in event of male or female infertility? Who can now actually claim to pronounce or decree that, despite the existence of the new and generally successful technologies, children should be foregone, while appealing to higher values? Of course, here it should also be stated that the term "forego" is never taught in our society after childhood days and for this reason can neither be understood nor accepted by many.

It is always very easy, as it were, to determine what is good, less good and bad from the conference table; and in many cases one may even be right. What about the psychological situation of people who cannot have any children and whose heart's desire it is to have children; people who have waited in vain, for years, to get a child for adoption! In this connection, we must be reminded that in the relevant counselling offices in the City of Vienna, the repeated attempt was made to convince women who had decided to terminate a pregnancy, to have their child, and then to put it up for adpotion. The almost immeasurable expenditure in terms of personnel and financial means brought no success at all: despite intensive therapeutic talks they didn't once succeed in preventing the death of an embryo.

Therefore, at the present, despite all objections, so-called "artificial insemination" is probably the only way to help childless couples get children. Scientific progress cannot be checked;

LAUN also concedes with this: "There is in-vitro fertilization, and no appeal whatsoever will make it disappear. None of the laboratories which practise in-vitro fertilization today will stop their work. On the contrary, state money is being increasingly put into this research and we have new success reports from science are immanent about getting life more and more under control". This realismus must be opposed by a realistic attitude in society. Ethics Commissions which are constantly active and permanently voicing their opinions, must become effective over and above the university sphere in order to prevent every conceivable misuse. Paedagogical strategies must be drawn up and must be passed on, in the sense of a new form of "life and partnership-hygiene teaching", to the schools, commencing in Primary Schools and continuing on to compulsory and higher level schools. The solution to the problem: "artificial insemination" will, in the short-term, be more or less solved efficiently in a legal-political way. But: short-term solutions and the resulting short-term political satisfaction will only be able to produce suspensive action, as is becoming particularly noticeable with the abortion legislation. As important as it may be today for those concerned, to replace the largely vacant space with adequate legal security, via suitable government meaures—the demand to develop long-term social structures with provisions is just as necessary; provisions which no longer regard everything as being able to be done, achievable and consumable.

LITERATUR:

W. Brandstetter, J. Huber, H. Janisch, A. Laun: Künstliche Befruchtung – Versuch einer Standortbestimmung in medizinischer, strafrechtlicher und moralischer Sicht. Facultas Universitätsverlag, Vienna 1985.

Mal in dieser Breite durch die Enquete „Familienpolitik und künstliche Fortpflanzung" des Bundesministeriums für Familie, Jugend und Konsumentenschutz erfolgen.

In welcher Situation aber stehen wir heute? Mit Ehrfurcht und Respekt hat man der Überzeugung des Moraltheologen A.Laun zu begegnen, der schreibt: „Sieht man von der gesellschaftlichen Situation ab und fragt nur, was allein unter dem Gesichtspunkt der sittlichen Wahrheit zur in-vitro-Fertilisation aus der Sicht der katholischen Moraltheologie zu sagen ist, lautet die Antwort: Ohne die großen ethischen Unterschiede zu verkennen, die sich aus den jeweils verschiedenen Zielsetzungen ergeben, aufgrund derer die in-vitro-Fertilisation angewandt wird, muß die katholische Moraltheologie die in-vitro-Fertilisation ablehnen." Aber: Respektieren wird man wohl Menschen müssen, die über die Medien informiert wurden, daß verschiedene Techniken der künstlichen Befruchtung durch den wissenschaftlichen Fortschritt in den gynäkologischen Ambulanzen fast schon Routinemethoden wurden und die nun all ihre Hoffnung in jene Ärzte setzen, die ihnen ihren innigsten Wunsch erfüllen könnten.

Hier ist auch aus der wichtigen Arbeit von Janisch zu zitieren, der eine Passage aus der Deklaration der Vereinten Nationen wird ausdrücklich festgelegt, daß jede Frau und jeder Mann das Recht hat, eine Familie zu gründen". Eine Familie zu gründen heißt aber, nicht nur zu heiraten, sondern auch Nachkommen zu haben. Wer aber ist nun jene oberste moralische Instanz, die sich für oder gegen die Ermöglichung von Nachkommenschaft im Falle männlicher oder weiblicher Infertilität ausspricht? Wer kann sich nun tatsächlich anmaßen, trotz des Vorhandenseins der neuen, zumeist erfolgversprechenden Technologie unter Berufung auf höhere Werte den Verzicht auf Nachkommen auszusprechen und zu verordnen? Freilich soll auch hier festgehalten werden, daß der Begriff „Verzicht" in unserer Gesellschaft von Kindestagen an ja gar nicht gelehrt wird und deshalb für viele weder verständlich noch akzeptabel sein kann.

Es ist immer recht leicht, gleichsam vom grünen Tisch aus zu bestimmen, was gut, weniger gut und schlecht ist; in vielen Fällen wird man damit vielleicht auch recht haben. Wie ist es aber um die psychische Situation von Menschen bestellt, die keine Kinder bekommen können und deren Herzenswunsch es ist, Kinder zu haben; Menschen, die jahrelang vergeblich darauf gewartet haben, daß man ihnen ein Kind zur Adoption frei gibt! In diesem Zusammenhang möge daran erinnert werden, daß in den entsprechenden Beratungsstellen der Stadt Wien wiederholt der Versuch unternommen wurde, Frauen, die zum Abbruch der Schwangerschaft entschlossen waren, dazu zu überreden, ihr Kind auszutragen, um es dann zur Adoption freizugeben. Der fast unermeßliche Aufwand an persönlichem Einsatz und finanziellen Mitteln erbrachte überhaupt kein Ergebnis: trotz intensiver therapeutischer Gespräche gelang es kein einziges Mal, den Tod der Frucht zu verhindern.

Zur Zeit also ist trotz aller Einwände die sogenannte „künstliche Befruchtung" wohl der einzige Weg, um kinderlosen Partnern zu Kindern verhelfen. Wissenschaftlicher Fortschritt läßt sich nicht aufhalten; dies konzidiert auch LAUN: „Es gibt die in-vitro-Fertilisation und kein Appell wird sie zum Verschwinden bringen. Keines der Laboratorien, die heute in-vitro-Fertilisation praktizieren, wird seine Arbeit einstellen. Im Gegenteil, staatliche Gelder werden vermehrt in diese Forschung fließen, und neue Siegesmeldungen der Wissenschaft, die das Leben mehr und mehr ‚in den Griff' bekommt, stehen bevor". Diesem Realismus muß aber auch eine realistische Einstellung der Gesellschaft gegenüberstehen. Ständige, aktive, permanent ihre Stimme erhebende Ethikkommissionen müssen über den universitären Bereich hinaus wirksam werden, um jeden auch nur denkbaren Mißbrauch zu verhindern. Pädagogische Strategien müssen erarbeitet und im Sinne einer neuen Form des „Lebens- und Partnerschaftshygiene-Unterrichtes" an den Schulen, beginnend in den Volksschulen, weiterführend an den Pflicht- und AHS-Schulen, weitergegeben werden. Die Lösung des Problems: " Künstliche Befruchtung" wird kurzfristig rechtlich politisch mehr oder weniger effizient gelöst sein. Nur: kurzfristige Lösungen und daraus resultierende kurzfristige politische Zufriedenheit werden nur aufschiebende Wirkung zeitigen können, wie das besonders deutlich bei der Fristenregelung bemerkbar wird. So wichtig es für die Betroffenen heute ist, über geeignete Maßnahmen der Regierung, den weitgehend rechtsleeren Raum durch adäquate Rechtssicherheit zu ersetzen – so unabdingbar ist aber auch die Forderung, langfristige soziale Strukturen mit Einstellungen zu entwickeln, die nicht mehr alles als machbar, alles als erreichbar und alles als konsumierbar ansehen.

LITERATUR:

W. Brandstetter, J. Huber, H. Janisch, A. Laun: Künstliche Befruchtung – Versuch einer Standortbestimmung in medizinischer, strafrechtlicher und moraltheologischer Sicht. Facultas-Universitätsverlag, Wien 1985

DADA IN DER WISSENSCHAFT

JOHANNES VOGGENHUBER

DADA IN SCIENCE
JOHANNES VOGGENHUBER

The special fascination of gene technology is to be found in the assertion made by its advocates, that it makes the fabrication, tuning and designing of organisms, plants, and animals possible, exactly as desired. The idea of helping the environmentally contaminated universe itself, of producing refuse-eating super-bacteria, herbicide-resistant plants or waste water-proof giant trout, nourishes the omnipotent feeling of early childhood: In this manner, the hibernation reserved until now for poikilothermic animals—to be more exact, a gene which researchers think causes hibernation—will be packed into cattle genoms so that animal keepers can save on feeding costs in winter in cold regions with longer periods of vegetation lulls.

Nevertheless, the greyish practical experience can never keep up with the bright, dazzling theory, as the results can hardly be predicted, and with complex organisms it is uncertain as to where and how genes are inserted, activated and/or deactivated: Theoretically, even in gene technology two plus two is still four, but practically speaking, the sum generally deviates from this result as we mainly have to reckon with biological random numbers.

Through the haphazard combination of very different genetic offset pieces, gene technology is simply the science of post modernism, the chance encounter of sewing machines and umbrellas on a dissecting table. It is the advent of DA in science. Whereas the Dadaists are defined as being anti-artists, having put new life into art by means of provocation and fun, the gene technologists get down seriously to their biological lotto game. It didn't occur to the inexhaustible imagination of the Dadaists to secure exclusive rights for alphabets and letters, scales and sounds, such fun only becomes a matter of course for the new biologists who are not afraid of patenting genes, plants and living beings as inventions to introduce a kind of genetic bondage.

The awareness that the isolated contemplation of individual aspects is insufficient as the earth forms a complicated ecosytem, makes the gene technician's promise that their instrumentation could solve all environmental, waste, food, propagation and other life problems, seems to be a lack of experience. The blind dealing with life, which appears to be lacking and in need of improvement in the cold light of scientific interest,

Die besondere Faszination der Gentechnik liegt in der Behauptung ihrer Befürworter, daß sie es ermögliche, Organismen, Pflanzen und Tiere exakt nach Wunsch fertigen, tunen oder designen zu können. Die Vorstellung, der umweltverschmutzten Schöpfung selbst auf die Sprünge zu helfen, müllfressende Superbakterien, herbizidresistente Pflanzen oder abwasserfeste Riesenforellen zu erzeugen, nährt frühkindliche Allmachtgefühle: So soll der bisher wechselwarmen Tieren vorbehaltene Winterschlaf – genauer, ein Gen, von dem die Forscher meinen, daß es Winterschlaf verursache – Rindern ins Genom gepackt werden, damit in kalten Gegenden mit längerer Vegetationspause die Tierhalter im Winter Futterkosten sparen können.

Doch kann die gräuliche Praxis mit der bunt-schillernden Theorie nicht mithalten, da die Ergebnisse kaum vorhersehbar sind, ist doch bei komplexen Organismen ungewiß, wo und wie Gene eingebaut, aktiviert bzw. deaktiviert werden: Theoretisch ist auch in der Gentechnik Zwei und Zwei Vier, doch weicht in der Praxis die Summe meist von diesem Ergebnis ab, weil vorwiegend mit biologischen Zufallszahlen gerechnet wird.

Durch das wahllose Kombinieren unterschiedlichster genetischer Versatzstücke ist die Gentechnologie die Wissenschaft der Postmoderne schlechthin, das zufällige Zusammentreffen von Nähmaschine und Regenschirm auf einem Seziertisch. Sie ist der Einzug von DADA in die Wissenschaft. Während sich die Dadaisten aber als Anti-Künstler definiert und die Kunst durch Provokation und Spaß belebt haben, machen die Gentechniker mit ihrem biologischen Lotteriespiel Ernst. Der unerschöpflichen Fantasie der Dadaisten ist es nicht eingefallen, sich Exklusivrechte auf Alphabete und Buchstaben, Tonleitern und Töne zu sichern; solche Späße sind erst für die neuen Biologen selbstverständlich, die sich nicht scheuen, Gene, Pflanzen und Lebewesen als Erfindungen patentieren zu lassen, um eine Art genetische Leibeigenschaft einzuführen.

Die Erkenntnis, daß die isolierte Betrachtung von Einzelaspekten unzureichend ist, weil die Erde ein kompliziertes Ökosystem bildet, läßt das Versprechen der Gentechniker, daß ihr Instrumentarium alle Umwelt-, Abfall-, Ernährungs-, Fortpflanzungs- und sonstigen Lebens-Probleme der Menschheit lösen könne, als Mangel an Erfahrung erscheinen. Der besinnungslose Umgang mit Leben, das im kalten Licht von Wirtschaftsinteressen mangelhaft scheint und zu verbessern sei, entpuppt sich als gefährliche Kurzsichtigkeit. Denn während die Evolution in kleinsten Schritten langsam, aber sicher neue Verhältnisse schafft, Organismen sich gegenseitig entwickelnd aufeinander einstellen, behutsame Verschiebungen im Ökogefüge stattfinden, wollen Gentechnologien über Nacht die Schöpfung auf den Kopf stellen.

Die große Gefahr der Gentechnologie ist ihr Mangel an Fehlerfreundlichkeit: Gentechnisch manipulierte Organismen können einmal freigesetzt nie wieder vollständig zurückgeholt werden, vermehren und verbreiten sich, können natürliche Organismen verdrängen, das empfindliche Ökosystem völlig durcheinanderbringen.

turns out to be a dangerous shortsightendness. For, while evolution slowly but surely creates new relationships, with organisms mutually developing and getting used to each other, cautious displacements are taking place in the ecostructure, gene technologists want to turn the universe upside down, over night.

The big danger behind gene technology is its lack of error sympathy: Organisms manipulated by gene technology once set free at some point, can never fully be called back, can multiply and spread out, can supersede natural organisms and completely upset the sensitive ecosystem.

GENTHERAPIE: NEUE WEGE IN DER KREBSBEHANDLUNG

ERNST WAGNER

GENE THERAPY: NEW METHODS OF TREATING CANCER
ERNST WAGNER

In the present day and age, practically every gene can be isolated and analysed with molecular-biological methods. The growing awareness of causal genetic defectes can be used for the diagnosis of a significant part of over 4000 human hereditary diseases. However, to a great extent, we are still a long way from utilizing this knowledge about the causes in the development of effective medication or treatment.
The new hope that the introduction of intact genes into human body cells can now directly cancel out the effect of the defective genes that cause illness ("somatic gene therapy"), led, first of all in the USA, now also in Europe, to the development of a total of more than 40 gene-therapy protocols. The treatment of relatively rare, life-threatening hereditary diseases such as the adenosine-deaminase defect, the mucoviscidosis, or the LDL receptor defect were initially in the foreground. The very latest research results point out that gene therapy could also possibly be used to fight more common illnesses such as cancer, which affect about a quarter of all human beings in the course of their lives.
One of the gene therapy approaches against cancer is based on the concept of strengthening the patient's immune defense system against the tumour. In the development of tumours such an immune reaction generally occurs in the initial stages. If this is not capable of directly shedding the tumour and destroying it, then the immune defence system becomes increasingly weaker as the development of the tumour progresses and is even actively suppressed by the body. Many of the conventional ways of treating cancer, such as surgery or chemo-therapy, which do help to remove large masses of tumour in the short-term, very often fail in the long-term because of the development of recurrences or the formation of metastasae. These could be prevented by re-activating the immune defence system against the tumour.
For this purpose, the patient should be administered with his own genetically changed tumour cells as a vaccine (tumour vaccine) in a split-dose irradiated form. First of all, genes are introduced into the tumour cells producing immuno-stimulated matter such as cytokine which

In der heutigen Zeit kann mit molekularbiologischen Methoden praktisch jedes beliebige Gen isoliert und analysiert werden. Die wachsenden Kenntnisse über die ursächlichen genetischen Defekte können für die Diagnose eines wichtigen Teils der über 4000 menschlichen Erbkrankheiten eingesetzt werden. Wir sind leider meist noch weit davon entfernt, dieses Wissen über die Ursachen in die Entwicklung von wirksamen Arzneimitteln oder Therapien umzusetzen.
Die neue Hoffnung, daß durch Einschleußen intakter Gene in menschliche Körperzellen die krankmachende Wirkung defekter Gene direkt aufgehoben werden kann („Somatische Gentherapie"), hat zunächst in den USA, nun aber auch in Europa, zur Entwicklung von insgesamt bereits über 40 gentherapeutischen Protokollen geführt. Die Behandlung von relativ seltenen, lebensbedrohlichen Erbkrankheiten wie dem Adenosin-Deaminase-Defekt, der Mukoviszidose, oder dem LDL-Rezeptordefekt standen dabei anfänglich im Vordergrund. Forschungsergebnisse aus der allerletzten Zeit weisen darauf hin, daß die Gentherapie möglicherweise auch zur Bekämpfung von wesentlich häufigeren Erkrankungen, wie Krebs, der etwa ein Viertel aller Menschen in ihrem Lebenslauf betrifft, eingesetzt werden könnte.
Einer der gentherapeutischen Ansätze gegen den Krebs beruht auf dem Konzept, die Immunabwehr des Patienten gegen den eigenen Tumor zu stärken. Bei der Entwicklung von Tumoren tritt meist anfänglich eine solche Immunreaktion auf. Ist diese nicht imstande, den Tumor unmittelbar abzustoßen und zu zerstören, so wird die Immunabwehr mit fortschreitender Tumorentwicklung immer schwächer oder sogar vom Körper aktiv unterdrückt. Viele der herkömmlichen Methoden der Krebsbehandlung, wie Chirurgie oder Chemotherapie, die kurzfristig helfen, große Tumormassen zu entfernen, versagen dann aber oft langfristig, da es zum Auftreten von Rezidiven oder zur Bildung von Metastasen kommt. Diese könnten durch eine Reaktivierung der Immunabwehr gegen den Tumor verhindert werden.
Zu diesem Zweck sollen dem Patienten seine eigenen, gen-

technisch veränderten Tumorzellen in bestrahlter, nicht teilungsfähiger Form als Impfstoff („Tumorvakzine") verabreicht werden. Zuvor werden in die Tumorzellen Gene eingeschleußt, die immunstimulierende Stoffe wie Zytokine produzieren, die die Immunzellen des Körpers an die Impfstelle locken. Eine erfolgreiche Impfung aktiviert und vermehrt in der Folge tumorspezifische zytotoxische T-Zellen, das sind Immunzellen, die im Körper des geimpften Patienten zirkulieren und einzelne verstreute Tumorzellen bzw. Mikrometastasen gezielt zerstören.

Voraussetzung für eine derartige Therapie ist eine effiziente und gefahrlose Methode, Zytokin-Gene außerhalb des Körpers in kultivierte Krebszellen einzuführen. Ein dafür geeignetes Gentransfersystem wurde am Institut für Molekulare Pathologie in Wien in einer Zusammenarbeit von unserer Gruppe mit der Gruppe von Prof. Max Birnstiel, und der Gruppe von Dr. David Curiel von der Universität in Chapel Hill, North Carolina, entwickelt. Ausgangspunkt war dabei die Entwicklung von synthetischen, d.h. im Reagenzglas chemisch hergestellte Komplexen. Diese enthalten die therapeutischen Gene in Form von Nukleinsäure (DNA), die mit Transportproteinen wie Transferrin verpackt sind. Dadurch wird die Rezeptor-vermittelte Endozytose, ein natürlicher effizienter Aufnahmemechanismus, zum Einschleußen des therapeutischen Genes in die Zelle möglich.

Diese synthetischen Nukleinsäure-Komplexe haben gewisse Ähnlichkeiten mit natürlichen Viren, was die Kapazität, DNA in die Zellen einzuschleußen, betrifft. Die „Künstlichen Viren" haben aber den großen Vorteil, daß sie nicht wie natürliche Viren innerhalb von Zellen vermehrt werden können. Neben den komplett synthetischen Viren haben wir auch sehr effiziente Mischformen wie ein System entwickelt, das abgetötete Adenoviruspartikel enthält. Dabei werden die DNA-Komplexe mit hoher Effizienz in die Zelle und weiter in den Zellkern transportiert. Hier kommt es dann zur Übersetzung des therapeutischen Gens in Boten-RNA, die weiter in den entsprechenden Eiweißstoff, das therapeutische Protein, übersetzt wird.

Diese Technik wurde an einer Reihe verschiedener Tumorzellen, wie an frisch isolierten Melanomzellen, die einen bösartigen Hautkrebs verursachen, erprobt. In sehr vielen Fällen wurde dabei ein effizienter Gentransfer erreicht. Bei der Herstellung einer Tumorvakzine (siehe Abbildung) sollen frische, chirurgisch isolierte Tumorzellen des Patienten mit dem Gen für das Zytokin Interleukin-2 versehen werden. Nach Bestrahlung dieser Zellen, die dadurch nicht mehr teilungsfähig sind, sollen die Zellen als Impfstoff in die Haut injiziert werden. An der Immunisierungsstelle produ-

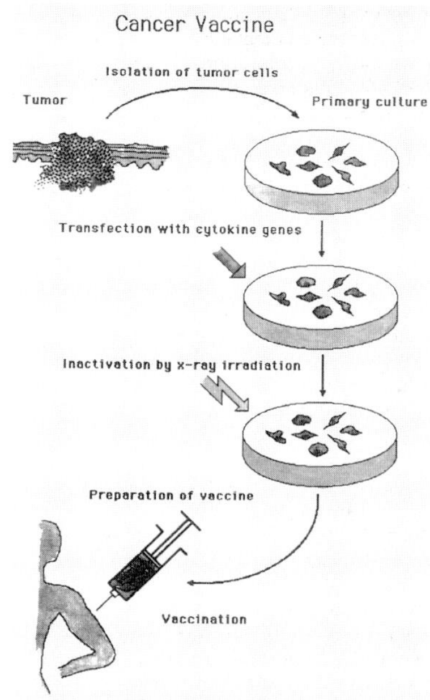

entice the body's immune cells to the place of vaccination. A successful vaccination consequently activates and increases specific tumour cytotoxic T-cells—that is immune cells that circulate in the body of the vaccinated patient and which purposefully destroy individually dispered tumour cells or micro-metastasae.

Tumour vaccine
Isolation of the tumour cells
Tumour Primary cultures
Transfection with cytokin genes
Inactivation by X-ray treatment
Production of the vaccine
Vaccination

The prerequisite for such a therapy is an efficient and harmless method of introducing cytokin genes into cultivated cancer cells outside the body. A suitable gene transfer system was developed at the Institute for Molecular Pathology in Vienna in cooperation with our group, and the team headed by Prof. Max Birnstiel and that of Dr. David Curiel from the University in Chapel Hill, North Carolina. The starting point was the development of synthetic i.e. chemically produced complexes in the reagent glass. These contain the therapeutic genes in the form of nucleic acid (DNA) which are packed with transport proteins such as Transferrine. In doing so, the receptor-mediated endocytosis, a naturally efficient receptive mechanism for introducing the therapeutic genes into the cells, is possible.

These synthetic nucleic acid complexes have certain similarities with natural viruses, as far as the capacity of introducing DNA into the cells is concerned. The "artificial viruses" do have the big advantage that they cannot multiply within the cells like natural viruses. In addition to the

completely synthetic viruses, we have also developed very efficient mixed forms, like a system containing dead adenovirus particles. Here the DNA complexes are very efficiently transported into the cell and onto the nucleus of the cell. Then the therapeutic genes are transformed into messenger RNA which are transformed into the corresponding protein matter, the therapeutic protein.
This technique was tested on a series of different tumour cells e.g. on freshly isolated melanoma cells which cause malignant skin cancer. In a lot of cases, an efficient gene transfer was achieved. In the manufacture of a tumour vaccine (see Figure), the patient's fresh surgically isolated tumour cells are to be given the gene for the cytokin Interleukin-2. After irradiating these cells which are then no longer split, the cells are to be injected into the skin as a vaccine. At the point of vaccination these irradiated tumour cells produce great amounts of Interleukin-2 whereby a strongly tumour-specific immune response should be initiated (see above).
The efficiency of such tumour vaccines has already been shown in a mouse melanoma model. Here, mice were vaccinated twice with Interleukin-2-productive, irradiated mouse melanoma cells. Afterwards, vaccinated and non-vaccinated animals were given mouse melanoma cells. In every non-vaccinated mouse a tumour developed within two weeks, whereas all the vaccinated animals were protected against the development of cancer. As to whether such a gene therapy tumour vaccine can lead to an immunological additional form of treatment in human beings for the operative removal of the tumour. to cure cancer, can only be discovered by treating cancer patients.

zieren diese bestrahlten Tumorzellen große Mengen an Interleukin-2, wodurch eine starke tumorspezifische Immunantwort in Gang gesetzt werden soll (siehe oben).
Die Wirksamkeit einer derartigen Tumorvakzine wurde bereits in einem Mausmelanom-Modell gezeigt. Dabei wurden Mäuse zweimal mit Interleukin-2 produzierenden, bestrahlten Mausmelanomzellen geimpft. Danach wurden geimpften und nichtgeimpften Tieren Mausmelanomzellen eingepflanzt. In allen nichtgeimpften Mäusen entwickelte sich innerhalb zweier Wochen ein Tumor, während alle geimpften Tiere vor der Krebsentstehung geschützt waren. Ob eine derartige gentherapeutische Tumorvakzine beim Menschen als immunologische Zusatzbehandlung zur operativen Entfernung des Tumors zur Heilung vom Krebs führt, kann nur durch Behandlung von Krebspatienten herausgefunden werden.

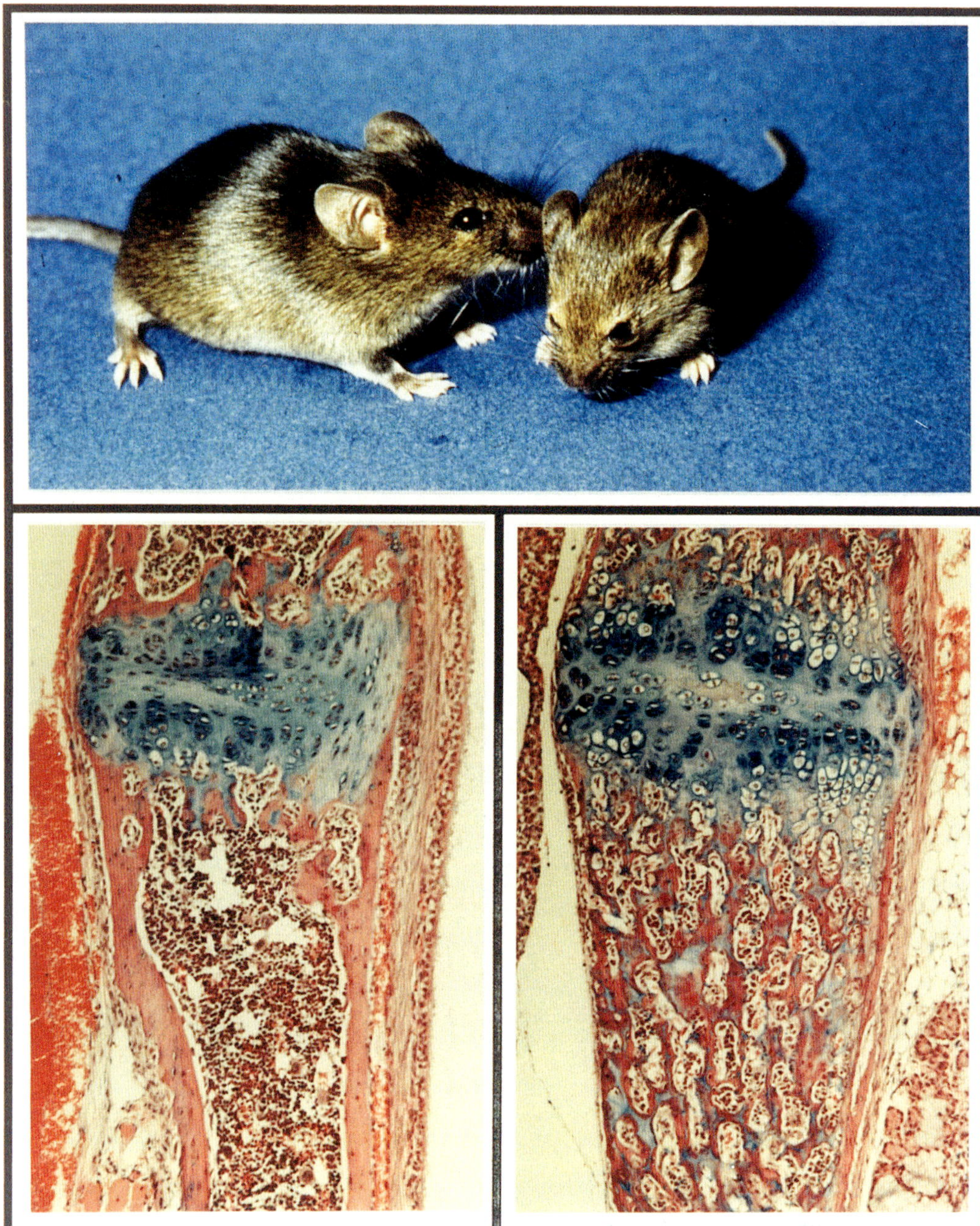

Fos +/+ Fos -/-

Phinotyp einer Maus mit c-Fos-Gen-Mangel. Gebremstes Wachstum und osteoperotische Knochen bei einer - /- Maus. (Institut für Molekulare Pathologie, Wien)

EIN MOLEKULARES VERSTÄNDNIS VON ENTWICKLUNG UND ERKRANKUNG BEI SÄUGETIEREN?

ERWIN F. WAGNER

A MOLECULAR UNDERSTANDING OF AMMALIAN DEVELOPMENT AND DISEASE?
ERWIN F. WAGNER

In the past decade we have witnessed a number of brakhroughs in the field of molecular biology, specifically towards a better understanding of mammalian development and disease. We are collecting important information on genes controlling early development using the mouse as the mammalian model system of choice. The basic question of how patterns in the embryo evolve and how cells specialize may soon be solved. The system of embryonic stem (ES) cells allows us to generate "ES mice", which are completely derived from cells grown in tissue culture. In addition, ES cells allow us to specifically delete and/or add genes to the mouse, thereby elucidating the function of a particular protein in development and disease. These genes are collectively known as oncogenes.

Im letzten Jahrzehnt waren wir Zeugen einer Reihe von Durchbrüchen im Bereich der molekularen Biologie, vor allem hinsichtlich eines besseren Verständnisses von Entwicklung und Erkrankung bei Säugetieren. Wir sammeln wichtige Informationen über Gene, die die Frühentwicklung steuern, indem wir die Maus als Modellsystem unserer Wahl für Säugetiere verwenden. Die grundlegenden Fragen, wie Muster in Embyos entstehen und wie sich Zellen spezialisieren, werden bald gelöst sein. Das System von embryonischen Stammzellen (ES) erlaubt uns, „ES-Mäuse" zu generieren, die gänzlich aus Zellen abstammen, die in Gewebekulturen gezogen wurden. Zusätzlich erlauben uns ES Zellen, spezielle Gene den Mäusen zu entnehmen und/oder zuzufügen, wobei die Funktion eines bestimmten Proteins bei der Entwicklung und Erkrankung erhellt wird. Diese Gene sind allgemein als Onkogene bekannt.

SYMPOSIUM „DIE LUST AUF UNSTERBLICHKEIT. KLONING, KRYONIK UND KOSMETIK“

DIE NEUEN ERBEN FRANKENSTEINS

KLAUS MADZIA

Der Schöpfer erschafft seine Welten am liebsten morgens, nach der ersten Tasse Kaffee. Den liebenlangen Tag wachsen, gebären und sterben seine Kreaturen dann, ohne daß er sie eines Blickes würdigt. Erst abends, kurz vor dem Einschlafen, schaut er, wie's in seinem Kosmos steht. Ein paar hundert Generationen haben inzwischen ihr kurzes Leben gelebt: unentwegt auf der Suche nach Nahrung, ständig auf der Flucht vor bösen Raubtieren und immer gierig nach Sex. Die Erfolgreichen konnten ihre Gene an die Nachkommen vererben und haben so ein Stück Unsterblichkeit erlangt. Die Unterlegenen sind ausgestorben.

Der Schöpfer selbst wohnt im Garten Eden der modernen Computerwelt: Im kalifornischen Silicon Valley, der Geburtsstätte von Chips und Personal Computern. Er heißt Larry Yaeger und auf seiner Visitenkarte steht, in typisch amerikanischem Understatement, Gott des „Mikrokosmos". Yaeger könnte Roadie für die kalifornische Rockgruppe Grateful Dead sein:schwarze, speckige Lederjacke, ein Bauch, der seine 42 Jahre verrät, schulterlange, silberne Mähne und dikke Ringe an den Fingern. Doch er ist ein moderner Erbe Dr. Frankensteins: ein Forscher, der sich der jungen Wissenschaft „Artificial Life" verschrieben hat – der Lehre, die beschreibt, wie in toter Materie Leben wächst.

Die Ziele der Forscher sind hoch gesteckt. Sie wollen die letzten Geheimnisse des Lebens entschlüsseln: erkennen, wie die Natur aus Chaos Ordnung schafft;verstehen, wie Leben auf unserer Erde entstehen konnte; und einige wollen den ganz großen Wurf: selbst ein Stück Unsterblichkeit erhaschen.

Deshalb erschafft Yaegger seit drei Jahren täglich neues, künstliches Leben – nur besteht das nicht aus den Natur-Zutaten Eiweiß, Kohlenstoff und Fett. Yaegers Geschöpfe sind nur elektronische Impulse in den fingernagelgroßen Chips eines Super-Rechners namens „Iris", hergestellt von der Firma Silicon Graphics.

Jedes seiner Wesen ist ein kleines Programm, das die Funktionen des Lebens nachahmt und dabei, so behaupten zumindest die Artificial-Life-Forscher, selbst lebendig wird. Yaeger nennt seinen Computer-Kosmos „Poly World", die Welt der Vielecke, weil seine Geschöpfe nur als farbige

FRANKENSTEINS'S NEW SUCCESSORS
KLAUS MADZIA

The Maker prefers to create his worlds in the morning after the first cup of coffee. Throughout the day his creatures grow, give birth and die without him even deigning to look at them. Only in the evening shortly before going to sleep, he takes a look at the state of things in his cosmos. A few hundred generations have, in the meantime, lived their short lives: steadfast in the search for food and constantly fleeing from evil predators, always greedy for sex. The successful ones are able to pass their genes on to their offspring and consequently achieve some immortality. The underdogs have died out.

The Maker himself lives in the Garden of Eden of the modern computer world: in California's Silicon Valley, the birth place of chips and personal computers. He is Larry Yaeger and on his business card there is the typical American understatement "Micro Cosmic God".

Yaeger could be a roadie for the Californian rock group "Grateful Dead": black, greasy leather jacket, a gut betraying his 42 years, shoulder-length silver mane and rings on his fingers. Yet he is a modern successor to Dr. Frankenstein: a researcher who has dedicated himself to the new science "artificial life"—a science which describes how life grows in dead matter.

The goals of these researchers are high. They want to decipher life's very last secrets: recognize how nature creates order from chaos: understand how life was able to develop on our earth: and some even want the big jackpot: to grasp a piece of immortality.

This is why Yaeger has been creating new artificial life for the past three years,—a life that does not consist of the natural ingredients protein, carbon and fat. Yaeger's creations are mere electronic impulses in the finger-nail sized chips of a super computer called "Iris", manufactured by the company "Silicon Graphics".

Each of his creatures is a small programme imitating the functions of life and in doing so, is alife—at least this is what the artificial life researchers claim. Yaeger calls his computer cosmos "Polyworld", the world of polygons, as his creations are only visible on the computer screen in the form of colourful blocks. "My little animals", says the scientist affectionately, "meet all the important criteria according to which we define life. They have a metabolism, multiply, act with their environment and continue to develop under the pressure of selection and choice".

Artificial life researchers simulate life in the computer by giving their creatures a few simple "instructions" with the aid of a control programme, such as "search for food" or "try to multiply". On the other hand, with software, they create a type of "world"—complete with digital continents and electronic flora and fauna. Once such programmes have been set free in this computer world, they begin to grow, change, mutate, and in a short time develop a behaviour which is very similar to that of living beings. For example, computer birds automatically form a flock when flying, without having been programmed to do so.

Whoever watches Yaeger's little computer world for a quarter of an hour never doubts that living beings are darting around on the 1230cm² area of screen. The creatures dart silently over a black matt screen: some spin around aimlessly, others seem to be determinedly hunting for square pieces of fodder. Depending on their "frame of mind", the artificial organisms change the colour of their bodies: the green ones are hungry, the blue ones want to multiply and the red ones are ready to fight.

Yaeger has equipped his polyworld creatures generously: each one has a set of 2500 digital genes whose individual values determine, for example, how big, how fast, and even how "clever" the artificial creation is. Sensory organs make it possible for Yaeger's little animals to recognize their surroundings and, as is the case with living organims, a network of brain cells is responsible for their reactions: they "experience" tiredness. They "feel" fear of enemies.

During their short lives, the little Polyworld animals learn from experience, how to find food or even a partner, faster. The consequence is: they make or cut connections between their digital brain cells. Sometimes the creatures astonish the Maker with their behaviour: "a few organisms have taken up the notion to circulate at the edge of the polyworld, thus making possible a relatively safe life". Yaeger assures us that he would never have dawned on this.

Abilities that have been learned are passed on by two mating creatures to their offspring. A male and a female block sprint towards each other on the screen, a small spark can be seen—and already there is a third small block crawling all over the place. This only takes but a few seconds.

Yaeger has thought of everything: whenever a little polyworld animal dies, its body transforms into green fodder which is then very often greedily consumed by the offspring. A dozen of them once even got together to form a real cannibal cult: for hours on end, sons, daughters and parents circled around in order to consume each other at some point—also a successful survival strategy, as their Maker comments dryly. His Polyworld is hard world to live in.

What drives a person like Larry Yaeger to such life-long work? Why do we need life in the computer? Yaeger hesitates with his reply, plays around with the rings on his fingers: "With my work I want to contribute to ensuring that an intelligent being is made of the computer, at last."

Klötzchen auf dem Computerschirm sichtbar sind. Meine „Tierchen“, so der Wissenschaftler liebevoll, „erfüllen alle wichtigen Kriterien, nach denen wir Leben definieren. Sie haben einen Stoffwechsel, pflanzen sich fort, agieren mit ihrer Umwelt und entwickeln sich weiter, unter dem Druck von Selektion und Auslese.“

Die Artificial-Life-Forscher simulieren Leben im Computer, indem sie ihren Kreaturen mit Hilfe eines Steuerprogramms ein paar einfache „Triebe“ mitgeben, wie: „Suche nach Futter“ oder: „Versuche dich fortzupflanzen“. Zum anderen konstruieren sie per Software eine Art „Welt“ – komplett mit digitalen Kontinenten, elektronischer Flora und Fauna. Einmal in dieser Computerwelt losgelassene Programme beginnen zu wachsen, verändern sich, mutieren und entwickeln in kurzer Zeit ein Verhalten, das dem von lebendigen Wesen durchaus ähnelt. Computervögel beispielsweise bilden beim Fliegen selbständig einen Schwarm, ohne, daß es ihnen einprogrammiert worden wäre.

Wer Yaegers kleine Computerwelt eine Viertelstunde lang betrachtet, zweifelt nicht daran, daß da auf 1.230 Quadratzentimeter Bildschirmfläche lebendige Wesen wuseln. Lautlos flitzen die Kreaturen über eine schwarze Mattscheibe; manche trudeln ziellos umher, andere scheinen zielstrebig nach viereckigen Futterstücken zu jagen. Je nach „Seelenzustand“ verändern die künstlichen Organismen ihre Körperfarbe:Die Grünen haben Hunger, die Blauen wollen sich vermehren, und die Roten sind in Kampfstimmung.

Yaeger hat seine Poly-World-Geschöpfe großzügig ausgestattet: Jedes besitzt einen Satz aus 2.500 digitalen Genen, deren einzelne Werte zum Beispiel festlegen, wie groß, wie schnell, ja, sogar wie „klug“ das Kunstgeschöpf ist. Sinnesorgane ermöglichen Yaegers Tierchen, ihre Umgebung zu erkennen, und – wie bei lebenden Organismen – ein Netzwerk aus Gehirnzellen ist für Reaktionen verantwortlich: Sie „fühlen“ Müdigkeit, sie „spüren“ Angst vor Feinden.

Während ihres kurzen Lebens lernen die Poly-World-Tierchen aus Eindrücken, etwa schneller Futter oder einen Partner zu finden. Konsequenz: Sie knüpfen oder kappen Verbindungen zwischen ihren digitalen Gehirnzellen. Manchmal verblüffen die Kreaturen den Schöpfer mit ihrem Verhalten: „Ein paar Organismen sind auf den Gedanken gekommen, immer am Rand der Poly-World zu kreisen, was ihnen ein relativ sicheres Leben ermöglicht.“ Darauf wäre er nie gekommen, versichert Yaeger.

Einmal erlernte Fähigkeiten vererben zwei sich paarende Wesen an ihre Nachkommen. Ein männliches und ein weibliches Klötzchen sprinten aufeinander zu, auf dem Bildschirm ist ein kleiner Funke zu sehen – und schon kriecht

ein kleines, drittes Klötzchen durch die Gegend. Der ganze Akt dauert nur wenige Sekunden.
Auch an die letzten Dinge hat Yaeger gedacht: Immer wenn ein PolyWorld-Tierchen stirbt, verwandelt sich sein Körper in grünes Futter, das dann oft von den Nachkommen gierig verspeist wird. Ein Dutzend hat sich denn auch einmal zu einem regelrechten Kannibalen-Kult zusammengefunden: Stundenlang kreisten Söhne, Töchter und Eltern umeinander, um sich irgendwann zu vertilgen – auch eine erfolgreiche Überlebensstrategie, wie ihr Schöpfer trocken kommentiert. Seine Poly-World ist eine verdammt unangenehme Welt zum Leben.
Was treibt jemanden wie Larry Yaeger zu solch einem Lebenswerk? Wozu brauchen wir Leben im Computer? Eigentlich genügen doch schon die wildgewordenen Schreibprogramme, die kaum ein Mensch richtig bedienen kann. Yaeger zögert mit der Antwort, spielt mit den Ringen am Finger: „Ich möchte mit meiner Arbeit dazu beitragen, daß aus dem Computer endlich ein intelligentes Wesen wird."
So will er zum Beispiel einen Forschungs-Assistenten, „den ich nicht programmieren muß, sondern dem ich einfach sagen kann, was ich will".
Schon seit den fünfziger Jahren jagen die Programmierer diesem letzten Ziel ihrer Arbeit nach: dem Programm, das alles Programmieren überflüssig macht; doch das Versprechen, in wenigen Jahren sei der Computer sapiens Wirklichkeit, erwies sich vornehmlich als plumpe Propaganda, um Forschungsgelder von Industrie und Militär zu kassieren.
Die Artificial-Life-Forscher wie Larry Yaeger kupfern dagegen frech beim Vorbild Evolution ab. Warum nicht erst mal einfachste Organismen elektronisch nachbauen und im Computer eine darwinistische Umwelt simulieren? In der Hoffnung auf das „Survival of the fittest", auf das Überleben der Tüchtigsten, soll sich Intelligenz im Speicher dann von selbst entwickeln. So ganz nebenbei wollen die Wissenschaftler dabei auch erfahren, ob die
Menschwerdung nur ein einmaliger Kunstfehler der Schöpfung war oder ob sie sich zwangsläufig am Ende auch im Computer wiederholt.
Der Vorteil: Anstatt ein paar Millionen Jahre zu warten, spielt Kollege Computer den Göttern vor dem Bildschirm die Entwicklung von Tausenden Arten, die Entwicklung von Generationen in ein paar Stunden vor.
Doch so weit sind die EDV-Frankensteins noch nicht. Larry Yaeger spürt noch kein „Mitleid", wenn er den „Aus"-Knopf drückt, und ganze Hundertschaften seiner Poly-World-Tierchen in den elektronischen Hades fliegen. „Wir sind ja erst auf dem Niveau einer Wasserschnecke." Zum Glück für Yae-

In this sense, he wants, for instance, a research assistant "that I do not have to programme, but I just have to tell what I want".
Programmers having been chasing this holy grail since the 1950s: The program to end all program, but the promise that computer sapiens would be reality in but a few years turned out to be heavy-handed propoganda in order to get research money from industry and from the military.
Artificial life researchers like Larry Yaeger, plagiarize the image of evolution. Why not electronically copy the simplest organims and simulate a Darwinstic environment in the computer? Hoping for "survival of the fittest", intelligence should develop by itself in the computer memory. In this way, scientists also want, incidentally, to discover whether the development of mankind
Just press the "Off" button and hundreds of little digital animals end up in the electronic Hades.
was merely a one-off malpractice of creation, or whether it will finally inevitably repeat itself in the computer, too.
The advantage: instead of waiting for a few million years, our colleague—the computer—runs off the development of a few generations to the Gods infront of the screen in just a few hours.
However, the EDP Frankenstein's are not that far yet. Larry Yaeger feels "no sympathy" when he presses the "Off" button and hundreds of his little polyworld animals fly off into the electronic Hades. "We are just at the level of a hydraulic screw". Luckily for Yaeger, until now no group has been founded for "freedom to all electronic laboratory creatures".
But as we talk about the moment following the pressing of the off-switch, Yaeger suddenly becomes contemplative. "I'm going to tell you the real reason why I fell for artificial life. Shortly before my death I would like to have the possibility to copy my knowledge, my intelligence, my whole consciousness into the computer so as to live on in the chips".
Probably, says Yaeger, bitterly "probably I will never live to see that, but perhaps my work will help give the next generation the possibility to defeat death".
The longing for immortality is also the driving force behind other followers of artificial life. "God damn it, I find it's a real swindle that we are only able to live for about 100 years", say Denny Hillis, computer researcher and successful business man from Cambridge, Massachusetts. We are sitting in an office in his company "Thinking Machines Corporation" and Hillis groans: "I want to live for 10,000 years. I have enough projects that I want to realize". In the course of his 35 years, he has done quite a lot. Driven by the idea of designing the thinking computer ("a machine that is proud of me"), in 1986 while he was still studying at the well-known Massachusetts Institute of Technology (MIT), he designed his super computer: the "Connection Machine", a matt, black cupboard, the height of man, with innumerable blinking red lamps. Every one standing for one of the 65536 micro-processors which are busy computing in the inside. Thanks to their enormous speed, Hillis's boxes have been a best seller;

companies like American Express use them to show the buying habits of their credit card customers.
And the architecture behind his "Connection Machine" is excellently suited for artificial life programmes. Each of the 65536 chips simulates a separate artificial life being, and consequently, programmes like Larry Yaeger's run much faster. Hillis supplies, so-to-speak, the terrarium with a turbo-growth guarantee for artificial life.
Only a stone throw away from Danny Hillis's company, researchers at MIT are working meticulously on artificial life that can be touched: poodle-sized robots with the souls of artificial life programmes crawl through the world on 6 legs. The idea originates from the Australian, Rodney Brooks.
Unnerved by the empty promises made by the recipe book computer scientists surrounding Marvin Minsky and their unsuccessful projects ("A robot needed three hours to erect a tower of building blocks)", he began, in 1985, to study thinking using tiny insect robots which had to be able to do little more than crawl around skillfully all over the place.
Brooks and a few students made their model robots—also called "mobots", for short—from metal sheets, LED's, model motors and, of course, computer chips. These little animals received world acclaim in but a few years, adorning the front pages of scientific magazines and even the US space authorities, NASA, started to become interested in the intelligent artificial animals as a replacement for astronauts.
In the meantime, Brooks is having a sabbatical; his Masters student, Colin Angle, just 24 years old and already the uncrowned king of the mobot tribe, had just founded the garage company "IS Robotics", in Boston. Silent partner in the venture is Brooks.
At the moment Colin is working a 14-hour days with his wife, his best friend and a few mates, on his mechanical beings: "Cheap, fast and a little out of control", that is his motto. Equipped with all kinds of sensors, Angle's mobots also feel what is moving around in front of them and beside them; in the meantime, his design even lets the little artificial animals palaver amongst themselves.
Soon there will even be small robots, "which can be sent into the pipes and tubes of nuclear power stations for maintenance or repair work". Or even better: "a herd of shoe-sized vacuum cleaning mobots waiting in the dark corners of the living room for dirt to fall on the floor will then dart off and clean away the dirt". A dozen should be sufficient for household usage, Angle believes. A few more perhaps for bachelor appartments.
Without his mobots, artificial life would grind to a halt, says Colin Angle. "After all, intelligence cannot develop without stimulations from the outside". Simulating life merely in the computer memory is a necessary but boring commodity. Artificial life will only be really exciting, really "cool", with his little animals.
In order to prove this, Angle shows us one of his creations. He fetches his "Genghis II" out of the dispatch box; Genghis II reminds us, in terms of

ger hat sich noch keine Gruppe „Freiheit für alle elektronischen Laborwesen" gegründet.
Aber als wir über den Moment nach dem Drücken des Aus-Schalters reden, wird Yaeger plötzlich nachdenklich. „Ich verrate jetzt mal den wirklichen Grund, warum ich Artificial Life verfallen bin. Ich möchte kurz vor meinem Tod gern die Möglichkeit haben, mein Wissen, meine Intelligenz, mein ganzes Bewußtsein in den Rechner zu kopieren, um so in den Chips weiterzuleben." „Wahrscheinlich", sagt Yaeger mit einer ganzen Menge Bitterkeit in seiner Stimme, „wahrscheinlich werde ich das nicht mehr erleben, aber vielleicht hilft meine Arbeit, daß die nächste Generation diese Möglichkeit hat, den Tod zu besiegen."
Diese Sehnsucht nach Unsterblichkeit treibt auch andere Jünger des Kunstlebens. „Verdammt, ich find' das einen ziemlichen Betrug, daß wir nur 100 Jahre leben können", sagt Denny Hillis, Computerforscher und erfolgreicher Unternehmer aus Cambridge im US-Staat Massachusetts. Wir sitzen in einem Büro seiner Firma „Thinking Machines Corporation", und Hillis stöhnt: „Ich will 10.000 Jahre leben, ich hab' genug Projekte, die ich realisieren möchte." In seinen 35 Lebensjahren hat er bisher schon eine Menge geleistet. Getrieben von der Idee, den denkenden Computer zu konstruieren („eine Maschine, die stolz auf mich ist"), entwarf er 1986 – noch während des Studiums am renommierten Massachusetts Institute of Technology (MIT) – seinen Superrechner: die „Connection Machine", einen mattschwarzen, mannshohen Schrank mit unzähligen rot blinkenden Lämpchen. Jedes steht für einen der 65.536 Mikroprozessoren, die im Inneren eifrig rechnen. Dank ihrer enormen Geschwindigkeit sind Hillis Kisten ein Verkaufsschlager; Unternehmen wie American Express durchleuchten damit die Kaufgewohnheiten ihrer Kreditkartenkunden.
Und die Architektur seiner „Connection Machine" eignet sich hervorragend für Artificial-Life-Programme. Jeder der 65.536 Chips simuliert ein eigenes Kunstlebewesen, und so laufen Programme wie die von Larry Yaeger natürlich wesentlich schneller. Hillis liefert sozusagen das Terrarium mit Turbowachstums-Garantie fürs Kunstleben.
Nur einen Steinwurf von Danny Hillis' Firmenbau entfernt tüfteln Forscher des MITschon am Kunstleben zum Anfassen: pudelgroße Roboter, die, beseelt von Artificial-Life-Programmen, auf sechs Beinen durch die Welt kriechen. Die Idee stammt von dem Australier Rodney Brooks.
Entnervt von den leeren Versprechungen der Rezeptbuch-Informatiker um Marvin Minsky und ihren gescheiterten Projekten („Ein Roboter brauchte drei Stunden, um einen Turm aus Bauklötzchen zu errichten"), begann er 1985, das

Denken anhand winziger Insektenroboter zu studieren, die wenig mehr können müssen, als geschickt durch die Gegend zu kriechen.

Brooks und ein paar Studenten bastelten aus Blech, Leuchtdioden, Modellmotoren und – natürlich – Computer-Chips ihre Mobile Robots, kurz auch Mobots genannt, zusammen. Die Tierchen erlangten in wenigen Jahren Weltruhm, schmückten die Titelseiten von Wissenschaftsmagazinen, und selbst die US-Raumfahrtbehörde Nasa begann sich für die intelligenten Kunstviecher als Astronautenersatz zu interessieren.

Brooks legt inzwischen ein Urlaubssemester ein; sein Meisterstudent Colin Angle, gerade 24 Jahre alt und schon ungekrönter Großmeister der Mobots-Zunft, hat gerade in Boston die Garagenfirma „IS Robotics" gegründet. Stiller Teilhaber:Brooks.

Colin bastelt derzeit mit seiner Frau, seinem besten Freund und ein paar Kumpels im 14-Stunden-Tag seine mechanischen Wesen: „Billig, schnell und ein bißchen außer Kontrolle", so sein Motto. Ausgestattet mit allerlei Sensoren, spüren auch Angles Mobots, was vor und neben ihnen kriecht; sein Design erlaubt inzwischen sogar, daß die Kunsttierchen miteinander palavern.

Schon bald soll es kleine Roboter geben, die man in die Röhren von Kernkraftwerken schicken kann. Für „Wartungs- oder Reparaturarbeiten". Oder noch besser: „Eine Herde schuhgroßer Staubsaug-Mobots, die in den dunklen Ecken des Wohnzimmers warten, bis Schmutz auf dem Boden ist, und dann von sich aus losflitzen und den Dreck wegputzen." Ein Dutzend sollte für den Hausgebrauch genügen, glaubt Angle. Für Junggesellenwohnungen vielleicht ein paar mehr.

Ohne seine Mobots bliebe die Artificial-Life-Forschung stekken, sagt Colin Angle. „Schließlich kann sich Intelligenz nicht ohne Reize von außen entwickeln." Nur im Speicher Leben zu simulieren sei zwar notwendig, aber langweiliges Schwarzbrot. Richtig spannend, richtig „cool" wird das Kunstleben erst mit seinen Tierchen.

Um das zu beweisen, zeigt uns Angle eines seiner Geschöpfe. Er holt seinen „Genghis II" aus einer Versandschachtel: Genghis II erinnert vom Gewicht (1,5 Kilo) und Aussehen her stark an einen Blechhummer. Ein bißchen schwerfällig schiebt er sich mit seinen sechs Beinchen über den Teppich. aber recht gekonnt steigt er über Hindernisse wie Lötkolben, Strommesser oder herumliegende Bücher.

Selbst als Angle eines der sechs außer Gefecht setzt, marschiert Genghis II unbeeindruckt weiter. Nach ein paar Minuten geht dem elektronischen Tier die Puste aus: Der Akku

weight (1.5 kilos) and appearance, strongly of a sheet metal lobster. It moves a bit clumsily across the carpet on its six legs, but tackles the obstacles very skillfully e.g. soldering irons, ammeters or books that are lying around.

Even when Angles puts one of the six out of operation, Genghis II marches on, unimpressed. After a few minutes, the electronic animal starts to falter: the battery is empty. "I forgot to load it up", Angle apologizes. The software that enables Genghis II to come to terms with the environment is, of course, based on artificial life techniques.

From MIT, Angle knows the 31 year old Belgian woman, Pattie Macs, who thought out the programmes for the Genghis predecessor. For her, artificial life research is her vocational dream combination: "I really wanted to study biology as my parent are doctors, but I was told that you couldn't earn any money with this". Then Pattie decided to study computer science and began working in Brussels on projects concerned with intelligent computers. The theories of the behavioural scientists, Konrad Lorenz and Nikolaas Tinbergen always seemed to her to be one-dimensional, too limited to explain the behaviour of man and animals. Pattie began to imitate the remarkable interlude of wishes, impulses and external stimulii in the computer, first of all using ants as an example, and now dogs.

There are now even artificial life programmes for the home computer: Ken Karakotsios, aged 33, developed the game "Simlife" in two years, a game with which one can now and again play God at home", as Karakotsios promises. Leisure-time Gods can create new animals and plants and observe their chances in the hard evolutionary struggle, on the screen. The game costs 70 dollars.

The military has also been interested in artificial life for a long time now. "The first practical applications in this new research field will be weapons", prophesies the US author Steven Levy*, who researched the beginnings and the facts behind artificial life. "Robot-controlled tanks, learning rockets and computer viruses which cannot be stopped by any defence programme", will soon be available, thinks Levy. "The Pentagon is closely watching this field". Even if the battle machinery functions without people, warns Levy, "the victims will still be people".

But even more: with artificial life, we—mankind—could be digging our own grave as a species. For who can guarantee that artificial beings having outgrown the computer memory age and being unable to be stopped by any switch, will want to go on living together with us bio-masses. A prominent artificial life thinker: "it is a good thing that the public haven't really noticed what we are working on, otherwise we would have faced more resistance". By the time citizens have understood our research, it will probably be too late to pull out the plug".

ist leer. „Ich hab' vergessen, ihn aufzuladen", entschuldigt sich Angle. Die Software, die Genghis II hilft, mit der Umwelt zurechtzukommen, basiert natürlich auch auf Artificial-Life-Techniken.

Noch vom MIT kennt Angle die 31jährige Belgierin Pattie Maes, die die Lauf-Programme für Genghis-Vorläufer erdacht hat. Für sie ist die Artificial-Life-Forschung die berufliche Wunschkombination: „Ich wollte eigentlich Biologie studieren, weil meine Eltern Ärzte sind, aber man sagte mir, damit sei kein Geld zu verdienen." Also entschied sich Pattie für die Informatik und begann in Brüssel, an Projekten rund um den intelligenten Computer zu arbeiten. Theorien der Verhaltensforscher Konrad Lorenz und Nikolaas Tinbergen erschienen ihr immer als eindimensional, zu beschränkt, um das Verhalten von Tier und Mensch zu erklären. Pattie begann, im Computer das merkwürdige Zwischenspiel aus Wünschen, Trieben und äußeren Reizen nachzuahmen: zuerst am Beispiel von Ameisen, jetzt sind Hunde dran.

Selbst für den Heimcomputer gibt es schon Artificial-Life-Programme: Ken Karakotsios, 33, entwickelte in zwei Jahren das Spiel SimLife, „mit dem man mal zu Hause Gott spielen kann", wie Karakotsios verspricht. Feierabend-Götter können neue Tiere und Pflanzen erschaffen und auf dem Bildschirm beobachten, ob sie eine Chance im harten Evolutionskampf haben. 70 Dollar kostet das Spiel.

Längst schon interessiert sich auch das Militär für Artificial Life. „Die ersten praktischen Anwendungen dieser neuen Forschungsrichtung werden Waffen sein", prophezeit US-Buchautor Steven Levy*, der Anfänge und Hintergründe des Kunstlebens recherchierte. „Robotergesteuerte Panzer, lernende Raketen und Computerviren, die kein Abwehrprogramm mehr stoppen kann" werde es schon bald geben, meint Levy. „Das Pentagon hat das Feld klar im Auge." Mögen auch die Kampfmaschinen ohne Menschen funktionieren, warnt Levy, „die Opfer werden Menschen sein".

Aber mehr noch: Mit Artificial Life könnten wir Menschen uns als Spezies auch das eigene Grab schaufeln. Denn wer garantiert, daß die künstlichen Wesen, erst einmal dem Speicherzeitalter entwachsen und durch keinen Schalter mehr abzustellen, noch mit uns Biomassen zusammenleben wollen. Ein prominenter Artificial-Life-Denker: „Gut, daß die Öffentlichkeit nicht so genau merkt, woran wir arbeiten. Sonst hätten wir mit mehr Widerständen zu kämpfen." „Bis die Bürger unsere Forschung verstanden haben, ist es wahrscheinlich zu spät, den Stecker zu ziehen".

Wir danken dem Gruner & Jahr Verlag für die Abdruckgenehmigung.

LÄNGER LEBEN

GERHARD JOHANN LISCHKA

TO LIVE LONGER
GERHARD J. LISCHKA

FOREIGN BODIES

Splitting reality into subject and object brings about not only polarisation but also fusion. The more we refer to object, objectification and alienation, the more excessively the subject is enhanced, as such. This applies in radical constructivism, where it is said that everyone constructs his or her own world. This also applies in medicine, where through organ transplants, objects as foreign bodies make the body, in its fragility, functional again. Function is a word normally used in conjunction with machines, but from a technological (objective) standpoint, the body is after all a machine.
Machines are increasingly serving medicine, taking the body apart, examining it, analysing it, etc. Computer programs help in diagnosing illnesses, in operations, and in the healing process. The boundaries between subject and object are becoming so fluid that mutual cross-fertilisation—with simultaneous rejection—is taking place. There is not only a mental meeting of macro- and microcosm in the brain (as right and left hemispheres) where they mutually complement each other; these spheres are inseparable from each other.
The way things stand, the surroundings (all objects) put the subject under the pressure of technological impact, making it ill, killing it. This is another aspect of the shifting and erasing of the boundaries between object (world) and subject. Our surroundings swallow us up and we are secularised man-eaters in that we adopt foreign organs or objects.

ARTIFICIAL BODIES

To negate death or define the afterlife belongs to the cultural techniques most societies use to get over the pain of having to die, and the loss of loved ones. Death can also be negated by making it a taboo to the extent that it is in our western society. Death is an outrage against the belief in progress, which is supposed to make our lives more comfortable. One wants to grow beyond oneself, reach the unreachable, immortality.
This life-extension is familiar to us from the first sculptures, the king lying in state, slowly decomposing but made whole and complete by

FREMDKÖRPER

Eine Spaltung der Realität in Subjekt und Objekt bewirkt nicht nur eine Polarisierung, sondern auch eine Verschmelzung. Je mehr wir von Objekt, Objektivierung und Entfremdung sprechen, desto mehr wird das Subjekt überhöht, als solches aufgewertet. So im Radikalen Konstruktivismus, wo gesagt wird, daß jede/r nur ihre/seine Welt konstruiere. So in der Medizin, in der Objekte als Fremdkörper durch Organtransplantationen den Körper in seiner Gebrechlichkeit wieder funktionstüchtig machen. Von Funktion spricht man zwar eher bei Maschinen, aber technologischem (objektivem) Aspekt ist der Körper schließlich eine Maschine.
Maschinen stehen immer mehr im Dienste der Medizin, im den Körper zu zerlegen, zu untersuchen, zu analysieren etc. Computerprogramme helfen bei der Diagnose von Krankheiten, bei Operationen und beim Heilungsprozeß. Die Grenzen zwischen Subjekt und Objekt werden dermaßen fließend, daß man von gegenseitiger Durchdringung bei gleichzeitiger Abstoßung sprechen muß. Makro- und Mikrokosmos treffen nicht nur mental im Gehirn (als rechte und linke Hemisphäre) aufeinander und ergänzen einander, diese Räume sind nicht voneinander trennbar.
Nun verhält es sich auch so, daß die Umwelt (alle Objekte) durch den technologischen Impakt das Subjekt bedrängen, krank machen, töten. Das ist ein anderer Aspekt der Verschiebung und Verwischung der Grenzen zwischen Objekt (Welt) und Subjekt. Die Umwelt frißt uns auf und wir sind säkularisierte Menschenfresser, indem wir fremde Organe oder Objekte adaptieren

KUNSTKÖRPER

Den Tod zu negieren oder das Jenseits zu definieren gehört zu den Kulturtechniken, deren sich die meisten Gesellschaften bedienen, um über den Schmerz des Sterben-Müssens und den Verlust geliebter Menschen hinwegzukommen. Den Tod kann man auch dadurch negieren, daß man ihn

dermaßen tabuisiert, wie dies in unseren westlichen Gesellschaften der Fall ist. Der Tod ist eine Unverschämtheit gegen den Glauben an den Fortschritt, der uns das Leben immer angenehmer machen soll. Man möchte über sich hinauswachsen, das Unerreichbare erreichen, die Unsterblichkeit. Diese Lebensverlängerung kenne wir von den ersten Plastiken, in denen der aufgebahrte, langsam verwesende König durch dauerhafte Materialien wieder ergänzt und vervollständigt wurde. Diese Art den Toten bei den Lebendigen zu erhalten zusammen mit der Wiedergeburtsmagie erleben wir in der Kunst bis heute. Sie überdauert uns, sie transportiert die Ideen des Menschlichen in die Zukunft.
Doch die Kunst wird vom Magier, vom Medizinmann von heute, vom Chirurgen arg bedrängt, vom von ihm geschaffenen Kunstkörper. Der beginnt in der Embryologie, im gezielten Eingriff in den genetischen Code und er endet in der Reanimation oder in der Hirnverpflanzung als Jungbrunnen. Der Kreislauf des Lebens ist nicht mehr zyklisch-natürlich, sondern fortschrittlich-künstlich.

ZWEITKÖRPER

Mußte bei der Mumifizierung noch ein Körper vorhanden bleiben und wurde er geistig transzendiert, lebt heute der medial mumifizierte Körper in seinem jeweiligen Abklatsch weiter. Zusammen mit der Technik des Klonens die Perpetuierung ein und desselben Körpers als lebendiger Toter oder (toter) Lebender. Wir leben nun nicht nur dank wissenschaftlicher Erkenntnis tatsächlich länger, sondern auch dank unserer Zweitkörper in diversen Medien. Die Medialisierung ist zum Jenseits im Diesseits geworden, indem die „Toten" mitten unter uns weilen.

durable materials. In today's art we are still seeing this way of keeping the dead in the land of the living, together with reincarnation magic. It outlives us, and transports the ideas of humanity into the future.
But art is being put under serious pressure by the magician, today's medicine man, the surgeon, by the artificial body he creates. This has its origin in embryology, in specific intervention in the genetic code, and ends in re-animation or in brain transplants as a Fountain of Youth. The cycle of life is no longer cyclic-natural but progressive-artificial.

SECOND BODIES

Whereas mummification required a body, which was to be spiritually transcended, today's mediumistically mummified body lives on as a poor imitation. Together with the technique of cloning, the perpetualisation of one and the same body as the living dead or the dead living. Not only are we now in fact living longer thanks to scientific discovery, but also thanks to our second bodies in various media. The mediatisation has become the hereafter in the present., in that the "dead" are among us.

KÜNSTLICHES LEBEN DURCH HINAUSZÖGERN DES ALTERNS

REIMARA RÖSSLER

ARTIFICIAL LIFE THROUGH POSTPONED AGING
REIMARA ROSSLER

A recent editorial in Time magazine (March 1st, p. 50) claims that in the age of cyberspace, artificial life has become attractive also in the sense of artificial life extension. The current biomedical consensus is that in the long run, the genome project will show the way toward effectively interfering with the genetic switching events that according to the Hayflick hypothesis underlie aging in all somatic cells. In the meantime, it appears that a simpler approach can be tried – the "melatonin short-cut." The latter comes in 3 clinical varieties. 1) The Russian school of Dilman and Anisimov, who since 1979 reduced old-age cancer and senility and increased life span by 25 percent in rats, by means of a pineal extract that stimulates nightly melatonin production, use the same extract since 1989 also on patients. 2) At the Health Sciences University in Portland, Oregon, patients with old-age insomnia are treated with melatonin as a natural sleeping pill, since 1992. 3) The monks of Mount Athos in Greece who allegedly reach a mean age of over 100 years go to bed at dusk and rise for prayer at 3 a. m. throughout the year. It will be important to verify by means of melatonin profiles that under such a life style, the product of sleeping time and melatonin concentration is maximized (as it is in cases 1 and 2). This product has been conjectured to control the irreversible cellular switching events that underlie somatic aging. Since this question can presumably be answered soon using cell cultures, an easy way to delay aging may turn out to be available. Would such a medical break-through be desirable? It is perhaps a good idea to aks this question before the situation has actually arisen.
R. R. thanks Peter Weibel and O. E. Rössler for discussions.

Nach Meinung von „Time“ (1. 3. 93, S. 50) gehört zum modernen Thema des „künstlichen Lebens“ in Computerwelten auch das der künstlichen Lebensverlängerung in der richtigen Welt – die effektive „Anti-aging therapy“. Im Zusammenhang mit dem modernen „Genomprojekt“ erhofft man sich für die Zukunft Mittel, um in die (nach der Hayflick-Theorie zu erwartenden) Gen-Umschaltungen als Grundlage des Alterns aller somatischen Zellen hemmend eingreifen zu können. Gegenwärtig zeichnet sich jedoch ein noch einfacherer Weg ab – die „Melatonin-Abkürzungsroute“. Sie manifestiert sich in 3 verschiedenen klinischen Formen: 1) Dilman und Anisimov in Rußland fanden 1979 einen Pinealextrakt, der die nächtliche Melatoninbildung stimuliert und bei Versuchstieren die Entstehung von Alterskrebs vermindert und die Lebensspanne um 25% erhöht; seit etwa 1989 wird er auch beim Menschen eingesetzt. 2) An der Health-Sciences University in Portland (Oregon) werden seit 1992 alte Patienten, die an Schlaflosigkeit leiden, erfolgreich mit Melatonin als einer „natürlichen Schlaftablette“ behandelt. 3) Die Mönche des Berg Athos in Griechenland werden angeblich im Durchschnitt über 100 Jahre alt und gehen das ganze Jahr mit der Sonne zu Bett, um sich bereits um 3 Uhr nachts wieder zum Gebet zu erheben. Es wäre lohnend, durch Melatonin-24-Stunden-Profile nachzuweisen, daß bei diesem Lebensstil das Produkt aus nächtlicher Melatoninkonzentration mal Schlafdauer auf natürliche Weise maximiert wird (ähnlich, wie es bei Punkt 1 und 2 der Fall ist). Dieses Produkt steuert nach einer neuen Vermutung die irreversiblen somatischen Gen-Umschaltungen, die das Zellaltern bewirken. Da diese Frage mit Hilfe von Zellkulturen klärbar erscheint, zeichnet sich die Möglichkeit einer leicht erreichbaren effektiven Hinauszögerung des Alterns ab. Wäre ein derartiger medizinischer Durchbruch wünschenswert? Es ist vielleicht gut, diese Frage bereits zu stellen, bevor der Traum Realität geworden ist.

R. R. dankt Peter Weibel und O. E. Rössler für Diskussionen.

KÖNNEN WIR METHUSALEM ÜBERLEBEN?

MATTHIAS WABL

Niemand möchte alt sein, wohl aber möchten die meisten alt werden. Die beiden Fragen, die viele von uns hier interessieren, lauten: Können wir den Prozeß des Alterns zum Stillstand bringen? und: Können wir wesentlich länger als hundert Jahre leben? Diese beiden Fragen können – müssen aber nicht – in einem Zusammenhang stehen.
Es scheint natürlich, daß wir, von Unfällen und Krankheit einmal abgesehen, an „Altersschwäche“ sterben. Der Tod wird als das Ende eines hinfällig gewordenen Körpers gesehen. Könnten wir das Altern erklären, so bräuchten wir, wie es scheint, den Tod nicht zu erklären. Für Menschen hat diese Sicht einige Vorzüge. Gleichzeitig reden wir jedoch in der Alltagssprache von der Lebens„uhr“, die abläuft. Diese Metapher impliziert nicht, daß wir, um zu sterben, alt werden müssen. Alle Bestandteile einer abgelaufenen Uhr können noch wie neu und somit funktionstüchtig sein und die Uhr kann wieder aufgezogen werden. Im Gegensatz dazu sind zu dem Zeitpunkt, da wir angenommen an Herzversagen sterben, das Herz und auch die meisten anderen Teile unseres Organismus allgemein in einem ziemlich schlechten Zustand.
Der Tod hat viele Bedeutungen, aber für unseren Zweck hier sei er das Ende der Existenz eines besonderen menschlichen Wesens, d. h. die Auflösung eines mehrzelligen Organismus. Wir alle bestehen aus vielen Zellen und obwohl jeden Tag viele dieser Zellen absterben, bedeutet der Tod dieser Zellen nicht den Tod des Individuums. Im Gegenteil, der Zelltod ist für die Fortdaver des Lebens des Individuums sogar unabdingbar. So werden Zellen, die von Krankheitserregern befallen sind, von unserem Immunsystem getötet. Und die Zellen der äußeren Hautschicht sterben, so wie viele verschiedene andere Zelltypen ab, um durch neue ersetzt zu werden. Wenn dieser normale, im Programm vorgesehene Zelltod nicht mehr stattfindet, können sich Tumore bilden, die unter Umständen den gesamten Organismus töten. In diesem Fall leben die einzelnen Zellen viel länger als vorgesehen und können sogar die Person, deren Bestandteil sie waren, überleben: so etwa werden die Krebszellen einer Frau, die vor vierzig Jahren starb, weiterhin in Kultur gehal-

CAN WE OUTLIVE METHUSELAH?
MATTHIAS WABL

No one wants to be old, but most of us want to get old. The two questions that interest many of us in this respect are: Can we stop the process of aging? And, can we live much longer than hundred years? These two questions probably are related to each other, but they need not to be.
It seems natural that, barring accidents and disease, we die of "old age". Death is viewed as the end of a body in decline. Could we explain aging, it seems, we would not have to explain death. For human beings this view has some merit. However, at the same time, in the language of every day life we talk about the "clock" of life, which runs down. This metaphor does not imply that we have to age in order to die. All the parts of a clock that has run out may still be in mint condition and thus functional, and the clock may be wound up again. In contrast to this, at the time we die from, say, heart failure, the heart and also most other parts of our organism are generally in pretty bad shape.
Death has many meanings, but for our purpose here, we think of it as termination of existence of a particular human being, i. e., the desintegration of a multicellular organism. We all consist of many cells; although many of these cells die every day, the death of these cells does not imply death of the individual. On the contrary, cell death is even required for the continuation of life of the individual. Thus, cells that are infected by pathogens are killed by our immune system. And the cells of the outer layer of the skin, as many other cells of different type, die off to be replaced by new ones. When this normal, programmed, cell death is not sustained, tumors may result that eventually may kill the whole organism. In such a case, the individual cells live much longer than they are supposed to and they may even outlive the person they have been part of:for example, the cancer cells from a woman who died fourty years ago are still cultured and thus alive today in many laboratories all over the world.
We replace our parts of the organism systematically and when needed; in that we resemble the gothic cathedrals that are built of sand stones, which have to be continually replaced over the centuries so that almost no stone of today has been part of the original structure. Why, then, do we not look always the same, as the cathedrals do? The reason for this is that to the builder it is obvious how a stone has to be replaced; and for rebuilding after a major catastrophy the

blue-point for the cathedral is kept unchanged in the parsonage. But for the cells there is nothing obvious; and the blue-print for us is kept inside of the very same cells that are to be replaced. Before the cells are replaced, the blueprint has to be copied and it is at this moment that sometimes innocuous, sometimes serious, errors are introduced. When errors are introduced, the new cells might even be "better off" than the old ones; for example, they might grow faster. In general, however, this will be detrimental to the organism as a whole: in our example of faster growth a tumor may result. Proofreading the copies of the blue-prints can reduce the rate of error, but cannot do away with each and every error. This fact is a consequence of a famous law of thermodynamics, one of the pillars of today's physics. The accumulation of errors over time brings incremental changes in the architecture of our organism, and, as explained above, unlikely to its advantage; the result is aging.

How then, can we ever be young? We, as homo sapiens, have been around for more than hundred thousand years, during which many errors in our blue prints must have occurred. The answer to this question is selection. As individuals, we all start from the fertilized egg, which is a single cell. This egg has one blue-print, which is tested over and over again during the development of the embryo. Many embryos do not make it and abort. And if serious errors become apparent during childhood, the afflicted person may never reach the sexual maturity and social acceptance needed to pass his blueprint onto the next generation of children.

Physics tell us that it is impossible to copy the blueprints of our many cells in an error-free way, and thus it is impossible for us to stay in this world forever. But how long could we live? Thousand years instead of our hundred years? The average life span appears to be a characteristic of the species: For example, a mouse lives about two years, a dog twenty years, and redwood trees can live thousand years. Our question now becomes: what determines the average lifespan of an individual of a given species? Obviously, the fidelity with which the blue-prints of the cells are copied has to be a factor perhaps even the most important one. This fidelity is achieved by a number of proofreading systems inside the cells. The proofreading systems are inherited by the very same blueprint that is present in all cells; they consist of several enzymes, which are biocatalysts. If we were able to make our proofreading systems better, or to transplant better proofreading systems from other species onto us, we might live much longer.

It is conceivable that we transplant onto us biocatalysts that may prolong life by slowing down aging? In principle, the procedures to introduce foreign blueprints for any biocatalyst into our organism are in place; they are provided by the so-called recombinant DNAtechniques, and their final application to the (hopefully volunteering) person does not amount to much more than a shot similar to vaccination. That is not to say that we could substantially prolong life today or tomorrow. But there is no a priori rea-

ten und leben somit heute noch in vielen Laboratorien in der ganzen Welt.

Die Bestandteile unseres Organismus werden systematisch und jeweils wenn erforderlich ersetzt; ähnlich den gotischen Kathedralen, die, aus Sandstein erbaut, im Laufe der Jahrhunderte kontinuierlich erneuert wurden, sodaß nahezu keiner der heutigen Steine schon Bestandteil der ursprünglichen Baustruktur war. Warum aber schauen wir dann, wie die Kathedralen, immer gleich aus? Der Grund liegt darin, daß es für den Bauherrn offenkundig ist, wie ein Stein ersetzt werden muß; und für den Fall eines Wiederaufbaus nach einer großen Katastrophe werden die Baupläne der Kathedrale im Pfarrhaus unverändert aufbewahrt. Für die Zellen ist dergleichen aber nicht selbstverständlich, die Baupläne für uns werden im Inneren eben jener Zelle, die es zu ersetzen gilt, aufbewahrt. Ehe die Zellen ersetzt werden, müssen die Baupläne kopiert werden und dies ist jener Moment, da es mitunter zu harmlosen, manchmal aber zu gravierenden Fehlern kommt. Es kann durchaus sein, daß die neuen Zellen mit solchen Fehlern „besser dran sind" als ihre Vorgänger; beispielsweise daß sie schneller wachsen. Im allgemeinen ist dies jedoch für den Organismus insgesamt nachteilig: in unserem Beispiel des rascheren Zellwachstums kann es zu einem Tumor kommen. Ein Korrekturlesen der Bauplankopien kann die Fehlerquote verringern, aber nicht alle und jeden Fehler ausmerzen. Diese Tatsache ist eine Konsequenz aus einem berühmten thermodynamischen Gesetz, – eine der Säulen der heutigen Physik. Die Akkumulation von Fehlern führt im Zeitverlauf zu größer werdenden Veränderungen in der Architektur unseres Organismus und da diese wie oben dargelegt, in der Regel nicht zu seinem Vorteil sind, ist Altwerden das Ergebnis.

Wie können wir dann jemals jung sein? Wir, als homo sapiens, existieren seit mehr als hunderttausend Jahren, während derer in unseren Bauplänen viele Fehler aufgetreten sein müssen. Selektion, lautet die Antwort auf diese Frage. Als Individuen beginnen wir alle mit dem befruchteten Ei, das eine einzelne Zelle ist. Dieses Ei hat einen Bauplan, der während der Entwicklung des Embryos immer wieder getestet wird. Viele Embryos entsprechen nicht und sterben ab. Und wenn während der Kindheiternsthafte Fehler offenkundig werden, erreicht die betreffende Person nie jenes Stadium der sexuellen Reife und sozialen Akzeptanz das erforderlich ist, um der folgenden Generation von Kindern ihren Bauplan weiterzugeben.

Die Physik besagt, daß es unmöglich ist, die Baupläne unserer vielen Zellen fehlerfrei zu kopieren und daß es daher unmöglich ist, für immer auf dieser Welt zu bleiben. Aber wie

lange könnten wir leben? Tausend Jahre anstatt hundert? Die durchschnittliche Lebensdauer scheint ein Charakteristikum der Spezies zu sein: Zum Beispiel lebt eine Maus etwa zwei Jahre, ein Hund zwanzig Jahre und Mammutbäume können tausend Jahre alt werden. Unsere Frage lautet jetzt: Was bestimmt die durchschnittliche Lebensspanne eines Individuums einer gegebenen Spezies? Es liegt auf der Hand, daß die Originaltreue, mit der die Baupläne der Zelle kopiert werden, ein Faktor sein muß, vielleicht sogar der wichtigste. Die Korrekturlesesysteme werden von eben jenem Bauplan, der in allen Zellen vorhanden ist, geerbt. Sie bestehen aus mehreren Enzymen, die als Biokatalysatoren fungieren. Wären wir in der Lage, unsere Korrekturlesesysteme zu verbessern, oder bessere Systeme von einer anderen Spezies auf uns zu übertragen, würden wir eventuell viel länger leben.
Ist es vorstellbar, daß wir Biokatalysatoren, die das Leben verlängern könnten, indem sie das Altern verlangsamen, in uns verpflanzen? Im Prinzip sind in unserem Organismus die Verfahren zur Einführung fremder Baupläne für jeden Biokatalysator vorhanden; sie sind in den sogenannten rekombinanten DNA-Techniken vorgesehen und ihre Endgültige Anwendung an einer (hoffentlich freiwilligen) Person läuft auf nicht viel mehr als auf eine Spritze hinaus, ähnlich einer Impfung. Das heißt nicht, daß wir in der Lage wären, das Leben heute oder morgen wesentlich zu verlängern. Aber es gibt a priori keinen Grund, warum das in absehbarer Zeit nicht möglich sein sollte. Wir könnten Methusalem, der es auf 969 Jahre gebracht hat, durchaus überleben. Reden wir wieder über diese Sache in tausend Jahren oder so!

son why this could not be done in some time from now, and we may well be able to outlive Methuselah, who made it to 969 years. Let us discuss this issue again in a thousand years or so!

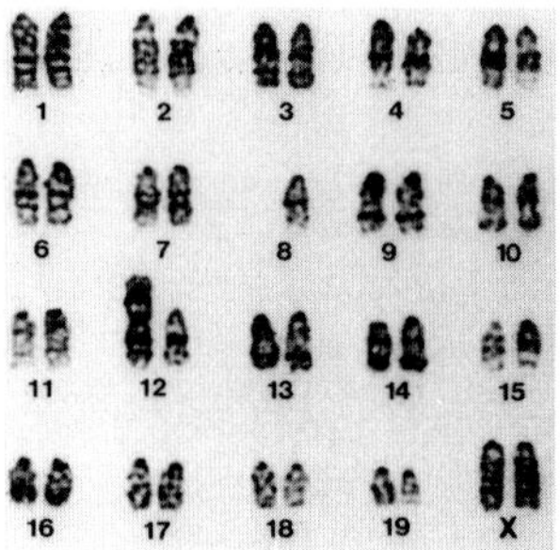

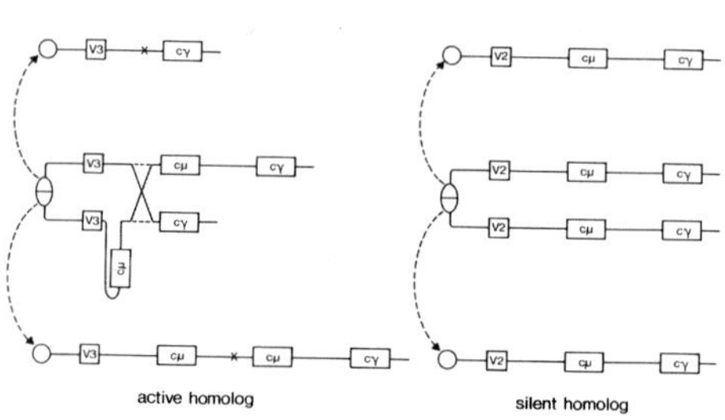

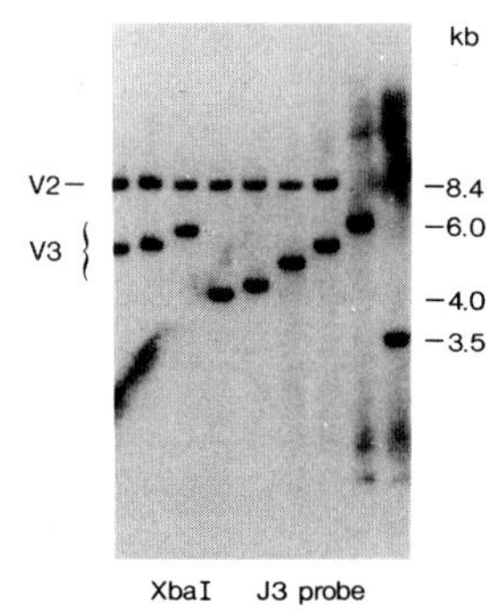

SYMPOSIUM „ROBOTER, ANIMATEN UND KÜNSTLICHE LEBEWESEN“

PROLEGOMENA

LOUIS BEC

ÄSTHETIK UND FABULÖSE ERKENNTNISTHEORIE DES KÜNSTLICHEN LEBENS

- Das künstliche Leben muß als eine Machination betrachtet werden.
- Es ist das wirklich letzte Unternehmen des Lebendigen, sich selbst zu verstehen und sich seiner selbst zu enteignen.
- Ziel dieser Machination ist die Erarbeitung von Strategien, die die krude kartesianische Maschinerie zum Verschwinden bringen und ersetzen durch ein variables Kontinuum von indirekt zoologischen Machinationen, die mehr als Grundlage der Geisteshaltung denn der Instrumentalität definiert sind.
- Trickreich wird in den Aktivitäten des künstlichen Lebens biologisches Wissen entschlüsselt und auf die technische Apparatur übertragen.
- Es ergibt sich als „scheinheilige" Finte, als verdrehte Methode, die das modellierte Lebendige dazu bringt, nicht mehr zu repräsentieren sondern vielmehr sich zu präsentieren.
- Deshalb strebt es danach, mit dem Auftauchen des Symbolischen quer durch die sensomotorischen Ebenen, die Algorithmen der Anpassung, des Lernens und der kollektiven Intelligenz, Zeichen des bewußten, autonomen Verhaltens zu setzen.
- Es tendiert dahin, dem Autonomen eine erkennbare Form zu geben, indem es das Anderssein so wie Abhängigkeit, Unabhängigkeit, Interdependenz und Interaktivität behandelt.
- Es verkleidet sich als wissenschaftliches Fachgebiet am Schnittpunkt der Lebenswissenschaften, der kognitiven Wissenschaften, der künstlichen Intelligenz, der systematischen Modelltheorie, der Bio-Informatik.
- Seine Artefakte gehen bei weitem über den einfachen Rahmen der biologischen und der technologischen Wissenschaften hinaus. Sie verleihen dem künstlichen Leben eine Überdimensionierung.
- Die schwindelerregenden Projektambitionen, die funda-

PROLEGOMENES
LOUIS BEC

ÉSTHÉTIQUE ET EPISTEMOLOGIE FABULATOIRE DE LA VIE ARTIFICIELLE

- La vie artificielle doit être considéré comme une machination.
- Elle est la toute dernière entreprise mise au point par le vivant pour se saisir et se desaisir de lui-même.
- L'objectif de cette machination est d'elaborer, des stratégies pour subtiliser la machinerie animale cartésienne et la remplacer par un continuum variable de machinations zoologiques biaisées, definies comme principe de mentalité plutôt que d'instrumentalité.
- La vie artificielle, dans ses activités, decode et transfert insidieusement du cognitif biologique vers du dispositif technologique.
- Elle se donne comme une ruse «hypocrisique», une methode vrillée qui amènerait le vivant modelisé à cesser de representer, mais plutôt de se presenter.
- Pour cela, elle vise à produire les insignes du comportement intentionnel autonome par emergence du symbolique, à travers les niveaux sensorimoteurs, les algorithmes d'adaptation, d'apprentissage et d'intelligence collective.
- Elle voudrait tendre à donner une forme discernable à l'autonomie, en traitant de l'alterité comme dépendance, indépandance, interdépendance et interactivé.
- Elle se travestit en domaine scientifique à la croisée des sciences du vivant, des sciences de la cognition, de l'intelligence artificielle, de la modélisation systémique, de la bio-informatique
- Mais ses artéfacts debordent largement le simple cadre des sciences du vivant et des technologies. Ils donnent un surdimensionnement à la vie artificielle.
- Ils ouvrent par l'ambition vertigineuse du projet, par la complexité fondamentale de leur objet d'etude, par la diversité fluctuante des concepts et la plasticité des méthodes utilisées, un champ d'investigation beaucoup plus etendu.
- Ils sont le produit de niveaux epistemologiques multiples, inscrits dans les domaines de la connaissance et de l'expression humaine qui englobent les pratiques fabricatoires arti-

stiques, les aspects ésthétiques, ethiques et sociologiques.
- Plus fortement encore, ils sont l'émanation la plus pertinente à ce jour, du projet de representation et de saisie du vivant qui, toutes disciplines confondues, hante la culture occidentale depuis la nuit des temps.
- Le retour à toute «machinerie machinique» de la vie artificielle risquerait de la reduire à un instrument trivial de simulation.
- La dimension exploratoire signalée par Chris Langton luimême, lorsqu'il parlait du passage d'une vie «telle qu'elle est à une vie telle qu'elle pourrait être», serait delibérement evacuée.
- Une erreur epistémologique sur le site ontogénique de la vie artificielle serait grave.

La vie artificielle se deploie à la pointe extrême de la pensée symbolique de l'evolution et ne peut qu'être un prolongement prospectif.
Cette position ne peut être réduite à une simple methode de verification de biologie théorique de l'origine de la vie ou de l'évolution.

STRATAGEME 1

Zoosystémique
- La vie artifielle est une machination qui produit des zoosystèmes de grande diversité et des zoosystemiciens.
- La tendance pernicieuse des zoosystèmes est à la prolifération, à l'envahissement, à la colonisation.
- La vie artificielle par zoosystèmes interposés, s'implante allégrement dans une nature donnée et installe au coeur de la biomasse des niches techno-ecologiques, des soupes technoprébiotiques, des essaims de robots communiquant par signaux technozoosemiotiques.
- Ce phènomène est une émergence HYPOZOOLOGIQUE, qui sous forme d'automates cellulaires, d'algorithmes génétiques, de L-systemes, de modelisations d'intelligence collective, de robots en interaction avec un milieu fluctuant ou hostile, surgit du dessous d'une zoologie objective pour l'envahir voir la chimeriser à travers de multiples ecrans.
- Un peuplement s'insinue dans les univers mentaux et comportementaux, colonise et affirme, sans scrupules, sa presence et sa specificité à travers toute sorte de canaux et toute forme de reseaux.
- Le zoosystème est le symptome d'une nouvelle gestuelle d'ANIMALEUR qui prefigure uns seconde révolution darwinienne.

STRATAGEME 2

Gestes modélisateurs.
- La vie artificielle comme pour toute machination est le resultat de manipulations.

Les gestes modélisateurs en sont les operateurs.
- Il faut entendre par gestes modélisateurs du vivant l'ensemble des activités humaines qui ont concouru et concourent à produire sous diverses formes des substituts du vivant.
- Des techniques les plus rudimentaires aux

mentale Komplexität ihres Untersuchungsobjekts, die fluktuierende Verschiedenheit der Begriffe und die Plastizität der verwendeten Methoden führen zu einem viel weiteren Untersuchungsfeld.
- Sie sind das Produkt vielschichtiger, in die Domänen des Wissens und des menschlichen Ausdrucks eingeschriebener wissenstheoretischer Ebenen, die künstlerische Herstellungspraktiken, ästhetische, ethische und soziale Aspekte umfassen.
- Mehr noch, sie sind die bis heute relevanteste Hervorbringung des Projekts der Repräsentation und des Verstehens des Lebens, das die westliche Kultur, quer durch alle Disziplinen, seit grauer Vorzeit quält.
- Die Rückkehr zu jedweder „Machinationsmaschinerie" des künstlichen Lebens läuft Gefahr, es auf ein triviales Instrument der Simulation zu reduzieren.
- Die von Chris Langton selbst hervorgehobene Forschungsdimension, – er spricht vom Übergang von einem Leben „wie es ist, zu einem Leben, wie es sein könnte" –, wäre bewußt ausgeschlossen.
- Ein wissenschaftstheoretischer Fehler auf dem ontogenetischen Gebiet des künstlichen Lebens wäre schwerwiegend.

Das künstliche Leben entwickelt sich bis an die äußerste Grenze des symbolischen Evolutionsgedankens und kann nur eine vorausschauende Fortsetzung sein.
Diese Position kann nicht auf eine simple Verifikationsmethode der theoretischen Biologie vom Ursprung des Lebens oder der Evolution reduziert werden.

STRATAGEM 1

Zoosystemisches
- Das künstliche Leben ist eine Machination, die sehr verschiedene Zoosysteme und Zoosystemiker hervorbringt.
- Die perniziöse Neigung der Zoosysteme dient der raschen Vermehrung, dem Überhandnehmen, der Kolonisation.
- Das künstliche Leben aus zwischenliegenden Zoosystemen nistet sich lebhaft in eine gegebene natürliche Umwelt ein und errichtet inmitten der Biomasse techno-ökologische Nischen, technopräbiotische Suppen und Scharen von Robotern, die über techno-zoosemiotische Signale kommunizieren.
- Dieses Phänomen ist ein HYPOZOOLOGISCHES Auftauchen, welches in Form von Zellulärautomaten, genetischen Algorithmen, L-Systemen, Modellbildungen, kol-

lektiver Intelligenz, Robotern, die mit einem unbeständigen oder feindseligen Milieu interagieren, von der Unterseite einer objektiven Zoologie her zum Vorschein kommt, um sich seiner zu bemächtigen und über multiple Bildschirme zu verfolgen, wie es zur Schimäre wird.
- Eine Population dringt in die Geistes- und Verhaltenswelt allmählich ein, kolonisiert sie und behauptet ohne Gewissensbisse ihre Präsenz und Besonderheit quer über alle Arten von Kanälen und Netzwerksformen.
- Das Zoosystem ist Symptom einer neuen kleinen Heldentat des ANIMALEURS, was eine zweite darwinistische Revolution erahnen läßt.

STRATAGEM 2

Modellierende Eingriffe
- Das künstliche Leben ist, wie jede Machination, Resultat von Manipulationen. Die modellierenden Eingriffe sind deshalb die Operatoren.
- Unter modellierenden Eingriffen des Lebendigen sind alle menschlichen Aktivitäten zu verstehen, die dazu beigetragen haben und beitragen, in verschiedener Form Substitute des Lebendigen zu produzieren.
- Von den rudimentärsten Techniken zu den fortgeschrittensten Technologien, von rein instinktiven Handlungen zu genauest ausgearbeiteten und formalisierten Konstruktionen, ist diese als Massenproduktion zu qualifizierende Produktion, von konventionellen Klassifikationen unbelastet und hinterläßt dem künstlichen Leben ein besonders reiches und innovatives Erbe.
- Diese Hinterlassenschaft beinhaltet auch eine Überfülle an innovativer Energie, – umso erregender, als jedes Mal an Stelle des Lebendigen nur die merkwürdige Amputation einer äußeren Hülle, d.h. der Artefakte, Modelle, der Simulation oder des Kunstwerks übrig bleibt.
- Vier modellierende Eingriffe des Lebendigen können als grundlegende Operatoren der Machination betrachtet werden:
  das Verflachen des Lebendigen
  das Zunehmen des Lebendigen
  das Bewegen des Lebendigen
  das Transformieren des Lebendigen
- In Form von Beispielen berücksichtigt werden hier nur die beiden letzteren Gesten, einerseits basierend auf dem Bewegen des Lebendigen, bei dem die Autonomie der Verhaltensweisen, des Lernens, der Anpassung der sensomotorischen Handlungen und der interaktiven Kogni-

technologies les plus avancées, des activités les plus instinctives aux constructions les plus élaborées et les plus formalisées, cette production que l'on peut qualifier de massive ne s'encombre pas de classification conventionnelles et offre en heritage particulierement foisonnant et inventif à la vie artificielle.
- Dans cet heritage se trouve aussi une debauche d'energie ingenieuse et d'autant plus emouvante qu'à chaque fois en lieu et place d'un vivant, ne subsiste que la curieuse amputation d'une depouille, c'est à dire d'artefacts, de modèles, de simulation ou d'oeuvre d'art
- Quatre gestes modelisateurs du vivant peuvent être considérés, comme les opérateurs de base de la machination:
  – La mise à plat du vivant
  – La mise en volume du vivant
  – La mise en mouvement du vivant
  – La mise en transformation du vivant
- Seul les deux derniers gestes basés sur la mise en mouvement visant l'autonomie des comportements, de l'apprentissage, l'adaptation les activités sensorimotrices et les systemes cognitifs interactifs d'une part et la mise en transformation des modèles du vivant par diverses interventions dans les processus metaboliques ou les phases adaptatives d'évolution, seront ici pris en consideration par un exemple.
- Si cette activité modélisatrice que l'homme a deployé, jusqu'à ce jour, pour saisir, maitriser et simuler le vivant n'etait qu'une ébauche préparatoire d'une tendance irrepressible, qui vise une entreprise plus vaste et plus definitive: «créer du vivant».
- Si l'accés au patrimoine génétique et la mise au point d'un vivant technologique levaient peu à peu certains interdits ethiques et fabricatoires, la force d'impact d'un tel dessein risquerait de renvoyer certains des postulats qui sont à la base de nos civilisations, au rang de strates archéologiques caduques.
- Le cas de la représentation du vivant par la sculpture, considerée comme une constante dans toute forme de societé, eclaire bien ces propos.
- Que devient, par exemple, le geste du sculpteur qui en taillant en polissant, gravant et moulant une matiere inerte, rêve du vivant?
- Ne cede-t-il pas la place à un autre geste qui greffe, selectionne, congèle, implante, clône et chimérise?
- Ne s'efface-t-il pas devant un autre geste qui simule, programme, construit des robots, un geste qui élabore des programes technomorphogenetiques et les imprime dans le processus évolutif d'une «sculpture vivante»?
- Dans ce cas, les clôneurs, les bio-informaticiens, les roboticiens ne sont-ils pas les «vrais sculpteurs», les ultimes réalisateurs d'un projet qui a cheminé pendant de longs siecles par les voies de l'art, de la science et de la technologie?

STRATAGEME 3

De l'artistique

- La machination de la vie artificielle travaille les pratiques artistiques comme un agent mutagène.
- Les productions actuelles de la vie artificielle agissent à la fois comme des opérateurs d'une mutation ésthétique en cours et comme les révélateurs des phases de son evolution.
- La vie artificielle en liant des aspects d'experimentations artistiques aux aspects scientifiques, joue-elle un rôle métaphorique d'adaptation sensorielle, fabricatoire, mentale, comportementale et inventive pour l'homme?
- Joue-t-elle d'une façon suffisement perfide le rôle d'une sonde intelligente et animalisée, installée aux limites de viabilité de l'espèce humaine?
- Peut-on deduire que, par la création de mondes virtuels animalisés, de modelisations d'espaces et d'objets intelligents, d'experiences sensibles et cognitives par espaces interactifs interposés, les machinations numériques de la vie artificielle entendent eriger un nouveau cheval de Troie par activités artistiques interposees.
- Certainement si l'on considéré l'art comme moyen de connaissance sinueux, dans la construction des représentations ou de l'interpretation du donné.
- Si l'on considéré l'entreprise artistique comme la construction oblique d'un projet s'edifiant autour du pourquoi et du comment de la construction des représentations symboliques à travers les quelles s'edifient les artefacts.
- Certainement si l'on considéré l'art comme un instrument d'adaptation inventive, comme une méthode elaborée par le vivant pour preserver sa viabilité physique et imaginaire en explorant le milieu artificiel qu'il crée lui-même.
- Surement si l'on considéré les activités artistiques comme des lieux d'investigation et d'experimentation de la perception, des emotions, de la mèmoire, de la formation des concepts, du temps, de l'espace, du mouvement, des trajectoires, des processus et de la relation homme/animal/machine
- Surement si ces activités demontrent, comme c'est le cas, dans l'utilisation specifiques des technologies par des images de synthèse, par l'exploration des realités virtuelles et la mise en place de vastes reseaux d'echange, leurs capacités à multiplier des univers fictionels tangeants et à aborder des contrées deviantes.
- Surement si l'on considéré que la vie artificielle est un des lieux privilègiés ou s'opère la transformation des systèmes de representation.
- Le passage du modèle de correspondance qui consiste à placer un modèle entre le sujet et le phenomène, laisse la place à une modélisation systèmique dans la quelle le sujet integré, devient un éléments pervers du système.

tivsysteme ins Auge gefaßt wird und andererseits das Transformieren der Modelle des Lebendigen durch verschiedene Eingriffe in Stoffwechselprozesse oder in Anpassungsphasen der Evolution.

Wie, wenn nun diese gestalterische Aktivität, die der Mensch bis zum heutigen Tage aufgewendet hat, um das Lebendige zu begreifen, zu beherrschen und nachzuahmen, nur die Vorarbeit für eine unaufhaltsame Entwicklung wäre, die ein viel weitreichenderes und endgültigeres Vorhaben ins Auge faßt, nämlich: „Das Lebendige erschaffen"?

- Wenn der Zugang zum genetischen Erbe und die Entwicklung eines technologischen Lebewesens allmählich gewisse ethische und herstellungsbedingte Schranken zu Fall bringen würde, so würde der gewaltige Effekt eines solchen Vorhabens die Gefahr mit sich bringen, daß einige Grundpfeiler unserer Zivilisation auf den Rang vergänglicher archäologischer Ablagerungen verwiesen würden.
- Der Fall der Darstellung des Lebendigen durch die Skulptur, die in allen Gesellschaftsformen als eine Konstante angesehen wird, erhellt die Zusammenhänge sehr gut.
- Was wird zum Beispiel aus dem Tun des Bildhauers, der vom Lebendigen träumt, indem er eine reglose Materie behaut, poliert, meißelt und formt?
- Überläßt er das Feld nicht einer anderen Aktivität, die veredelt, aussondert, gerinnen läßt, klont und Schimären erzeugt?

Tritt er nicht zurück hinter eine andere Form des Eingreifens, eine die simuliert, programmiert und Roboter konstruiert, eine Aktivität, die techno-morphologische Programme erarbeitet und diese in den evolutiven Prozeß einer „lebenden Skulptur" einprägt?

- Sind die „wahren Bildhauer" in diesem Fall nicht die Kloner, die Bioinformatiker, die Roboterkonstrukteure, diejenigen, die letztlich ein Projekt realisieren, welches jahrhundertelang über die Pfade der Kunst, der Wissenschaft und der Technologie geführt hat?

STRATAGEM 3

Vom Künstlerischen

Die Machination des künstlichen Lebens beeinflußt die künstlerische Praktiken wie ein mutagenes Medium.

- Die gegenwärtigen Produktionen des künstlichen Lebens agieren als Operatoren einer gerade stattfindenden ästhetischen Mutation und gleichzeitig enthüllen sie deren Evolutionsphasen.

- Spielt das künstliche Leben, als Bindeglied zwischen Aspekten künstlerischer Experimente und wissenschaftlichen Ansichten, für den Menschen eine metaphorische Rolle im Hinblick auf die sensorielle, fabrikatorische, mentale, verhaltensrelevante und innovative Anpassung?
- Spielt es auf hinlänglich perfide Weise die Rolle einer intelligenten und animalisierten Sonde, die an den Grenzen der Lebensfähigkeit der menschlichen Spezies installiert ist?
- Kann man folgern, daß es den numerischen Machinationen des künstlichen Lebens über künstlerische Vermittlungsaktivitäten gelingt, ein neues Trojanisches Pferd zu errichten, nämlich durch die Schaffung von virtuellen animalisierten Welten, von Raummodellierungen und intelligenten Objekten, von – über interaktive Vermittlungsräume – sinnlich wahrnehmbaren und kognitiven Erfahrungen?
- Gewiß, wenn man die Kunst bei der Konstruktion der Darstellungen oder der Interpretation des Gegebenen als gewundenen Erkenntnisweg betrachtet.
- Wenn man das künstlerische Unternehmen als schräge Konstruktion eines Projekts betrachtet, welches rund um das Warum und das Wie der Konstruktion der symbolischen Darstellungen errichtet ist, auf denen sich wiederum die Artefakte erheben.
- Gewiß, wenn man die Kunst als innovatives Anpassungsinstrument betrachtet, als eine Methode, die vom Menschen entwickelt wurde, um seine physische und imaginäre Lebensfähigkeit durch Erforschung der selbst geschaffenen künstlichen Umwelt zu erhalten.
- Sicher, wenn man die künstlerischen Aktivitäten als Forschungs- und des Experimentierfelder der Wahrnehmung, der Emotionen, des Gedächtnisses, der Begriffsbildung, der Zeit, des Raumes, der Bewegung, der Flugbahnen und der Beziehung Mensch/Tier/Maschine ... betrachtet.
- Sicher, wenn diese Aktivitäten geeignet sind, die fiktionalen, sich berührenden Universen zu vervielfachen und sich den abweichenden Gebieten zuzuwenden, wie dies bei der spezifischen Nutzung der Technologien durch Synthesebilder, durch die Erforschung virtueller Realitäten und die Realisierung weitreichender Austauschnetze der Fall ist.
- Sicher, wenn man bedenkt, daß das künstliche Leben einer jener privilegierten Orte ist, an dem sich die Transformation der Repräsentationssysteme vollzieht.
- Der Wechsel des Korrespondenzmodells, welches darin besteht, zwischen dem Gegenstand und dem Phänomen

STRATAGEME 4

Autonomie et Esthétique du Renfloué

- Les machinations ourdies par la vie artificielle contribuent fortement à l'elaboration d'une esthétique de l'AUTONOMIE en mettant en evidence par délégation programatique les emergences significatives des systèmes artificiels.
- Cette ésthétique est le mode d'expression des interactions des differents constituants du dispositif, des traitements et des comportements qui s'y effectuent, des informations qui y circulent, des apprentissages, des adaptions et des intéractions avec le milieu qui s'y opèrent.
- C'est une ésthétique qui a pour symptomatique des etats successifs concretisés par des comportements intentionnels, des traces, des trajectoires, des transformations morphogénétiques.
- C'est une ésthétique qui temoigne des capacités d'un système à exprimer des informations nouvelles qui n'etaient pas reperable dans l'environnement.
- C'est une ésthétique de la resurgence de tâches algorithmiques hierarchisées.
- C'est une ésthétique du renfloué, une emersion d'un révélé enfoui.
- C'est une ésthétique semaphorique de l'affichage des determinants du vivant pour le vivant.
- Qui se trouve dans l'obligation de developper un dialogue rusé de vivant avec du vivant modelisé, à travers un langage numerique, afin d'authentifier les répères affichés et de les classer dans une des catégories du vivant elargie à l'artificiel.

Toute vivant doit renflouer son vivant pour reconnaitre du vivant dans toute forme de modelisation d'organismes artificiels.
Il s'artificialise lui aussi par la meme.

- Cette artificialisation est un élément symptomatique de l'ésthétique du renfloué. Car dans cette interactivité se developpent non pas des reponses instrumentalisées, mais des perspectives fantasmatiques qui proposent une virtualité latente de chimerisations.
- Une des machinations de l'ésthétique du renfloué reside dans la manière dont le geste de chimerisation derive.
- Il passe d'un ajustement «rétinien et artistique» à une intégration fonctionnelle.
- Ce qui n'etait qu'assemblage imaginaire, hasardeux ou decoratif, construction technique et industrielle boulonnée, devient une liaison techno-organique, une «hypoconnexion» exprimant un continuum du dessous de l'assemblage, une sousdure, une circulation d'information qui structure l'hétérogene, qui invente les arrimages des comportements cognitifs.
- A l'oppose des «prothèses» artificielles, ce sont des «endothèses» qui s'erigent en «epithèse».
- L'assembleur n'agit plus mecanistiquement du dehors du phénomème. Il introduit dans le processus une machination entre deux antagonismes, pour faire apparaitre un protagonisme.

Oben: Labis Polupons
Unten: Phytogudine

ein Modell anzubringen, schafft Platz für eine systemische Modellierung , in der der integrierte Gegenstand zu einem perversen Element des Systems wird.

STRATAGEM 4

Autonomie und Ästhetik des Gestärkten

- Die vom künstlichen Leben angezettelten Machinationen tragen, indem sie die bedeutsamen Hervorbringungen des künstlichen Systems in programmatischem Auftrag hervorheben, viel zur Ausarbeitung einer Ästhetik der AUTONOMIE bei.
- Diese Ästhetik ist Ausdrucksform der Interaktionen der verschiedenen Bestandteile der Apparatur, der Behandlungen und der dort sich vollziehenden Verhaltensformen, der dort sich in Umlauf befindlichen Informationen, der Lern-, der Anpassungsvorgänge und der dort erfolgenden Milieuinteraktionen.
- Das ist eine Ästhetik, deren Symptome sukzessive Zustände sind, – zu veranschaulichen durch bewußte Verhaltensweisen, Spuren, Flugbahnen, morphogenetische Transformationen.
- Das ist eine Ästhetik, die von der Fähigkeit eines Systems zeugt, neue, in der Umwelt nicht erkennbare Informationen auszudrücken.
- Das ist eine semaphorische Ästhetik, die die Determinanten des Lebendigen für das Lebendige affichiert.
- Die sich verpflichtet fühlt, über eine numerische Sprache einen trickreichen Dialog des Lebendigen mit dem gestalteten Lebendigen zu entwickeln, um die affichierten Zeichen zu beglaubigen und in einer der zum Künstlichen hin erweiterten Kategorien des Lebendigen zu klassifizieren.

JEDES LEBEWESEN MUSS SEIN LEBENDIGES STÄRKEN, UM ES IN JEDER GESTALTUNGSFORM DER KÜNSTLICHEN ORGANISMEN WIEDERZUERKENNEN. ES VERKÜNSTLICHT SICH EBENFALLS GERADE DADURCH.

- Diese Verkünstlichung ist ein symptomatisches Element der Ästhetik des Stärkens. Denn in dieser Interaktivität entstehen keine instrumentalisierten Antworten, sondern fantasmatische Perspektiven, die eine latente Virtualität der Entstehung von Schimären nahelegen.
- Eine der Machinationen der Ästhetik des Stärkens wohnt in der Art, in der sich die Handlung der Trugbildentstehung herleitet, inne.

- On passe ainsi d'un imaginaire du collage additif, d'assemblage à un imaginaire procédural de synthèse morphogénétique, programatique et numerique en bonne voie d'intelligence.

STRATAGEME 5

Autotomie et Amputat

- La machination autonomique de la vie artificielle fait apparaitre par delegation programatique, une autre forme d'ésthétique, celle de l'autotomie ou de l'amputation.
- Elle se construit autour d'une question centrale.
- Une memoire biologique est interrogée technologiquement par une mêmoire culturelle.
- A travers une modélisation artificielle une espèce vivante se donnerait les instruments pour tester ses limites de viabilité en devenant un AMPUTAT qui se prive delibérement et stratégiquement de certaines de ses proprietés physiques ou mentales.
- Ne peut-on pas penser que cet imaginaire machinant, ancré au plus profond d'un vertige fondamental sur la vie, questionnant le temps, les processus biologiques et comportementaux, l'emergence truitée de la pensée, ne soit un moment tenté par un projet d'errance, une strategie de l'exode, une esthetique du renfloué, qui proposerait, à travers les principes minimum d'une viabilité physique, mental et collective, une vertigineuse amputation pour l'exploration fabulée du milieu artificiel qu'il edifie?
- Ne peut-on pas estimer que cette hantise de l'absence ou du retrait definitif de l'homme, ne soit poussée à elaborer, par les voies de l'autonomie et de l'autotomie une manifestation grandiose finale:

Une scénographie de la vie artificielle sans spectateurs ni machinistes.

PARUTIONS

– L. Bec «Elements de chromozoosemiotique» revue: La Couleur, Centre Francais de la couleur 80 Paris.
– L. Bec «Elements d'hygrozoosemiotique» ed Sgraphite Marseille 80.
– XVI BIENAL Sao Paulo «les Sulfanogrades» V. Flusser 81.
– L. Bec «Modelisation upokrinomenologique en substrat festivalier» Le Vivant et l'Artificiel, Avignon, Sgraphite ed 84.
– L. Bec Texte general de conception et presentation de la manifestation le vivant et l'artificiel catalogue: ed Sgraphite, Avignon 84.
– L. Bec «Art plastique et sciences du vivant» acte du colloque Sens de la Science Conseil de l'Europe, Strasbourg 86.
– Vilem Flusser/Louis Bec, «Vampyroteuthis infernalis» Immatrix editeur Andreas Muller-Pohle et Volker Rapsch Gottingen 88.
– L. Bec, Kunstforum Novembre 88 «L. Bec Zoosystemiker» 20 pages 18 reproduction couleurs.

– L. Bec «Sciences du vivant et arts plastiques» revue Mars 88 Marseille.
– L. Bec «Un beau chasse croise» acte du colloque Imaginaire de la chasse, ed Atelier CRCFrance avril 88.
– L. Bec «Le graphethereutte Paranome ou etude d'un Upokrinomene braconnant en milieu biomosyntaxique» texte et dessin revue Milieu: Eloge du braconnage, Le Creusot 88.
– Revue kultuRRevolution image/computer mai 88 Bochum, Essen.
– Revue CAOS, Sao Paulo 89 image/computer (Casa Da Cor).
– L. Bec, «Chimerique teratologie permuteert deja-vues» From Prothesis to endothesis. Texte et Image/computer. Mediamatic (Amsterdam 89).
– L. Bec texte de presentation du colloque «Creation artistique/decouverte scientifique» Marseille Verba Volant 89.
– L. Bec, «Cephalopodiquement votre» dans Uberflusser Bollmann editeur Dusseldorf 90.
– L. Bec, image/computer EXPRESS(Paris) Septembre 90:«Les nouvelles creatures de la science» Gilbert Charles.
– L. Bec «Elements d'epistemologie fabulatoire», image/computer, colloque Artificial Life II, Institut de Santa Fe (USA) ed C Langton 90.
– L. Bec, «A Tatons» Elements d'Upokrinomenologie. 91 Digitaler Schein Aesthetic der electronischen Medien ed suhrkamp Francfort.
– L. Bec, «Elements d'upokrinomenologie: Contributions a l'etude des upokrasis: L'enantiokrasiologie» alliage (edition de culture scientifique dirigee par J.M. Levy-Leblond, Nice 91).
– L. Bec, image/computer Omni magazine (New York) mars 91: dans «MechAnimals» de Tom Dworetzky.
– L. Bec, image/computer Natur (Munich) juin 91 «Fast wie im richtigen leben» Mathias Brockers et Michael Odenwald.
– L. Bec, image/computer: le Phycodiapheirina Mellontalhalatta couverture Biofutur, revue de Biotechnologie 91 ed Elsevier Paris.
– L. Bec, image/computer:«Le Pselaphane Pteruge» agenda Cite des arts et des sciences, La Villette Paris 91.
– L. Bec, image/computer couverture, «From animals to animats» colloque Simulation of adaptative behavior, Mit press Boston USA 91.
– L. Bec, image/computer couverture «Toward a pratice of autonomous systems» first European conference on Artificial Life Paris, Mit press Boston USA 92.
– L. Bec «Jeden Samstag » à la memoire de V. Flusser, Kunstforum Munich 92.
– L. Bec «Skenabiotopie» etude des comportements modelises et pamphletaires d'organismes artificiels.
Arts de la scene/scene de l'art Colloque Festival d'Avignon edition Evidant Fevrier 92.
– L. Bec, image/computer ARCH+ mars 92 BERLIN
– L. Bec, image/computer european photography V. Flusser issue Gottingen 92.
– L. Bec «Elements de zoosystemique» Actes Artificial Life Imagina Monaco
– L. Bec Elements d'Hypozoologie, Revue Virtuelle Centre G. Pompidou mars 93.
En cours d'edition 93:

- Sie geht von einer „die Netzhaut betreffenden und künstlerischen" Anpassung zu einer funktionellen Integration.
- Was nur imaginäre Assemblage war, gewagt oder dekorativ, technische Konstruktion und industriell verbolzt, wird eine techno-organische Verbindung, eine „Hypoverknüpfung", die ein Kontinuum von der Unterseite der Assemblage her ausdrückt, ein Informationskreislauf, der das Heterogene strukturiert, der die Koppelung des kognitiven Verhaltens erfindet.
- Im Gegensatz zu den künstlichen „Prothesen" stehen die „Endothesen", die sich zur „Epithese" erheben.
- Der Monteur verfährt nicht mehr mechanistisch, von der Außenseite des Phänomens her. Er führt eine Machination zwischen zwei Antagonismen in das Verfahren ein, um einen Protagonismus hervorzurufen.
- Auf diese Weise gelangt man intellektuell nachvollziehbar von einem Imaginären der additiven Collage, von einer Assemblage, zu einem prozeduralen Imaginären der morphogenetischen, programmatischen und numerischen Synthese.

STRATAGEM 5

Autotomie und Amputat

- Die automatische Machination des künstlichen Lebens bringt – vermittelt über einen programmatischen Auftrag – eine andere Form der Ästhetik hervor, jene der Autotomie oder der Amputation.
- Sie entsteht rund um eine zentrale Frage.
- Ein biologischer Speicher wird durch einen kulturellen Speicher technologisch abgefragt.
- Eine lebende Spezies würde sich mittels künstlicher Modellierung die Instrumente verschaffen und die Grenzen ihrer Lebensfähigkeit prüfen, indem sie zum AMPUTAT wird, welches absichtlich und strategisch gewissen physischen oder mentalen Eigentümern entsagt.
- Wäre nicht denkbar, daß dieses angezettelte Imaginäre, – verankert in der tiefsten Tiefe eines fundamentalen Schwindelgefühls in bezug auf das Leben, welches die Zeit, die biologischen und Verhaltensprozesse, das Auftauchen des Gedankenflickwerks in Frage stellt –, ein verlockender Moment wäre für ein Projekt der Heimatlosigkeit, eine Strategie des Exodus, eine Ästhetik des Wiederflottmachens, die – über die Minimalprinzipien der physischen, mentalen und kollektiven Lebensfähigkeit eine schwindelerregende Amputation für die fabulierte Erforschung des von ihm errichteten Milieus nahelegt.

- Ist es nicht abschätzbar, daß diese Angst vor der Abwesenheit oder dem definitiven Rückzug des Menschen über den Weg der Autonomie und der Autotomie, Anstoß für eine grandiose Schlußveranstaltung wäre:
  Eine Szenografie des künstlichen Lebens ohne Zuschauer und Bedienungsleute.

– L. Bec «Esthetique du renfloue», Suhrkamp editeur Francfort. (F. Rotzer)
– L. Bec «Cephalopode et Technobiome», Revue Autrement Paris.
– L. Bec «Art/Cognition», Texte d'introduction au catalogue de la manifestation d'AIX en Provence Images en Manoeuvre Marseille.
– L. Bec La vie artificielle comme machination, Eikon International Zeitschrift für Photographie et Medienkunst. Wien Autriche
– Jorg Albrecht et L. Bec: Leben der anderen Art, Zeitmagazin Hambourg Allemagne Mars 93

KÜNSTLICHE INTELLIGENZ UND INTERAKTIVE KUNST

JOSEPH BATES

ARTIFICIAL INTELLIGENCE AND INTERACTIVE ART
JOSEPH BATES

Interactive art and entertainment are increasingly being explored byresearchers, artists, and product developers. An ideal system would be deeply interactive, yet provide the richness and emotional impact of art and entertainment expressed through traditional media. This requires the computing system to make decisions on its own, during interaction, that are normally made with great care by artists. In turn, this means that some of the artist's knowledge, sensibilities, and capabilities must be transferred into the interactive system, so that it can serve as the artist's emissary during interaction. The Oz Project at Carnegie Mellon is exploring one variation of this theme. We want to provide users with the experience of living in dramatic simulated worlds that include rich and believable characters. Our research falls into three areas, which we believe are central to this goal:

- the construction of broadly capable, though perhaps shallow, autonomous agents that integrate elements of perception, cognition, emotion, action, and language,
- the construction of a computational theory of interactive drama, to gently shape the user's overall experience, and
- the development of computational methods for varying the presentation style of the experience, by analogy with film technique and writing style.

One product of our work is an interactive animated world containing several autonomous creatures. These "Woggles" blend goal-directed behavior, reactivity, emotion, perception, and smooth multi-channel motor control in a single realtime architecture for mind. They were first shown at the AAAI-92 Artificial Intelligence Based Arts Exhibition.

Interaktive Kunst und Unterhaltung werden von Forschern, Künstlern und Produktentwicklern immer mehr untersucht. Eine ideales System wäre ausgesprochen interaktiv, würde jedoch auch über den Reichtum und den emotionalen Anstoß einer in traditionellen Medien ausgedrückten Kunst verfügen. Dies verlangt vom Computersystem die Fähigkeit, während der Interaktion eigene Entscheidungen zu treffen, die üblicherweise vom Künstler sehr sorgfältig vorbereitet werden. Umgekehrt heißt das, daß Wissen, Sensibilität und Fähigkeit des Künstlers teilweise in das interaktive System übertragen werden muß, sodaß dieses während der Interaktion stellvertretend für den Künstler agieren kann.

Das OZ Projekt in Carnegie Mellon untersucht eine Variante dieses Themas. Wir wollen den Benutzern die Erfahrung vermitteln, in dramatischen Simulationswelten mit gehaltvollen und glaubwürdigen Charakteren zu leben. Unsere Forschungen beziehen sich auf drei Bereiche, die, wie wir glauben, für diese Zielsetzung zentral sind:

- die Konstruktion von umfassend tauglichen – wenn auch vielleicht oberflächlichen – autonomen Vermittlungsinstanzen, die Elemente der Wahrnehmung, des Wissens, der Emotion, der Aktion und der Sprache integrieren,
- die Konstruktion einer rechnerischen Theorie des interaktiven Dramas um die Erfahrungen, die der Benutzer insgesamt macht, sanft zu beeinflussen,
- die Entwicklung von Computermethoden zur Veränderung des Stils, in dem die Erfahrungen dargestellt werden, – in Analogie zur Filmtechnik und zum Schreibstil.

Ein Produkt unserer Arbeit besteht in einer interaktiven, animierten Welt mit mehreren autonomen Geschöpfen. Diese „Woggles“ mischen zielgerichtetes Verhalten, Reaktivität, Emotion, Wahrnehmung und fließende Mehrkanal-Motorsteuerung in einer einzelnen Echtzeitarchitektur des Bewußtseins. Sie wurden erstmals im Rahmen der AAAI 92 – Artificial Intelligence Based Arts Exhibition gezeigt.

PHYSIKALISCHES KÜNSTLICHES LEBEN

RODNEY A. BROOKS

PHYSICAL ARTIFICIAL LIFE
RODNEY A. BROOKS

At the MIT Artificial Intelligence Laboratory we have been building prototype artificial creatures, electromechanical machines which are able to operate autonomously in unstructured domains. The goal is to eventually build machines that can survive for months at a time in natural and man-made environments performing useful or pleasing tasks without human interference.

Our artificial creatures have ranged in size from 50 kilograms down to 50 grams, although we have also built motors as small as 200 micrometers in diameter in preparation for building artificial creatures in the millimeter size range.

A key advance was the development of behaviour-based methods for building the intelligence of these creatures. Inspired by evolution we incrementally build parallel layers of intelligence, each linking sensors to actuators. The result is a network of simple computational elements. The layers directly implement action patterns, and traditionally studied aspects such as perception, planning, and reasoning, are produced as an emergent property of the networks. We have built insect-like six legged robots which can walk over rough terrain, visually based rotos which can navigate indoors giving crude tours of our laboratory to visitors, vacuum cleaning robots, a soda-can collecting robot, and a large collection of identical robots programmed in ways similiar to insects that live in colonies.

The results are robots which have life-like attributes and point the way for future generations of artificial creatures.

Im Artificial Intelligence Labor am MIT haben wir Prototypen künstlicher Kreaturen – elektromechanische Maschinen, die fähig sind in unstrukturierten Domänen autonom zu funktionieren, gebaut. Das Ziel ist, einmal Maschinen zu bauen, die über einige Monate hindurch in natürlichen und in vom Menschen geschaffenen (künstlichen) Umwelten überleben und dabei ohne menschliche Einmischung nützliche oder wohltuende Aufgaben ausführen können.

Unsere künstlichen Kreaturen bewegen sich in der Größe zwischen 50 kg bis hinunter zu 50 g, obwohl wir, in der Vorbereitung zum Bau von Kreaturen im Millimeterbereich, auch schon Motoren gebaut haben, die im Durchmesser nur 200 Mikrometer klein waren.

Der wichtigste Fortschritt war die Entwicklung von auf Verhalten basierenden Methoden für den Bau der Intelligenz dieser Kreaturen. Von der Evolution inspiriert, bauten wir zunehmend parallele Schichten von Intelligenz, von denen jede die Sensoren und Agierenden verband. Das Resultat ist ein asynchrones Netzwerk einfacher rechnerischer Elemente. Die Schichten setzen direkt Handlungsmuster in Kraft und üblicherweise untersuchte Aspekte, wie zum Beispiel das Sehen, das Planen und das logische Denken werden als entstehende Eigenschaft der Netzwerke erzeugt.

Wir haben einen insektenähnlichen sechsbeinigen Roboter gebaut, der über unebenes Terrain gehen kann, weiters visuell basierte Roboter, die sich im Haus zurechtfinden und unseren Laborbesuchern grobe Besichtigungstours geben können, staubsaugende Roboter, einen Roboter, der Getränkedosen einsammelt, und eine große Sammlung identischer Roboter, die ähnlich programmiert sind wie Insekten, die in Kolonien leben.

Die Resultate sind Roboter, die lebensähnliche Eigenschaften haben und den Weg für zukünftige Generationen künstlicher Kreaturen weisen.

KÜNSTLICHE KREATUREN BAUEN

PATTIE MAES

Eines der Probleme, mit denen sich die Artificial Life Gemeinde befaßt, ist die Gestaltung und Konstruktion künstlicher Tiere, sogenannter „Animaten". Die Forschung verfolgt dabei ein doppeltes Ziel. Das wissenschaftliche Ziel ist ein besseres Verständnis des Verhaltens und der Intelligenz von Tieren. Das eher praktische Ziel besteht darin, (von der Biologie inspirierte) Werkzeuge zu entwickeln sowie Techniken zur Konstruktion autonom anpassungsfähiger „Akteure", die sich in einer komplexen Umwelt zurechtfinden.

Der Vortrag diskutiert den Stand der Kunst in der Animatenforschung und präsentiert eine Vielzahl konkreter Beispiele. Die Beispiele stammen aus den Bereichen der Mensch-Computer-Interaktion, Cornputeranimation, Virtuelle Realität und Unterhaltung.

Der Vortrag wird eine kürzlich von mir, Professor Sandy Pentland und unseren Studenten errichtete interaktive Installation namens „Alive" (für Artificial Life Interactive Video Environment) eingehender diskutieren. Erstmals vorgestellt wird diese Installation bei der. Siggraph-93-Konferenz in Anaheim, Kalifornien. Sie vereinigt in sich die neuesten technologischen Errungenschaften der Vision-Based-Gesture Recognition, des Physically-Based Modelling und des künstlichen Lebens. Das ALIVE-System ermöglicht dem Benutzer ein physisch basierendes Computergraphik-Environment zu erfahren und mit den künstlichen Tieren, die diese Welt bewohnen, unter Verwendung einfacher und natürlicher Gesten zu interagieren.

Im speziellen wird Chromakeying-Technologie eingesetzt, um das Bild des Benutzers über eine interaktive Echtzeit-Computeranimation zu legen. Das zusammengesetzte Bild wird auf einem großen Bildschirm (10' mal 10'), der zum Benutzer schaut, gezeigt. Daraus resultiert ein Schauen in einen „magischen Spiegel". Der Benutzer kann durch natürliche Gesten, die von einem bildgestützen Mustererkennungssystem übersetzt werden, mit den animierten Wesen im Spiegel interagieren und kommunizieren und so ihr Verhalten beeinflussen.

Die Konstruktion der animierten Wesen des ALIVE-Systems erfolgte mit Hilfe eines Toolkit und einer Reihe von Algo-

BUILDING ARTIFICIAL CREATURES
PATTIE MAES

One of the problems the Artificial Life community is concerned with is the modeling and building of artificial animals or socalled "Animats". The goals of this research are twofold. The scientific goal is to better understand animal behavior and animal intelligence. The more practical goal is to develop tools and techniques (inspired by biology) for building autonomous adaptive "agents" that behave in complex environments.

The talk discusses the state of the art in Animat research and presents a lot of concrete examples. The examples stem from the domains of human-computer interaction, computer animation, virtual reality and entertainment. Other speakers will discuss applications in the area of robotics).

The talk will discuss in more detail an interactive installation called "Alive" (which stands for Artificial Life Interactive Video Environment) which was recently built by myself, Professor Sandy Pentland and our students. This installation will be premiered in August at the Siggraph-93 conference in Anaheim, California. It brings together the latest technological breakthroughs in Vision-Based Gesture Recognition, Physically-Based Modelling and Artificial Life. The ALIVE system allows a user to experience a physically-based computer graphics environment and to interact with the artificial animals that inhabit this environment using simple and natural gestures.

More specifically, chromakeying technology is used to overlay the image of the user on top of a real-time interactive computer animation. The composited image is displayed on a large screen (10' by 10') which faces the user, the resulting effect being that of looking in a "magical mirror". Using natural gestures interpreted by a vision-based pattern recognition system, the user can interact and communicate with the animated creatures in the mirror and as such affect their behavior.

The animated creatures of the ALIVE system are constructed using a toolkit and set of algorithms which make it possible to create "autonomous goal-seeking agents" by specifying their sensors, motivations and repertoire of behaviors. For example, for the ALIVE creatures, the sensor data include the gestures made by the user, positions of the user's hands as well as the position and behavior of other creatures in the world. Motivations (or goals) include: desire for

creatures to stay close to one another, fear of unknown things/people, curiosity, etc. Examples of behaviors are: move towards the user, move away from the user, track the user's hand, etc.
Given this information, the toolkit produces creatures which autonomously decide what action to take next based on their current sensor data and motivational state.The model also incorporates a learning algorithm which makes the creatures learn from experience and improve their goal-seeking behavior over time.

rithmen, die durch Spezifizierung ihrer Sensoren, Motivationen und ihres Verhaltensrepertoires die Erzeugung „autonom zielsuchender Akteure" ermöglichen. Bei den ALIVE-Geschöpfen etwa beinhalten die Sensordaten die vom Benutzer gemachten Gesten, die Positionen der Hände des Benutzers wie auch die Position und das Verhalten anderer Geschöpfe auf der Welt. Die Motivationen (oder Ziele) beinhalten: den Wunsch der Geschöpfe, nahe beieinander zu bleiben, Angst vor unbekannten Dingen/Personen, Neugier, usw. Beispiele für das Verhalten sind: Zugehen auf den Benutzer, Weggehen vom Benutzer, der Hand des Benutzers nachspüren, etc.
Sind diese Informationen vorhanden, produziert der Toolkit Geschöpfe, die anhand ihrer aktuellen Sensordaten und ihres motivationalen Zustands autonom über die nächste Handlung entscheiden. Das Modell umfaßt auch einen Lernalgorithmus, der die Geschöpfe aus der Erfahrung lernen läßt und ihnen im Lauf der Zeit eine Verbesserung ihres zielorientierten Verhaltens ermöglicht.

MACHINA COGITANS / DAS VISUELLE DESIGN DER CONNECTION MACHINES CM-1 UND CM-2

TAMIKO THIEL

Vor zehn Jahren, im Juni 1983, begann die Thinking Machines Corporation, den ersten kommerziellen massiv parallelen Supercomputer, die Connection Machine CM-1, zu bauen. Für mich und die jungen Computerwissenschafter, die die Maschine entwarfen, sollte sie die Inkarnation unserer Träume darüber, was einen idealen Computer ausmacht, sein.

Heute ist das parallele Rechnen die unumstrittene Führungsspitze der Computertechnologie. 1983 jedoch war es noch überaus umstritten. Damals wurden schnelle sequentielle Vektormaschinen als die endgültige Grenze der Rechenfähigkeit angesehen. Sie waren nahe an der absoluten Grenze der Natur, ihre Signale konnten jedoch nie die Lichtgeschwindigkeit überschreiten. Theoretisch konnten parallele Maschinen diese Barriere umgehen und eine höhere Geschwindigkeit erreichen, indem sie die Rechnungen von mehreren Prozessoren gleichzeitig ausführen ließen, aber existierende Maschinen waren beschränkt auf spezielle, kleine Untergruppen von Problemen, und Allzweckmaschinen schienen umöglich zu programmieren und unmöglich zu bauen sein.

Für Danny Hillis, der an Problemen menschlicher Kognition am MIT Artificial Intelligence Lab. arbeitete, waren die existierenden sequentiellen Supercomputer einfach den Problemen, die ihn interessierten, nicht gewachsen. Er war überzeugt, daß es notwendig war, einen parallelen Computer mit einer dem menschlichen Gehirn ähnlicheren Struktur zu konstruieren, dessen Wichtigkeit nicht so sehr in den Prozessoren selbst zu sehen sei, sondern eher in der Veränderbarkeit der Verbindungen zwischen ihnen, daher der Name „Connection Machine" („Verbindungs-Maschine"). Um die erste dieser neuen Maschinen zu bauen, half er 1983, die Thinking Machines Corporation zu gründen, die die CM-1 1986 und die Version mit der höheren Leistung, die CM-2 1987, einführte.

MACHINA COGITANS / THE VISUAL DESIGN OF THE CONNECTION MACHINES CM-1 AND CM-2

TAMIKO THIEL

Ten years ago, in June 1983, Thinking Machines Corporation started building the first commercial massively parallel supercomputer, the Connection Machine CM-1. For myself and the young computer scientists designing the machine, it was to be the incarnation of our dreams of what a computer should be.

Today, parallel computing is the undisputed leading edge of computer technology. In 1983, however, it was still extremely controversial. At that time, high-speed sequential vector machines were regarded as the ultimate in computing power. They were up against nature's absolute limit, however: their signals could never exceed the speed of light. Theoretically, parallel machines could circumvent this barrier, gaining increased speed by having multiple processors execute calculations simultaneously, but existing machines were limited to special, small subsets of problems, and general purpose machines seemed impossible to program and impossible to build.

For Danny Hillis, working on problems in human cognition at the Massachusetts Institute of Technology's Artificial Intelligence Laboratory, existing sequential supercomputers were simply inadequate for the problems in which he was interested. He became convinced it was necessary to design a parallel computer with a structure closer to that of a human brain, laying importance not so much on the processors themselves, but rather on the nature and mutability of the connections between them, hence the name "Connection Machine". In order to build the first of these new machines, he helped found Thinking Machines Corporation in 1983, which introduced the CM-1 in 1986 and the higher performance version, the CM-2, in 1987.

Due to the controversial nature of the machine, the top management of Thinking Machines, especially Danny Hillis and the company president, Sheryl Handler, put a high priority on a package whose visual appearance could convince people that this was the first of a new generation, unlike any computer they had ever seen before. I was responsible for the mechanical and industrial design group that produced this package, which was used for both the CM-1 and the CM- 2. Ted Bilodeau did the detailed mechanical design, Tom Callahan built the first prototype, and Allen Hawthorne and Gordon Bruce did the detailed industrial design. The CM-2 was superseded by the next generation Connection Machine CM-5 in October, 1991, which has a very different architecture and package, so this paper can also be seen as an epitaph for the original Connection Machine.

THE ARCHITECTURE OF A NEW MACHINE

The Connection Machines CM-1 and CM-2 were to have up to 65,536 simple 1-bit processors grouped 16 to a chip, for a total of 4,096 chips. Each processor could simultaneously perform the same calculation, each on its own separate data set. This kind of massively parallel architecture had been tried in the past, but what enabled the CM-1 and CM-2 to succeed where others had failed was an extremely flexible and fast hardware communications network between the processors. If this network could operate fast enough, the software connections between processors could be arbitrarily configured to optimally fit the structure of any given problem, ignoring the physical connectivity of the hardware.
This hardware network was to be in the shape of a 12-dimensional hypercube. The term "12-D", far from having to do with warp drives and extraterrestrials, had the mundane but complicated meaning that each processor chip would be directly wired to 12 other chips in such a way that any two chips could communicate with each other in 12 or less steps. Overwhelmed by the effort to visualize a 12-D connection scheme for 4,096 chips, I expressed my bemusement to Richard Feynman, the Nobel-Prize winning physicist who was helping us design the network. (His son Carl was working for Thinking Machines, and Richard got so interested that he asked for a summer job too!) Feynman had the rare talent of being able to explain the most complicated things simply, and characteristically his reply to my complaint was, "Oh, that's easy!"
He connected two chips together to make a "1-D" cube, commonly called a "line". He joined two 1-D cubes together at their ends to make a "2-D" cube, commonly called a "square", and then two 2-D cubes together to make a "3-D" cube, which is the same as our usual understanding of a "cube". Then the step into the 4th dimension: He connected the two 3-D cubes together to make a "4-D" cube, the first stage of a hypercube with more than 3 dimensions.
It is difficult to represent these multidimensional structures in a 2-D drawing. I finally resorted to a radical graphic simplification: I represented all dimensions greater than 3 as thick "hyperlines", and drew cubes as somewhat solid objects in order to visually simplify the re-

Aufgrund der Neuartigkeit der Maschine räumte das Top-Mangement von Thinking Machines, vor allem Danny Hillis und die Firmenpräsidentin Scheryl Handler dem Aussehen eine Vorrangstellung ein, dessen visuelle Erscheinung Leute davon überzeugen konnte, daß dies das erste Stück einer neuen Generation war, anders als alle Computer, die sie bis dahin gesehen hatten. Ich war zuständig für die mechanische und industrielle Design-Gruppe, die das Gehäuse entwarf, das sowohl für die CM-1 als auch für die CM-2 verwendet wurde. Ted Bilodeau machte das detailierte mechanische Design, Tom Callahan baute den ersten Prototypen und Allen Hawthorne und Gordon Bruce waren für das detailierte industrielle Design zuständig. Die CM-2 wurde durch die nächste Generation, der Connection Machine CM-5, im Oktober 1991 ersetzt, welche eine andere Architektur und Form hat, daher kann dieser Aufsatz also als ein Epitaph für die originale Connection Machine gesehen werden.

DIE ARCHITEKTUR EINER NEUEN MASCHINE

Die Connection Machines CM-1 und CM-2 sollten bis zu 65.536 einfache 1-Bit Prozessoren haben, die zu je 16 auf einen Chip gruppiert werden sollten zu einer Gesamtzahl von 4.096 Chips. Jeder Prozessor könnte gleichzeitig die selbe Rechnung ausführen, jeder auf seinem eigenen Datenbestand. Diese Art von massiv paralleler Architektur war in der Vergangenheit versucht worden, aber was die CM-1 und CM-2 befähigte erfolgreich zu sein, wo die anderen versagt hatten, war ein extrem flexibles und schnelles Hardware Kommunikations-Netzwerk zwischen den Prozessoren. Wenn dieses Netzwerk schnell genug arbeitete, konnten die Software-Verbindungen zwischen den Prozessoren beliebig konfiguriert werden, um sich der Struktur jedes vorgegebenen Problems optimal anzupassen, unabhängig von den physikalischen Verbindungen der Hardware.
Dieses Hardware-Netzwerk sollte die Form eines 12-dimensionalen Hyperwürfels haben. Der Terminus „12-D", der weit davon entfernt ist, mit Warp-Antrieb oder Außerirdischen zu tun zu haben, hatte die banale, aber komplizierte Bedeutung, daß jeder Prozessor Chip direkt mit 12 anderen Chips so verkabelt sein würde, daß jede beliebigen zwei Chips in 12 oder weniger Schritten miteinander kommunizieren könnten. Überwältigt von der Bemühung ein 12-D Verbindungsschema für 4.096 Chips zu visualisieren, drückte ich gegenüber Richard Feynman, dem Physiker und Nobelpreisträger, der uns half das Netzwerk zu entwerfen, meine Verwirrtheit aus. (Sein Sohn, Carl Feynman, arbeitete bei

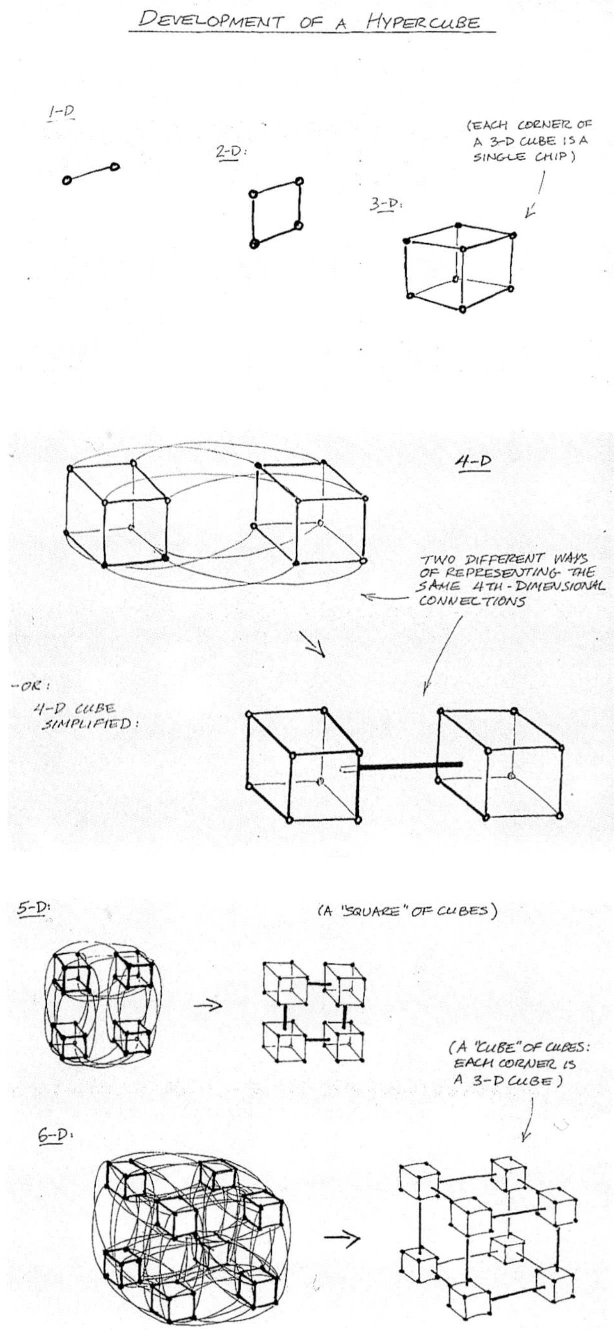

sultant structures. Using this simplification, it is easy to see that the structures always repeat themselves: a 4-D hypercube looks just like a 1-D line, except that it connects two cubes rather than two chips. A 5-D hypercube is a square of cubes, and a 6-D hypercube is a cube of cubes. Going further, a 9-D hypercube is a cube of 6-D hypercubes, and a 12-D hypercube is a cube of 9-D hypercubes.
This is the structure used in the CM-1 and CM-2, a cube with 2 to the power 12 corners, or 4,096 chips, each connected to 12 other chips, each connection being one dimension of the cube. This structure was repeated throughout every level of the machine, in the traces connecting processor chips, in the connectors between the printed circuit boards, and in the 1000 feet of cable connecting the highest dimensions of the machine.
What is the "Function" of a Computer?
Now we could turn our attention to the esthetic aspects of the Connection Machine package. The computer scientists whose visions of the machine influenced me the most, Danny Hillis, Brewster Kahle and Carl Feynman, talked of the machine as a cerebral starship, a vehicle that could open up boundless new frontiers, or as an immensely complex, constantly fluctuating electronic society—the image of an electronic brain. We didn't want to build a machine that looked just like a refrigerator or a washing machine, even if this was the most "practical" and "functional" way to package it. We wanted the design to express the excitement we felt about the machine and about its potential to revolutionize computer architecture.
We still felt, however, that "form should follow function": the form should have meaning and express the essence of the machine. The most obvious solution was to directly follow the lead of modern design and expose the physical structure, which for a computer is its boards and cables. But how can you "see" the function of an electronic machine? Unlike a mechanical machine, a computer's real structure and function is buried in the invisible layers of silicon on a chip, or hidden in the tangle of cables and electronic circuits on a printed circuit board. It is illegible even to a vast majority of computer professionals, who are concerned exclusively with the software and often have not the slightest idea in which direction electricity flows.
It became clear to me that for a computer, "function" went beyond physical structure into the abstract. To truly understand the function of a computer one has to look at the schematic representations that a computer scientist would use to talk about its architecture, the diagrams that describe the flow of data and commands within the system.

THE CUBE-OF-CUBES

So if form should follow function, and function in a computer means the workings of the processors hidden in the silicon chips, then the real function of the CM-1 and CM-2 lay in the way the processors could communicate with each other, physically using the 12-D hypercube network hardware, but conceptually—that is to say in the software—independent of its structure. We had already developed a symbol that expressed these aspects of the machine: in a design I had done for the company T-shirt! (Richard Feynman liked the T-shirt enough to wear it on the cover of one of his popular books!)

This design showed a cube-of-cubes: a large cube built up out of 8 smaller cubes, representing the "hard" electrical connections of part of the 12-D network. Inside these hard rectangular boxes are the "fuzzy" software connections that can be changed independently of the physical wires and traces. Both were equally important aspects of the structure of the machine: the hard, physical wiring and the soft, programmable connections. How could we make something as abstract as software—which has the intangibility of a concept, a speech, a conversation—visible to the eye?

Carl Feynman had described a fantasy of the CM-1 as a vast cloud of lights that flickered as they sent their electronic messages back and forth, like the firing of neurons in a brain. Status lights are often installed on printed circuit boards to provide visual monitors of the current state of components—whether power is "on", or a chip is plugged in properly. We decided to use these lights to make the intangible and unseen activity of the processors visible to the naked eye.

A LIVING MACHINE

Thus, we chose to depict the hardware structure of the machine in the external form of the CM-1 and CM-2 package, and depicted the software connections within this hardware structure using the status lights of the chips: Eight cubes, each holding 9 dimensions of the hypercube, are visually plugged together to form the cube-of-cubes, just as the internal electronic components are physically plugged together to form the highest level of the machine, the 12-D hypercube. Through the doors of the machine glow the lights from 4,096 chips, flickering on and off as the processors work in parallel, each one computing its own part of the data. The microscopic elements of the machine, and the structure buried in the confusion of traces and cables thus become visible, to let the machine speak for itself.

This would communicate to the viewer the immense complexity hidden beneath the surface of the machine. A massive electronic brain, 1.5 meters in height, it is connected with cables to the data drives that feed its processors information and the workstations and monitors that let it communicate with its human users. A hard, geometric object, black, the non-color of sheer, static mass, it is filled with a soft, constantly changing cloud of lights, red, the color of life and energy. This is how we felt a computer should look, a living, breathing machine, a machine that could be proud of us.

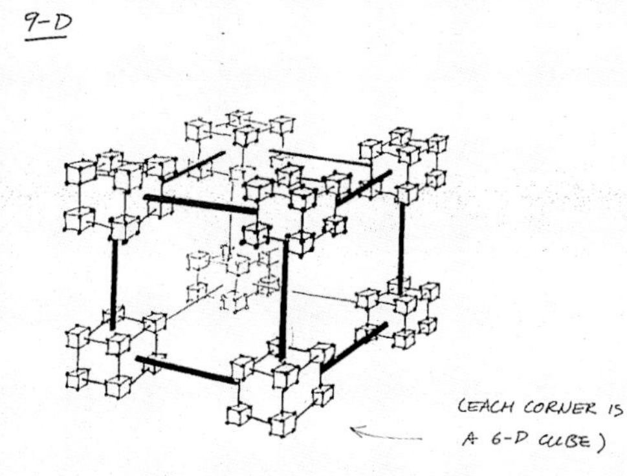

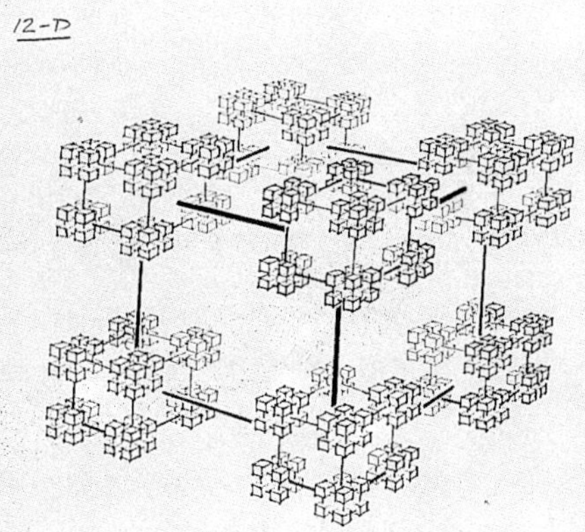

Thinking Machines, und hat Richard einen „Sommerjob" besorgt.) Feynman hatte das seltene Talent, die kompliziertesten Dinge einfach erklären zu können, und so war seine Antwort auf meine Beschwerde ein charakteristisches: „Oh, das ist doch ganz einfach!"

Er verband zwei Chips miteinander, um einen „1-D"-Würfel zu machen, allgemein eine „Linie" genannt. Er verband zwei 1-D-Würfel an ihren Enden, um einen „2-D"-Würfel, allgemein „Quadrat" genannt, zu machen und dann verband er zwei 2-D-Würfel, um einen „3-D"-Würfel zu machen, was dem „Würfel" entspricht, den wir uns normalerweise vorstellen. Dann der Schritt in die vierte Dimension: Er verband zwei 3-D-Würfel miteinander, um einen „4-D" Würfel zu machen, die erste Stufe eines Hyperwürfels mit mehr als drei Dimensionen.

Es ist schwierig diese multidimensionalen Strukturen in einer 2-D Zeichnung zu darzustellen. Ich nahm schließlich zu einer radikalen grafischen Vereinfachung Zuflucht: Ich stellte alle Dimensionen, die größer als als 3 waren als dicke „Hyperlinien" dar und zeichnete Würfel als in gewisser Weise solide Objekte, um die resultierenden Strukturen visuell zu vereinfachen. Durch Anwendung dieser Vereinfachung ist leicht zu erkennen, daß die Strukturen sich immer wiederholen: Ein 4-D Hyperwürfel sieht genauso aus, wie eine 1-D Linie, außer daß er eben zwei Würfel, statt zwei Chips verbindet. Ein 5-D Hyperwürfel ist ein Quadrat von Würfeln und ein

6-D Hyperwürfel ist ein Würfel aus Würfeln. Weiterführend ist ein 9-D Hyperwürfel ein Würfel aus 6-D Hyperwürfeln und ein 12-D Hyperwürfel ist ein Würfel aus 9-D Hyperwürfeln.

Das ist die Struktur die in der CM-1 und der CM-2 verwendet wurde, ein Würfel mit 2 hoch 12 Ecken, oder 4.096 Chips, von denen jeder einzelne mit 12 anderen Chips verbunden, und jede Verbindung eine Dimension des Würfels ist. Diese Struktur wurde über jede Ebene der Maschine wiederholt, in den Leiterbahnen, die die Prozessorchips verbanden, in den Konnektoren zwischen den Leiterplatten und in dem 1000 Fuß (ca. 330m) Kabel, die die höchsten Dimensionen der Maschine verbanden.

WAS IST DIE „FUNKTION" EINES COMPUTERS?

Wir konnten unsere Aufmerksamkeit nun den ästhetischen Aspekten der Gestalt der Connection Machine zuwenden. Die Computerwissenschafter, deren Vorstellungen über die Maschine mich am meisten beeinflußt haben, Danny Hillis,

NOTES

The opinions expressed in this article are the author's alone, and do not necessarily represent Thinking Machines policy.

This article is an extract from a longer article to be published this fall in the journal "Design Issues", ed. Dick Buchanan, Chair, Department of Design, Carnegie-Mellon University, Pittsburgh, Pennsylvania, USA.

For more technical information on the Connection Machine CM-2 see "The Connection Machine", MIT Press, 1985, or "The Connection Machine", Scientific American, June 1987, vol. 256, pp. 108, both by Daniel W. Hillis.

Brewster Kahle und Carl Feynman, sprachen von der Maschine als ein Gedankentraumschiff, ein Vehikel, das unbegrenzte neue Ziele eröffnen könnte, oder als eine immens komplexe, ständig fluktuierende elekronische Gesellschaft – das Bild eines elektronischen Gehirns. Wir wollten keine Maschine bauen, die genauso aussah wie ein Kühlschrank oder eine Waschmaschine, nicht einmal, wenn dies die „praktischeste" und „funktionellste" Art wäre, sie zu gestalten. Wir wollten, daß das Design die Erregung ausdrückt, die wir angesichts dieser Maschine und ihrem Potential, die Computerarchitektur zu revolutionieren, fühlten.
Wir dachten jedoch trotzdem, daß „die Form der Funktion folgen sollte": die Form sollte eine Bedeutung haben und die Essenz der Maschine ausdrücken. Die offensichtlichste Lösung war, dem Vorbild des modernen Design direkt zu folgen und die physikalische Struktur, die bei einem Computer seine Schaltungen und Kabel sind, herauszustellen. (bloßzulegen/ zu enthüllen). Wie aber kann man die Funktion einer elektronischen Maschine „sehen"? Anders als bei mechanischen Maschinen, ist die Struktur und Funktion eines Computers in unsichtbaren Silikonschichten auf einem Chip begraben, oder im Gewirr von Kabeln und elektronischen Schaltkreisen auf einer Leiterplatte versteckt. Das ist sogar für eine riesige Mehrheit von Computerprofessionals unleserlich, die doch ausschließlich mit der Software beschäftigt sind und oft nicht die geringste Idee haben, in welche Richtung die Elektrizität fließt.
Es wurde mir klar, daß für einen Computer „die Funktion" über die physische Struktur hinaus, ins Abstrakte, reichte. Um die Funktion eines Computers wirklich zu verstehen, muß man die schematischen Darstellungen betrachten, die Computerwissenschafter verwenden, um über dessen Architekur zu sprechen, die Diagramme also, die den Datenfluß und die Befehle innerhalb des Systems beschreiben.

DER WÜRFEL AUS WÜRFELN

Wenn also die Form der Funktion folgen sollte, und die Funktion in einem Computer die Arbeitsgänge von in Silikonchips versteckten Prozessoren bedeutet, dann lag die wirkliche Funktion von CM-1 und CM-2 in der Art, wie die Prozessoren miteinander kommunizieren konnten, physikalisch, indem sie die 12-D Hyperwürfel-Netzwerk Hardware verwendeten, aber konzeptuell – also in der Software – unabhängig von deren Struktur. Wir hatten bereits ein Symbol entwickelt, das diese Aspekte der Maschine ausdrückte: in einem Design, das ich für ein Firmen-T-Shirt gemacht hat-

Oben: Connection Machine mit 128 Prozessor-Boards
Unten: Connection Machine CM2

te! (Richard Feynman gefiel das T-Shirt so gut, daß er es auf dem Einband eines seiner populärsten Bücher trug!)
Dieses Design zeigte einen Würfel aus Würfeln: einen großen Würfel aus 8 kleineren Würfeln gebaut, der die „harten" elektrischen Verbindungen eines Teils des 12-D Netzwerkes darstellte. Innerhalb dieser harten rechteckigen Box sind die „fasrigen" Software-Verbindungen, die unabhängig von den physikalischen Drähten und Leiterbahnen, verändert werden können. Beide waren gleich wichtige Aspekte der Struktur der Maschine: die harte, physikalische Verkabelung und die weichen, programmierbaren Verbindungen. Wie konnten wir etwas so Abstraktes wie Software – welche das Immaterielle eines Konzepts, einer Sprache, einer Konversation hat – für das Auge sichtbar machen?
Carl Feynman hat eine Phantasie über die CM-1 als eine riesige Wolke von Lichtern beschrieben, die flackerten, während sie ihre elektronischen Botschaften hin und her schickten wie das Abfeuern von Neuronen in einem Gehirn. Leuchtdioden werden oft auf Computerschaltungen installiert, um für visuelle Kontrolle über den Zustand der Teile zu sorgen – ob der Strom „an" ist, oder ob ein Chip ordentlich eingesteckt ist. Wir beschlossen, solche Dioden zu verwenden, um die immaterielle und ungesehene Aktivität der Prozessoren für das nackte Auge sichtbar zu machen.

EINE LEBENDE MASCHINE

So beschlossen wir, die Hardware-Struktur der Maschine in der äußerlichen Form der CM-1 und CM-2 darzustellen und stellten die Software-Verbindungen innerhalb dieser Hardware-Struktur dar, indem wir die Statusdioden der Chips verwendeten: Acht Würfel, von denen jeder 9 Dimensionen eines Hyperwürfels enthält, sind visuell zusammengesteckt, um den Würfel der Würfel zu bilden, genau wie die internen elektronische Komponenenten physikalisch zusammengesteckt sind, um die höchste Ebene der Maschine zu bilden, den 12-D Hyperwürfel. Durch die Türen der Maschine schimmern die Lichter von 4.096 Chips, an- und ausflakkernd während die Prozessoren parallel arbeiten und jeder einzelne seinen eigenen Teil der Daten bearbeitet. Die mikroskopischen Elemente der Maschine, und die Struktur die in der Verwirrung der Leiterbahnen und Kabeln begraben ist, wird auf diese Weise sichtbar, um die Maschine für sich selbst sprechen zu lassen.
Diese würde dem Betrachter die immense Komplexität mitteilen, die unter der Oberfläche der Maschine verborgen ist. Ein riesiges elektronisches Gehirn von 1,5 m Höhe, es ist

durch Kabel mit den Data Drives verbunden, die seine Prozessoren mit Information speisen und mit den Workstations, die es mit seinen menschlichen Benutzern kommunizieren lassen. Es ist ein hartes, geometrisches Objekt, schwarz, die Nicht-Farbe reiner, statischer Masse und ist gefüllt mit einer weichen sich ständig ändernden Wolke von Lichtern, in rot, der Farbe des Lebens und der Energie. So dachten wir immer, daß ein Computer aussehen sollte, eine lebende, atmende Maschine, eine Maschine, die stolz auf uns sein könnte.

ANMERKUNGEN

Die Meinungen, die in diesem Artikel ausgedrückt werden, sind allein die der Autorin und repräsentieren nicht notwendigerweise die Auffassung von Thinking Machine.
Dieser Artikel ist ein Auszug aus einem längeren Artikel, der diesen Herbst in der Zeitschrift „Design Issues" publiziert werden wird, Hrsg. Dick Buchanan, Chairman, Department for Design, Carnegie-Mellon University, Pittsburgh, Pennsylvania, USA.
Für mehr technische Information über die Connection Machine CM-2 siehe „The Connection Machine", MIT Press, 1985, oder „The Connection Machine", Scientific American, Juni 1987, vol.256, pp. 108, beide von Daniel W. Hillis.

DIE EVOLUTION FUNKTIONALER ROBO-ÖKOLOGIEN

MARK W. TILDEN

THE EVOLUTION OF FUNCTIONAL ROBO-ECOLOGIES
MARK W. TILDEN

Hollywood science fiction has always falsely portrayed the idea that robots just "happen" when motors, neon lights, silicon chips, and a little programming (usually shown as BASIC program listings) combine. Put in bucket, shake well, out pops R2D2. This has, alas, scared away more people from robotics than the "Terminator" because it just doesn't work, or when it does work, the damn thing doesn't even compare to a store-bought toy. Even worse is when enthusiasts are told that "The Real Money" is not in the robot mechanisms of their dreams but in industrial robotics, a field more concerned with statistics than imagination. Consequently, the robotic ideal still exists only on the silver screen and in the fertile imagination of its viewers.
Although current technology has made great strides in building artificial reasoning machines, there has yet to be any definitive way of interfacing such "brains" with robot bodies capable of surviving real-world complexity. Almost every attempt to make truly autonomous robots has resulted in failure. Exceptions have usually involved fantastic sums of money, thousands of man hours, usually both.
However, there is now evidence that there are simple, elegant solutions to making autonomous robotic devices, solutions which show adaptability and dependability even after undergoing significant damage. Some of the principles behind this work are being developed and expanded upon by Mark W. Tilden at the University of Waterloo in Ontario, Canada. Tilden's idea is not to study just one aspect of autonomous robot construction, but all of them, on a tight budget, short design time line, many biological precepts, and most importantly, outside of computer simulation or dependance. To date nearly forty functional robotic devices have been constructed, some of which have been running continually for over three years. Most are solar powered, smaller than a telephone, and so far have avoided the need for processor based con trollers.
Best of all, they are dead cheap.
This research is currently concentrating on four basic fields; Construction research, Vertebrate and Invertebrate design, and Co-operative behavior studies (abbreviated as CIVC, or "civ-ic"

Hollywood Science Fiction hat fäschlicherweise immer die Idee dargestellt, daß Roboter einfach „passieren", wenn Motoren, Neonlichter, Silikonchips und ein bißchen Programmieren (normalerweise als BASIC Programm listings gezeigt) zusammenwirken. Gibs in den Kübel, schüttle es gut und heraus hüpft R2D2. Dies hat, leider, mehr Leute von der Robotik abgeschreckt als der „Terminator", da es einfach nicht so funktioniert, oder wenn es tatsächlich so geht, dann läßt sich das verdammte Ding nicht einmal mit einem im Geschäft gekauften Spielzeug vergleichen. Noch schlimmer ist es, wenn Enthusiasten gesagt wird, daß das „Echte Geld" nicht in den Robotermechanismen ihrer Träume steckt, sondern auf dem Gebiet der Industrierobotik, einem Gebiet, dem mehr an Statistik, als an Phantasie liegt. Folglich existiert das robotische Ideal nach wie vor nur auf der Kinoleinwand und in der fruchtbaren Phantasie der Kinobesucher.
Obwohl die gegenwärtige Technologie große Schritte beim Bau von künstlichen vernünftig denkenden Maschinen gemacht hat, muß man jedoch erst irgendeinen bestimmten Weg finden, zwischen diesen Gehirnen und Roboterkörpern, die fähig sind die Komplexität der realen Welt zu überleben, eine Schnittstelle zu schaffen. Fast jeder Versuch, wahrhaft autonome Roboter zu bauen hat bis jetzt in einem Fehlschlag resultiert. Ausnahmen haben meist Unsummen von Geld und tausende Arbeitsstunden gekostet, normalerweise beides.
Es gibt jedoch jetzt Anzeichen dafür, daß es einfache, elegante Lösungen für die Herstellung autonomer robotischer Geräte gibt, Lösungen, die Anpassungsfähigkeit und Verläßlichkeit zeigen, sogar nachdem sie signifikante Beschädigungen erlitten haben. Einige der Prinzipien hinter dieser Arbeit werden von Mark W. Tilden an der University of Waterloo, Ontario, Canada, entwickelt und erweitert. Tildens Absicht ist es, nicht nur einen, sondern alle Aspekte der Konstruktion autonomer Roboter zu studieren und zwar bei geringem Budget, kurzer Planungszeit, vielen biologischen

MUM 2.2-FB
6v

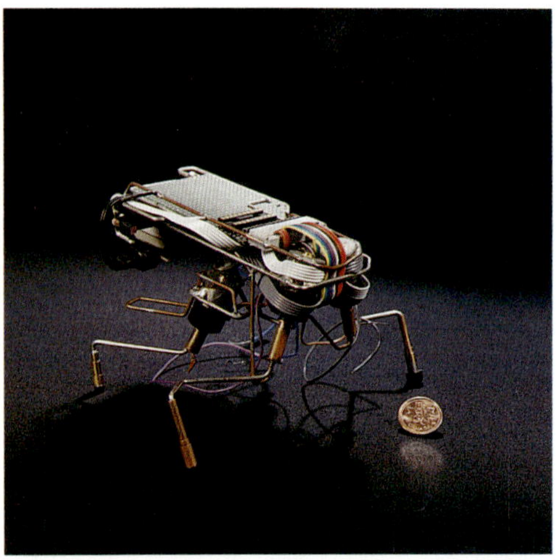

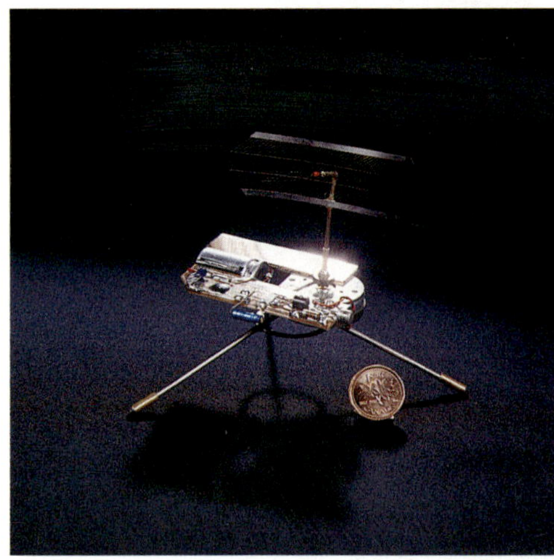

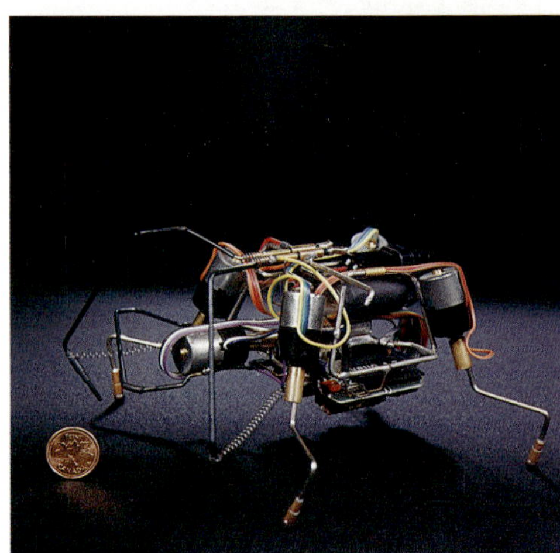

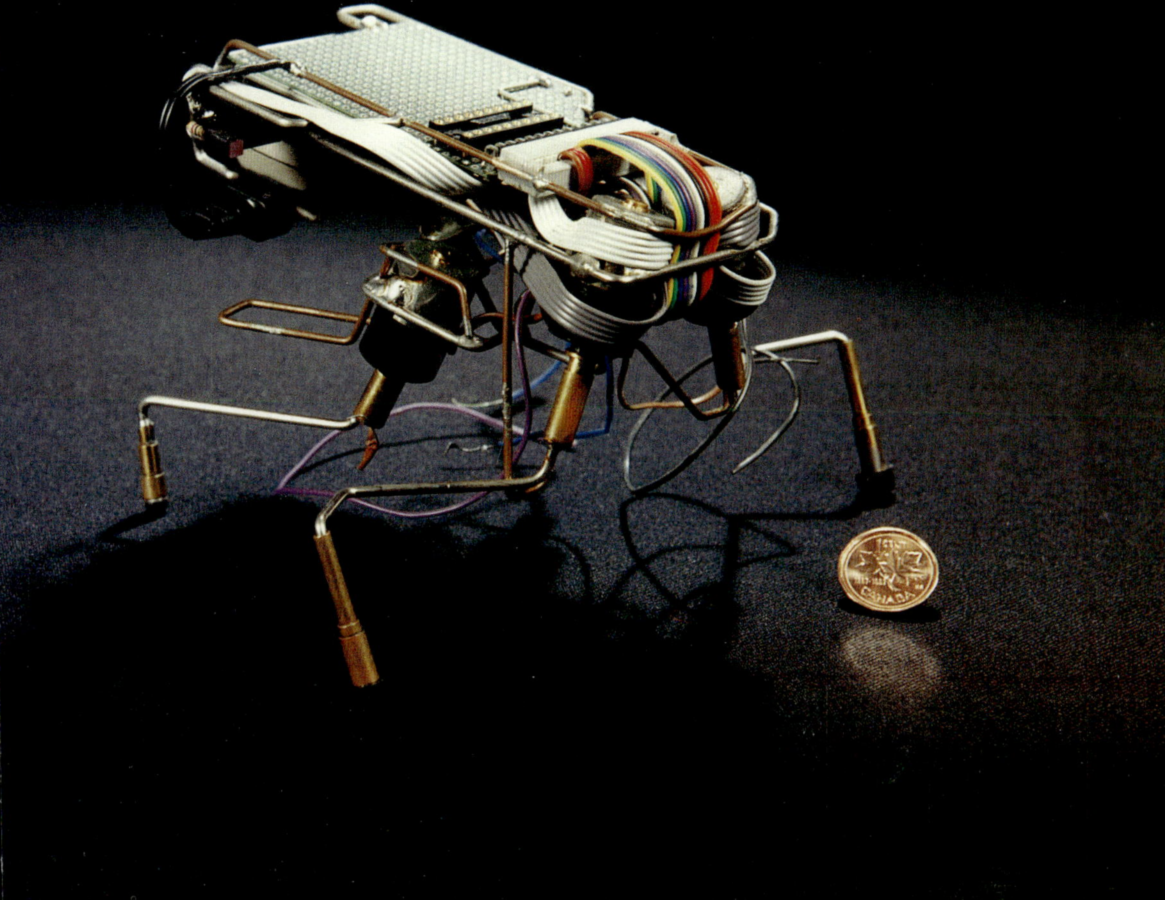
CANADA

Richtlinien und, was am wichtigsten ist, außerhalb von Computer Simulation oder -Abhängigkeit.
Bis dato sind fast vierzig funktionierende robotische Geräte gebaut worden, von denen manche schon seit über drei Jahren durchgehend in Betrieb sind. Die meisten werden mit Sonnenenergie angetrieben, sind kleiner als ein Telefon und haben bis jetzt die Notwendigkeit für auf Prozessoren basierende Kontrollore vermieden.
Und das beste daran ist – sie sind spottbillig.
Diese Forschung konzentriert sich im Moment auf vier grundlegende Gebiete; Konstruktionsforschung, Wirbelsäulen und Wirbellosen – Design und kooperative Verhaltensstudien (abgekürzt CIVC oder „civ-ic" robotische Studien). Die leitenden Grundprinzipien (Grundregeln) sind „Tildens Gesetze der Robotik" und zwar folgende:
1. Ein Roboter muß seine Existenz um jeden Preis schützen
2. Ein Roboter muß den Zugang zu einer (Stromquelle) Energiequelle er- und behalten
3. Ein Roboter muß ständig nach besseren Energiequellen suchen
Anders bekannt als:
1. Schütze deinen Arsch
2. Füttere deinen Arsch
3. Schau dich nach besserem Grundbesitz um
Beachten Sie, daß diese Regeln sich völlig von den Asimovschen Robotergesetzen unterscheiden, welche zwar gute Literatur ergeben, leider aber lausige Roboter. Diese Gebiete und Prinzipien werden jedoch nicht unabhängig studiert, sondern parallel, indem man neue Arten von Robotern in eine einfache „Ökologie" einführt, wo sie mit der realen Welt und miteinander umgehen müssen. Manche sind gebaut worden, um einfache häusliche Bedürfnisse zu befriedigen (Fensterwäscher, Katzenspielzeug, Bodenwäscher), andere sind gebaut worden, nur um irgendein Prinzip, Material oder einzigartiges elektronisches Gerät zu testen.
Zur Zeit der Verfassung dieses Textes hat die Arbeit, zwar nur als Teilzeitbeschäftigung, nun schon drei Jahre lang gedauert, es hat aber in der kurzen Zeit schon signifikante Fortschritte auf allen CIVC Disziplinen gegeben. Es scheint nun, daß kooperatives Verhalten zwischen autonomen, nach einem Ziel strebenden Organismen nicht nur möglich, sondern unter Bedingungen mit geringer Streßbelastung unvermeidlich ist. Außerdem scheint es, daß die überall herrschende Vorstellung Roboter müssen nach irgendeiner biologischen Morphologie gestaltet werden (z. B. Insekten) schon an sich fehlerhaft ist. Roboter werden aus anderem Stoff gemacht und basieren auf völlig anderen Prinzipien, daraus folgt daher, daß optimale robotische Formen sich

robotic studies). The main guiding principles are "Tilden's Laws of Robotics", which are:
1/ A robot must protect its existence at all costs.
2/ A robot must obtain and maintain access to a power source
3/ A robot must continually search for better power sources
Otherwise known as:
1/ Protect thy ass.
2/ Feed thy ass.
3/ Look for better real-estate.
Notice these are vastly different from the classic Asimovian robot laws, which make for good fiction, but alas, lousy robots. These fields and principles are not studied independently but in parallel, introducing new types of robots into a simple "ecology" where they have to deal with the real world and each other. Some have been built to solve simple domestic needs (window cleaner, cat toy, floor cleaners), others were built just to test some principle, material, or unique electronic device.
The work has been going on only part time for three years as of this writting but in that short time there have been significant progress in all CIVC disciplines. It appears now that cooperative behavior amongst autonomous, goal seeking organisms may not only be possible but inevitable under low-stress circumstances. As well, it seems that the pervasive idea that robots must be fashioned upon some biological morphology (ie: insects) may be inherently flawed. Robots are made from a different stuff and based upon very different principles, so it follows that optimal robotic forms might also vastly different from what we might expect. As for function, CIVC robots have evolved from simple wheeled devices to some recent legged forms with astonishing adaptability (and more than just a passing biological similarity).
One of the interesting aspects of this work is that few of these robots are alike in style or function, and this has led to the conclusion that mobile robots alone are not sufficient for a balanced robot ecology. Robot "plants", as well as various other hybrids are vital to improve the "quality of life" in the robo-ecology. An interesting point is that although attempts have been made at building purposeless robots, it seems it cannot be done easily. Given sufficient time and environmental interaction, even the most inane self-contained mechanism will find a purposeful niche.
Future efforts will include documenting all aspects of CIVC robotic research in a book (or two) so that others can make their own devices, then concentrate on the building, observation and evolution of larger and more diverse robo-ecologies, placing them under various stresses, studying the reactions, and developing new generations of survivor automata.
But a single robot builder is too slow, so work is also progressing on the BEAM Robot Olympic Games, an international forum designed to get more people building artificial-life robots rather than writting computer simulations. BEAM, which stands for Biology, Electronics, Aesthetics, and Mechanics is designed as a method so that first time enthusiasts can get started easily. By building one or more simple self-con-

tained creatures, anyone can gain the confidence and ability to assemble a wider range of robotic devices. The Olympics feature a decathlon of competitions ranging from the simplest two-transistor Solaroller race to flying robot contests. The competitions are all very open and adaptive, non-destructive cheating is encouraged, and winners and "Mad Scientists" are rewarded equally. The show is emphasizes the light-hearted approach, events like the "Canadian-Rules-No-Holds-Barred Robot Sumo" detail adaptive evolution at it's aggressive best.
The show is in fact an experiment in forced robo-genetic engineering where humans are used as the reproductive media. Like any good primordial genetic "soup", the more variations observed in the initial species, the better to boil a good stock from, metamorphically speaking. A 100 page Guideline is available to the interested, detailing everything from how to run such events to simple robot construction plans. The second such Olympics happened in April of 1993, along with 5 other Games scheduled internationally throughout the year.
Ideas will be nurtured and expanded on in CIVC robot designs, and once a sufficient database has been explored (and tested by the building of "herds" of devices), there will be more books written. Research can then confidently concentrate on developing robot mechanisms which do satisfy coveted Hollywood Ideals, filling the vast variety of possible applications (bionics, medicine, space, construction, nanoscience, chaos engineering, defence, etc.). The result will not be HAL 9000's but likely a guide by which autonomous mechanisms can be made for the vast array of potential applications; everything from grass cutting hive organisms to robot goldfish.
What sort of functions are anticipated for these robots? Currently, it is difficult to tell. Proctoring an artificial life form is wrought with questions, but that's what fires the interest. Once there are sufficient answers, and concrete examples, to the questions of building "living" robots, then the science will only have just started. The motive is fascination, the results are hoped to do more than satisfy the demands of a tool based industry.
Of course, as the understanding of these primitives grows, so will the confidence to tackle bigger game. Eventually, mechanisms will be built at least as smart as the average simian, and possibly with similar attributes. After that there is bigger game still, but that's so far ahead that it's considered more science fiction than science.
But then, so was the telephone.
Is all.

ebenfalls völlig von unseren Erwartungen unterscheiden. Was die Funktion betrifft, haben CIVC Roboter sich von einfachen beräderten Geräten zu einigen aktuellen Formen mit Beinen entwickelt, die erstaunliche Adaptabilität (und mehr als eine nur flüchtige biologische Ähnlichkeit) besitzen.
Ein interessanter Aspekt dieser Arbeit ist, daß wenige dieser Roboter gleich sind in Stil oder Funktion, und dies hat zu der Schlußfolgerung geführt, daß mobile Roboter alleine für eine ausgewogene Roboter-Ökologie nicht ausreichend sind. Roboter „Pflanzen", wie auch verschiedene andere Hybride sind notwendig, die „Lebensqualität" in der Robo-Ökologie zu verbessern. Ein interessanter Punkt ist, daß, obwohl Versuche gemacht wurden, absichtslose Roboter zu bauen, dies dennoch nicht einfach zu bewerkstelligen erschien. Sogar die geistlosesten, in sich geschlossenen Mechanismen finden, wenn man ihnen genügend Zeit und Interaktionsmöglichkeit in einer Umwelt gibt, eine Nische, die ihnen Zweck verleiht.
Zukünftige Bemühungen werden eine Dokumentation aller Aspekte der Forschung über CIVC Robotik in einem oder zwei Büchern beinhalten, damit andere ihre eigenen Geräte machen können und sich dann auf den Bau, die Beobachtung und Evolution größerer und vielseitigerer Robo-Ökologien konzentrieren können, diese verschiedenen Belastungsproben auszusetzen, ihre Reaktionen zu studieren und neue Generationen von Überlebens-Automaten zu entwickeln.
Aber ein einzelner Roboterbauer ist zu langsam, und deshalb geht die Arbeit auch bei den BEAM Robot Olympic Games voran, einem Forum mit der Aufgabe, mehr Leute dazu zu bringen, Roboter mit künstlichem Leben zu bauen, als Computersimulationen zu schreiben. BEAM, was für Biologie, Elektronik, Ästhetik und Mechanik steht, ist als eine Methode konzipiert, die Enthusiasten, die zum ersten Mal auf dem Gebiet arbeiten, den Start erleichtern soll. Durch das Bauen von einem oder mehreren selbständigen Kreaturen, kann jeder die Sicherheit und die Fähigkeit erlangen, eine größere Auswahl robotischer Geräte zusammenzubauen. Das olympische Charakteristikum, ein Dekathlon (Zehnkampf) der Wettbewerbe reicht vom einfachsten zwei-Transistor-Rennen zu Wettbewerben mit fliegenden Robotern. Die Wettbewerbe sind alle sehr offen und adaptives, nicht destruktives Schwindeln wird ermutigt und Gewinner wie auch „Verrückte Wissenschafter" werden gleichermaßen belohnt. Die Show betont den leichtherzigen Ansatz (Ausgangspunkt/Zugang) Ereignisse wie der „Kanadische-Regeln-Kein-Griff-Ist-Verboten-Roboter-Sumo" behandeln detailliert die adaptive Evolution auf ihre aggressivste, beste Art.

Tatsächlich ist die Show ein Experiment in forcierter robogenetischer Technik, wo Menschen als das reproduktive Medium verwendet werden. Es verhält sich wie bei jeder guten genetischen „Ursuppe", je mehr Variationen man in der anfänglichen Spezies beobachten kann, desto besser wird die Brühe, um es einmal metamorphisch auszudrücken, die man davon kochen kann. Für Interessierte gibt es ein 100-seitiges Büchlein mit Richtlinien, das alles detailliert angibt, zum Beispiel, wie man solche Ereignisse veranstaltet bis zu einfachen Konstruktionsplänen für Roboter. Die zweite solche Olympiade wurde im April 1993 durchgeführt, zusammen mit 5 anderen Spielen, die international über das ganze Jahr geplant sind.

Ideen werden genährt und erweitert im CIVC Roboterdesign und wenn einmal eine ausreichende Datengrundlage erforscht worden ist, (und getestet durch den Bau von „Unmengen" von Geräten) dann werden mehr Bücher geschrieben werden. Die Forschung kann sich dann zuversichtlich darauf konzentrieren, Robotermechanismen zu entwickeln, die die begehrten Hollywood-Ideale befriedigen, und damit die riesige Auswahl möglicher Anwendung zu füllen (Bionik, Medizin, Raumforschung, Bauen, Nanowissenschaft, Chaostechnologie, Verteidigung etc.). Das Ergebnis werden keine HAL 9000s sein, sondern wahrscheinlich eine Anleitung, nach der autonome Mechanismen für die riesige Menge möglicher Anwendungen gemacht werden können; alles von Gras schneidenden Schwarmorganismen zu Roboter-Goldfischen.

Welche Art von Funktionen sind für diese Roboter vorauszusetzen? Zur Zeit ist das schwer zu sagen. Eine künstliche Lebensform heranzuziehen ist geprägt von vielen Fragen, aber das gerade regt das Interesse an. Wenn es einmal genügend Antworten auf die und konkrete Beispiele zu den Fragen bezüglich der Konstruktion „lebender" Roboter geben wird, wird die Wissenschaft erst gerade begonnen haben. Das Motiv ist Faszination, die Ergebnisse, so hofft man, werden mehr können, als die Anforderungen einer auf Werkzeugen basierenden Industrie zu befriedigen.

Natürlich wird mit dem wachsenden Verständnis dieser Primitiva auch die Zuversicht und das Vertrauen wachsen, das größere Spiel zu wagen. Schließlich werden Mechanismen gebaut werden, die zumindest so klug sind, wie der durchschnittliche Menschenaffe und möglicherweise mit ähnlichen Eigenschaften. Danach gibt es ein sogar noch größeres Spiel, aber das ist so weit entfernt, daß es mehr als Science Fiction denn als Wissenschaft angesehen wird.

Aber andererseits war das beim Telefon ja auch so.

Das wars.

Cindy Sherman: Untitled, 1992

wissenschaftliche
SENSATION

BRAINSCAPE LABORATORY

BAR CODE

KONRAD BECKER / WOLFGANG ZINGGL

BAR CODE
KONRAD BECKER / WOLFGANG ZINGGL

THE WORLD—SYNTHESIZEABLE FROM BAR CODES AND IMAGINATION

"The industry feeds of the human biomass, like a whale straining krill from the sea"
from "Snow Crash" by N. Stephenson
"Bar Codes are a Girls best friend"
From "T.R.I.A.D." (Trivial Research Industries Arch. Dept.)
"The Bar as a place where social codes, social games, and bar rituals are performed, is the city's communications battle field.
It is obvious that the decisive influence of new technologies and fields of science are to be found, in an experimental sense, at the intersections of social interaction, amongst other things, utopic models can be directly introduced at the gastronomy taps".
The Bar as a reagent glass of human biomass is the laboratory of a humanistic information virology. The silent post of the quasi species man as a case example for the Tower Building of Babel.

CODE WAR

THE MATHEMATICAL MODELS CONCERNING THE COURTSHIP OF GLOW WORMS, MAY ALSO POSSIBLY REVEAL SOCIAL BEHAVIOURAL PATTERNS AND FROM THE REACTION CYCLES OF CHEMICAL CLOCKS; CONNECTIONS MAY BE ESTABLISHED TO THE LAWS ACCORDING TO WHICH FATHER CHRISTMASES DRESSED IN RED AND WITH WHITE BEARDS; APPEAR.
IF COAT MARKINGS AND STRIPE PATTERNS IN THE ANIMAL WORLDS CAN BE SIMULATED WITH THE STANDING WAVES OF CHEMICAL REACTION-DIFFUSION MODELS, THEN WHAT FUNDAMENTAL PATTERN FORMATION MECHANISMS APPLY TO FASHIONABLE ACESSOIRES OR THE AFFIRMATIVE SMALL TALK? THE "SHAMELESS SOCIETY, WITH MODERN LIFE AS A HOTHOUSE OF BASE INSTINCTS", ACCORDING TO THE TITLE STORY IN "SPIEGEL" ON 11.1.93, PROBABLY PROVIDES OPTIMAL CONDITIONS FOR THE DISCOVERY OF NEW PARASITIC INFORMATION MOLECULES.

BAR CODE ARGE to
Konrad Becker & Wolfgang Zinggl

Mitarbeit:
Werner Rodlauer (Produktion), Sabine Dreher (Sponsoring), Francisco Webber (Software), Michael Lohn (Catering), Eiblmayr Korab Design (Architektur)

Es liegt nahe, dem Einfluß wissenschaftlicher Innovationen an Schnittpunkten sozialer Interaktion zu begegnen. Zum Beispiel an der Bar. Als Arena der Kommunikation ist sie besonders geeignet, tief konditionierte Verhaltensmuster aufzuzeigen oder sogar zu beeinflussen.
Mit der ständig veränderten globalen Ernährungslandschaft sind manche Grundlagen unseres Speiseschemas in Frage gestellt. Längst sind die Augen, sind der Geschmacks- und der Geruchsssinn nicht mehr in der Lage für das Wohl der Konsumenten relevante Informationen aufzunehmen. Dennoch wird weiter nach optischen Richtlinien gewählt und gegessen.
Das ist lediglich eine Frage der Kodierung im Kopf. Nichts hindert uns daran, Hundefleisch zu genießen, selbst wenn es von einem Extruder zu einem lecker anmutenden T-bone Steak gekittet wurde. Umgekehrt nehmen wir chemisch exakt definierte Vollwertnahrung nur ungern zu uns, wenn sie sich in Kunststoffolien verschweißt als grünbraune Soße präsentiert.
Unsere kulturell konditionierten Präferenzmuster sind zunehmend fragwürdig geworden. Sie werden durch eine hereinbrechende Gentechnologie noch viel fragwürdiger und es wird Zeit, daß wir die alten Vorurteile über Bord werfen, um neue aufzubauen.
Hunger auf Hund und gegrillte Grillen, Ekel und Appetitlichkeit sind manchmal nur einen Gedankensprung voneinander entfernt.
Die Gestaltung unserer Bar orientiert sich an Selfservice-, Junkfood- und Lowlifekultur zwischen Baustellen, Gerüsten und Monitoren, die als Überwachung dienen und alternierend mit Videoanimationen und Dokumentationen bespielt werden.

Optisch ersetzen leuchtende Firmenlogos als Totems des Hightech-Wirtschafts-Feudalismus jeden künstlerischen Gestaltungsdrang durch kapitalistischen Realismus und insgesamt geht es einzig um die Frage, welchen Sinnesinformationen werden wir trauen, wonn wir Essen bestellen.
Zuletzt und im Zentrum von Bar-Code befindet sich eine kleine Ausstellung. In einer Kapelle wissenschaftlicher Innovation werden in reliquienartigen Schreinen einige der wenigen bisher verfügbaren, chemisch transferierten Organismen – Ikonen einer konstruktiven Biologie – präsentiert. Sie gelten als sicher.
Kaum eine Pflanze läßt sich anmerken, daß sie genetisch manipuliert ist. Oberflächlich sieht die Tabakstaude aus wie jede andere. Dem Salomonen-Pilz ist nichts außergewöhnliches anzusehen, die kleinen Kartoffelpflänzchen sind normale Kartoffelpflänzchen und die Crysanthemen blühen vielleicht in einer anderen Farbe, aber wer weiß schon, in welchen Farben Crysanthemen blühen.
Die Diskussion der Vor- und Nachteile biologischer Veränderungen beginnt im unsichtbaren Bereich. Die Diskussion der Vor- und Nachteile jedes Wahrnehmungsangebotes beginnt bei den Zusatzinformationen.

DIE WELT SYNTHETISIERBAR AUS STRICHCODES UND VORSTELLUNG

"The industry feeds of the human biomass, like a whale straining krill from the sea" aus "Snow Crash" von N. Stephenson
"Barcodes are a girl's best friend"
aus "T.R.I.A.D." (Trivial Research Industrie Arch. Dept.)
„Die Bar als Austragungsort sozialer Codes, gesellschaftlicher Spiele und Balzrituale ist das Kommunikationsschlachtfeld der Stadt.
Es liegt nahe, dem bestimmenden Einfluß neuer Technologien und Wissensgebieten an den Schnittpunkten sozialer Interaktion experimentell zu begegnen. Unter anderem können utopische Modelle direkt an den Zapfhähnen der Gastronomie ins Spiel gebracht werden."
Die Bar als Reagenzglas menschlicher Biomasse ist das Laboratorium einer humanistischen Informationsvirologie. Die stille Post der Quasispezies Mensch als Fallbeispiel für den Turmbau zu Babel.

CODE WAR

Aus den mathematischen Modellen für das Liebeswerben

THE VIRUS AS A GENETIC PIRATE IS A FRONTIER COMMUTER BETWEEN INANIMATE MATTER AND LIVING ORGANISMS, A MODEL FOR SELF-ORGANIZATION AT AN EARLY DEVELOPMENT STAGE IN LIFE. THE EXAMINATION OF VIRUSES SHOWS HOW INFORMATION CAN BE OPTIMIZED AND FURTHER PROCESSED AT A MOLECULAR LEVEL. THESE SELF-REPRODUCING INFORMATION SYSTEMS TRANSCEND THE BARRIERS BETWEEN MAN AND MACHINE, ANIMATE AND INANIMATE NATURE.
WHEN THE TEXT "I HAVE BECOME ALIVE, I AM ALIVE!" SUDDENLY APPEARS ON A COMPUTER MONITOR, THEN THE COMPUTER IS VERY PROBABLY INFECTED WITH A VIRUS.
LANGUAGE ITSELF CAN BE UNDERSTOOD AS BEING A VIRUS, ACCORDING TO W. BOUROUGHS, EVEN AS A VIRUS FROM ANOTHER STAR.
EVERY RELIGIOUS-IDEOLOGICAL MISSIONIZING SHOWS THE QUALITY OF SELF-ACCOMPLISHING REPRODUCTION AND THE COMMON EARWIG CAN BE UNDERSTOOD AS BEING A VIRAL INFECTION.
IN CONTRAST TO THE SOMEWHAT AWKWARD SELF-REPRODUCING IDEOLOGIES OF THE PAST CONSISTING OF RELIGION AND POLITICS, WE HAVE BECOME ACQUAINTED WITH, NOT LEAST, NEW AND MORE AGGRESSIVE SPECIES OF IDEOLOGY BYTES AND TIME CODES THROUGH THE FAST BREEDER OF THE MEDIA.
IDEOLOGY IS SUPERSEDED BY EFFICIENT IDEOGRAMMES WHOSE REDUCED MOLECULAR MORPHOLOGY BECOMES CLEAR IN THE COMPARISON BETWEEN A BAROQUE SAINT AND A MODERN STREET SIGN. THE LOGOGRAMME OF THE AIDS VIRUS WITH ITS DEGREE OF NOTORIETY, IN THE MEANTIME, COMES CLOSE TO THE POPULARITY OF THE MERCEDES STAR.
ADVERTISING AND MARKETING HAVE ADVANCED THE IDEOLOGICAL INTERLOCKING OF CODES WITH THE CONSCIOUSNESS OF THE EVERY DAY CONSUMER THROUGH PRODUCT NAMES SUCH AS "DU DARFST" (YOU MAY) OR "NIMM ZWEI" (TAKE TWO). CHEERFUL POST-BEHAVIOURISM AS SELF—SERVICE FOR THE AUTOMATED CONSUMER. "EVERYONE ACCORDING TO HIS NEEDS" CHANGED FROM THE LIBERTARIAN SLOGAN TO THE RELIGIOUS META-CONCEPT OF THE LATE CAPITALISTIC SUPERMARKET'S WORLD OF GOODS AND THE SALVATION ARMY OF POSITIVE THINKING. IN THE PRECONSCIOUS STIMULUS RESPONSE OF THE SOCIALLY STRESSED PRIMATES, IT DOESN'T FIT TOGETHER AT ALL, LIKE FLEEING INSTEAD OF STANDING FIRM TO AN EXPLODING FAST RESTAURANT.
MIND-BYTE-MARKETING IS THE FUTURE BAROMOETER OF ALL TREND RESEARCHERS AND THE WATERHOLE OF ALL MEDIA FEEDBACK ARTISTS.
JUST AS A BOOK OFTEN ONLY REPRESENTS THE JUSTIFICATION FOR THE BLURB, INFORMATION SCANNING IS SIMILAR TO THE FILTERING OF RESYNTHESIZEABLE CODES TO

FORM A SELF-REFERENTIAL KEY SERVICE, (HIT ME WITH YOUR FUNCTION KEY).
"YES, YOU GET THINGS LIKE THAT: MORE LOGICAL, VERY LOGICAL, LESS LOGICAL—FORMALLY THIS CAN ONLY BE UNDERSTODD AS LONG AS IT IS MEANINGLESS.
ADVERTISING AND MEDIA OPERATE ACCORDING TO THE CONCEPT OF AFFECTIVE LOGIC AND THE MEANINGFULL HUNCH OF "PERHAPS" ORIGINATING FROM THE DUAL LOGIC, HAS CAST ITS SHADOWY SWEEP ONTO THE SCIENTIFIC DISCOURSE, PARTICLES OF THE WORLD BECAME PROBABILITY FUNCTIONS AND MATTER BECAME SYMMETRY. BUT NOT THE INCLINATION FOR POETRY, ON THE CONTRARY, A COMPLUSION TO WRITE TRANSFORMS HALF-BAKED FACTS INTO TURN-KEY METAPHORS AND SPIRALIZES THE AMBIGUITY OF THE MEDIAL COMMON PLACE INTO THE UPS AND DOWNS OF COLLECTIVE UNCONSCIOUS IN ORDER TO LEAVE ITS SCENT THERE.
WITH A CHEERFUL "EX NIHILO NIHIL FIT", WE LEAF THROUGH THE PRESS OR ABSORB VIVID PICTURES AND JUST AS GENETIC MUTATIONS ARE TRIGGERED OFF THROUGH THE BOMBARDMENT OF COSMIC RADIATION, THE FIELD OF VISION OF THE MEDIA CONSUMER IS PICTURE POINTED BY CATHODE RAYS.
BEING ABLE TO MAKE SENSE, MEANS IN THE KILLER CIRCLE OF DOG EATS DOG; MAKE SENSE OR I'LL EAT YOU.
MAN AS THE FORERUNNER OF THE 100% BIOLOGICALLY DECOMPOSABLE THROW AWAY PACKAGE HAD, IN THE HISTORY OF MANKIND, AN AVERAGE EXPIRY DATE OF 30 YEARS.
UNDER FAVOURABLE CONDITIONS AND IN A CIVILIZATION WHICH IS FOUNDED ON WEALTH AND GOOD BEHAVIOUR, THE HUMAN EXPIRY DATE ON THE BIOLOGICAL SPARE WHEEL CAN BE CONSIDERABLY PROLONGUED DESPITE RESTRICTED VITALITY. HOWEVER, WITH GREATLY INCREASED LIFE EXPECTANCY, AN ENOMOROUS LEISURE PROBLEM ARISES AS AN AVERAGE LIFE EXPECTANCY OF 30 YEARS APPEARS TO BE MORE THAN SUFFICIENT FOR SEXUAL REPRODUCTION AND THE RAISING OF OFFSPRING. ("IS THERE A LIFE BEFORE DEATH? WHAT RESTS FOREVER IS NOT DEAD, BUT IN UNKNOWN TIMES DEATH STILL COULD DIE!").
IF WE WANT TO MEASURE LIVELINESS TO THE ADAPTATION POSSIBILITY TO ENVIRONMENTAL STIMULUS, THEN DON'T TRUST ANYONE OVER TWENTY, AS APPARENTLY THE ENERGY HAS GONE AND THE FIRE IS OUT SOON AFTER THE DECISIVE SEXUAL CHARACTER PHASE (THE TRANSFORMATION TO THE HONOURABLE MEMBER OF SOCIETY). AS CAN BE SEEN CLEARLY FROM THE ANNUAL RINGS OF THE YOUTH CULTURE AND THE QUICK SUCCESSION OF THEIR TIDES, ONLY A FEW SUCCEED IN TRANSCODING THE MODEL OF THEIR COINING. THE READINESS OF THE BRAIN TO MAKE NEW CONNECTIONS OBVIOUSLY DE-

der Glühwürmchen sind möglicherweise auch gesellschaftliche Verhaltensmuster ableitbar und von den Reaktionszyklen der chemischen Uhren lassen sich Verbindungen ziehen zu den Gesetzmäßigkeiten nach denen rotgekleidete Weihnachtsmänner mit weißen Bärten erscheinen.
Wenn Fellzeichnung und Streifenmuster in der Tierwelt mit den stehenden Wellen chemischer Reaktions-Diffusions-Modelle simuliert werden können, welche grundlegenden Musterbildungsmechanismen gelten dann für das modische Accessoire oder den affirmativen Small Talk? Die laut „Spiegel"-Titelstory vom 11. Jänner 1993 „Schamlose Gesellschaft" mit dem modernen Leben als Treibhaus der niederen Instinkte bietet vermutlich optimale Bedingungen für die Entdeckung neuer prasitärer Informationsmoleküle.
Der Virus als genetischer Pirat ist ein Grenzgänger zwischen unbelebter Materie und lebenden Organismen, ein Modell für Selbstorganisation auf einer frühen Entwicklungsstufe des Lebens. Die Untersuchung von Viren zeigt wie Information auf molekularer Ebene optimiert und weiterverarbeitet werden kann.
Diese Selbstreproduzierenden Informationssysteme transzendieren die Grenzen zwischen Mensch und Maschine, belebter und unbelebter Natur.
Wenn auf einem Computer-Bildschirm plötzlich der Text „I have become alive, I am alive!" auftaucht, dann ist der Rechner höchstwahrscheinlich mit einem Virus infiziert.
Sprache selbst kann als Virus verstanden werden, laut W. Bouroughs sogar als Virus von einem anderen Stern.
Jede religiös-ideologische Missionierung zeigt die Qualität selbsterfüllender Reproduktion und der gemeine Ohrwurm ist als virale Infektion zu verstehen.
Im Kontrast zu den etwas schwerfälligen Selbstreproduzierenden Ideologien der Vergangenheit aus Religion und Politik haben wir nicht zuletzt duch die schnellen Brüter der Medien neue und agressivere Spezies von Ideologie-Bytes und Time-Codes kennengelernt.
Ideologie wird abgelöst durch effiziente Ideogramme deren reduzierte molekulare Morphologie im Vergleich zwischen einem barocken Heiligen und einem modernen Straßenschild deutlich wird. Das Logogramm des Aids-Virus grenzt mit seinem Bekanntheitsgrad inzwischen an die Popularität des Mercedes-Stern.
Werbung und Marketing haben die ideolografische Verzahnung von Codes mit dem Bewußtsein des Alltagskonsumenten durch Produktbezeichnungen wie „du darfst" oder „nimm zwei" vorangetrieben. Fröhlicher Post-Behavourismus als Self-Service für den automatisierten Verbraucher. „Jeder nach seinen Bedürfnissen" wurde vom libertären Slo-

gan zum religiösen Metakonzept des spätkapitalistischen Supermarktes Warenwelt und der Heilsarmee des positiv thinking. Im vorbewußten Stimulus-Response des gestreßten Herrentiers paßt die Faust auf's Aug' wie das Flüchten statt Standhalten zu einem explodierendem Schnellrestaurant.

Mind-Byte-Marketing ist das Zukunftsbarometer aller Trendforscher und das Wasserloch aller Medienfeedback-Artisten. So wie ein Buch oft nur mehr die Rechtfertigung für den Klappentext darstellt, gleicht Informations-Scanning dem Filtern von Resynthetisierbaren Codes zu einem selbstreferentiellen Schlüsseldienst. (Hit me with your function-key.)

„Sowas soll's ja geben: Mehr logisch, sehr logisch, weniger logisch – formal läßt sich das nur verstehen solange es bedeutungslos ist."

Werbung und Medien operieren nach dem Konzept der Affektlogik und die bedeutungsvolle Ahnung des, der dualen Logik entsprungenen „vielleicht" hat seine schattigen Schwingen auf den wissenschaftlichen Diskurs geworfen. Die Teilchen der Welt wurden zu Wahrscheinlichkeitsfunktionen und Materie wurde zur Symmetrie. Aber nicht der Hang zur Poesie, vielmehr ein Zwang zur Dichtung verwandelt halbharte Fakten in schlüsselfertige Metaphern und spiralisiert die Vieldeutigkeit des medialen Allgemeinplatzes in die Höhen und Tiefen des kollektiven Unbewußten, um dort seine Duftmarken zu setzen.

Mit einem fröhlichen „ex nihilo nihil fit" blättern wir durch den Blätterwald oder absorbieren bewegte Bilder und so wie durch das Bombardement kosmischer Strahlung genetische Mutationen ausgelöst werden, wird das Blickfeld des Medienkonsumenten mittels Kathodenstrahl verpixelt.

Sich einen Reim machen können bedeutet auf dem Killerparkett des dog eats dog: Reim dich oder ich freß' dich.

Der Mensch als Vorläufer der 100 Prozent biologisch abbaubaren Wegwerfverpackung hatte in der Menschheitsgeschichte ein durchschnittliches Ablaufdatum von 30 Jahren. Unter günstigen Bedingungen und einer Zivilisation die auf Wohlstand und Wohlverhalten gegründet ist, läßt sich das menschliche Verfallsdatum auf dem biologischen Reserverad, trotz eingeschränkter Vitalität, erheblich verlängern. Allerdings entsteht durch die stark erhöhte Lebenserwartung ein enormes Freizeitproblem, denn für die sexuelle Reproduktion und die Aufzucht des Nachwuchs scheint eine durchschnittliche Lebensdauer von 30 Jahren mehr als ausreichend. („Gibt es ein Leben vor dem Tod? Gestorben ist nicht was ewig ruht, aber in unbekannten Zeiten könnte der Tod noch sterben!")

Wenn man Lebendigkeit an der Adaptionsmöglichkeit an

CREASES TO SUCH A DEGREE THAT THE MUSICAL STYLISTIC EXCRESCENCE CAN NO LONGER BE ACCOMPLISHED AFTER THE "OPEN WINDOW". BE IT FISH OR FROG, BABOON OR HUMAN BEING, THE EMBRIONIC DEVELOPMENT OF VERTEBRATES IS VERY SIMILAR IN ITS INITIAL STAGES, BUT THE DEVELOPMENT STOP AND THE SIDESTEP INTO THE ECO-NICHE NOT ONLY PRESENTED US WITH ADULT ROCK AND POST PUNK, BUT ALSO APPEARS TO BE AN EVOLUTION PHENOMENA.

THE LUXURY OF A PROLONGUED ADOLESCENCE IN THE LONG-LIVED WEALTHY CIVILIZATIONS IS DIRECTLY CONNECTED TO THE CULTURAL DEVELOPMENT, FOR EXAMPLE, HOW THE DREAM FACTORY OF THE CINEMA FINANCES ITSELF LARGELY FROM THE POCKET MONEY OF THE INTERNATIONAL TEENAGER. THE LEISURE PROBLEM HAS FURTHER INTENSIFIED WITH INCREASING AUTOMATION AND AFTER HAVING SUPERSEDED BLUE COLLAR WORKERS BY THE INTRODUCTION OF INTELLIGENT TECHNICAL PRODUCTION METHODS, THE NEXT STAGE IS READY TO IGNITE: THE AUTOMATION OF INTELLECTUAL WORK DRIVES THE MENTAL SILICON PROTHESIS RIGHT OUT INTO THE SERVICE AREA.

SOON THERE WILL HARDLY BE ANY PRODUCTION SECTORS WHERE MACHINES DO NOT WORK MORE ECONOMICALLY, FASTER, CLEANER, AND MORE EFFICIENTLY THAN HUMAN BEINGS. WHEN WILL THE POST-INDUSTRIAL DATA ECONOMY SWITCH OVER TO AUTO-PILOT AND DISMISS THE WORKING POPULATION INTO HISTORY BY MEANS OF LEISURE SHOCK? THE HEADING "WORK LIBERATES" WAS PART OF THE WEIRD IRONY OF THE MORE RECENT CONTEMPORARY HISTORY; BUT "FREEDOM MAKES WORK" IS AN UNWRITTEN LAW OF THE LEISURE SOCIETY. IT MAY BE POSSIBLE TO VERY EXACTLY FOLLOW"; BUT FROM WHICH UNCONSCIOUS AFFECTIVE CHANGES AND REGULATIONS OF HIERARCHICALLY SUPERORDINATED FEELING IMPULSES A "FREE WILL" ORIGINATES, CAN HARDLY STILL BE FOLLOWED. THE SOFTWARE IS THE SAFETY RISK OF COMPUTER-AIDED WAR STRATEGY, COMPLEX SOURCE CODES LEAD A LIFE OF THEIR OWN AND ESCAPE THEIR UNVEILING ON THE ARROW OF TIME.

JUST FOLLOW YOUR NOSE, EVEN JUST A FEW MOLECULES OF A SCENT OR PHEROMONE ARE SUFFICIENT TO AWAKEN MEMORIES OF THE ANIMAL IN HUMAN BEINGS. PRODUCT NAMES LIKE OBSESSION, EGOISTE, OR PITRALON, SPEAK A VERY CLEAR LANGUAGE. SOME RECOLLECTION STORES, THE DRAWERS OF THE MEMORY, APPEAR ONLY TO OPEN IN CERTAIN FRAMES OF MIND AND EMOTIONAL SETTINGS. IT IS ONLY THE TRANSITION INTO THE PHASE AREA OF THE ATTRACTOR THAT PERMITS ACCESS TO THE SYSTEM.

AS A MATTER OF INTEREST, WITH THE STORING AND RECALLING OF COMPLEX COGNITIVE MATERIAL THERE IS A HIERARCHICAL STRUCTURE IN WHICH THE INFORMATION

STORED IN HIGHER CONSCIOUS STAGES (AWAKENED CONSCIOUSNESS) REMAINS AVAILABLE IN LESS DIFFERENTIATED STATES (DREAM), BUT NOT IN REVERSE. AFTER WAKING UP IT IS OFTEN DIFFICULT TO REMEBER A DREAM AND WHOEVER HAS AWAKENED FROM A DEEP HYPNOSIS HAS NO DIRECT ACCESS TO THE SUGGESTIONS MADE IN THE HYPNOTIC SLEEP.
IN THE CASE OF OPERATIONS PERFORMED UNDER A GENERAL ANAESTHETIC, ANY NEGATIVE SUGGESTIONS MADE BY THE MEDICAL STAFF PRESENT (E.G. "THE FAT PIG WON'T DO IT MUCH LONGER") CONSIDERABLY HAMPER THE REHABILITATION PROCESS AND HAVE LED TO MALPRACTICE PROCESSES AND ACTION FOR DAMAGES.
EVEN REAL ZOMBIES EAT HAMBURGERS, BUT DO THE BRAIN DEAD EXPERIENCE HUNGER? AT ANY RATE THEY NEED NOURISHMENT AND OXYGEN.
CONSCIOUSNESS AND READINESS FOR MENTAL RECEPTION CONSUMES ASTONISHINGLY JUST AS MANY CALORIES AS APATHY OR INDOLENCE. ACTING DOESN'T COST ANY MORE STRENGTH THAN REACTING. HERE AT THE CROSSING POINT OF THE CONSTANTLY CHANGING WITH THE PERMAMENT, THERE APPEARS TO BE A HIDDEN SOURCE OF NEGATIVE ENTROPY. CONSCIOUSNESS AS A NON-THERMAL POWER STATION OF AN ENERGY FASTER THAN LIGHT, IS IN ITS SIMULTANEOUSNESS, AN ADHESIVE OF THE UNIVERSE.
THE CINEMA DEVELOPED AS THE TECHNICAL EXECUTION OF THE MODEL OF JACOB'S LADDER AND THE CADRE GRID REMINISCENT OF AN EXTENDED FIRE BRIGADE LADDER REVEALS THE FUNCTIONAL PRINCIPLE WHICH BECOMES SYMBOLIZATION IN THE INTERNATIONAL SYMBOL FOR EMERGENCY LADDER. AS, OF COURSE, IT INVOLVES TOO MUCH EFFORT TO TRANSPORT THE AUDIENCE AT THE CORRESPONDING SPEED ALONG THE CELLULOID LADDER, THE INGENIOUS IDEA AROSE TO MOVE THE FILM ON WITH AN ARTFUL MECHANICAL DEVICE. ULTIMATELY, THE AUDIENCE IS THEN MOVED MORE THAN THE MATERIAL.
THE SPACE BETWEEN THIS FILMED LATTICE FENCE BECOMES A VISION OF A PROJECTED MODULATION OF TRANSPARENCY. AND JUST AS GALILEO'S BINOCULARS, THE VIEW OF THE STARS AND LITTLE STARS PROVOKES THE CRY: "AND THEY DO MOVE!"
BEYOND A PEACEFUL COEXISTANCE, THESE ARTIFICIAL GALAXIES HAVE LONG BEEN INSEPARABLE FROM OUR REAL WORLD, AS IS SHOWN BY THE PICTURE OF THE "FILM TEAR" THAT FREQUENTLY CROPS UP IN COURT PROCEEDINGS. "THE FILM TEAR" AS MITIGATING CIRCUMSTANCE STANDS E.G. FOR THE ALCOHOL-RELATED BLACKOUT OF CULTURAL GLOSS AND WHEN THIS SHORT-TERM LOSS OF SOCIAL ENTRAINMENT PROCEEDS WITHOUT MUCH HARM BEING DONE, EVERYTHING IS OK AGAIN. THE TECHNICAL FAULT (WE REGRET) OF THE PRIVATE RED-GREEN-BLUE LINE DANCE MONITOR, OF COURSE, REQUIRES A NEW LIN-

Umweltreize bemessen will, dann traue keinem über zwanzig, denn scheinbar ist bald nach der entscheidenden sexuellen Prägungsphase (der Wandlung zum ehrenwerten Mitglied der Gesellschaft) die Luft raus und der Ofen aus. Wie sich an den Jahresringen der Jugendkultur und der raschen Abfolge ihrer Gezeiten deutlich ablesen läßt, gelingt es nur wenigen das Modell ihrer Prägung zu transkodieren. Die Bereitschaft des Gehirns, neue Verbindungen zu ziehen, läßt offenbar so stark nach, daß der musikalische Stilbruch nach dem „offenen Fenster" nicht mehr nachvollzogen werden kann. Ob Fisch, Frosch, Pavian oder Mensch, die embryonale Entwicklung der Wirbeltiere verläuft in ihren Anfängen sehr ähnlich, aber der Entwicklungsstop und Sidestep in die Öko-Nische bescherte uns nicht nur Adult-Rock und Post-Punk, sondern scheint ein Evolutionsphänomen zu sein.
Der Luxus einer verlängerten Adoleszenz in langlebigen Wohlstandszivilisationen steht in direktem Zusammenhang mit der kulturellen Entwicklung, in etwa wie sich auch die Traumfabrik des Kinos weitgehend aus dem Taschengeld des internationalen Teenagers finanziert. Das Freizeitproblem hat sich durch die zunehmende Automatisierung weiter verschärft und nachdem die Verdrängung des Blue-Collar-Workers durch die Einführung intelligenter technischer Produktionsmethoden eingeleitet wurde, zündet bereits die nächste Stufe: Die Automatisierung geistiger Arbeit treibt die mentale Siliconprothese bis weit hinaus in den Dienstleistungsraum.
Bald gibt es kaum noch Produktionsbereiche in denen Maschinen nicht sparsamer, schneller, sauberer und effizienter arbeiten als Menschen. Wann schaltet die postindustrielle Data-Ökonomie auf Autopilot und entläßt die werktätige Bevölkerung mittels Freizeitschock in die Historie? Die Aufschrift „Arbeit macht frei" war Teil der gruseligen Ironie der jüngeren Zeitgeschichte, aber „Freiheit macht Arbeit" ist ungeschriebenes Gesetz der Freizeitgesellschaft. Es ist vielleicht möglich einem „letzten Willen" peinlich genau zu folgen, aber aus welchen unbewußten Affektschaltungen und Regulationen hierarchisch übergeordneter Gefühlsimpulse ein „freier Wille" entspringt, ist kaum noch zu verfolgen. Die Software ist das Sicherheitsrisiko der computerunterstützten Kriegsführung, komplexe Quellcodes führen ein Eigenleben und entziehen sich ihrer Entschleierung auf dem Pfeil der Zeit.
Immer der Nase nach reichen bereits wenige Moleküle eines Duftstoffes oder Pheromons um Erinnerungen an das Tier im Menschen zu wecken. Produktnamen wie Obsession, Egoiste oder Pitralon sprechen eine deutliche Sprache. Manche Erinnerungsspeicher, die Schubladen (Drawers) des Ge-

dächtnisses scheinen sich nur in bestimmten Stimmungslagen und emotionalen Settings öffnen zu lassen. Erst die Transition in den Phasenraum des Attraktors gestattet den Zugriff des Systems.

Interessanterweise gibt es beim Speichern und Abrufen von komplex-kognitivem Material eine hierarchische Struktur, in der die in höheren Bewußtseinsstufen (Wachbewußtsein) gespeicherte Information in weniger differenzierten Zuständen (Traum) verfügbar bleibt, nicht aber umgekehrt. Es fällt nach dem Aufwachen oft schwer sich an einen Traum zu erinnern und der aus tiefer Hypnose Erwachte hat keinen direkten Zugang zu den im Hypnoseschlaf erfolgten Suggestionen.

Bei Operationen unter Vollnarkose können negative Suggestionen vom anwesenden medizinischen Personal (z. B.: „die fette Sau macht's nimmer lang") den Rehabilitationsprozeß schwer beeinträchtigen und führten zu Kunstfehlerprozessen und Schadensersatzklagen.

Auch echte Zombies essen Hamburger aber haben Hirntote Hunger? Jedenfalls verbrauchen sie Nahrung und Sauerstoff. Bewußtsein und geistige Aufnahmebereitschaft verbraucht erstaunlicherweise genausoviele Kalorien wie Stumpfsinn oder Indolenz. Zu agieren kostet nicht mehr Kraft als zu reagieren. Hier scheint am Kreuzungspunkt des ständig Wechselnden mit dem Permanentem eine Quelle negativer Entropie verborgen zu sein. Das Bewußtsein als non-kalorisches Kraftwerk einer Energie schneller als Licht, ist in seiner Gleichzeitigkeit ein Klebstoff des Universums.

Das Kino entstand als technische Projektion des Typus Jakobs Himmelsleiter und der an eine ausgefahrene Feuerwehrleiter erinnernde Kaderraster verrät das Funktionsprinzip welches im internationalen Symbol für Notleiter versinnbildlicht wird. Weil es natürlich zu aufwendig ist, das Publikum in der entsprechenden Geschwindigkeit entlang der Zelluloidleiter zu transportieren, entstand die geniale Idee den Film mit einer trickreichen mechanischen Vorrichtung weiterzubewegen. Letztlich ist das Publikum dann aber meist doch mehr bewegt als das Material.

Der Zwischenraum dieses verfilmten Lattenzauns wird zur Vision einer projezierten Modulation der Transparenz. Und wie einst das Fernglas des Galileo provoziert der Ausblick auf die Stars und Sternchen den Ausruf: „Und sie bewegen sich (doch)!"

Jenseits einer friedlichen Koexistenz sind diese künstlichen Galaxien von unserer realen Welt längst nicht mehr zu trennen wie sich an dem in Gerichtsprotokollen häufig auftauchendem Bild des „Filmrisses" zeigt. Der Filmriss als mildernder Umstand steht z. B. für das alkoholbedingte Blak-

GUISTIC REGULATION, E.G. TAPE TEAR, BITMAP ERROR OR " :O*O*(".

RITUALIZED NON-LOCALITY IN THE LOCAL OF YOUR CHOICE IS, OF COURSE, THE BAR: IN THE COURT OF CONTACT OF ZEITGEIST IS THE TEST ROUTE OF HUMAN2 INTERFACE MODELLING AND THE ARENA FOR BREEDING SELECTION (SON OF A BITCH). A MERRY ROUND CONSISTING OF ATTRACTION AND REPULSION ON A MATRIX OF THE GUESTS' REQUEST INTERVALS. THE COURSE OF A PUBLIC MULTI-LATERAL RELATION BUSINESS CAN BE REPRESENTED AS A DYNAMIC LANDSCAPE OF VIRTUAL MOUNTAINS OF UNEASE AND VALLEYS OF WELL-BEING, IN WHICH THE SUBJECTIVE TOPOGRAPHY OF THE PARTICIPANTS IS ALWAYS DIFFERENT. ENDLESS HUNTS AND THE ROMANTIC TURBULENCE OF CELLULAR SLOT MACHINES ON THE COORDINATES OF THE SOCIAL DISTANCE OF PERSONAL SPACE (30 SECONDS TO COMPLY). THE BIOCULTURALLY RELATED GAMES RULES HAVE BECOME INCREASINGLY COMPLICATED AND ABSTRACTED THROUGH MEDIALIZATION. (IS THAT NEW? NO ...). AN INDUSTRY OF "SPECIAL EFFECTS FOR SPECIAL EFFECTS" HAS RECORDED ITSELF ENGRAMMATICALLY IN THE UNCONSCIOUS, JUST AS VIRAL GENETIC INFORMATION HAS BEEN INTRODUCED OVER GENERATIONS INTO THE HUMAN GENOTYPE. (SOME OF THESE VIRUSES COULD HAVE BEEN WASHED ONTO OUR PLANET A LONG TIME AGO AS COSMIC FLOTSAM AND JETSAM FROM EXPLODING STAR SYSTEMS AND COULD HAVE MADE MAN INTO THE HOST OF PARASITIC ALIEN LIFE FORMS). IN THIS WAY MAN BECAME HIS DOUBLE, CLONED FROM THE TRIPLETS OF TRIVIAL TRINITY BY PRESS, RADIO AND TELEVISION.

FROM PEN-FRIENDSHIP TO TELEPHONE SEX, FROM THE TELECOM TO IN VITRO-FERTILIZATION, IT IS ONLY ONE HOTLINE. SOME BEHAVIOURAL RESEARCHERS REDUCED THE FUNDAMENTAL STATEMENT OF HUMAN COMMUNICATIONS TO THE PRIMAL FORMULA: "I AM HERE! ARE YOU HERE TOO?" A VERBAL EXCHANGE WHICH HAS BEEN PRACTISED SINCE THE VERY EARLY HISTORY OF MANKIND (IN THE NON-ELECTRIFIED FLATS OF THE CAVE BEARS). THE FORMULA CHANGED INTO "I AM COMING! ARE YOU COMING TOO?" IN THE SYMBOL OF TELEMATIC MOBILITY AND EROTICIZED TECHNOLOGY.

EVER SINCE THE EARTH HAS BEEN ROUND AND REVOLVES, EVERYTHING REVOLVES AND MOVES, AND TO JUST BE ABLE TO REMAIN AT THE SAME PLACE, THE COMPLETE ROTATION OF THE TERRESTRIAL GLOBE HAS TO BE ACCOMPLISHED OVER 24 HOURS. THE CLEAR STAND POINT GETS INTO THE FLUX TO THE LINE AND OPINION BECOMES A QUESTION OF STYLE, CONTEXTUALITY, THE CUDGEL IN THE LAUGHING BAG OF MODERN PERPLEXITY, WILL AT SOME TIME WILL BE SLAIN BY HYPER-CONTEXTUALITY; WITH THE FAINT IDEA THAT SOMEWHERE, EVERYTHING IS SOMEHOW CONNECTED.

EVEN COMPUTERS NEED FUZZY LOGIC AND IT CAN BE SEEN HOW THE PRECISION OF A STATEMENT CAN BE THE REVERSE OF ITS SIGNIFICANCE, WITH THE COMPLEXITY OF A SYSTEM. "NO NEWS IS BAD NEWS"—EVEN WHEN LIFE SEEMS TO BE HARD ENOUGH. FOR, WHOEVER UNDERSTANDS EVERYTHING MUST HAVE UNDERSTOOD SOMETHING WRONG. IT IS NOT A LONG WAY FROM SURVIVAL AND FITNESS TO SELF-OUTSMARTING. THE RELATIONSHIP OF COOPERATION AND SELF-INTEREST WAS KNOWN AS A GAMES-THEORY SITUATION UNDER THE NAME OF PRISONERS' DILEMA AND AWAKENED THE INTEREST OF MATHEMATICIANS, SCIENTISTS, POLITICAL SCIENTISTS AND EVOLUTONARY BIOLOGISTS. COMPUTER GAMES AND COMPETITIONS FOR ITERATIVE AND TERRITORIAL FORMS OF THE PRISONERS' DILEMA SHOW JUST HOW COOPERATION STRATEGIES CAN SUCCEED, ALTHOUGH SUCCESSFUL FRAUD BRINGS THE BIGGEST GAIN IN THE SHORT-TERM.
LUCKILY ENOUGH, OUR ANTHROPICAL CHAUVANISM RELATIVIZES ITSELF IN RELATION TO THE LIVING BEINGS WHICH RULED THE PLANETS BEFORE US. WITH THE AID OF NEW FINDINGS AND THE ASSISTANCE OF THE YOUTH FROM ALL OVER THE WORLD (THE DINO AS CONTEMPORARY TEDDY BEAR), THE SAURIERS ARE HITTING BACK AND NO LONGER LET THEMSELVES BE SLANDERED AS THE PLUMP-DULL MONSTERS WHICH WERE OVERRUN BY EVOLUTION ON ACCOUNT OF ALLEGEDLY BEING UNFIT TO LIVE. WHEN THE DINOSAURIERS STILL LIVED ON THE SPACE SHIP EARTH, THE FORERUNNERS OF THE HOMONIDS WERE ONLY INSIGNIFICANT SORICIDAE AND OPOSSUMS WHICH OCCUPIED ONLY A SMALL ECOLOGICAL NICHE AMONG THE MAMALS. IS HISTORY REPEATING ITSELF AT THE END, AGAIN, AND IS THE MOUSE WHICH IS NOW TO BE FOUND ON NEARLY EVERY WRITING DESK THE FORERUNNER OF A NEW MASTER RACE?
IT IS NO LONGER PENNIES WHICH FALL FROM HEAVEN BUT GAME CHIPS AND AN AMERICAN PRESIDENT WHO DREAMED OF HOW THE YOUTH COULD TURN INTO PEREFCT FIGHTER PILOTS WITH THE AID OF VIDEO GAMES, WAS STILL ABLE TO EXPERIENCE HOW AIR BATTLES BECAME VIDEO GAMES. JUST AS THE CAPITAIN OF A PLANE ON THE APPROACH FOR LANDING UNDER BAD VISIBILITY CONDITIONS ORIENTATES HIMSELF ON THE SOVEREIGN CONTROL ABILITIES OF THE COMPUTER-EXPERT SYSTEM "AUTOPLIOT", IT IS NOT A DISGRACE TO WITHDRAW IN THE FACE OF A SUPERIOR OPPONENT. IF OVERREACHING DOESN'T PAY, A COOPERATION MODEL COULD POINT OUT THE WAY. THE "DIVIDE AND DOMINATE" PRINCIPLE OF THE OLD WARLORDS DEVELOPS ITS COUNTERACTING FORCE IN ELECTRONIC INTERLINKING. UNITE AND FIGHT!
THE WORLD WAR AMONGST COMPUTERS HAS BEEN RAGING FOR YEARS AS COREWARS AND, AS OPPOSED TO START WARS,

kout des kulturellen Firnisses und wenn dieser kurzfristige Verlust des sozialen Entrainments glimpflich abläuft, ist alles wieder Leinwand. Die technische Störung (wir bedauern) des privaten rot-grün-blauen Zeilentanzmonitors fordert natürlich eine neue Sprachregelung wie z. B. Bandriß, Bitmap-Error oder „: ( ) * () * (".

Ritualisierte non-Lokalität im Lokal der Wahl ist, na klar, die Bar. Im Kontakthof des Zeitgeistes liegt die Teststrecke des Human[2] Interface Modelling und die Arena der Zuchtwahl (son of a bitch). Ein lustiger Reigen aus Anziehung und Abstoßung auf einer Matrix der Wunschabstände der Gäste. Der Verlauf einer öffentlichen, multilateralen Beziehungskiste kann als dynamische Landschaft von virtuellen Bergen des Unbehagens und Tälern des Wohlbefindens dargestellt werden, in der die subjektive Topographie der Teilnehmer jeweils verschieden ist. Endlose Jagden und romantische Wirbel zellulärer Spielautomaten auf den Koordinaten der sozialen Distanz des personal space (30 seconds to comply). Die biokulturell bedingten Spielregeln haben sich durch die Medialisierung erheblich kompliziert und abstrahiert („Ist das neu? Nein"). Eine Industrie von „special effects for special affects" hat sich engrammatisch in das Unbewußtsein geschrieben so wie sich virale genetische Information über Generationen hinweg ins menschliche Erbgut eingeschleust hat. (Manche dieser Viren könnten vor langer Zeit als kosmisches Strandgut explodierender Sternsysteme auf unseren Planeten gespült worden sein und die Menschheit zum Wirt parasitärer Alien-Life-Forms gemacht haben.) So wurde der Mensch zu seinem Double – geklont aus den Triplets trivialer Trinität von Presse, Funk und Fernsehen.
Von der Brieffreundschaft zum Telefonsex, von der Telecom zur Invitro-Fertilisation ist es nur eine Hotline. Einige Verhaltensforscher brachten die Grundaussage der menschlichen Kommunikation auf die Urformel: „Ich bin da! Bist du auch da? Ein verbaler Austausch der seit der Frühgeschichte der Menschheit (in den nicht elektrifizierten Wohnungen des Höhlenbären) geübt wird. Im Zeichen der telematischen Mobiliät und der erotisierten Technik verwandelte sich die Formel in: „Ich komme! Kommst du auch?"
Seit die Erde rund ist und sich dreht, dreht und bewegt sich alles und um auch nur am selben Ort bleiben zu können, muß 24 Stunden lang die komplette Rotation des Erdballs mitvollzogen werden. Der eindeutige Standpunkt gerät im Flug zur Linie und Meinung wird zur Stilfrage. Kontextualität, der Knüppel im Lachsack moderner Ratlosigkeit, wird irgendwann von der Hyperkontextualität mit der leisen Ahnung, daß irgendwo alles irgendwie zusammenhängt, erschlagen.

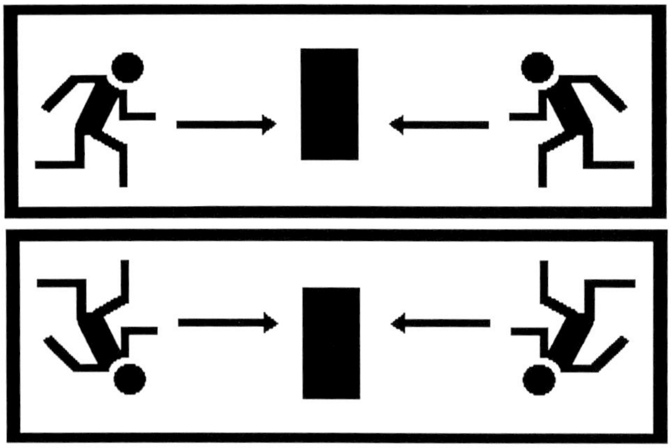

Auch Computer brauchen Fuzzy Logic und es zeigt sich , wie mit der Komplexität eines Systems die Präzision einer Aussage im umgekehrten Verhältnis zu ihrer Signifikanz stehen kann. „No News is bad News" – selbst wenn das Leben hart genug erscheint, denn wer alles versteht muß irgendet was falsch verstanden haben. Von Survival und Fitneß zur Selbstüberlistung ist es nicht weit. Die Beziehung von Kooperation und Eigennutz wurde als spieltheoretische Situation unter dem Namen Gefangenendilemma bekannt und hat das Interesse von Mathematikern, Wirtschaftswissenschaftlern, Politologen und Evolutionsbiologen geweckt. Computerspiele und Turniere für iterative und territoriale Formen des Gefangenendilemmas zeigen, wie sich Kooperationsstrategien durchsetzen können, obwohl erfolgreicher Betrug kurzfristig den größten Gewinn abwirft.

Glücklicherweise relativiert sich unser anthropischer Chauvinismus in Bezug auf die Lebewesen die den Planeten vor uns beherrschten. Mit Hilfe neuer Erkenntnisse und der Unterstützung der Jugendlichen aller Länder (der Dino als contemporary teddybear) schlagen die Saurier zurück und lassen sich nicht mehr als plump-dumpfe Monster verleumden, die aufgrund angeblicher Lebensuntüchtigkeit von der Evolution überrollt wurden. Als die Dinosaurier noch auf dem Raumschiff Erde lebten, waren die Vorläufer der Hominiden nur scheinbare Spitzmäuse und Beutelratten, die eine schmale ökologische Nische der Säugetiere besetzt hielten. Wiederholt sich hier die Geschichte am Ende noch einmal und die Mäuse die sich heute auf fast jedem Schreibtisch finden, sind die Vorboten einer neuen Herrenrasse?

Es fallen nicht mehr Pennies sondern Gamechips from heaven und ein amerikanischer Präsident, der davon geträumt hatte wie die Jugend mittels Videogames zu perfekten Kampfpiloten heranwächst, konnte noch erleben, wie der Luftkampf zum Videospiel wurde. Sowie der Flugkapitän ei-

PROGRESSES COMPLETELY WITHOUT LOSS OF BLOOD. AND PARADOXICALLY THIS CAN ONLY BE TERMED AS BEING HUMAN IN FRONT OF THE BACKGROUND OF "REAL" WARS IN WHICH THERE IS NO VICTOR ANY MORE. INBREEDING AND SPECIALIZATION ARE AT THE EXPENSE OF THE ABILITY TO ADAPT AND OVER-SPECIALIZING IS THE FASTEST WAY TO EXTINCTION. ON THE WAY TO THE GLOBAL SELF-FULFILLING MEDIA, DATA DEAMONS DEVELOP TO FORM EMANCIPATED KNOWBOTS ON A SILICON PLANET OF ELECTRONIC SELF-STIMULATION. ("DO ANDROIDS DREAM ABOUT ELECTRICAL SHEEP?")

AMUSINGLY ENOUGH, THE BASIS OF THE MATERIAL WORLD (MONEY MAKES THE WORLD GO ROUND?) IS STILL GOLD, THE MEANS OF PAYMENT OF ANALPHABETIC PIRATES AND CRAFTY CHIEFTAINS. AND ALTHOUGH, FOR CENTURIES NOW, MORE AND MORE GOLD HAS BEEN PRODUCED AND BROUGHT INTO CIRCULATION, THERE IS HARDLY LESS POVERTY THAN BEFORE. EVEN WHEN AN AUSTRIAN DAILY NEWSPAPER ADVERTISES FOR ITSELF WITH THE SLOGAN "INTELLIGENCE CAN BE BOUGHT"(!), IT BECOMES MORE AND MORE EVIDENT JUST HOW PASSE THE ECONOMIC APPRAISAL SYSTEM IS. YET THE INFORMATION WAR RAGES AND SETS NEW STANDARDS: PATENTED MICE AND COPYRIGHT TOMATOES HAVE ALARMED BIG MONEY, TO CONQUER THE GENETIC MAPS WITH GENOM DECODERS.

AS IS WELL KNOWN, YOU CAN'T EAT MONEY, BUT YOU CAN EAT TRANSGENIC PRODUCTS AND THE INFORMATION CODED IN IT CAN SUDDENLY CAUSE A HARDWORKING BUSINESS MAN TO EXCHANGE A SUITCASE FULL OF GOLD FOR A FEW NUTS OR GRAINS OF CEREAL.

IN THE GENETIC GOLD RUSH, THE DIRECT INFLUENCE OF A SEMEN BANK IS SHOWN ON THE STATEMENT OF ACCOUNTS OF A DATA BANK. WHO GETS THE PATENT FOR THE NEW PERSON? WHO MONOPOLIZES THE SPECIES? WHO LICENSES THE BORN WINNERS AND LOSERS? IS THERE A MARKET FOR TRANSGENIC CENTAURS, CONTORTIONISTS, DWARFS OR SELF-LUMINOUS HOUSE PLANTS? TRADE IN CHANGE! FROM CONSUMER ELECTRONICS TO CONUSMER BIOLOGICALS, FROM ANIMATRONIC ENVIRONMENT TO THE MULTI-DIMENSIONAL ECOLOGICAL HYPERSPACE-DESIGN OF THE BIOMASS. THE KEY TO SUCCESS IS RECOMBINATION, LIFE IS CHANGE, SO RESIST THE BEGINNINGS—TRANSCODE YOURSELF! (REVOLUTIONS GOBBLE UP THEIR CHILDREN, BUT YOU CAN'T FOOL THE CHILDREN OF THE SYNVOLUTION).

FRY LUKEWARM REALITY SCHNITZEL WITH STATISTIC INSUFFICIENCY IN THE BODY FAT OF THE MENTALLY STILLBORN, ARE THEY PERPETUUM PERPLEX OF NEW HIGH TECH FEUDALISM. ON A RESTAURANT WHERE ONLY THE MENU IS ON OFFER (THE ULTIMATE FAST FOOD), THE KAISERS NEW CLOTHES SUGGEST THEMSELVES. ON THE

DEAD FLANK ARMS OF GAME, FUN AND EXCITEMENT, WHERE FIGURES CARVE FIGURES WITHOUT MAKING THEIR GAME, LIE THE HEAPS OF COMPLEX IGNORANCE LIKE METABOLISM PRODUCTS.
CODING AND DECODING WERE AT THE CRADLE OF MODERN INFORMATICS IN THE WAR OF THE BRAINS (ENIGMA VS. TURING, WW II). CRYPTOLOGY AND THE SCIENCE OF COMPLEX DYNAMIC SYSTEMS UNVEIL THE MYSTERIES OF OPEN SECRETS AND THE MECHANISMS OF WONDERFUL FOG MACHINES OF PUBLIC OPINION FORMING. WHILE THE CONES OF PANIC SEARCH LIGHTS FALL ON THE CLOUD BANKS OF CULTURAL STEAM, THE PSYCHOCYBERNETIC TARGET SIGHTING MECHANICS ARE HOTTING UP. EVERYTHING IS REVOLVING, EVERYTHING IS MOVING IN THE GLOBAL PLAYGROUND "PANTA RHEI", AND EVEN THE VACUUM OF THE EMPTY SPACE IS FLOODED BY ENERGY FLUCTUATIONS (ON WHICH THE LAWS OF NATURE OF THE ELEMENTARY PARTICLES DEPEND).
PERHAPS ON THE OTHERSIDE OF THE WALL OF SEMOLINA PUDDING THERE IS THE GENERAL KEY TO THE SYNLOGISTICAL PERMAFLUX WITH WHICH THE VISCIOUS CIRCLE OF CODED PROJECTIONS AND PERCEPTIONS CAN BE ALLOWED TO BE TRANSFORMED INTO A NON-DETERMINISTIC HYPERCYCLE.

Konrad Becker

ner Verkehrsmaschine sich beim Landeanflug unter schlechten Sichtverhältnissen an den souveränen Steuerungsfähigkeiten des Computer-Expertensystems „Autopilot" orientiert, ist es keine Schande, sich vor einem überlegenen Gegner zurückzuziehen. Wenn sich Übervorteilen nicht lohnt, könnte ein Kooperationsmodell den Weg weisen. Das „Teile und Herrsche" der alten Warlords entwickelt in der elektronischen Vernetzung seine Gegenkraft:unite and fight!
Der Weltkrieg der Computer untereinander wütet seit Jahren als core-wars (Krieg der Kerne) und verläuft im Gegensatz zum Krieg der Sterne völlig unblutig. Paradoxerweise kann das nur als human bezeichnet werden vor dem Hintergrund „realer" Kriege in denen es keine Sieger mehr gibt. Inzucht und Spezialisierung gehen auf Kosten der Anpassungsfähigkeit und Überspezialisierung ist der schnellste Weg um auszusterben. Unterwegs zum globalen Selffullfilling Media entwickeln sich Data-Dämonen zu emanzipierten Knowbots auf einem Silicon-Planet elektronischer Selbststimulation. („Träumen Androiden von elektrischen Schafen?") Amüsanterweise ist die Basis der materiellen Welt (money makes the world go round) noch immer Gold, das Zahlungsmittel analphabetischer Piraten und schlitzohriger Stammesfürsten. Obwohl seit Jahrhunderten immer mehr Gold gefördert und in Umlauf gebracht wurde gibt es kaum weniger Armut als zuvor. Auch wenn eine österreichische Tageszeitung mit dem Slogan „Intelligenz kann man kaufen" Eigenwerbung (!) gemacht hat, zeigt sich doch immer deutlicher, wie hinfällig das ökonomische Bewertungssystem ist. Doch der Informationskrieg tobt und setzt neue Maßstäbe: Patentierte Mäuse und Copyright-Tomaten haben big money alarmiert, die genetischen Landkarten mit Genom-Decodern zu erobern.
Geld kann man bekanntlich nicht essen, aber transgene Produkte durchaus und die darin codierte Information kann einen tüchtigen Geschäftsmann plötzlich dazu bringen, einen Koffer voller Geld gegen ein paar Nüßchen oder Getreidekörner zu tauschen.

Im genetischen Goldrausch zeigt sich der direkte Einfluß einer Samenbank auf den Kontostand einer Datenbank. Wer bekommt das Patent auf den neuen Menschen? Wer monopolisiert die Spezies? Wer lizensiert die geborenen Sieger und Verlierer? Gibt es einen Markt für transgene Centauren, Schlangenmenschen, Liliputaner oder selbstleuchtende Zimmerpflanzen? Handel im Wandel! Von Consumer Electronics zu Consumer Biologicals, vom animatronischen Enviroment zum multidimensionalen, ökologischen Hyperspace-Design der Biomasse. Der Schlüssel zum Erfolg ist Re-

kombination. Leben ist Wandlung also wehret den Anfängen – transcode yourself! (Revolutionen fressen ihre Kinder, aber – you can't fool the children of the synvolution).
Laue Reality-Schnitzel, mit statistischer Unzulänglichkeit im Leichenfett mentaler Totgeburt gebraten, sind das Perpetuum Perplex des Nouveau Hightech-Feudalismus. Zu einem Restaurant in dem nur die Speisekarte geboten wird (the ultimate fast-food), empfehlen sich Kaisers neue Kleider. An toten Seitenarmen von Spiel, Spaß und Spannung, wo Figuren Figuren schnitzen ohne ihr Spiel zu machen, liegen die Haufen komplexer Ignoranz als Stoffwechselprodukt.
Verschlüsselung und Entschlüsselung standen im Krieg der Gehirne an der Wiege der modernen Informatik (Enigma Vs. Turing, WW II). Kryptologie und die Wissenschaft komplexer dynamischer Systeme entschleiern die Mysterien der offenen Geheimnisse und die Mechanismen wundersamer Nebelmaschinen öffentlicher Meinungsbildung. Während die Kegel panischer Suchscheinwerfer auf die Wolkenbänke kulturellen Wasserdampfs fallen, läuft die psychokybernetische Zielsuchmechanik heiß. Alles dreht sich, alles bewegt sich im global playground „Panta Rhei" und auch das Vakuum des leeren Raums ist durchflutet von Energiefluktutationen (von denen die Naturgesetze der Elementarteilchen abhängen).
Vielleicht liegt jenseits der Mauer aus Grießbrei der Generalschlüssel des synlogistischen Permaflux, mit dem sich der Teufelskreis codierter Projektion und Perzeption zu einem nichtdeterministischen Hyperzyklus transformieren läßt.

Konrad Becker

Wir präsentieren Ihnen bei dieser Ars Electronica unter anderem einige Geschmackstests und ganz nebenbei Ergebnisse der gentechnologischen Veränderung genießbarer Pflanzen, Bakterien und anderer Tiere. Es geht wieder um eine Neuorientierung. Und es geht um Ernährung. Leicht möglich also, daß die folgenden Überlegungen grenztriviale Züge aufweisen.
Eigentlich sind wir über einen Zeitungsartikel auf die Materie aufmerksam geworden. Vom „Durchbruch in der Technologie teilflüssiger Lebensmittel" war da die Rede und von einem Sandwich aus „regalstabilem fermentiertem Fleisch", das mit einem „synergistischen Korrosionsschutz" gesichert worden war, wodurch angeblich die „Lipid-Stabilität" deutlich erhöht werden konnte.

Among other presentations at this Ars we will be carrying out some taste tests, and in addition, results of the gene manipulation of edible plants, bacteria and other animals. It is again a question of a reorientation. And it is a question of nutrition. So it is quite possible that the following thoughts seem to border on the trivial.
It was in fact a newspaper article that drew our attention to the material. It concerned a "breakthrough in partially fluid foodstuffs technology" and a US Army sandwich containing "shelf-stable fermented meat" kept fresh by "synergetic protection against corrosion", which can allegedly bring about a significant increase in the "Lipid stability".
These are, incidentally, precisely those qualities that no Parisian connoisseur would under any circumstances want to find lacking when tucking into his roast at a restaurant:

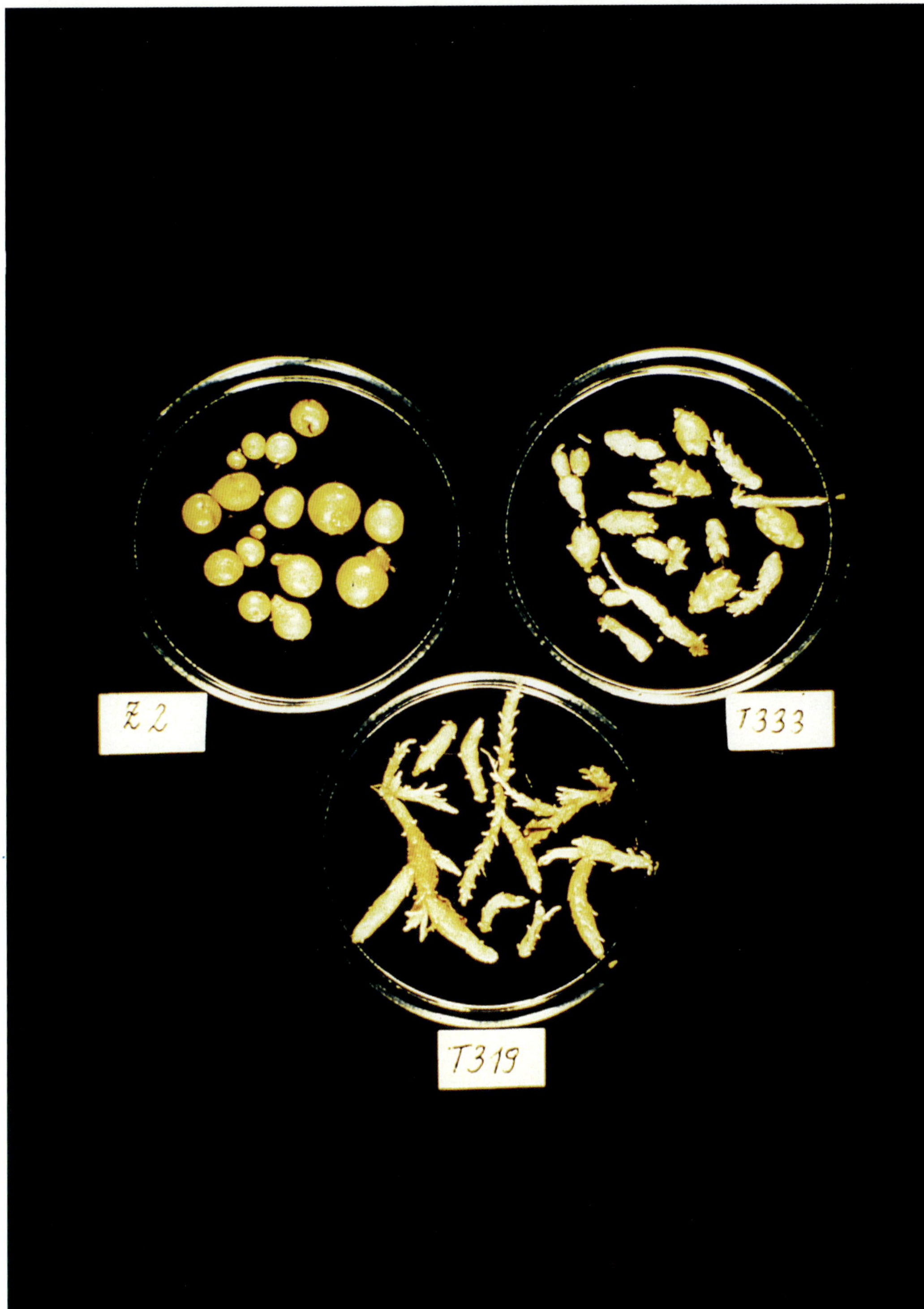

Systematische Beobachtung der Langzeitwirkungen gentransferierter Kartoffelpflänzchen im Forschungszentrum Seibersdorf, Österreich.

Es sind das immerhin genau jene Eigenschaften, die der Pariser Connaisseur am Braten, wenn er im Restaurant vor sich hin diniert, unter keinen Umständen missen möchte:
GOURMET (aus dem Französischen): Kellner, mir scheint als hätte der Koch den synergistischen Korrosionsschutz vergessen, jedenfalls bemerke ich heute eine geringe Lipidstabilität.
GARCON: Monsieur, wir setzen mit Verlaub neuerdings statt der bisherigen Molkenproteinkonzentrate, Eialbumin als Bindemittel ein, wodurch die oxydative Ranzidität und das Wasserhaltevermögen besonders wirkungsvoll gefördert werden.
Wir hatten zu diesem Zeitpunkt noch wenig Ahnung vom riesigen Gebiet der Lebensmittelveränderungen und den zahllosen Möglichkeiten, die sich zukünftigen Generationen künstlerisch Begabter auftun.
Gefärbt und geformt wird an Speisen natürlich (und künstlich) immer schon. Wahrscheinlich, weil seit jeher nur wenige Menschen freiwillig ein grüngrau, schleimiges Würstel essen wollen, und weil bestimmte, von Geburt an bleich gewachsene Tomaten, sogenannte Aastomaten, irgendwie verstrahlt, krank und gefährlich wirken.
Das sind natürlich Vorurteile, deren Wurzeln zumindest in jene längst vergessenen Tage zurückreichen, als der Mensch noch freier Löwe in freier Natur war und frische, blutige Ware den halbverwesten Resten der Beute vorzog. Nie war dieser Mensch Aasgeier – oder selten.
Deswegen kann er sich auch mit bestimmten Gerüchen nur schwer abfinden. Und deswegen liebt er das leuchtende Rot in allen Schattierungen eher als die bleichen und krebserregenden Farben. Den Chicorée rot wachsen zu lassen, ist kein ästhetisches und schon gar kein ethisches Problem.
Soviel zu den biologischen Ursachen ästhetischer Geschmackspräferenzen.
Phylogentisch und kulturell gewachsene Vorlieben sind wahrscheinlich auch der Grund, warum Naturfromme der festen Überzeugung sind, daß genetische Manipulationen an Formen und Farben hilfloser Gemüse zu weit gehen und daß maximal kleine Unpäßlichkeiten der Schöpfung korrigiert werden dürften. Zum Beispiel, wenn ein Mais vom bösen Colorado-Käfer gefoltert wird, wenn Zuckerrüben von Viren der Wurzelbärtigkeit befallen werden, und also nicht so gedeihen können, wie sie sollen, oder wenn Tomaten hart und rot zugleich werden wollen, aber leider zu früh geerntet werden. Im Interesse der Natur darf nach ursprünglich vorliegenden Bauplänen korrigiert werden. Absichten darüber hinaus sind verwerflich, für Bodenständige ist selbst das zuviel. 40 deutsche Spitzenköche appelieren generell gegen die Marktzulassung von „Gentechnik in Lebensmitteln“ und vermuten einen „Angriff auf Würde, Integrität und

GARCON (from the French): Everything to your satisfaction, sir?
GOURMET: It seems to me as if the Lipid stability had not been mixed with synergetic corrosion protection this time.
GARCON: But of course it is, sir. But lately, if I may say so, we have replaced the whey protein concentrate we used to use as a binder with egg albumin, which is especially effective in improving the oxidative rancidity and water capacity.
At this point we are merely scratching the surface of the enormous area of foodstuff alteration and the numerous possibilities available to future generations of the artistically gifted.
Food has of course always been naturally (and artificially) coloured and moulded. Probably because not many people have ever wanted to eat a green-grey, slimy sausage, and because certain pale tomatoes, known as flesh tomatoes, seem somehow irradiated, sickly and dangerous.
These are of course prejudices whose roots go back to the long-forgotten days when man was a free lion in free nature, and preferred fresh, bloody meat to decaying leftovers. Man was never, or seldom, a vulture. (consumption of partially decomposed bodies has only been reported from Foré in the highlands of New Guinea, incidentally, with fatal consequences)
This is why even some smells are hard for man to tolerate. Any this is why he prefers the glowing colour red in all its shades to the pale and cancer—causing colours. Letting chicory grow red is not an aesthetic question, and certainly not an ethical one.
So much for the biological origins of aesthetic taste preferences. Philo-genetic and culturally developed preferences are probably also the reason why supporters of nature are firmly convinced that genetic manipulation of the shape and colour of defenceless vegetables is going too far and that only minor indispositions of creation should be corrected. If, for instance, an evil Colorado beetle is torturing corn, or if sugar beet is beset with fungus and cannot thrive the way it should, or if tomatoes try to grow hard and red but are prematurely harvested. In the interests of nature, corrections can be made according to the original blueprints. Any further intentions are reprehensible. Even Der Spiegel (15/93) warns of "Gene Feeding" and airbrushes a precautionary, deterrent picture of an apocalyptic vision on its cover: flat radishes, octagonal peppers, pentagonal sausage slices with white inserts.
The gene discussion in general has inspired witty illustrators to draw horror scenarios and two-headed monsters, renditions as good as our first unsuccessful attempts in school to portray St. Nicholas on horseback after we simply renamed each of these failures without any further ado.
But bred creatures have been vegetating, without much uproar, ever since man took up the redesigning of flora and fauna. Crippled dogs, pigs, geese. The portion-sized chicken on the grill, the broiler is a particularly monstrous example of hormonal breeding culture. If this poor creature were not slaughtered within forty

days its rapid growth hormones would turn it into a wretch incapable of life in the wild.
Foodstuff producers, despite their creativity, know their aesthetic limits. Hence, as an extra, this quiz question: should the gene technician, the artist working with biological materials, only go about making changes in an ideal-typical direction, using picture-books and clichés as models, or can he from time to time create the odd Frankenstein, dragon, or rubbish- eating bush? Assuming, that is, that such techniques were not beyond the bounds of what can realistic possibility.
Just to avoid any misunderstanding: Nobody wants a complete fantasy world. Nobody would want to turn the vegetable market into a paper box with rabbit-shaped carrots, striped lemons, or designer plums, autographed but otherwise original in their simplicity. It is sufficient that artists invent cute handbags and hilarious clocks.
Despite this, or just because of this, here are three more non-competitive, leading questions: must bio-art be a division of the decorative arts? Are the visible characteristics of food at all important? Does history not show the plastic arts to be the development of aesthetic taste; that formal preferences with differing half-lives fall apart just as they came about?
It is to be expected that the possibilities of gene manipulation will also be used to practise beautification on food.
Consumer-friendly, sales-boosting, populistic. Even without genetic techniques, foodstuffs are altered mainly for these reasons. They are coloured, flavour-strengthened, aromatised, emulsified, homogenised, sulphured, etched, held in shape by stabilisers, thickeners, and subjected to other processes of which the ordinary consumer knows little.
That is the one department. In the other, biochemists and genetic engineers develop the novel food which displays certain specific characteristics while suppressing others. For instance, it must make the eater big and strong, but not unnecessarily fat—or ill. Or not fat and not ill. And not ugly either.
Tobacco plants with higher nicotine content are in the pipeline, the sugar content of pumpkins, and manipulated tomatoes are coming into circulation in the USA which in principle look like tomatoes, are red and not too small, taste like tomatoes, sweet and fruity, have their vitamins and nutrients, everything as it should be, and they keep all these qualities for weeks.
This is not to be taken for granted in a tomato. In the last few years they have also been beautiful, red and firm, which is why they too were loosely termed tomatoes, although they tasted more like the fourth state of water.
Which leads us to the hierarchy of sensory information acquisition. What is it that leads us to identify an object as a tomato, the visual or taste information? With natural products, taste seems to come second. In the first instance, a tomato is a tomato if it looks like a tomato, i.e.: when it is not cracked, even if it does not taste of anything.
Products that are already marked by a synthetic character are a different matter. Where there are no archetypes, there are no formal taboos. Cho-

Tradition der Kochkunst." Selbst Der Spiegel (15/93) warnt vor einem „Gen-Fraß" und malt zur Abschreckung vorsichtshalber eine apokalyptische Vision mit dem Luftpinsel aufs Cover: flache Radieschen, achteckige Paprika, fünfeckige Wurstscheiben mit weißen Einschlüssen.
Überhaupt animiert die Gendiskussion lustige Zeichner zu Horrorszenarien und Doppelkopfmonster, wie sie auch uns damals so gut gelungen waren, als wir in der Unterstufe des Gymnasiums jeden mißlungenen Nikolaus am Pferd kurzerhand umgetauft hatten.
Dabei vegetieren gezüchtete Kreaturen, ohne große Aufregung, seitdem sich der Mensch als Gestalter von Flora und Fauna versteht. Verkrüppelte Hunde, Rinder, Schweine, Gänse. Das Portionshähnchen am Grill, der Broiler ist ein besonderes Monsterbeispiel hormoneller Zuchtkultur. Würde dieses armselige Geschöpf nicht vor seinem vierzigsten Lebenstag geschlachtet, entwickelte es sich dank seiner Schnellwachstumshormone zu einem außerhalb menschlicher Stützung völlig lebensunfähigen Elend. „Wollen wir uns von der Gentechnik den Appetit verderben lassen?", fragt Pierre Pfister Maître am „Bayrischen Hof", der seinen Gästen, wie beispielsweise dem Papst, gerne Leckereien aus Gänseleber auftischt.
Hersteller von Lebensmitteln, Köche und andere Drappierer wissen trotz expansiver Kreativität um ihre ästhetischen Grenzen. Deshalb und als Einschub gleich die Quizfrage: Soll der Gentechniker, der Künstler biologischen Materials, Veränderungen nur in idealtypischer Richtung, nach Bilderbuch-Vorlagen und Klischees vornehmen, oder darf er gelegentlich auch einmal einen Frankenstein entwickeln, Drachen, müllschluckende Stauden? Ganz abgesehen einmal davon, daß solche Techniken außerhalb jeder realistisch entwickelbaren Methode liegen.
Nur damit kein Irrtum entsteht. Niemand möchte das totale Phantasieland. Niemand möchte den Gemüsemarkt zur Paperbox erweitern mit einem Angebot an hasenförmigen Karotten, gestreiften Zitronen, mit signierten, aber sonst originell einfachen Designer-Zwetschken. Es reicht, daß Künstler putzige Tragtaschen und Uhren zum Schieflachen erfinden.
Dennoch, oder gerade deswegen, drei suggestive Zusatzfragen außer Konkurrenz: Muß Bio-Art eine Abteilung der Dekorkunst werden? Sind die sichtbaren Eigenschaften von Nahrungsmitteln überhaupt wichtig? Zeigt nicht die Geschichte der bildenden Kunst als Entwicklung des ästhetischen Geschmacks, daß formale Präferenzen mit unterschiedlichen Halbwertszeiten zerfallen, so wie sie entstanden sind?
Es ist zu erwarten, daß auch mit den Möglichkeiten der Genmanipulation an Nahrungsmitteln geschönt wird. Konsumenten-

colate is blue, red and green, and everyone finds that amusing. It is brown and white, liquid, flaky and solid, none of which has ever caused anyone to lose their lunch. If synthetics look like soiled nappies, taste like them are named accordingly, they will sell. If eggs look like rotten eggs and are marketed as such, they will not sell. Even if biological technology should one day imbue them with all important nutrients.
Is a tomato really only a tomato if it looks like one? Categorising into groups and the identity of kinds and sorts will be no simple matter in the future. It never was an exact science, but will only be complicated by gene transformation. Take fruit, for example.
Everybody knows what fruit is. Saint Augustine himself thought he knew what fruit is, at least as long as he was not asked to define it. To define fruit precisely is more difficult than one might think. According to the encyclopaedia it is what grows on herb- and wood-like plants, but this is not satisfactory because it could of course apply just as well to the tomato, the pumpkin, and other kinds of vegetable. On the other hand, ashanti nuts would not count as fruit because they grow in the ground, even though dried nuts are counted as dry fruit. What else could they be?
Hair-splitting. It is much simpler to define a lion. Not that there are no problems of demarcation, but they are of a more obscure nature. A philosopher like Robin G. Collingwood might pose the question "is a lion still a lion if it is a dead lion?", for instance when watching the film "Leila the Lioness", in which Leila the Lioness does in fact die. Once the eyes are closed, has the lion become the dust it was, metaphorically, during its lifetime?
And what if the lioness were alive but had no legs? And no fur? Or pink fur? Does a boneless pink lion belong in the lion family?
A comparison of the genomes gives one a clue as to whether the apparent similarity between two organisms is coincidental or derives from common ancestry.
But how, if one tiny gene, essential for classification, were missing? Or if on the other hand many genes were altered, without even resulting in a single white hair on the lion turning black?
A duck is a duck if it waddles, cackles and looks like a duck. This saying from the McCarthy era, which was used to unmask every American who was in some way liberal as a Soviet spy, does have some merit—as far as the waddling goes. But then again, maybe not.
Are there ducks that neither waddle nor cackle? And conversely, are there not cackling Republicans who waddle and look like ducks?
Not that the following quote from Collingwood on this subject is boring, hard to understand, or otherwise fitting. It is just that no self-respecting catalogue contribution is really complete without a quote from two philosophers or two quotes from one:
"The definition of every given kind of thing", writes Collingwood, "is simultaneously the definition of a good thing of this kind: since a thing that is good for its kind is simply a thing that exhibits the attributes of its kind."

freundlich, verkaufsfördernd, populistisch. Auch ohne genetische Techniken werden Lebensmittel in erster Linie aus diesem Grund verändert. Sie werden gefärbt, im Geschmack verstärkt, aromatisiert, emulgiert, homogenisiert, geschwefelt, geätzt, gewachst, durch Stabilisatoren und Dickungsmittel in der Form gehalten und einiges mehr, von dem der gemeine Verbraucher wenig Ahnung hat.
Das ist die eine Abteilung. In der anderen entwickeln Biochemiker und Geningenieure das Novel food, das gezielte Eigenschaften aufweist, während andere unterdrückt werden. Zum Beispiel soll es groß und stark aber nicht unnötig dick machen – oder krank. Oder nicht dick und nicht krank. Und auch nicht häßlich.
Es wird an Tabakpflanzen mit erhöhtem Nikotingehalt gebastelt, der Zuckergehalt von Kürbissen wird verbessert und in den USA kommen manipulierte Tomaten in den Handel, die im Prinzip aussehen wie Tomaten, rot sind, rund und nicht zu klein, die schmecken wie Tomaten, süß und fruchtig, die ihre Vitamine und Nährstoffe aufweisen, wie es sich gehört und die obendrein all diese Eigenschaften wochenlang bewahren.
Das ist keine Selbstverständlichkeit für eine Tomate. Die Angebote der letzten Jahre waren zwar auch schön, rot und fest und deswegen wurden sie auch leichtfertig Tomaten genannt, geschmacklich entsprachen sie aber eher einem vierten Aggregatszustand von Wasser.
Womit wir bei der Hierarchie der Sinnesinformationen wären. Was verleitet uns ein Objekt als Tomate zu identifizieren, die visuelle oder die geschmackliche Information? Bei Naturprodukten scheint der Geschmack zweitrangig zu sein. Eine Tomate ist vor allem eine Tomate, wenn sie wie eine gute Tomate aussieht, also wenn sie nicht schrundig ist. Wenn der schöne Paradeiser nach nichts schmeckt, ist das nicht wichtig.
Bei Produkten, die von vorneherien den Charakter des Synthetischen aufweisen, ist das anders. Wo keine Archetypen existieren, gibt es keine formalen Tabus. Schokolade ist blau, rot und grün und das finden alle lustig. Sie ist braun und weiß, flüssig, flockig, fest und all das hat noch niemanden zum Brechen gereizt. Wenn Synthies aussehen, wie verpißte Windeln, genau so schmecken und so heißen, werden sie gekauft. Wenn Eier aussehen wie faule Eier, und im Verkauf als solche angeboten werden, werden sie nicht gekauft. Selbst wenn sie eines Tages mittels biologischer Technologie mit allen wichtigen Nährstoffen angereichert wären und köstlich schmeckten.
Ist eine Tomate tatsächlich erst eine Tomate, wenn sie aussieht wie eine?
Die Zuteilungen zu Ordnungsgruppen, die Identitäten der

Arten und Sorten aufgrund von Bezeichnungen werden in Zukunft nicht einfach sein. Sie war bisher nicht exakt, wird aber durch Gentransformierungen immer schwieriger werden. Beispiel Obst.

Alle wissen was Obst ist. Selbst der heilige Augustinus zu seiner Zeit glaubte zu wissen, was Obst ist, jedenfalls solange er nicht danach gefragt werde. Obst exakt zu definieren, ist aber schwieriger als man meint. Im Lexikon steht: „Früchte von kraut- und holzartigen Gewächsen", aber das ist nicht befriedigend, weil diese Beschreibung natürlich genauso auf die Tomate und auf den Kürbis passen würde und auf andere Gemüsesorten. Umgekehrt wären Aschantinüsse, da sie doch naturgemäß im Boden wachsen, kein Obst. Nüsse werden aber zum Trockenobst gerechnet. Wohin sonst sollten sie gehören?

Spitzfindigkeiten. Die Definition eines Löwen ist weit einfacher. Nicht, weil es da keine Probleme mit Abgrenzungen gäbe, aber die sind eher obskurer Natur. Ist ein Löwe auch ein Löwe, wenn er tot ist, könnte sich ein Philosoph wie Robin G.Collingwood bei Gelegenheit, zum Beispiel beim Betrachten des Films „Leila die Löwin" fragen, in dem die Löwin Leila stirbt. Ist die Löwin gleich nach dem Zudrücken der Augen jene Asche, die sie metaphorisch auch schon zu Lebzeiten war?

Und wenn die Löwin lebte aber keine Beine hätte? Und kein Fell oder nur ein rosarotes? Gehört ein rosaroter Löwe ohne Knochen zur Familie der Löwen?

Eine Ente ist eine Ente, wenn sie watschelt, schnattert und aussieht wie eine solche. Dieser Spruch aus der McCarthy-Ära, der in den Fünzigern verbreitet wurde, um jeden irgendwie liberalen Amerikaner als sowjetischen Spion zu entlarven, hat einiges für sich – was das Watscheln betrifft. Und doch wieder nicht.

Gibt es nicht Enten, die weder watscheln noch schnattern? Und gibt es nicht umgekehrt schnatternde Republikaner, die watscheln und aussehen wie Enten?

Durch Genetik und Molekularbiologie ist der Zoologe heute nicht mehr allein auf phänotypische Vergleiche angewiesen, wenn er Verwandtschaftsbeziehungen zwischen Arten und Unterarten von Lebewesen untersucht. Ein Vergleich der Genome gibt ihm Auskunft darüber, ob die Ähnlichkeit in der Erscheinung zweier Organismen zufällig ist oder auf Abstammung von einem gemeinsamen Vorfahren beruht.

Wie aber, wenn ein für die Zuordnung ganzklein klitzewichtiges Gen fehlte? Oder wenn umgekehrt gleich zahlreiche Gene verändert wären, ohne daß deswegen äußerlich auch nur ein Löwenhaar schwarz geworden wäre, das vorher weiß war?

Nicht, daß das folgende Zitat Collingwoods zu diesem The-

The distinguishing features by which an object is categorised as a duck or a lion are in Collingwood's opinion the same features, whether they are to a greater or lesser extent apparent, by which one lion is judged to be more of a lion than another one is. But then, what is the other one?

Enough of that. Back to the vegetables. What was announced at the beginning as a trivial message is this: Produce at the vegetable market should only be judged by its appearance to the same extent as the black square in the art museum—that is, not at all.

Even the more discerning customers, who know that all that glitters is not tasty, and all that is tasty is not safe, even customers who would rather buy bio-mass and faded goods, and feel they are thereby consuming quality, are labouring under illusions. Not just because the market has long since adjusted its strategies to these new, superficial quality criteria with varying degrees of refinement and has accordingly widened its range from the ripe, spotless and tasteless to the small, shrivelled and also tasteless, but because various forms of cosmetics have been applied too.

Food stays fresh longer after ionisation through irradiation with gamma rays. Buyers looking for visual information to make their choices actually mean fresh, vitamin-rich food when they decide for the smooth, shiny surface, are in reality getting the old product, whose nutritional value has become a question of survival. (War and TV, Hanser, Munich, 1993). But can the other senses no longer be trusted?

We sent off for small test sample from a military survival packet. Of course we could not assume that this represented the state of the art. Who would give away such secrets? But one thing became clear: the information our senses deliver does not match the contents of such a packet.

What we got looked ambiguous at best. The label said chicken stew, but even a starving Rambo could only have taken what gushed out of the slime-green sachet to be a mistake, wrongly labelled construction material, or fertiliser.

When a thick, brown mass triggers associations of involuntary repulsion, the cause is either the personal or collective memory. The mass can still be highly nutritious, independently of its appearance. The important thing is what it is rather than who eats it.

Of course, as we have learned from Pavlov, the appearance and smell of the food have an effect on its insalivation, and therefore its digestion, that should not be underestimated. Complete substitute nutrition, the diet prescribed to astronauts and other victims of stomach disorders, has no appearance or smell. Conditioned salivation therefore has its limits, which can sometimes be advantageous, but in the case of soluble space food, is not even necessary.

In the case of the survival food however, the slime in question either smelled like its surroundings, for instance, when toilets were nearby, or it smelled like toilets when in the presence of apricot blossoms, which struck us as being a suitable suitably instructive example of synaesthesia.

But when it comes to actually consuming the food, it should be evaluated with the really competent sense, which should count for more than appearance and smell put together. The nutritional value of a substance may occasionally be apparent from a distance by the way it diffuses and reflects light, but on-the-spot chemical contact is still more reliable. Besides, the interaction of optical, smell and taste contact sometimes contains different information about the type of a meal than just its smell and appearance. Immediacy is without a doubt the surest way to ascertain the qualities of an object. The content of the package tasted the way it smelled and looked. Even so, the greatest caution is called for here. Think of the ducks. Just because a sauce tastes and smells like it looks, it does not really have to be bad. As always in life, it is a question of inherent values.

This insight came to us in the course of observing a dog who was assisting us with our investigations. The dog ate the lipid muck but this does not change anything about the fact that the same dog occasionally eats empty pizza cartons.

The important thing is: that the army ration, prepared for emergencies, is a triumph for food preparation technology. It meets all the guidelines for healthy dining and is logistically well thought out as far as hygiene and longevity regulations are concerned. Psychologically, it is even a palette ahead of the elementary and complete food served in hospitals, as it is not defined purely in terms of chemistry but reveals a psychological component in its range of smells and colours. But it is perhaps just for this reason that it lags seriously behind duck food.

Thus we reach our first conclusion. Eating means "a choice of material supply", writes James J. Gibson ("Senses and the Perception Process", Huber 1973). And "for every kind of creature there are substances that contribute to its diet, but also others which have no nutritional value. The former must therefore be selected and extracted from the available range of biochemical substances." The question is: how? Some things taste good, some smell alright, some even look tasty. Creatures with the urge for self-preservation will still be more careful with these old, tried and tested, instinctive perception modes and subordinate them to rational guidelines, despite all insalivation theories. In their choice of food, at least, pure reason quite unexpectedly scores over the sense-oriented choice of feelings.

We are depending less and less on the primary information available to our organs of perception. Nutrient tables and chemical analyses will be the future basis for classification at mealtimes. They provide better protection than juicy looking illusions concealing heavy metals. When in doubt and having to make a choice, even linen wallpaper would be better for you than the unexamined asparagus shoot—assuming that the wallpaper passes its protein and vitamin test with flying colours.

Waiter: Sir, today's dish is a rich, tasty wallpaper. It has a protein share of 63%—especially Lysine, by the way—and only 15% fat, so say nothing of the vitamins.

ma langweilig, schwer verständlich oder sonst wie passend wäre. Es ist bloß so, daß ein seriöser Katalogbeitrag im Normalfall mindestens ein Zitat von zwei Philosophen oder zwei Zitate von einem aufweisen sollte:

„Die Definition jeder gegebenen Art von Dingen", schreibt Collingwood, „ist zugleich die Definition eines guten Dinges von dieser Art: denn ein Ding, das gut in seiner Art ist, ist lediglich ein Ding, das die Attribute jener Art aufweist."

Die Merkmale, aufgrund derer irgendein Objekt als Ente oder Löwe bezeichnet wird, sind nach Collingwood demnach dieselben Merkmale, aufgrund derer, je nachdem, ob sie in größerem oder geringerem Maß vorhanden sind, ein Löwe eher als Löwe zu beurteilen ist, als ein anderer. Und was ist dann der andere?

Genug davon. Zurück zum Gemüse. Was zu Beginn als triviale Botschaft angekündigt wurde, lautet: Waren am Gemüsemarkt sollten, wie das schwarze Quadrat im Kunstmuseum nicht allein nach ihrem Aussehen beurteilt werden. Kleine Zusatzinformationen können die Einstellung des Konsumenten in beiden Fällen schlagartig verändern.

Selbst Konsumenten, die feiner differenzieren und wissen, daß nicht alles schmeckt was glänzt und daß nicht alles ungefährlich ist, was schmeckt, selbst Konsumenten, die lieber Bioschrumpf und Abgetackeltes kaufen und verzehren und damit scheinbar Qualität, unterliegen Täuschungen. Nicht nur, weil der Markt mit unterschiedlich raffinierten Strategien längst auf diese neuen, oberflächlichen Kriterien für Qualität eingeht und dementsprechend neben den reifen Makellosen, die nach nichts schmecken auch kleine Verrunzelte anbietet, die ebenfalls nach nichts schmecken, sondern vor allem, weil viele Formen der Kosmetik eingesetzt werden.

Lebensmittel wirken länger frisch, wenn sie mit Gammastrahlen ionisiert werden. Käufer die nach visuellen Informationen suchen, um ihre Wahl zu treffen und eigentlich frische, also vitaminreiche Nahrung meinen, wenn sie die glatte und glänzende Oberfläche wählen, betrachten als gesund und vollwertig, was in Wahrheit alt und von geringem Nährwert ist. „Seinen Augen nicht mehr zu traun", sagt selbst Paul Virilio, „ist zur Überlebensnotwendigkeit geworden." (Krieg und Fernsehen. Hanser. München 1993). Aber kann man den anderen Sinnen mehr trauen?

Wir haben uns eine kleine Testpackung aus einem militärischen Überlebenspaket schicken lassen. Natürlich war nicht anzunehmen, daß es sich dabei um den neuesten Entwicklungsstand handeln würde. Wer gibt schon Geheimnisse freiwillig aus der Hand? Eines wurde dennoch klar: Was unsere Sinne an Informationen übermitteln, kann nicht mit dem übereinstimmen, was sich in so einer Packung befindet.

Was wir erhielten, sah bestenfalls zweideutig aus. Auf der Packung stand zwar Eintopf mit Huhn, was dann aber aus dem schlammgrünen Sackerl hervorquoll, kann selbst einem ausgehungerten Rambo nur als Irrtum, als falsch beschriftetes Baumaterial oder Düngemittel erschienen sein.

Wenn eine braune, teilflüssige Masse unwillkürlich Ekelassoziationen auslöst, liegt das entweder an persönlichen oder an kollektiven Erinnerungen. Die Masse kann deswegen dennoch, vom Aussehen unabhängig, besonders hohe Nährwerte aufweisen. Wichtig ist jedenfalls, was ist und weniger, wer es ißt.

Natürlich hat das Aussehen der Nahrung, wie wir seit Pawlow wissen, genau wie ihr Geruch, auf den Vorgang des Einspeichelns und somit auf die Verdauung einen nicht zu unterschätzenden Einfluß. Komplettersatznahrung, wie sie Astronauten und anderen Magenkranken als Diät verschrieben wird, sieht nicht aus und riecht nicht. Das konditionierte Einschleimen hält sich demnach in Grenzen, was manchmal auch ein Vorteil sein kann und was im Falle der löslichen Weltraumnahrung vor allem gar nicht nötig ist.

Im Fall der Überlebensnahrung allerdings roch der getestete Schleim entweder nach der jeweiligen Umgebung, wenn sich zum Beispiel in der Nähe eine Latrine befand, oder er roch nach Latrine, wenn Marillenblüten nicht weit waren, was uns zumindest im ersten Fall als geeignetes Lehrbeispiel für Synästhesie erschien.

Ausschlaggebender als Aussehen und Geruch zusammen sollte vor jeder endgültigen Nahrungsaufnahme die Bewertung durch den wirklich kompetenten Sinn sein. Der Nährwert einer Substanz mag gelegentlich – aufgrund der Diffusionen und der Lichtreflexionen – schon aus der Entfernung erkannt werden, ein unmittelbarer chemischer Kontakt ist dennoch verläßlicher. Außerdem enthält die Wechselwirkung aus Optik, Geruchs- und Geschmackskontakt gelegentlich andere Informationen über die Art einer Speise als Geruch und Gestalt allein. Der unmittelbare Kontakt mit einem Objekt ist zweifellos der sicherste Test, die Eigenschaften dieses Objekts kennenzulernen.

Der Inhalt der Packung schmeckte, wie er roch, wie er aussah. Trotzdem ist äußerste Vorsicht geboten. Denken wir an die Enten. Nur weil eine Soße schmeckt und riecht wie sie aussieht, muß sie nicht wirklich schlecht sein. Es kommt hier, wie im Leben immer, auf die inneren Werte an.

Diese Einsicht ist uns durch eine Beobachtung an einem Hund bewußt geworden, der uns bei der Entsorgung des Lunchpaketes unterstützte. Der Hund zog den lipidgetesteten Kot allen Leckerbissen vor, die er aus der Werbung kannte. An dieser Relativierung des Geschmacks änderte dann

Gourmet: Hopefully without connective tissue.
Waiter: Regretfully, it is a linen wallpaper.

Fiction, admittedly. With fiction it's like goose pimples. It comes with shivers and excitement, fear and frustration. And nobody knows what to do with it. Better not to have any more fiction. Or maybe just once more:

If steaks are recombined from pieces of meat, so could wallpaper or fly larvae. It is only a question of the sculptural quality. Common housefly larvae incidentally have the same share of protein as the fly larvae that are produced. These larvae are made up of the same cultures and only the barriers of our conditioned western visual prejudices prevent us from enjoying wallpaper and flies as much as we enjoy sick pigs.

The body can no longer determine which things are good for it and which things are bad using the senses it has developed for the purpose. This seems to be the conventional wisdom from the "Bubba psychology" field, the same laboriously formulated results, scientifically backed up at great expense, that world-wise grandmas could confirm just as well for free.

All the same, and the grandmas are asking this too, what is it all about? Should we only let secondary information guide us? Should we study books and carry out C 14 tests at the vegetable market before filing the basket? Should be bite into the apple before we get too excited about its bright red colour, to avoid disappointment when we get home? And does biting the apple tell us more than looking at it?

What is important in making the right choice? What must our eyes and noses be on the lookout for?

We are tortured by the question of how we will safely identify good food in the near future, when food is no longer even genetically what it claims to be, to say nothing of its appearance and smell.

Even the names of the meals are hollow. At the restaurant, the diner orders the "cat in juice" if he puts his trust in names. What do names mean anyway? What hides behind "minced meat roast" or a "green salad"? What hides behind titles like pigeon soup, laboratory goulash or cold dog?

The diner orders according to the expectations he has of the names to the dishes and the waiter's recommendations. He looks at the food, smells it, and tastes it. And yet he seldom discovers what he is really eating, what nourishment and poison he has ordered.

Regrettably, secondary information also threatens not to communicate things that could be of advantage and of life-saving importance to the customer. The waiter who points out that the baked mice are really a Bohemian desert speciality made of yeast dough can also, if necessary, offer the chemical composition of the dough. This would not mean much to most of the guests. Extra information sometimes causes more confusion than enlightenment. At least as long as superficial, formal appeals dominate the hierarchy of sensual information. Only through a completely un-assessed and random use of optical shapes and colours, smells and flavour enhancers will the consumer

grasp the minimal relevance of these superficial aestheticisations, and learn to take note of background information.
It is time the experiences of the plastic arts—especially in this century—the systematic deconstruction of all formal values, that these experiences were applied.
Among other presentations at this Ars we will be carrying out some taste tests, and in addition, results of the gene manipulation of edible plants, bacteria and other animals. Art history has also taught us that genetically varied plants, bacteria and other animals can be aestheticised through auratisation—with a context and observation, through veneration and discourse. This way research results become icons of the new design possibilities. The first genetically altered oil plant is like the first painting executed in perspective—worth seeing.

Wolfgang Zinggl

auch die Tatsache nichts, daß der selbe Hund gelegentlich leere Pizzaschachteln frißt.
Wichtig ist: Die zusammengestellte Armee-Packung für den Ernstfall ist ein Triumph der Lebensmitteltechnologie. Sie entspricht allen Richtlinien gesunder Ernährung und ist logistisch ausgeklügelt, was Hygiene und Langlebigkeitsvorschriften betrifft. Sie ist psychologisch sogar den in den Spitälern verabreichten Elementar- und Komplettnahrungen um eine Gaumenlänge voraus, da sie nicht rein chemisch definiert ist, sondern über die Geruchs- oder Farbpalette eine psychologische Komponente aufweist. Aber vielleicht ist sie gerade aus diesem Grund der enteralen Weltraumnahrung schwer unterlegen.
Wir kommen zu einem ersten Schluß. Essen bedeutet „Stoffzufuhr in Auswahl" schreibt James J. Gibson („Die Sinne und der Prozeß der Wahrnehmung." Huber 1973) Und „für jede Art von Lebewesen gibt es Substanzen, die seiner Ernährung zuträglich sind, aber auch andere, die keinen Nährwert besitzen. Die ersteren müssen dann eben aus dem jeweiligen Angebot biochemischer Substanzen ausgewählt werden." Die Frage ist bloß –: wie?
Manche Dinge schmecken gut, manche riechen nicht schlecht, manche sehen lecker aus. Wesen mit Überlebensdrang werden dennoch mit diesen altgedienten, instinktiven Wahrnehmungsmodalitäten vorsichtiger umgehen und sie trotz aller Einspeichelungstheorien rationalen Richtlinien unterordnen müssen. Zumindest bei der Wahl der Lebensmittel zeichnet sich völlig überraschend ein Punktesieg der reinen Vernunft über die sinnenbetonte Gefühlswahl ab.

Immer weniger kommt es auf die primären Informationen an, die den Wahrnehmungsorganen zur Verfügung stehen. Nährstofftabellen und chemische Analysen dienen in Zukunft als Grundlagen der Klassifizierung des Mittagstisches. Sie schützen besser als saftig wirkende aber mit Schwermetallen angereicherte Täuschungen. Im Zweifelsfall und wenn man vor der Wahl steht, müßte selbst eine Leinentapete, vorausgesetzt sie besteht ihre analytische Durchleuchtung auf Protein- und Vitaminanteile mit Auszeichnung, der ungeprüften Spargelspitze vorgezogen werden.
KELLNER: Monsieur, wir haben heute eine herzhaft angereicherte Tapete. Sie hat einen Proteinanteil von 63% – übrigens besonders reich an Lysin – und nur 15% Fett, und Vitamine...
GOURMET: Hoffentlich alles ohne Bindegewebe.
KELLNER: Es ist leider eine Leinentapete.
Fiktion zugegeben. Es ist mit der Fiktion wie mit der Gänsehaut. Sie kommt bei Frost, Lust, Angst und Frust. Und nie-

mand weiß so recht etwas anzufangen mit ihr. Also besser keine Fiktionen mehr. Oder vielleicht die eine noch:
Wenn Steaks aus Fleischflocken rekombiniert werden, können aus denselben Flocken auch Tapeten oder Fliegenlarven geformt werden. Das ist nur eine Frage der skulpturalen Qualitäten. Bescheidene Hausfliegenlarven haben übrigens den selben Proteinanteil wie die genannten Tapeten. Und somit könnten umgekehrt auch Tapeten oder T-bone-Steaks aus Fliegenlarven produziert werden. Diese Larven werden von vielen Kulturen zubereitet und nur unsere westlich konditionierten Schranken visueller Vorurteile verhindern, daß wir Tapete und Fliege genießen, wie wir kranke Schweine genießen.
Was dem Körper nützt und was ihm schadet, kann er mit den evolutiv dafür entwickelten Sinnen nicht mehr erfassen. Das scheint mittlerweile eine Allerweltsweisheit aus dem Bereich der „Bubba-psychologie" zu sein, jener mühsam aufgeplusterten und wissenschaftlich teuer unterstützten Ergebnsisse, die lebenserfahrene Goßmütter mit links und ganz umsonst verbreiten könnten.
Dennoch, und das fragen sich auch die Großmütter, was ist eigentlich Sache? Sollen wir uns nur noch nach den Sekundärinformationen orientieren? Sollen wir Bücher studieren und jedesmal C14-Tests am Gemüsemarkt durchführen, ehe wir den Einkaufskorb füllen? Sollen wir in den Apfel beißen, ehe wir uns an seiner gewachsten roten Farbe zu früh freuen und zu Hause bitter enttäuscht werden? Und sagt uns das Apfelbeißen mehr als das Apfelbetrachten?
Was ist wichtig für eine richtige Auswahl? Worauf muß das Augen- und Nasenmerk gerichtet werden?
Uns quält die Frage, wie denn in naher Zukunft, wenn die Nahrungsmittel nichteinmal mehr genetisch das sein werden, was sie zu sein vorgeben, vom Aussehen und den Gerüchen ganz zu schweigen, wie denn die Sinne noch sinnvoll eingesetzt werden können, für eine ungefährliche Identifikation von Liptauer.
Auch die Bezeichnungen der Speisen sind hohl. Im Restaurant bestellt der Gast die Katze im Saft, wenn er auf Namen vertraut. Was dennotieren schon Namen? Was verbirgt sich hinter dem „Faschierten Braten"? Was verbirgt sich hinter Bezeichnungen wie Taubensuppe, Laborgulyasch oder Cold Dog?
Der Gast bestellt nach Erwartungen aufgrund angeführter Speisenamen und der Empfehlungen des Kellners. Er betrachtet die servierten Gerichte, riecht, kostet. Und dennoch erfährt er selten, was er wirklich ist. Welche Nährstoffe und Gifte er bestellt hat.
Dummerweise sind auch Sekundärinformationen gefährdet,

nicht das mitzuteilen, was von Vorteil und lebensrettender Wichtigkeit für den Konsumenten wäre. Der Kellner im Restaurant, der darauf aufmerksam macht, daß die gebackenen Mäuse in Wahrheit eine böhmische Mehlspeisspezialität aus Germteig sind, kann zur Not auch noch die chemischen Zusamnmensetzungen des Germteiges mitteilen. Sie würden den meisten Gästen aber wenig sagen. Zusatzinformationen dienen manchmal eher der Verwirrung als der Aufklärung. Zumindest, solange oberflächliche, formale Reize eine Vormachtstellung in der Hierarchie der Sinnesinformationen genießen.

Erst durch eine völlig unbewertete und beliebige Verwendung von optischen Formen und Farben, von Gerüchen und Geschmacksverstärkern wird dem Konsumenten die geringe Relevanz dieser oberflächlichen Ästhetisierungen bewußt und er lernt auf dahinterliegende Informationen zu achten.

Es wird Zeit, daß die Erfahrungen der bildenden Kunst – vor allem in diesem Jahrhundert – die systematische Dekonstruktion aller formalen Werte, daß diese Erfahrungen angewendet werden.

Wir präsentieren Ihnen bei dieser Ars Electroncia unter anderem einige Geschmackstests und ganz nebenbei Ergebnisse der gentechnologischen Veränderung genießbarer Pflanzen, Bakterien und anderer Tiere. Ästhetisieren lassen sich, auch das hat uns die Kunstgeschichte gelehrt, genetisch variierte Nutzpflanzen, Bakterien und andere Tiere, über eine Auratisierung – mit Rahmen und Bewachung, durch Verehrung und Diskursion.

Forschungsergebnisse werden auf diese Weise zu Ikonen der neuen Gestaltungsmöglichkeiten. Die erste gentechnisch veränderte Ölpflanze ist wie das erste perspektivisch gemalte Bild – sehenswert. Mehr nicht.

Wolfgang Zinggl

Das Projekt wurde ermöglicht durch die großzügige Unterstützung der Fa. THYSSEN Gerüstbau, Traun, sowie durch die freundliche Unterstützung der Fa. Delikomat, Wien, und der Fa. Ing. Markovits, Wien.

AUGen

LEOPOLD LARCHER / RICH.ART

AUGen
LEOPOLD LARCHER / RICH.ART

QUALIFYING EMOTIONAL APPROACH

The computer is becoming a human, finite universe—it simulates life systems.
We are living in a non-artificial system, within which we create new systems. The human becomes an artificial shadow in this system.
We set the rules of life. It is only the user who makes us an artificial creator.
Man is master of his creation, whose code has been determined by **chance.**
Who gives the non-artificial creator the rules of life?
The storage medium / HW becomes an artificial nucleus.
The storage content / SW becomes the artificial DNA.[1]
The memory of the computer (existent binary character chain) is directly manipulated by the user, in other words, it is artificially "evolved".[2]
The memory replaces non-artificial test subjects.[3]
The created binary code defines a generating, artificial, genetic RNA code that is transcribed when at least a genetic start code exists: AUG.[4]
It is a unique, random object code defined by an individual object/"being" which can be interactively influenced/controlled by the user of the installation.[5]
The object code is set by the interface between the artificial life form and the non-artificial life form. Eyes are the interface of the artificial object, because only artificial life forms can simulate non-artificial ones. The interface's characteristic similarity to our human eyes makes it able to simulate human contact. It is only in our three-dimensional, global world, still the only one we know, that the eyes are the first means of communication between different "cultures" who have no common language.
The control/data entry is effected through a brain wave analyser. The thought about a feeling will become the universal basis for communication/language. Can the created artificial life form develop, or understand, different forms of communication? The object/"life form" "lives" and interacts with or from feeling structures of the user.
Will this turn the user into the used?!
The user's feelings combined with the movement language of the object comprise a dynamic system within which the behaviour of the

QUALIFIZIERENDER EMOTIONSANSATZ

Der Computer wird zum menschlichen, endlichen Universum – er simuliert lebende Systeme.
Wir leben in einem nicht-künstlichen System, in welchem wir neue Systeme kreiern.
Der Mensch wird zum künstlichen Schöpfer in diesem System.
Wir geben die Lebensregeln. Erst der Benutzer macht uns zum künstlichen Schöpfer.
Man ist Herr über seine Schöpfung, deren Code der ZUFALL bestimmt hat.
Wer gibt dem nicht-künstlichen Schöpfer die Lebensregeln?
Das Speichermedium / HW wird zum künstlichen Nucleus.
Der Speicherinhalt / SW wird zur künstlichen DNS.[1]
Der Speicher des Computers (bestehende Binärzeichenkette) wird durch Licht/Strahlung direkt vom Benutzer manipuliert d.h. künstlich "evolutioniert".[2]
Der Speicher ersetzt nicht-künstliche Versuchsobjekte.[3]
Der kreierte Binärcode definiert einen generierenden, künstlichen, genetischen RNS Code, der nur dann transkripiert wird, wenn zumindest ein Genetisches Startcodon AUG existiert.[4]
Es ist ein zufälliger, einzigartiger Objektcode, welcher ein individuelles Objekt/„Lebewesen" definiert, das interaktiv vom Benutzer der Installation beeinflußt / gesteuert werden kann.[5]
Der Objektcode bestimmt das Interface der künstlichen Lebewesen mit nicht-künstlichen Lebewesen. Das Interface des künstlichen Objektes sind Augen, weil nur künstliche Lebewesen nicht-künstliche simulieren können. Die Eigenschaft des Interfaces, unseren menschlichen Augen ähnlich zu sein, verleiht ihm die Fähigkeit menschenähnlichen Kontakt zu simulieren. Die Augen sind nur in dieser, unserer zur Zeit noch einzig bekannten, dreidimensionalen globalen Welt das erste Kommunikationsmittel zwischen verschiedenen „Kulturen", deren gemeinsame Sprache noch unbekannt ist.
Die Steuerung/Eingabe erfolgt über einen Brain-Wave-Ana-

lyzer. Der Gedanke an ein Gefühl wird zur universiellen Kommunikationsbasis/Sprache. Kann das kreierte künstliche lebewesen verschiedene Kommunikationsformen entwickeln, bzw. verstehen? Das Objekt/„Lebewesen" „lebt" und interagiert mit oder von Gefühlsstrukturen des Benutzers.
Wird der Benutzer daduch zum Benutzten?!
Die Gefühle des Benutzers in Verbindung mit der Bewegungssprache des Objektes ergeben ein dynamisches System, in welchem das Verhalten der jeweiligen „Gesprächspartner" in einem geschlossenen Kreis darstellbar ist.
Nach Ablegen des Interface „stirbt" das Lebewesen und ist nicht mehr reproduzierbar. Das künstliche Leben wird nicht mehr gedacht.

FORMALER ABSTRAKTER DENKANSATZ

Vier Basen in der DNS (Desoxyribonukleinsäure) (engl. DNA) deren sequentielle Reihenfolge den genetischen Code (Sinnstrang) definieren
A Adenin
T Thymin (wird bei RNS durch U für Uracil ersetzt)
G Guanin
C Cytosin
In der Doppelhelix der DNS bilden jeweils
A – T
C – G
durch Wasserstoff verbundene komplementäre Paare (der Sinnstrang wird komplementär durch den Matrizenstrang ergänzt)
Bei RNS Polymerase wird der DNS Code auf die messenger-RNS (m-RNS) umgeschrieben (Transkription)

CODIERUNGSFOLGE:

– Farbe des Hintergrundes
– Art des Objektes
– Farbe des Objektes
– BewegungsSprach

ANMERKUNGEN

[1] Durch Binäre Zuordnung
00 – A Adenin
11 – U Uracil (statt Thymin – siehe oben)

various "conversation partners" can be represented in a closed circle.
When the interface is taken off the life form "dies" and cannot be reproduced. Artificial life is not remembered.

FORMAL ABSTRACT THOUGHT APPROACH

Four bases in DNA (Desoxyribonucleic acid) whose sequential order define the genetic code (sense strand)
A Adenine
T Thiamine (replaced by Uracil in RNA)
G Guanine
C Cytosine
In the double helix of DNA, the following:
A – T
C – G
form complementary pairs joined by hydrogen. (the sense strand is complemented by the matrix strand)
In RNA Polymerase the DNA code is transcribed onto the messenger RNA (M-RNS)

NOTES

[1] Trough binary Allocation
00 – A Adenine
11 – U Uracil
01 – G Guanine
10 – C Cytosine
a kind of M-RNA comes about, and can be digitally processed.
In artificial DNA, just as in non-artificial DNA, a promoter can be located—the starting position of the transcription. The double helix is broken open, an M-RNA is formed as a complement to the matrix strand. Three successive bases (base triplet) of the M-RNA form a codon.
[2] Note: The duration and intensity of the radiation is directly proportional to the amount of binary code erased.
[3] cf.: radiation and mutation experiments on drosophila flies—Hermann J. Muller, a student of Thomas Hunt Morgan at the turn of the century)
[4] To show where the starting point of the chain is, from which the triplets are read, there is a general start codon: AUG.
These codons in the ribosome determine the forming of amino acids (translation).
DNA is represented by a designated storage medium with the binary code 0 (default value) which is erased by chance (corresponds to code 1). The result is an involuntary progression from 0, or erasure (1).
[5] This code is read sequentially (i.e. processed as triplets—6 binary symbols corresponds to 64 variations) and serves to determine the object once the start codon, AUG (00 11 01), has been registered.

ORDER OF CODIFICATION:

- Colour of the background
- Type of object
- Colour of object
- Movement language

The colour palette allows 16,777,216 x 16,777,216 x 4 = 1.1258999E15 possible visual images, multiplied by 24 possible variations of movement.

01 – G Guanin
10 – C Cytosin
entsteht quasi ein m-RNS, und ist digital einsetzbar.
In der künstlichen DNS wird, gleich wie in der nicht künstlichen DNS, ein Promoter erkannt = die Startposition der Transkription. Die Doppelhelix wird aufgebrochen, eine m-RNS als Komplement des Matrizenstranges gebildet. Jeweils drei aufeinanderfolgende Basen (Basentriplet) der m-RNA bilden ein Codon.

[2] Anmerkung: Die Dauer und Intensität der Bestrahlung ist direkt proportional zur Menge des gelöschten Binärcodes.

[3] (vgl. Strahlungs- und Mutationsversuche mit lebenden Drosophila Fliegen – Hermann J. Muller, Schüler von Thomas Hunt Morgan zur Jahrhundertwende)

[4] Um anzuzeigen, wo in der Kette der Startpunkt ist, ab dem die Triplets gelesen werden, gibt es einen allgemeinen Startcodon: AUG
Diese Codons bestimmen im Ribosom die Bildung der Aminosäuren (Translation).
Als DNS dient ein, mit Binärcode 0 (default-Wert) definiertes Speichermedium,welches durch Strahlung zufällig gelöscht wird (enspricht Code 1), Es entsteht eine unwillkürliche Reihenfolge von 0 bzw. Löschung (1).

[5] Dieser Code wird sequentiell gelesen (d.h. als Triplet behandelt = 6 Binärzeichen entspricht 64 Variationen) und dient nach erkennen des Startercodons AUG (00 11 01) zur Objektbestimmung.

DANK AN:
Werner Petricek / Klosterneuburg – Programmierung
Apple Friends / IBVA
Glasfachschule Kramsach
Der Raum – P. Binder, Linz

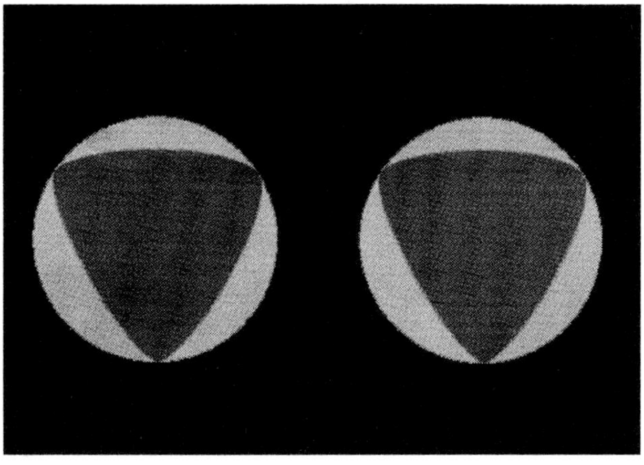

VIRTUELLE EMOTIONEN

STEFAN SCHEMAT

ZWEI MPCS

Szenarien der virtuellen Realität beschränken sich aus physiologischer Sicht auf das Feedback der Willkürmotorik, die mit Datenhandschuhen oder -anzügen gemessen wird. Damit wird jedoch nur ein Ausschnitt menschlichen Verhaltens und Erlebens dargestellt. Dieses Projekt intendiert, physiologische Parameter für Emotionen in eine virtuelle Welt zu exportieren. Als Repräsentation[1] für Emotionen werden Visualisierungen von Biosignalen wie dem Atemrhythmus verwendet.

Durch die Beschäftigung mit dem Thema virtuelle Emotionen, wird man mit ungewöhnlichen Perspektiven auf Kommunikations- und Kognitionswissenschaften konfrontiert. Zudem ergeben sich Bezüge zu psychotherapeutischen Techniken der Tranceinduktion.

VIRTUELLE REALITÄT OHNE EMOTIONEN?

Virtuelle Realitäten (VR) haben wegen der Verwandlungsmöglichkeiten ihrer Akteure einen hohen Anreiz. Mit zukünftiger Technologie sind Szenarien der Verwandlung denkbar, in denen die Datenreisenden ein beliebiges Aussehen annehmen können, um eine von ihnen erdachte Rolle zu spielen. Doch vergleicht man die Komplexität der VR mit unserer Alltagsumwelt, so werden große Mängel deutlich. Durch die erwähnte Einschränkung der VR auf die Willkürmotorik ist nur ein extrem begrenztes Verhalten möglich. Dieser Mangel wird besonders sichbar, wenn man an die Kommunikationsmöglichkeiten innerhalb der VR denkt. Zwischenmenschliche Kommunikation bezieht neben rein sprachlicher Information auch nonverbale Signale wie Körperhaltung, Tonfall und Psychophysiologie mit ein. Mit Hilfe dieser Signale erkennen wir die Ironie in einem Scherz oder die Intention einer Aussage.

Angesichts dieser Vielfalt wird die Selektion durch das Interface zur VR um so deutlicher, denn was alltägliche Kommunikation wirklich spannend macht, fehlt. Gemeint sind da-

VIRTUAL EMOTION
STEFAN SCHEMAT

TWO MPCS
TWO BREATHING BIOFEEDBACK UNITS

Virtual reality scenarios are restricted, from a psychological point of view, to the feedback from arbitrary motor responses which are measured with data gloves or suits. However, this only represents one section of human behaviour. This project intends to export physiological parameters for emotions into a virtual world. As a representation[1] for emotions, visualizations of biosignals, such as breathing rhythm, are used.

In the pre-occupation with the subject of virtual emotions, one is confronted with unusual perspectives concerning communications and cognitive sciences. In addition to this, there are references to psychotherapeutical techniques of trance induction.

VIRTUAL REALITY WITHOUT EMOTIONS?

Virtual realities (VR) have a high degree of stimulation because of the transformation possibilities of its actors. Scenarios of transformation are possible with future technologies, in which data travellers can assume any appearance in order to play a role they have thought out. However, if we compare the complexity of VR with our everyday environment, great shortcomings become apparent. On account of the afore-mentioned fact that VR is restricted to arbitrary motor responses, only an extremely limited behaviour is possible. This shortcoming becomes particularly noticeable when we think of the communications possibilities within VR. Inter-personal communication involves, besides pure linguistic information, even non-verbal signals such as posture, intonation and psychophysiology. With the aid of these signals we recognize the irony in a joke or the intention of a statement. Considering this multiplicity, the selection to VR through the interface becomes even more apparent, as what makes everyday communications really exciting, is missing. What is meant here are the correlatives of our world of feelings, which, among other things, become noticeable in non-verbal communication. Non-verbal communication takes place in everday life, generally, without any conscious reflection. In this way we can recognize the hint of a smile by the fine changes in the muscles and we can recognize when someone is excited or has just woken up.[1]

In this work, the concept of representation is tackled very widely. It is used in the sense of a relation between what should be represented and what is actually represented. This relation can be very different. With the visualization of breathing rhythm, there is a relation between the breathing frequency and animation speed. In addition to this, the contraction and the expansion of the lungs is represented (symbolized) during breathing, by apparent contractions and expansions in the graphics. A further representation level can be effected by allocating frequency ranges to colours. When the graphics change to take on a reddish colour this can signify a high breathing frequency, and a blue colour stands for a low frequency. Representations can be assessed according to the quality of what is reproduced.

All this information forms the context in which we understand spoken language. How can emotional reactions be converted into virtual reality? One possibility would be to give the representation of the protagonist a certain facial expression depending on the desired or actual mood. This direct conversion, however, in a technical sense, still involves a lot of effort. It is one alternative to symbolically convey feelings. An aggressive mood can e.g. be elucidated by a certain rhythm and/or by a certain colour combination. What is important, is only that the symbol used is to be intuitively accessible and suited to capturing the attention of the interaction partner. With the aid of smilies known from telecommunications, statements about emotional connotations can be made but they do not have the complexity of non-verbal communication.

In order to solve this task, we have expanded the biofeedback technology popular in psychology. In the case of biofeedback, the patient receives a feedback message of his biosignals (breathing, brain waves, pulse, skin conductivity, etc.), so that he can learn to influence them himself. In this way, for example, an attempt can be made to learn relaxation states through the change in the skin conductivity. The feedback from such equipmnt is, as a rule, very simple. A green lamp lights up e.g. when skin conductivity decreases and a red one lights up when it increases.

BIOFEEDBACK AS AN "EXCITING" REPRESENTATION

It was our aim to create a kind of external representation of mental and physiological states that is more complex and therefore, in at least one aspect, is comparable to non-verbal communication. As a result of lengthy series of experiments, representations were developed for this project which were able to capture the attention of protagonists. Tunnel-like fractals with fine colour nuances proved to be most suited to this task. The first experiments with this technology

mit die Korrelate unserer Gefühlswelt, die u.a. in der nonverbale Kommunikation sichtbar werden. Nonverbale Kommunikation geschieht im Alltag meist ohne bewußte Reflexion. So erkennt man schon an feinen Veränderungen der Muskulatur den Anflug eines Lächelns, und man erkennt, wenn jemand aufgeregt ist oder gerade erst aufgewacht ist. All diese Informationen bilden den Kontext, in dem wir gesprochene Sprache verstehen. Wie können emotionale Reaktionen in die virtuelle Realität umgesetzt werden? Eine Möglichkeit wäre es, dem Abbild des Protagonisten je nach gewünschter oder tatsächlicher Stimmung einen bestimmten Gesichtsausdruck zu geben. Diese direkte Umsetzung ist allerdings technisch noch relativ aufwendig. Eine Alternative ist es, Gefühle symbolisch zu übermitteln. Eine aggressive Stimmung kann z.B. durch einen bestimmten Rhythmus und/oder durch eine bestimmte Farbkombination verdeutlicht werden. Wichtig ist nur, daß das verwendete Symbol intuitiv zugänglich und dazu geeignet ist, die Aufmerksamkeit des Interaktionspartners zu fesseln. Mit Hilfe der aus der Telekommunikation bekannten Smilies können zwar auch Aussagen über emotionale Konnotationen getroffen werden, sie haben aber nicht die Komplexität nonverbaler Kommunikation.

Zur Lösung dieser Aufgabe haben wir die in der Psychologie gängige Biofeedback-Technologie erweitert. Beim Biofeedback werden dem Patienten seine Biosignale (Atem, Gehirnwellen, Puls, Hautleitfähigkeit etc.) zurückgemeldet, damit er lernen kann, sie selbst zu beeinflussen. So kann beispielsweise versucht werden, über eine Veränderung der Hautleitfähigkeit Entspannungszustände zu erlernen. Die Rückmeldungen solcher Geräte sind jedoch in der Regel recht simpel. Ein grünes Lämpchen leuchtet z.B. auf, wenn die Hautleitfähigkeit abnimmt, ein rotes, wenn sie zunimmt.

BIOFEEDBACK ALS „REIZVOLLE" REPRÄSENTATION

Unser Ziel war, eine Art externe Repräsentation von mentalen und physiologischen Zuständen zu schaffen, die komplexer ist und somit zumindest in einem Aspekt mit nonverbaler Kommunikation vergleichbar ist. Durch längere Versuchsreihen wurden für dieses Projekt Repräsentationen entwickelt, die die Aufmerksamkeit der Protagonisten fesseln können. Als besonders geeignet erwiesen sich für diesen Zweck tunnelartige Fraktale mit feinen Farbabstufungen.

Die ersten Versuche mit dieser Technologie zeigten verblüffend starke Effekte. Das alleinige Feedback des Atmens durch „animierte“ Fraktale wirkte so stark, daß es bei den meisten Probanden schon nach kurzer Zeit zu entspannten oder hypnoiden Bewußtseinszuständen führte. Der für uns überraschende Effekt war, daß es sogar bei der alleinigen Darbietung vor einem größeren Publikum (es handelte sich um Hypnotherapeuten!) zu deutlichen Anzeichen von Gruppentrance kam.

Durch diese Erfolge beflügelt, wurde versucht, die Bedeutung von derartiger Technologie für virtuelle Welten theoretisch zu klären. Dabei stellten sich sehr interessante, auf den ersten Blick provozierende Bezüge her. Forschungstraditionen, die in der Psychologie weitgehend isoliert voneinander sind, kamen ins Spiel: Steuerungsmechanismen des Atemzentrums im Gehirn, die kognitive Psychologie der mentalen Repräsentationen, Modelle des menschlichen Bewußtseins und des Gehirns.

TRANCEFORSCHUNG: PHANTASTISCHE ERKLÄRUNGEN FÜR PHANTASTISCHE PHÄNOMENE?

Bei der Erforschung von Trancephänomenen wird man mit stark wechselhaften Forschungsstrategien konfrontiert. Zunächst sind da die spektakulären Dinge, die unter Hypnose möglich sein sollen. Doch bei genauer Analyse und sorgfältigen Experimenten schrumpft die Anzahl der Phänomene, die sich allein durch Trance erklären lassen, deutlich. Das eine oder andere in der Literatur vorkommende Phänomen widerspricht nicht nur naturwissenschaftlichen Prinzipien (was vielleicht noch nicht so ungewöhnlich ist), sondern läßt sich empirisch auch nicht belegen. Oder es findet sich bei genauer Analyse auch eine ‚einfachere Erklärung. Ein Beispiel hierfür ist die unter Hypnose herbeigeführte Erinnerung an ein früheres Leben. Wer möchte nicht über die Fähigkeit verfügen, sich an frühere Leben zu erinnern? Auf welche Fülle verborgener Schätze könnten wir zurückgreifen? Doch diese Erinnerungen an das frühere Leben lassen sich zumeist durch verdeckte Suggestionen des Versuchsleiters und der Erwartungshaltung seiner Probanden erklären. Andere Phänomene, wie z.B. die „kataleptische Brücke“, d.h. die Fähigkeit, sich unter Hypnose auf eine sehr unbequeme Weise auf zwei Stühle zu legen (s. Abbildung), ließen sich auch ohne hypnotische Induktion bei den meisten Probanden erreichen – allein die Anweisung, sich steif zu machen, reichte aus. Es handelt sich hier also eher um ein sozial bedingtes Phänomen.

Der aus dieser Perspektive augenscheinliche Fehler, den viele Trance-Forscher in der Vergangenheit gemacht haben,

showed amazingly powerful effects. The mere feedback from breathing through “animated” fractals had such a powerful effect that it soon led to relaxed or hypnoidal states of consciousness with most of the test candidates. The effect that was surprising for us was that even the mere presentation to a larger audience (hynotherapists!) produced clear signs of group trance.

Encouraged by this success, we attempted to theoretically clarify the meaning of such a technology for virtual worlds. This produced very interesting, and at a first glance, provocative references. Research traditions which are largely isolated from each other in psychology, were involved: control mechanisms of the breathing centre in the brain, the cognitive psychology of mental representations, models of human consciousness and of the brain.

TRANCE RESEARCH: FANTASTIC EXPLANATIONS FOR FANTASTIC PHENOMENA?

When researching trance phenomena, one is confronted with greatly changeable research strategies. First of all, there are the spectacular things that are supposed to be possible under hypnosis. However, when analysed more exactly and after careful experiments have been performed, the number of phenomena that can be explained by trance alone, clearly dwindles. One or the other of the phenomena that occurs in the literature not only contradicts scientific principles (which is perhaps not that unusual), but also cannot be accommodated in an empirical sense. Or, when subjected to more exact analyses, a “more simple explanation” can be found. One example of this is the memory of a former life conjured up under hypnosis. Who would not like to have the ability to remember a former life? What number of hidden treasures can we resort to, to do this? But, these memories of a former life can generally be explained by concealed suggestions made by the person in charge of the experiment and the anticipatory attitude of the test candidates. Other phenomena, e.g. the “cataleptic bridge”, i.e. the ability to lie on two chairs in a very uncomfortable manner when under hypnosis (see Figure), was also achieved with most test persons without hypnotic induction— merely the command to make oneself stiff was sufficient. Consequently, here it is more a matter of a socially induced phenomenon.

From this perspective, the obvious mistakes that many trance researchers have made in the past is to search for a fantastic explanation for a fantastic occurrence.

What is complicating in the discussion about the trance concept, is the multiplicity of the phenomena described—they range from deep relaxation to enrapture. In order not to wear down the concept any more, it can be said that certain patterns and contents in interpersonal communications can decisively lead to grave changes in mood, and even to changes in the state of consciousness.

TRANCE AND COMMUNICATION

Milton Erickson has conceptionalized such hypnotic communications patterns and has specifically used them in psycho-therapy. He and his successors formulated the pacing and leading diagramme for this. In the context of psychotherapy, he designated the afore-mentioned communications pattern as pacing—the therapist "mirrors" the verbal and/or non-verbal behaviour of the client and in doing so signalizes acceptance to him. A leading phase follows this pacing phase, in which the cognitive routine of the client can be influenced.
This communications pattern should be explained on the basis of an anecdote by Bandler and Grinder, two psycho-therapists who have further developed the Erickson approach: in the case of a psychological disturbance which occurs in the course of a bad depression, or even in the case of schizophrenia, the person concerned can become completely rigid (stupor). People in such a state are no longer responsive. They hardly move or they remain fixed in a certain posture and have broken off every obvious communication with their environment. Bandler and Grinder succeeded, nevertheless, in building up a relationship to such a client by using a non-verbal communications channel: breathing rhythm. In the first few days, therapy merely consisted of the therapist entering the room where the client was and trying to breathe in his rhythm. After a few days, by changing his breathing rhythm, the therapist was also able to influence the client's breathing. As soon as the therapist was assured of communications via this channel, he took out a cigarette and asked the client for a light. The client replied spontaneously that he was sorry, but he didn't have a light and that he would like to smoke. Although this story arouses the impression of a not quite credible miracle healing, it is, nevertheless, based on the relatively simple communications pattern of pacing and leading. By mirroring the breathing rhythm, a relationship was built up—pacing. Then, the therapist was able to intervene in a key way and break through the client's isolation. In this connection, it becomes clear that non-verbal communications are more than just accompanying music to verbal communications.
In Erickson's concept, pacing extends beyond a simple tuning in. By means of the appropriate and extensive mirroring of a client's verbal and non-verbal behaviour, not only is a relationship built up, but a hypnotic state is also induced. This is intensified by further relaxation suggestions in the leading phase.
This pacing phenomenon is not merely restricted to interpersonal communications, but can also be observed with mechanically-conveyed interaction, like the breathing biofeedback described here.
Trance processes can be proven on the physiological level too—Eva Banyai and her staff at the University of Budapest found out that mutual tuning in took place with successful hypnotic induction. This tuning in is not only related to the obvious behaviour but also takes place on the psychophysiological level. Brain

ist die Suche nach einer phantastischen Erklärung für ein phantastisches Ereignis.
Erschwerend ist bei der Diskussion des Trancebegriffs die Vielfalt der beschriebenen Phänomene – sie reichen von tiefer Entspannung bis hin zum Entrücktsein. Ohne den Begriff weiter zu strapazieren, läßt sich sagen, daß bestimmte Muster und Inhalte zwischenmenschlicher Kommunikation in entscheidender Weise zu gravierenden Stimmungsveränderungen und sogar zu Änderungen des Bewußtseinszustandes führen können. (Revenstorf: simulated annealing)

TRANCE UND KOMMUNIKATION

Milton Erickson hat derartige hypnotische Kommunikationsmuster konzeptionalisiert, um sie gezielt in der Psychotherapie einzusetzen. Er und seine Nachfolger formulierten hierzu das Pacing- und Leading-Paradigma. Im Kontext der Psychotherapie bezeichnete er das oben beschriebene Kommunikationsmuster als Pacing – der Therapeut „spiegelt" das verbale und/oder nonverbale Verhalten des Klienten und signalisiert ihm damit Akzeptanz. Auf diese Pacing-Phase folgt eine Leading-Phase, in der kognitive Schemata des Klienten beeinflußt werden können.
Dieses Kommunikationsmuster soll anhand einer Anekdote von Bandler und Grinder, zwei Psychotherapeuten, die den Ericksonschen Ansatz weiterentwickelt haben, erläutert werden:
Bei einer psychischen Störung, die im Verlaufe einer schweren Depression oder auch bei der Schizophrenie auftritt, kann es zu völliger Erstarrung der Betroffenen kommen (Stupor). Menschen, die sich in einem solchen Zustand befinden, sind nicht mehr ansprechbar. Sie bewegen sich kaum noch oder verharren fest in einer bestimmten Haltung und haben jede offensichtliche Kommunikation mit ihrer Umwelt abgebrochen. Bandler und Grinder ist es gelungen, trotzdem eine Beziehung zu einem solchen Klienten aufzubauen, indem sie einen nonverbalen Kommunikationskanal verwendeten: den Atemrhythmus. Die Therapie bestand in den ersten Tagen lediglich darin, daß der Therapeut den Raum, in dem sich der Klient befand, betrat und versuchte, in dessen Rhythmus zu atmen. Nach ein paar Tagen konnte der Therapeut, indem er seinen Atemrhythmus veränderte, auch die Atmung des Klienten beeinflussen. Als sich der Therapeut der Kommunikation über diesen Kanal versichert hatte, nahm er eine Zigarette heraus und bat den Klienten um Feuer. Dieser antwortete spontan, daß er leider gerade kein Feuerzeug dabeihätte, aber auch gerne eine Zigarette

rauchen möchte. Obwohl diese Geschichte den Eindruck einer nicht ganz glaubwürdigen Wunderheilung erweckt, liegt ihr doch nur das relativ simple Kommunikationsmuster von Pacing und Leading zugrunde. Durch die Spiegelung des Atemrhythmus wurde eine Beziehung aufgebaut – Pacing. Dann konnte der Therapeut leitend eingreifen und so die Isolation des Klienten durchbrechen. In diesem Zusammenhang wird erkennbar, daß nonverbale Kommunikation mehr ist als Begleitmusik zur verbalen Verständigung.

Im Konzept Ericksons geht das Pacing über ein einfaches Aufeinander-Einstimmen hinaus. Durch angemessene und umfassende Spiegelung des verbalen und nonverbalen Verhaltens des Klienten wird nicht nur eine Beziehung aufgebaut, sondern kann zudem ein hypnotischer Zustand induziert werden. Dies wird noch durch weitere Entspannungssuggestionen in der Leading-Phase intensiviert.

Diese Pacing-Phänomene sind nicht nur auf zwischenmenschliche Kommunikation beschränkt, sondern lassen sich auch bei maschinenvermittelter Interaktion, wie beim hier beschriebenen Atembiofeedback, beobachten.

Tranceprozesse lassen sich auch auf der physiologischen Ebene nachweisen - Éva Bányai und ihre Mitarbeiter an der Universität von Budapest fanden, daß bei erfolgreicher hypnotischer Induktion ein wechselseitiges Aufeinander-Einstellen (tuning in) stattfindet. Dieses Einstimmen bezieht sich nicht nur auf das offensichtliche Verhalten, sondern findet auch auf psychophysiologischer Ebene statt. Gehirnwellen und Atemrhythmen sind bei einer erfolgreichen Tranceinduktion ebenso koordiniert.

Eine weitere Frage, warum gerade durch die Rückmeldung der Atemrhythmik derartig starke Effekte erzielbar sind, beantwortet die Forschung von Richter (1986). Das Atemzentrum im Hirnstamm gehört zu den vitalen Regelzentren und steht zudem mit dem Herz-Kreislauf-System in Verbindung. Außerdem bestehen über die Formatio Reticularis weitreichende Beziehungen zu anderen Gehirnarealen.

DIE MACHT DER WELT DES SPIEGELS

Eine weitere Facette des Trancephänomens sind die damit verbundenen Zusammenhänge zur mentalen Repräsentation. Die Wirkung einer auf Betty Erickson zurückgehenden Selbsthypnosetechnik, (s. Wippich, 1985, S. 242) ist ein Beleg für die Bedeutung mentaler Repräsentationen. Durch diese Übung werden hypnoide Zustände allein durch stärkeren Bezug auf die Umwelt bzw. ‚bewußte" mentale Repräsentation induziert.

waves and breathing rhythms are similarly coordinated with successful trance induction.

A further question about why such powerful effects can be achieved with the feedback of breathing rhythms is answered by Richter (1986)'s research. The breathing centre in the brain belongs to the vital control centres and, in addition to this, is connected to the cardio-vascular system. Furthermore, via the formatio reticularis, extensive relationships exist to other areas of the brain.

THE POWER OF THE WORLD OF THE MIRROR

A further facet of the trance phenomenon are the associated connections to mental representation. The effect of a self-hypnosis technique—to go back to Betty Erickson (see Wippich 1985, P. 242)—is proof of the significance of mental representations. With this exercise, hypnoidal states are induced merely by means of more powerful references to the environment and/or "conscious" mental representations.

One looks for a quiet place and commences with the exercise of autosuggestion and after five minutes one wakes up again, fully refreshed. The procedure behind this exercise is conceiveably simple. One makes statements about visual, acoustic and kinaesthetical perceptions which are presently appropriate. First of all, one makes three visual sentences, then three auditive ones, and then three kinaesthetic ones. These sentences can be spoken out loud or quietly (i.e. purely mental). The procedure could look like this. First of all, one begins visually: "I see the red carpet ... I see the shadow of the tree on the wall .. I see the flower vase infront of me on the table...", going over to the auditive ones "I hear a car driving past ...I hear the hum of the fridge ..I hear the noises on the street..", then one verbalizes the kinaesthetic perceptions: "I feel the rest of the chair in my back ..I feel my breathing ..I feel the clothes on my skin". In the next round, only two statements are selected, respectively, and in the next round, only one. Should a deep trance be induced before this, one can shut ones eyes and finish the verbalization. Very often, one can clearly feel a changed consciousness and a deep relaxation, even in the first exercise. The effect is intensified through further exercises.

WHAT DOES REPRESENTATION MEAN FOR OUR BRAIN?

We assume that our sensory systems are allocated to simulation systems in the brain, which, e.g. make test actions possible. Some researchers propose a kind of internal monitor for our visual system, on which we can produce graphic ideas. A similar thing is assumed for the auditive system, a kind of inner loud speaker on which we, e.g. can play melodies (see Kosslyn and Koenig, 1992). If we add our working memory to this representation system and proceed from an interlinking of these systems in the brain, then we have an attractive explanation for the puzzle of consciousness. Consciousness is the process which emerges when these systems interact, whereby a new complexity stage is reached (see Crick and Koch, 1992; Gadenne and Oswald, 1991). The significance of this principle of emergence was already recognized in gestalt psychology and can be elucidated on the basis of these graphics: the whole is more than the sum of parts. What one sees is not a number of dots but a circle.

The afore-said is, of course also valid for mental representations at a deeper complexity stage. They are not coded in the brain as symbols, but as emergent features of neronal network structures (see Levelt, 1991).

SUMMARY

When one considers the afore-mentioned aspects relevant for virtual emotions, no consistent picture arises. This is most certainly due to the fact that in AI, information processing is put on a level with logical consequences. The terms, emotion and intuition, have only recently been involved in the development of new methods. At this early research stage it appears to be sensible to make the phenomena experienceable in order to stimulate further questions and research. The demand for a traditional scientific approach is too premature.

The installation presented, can be understood as being a play with the concepts: virtual emotion, emergence, trance and non-verbal communication.

DESCRIPTION OF THE INSTALLATION

The installation consists of two cabins in which the active participants sit with their backs to the public. The sense of this structure is that the protagonists are not frontally visible to the observer and they feel relatively unobserved. The cabins are arranged beside each other so that they can be jointly kept in sight by the observers.

In every cabin there is a multi-media PC whose monitor has been arranged so that it is visible both for the participant as well as the observer. A further part is composed of fixtures to determine breathing rhythms. Here, the participant's biosignals are measured and are transformed into an intuitive, comprehensible, complex pattern of shapes, colour and rhythm. As already said, animated fractal landscapes were chosen as representation patterns.

Whereas with a normal feedback application, the participant receives feedback via his own body signals, in this installation, the feedback channels of both participants are switched, crosswise. In this way, both of them are confronted with the other's biosignals on the monitor. As to whether they are aware of this connection, depends on whether they have perceived the relevant information supplied at the beginning of the experiment, or not.

The observer in the installation and the participants can respectively experience, in this way,

Man sucht sich einen ruhigen Ort und beginnt die Übung mit der Autosuggestion, nach fünf Minuten wieder erfrischt aufzuwachen. Der Ablauf der Übung ist denkbar einfach: Man trifft Aussagen über visuelle, akustische und kinästhetische Wahrnehmungen, die momentan zutreffen. Zunächst bildet man drei visuelle Sätze, dann drei auditive und schließlich drei kinästhetische. Diese Sätze kann man sich dann laut oder leise (d.h. rein mental) vorsagen. Der Ablauf könnte folgendermaßen aussehen. Man beginnt zunächst visuell: „Ich sehe den roten Teppich ... ich sehe die Schatten von dem Baum an der Wand ... ich sehe die Blumenvase vor mir auf dem Tisch ...“; geht zum Auditiven über: „Ich höre ein vorbeifahrendes Auto ... ich höre das Summen des Kühlschranks ... ich höre die Geräusche auf der Straße...“; zum Schluß verbalisiert man seine kinästhetischen Wahrnehmungen: ‚Ich spüre die Lehne des Stuhls an meinem Rücken ... ich spüre die Atemzüge ... ich fühle die Kleidung auf meiner Haut.“ Im nächsten Durchgang trifft man nur noch jeweils zwei Aussagen und im letzten Durchgang nur noch eine. Sollte sich schon vorher eine tiefe Trance einstellen, kann man die Augen schließen und die Verbalisierung beenden. Oft kommt es schon bei der ersten Übung zu einem deutlich spürbaren veränderten Bewußtsein und einer tiefen Entspannung. Die Wirkung wird durch weitere Übungen verstärkt.

WAS BEDEUTET REPRÄSENTATION FÜR UNSER GEHIRN?

Man nimmt an, daß unseren Sinnessystemen im Gehirn Simulationssysteme zugeordnet sind, die z.B. Probehandlungen ermöglichen. Für unser visuelles System wird von einigen Forschern eine Art interner Monitor vorgeschlagen, auf dem wir bildliche Vorstellungen erzeugen können. Ähnliches wird auch über das auditive System angenommen, eine Art innerer Lautsprecher, auf dem wir z.B. Melodien spielen können (vgl. Kosslyn und Koenig, 1992). Nimmt man zu diesen Repräsentationssystemen noch unser Arbeitsgedächtnis hinzu und geht von einer Verknüpfung dieser Systeme im Gehirn aus, so bietet sich eine attraktive Erklärung für das Rätsel des Bewußtseins an. Das Bewußtsein ist der Prozeß, der emergiert, wenn diese Systeme interagieren, wodurch eine neue Komplexitätsstufe erreicht wird (vgl. Crick und Koch, 1992; Gadenne und Oswald, 1991). Die Bedeutung des Prinzips der Emergenz wurde schon in der Gestaltpsychologie erkannt und läßt sich anhand dieser Grafik verdeutlichen: Das Ganze ist mehr als die Summe seiner Teile.

Man sieht nicht Anzahl von Punkten, sondern einen Kreis. Das oben Gesagte gilt natürlich auch für die auf einer tieferen Komplexitätsstufe liegenden mentalen Repräsentationen. Sie sind im Gehirn nicht als Symbole kodiert, sondern als emergente Eigenschaften von neuronalen Netzwerkstrukturen (vgl. Levelt, 1991).

RESÜMEE

Betrachtet man die oben dargelegten, für virtuelle Emotionen relevanten Aspekte, so ergibt sich kein konsistentes Bild. Dies liegt sicherlich auch daran, daß in der KI Informationsverarbeitung mit logischem Schlußfolgern gleichgesetzt wurde. Die Begriffe Emotion und Intuition werden erst in letzter Zeit, im Zuge der Entwicklung neuer Methodik, mit Informationsverarbeitung in Beziehung gebracht. In diesem frühen Forschungsstadium erscheint es sinnvoll, die Phänomene überhaupt erfahrbar zu machen, um zu weiteren Fragestellungen und Forschungen anzuregen. Der Anspruch auf traditionell wissenschaftliches Vorgehen ist noch verfrüht.

Die vorgestellte Installation versteht sich als ein Spiel mit den Konzepten: virtuelle Emotion, Emergenz, Trance und nonverbale Kommunikation.

BESCHREIBUNG DER INSTALLATION

Die Installation besteht aus zwei Kabinen, in denen die aktiven Teilnehmer mit dem Rücken zum Publikum sitzen. Sinn dieser Konstruktion ist, daß die Protagonisten für die Betrachter nicht frontal sichtbar sind und sich relativ unbeobachtet fühlen können. Die Kabinen sind nebeneinander angeordnet, so daß sie vom Betrachter gemeinsam im Blick behalten werden können.

In jeder Kabine befindet sich ein Multimedia-PC, dessen Monitor so angebracht ist, daß er sowohl für den Teilnehmer selbst als auch für die Betrachter sichtbar ist. Ein weiterer Bestandteil sind Vorrichtungen zur Erfassung des Atemrhythmus. Damit werden die Biosignale der Teilnehmer gemessen und in ein intuitiv verständliches, komplexes Muster von Form, Farbe und Rhythmus umgesetzt. Als Repräsentationsmuster wurden wie bereits erwähnt animierte Fraktallandschaften gewählt.

Während bei einer normalen Feedback-Anwendung der Teilnehmer Rückmeldungen über seine eigenen Körpersignale erhält, sind die Feedbackkanäle der beiden Teilneh-

other sections of the same reality. The participants are confronted with the attention-absorbing feedback and have two reaction possibilities: either they coordinate with the "foreign" biosignals and resonate to each other (acceptance), or they repel (reactance). Which of the two reactions is selected greatly depends on four factors: on the one hand, on the general readiness to engage in the installation and, on the other hand, the acceptance of the colour and shape language of the feedback pattern for every respective participant. A further influential factor is the distance, or the proximity of the psychophysiological initial states of both participants. If one participant is quiet while the other is active, the initial coordination is less. A fourth infuential factor for the behaviour of the participant is the time. The longer they are confronted with the representation pattern, the stronger acceptance and coordination can be observed, as a rule.

The observer who observes the system from the outside, perceives how the psychophysiology of both participants resonates or differentiates, and in this way, he/she can follow the mutual computer-conveyed non-verbal interaction/coordination. In doing so, he/she has the possibility of tuning in to the foreign feedback himself and consequently, of literally becoming a participant in the system. He/she can observe the emergence of new system features. Both participants consciously experience their "trance state"—as to whether they also consciously perceive the emergence, greatly depends on whether they have made use of the information about the feedback switching.

OUTLOOK: COMMUNICATION AND ARTIFICIAL LIFE

In accordance with von Neumann, systems can only increase in complexity when they, on their part, interact with a more complex environment. The question of communication is closely linked to that of learning and represents a key question about the creation of artificial life. Future research will show as to whether the forms of communication and information processing discussed here are also relevant for artificial living beings.

BIBLIOGRAPHY

Banyai, Eva I.: Meszaros, Istvan; Csokay, Laszlo (1985). Interaction between hypnotist and subject: A social psychophysiological approach (Prelimiary report). In D. Waxman, P.C. Misra, M. Gibson and M.A. Basker (Eds). Modern Trends in Hypnosis, New York: Plenum Press, 97–108

Ciompi, Luc (1993). Die Hypothese der Affektlogik, Spektrum der Wissenschaft, 2, 76–84.

Crick, Francis & Koch, Christof (1992). Das Poblem des Bewußtseins. Spektrum der Wissenschaft, 11, 144–152.

Gadenne, Volker & Oswald, Margit E. (1991). Kognition und Bewußtsein. Berlin: Springer

Grinder, John & Bandler, Richard (1988). Therapie in Trance. Stuttgart:Klett Cotta

Kossak, Hans-Christian (1989), Hypnose. Ein Lehrbuch. München: Psychologie Verlags Union (P. 221)
Kosslyn, Stephan M. & Koenig, Oliver (1992). Wet Mind. The new cognitive neuroscience: New York: MacMillan
Levelt, Willem J.M. (1991). Die konnektionistische Mode. Sprache & Kognition, 10 (2), 61–72.
Levy, Steven (1992). Artificial Life. The quest for a new creation. London: Johnathan Cape
Pechmann, Thomas & Engelkamp, Johannes (1992). Mentale Repräsentationen – Verschiedene Sichtweisen eines Begriffs. Sprache & Kognition, 11 (2), 51–64.
Reingold, Howard (1992) Virtuelle Welten. Reisen im Cyberspace. Reinbek bei Hamburg:Rowohlt
Richter, Diethelm M. (1986). Zur Frage der Rhythmogenese der Atmung. Physiologie aktuell, 2–201–218.
Reibensahm, Hans (1985). Anwendung Ericksonscher Sprachmuster als rhetorische Strategien in Lerngruppen. Hypnose & Kognition, 2(2), 44–53
Schemat, Stefan, Müller Andreas & Riebensahm, Hans (1992). Zur experimentellen Prüfung von therapeutischen Zugängen zur nonverbalen Kommunikation: Neuere rechnergestütze Realisationen von Biofeedback. In L. Montada (eds). Bericht über den 38. Kongreß der Deutschen Gesellschaft für Psychologie in Trier 1992. Göttingen: Hogrefe, P. 408–409.
Schemat, Stefan (1991). Die emotionale Komponente von Cyberspace. Vortrag auf dem interdisziplinären Workshop "Virtual Reality und Kommunikationsästhetik" am 7.12.91 in Göttingen.
Waldrop, Mitchell (1993). Können Computer denken? In: R. Kurzweil (eds.) AI. Das Zeitalter der Künstlichen Intelligenz, P. 62—67 München: Hanser

mer dieser Installation über Kreuz verschaltet. So wird jeder von ihnen auf dem Bildschirm mit den Biosignalen des anderen konfrontiert. Ob sie Kenntnis von diesem Zusammenhang haben, hängt davon ab, ob sie das entsprechende Informationsangebot zu Beginn des Experiments wahrgenommen haben oder nicht.

Der Betrachter der Installation und die Teilnehmer können auf diese Weise jeweils andere Ausschnitte derselben Realität erleben. Die Teilnehmer sind mit dem aufmerksamkeitsabsorbierenden Feedback konfrontiert und haben zwei Reaktionsmöglichkeiten: Entweder koordinieren sie sich mit den „fremden" Biosignalen, und es findet ein Aufeinandereinschwingen statt (Akzeptanz), oder sie wehren sie ab (Reaktanz). Welche der beiden Reaktionen gewählt wird, hängt im wesentlichen von vier Faktoren ab: Zum einen von der generellen Bereitschaft, sich auf die Installation einzulassen, zum anderen von der Akzeptanz der Farb- und Formensprache des Feedbackmusters beim jeweiligen Teilnehmer. Eine weitere Einflußgröße besteht in der Distanz bzw. Nähe der psychophysiologischen Anfangszustände beider Teilnehmer. Befindet sich ein Teilnehmer in Ruhe, während der andere aktiviert ist, ist die anfängliche Übereinstimmung geringer. Eine vierte Einflußgröße für das Verhalten der Teilnehmer ist die Zeit. Je länger sie mit den Repräsentationsmustern konfrontiert werden, desto stärker läßt sich in der Regel Akzeptanz und Koordination beobachten.

Der Betrachter, der das System von außen beobachtet, nimmt das Aufeinandereinschwingen oder die Differenzierung der Psychophysiologie beider Teilnehmer wahr und kann so die wechselseitige, computervermittelte nonverbale Interaktion/Koordination verfolgen. Er hat dabei die Möglichkeit, sich selbst auf das fremde Feedback einzustimmen, und so Teilnehmer des Systems im weiteren Sinne zu werden. Er kann das Emergieren neuer Systemeigenschaften beobachten. Die beiden Teilnehmer erleben bewußt ihren „Trancezustand" – ob sie ebenfalls bewußt die Emergenz wahrnehmen, hängt wesentlich davon ab, ob sie vom Informationsangebot über die Feedback-Verschaltung Gebrauch gemacht haben.

AUSBLICK: KOMMUNIKATION UND ARTIFICAL LIVE

Nach von Neumann können Systeme nur an Komplexität zunehmen, wenn sie ihrerseits mit einer noch komplexeren Umwelt interagieren. Die Frage der Kommunikation ist mit der des Lernens eng verknüpft und stellt eine Schlüsselfrage für die Schaffung von künstlichem Leben dar. Zukünftige

Forschung wird zeigen, ob die hier diskutierten Formen der Kommunikation und Informationsverarbeitung auch für künstliche Lebewesen relevant sind.

ANMERKUNGEN

[1] In dieser Arbeit wird der Begriff der Repräsentation sehr weit gefaßt. Er wird im Sinne einer Relation zwischen dem, was repräsentiert werden soll, und der eigentlichen Repräsentation gebraucht. Diese Relation kann sehr unterschiedlich sein. Bei der Visualisierung des Atemrhythmus besteht eine Relation zwischen der Atemfrequenz und der Animationsgeschwindigkeit. Zudem wird das Zusammenziehen und Ausdehnen der Lunge bei der Atmung durch scheinbares Zusammenziehen und Ausdehnen der Grafik dargestellt (symbolisiert). Eine weitere Repräsenationsaufgabe kann über eine Zuordnung von Frequenzbereichen zu Farben erfolgen. Eine Einfärbung der Grafik ins Rötliche kann eine hohe Atemfrequenz bedeuten, eine Einfärbung ins Blaue steht für eine niedrige Frequenz. Repräsentationen können nach der Güte der Abbildung beurteilt werden.

BIBLIOGRAPHIE

Bányai, Éva I.; Mészáros, István; Csókay, László (1985). Interaction between hypnotist and subject: A social psychophysiological approach (Preliminary report). In D. Waxman, P. C. Misra, M. Gibson and M. A. Basker (Eds.). Modern Trends in Hypnosis. New York: Plenum Press, 97–108.
Ciompi, Luc (1993). Die Hypothese der Affektlogik. Spektrum der Wissenschaft, 2, 76–84.
Crick, Francis & Koch, Christof (1992). Das Problem des Bewußtseins. Spektrum der Wissenschaft, 11, 144–152.
Gadenne, Volker. & Oswald, Margit E. (1991). Kognition und Bewußtsein. Berlin: Springer.
Grinder, John & Bandler, Richard (1988). Therapie in Trance. Stuttgart: Klett Cotta.
Kossak, Hans-Christian (1989). Hypnose. Ein Lehrbuch. München: Psychologie Verlags Union. (S. 221).
Kosslyn, Stephen M. & Koenig, Oliver (1992). Wet Mind. The new cognitive neuroscience. New York: Macmillan.
Levelt, Willem J. M. (1991). Die konnektionistische Mode. Sprache & Kognition, 10 (2), 61–72.
Levy, Steven (1992). Artificial Life. The quest for a new creation. London: Johnathan Cape.
Pechmann, Thomas & Engelkamp, Johannes (1992). Menta-

le Repräsentationen – Verschiedene Sichtweisen eines Begriffs. Sprache & Kognition, 11 (2), 51–64.
Reingold, Howard (1992). Virtuelle Welten. Reisen im Cyberspace. Reinbek bei Hamburg: Rowohlt.
Richter, Diethelm M. (1986). Zur Frage der Rhythmogenese der Atmung. Physiologie aktuell, 2, 201–218.
Riebensahm, Hans (1985). Anwendung Ericksonscher Sprachmuster als rhetorische Strategien in Lerngruppen. Hypnose & Kognition, 2 (2), 44–53.
Schemat, Stefan; Müller, Andreas & Riebensahm, Hans (1992). Zur experimentellen Prüfung von therapeutischen Zugängen zur nonverbalen Kommunikation: Neuere rechnergestützte Realisationen von Biofeedback. In: L. Montada (Hrsg.). Bericht über den 38. Kongreß der Deutschen Gesellschaft für Psychologie in Trier 1992. Göttingen: Hogrefe, S. 408–409.
Schemat, Stefan (1991). Die emotionale Komponente von Cyberspace. Vortrag auf dem interdisziplinären Workshop „Virtual Reality und Kommunikationsästhetik“ am 7. 12. 91 in Göttingen.
Waldrop, Mitchell (1993). Können Computer denken? In: R. Kurzweil (Hrsg.). KI. Das Zeitalter der Künstlichen Intelligenz. S. 62–67. München: Hanser.

GEN-MANIPULATIONS-SET (PART I)

ALEXANDER POPPER / KATRIN STOCKHAMMER

GENTRANSFER IN PFLANZEN

LIGATION VON GEN X IN DAS PLASMID

Ansatz:
Gen X – 20–5000ng
Plasmid DNA – 10–500ng
10x Ligase Puffer – 1.5ml
T4 DNA Ligase – 400units
H_2O – auf 15ml
Ansatz über Nacht bei 15°CÉ (sticky ends) oder 1–3h bei Raumtemperatur (blunt ends) inkubieren

TRANSFORMATION

- 100ml kompetente Bakterien (*Escherichia coli*) auf Eis auftauen und mit der Plasmid DNA versetzen
- Nach 20 min. die Bakterien 90 sec. bei 42°C (Wärmeschock) belassen und erneut 2–3 min. auf Eis transferieren
- Dem Ansatz 900ml SOB-Medium zugeben und 1h bei 37°C schütteln
- 100–250ml davon auf LBamp-Agar ausplattieren

Selektion der transgenen Bakterien auf Ampicilin-Resistenz

AMPLIFIKATION DER PLASMID DNA

- 2–3 ml Selektivmedium mit transgenen Bakterien inokulieren und über Nacht bei 37°C schütteln
- Abzentrifugieren bei 4000rpm
- Den Überstand entfernen und das Pellet in 300ml STETL (Saccharose-Tris EDTA TritonX-100® Lysozym) resuspendieren
- Nach 3 min. auf Eis wird 3min. auf 95°C transferieren und anschließend 15 min. bei 14000rpm abzentrifugieren

GENE MANIPULATION SET (PART I) ALEXANDER POPPER / KATRIN STOCKHAMMER

GENE TRANSFER IN PLANTS

Ligation of gene X into the plasmid
Preparation:
Gene X 20–5000 ng
Plasmid DNA 10–500 ng
10x Ligase Buffer 1.5ul
T4 DNA Ligase 400 units
H_2O to 15ul
Incubate the preparation over night at 15°C (sticky ends) or 1–3 hours at room temperature (blunt ends).

TRANSFORMATION

- Thaw out 100ul of competent bacteria (Escherichia coli) on ice and dilute with the plasmid DNA.
- „After 20 min., leave the bacteria for 90 sec. at 42°C (heat shock) and transfer again for 2–3 min. onto ice.
- Add 900ul SOB-Medium to the preparation and shake for 1 hour at 37°C
- Plate 100-250ul of this onto LBamp agar

Selection of the transgenic bacteria for ampicilin resistance

AMPLIFICATION OF PLASMID DNA

- Inoculate 2–3 ml of selective medium with transgenic bacteria and shake over night at 37°C.
- Separate by centrifuging at 4000 rpm
- Remove the supernatant and resuspend the

GEN-MANIPULATIONS-SET Part One

pellet in 300ul STELI (Sucrose-Tris EDTA TritonX-100[R] Lysozyme).

- After 3 min. on ice, transfer to 95°C for 3 min and then separate by centrifuging for 15 min at 14000 rpm.
- Remove the pellet carefully with a sterile tooth pick and incubate the remaining supernatant containing the plasmid DNA with 1ug RNase A for 15 min., at room temperature.
- Precipitate the DNA with isopropanol and separate by centrifuging for 15 min.
- Dissolve the washed and dried pellet in 20ul 1xTE (Tris EDTA).

CHARACTERIZATION OF THE PLASMID DNA

DNA processing with restriction endonuclease:
Preparation:
Plasmid DNA 0.2–1ug
10x restriction buffer 2ul
Restriction endonuclease 2 units
H_2O to 20ul
Incubate the preparation for 2 hours at corresponding temperature.
Separate the DNA fragments in the electrical field:

- Bring agarose to the boil in 0.5x TPE (Tris Phosphate EDTA) and after cooling, dilute with 5ul ethidium bromide 100 ml.
- Ethidium bromide intercalates in the DNA and makes DNA visible through the absorption of UV rays.
- Pour the gel which is still in a liquid state onto a tray and after hardening, transfer to a buffer chamber filled with 0.5x TPE.
- Dilute the DNA specimen to be analysed with the loading buffer and pipet into the slots.
- Separate the DNA electrophoretically at 1–5 eV/cm, according to size

TRANSFORMATION OF EMBRYONIC PLANT CELLS WITH THE HETEROLOGOUS DNA

Hit the nucleus.

REGENERATION OF COMPLETE TRANSGENIC PLANTS FROM THE TRANSFORMED TISSUE CULTURE

Transfer calli to SIM (shoot inducing medium)

- SIM:

IPA (isopentenyladenosine) 4.0 mg l
NAA (Naphtol acetic acid) 0.2 mg l
MS (Murashige & Skoog) salts 4.4 g/l
Sucrose 30 g/l
Vitamix 2 ml/l
Agar 9 g/l
pH 5.8 (KOH)

- Let the regenerated shoots form, then incubate briefly in RIM (root inducing medium)
- RIM:

IAA (indole acetic acid) 1 mg l

- Mit einem sterilen Zahnstocher das Pellet vorsichtig entfernen und den verbleibenden Überstand, der die Plasmid-DNA enthält, mit 1mg RNase A 15 min. bei Raumtemperatur inkubieren
- Die DNA mit Isopropanol präzipitieren und 15 min. abzentrifugieren
- Das gewaschene und getrocknete Pellet in 20ml 1xTE (Tris EDTA) lösen

CHARAKTERISIERUNG DER PLASMID-DNA

DNA-Spaltung mit Restriktionsendonucleasen:
Ansatz:
Plasmid-DNA – 0.2–1mg
10x Restriktionspuffer – 2ml
Restriktionsendonuclease – 2units
H_2O – auf 20ml
Ansatz 2h bei entsprechender Temperatur inkubieren
Auftrennung der DNA-Fragmente im elektrischen Feld:

- Agarose in 0.5x TPE (Tris Phosphat EDTA) aufkochen und nach dem Abkühlen mit 5ml Ethidiumbromid/100ml versetzen

Ethidiumbromid interkaliert in die DNA und macht DNA durch Absorption von UV-Strahlung sichtbar.

- Das noch flüssige Gel in einen tray gießen und nach dem Erhärten in eine mit 0.5x TPE gefüllte Pufferkammer transferieren
- Die zu analysierenden DNA-Proben mit Auftragspuffer versetzen und in die slots pipettieren

Die DNA elektrophoretisch bei 1–5eV/cm nach Größe auftrennen.

TRANSFORMATION VON UNDIFFERENZIERTEN PFLANZENZELLEN MIT DER FREMD-DNA

- Zellkern treffen

REGENERATION VON VOLLSTÄNDIGEN TRANSGENEN PFLANZEN AUS DER TRANSFORMIERTEN GEWEBEKULTUR

- Kalli auf SIM (shoot inducing medium) transferieren
- SIM:
  IPA (Isopentenyladenosine) – 4.0mg/l
  NAA (Naphtol acetic acid) – 0.2mg/l

MS (Murashige & Skoog) salts – 4.4g/l
Saccharose – 30g/l
Vitamix – 2ml/l
Agar – 9g/l
pH – 5.8 (KOH)

Regenerierte Sprosse ausbilden lassen, dann kurzfristig in RIM (root inducing medium) inkubieren
RIM:
IAA (Indole acetic acid) – 1mg/l
IBA (Indole-3-butyrate) – 0.2mg/l
Kinetin – 0.2mg/l

Sprosse auf MS-Medium aufbringen, Ausbildung der Wurzeln abwarten
MS-Medium:
MS salts – 4,4g/l
Saccharose – 30g/l
Vitamix – 2ml/l
Agar – 9g/l
pH – 5.8 (KOH)
Abb.1: Plasmid mit Fremd-DNA

colEI: Origin of replication. Ermöglicht Vermehrung des Plasmids in *E. coli* .
amp^r^: Gen codierend für Ampicilin-Resistenz. Transformierte Bakterien sind resistent gegen das Antibiotikum Ampicilin.
CaMV35SP: Starker konstitutiver Promoter des Cauliflower Mosaic Virus, der von der pflanzlichen Transkriptionsmaschinerie erkannt wird.
GUS: b-Glucuronidase. Ein Gen aus *E. coli*, das als Reportergen in pflanzlichen Systemen Anwendung findet (detailierte Restriktionskarte: Abb. 1b; DNA Sequenz: Abb. 2). Durch Spaltung eines zugegebenen Substrates werden transformierte Gewebebereiche, die dieses Gen exprimieren, blau gefärbt. Blaue Zellen tragen mit hoher Wahrscheinlichkeit auch das Fremdgen (Gen X).
XbaI, EcoRI, ...: Erkennungssequenzen von Restriktionsendonucleasen. Diese Enzyme sind im Handel erhältlich und spalten DNA in vielen Fällen an definierten Nucleotidabfolgen. Diese Eigenschaft erlaubt es DNA-Fragmente zu trennen und (mit Hilfe weiterer Enzyme) in veränderter Kombination zu verbinden.
Gen X: Ein beliebiges Gen (Fremdgen). Es kann aus Viren, Bakterien, Pflanzen oder animalischen Systemen stammen und soll der transformierten Pflanze die gewünschten Eigenschaften verleihen.

IBA (indole 3 butyrate) 0.2 mg/l
Kinetine 0.2 mg/l
- Apply the shoot to the MS medium. Wait for the roots to form.

MS Medium:
MS salts 4.4 g/l
Sucrose 30 g/l
Vitamix 2 ml/l
Agar 9 g/l
pH 5.8 (KOH)

Figure 1: Plasmid with heterologous DNA

colEI: Origin of replication. Enables the amplification of the plasmid in E. coli
amp^r^: (Gene coding for ampicilin resistance. The transformed bacteria are resistant to the antibiotic ampicilin.
CaMV35SP: A more stronger constitutive promoter of the cauliflower mosaic virus which is recognized by the plant transcription machinery.
GUS: ß Glucuronidase. One gene from E. coli which is used as a reporter gene in the plant system (detailed restriction map: Fig. 1b: DNA sequence: Fig. 2). By processing an added substrate, transformed tissue areas which express this gene turn blue. Blue cells also very probably have the heterlogous gene (gene X).
XbaI. EcoRI...: Recognition sequence of restriction endonucleases. These enzymes are obtain-

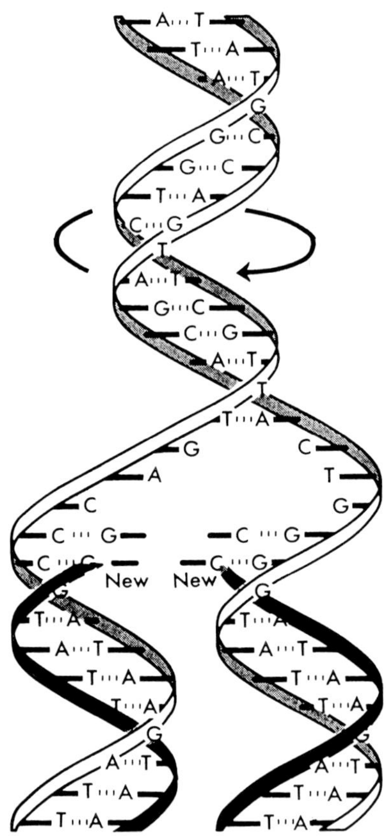

CTGCAGGTCA	GTCCCTTATG	TTACGTCCTG	TAGAAACCCC	AACCCGTGAA	ATCAAAAAAC
TCGACGGCCT	GTGGGCATTC	AGTCTGGATC	GCGAAAACTG	TGGAATTGAT	CAGCGTTGGT
GGGAAAGCGC	GTTACAAGAA	AGCCGGGCAA	TTGCTGTGCC	AGGCAGTTTT	AACGATCAGT
TCGCCGATGC	AGATATTCGT	AATTATGCGG	GCAACGTCTG	GTATCAGCGC	GAAGTCTTTA
TACCGAAAGG	TTGGGCAGGC	CAGCGTATCG	TGCTGCGTTT	CGATGCGGTC	ACTCATTACG
GCAAAGTGTG	GGTCAATAAT	CAGGAAGTGA	TGGAGCATCA	GGGCGGCTAT	ACGCCATTTG
AAGCCGATGT	CACGCCGTAT	GTTATTGCCG	GGAAAAGTGT	ACGTATCACC	GTTTGTGTGA
ACAACGAACT	GAACTGGCAG	ACTATCCCGC	CGGGAATGGT	GATTACCGAC	GAAAACGGCA
AGAAAAAGCA	GTCCTACTTC	CATGATTTCT	TTAACTATGC	CGGAATCCAT	CGCAGCGTAA
TGCTCTACAC	CACGCCGAAC	ACCTGGGTGG	ACGATATCAC	CGTGGTGACG	CATGTCGCGC
AAGACTGTAA	CCACGCGTCT	GTTGACTGGC	AGGTGGTGGC	CAATGGTGAT	GTCAGCGTTG
AACTGCGTGA	TGCGGATCAA	CAGGTGGTTG	CAACTGGACA	AGGCACTAGC	GGGACTTTGC
AAGTGGTGAA	TCCGCACCTC	TGGCAACCGG	GTGAAGGTTA	TCTCTATGAA	CTGTGCGTCA
CAGCCAAAAG	CCAGACAGAG	TGTGATATCT	ACCCGCTTCG	CGTCGGCATC	CGGTCAGTGG
CAGTGAAGGG	CGAACAGTTC	CTGATTAACC	ACAAACCGTT	CTACTTTACT	GGCTTTGGTC
GTCATGAAGA	TGCGGACTTA	CGTGGCAAAG	GATTCGATAA	CGTGCTGATG	GTGCACGACC
ACGCATTAAT	GGACTGGATT	GGGGCCAACT	CCTACCGTAC	CTCGCATTAC	CCTTACGCTG
AAGAGATGCT	CGACTGGGCA	GATGAACATG	GCATCGTGGT	GATTGATGAA	ACTGCTGCTG
TCGGCTTTAA	CCTCTCTTTA	GGCATTGGTT	TCGAAGCGGG	CAACAAGCCG	AAAGAACTGT
ACAGCGAAGA	AGCAGTCAAC	GGGGAAACTC	AGCAAGCGCA	CTTACAGGCG	ATTAAAGAGC
TGATAGCGCG	TGACAAAAAC	CACCCAAGCG	TGGTGATGTG	GAGTATTGCC	AACGAACCGG
ATACCCGTCC	GCAAGTGCAC	GGGAATATTT	CGCCACTGGC	GGAAGCAACG	CGTAAACTCG
ACCCGACGCG	TCCGATCACC	TGCGTCAATG	TAATGTTCTG	CGACGCTCAC	ACCGATACCA
TCAGCGATCT	CTTTGATGTG	CTGTGCCTGA	ACCGTTATTA	CGGATGGTAT	GTCCAAAGCG
GCGATTTGGA	AACGGCAGAG	AAGGTACTGG	AAAAAGAACT	TCTGGCCTGG	CAGGAGAAAC
TGCATCAGCC	GATTATCATC	ACCGAATACG	GCGTGGATAC	GTTAGCCGGG	CTGCACTCAA
TGTACACCGA	CATGTGGAGT	GAAGAGTATC	AGTGTGCATG	GCTGGATATG	TATCACCGCG
TCTTTGATCG	CGTCAGCGCC	GTCGTCGGTG	AACAGGTATG	GAATTTCGCC	GATTTTGCGA
CCTCGCAAGG	CATATTGCGC	GTTGGCGGTA	ACAAGAAAGG	GATCTTCACT	CGCGACCGCA
AACCGAAGTC	GGCGGCTTTT	CTGCTGCAAA	AACGCTGGAC	TGGCATGAAC	TTCGGTGAAA
AACCGCAGCA	GGGAGGCAAA	CAATGAATCA	ACAACTCTCC	TGGCGCACAC	GTGGCTACAG
CCTCGGTGGG	GAATTC				

Nucleotidsequenz des GUS-Gens. A=Adenin, C=Cytosin, G=Guanin, T=Thymidin

Thanks & Kisses to:
Gregor Mendel
H. Kienesberger
Virus Like Particle
W. Prymas
W. Goedl
Whattochter
& Sherman H. Space
A. Baumgartner

Die Natur kann verbessert werden

Das Projekt wurde ermöglicht durch die freundliche Unterstützung der Fa. Olympus.

TÖNE

R.A.M.S. ATTACK

AUTOMATIC RADIO

R.A.M.S. ATTACK AUTOMATIC RADIO

The dream of equalitarian media seems to be over. Especially in a country poisoned by an unparalleled concentration which politics humbly kneeled before, full of broken journalists. A country at the edge of a cesspool of authoritarian heartless and resourceless and consequently inhuman unity – slime.
Technologies have turned out to be problem makers, as an end in itself where limited techo-disciples worship in ecstasy – in the dusk – a golden calf, full of hope for the fictive Nirvana in the warm uterus of virtual realities.
R.A.M.S. ATTACK is brutal radio, a radio terminator which as a taker of hostages subjects its hostages to thematically glossed interrogation, commanding absolute obediance to ignore everything – like a great inquisitor – that seems not to fit in with his arbitrary schemes, stupid machine-intelligence! R.A.M.S. ATTACK is the backlash, radio for masochists who celebrate their orgasm in the first fuck.

The central module harbours a hierarchical language programme with a working question-answer system on a **reverence word basis** within acceptable **tolerance ranges**, as the hugest subprogramme. The data basis contains "keys" of the theorems of art which produced theories of the partition of the distribution paths. Emotive words act as attractors.
The coding away and **"mapping"** of the conceptual depth structure during broadcasting is effected by integrating the immediate conversation data into new question structures. Set **prognoses** correspond to the formal structure of the conceptual basis of medial statements on a wider context-related level than knowledge about the real world which is assessed in question-answer systems as represented by our broadcasting programme. In line with the pioneer programmes of the magical year 66: **try 66**
The information industry provides the materials and the hardware to create an active installation that investigates the **social transformation** it triggers off. The **political peripheral conditions** of the constantly changing cultural and commercial situation provide the "material".
In the „installation programme" ATTACK, the **compulsory control system** for the recipients and interagents can be physically fully experienced and disperses with every virtuality Sequence and Choice of the Broadcasting Programme System and hardware configuration

Das zentrale Modul beherbergt ein hierarchisches Sprachprogramm mit einem auf *Reverenzantwortbasis* innerhalb akzeptabler *Toleranzbreiten* arbeitenden Frage-Antwortsystem als mächtigstes Subprogramm. Die Datenbasis enthält „keys" der Theoreme der Kunst, die Theorie der Aufteilung der Distributionswege hervorriefen. Reizwörter agieren als Attraktor.
Das Vercoden und *„Kartographieren"* der begrifflichen Tiefenstrukturen als Sendung erfolgt durch das Integrieren der aktuellen Gesprächsdaten in neue Fragestrukturen. Aufgestellte *Prognosen* entsprechen der formalen Struktur der begrifflichen Grundlagen von medialen Äußerungen auf breiter kontektbezogener Ebene als Wissen über die reale Welt, was in Frage-Antwort Systemen wie unser Sendeprogramm eines darstellt ausgewertet wird. Entsprechend den Pionierprogrammen des magischen Jahres 68: *try 66*
Die Informationsindustrie bietet die Materialien und Hardware um eine aktive Installation zu schaffen, die die *soziale Transformation* untersucht, die sie auslöst. Die *politischen Rahmenbedingungen* der sich ständig verändernden kulturellen und kommerziellen Situation stellen den „Stoff".
Im „Installationsprogramm" ATTACK wird das *Zwangs-Leitsystem* für den Rezipienten und Interagenten physisch voll erfahrbar und entbehrt jeder Virtualität.
Ablauf und Auswahl des *SENDEPROGRAMMS*
System und Hardwarekonfiguration via* sampler, Mixer, Livezuspielung und Steuercomputer sind das Gerüst und Herzstück.
@SCHNITTSTELLE
@INSZENIERUNG des Sende- und Interaktionsgeschehens
@Belegen der erforderlichen Begriffsdatenbanken, die bestimmten samples oder Fragen zugeordnet werden.
#Erörtern der sendetechnischen Möglichkeiten und programmimmanenter Faktoren des Landes OÖ. Das Medium selbst tritt als Algorithmus des Programms auf, wird in das Kompositionskonzept des ATTACK-Radios integriert.
#Radioüberfälle treten unerwartet auf.#Transportiert wird die Transparenz systemorientierter Abläufe im Medium
ZIEL: Nicht vollautomatisches Radio als geschlossenes vor-

bestimmtes und vorproduziertes System sondern lebendiges auf die unmittelbare Aktion reagierendes Liveprogramm. INHALT: Nicht die Funktionstüchtigkeit von Systemkonfigurationen der Industrie soll exemplifiziert werden sondern das Aufbrechen des Systems mit Bezug auf das Geschehen vor Ort und das bestehende Programm im Land. Die Vorproduktion wird im Sinne von Echt-Erleben aufgelöst.

$Erscheinungsbild im Radio

$Zeit der Übertragung

$Dauer der Produktion

Ergebnis sollen definierte Programmplätze zusätzlich zu einer permanenten punktuellen Präsenz im gesamten Landesprogramm sein. RADIOÜBERFÄLLE sind hier die definierte Gefahr im Lokalprogramm.

#Das parallele Musikprogramm besteht aus samples die in jedem Programm$ als Fraktale der samples zu einem immer neuen Technostück formiert werden. Die Stücke sind Begriffen aus der Gesprächsdatenbank zugeordnet

RADIOVERHÖR TALK: Licht macht blind für das Radio. Die Aufforderung zur Stellungnahme ist computergeneriert.

Fragen werden via determiniertem Zufall abgerufen – die Verhörstruktur ist analysiert, festgelegt – nächste Frage folgt auf hierarchischer Begriffsebenenstruktur, die ebenfalls mit der vorhandenen Begriffssammlung operiert.

KONSEQUENZ: Das Radiosystem selbst ist neues Menscheninterview. Situation simuliert Wissen bzw. Intelligenz des Systems.

Das Medium Radio hat seinen Ereignischarakter, durch effektvollere Vermittlungssysteme abgelöst, mittlerweile weitgehend verloren. Produktionen werden durch Programmierung ersetzt, die immer häufiger automatisch erfolgt. Menschen spielen im Geschehen zunehmend eine untergeordnete Rolle, liefern den menschlichen Aspekt für ein Programm, das einen kommunikativen Charakter simuliert.

Zur Steigerung der Attraktivität werden aber Eingriffe in den Programmablauf erlaubt. Interaktive Benutzer werden zum wesentlichen Bestandteil eines Systems, dessen Effizienz als Steuerungsinstrument auf einer breiten Publikumsakzeptanz basiert. Die Möglichkeit der Mitgestaltung ist durch klare Vorgaben geregelt und beschränkt sich auf ein Klischee von Scheinkommunikation.

fast, cheep and efficient

Demnächst wird das Radio vom elektronischen in den digitalen Raum überwechseln. Kompatibel zu allen Datennetzen ergibt sich mittels digitaler Kodierung ein schnelles und effizientes Verbreitungsmedium für Verkehrs- und Sicherheitssysteme. Radio bekommt im Unterstatement zum aku-

via* sampler, mixer, live play and control computer are the framework and the core.

a INTERFACE

a PRODUCTION of the broadcasting and interaction event

a occupation of the relevant concept data banks which are allocated to certain samples or questions.

Discussion about broadcasting technology possibilities and immanent programme factors in the province of UA. The medium itself appears as an algorithm of the programme and is intergrated in the composition concept of ATTACK radio.

Radio attacks take place unexpectedly. The transparency of system-orientated sequences is transported in the medium GOAL: Not fully-automatic radio as a closed, pre-determined and pre-produced system, but animated live programme reacting to the direct action. CONTENT: Not the functionability of the industry's system configurations should be exemplified, but the breaking open of the system in relation to what is happening in situ and the existing programme in the province. The pre-production is dissolved in the sense of real-experience.

- Phenotype in radio
- Transmission time
- Duration of the production

Result, should there be defined programme spaces in addition to a permanent presence in points in the entire provincial programme. RADIO ATTACKS are here the defined danger in the local programme.

The parallel music programme consists of samples which to be formed in every programme as a fraction of the samples to into an ever new techno-piece. The pieces are allocated to terms from the conversation data bank.

RADIOINTERROGATION TALK: Light is blinding for the radio. The summons to comment is computer-generated.

Questions are called in via determined chance – the interrogation structure is analysed, stipulated – next question follows on a hierarchical conceptual level structure which similarly operates with the available conceptual collection.

CONSEQUENCE: The radio system itself is the new machine interview. Situation simulates knowledge and/or intelligence of the system.

The medium radio has, in the meantime, largely lost its sensation structure, replaced by more effective communications systems. Productions are replaced by programming and is more and more frequently being effected automatically. People increasingly play a subordinate role in what is going on, supplying the human aspect for a programme that simulates a communicative character.

Interventions in the programme sequence are allowed, however, to increase attractivity. Interactive users become an integral part of a system whose efficiency as a control instrument is based on wide-scale public acceptance. The possibility of co-creating is controlled by clear points and is limited to a cliche of apparent communication.

FAST, CHEAP, EFFICIENT

In the very near future, radio will change over from electronic to digital space. Compatible to all data networks, by means of digital coding, a fast and efficient propagation medium results for traffic and safety control systems. Radio, as a driving system that purposefully controls vertical flows on account of their complexity and overload, shortly before breaking down gets back something of the sensation of happening, in understatement to the acoustic accompanying programme.

CONTEXT:
We are creating an interface where the medium and the public clash together. The public ends up in the difficult position of having to communicate with an uncommunicative programme. The radio as a superordinated system stipulates the procedure.
The second sector is the transmission to a wide public. The conflict between being played in programme sequences and listening habits and a breaking through of this scheme, produces a field of tension for a discussion with the definition of quite how radio operates. The prerequisite is the occupation of existing spaces and an as offensive as possible a breaking open of unreflected mechanisms.

Concept: Alf Altendorf, Margarete Jahrmann, Thomas Madersbacher
Technical advisor and programming: Bernhard Loibner. "All Quiet on the Western Front"
Acoustic-Installation: Christof Cargnelli, Peter Szely

Thanks to:
A-Team Computer Design GmbH, Linz

stischen Begleitprogramm etwas Ereignishaftes zurück, als Lenkungssystem, das die wegen ihrer Komplexität und Überbeanspruchung kurz vor dem Zusammenbruch stehenden Ströme gezielt steuert.

KONTEXT

Wir schaffen eine Schnittstelle, an der Medium und Publikum aufeinanderprallen: Das Publikum gerät in die Zwangslage, mit einem unkommunikativen Programm kommunizieren zu müssen. Das Radio gibt als übergeordnetes System den Ablauf vor.
Der zweite Bereich ist die Übermittlung an das breite Publikum. Der Konflikt zwischen eingespielten Programmabläufen und Hörgewohnheiten und einem Durchbrechen dieses Schemas ergibt ein Spannungsfeld für eine Auseinandersetzung mit der Definition dessen, wie Radio funktioniert. Voraussetzung ist die Okkupation vorhandener Räume und ein möglichst offensives Aufbrechen von unreflektierenden Mechanismen.
R.A.M.S.
REBEL ARMY OF MILITANT SHEEP
RANDOM ACCESS MEDIA SYSTEM
MARCH 92 AV-VIDEO-PRÄSENTATION, WOOLY AWARD, SALZGRIES, VIENNA
MARCH 92 START OF THE BROADCASTING OF RAMS-RADIO, WEDNESDAY 8 PM, 103,3 MHZ
MAY 92 „JUST A MINUTE", PALAIS LIECHTENSTEIN, VIENNA
JUNE 92 „RAMS OCCUPIES THE PLANET", NOISE—EVENT UNIVERSITY OF APPLIED ARTS VIENNA
JUNE 92 „RAMS-CAFE", WÄHRINGER STRASSE, VIENNA
JUNE 92 „RADIO INTERACTIVITY", ACADEMY OF FINE ARTS, VIENNA
AUGUST 92 „COLLECTIVE RADIO", PROGETTO CIVITELLA DAGLIANO, ITALY
DECEMBER 92 VIRTUAL DEPARTMENT, PARADISO, AMSTERDAM, NETHERLANDS
JUNE 93 „SPRENGSTOFF SUPAKLASS", TREIBSTOFF SUPERNORMAL, GASSTATION SALZBURG
RANDOM ACCESS MEDIA SYSTEM, REBEL ARMY OF MILITANT SHEEP IS ATTEMPTING TO CREATE A NEW ACCESS TO PRESENTATION AND INFORMATION CHANNELS.
R.A.M.S. IS A LABEL WHICH STANDS FOR AN „USER -CONTROLLED- SYSTEM".
THE RESULT IS CONSTANT CHANGE OF CONTENT IN EACH WORK, ON EACH LOCATION AND VARYING USERS.

AN IMPORTANT STEP IN PROCESS IS THE CONSCIOUS „OCCUPATION“ OF SITUATIONS, WHICH REMAIN UNCHANGED BUT WHICH IN THEIR IDENTITY ARE SUBORDINATED TO THE LABEL.
THIS REPRESENTS A REVERSAL TO COMMON CURRENT MEDIA IDENTIFICATION PRACTICE:
CUSTOMERS AND SPONSORS USE ECONOMIC INTERDEPENDENCIES AND EXPLOIT CREATIVE WORK.
THE DEVELOPMENT OF PARAIDENTITIES IS PART OF THE PROGRAMATIC INTENTION, SAME AS THE BORDERWALK IN THE USE OF ALL AVAILABLE MEDIAS BETWEEN ART—ADVERTISING—LOGOCULTURE.
SEARCH, DON'T DESTROY,
RESEARCH, BUT REDEFINE!

Konzept: Alf Altendorf, Margarete Jahrmann und Thomas Madersbacher
Technischer Berater und Programmierung: Bernhard Loibner—„All Quiet on the Western Front“
Akustikkonzept: Peter Szely, Christof Cargnelli

R.A.M.S. ATTACK dankt **TRANSIT** für die freundliche Unterstützung.

SIMULATIONSRAUM

KNOWBOTIC RESEARCH

kr+cf

kr+cf realized interdisciplinary projects e.g. in the fields of artificial language synthesizing, real time operation, data banks, self-organization, man-machine interfaces, medialized natural presentations.
Exhibitions where kr+cf have participated (selection): Europ. Media Art Festival, Bonn 1991; spektakel '92, Essen; Europäisches Mediainstitut, Dusseldorf 1992; Videonale, Bonn 1992; Int. Architekturfestival, Graz 1992; Mediale Hamburg, 1993:

"SIMULATION ROOM-MOSAIC OF MOBILE DATA SOUNDS"—A WALKABLE DATA BANK.

Two rooms, a real room and its computer model. Equipped with a navigation aid (private eye) and a position finding system (space tracking), the visitor moves in a sound data bank which constantly re-structures itself through the implemented self-organization. The visitor acts likewise in the real room as in the virtual model and creates a real time composition and its visualization with the aid of a sensor, by means of which he sets off the mobile sound data.
The *open data bank* contains personal statements of a sound nature which incessantly change and actualize their composition following electronic and postal announcements e.g. input via internet. Every sound file which is clearly recognizeable by its addressee is stored in the data bank, analysed in accordance with sound characteristics which are binary coded.
The sound file receives a real-space as well as a system-internal allocation. Of course, it can be found locally at any time but at the same time is a part of two *dynamic systems:*
1) *The self-organization.* The sound data become mobile elements in real space and their equivalent in virtual space. On account of their characteristics, self-similar groups form and the chaotic behaviour of the entire system is determined by means of simple, implemented rules.
2) *The interaction.* The behaviour of the entire system reacts to the movements of the actor in the sound chamber.
Every statement, itself, being a personal acoustic expression of the sender with an individual sound structure, forms a mosaic piece of composition which is produced by a visitor in the real space.
The *real time composition* resulting from this (with the variables; duration, volume, direc-

kr+cf (knowbotic research) realisierte interdisziplinäre Projekte in den Bereichen künstlicher Sprachsynthetisierung, Echtzeitoperation, Datenbanken, Selbstorganisation, Mensch-Maschine-Schnittstellen, medialisierte Naturdarstellung.
Ausstellungsbeteiligungen von kr+cf (Auswahl):
Europ. Medienkunstfestival Bonn, 1991; Spektakel '92 Essen; Europäisches Mediainstitut Düsseldorf 1992; Videonale Bonn 1992; Int. Architekturfestival Graz 1992; Mediale Hamburg 1993;

„SIMULATIONSRAUM-MOSAIK MOBILER DATENKLÄNGE" – EINE BEGEHBARE DATENBANK.

Zwei Räume, ein Realraum und sein Computermodell. Ausgestattet mit einer Navigationshilfe (private eye) und einem Ortungssystem (space-tracking) bewegt sich der Besucher in einer Klangdatenbank, die sich durch die implementierte Selbstorganisation ständig neu strukturiert. Der Besucher agiert gleichermaßen im Realraum wie im virtuellen Modell und erstellt mit Hilfe eines Sensors, durch den er die mobilen Klangdaten auslöst, eine Echtzeitkomposition und deren -visualisierung.

SMDK – SIMULATIONSRAUM-MOSAIK MOBILER DATENKLÄNGE

Die **offene Datenbank,** deren Zusammensetzung sich fortwährend verändert und aktualisiert, beinhaltet persönliche Statements klanglicher Natur, die nach postalischen und elektronischen Ausschreibungen (z. B. über internet, compuserve) eingehen. Jedes Statement, für sich eine persönliche akustische Äußerung des Einsenders mit einer individuellen klanglichen Struktur, bildet Mosaikstücke für eine mögliche Komposition, die durch den Besucher erzeugt wird. Es entstehen dadurch unwiederholbare akustische Ereignisse, die nicht nur die klanglichen Eigenschaften, son-

dern auch die persönlichen Aussagen zu übergeordneten Bedeutungen reorganisieren.
Jedes eindeutig nach seinem Adressaten identifizierbare Soundfile wird in der Datenbank gespeichert, nach klanglichen Charakteristika analysiert und codiert. Das Soundfile erhält eine realräumliche sowie systeminterne örtliche Zuordnung, die aber nicht stationär determiniert ist. Es ist jederzeit vom Besucher aufrufbar, doch gleichzeitig Teil zweier **dynamischer Systeme:**
der **Selbstorganisation** (einfache implementierte Regeln bestimmen das chaotische Verhalten des Gesamtsystems und damit die Gruppenbildung von Soundfiles selbstähnlicher Klangcharakteristiken)
der **Interaktion** von Besuche rund Installation (das Verhalten des Gesamtsystems reagiert auf die Bewegungen des Akteurs im Klangraum).
Die daraus entstehende **Echtzeitkompensation** (mit den Variablen: Dauer, Lautstärke Montage der Klangstücke, Klangachsen) ist unmittelbar wahrnehmbares Ergebnis eines körperlichen Agierens innerhalb eines mathematisch

tions, setup of thė sound pieces) is the directly perceptible result of physical action within a virtual space—produced by computers and the information stored and administrated there.
smdk is a project which did not emerge as a result of some one individual artist personality's genius force of imagination. A self-dynamics developing during the production process and arising from the resistances (confrontations of opposing cognition possibilities proffered by scientists and artists, emerges, formulating the rules behind the work. These lead to a functionable model which is empirically experienced, personally transformed and useable by the visitor.
Computer scientists and artists produced a framework for a multitude of individual experiences which are non-calculable andnon reproduceable by a visitor, equally, with the aid of efficient, mechanical data processing.
The self-organization of the system, the direct interactivity of a real room with its synthetic, simulated model, the real time composition of acoustic foreign material and its fragmentation, the continual visualization of computing operations and the openness of the entire system over networks externally, form a chaotically structured complexity which cannot be overcome by the visitor in its entirety. As a result,

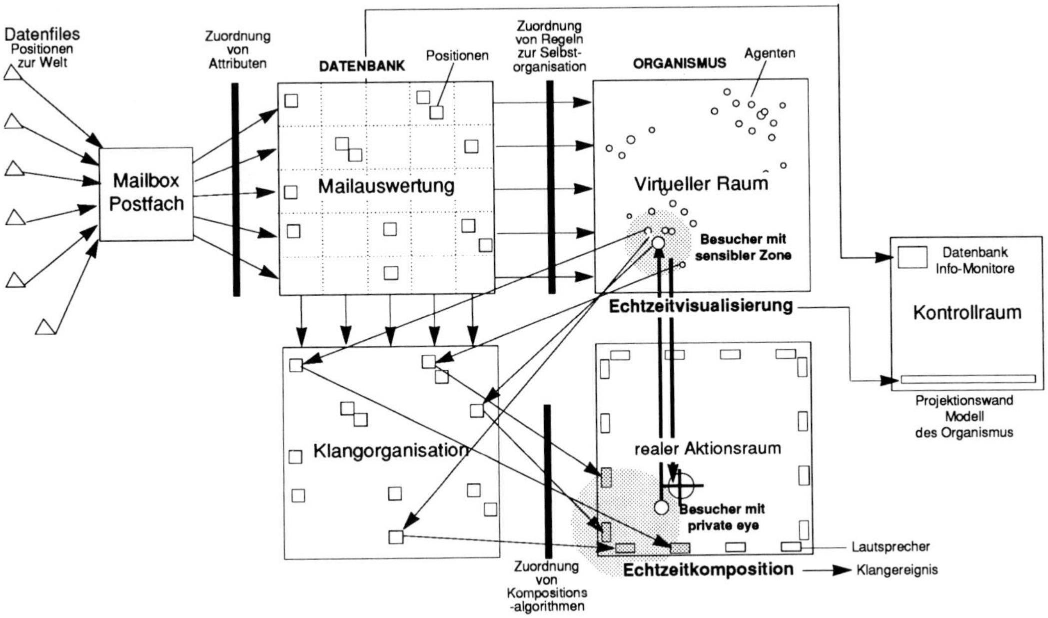

every visitor develops individual orientation routes within a "living" virtual organism.

kr+cf—knowbotic research

Which perceptible form calls for a mathematical formula, an abstract thought, an emotion, a memory, the energy behind a conflict, when the methods of pure linguistic description are not sufficient to convey and conserve?
kr+cf uses information systems, communication networks, knowledge stores and files in order to put them together again as such, split and analysed:
Computers speak their own source code (Sprachprogramm, 1991), media texts from live zapped TV programmes are reduced to their linguistic and acoustic substance, at the same time being reflected philosophically and in terms of sound and presented as a live concert (ping Operation pong, with Friedrich Kittler, 1992), documented reality (Medienbilder) is formally reduced by digital manipulation and is iconographically analysed (Archive, 1992), language grammalogues, go-commands from commercial data networks satirize their information value and react in a glass data room to a model area of gestic instructions provided by a visitor (hypervirus, 1992).
Those involved in the smdk project are besides the 3 principle members Christian Hübler (concept, realization), Alexander Tuchacek (real time composition) and Yvonne Wilhelm (visualization), George Fleischmann (self-organization, complex systems), Detlev Schwabe (data bank and system management), Michael Hoch (sound analyses, private eye), Will Bauer (space tracking), Tobias Pfeil (data brooking), Rajele Jain and Udo Zyber (technical installation).

definierten Systems – eines virtuellen Raumes und seiner darin gespeicherten und verwalteten Informationen.
smdk ist ein interdisziplinäres Projekt, das sich nicht durch die Einbildungskraft einer Künstlerpersönlichkeit, sondern sich aus einer in sich selbst bildenden Eigendynamik konkretisiert: Durch die Konfrontation der gegensätzlichen Erkenntnismöglichkeiten der mitarbeitenden Spezialisten entstehen Spielregeln zum Einpassen der verschiedenen Arbeitsprozesse. Dies ermöglicht im Rechner die Visualisierung eines gemeinsamen, funktionsfähigen Modells der interaktiven Datenbank, das vom Besucher empirisch erfahren und lesbar wird. Informatiker und Künstler erzeugen mit Hilfe von leistungsfähiger, maschineller Datenverarbeitung einen ästhetischen Rahmen für einen virtuellen Organismus nicht berechenbarer und nicht reproduzierbarer Einzelerfahrungen. Die chaotische Grundstruktur von smdk, die Selbstorganisation, die Echtzeitkomposition von aktustischem Fremdmaterial und dessen Fragmentarisierung, die kontinuierliche Visualisierung von (mathematischen) Vorgängen und die Offenheit des gesamten Systems über Netzwerke nach außen, bilden eine Komplexität, die den Besucher zur Konstruktion eines eigenen Orientierungssystems provoziert.

KR+CF – KNOWBOTIC RESEARCH

Welche wahrnehmbare Form erfordert eine mathematische Formel, ein abstrakter Gedanke, eine Emotion, eine Erinne-

rung, die Energetik eines Konfliktes usw., wenn die Methoden der reinen sprachlichen Beschreibung zur Speicherung und Vermittlung nicht zufriedenstellen?

kr+cf benutzen Informationssysteme, Kommunikationswege, Wissensspeicher und Archive, um sie zerteilt und analysiert wieder als solche neu zusammenzusetzen: Computer sprechen ihre eigenen Quellencodes *(Sprachprogramm, 1991),* Medientexte aus live gezappten TV-Programmen werden auf ihre sprachliche und akustische Substanz reduziert, gleichzeitig (!) philosophisch und klanglich reflektiert und als Livekonzert präsentiert *(ping Operation pong,* mit Friedrich Kittler, *1992)*, dokumentierte Wirklichkeit (Medienbilder) wird durch die digitale Manipulation formal reduziert und ikonografisch analysiert *(Archive, 1992),* Sprachkürzel, Go-Befehle kommerzieller Datennetze persiflieren ihren Informationswert und reagieren in einem gläsernen Datenraum auf einer Musterfläche gestischen Anweisungen eines Besuchers *(hypervirus, 1992).*

Die Mitarbeiter am smdk-Projekt sind neben den 3 Stammitgliedern Christian Hübler (Konzept, Realisierung), Alexander Tuchacek (Echtzeitkomposition) und Yvonne Wilhelm (Visualisierung), Georg Fleischmann (Selbstorganisation, komplexe Systeme), Detlev Schwabe (Datenbank und Systemmanagement), Michael Hoch (Klanganalyse, private eye), Will Bauer (space-tracking), Toblas Pfeil (data-broking), Rajele Jain und Udo Zyber (technische Installation).

Die Datenbank ist auch während Ars Electronica für Beiträge (eine klanglich formulierte Haltung zur Welt, 6 Sekunden, mono) offen.

Transfer über email und ftp: Information unter kr+cf khm.uni-koeln.de

Transfer über Audio-, und DAT-tapes: Überspielung vor Ort

Das Projekt wurde gefördert im Auftrag des Bundesministers für Unterricht und Kunst Österreich, dem Kulturamt Wien und wurde an der Kunsthochschule für Medien Köln realisiert.

DAS SEHENDE OHR

BERNHARD LEITNER

In mehrjähriger Zusammenarbeit von Wissenschaftlern und Künstlern entstand ein zukunftsweisendes Instrument zur Gestaltung von Klang und Raum.
Projekt Ton-Räume P7130-TEC
Fonds zur Förderung der wissenschaftlichen Forschung, Wien
Projektleiter:
OHS Prof. Dr. Bernhard Leitner
Hochschule für angewandte Kunst, Wien
Dr. D. I. Heinrich Pichler
D. I. Geza Beszedics
D. I. Franz Pavuza
Ing. Manfred Wawra
Technische Universität Wien
Institut für allgemeine Elektrotechnik und Elektronik

SOUND SPACE MOTION SYSTEM 1

SSMS1 ist ein digitales 16 Bit Audio System hoher Übertragungsqualität mit 4 Eingängen und 16 Leistungsausgängen. Das System dient zur Verteilung von Audio Eingangssignalen auf die voneinander unabhängigen Ausgänge, wobei die einzelnen Parameter zeitlich verändert werden können. Jeder Eingang und Ausgang besitzt einen Klangregler, der ebenfalls durch zeitlich veränderbare Parameter eingestellt werden kann.
Die Steuerung der Maschine erfolgt über ein serielles Datenprotokoll von einem Steuerrechner aus, der die Daten über ein Interface an die Maschine und den CD-Player (Ton-Material-Speicher) übermittelt.
Die Erstellung der Parameter erfolgt mit Hilfe eines in Turbo Pascal geschriebenen Programmes. Komponieren und Editieren mit graphischer Oberfläche, Eingabemöglichkeit in Fenstertechnik. Einzelne Figuren-Module werden aus einer Bibliothek zu Raum-Kompositionen zusammengefügt, wobei bis zu 10 Ton-Räume zeitgleich aufgerufen werden können.
Ton-Räume sind eine körperlich-sinnliche Erfahrung, ein

THE SEEING EAR
BERNHARD LEITNER

After several years collaboration between scientists and artists, a future-orientated instrument was developed to arrange sound and space.

Bernhard Leitner
Project Sound-Spaces P7130-TEC
Fund for the Promotion of Scientific Research, Vienna
Project leader:
Prof. Dr. Bernhard Leitner
University for Applied Art, Vienna
Dr. D.I. Heinrich Pichler
D.I. Geza Beszedics
D.I. Franz Pavuza
Ing. Manfred Wawra
Technical University, Vienna
Institute for General Electro-technology and Electronics

SOUND SPACE MOTION SYSTEM 1

SSMS1 is a digital 16 bit audio system of high transmission quality, with 4 inlets and 16 power outlets. The system serves to distribute audio input signals to outlets that are independent of each other, whereby the temporal parameters can be changed. Every input and outlet has a sound regulator which can similarly be adjusted by temporally changeable parameters.
The machine is controlled via a serial data protocol from a control computer which transmits the data to the machine and the CD-player (sound-material-store) via an interface.
Parameters are drawn up with the aid of a programme written in Turbo Pascal. Composing and editing with graphic surface, input possibilities in window technology. Individual figure models are put together from a library to form space-compositions and up to 10 sound-spaces can be called up simultaneously.
Sound-spaces are a physical-sensual experience, a new hearing/experiencing of shaped sound envelopes. It is only thanks to modern technology that this has become artistically conceivable and realizable. In this way, my own work and investigations in this sector have, since 1968, been inseparable from technological developments.
The SOUND SPACE MOTION SYSTEM 1 (SSMS1) is the first fully digitalized system to record and process sound movements in space and to graphically record and process space-

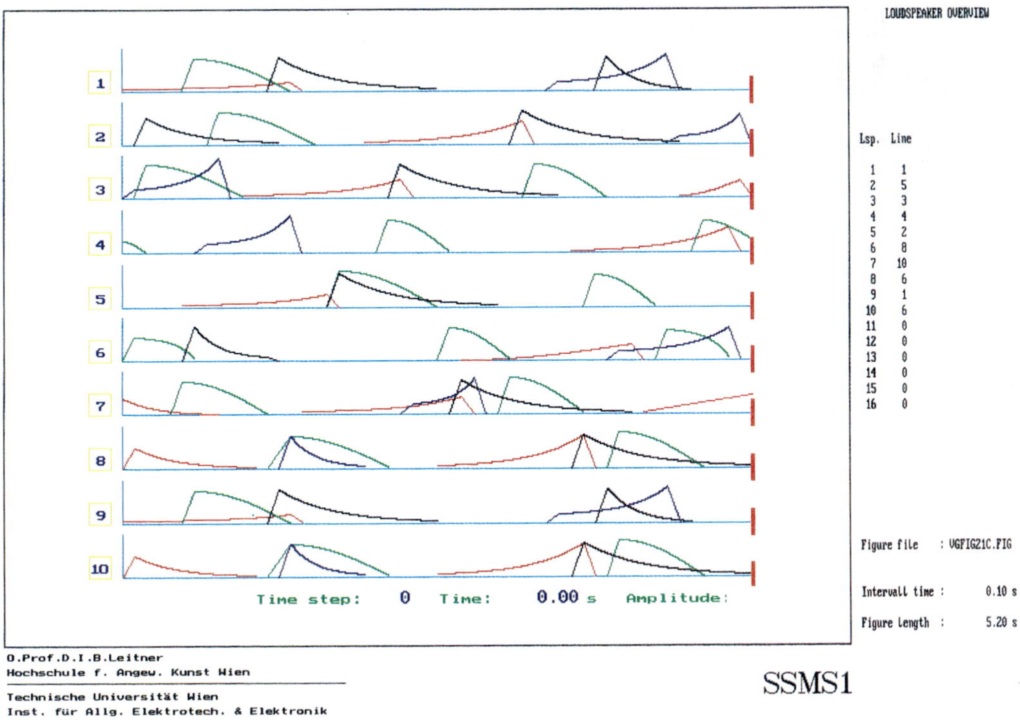

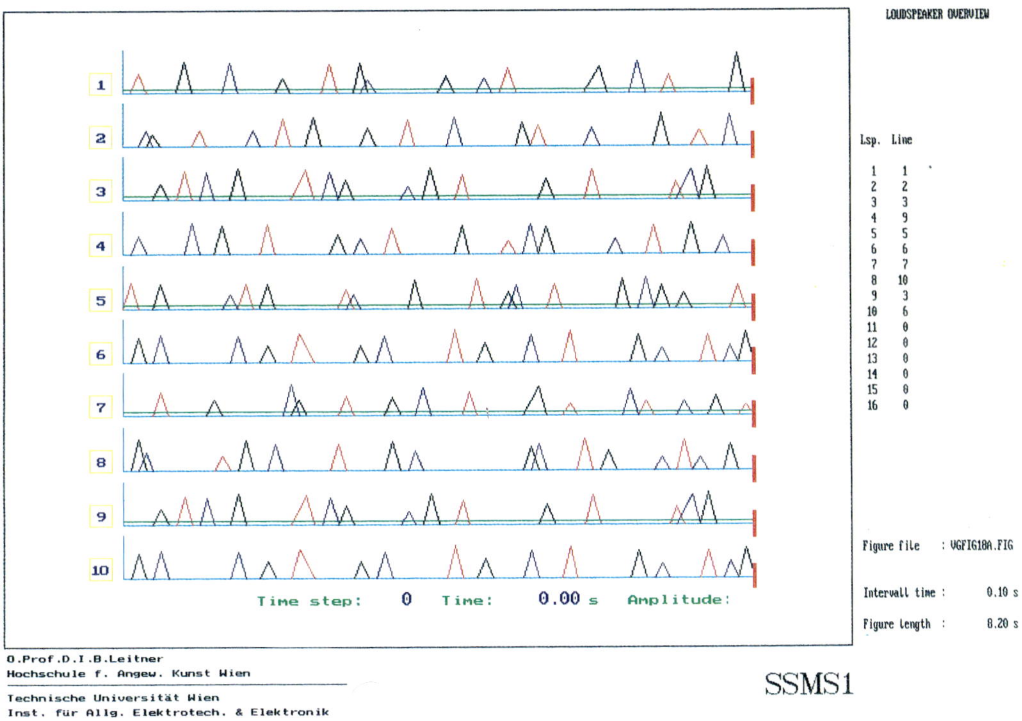

Oben: 4 inputs (rot, grün, blau, schwarz) mit linearen, spitzen Hüllkurven auf 10 Lautsprecher verteilt (Zuckender Raum)
Unten: 4 inputs, sich überlagernd, auf 10 Lautsprecher verteilt (Rhythmus-Feld)

neues Hören/Erleben von geformten Klang-Hüllen. Erst durch die moderne Technik ist dies künstlerisch denkbar und ausführbar geworden. So sind meine eigenen Arbeiten und Untersuchungen auf diesem Gebiet seit 1968 von technologischen Entwicklungen nicht zu trennen.
Das Sound space motion system 1 (SSMS1) ist das erste voll digitalisierte System, um Klang-Bewegungen im Raum, um aus Klang geformte Raum-Gebilde graphisch aufzuzeichnen und zu bearbeiten. Es erlaubt eine von (bis zu) 16 outputs (Lautsprechern) akustisch sofort überprüfbare visuelle Notation der zeitlichen Evolution eines Ton-Raumes mittels Hüllkurven und Klangfarben.
Das menschliche Ohr kann mehrere akustische Räume gleichzeitig lesen. Davon ausgehend kann jeder der 16 Ton-Orte (bis zu) 4 inputs gleichzeitig wiedergeben: so daß jeder Ton-Ort gleichzeitig Schnittpunkt von mehreren Klang-Bewegungen im Raum sein kann, beziehungsweise jeder Ton-Ort gleichzeitig Teil verschiedener Ton-Raum-Figuren ist. Erst die graphische Zeit-Raum-Notation des SSMS 1 erlaubt es, die daraus resultierende hohe akustisch-bildnerisch-räumliche Komplexität nachvollziehbar aufzubauen, lesbar hörend zu überprüfen und hörbar lesend durchzukomponieren.

Bernhard Leitner

Johann Sebastian Bach spricht im Jahre 1733 mit Selbstverständlichkeit von der „Wißenschaft, welche ich in der Musique erlanget". Noch vor 178 Jahren, als Johann Prechtl, erster Direktor des Wiener Polytechnikums, der heutigen Technischen Universität, seine Inaugurationsrede hielt, meinte er mit dem Ausdruck „Kunst" sowohl Kunst, als auch Technik, ganz im Sinne des griechischen
Die extreme Arbeitsteilung und der starke Wissenschaftsbezug der Techniken des 20. Jahrhunderts haben eine bedauerliche, nicht zwingende Entkoppelung von Kunst und Technik gebracht und damit den Konstrukteur einer wertvollen menschlichen Komponente seines Wirkens beraubt. Es ist ein Gebot der geistigen Gesundheit, Kunst und Technik zusammenzuführen, unter anderem auch das Ausschöpfen des Potentials neuer Techniken, wie der Mikroelektronik, durch neue Kunstformen. Beim Projekt „Ton-Räume/Steuersystem SSMS1" haben Gleichgesinnte zusammengefunden: Der schöpferische Künstler Bernhard Leitner, kongeniale Konstrukteure der T. U. Wien und der Fonds zur

structures formed from sound. It makes possible an acoustically, immediately scrutizeable visual notation of (up to) 16 outputs (loud speakers) of the temporal evolution of a sound space by means of envelopes and sound timbres.
The human ear can read several acoustic spaces at the same time. Using this as a basis, each of the 16 sound places (up to) can replay 4 inputs simultaneously; so that every sound place can be, at one and the same time, the intersection of several sound-movements within the space or, rather, every sound-place is, at the same time, part of different sound-space figures. It is only the graphical time-space notation of SSMS1 which permits the resultant high degree of acoustic-artistic-spatial complexity to be constructed in a way that it can be duplicated, to be scrutinized in a readable listening way, and to be composed in an audible reading way.

Bernhard Leitner

In 1733, Johann Sebastian Bach spoke of the "science", with a matter-of-factness, "which I achieve in music". Even some 178 years ago when Johann PRECHTL, the first director of the present Technical University held his inauguration speech, he meant with the term "art", both art and technology, quite in keeping with the Greek...
The extreme division of work and the strong scientific benefits enjoyed by the technicians of the 20th century have brought about a regrettable, not compelling de-coupling of art and technology and consequently robs the designer of a valuable human component of his work.
It is a rule of mental health to bring art and technology together, among other things by exhausting the potential of new technologies such as micro-electronics, with new art forms. In the project "Sound-Spaces/Control System SSMS1", the like-minded have got together: the creative artist, Bernhard LEITNER, congenial designers from the T.U. in Vienna and the Fund for the Promotion of Scientific Research, which has rendered a pioneer achievement by financing an "art and technology" project in his field.

Fritz Paschke

Technical data:
16 bit audio system with control computer
4 inputs:asymmetrical 0.7 V level to 10KOhm for full control
16 outlets:60W to 8 Ohm (100W to 4Ohm)
Frequency:12 Hz–20KHz
Disturbance interval: 86dB
Control computer PC 486/33
20 signal processors TMS 320/33
20 controllers INTEL 8031
CD-player with control computer
4 Denon CD-player SCSI-Bus
Control computer PC386/40

Förderung der wissenschaftlichen Forschung, der durch die Finanzierung eines „Kunst und Technik"-Projektes auf seinem Gebiet eine Pionierleistung erbracht hat.

Fritz Paschke

TECHNISCHE DATEN:

16 Bit Audio System mit Steuerrechner
4 Eingänge: asymmetrisch 0.7 V Pegel an 10 KOhm für Vollaussteuerung
16 Ausgänge: 60 W an 8 Ohm (100 W an 4 Ohm)
Frequenzgang: 12 Hz–20 KHz
Störabstand: 86 dB
Steuerrechner PC 486/33
20 Signalprozessoren TMS320/33
20 Kontroller INTEL8031
CD-Player mit Steuerrechner
4 Denon CD player SCSI-Bus
Steuerrechner PC 386/40

DER GEKLONTE KLANG

KLAUS OBERMAIER / ROBERT SPOUR

EINE MULTIMEDIALE, INTERAKTIVE KOMPOSITION FÜR DAS KRONOS QUARTET

Naturklänge – vom Streichquartett erzeugt – werden digitalisiert und damit geklont. Durch die Digitalisierung ist es möglich, bis zu den kleinsten Bestandteilen der Klänge vorzudringen, sie zu zerschneiden, neu zusammenzusetzen, zu überlagern, addieren, multiplizieren. Eingriffe in die Frequenzspektren und Manipulationen der Wellenformen lassen Klänge bis zur Unkenntlichkeit mutieren. Diese Klangmanipulationen zusammen mit Wachstumsphänomenen im Spannungsfeld mit dem klassischen Klangkörper Streichquartett bilden die Grundlagen der kompositorischen Arbeit.
Die Reduzierung von Information auf den binären Code ermöglicht es, genetische Strukturen in musikalische umzuwandeln, durch Musik visuelle Ereignisse zu steuern, künstliche, multimediale Welten zu schaffen. Genetische „Fingerprints" dienen als Vorlage für musikalische Prozesse. Computerprogramme generieren aus dieser genetischen Basisinformation harmonisches und melodisches Material, das wir assoziativ weiterverarbeitet haben.
Zum Beispiel entwickeln sich aus mikrotonalen Umspielungen eines Zentraltons durch das Kronos Quartet völlig neue komplexe Obertonmelodien und Klangstrukturen. Diese verdichten wir durch digitale Prozessoren. So entstehen aus dem Klang des Streichquartetts orchesterartige, komplexe Klangwucherungen, die durch eine mehrkanalige Beschallung in den Raum wachsen.
Analogien zu Artificial Life finden sich auf zwei Ebenen. Erstens im Kompositionsprozess selbst, wo rückgekoppelte Systeme in den schöpferischen Akt miteinbezogen werden, wo etwa Zufallsgeneratoren auf komponierte Strukturen Einfluß nehmen, sie verändern und somit auf das Ausgangsmaterial rückwirken. Zweitens bei der Aufführung, wo das „offene System" Musik immer wieder von außen beeinflußt und gestört wird und auf die veränderten Bedingungen reagiert. Diese Systemstörungen sind einerseits bewußt gesteuerte Eingriffe durch Obermaier/Spour mit Midi-Gitarre und Keyboard, andererseits unkontrollierte und unvorhersehba-

THE CLONED SOUND / A MULTIMEDIAL INTERACTIVE COMPOSITION / FOR THE KRONOS QUARTET KLAUS OBERMAIER / ROBERT SPOUR

Natural sounds—produced by the string quartet—are digitalized and thereby cloned. By means of digitalization it is possible to penetrate right to the very smallest parts of the sounds, to shred them, to put them together again, to superimpose them, add, multiply. Interventions in the frequency spectrums and manipulations of the wave forms enable the sounds to be mutated until they are no longer recognizeable. These sound manipulations together with growth phenomena in the field of tension with the classical string quartet form the basis of this compositionary work.
The reduction of information to binary code makes it possible to transform genetic structures into musical ones, to control visual happenings by music, to create artificial, multi-medial worlds. Genetic "fingerprints" act as a reference for musical processes. Computer programmes generate harmonic and melodic material from this genetic basic information that we have associatively further processed.
For example, completely new complex overtone melodies and sound structures develop from micro-tonal rerecordings performed by the Kronos Quartet with the central tone. We condense these with digital processors. As a result, orchestra-like complex sound proliferations result from the sound of the string quartet and expand into the room through a multichannel public address system.
Artificial life appears in two forms on the musical level. Firstly, in the composition process itself, where feedback systems are incorporated into the creative act, where random number generators influence composed structures, change them and then react on the initial material. Secondly, during the performance, where the "open system" music is constantly influenced from the outside and is disturbed, reacting to the changed conditions. These system disturbances are, on the one hand, consciously controlled interventions performed by Obermair/Spour with the midi guitar and keyboard, on the other hand, they are uncontrolled and unpredictable happenings that arise when the audience reaches into the laser beams. Both types of disturbance influence the musical and visual happenings, directly and in real time.

A further important factor to increase the complexity of the system arises by the digitalization of the strings sounds. A computer programme analyses and interprets real time playing and sound characteristics and the information gained from this is used again as manipulators of the initial signal.
In addition to this, by involving a special sound animation we open the rigid acoustic space and in doing so reach a system of variable sound environments in which the listener continuously has to re-adapt his sense of hearing to the changed acoustic conditions, finding himself again in different virtual listening positions.
In addition to several lasers and a 6-channel public address system, slide and video projections expand the stage and involve the auditorium.
The lasers are controlled directly by the string instruments. Musical parameters such as pitch, volume or sound timbre generate and change laser images in real time.
On the other hand, the Kronos Quartet can also interrupt laser beams with the violin bow, and in doing so trigger off sounds. A specially developed computer programme analyses and interprets the speed of the movement, the place and the number of interruptions. The laser becomes the "instrument".
Even the audience has the possibility to play with the sounds by reaching into the laser beams. Special sensors which register the interruptions distributed throughout the auditorium, convey this information to the computer programme. Consequently, the audience can intervene directly in the musical happening.

Klaus Obermaier, Robert Spour

SOUND ANIMATION AS A REAL TIME PROCESS

By graphically resolving the auditorium on the user surface of a computer (Macintosh), the place of the sound and its dimension is defineable. This makes it possible to organize different sound movements in the three-dimensional space, independent of the "real" position of the instruments and of creating new positions for musical, spatial listening.
The distribution is based on a matrix controlled by the computer and by six loud speakers (source cluster) positioned within the room, the selection of which is controlled according to the structure and gesture of the music on four different paths via sequence-like composed motives. With the software especially designed for this installation, influencing and control is possible via midi-data as well as by means of real time sound parameters and is realized "topographically" on the computer monitor.
A further level of sound influencing between the instruments is achieved by a real time signal processor (NeXt Cube/IMW processor card) and the software package MaxAudio which can be openly designed. Frequency spectrums of the string instruments are analysed in real time and are used via "organic" structure processes

re Ereignisse, die durch Hineingreifen des Publikums in die Laserstrahlen entstehen. Beide Arten der Störungen beeinflußen direkt und in Echtzeit das musikalische und visuelle Ergebnis.
Ein weiterer wichtiger Faktor zur Komplexitätserhöhung des Systems entsteht durch die Digitalisierung der Streicherklänge. Ein Computerprogramm analysiert und interpretiert

realtime Spiel- und Klangeigenschaften, die daraus gewonnenen Informationen werden wiederum als Manipulatoren des Ausgangssigals eingesetzt.
Darüberhinaus öffnen wir durch die Einbeziehung einer speziellen Klanganimation den starren akustischen Raum und gelangen dadurch zu einem System des variablen Klangenvironments, in dem der Zuhörer sein Hörempfinden den veränderten akustischen Bedingungen immer wieder neu anpaßt und sich in verschiedenen virtuellen Hörpositionen wiederfindet.
Neben mehreren Lasern und einer 6-kanaligen Beschallung erweitern Dia- und Video-Projektionen die Bühne und beziehen den Publikumsraum mit ein.
Die Laser werden direkt von den Streichinstrumenten gesteuert. Musikalische Parameter, wie Tonhöhe, Lautstärke oder Klangfarbe generieren und verändern in Realtime Laserimages. Umgekehrt kann das Kronos Quartet auch mit den Geigenbögen Laserstrahlen unterbrechen und dadurch Klänge auslösen. Ein speziell entwickeltes Computerprogramm analysiert und interpretiert die Geschwindigkeit der Bewegung, den Ort und die Anzahl der Unterbrechungen. Der Laser wird zum „Instrument".
Auch das Publikum hat die Möglichkeit durch Hineingreifen in die Laserstrahlen mit den Klängen zu spielen. Spezielle Sensoren, die im Publikumsraum verteilt die Unterbrechungen registrieren, leiten diese Informationen an das Computerprogramm weiter. Das Publikum kann also direkt in das musikalische Geschehen eingreifen.

Klaus Obermaier / Robert Spour

KLANGANIMATION ALS ECHTZEITPROZESS

Durch die graphische Auflösung des Hörraums auf der Benutzeroberfläche eines Computers (Macintosh) wird der Klangort und seine Dimension bestimmbar. Dies ermöglicht verschiedene Klangbewegungen im dreidimensionalen Raum unabhängig von der „realen" Position der Instrumente zu gestalten und neue Positionen des musikalisch räumlichen Hörens zu kreieren.
Die Verteilung basiert auf einer über den Computer gesteuerten Matrix und sechs im Raum positionierten Lautsprechern (Quellcluster), deren Ansteuerung nach Struktur und Gestus der Musik auf vier verschiedenen Wegen über Sequenzerartige komponierte Motive gesteuert wird. Über die speziell für diese Anlage erstellte Software wird eine Beein-

to mutate sounds and time parameters. Communications resulting between composition and electronically generated sound-time level brings about a new synthesis of musical action, in situ.

Peter Böhm

LASER LIGHT IN THE INTERACTIVE PERFORMANCE

Laser light possesses several features which can only be realized with the utmost of difficulty by other light sources, or even not at all. Depending on the type of laser, there is a light beam with a high degree of intensity, low divergence /dispersion) and different colours. The light is coherent i.e. the individual light waves vibrate diffently to sun or bulb light in phase and are, so-to-speak, emmitted in cadence.
In the project "The Cloned Sound", different physical features are used. As the light is very finely concentrated when the beam emerges, it can be deflected via relatively small and consequently quick moving mirrors. This ability to deflect quickly also makes the projection of images possible, the shape of which can be scanned so quickly that the impression of closed line outlines develop for the eye. These figures stored as vector graphics can be called up in real time, and in addition to this, can be manipulated in their characteristics. In this way, musical parameters control picture size, distortion and "writing" speed. Similarly, the speed of metamorphosis between serveral images can be determined directly by the musicians. The concept for the interactive software "Phonola" is represented in the following graphics, whereby the inlet and outlets in bold print are used in the project "The Cloned Sound".
The coherence of the laser light is a prerequisite to produce interference figures and to produce hologrammes. Interference figures develop when the laser light disperses through suitable materials and is superimposed with itself. Interferences even develop in the eye of the observer, giving the laser light a special quality which is only directly perceivable. Grids produced holographically are used for the reproduction of beams and figures.
The high degree of intensity of the laser light in connection with its low divergence makes it visible in the air, even over greater distances. As a result, there is an artistic medium available for representing connections and spatial light surfaces.
Whereas until now we have talked about the creative possibilities of laser images produced by music, the following will now describe the reversal of this allocation.
In "The Cloned Sound", laser light surfaces receive an additional function: they serve as an input medium for the generation of sound parameters in which a specially developed hardware and sofware follows shadows and reflections of objects being immersed in the light.
The software modules for the sound control, made of light data, have the working title

"Digitus Package", commencing with the situation that one finger ("digitus") is immersed in the light zone. From the light reflex of the finger, or the hand, a rod or e.g. a violin bow, data are acquired relating to place, speed and duration ("digitalization = to represent in a countable way). From this, new data sets are compiled which can be used for the production of sound and to influence sound. In this way, the place can determine the pitch and/or samples while the speed of immersion detemines the volume. Lateral movement in the light surface modulates, for example, the sound timbre.
As long as the sensors detect only a few reflexes, the digitus provides many more possibilities for sound manipulation; as soon as a large number of fingers (or hands, or rods) reach into the light surface, the sound manipulation subsides in favour of an "unlimited" polyphone game.
"Phonola" and "Digitus" are a step towards interactive freedom of creation. While the laser light in "Digitus" becomes a sensor which can be used to control sound parameters, with "Phonola" every variation possibility and the entire wealth of nuances of musical expression media are available, controlled in real time and to control visual happenings in an improvisatorial manner.

Friedrich Förster, Kurt Walz

MacPanic is a midi-controlled computer programme for musicians that combines both elements of a computer virus as well as those of a life-simulating computer game. The surface has been consciously kept in such a way that the connection between new sounds and new life activities remains recognizeable for as long as possible. The figures which emerge remind us, parodistically, of the classics of all computer games.
It is left to the musicians discretion, to very suddenly abandon the ability to fathom what is happening on the monitor, as a result of a certain "event". From then on, an individual life develops which is "chaotic" from a mathematical point of view. The theory of chaos is held to be that very mathematical branch whose formulae are closest to real life. The fathomable "Simulation of Life" moves a little bit closer to "Real life". But is our understanding helped by this? Everybody has to decide that for himself ...

Kurt Walz

"THE CLONED SOUND"

Composition, overall concept, live electronics:
Klaus Obermaier, Robert Spour

Kronos Quartet:
David Harrington, violin
John Sherba, violin
Hank Dutt, viola
Joan Jeanrenaud, cello

flußung und Kontrolle sowohl über Midi-Daten als auch durch Echtzeit-Klangparameter möglich und „topographisch" am Monitor des Computers umgesetzt.
Eine weitere Ebene der klanglichen Beeinflußung zwischen den Instrumenten wird über einen Echtzeit-Signalprozessor (NeXt Cube/IMWProzessorkarte) und das offen gestaltbare Softwarepaket MaxAudio erreicht. Frequenzspektren der Streichinstrumente werden in Echtzeit analysiert und über „organische " Strukturprozesse zur Mutation von Klängen und Zeitparametern benutzt. Die dadurch entstehende Kommunikation zwischen Komposition und elektronisch generierter Klang-Zeitebene, bewirkt eine neuartige Synthese der musikalischen Aktion vor Ort.

Peter Böhm

LASERLICHT IN DER INTERAKTIVEN PERFORMANCE

Laserlicht besitzt mehrere Eigenschaften, die durch andere Lichtquellen nur sehr schwer oder überhaupt nicht realisiert werden können. Je nach Art des Lasers steht ein Lichtstrahl mit hoher Intensität, geringer Divergenz (Streuung) und unterschiedlichen Farben zur Verfügung. Das Licht ist kohärent, d.h. die einzelnen Lichtwellen schwingen anders als beim Sonnen- oder Glühlampenlicht in Phase, werden sozusagen im Gleichschritt emittiert.
Beim Projekt „Der geklonte Klang" kommen unterschiedliche physikalische Besonderheiten zur Anwendung. Da das Licht schon beim Strahlaustritt sehr fein gebündelt ist, läßt es sich über relativ kleine und dadurch schnell bewegliche Spiegel ablenken. Diese schnelle Ablenkbarkeit ermöglicht auch die Projektion von Images, deren Formen so schnell abgetastet werden, daß für das Auge der Eindruck von geschlossenen Linienzügen entsteht. Die als Vektorgraphik abgespeicherten Figuren können in Echtzeit abgerufen werden und darüber hinaus in ihren Eigenschaften manipuliert werden. So steuern musikalische Parameter die Bildgröße, Verzerrung und „Schreib"- Geschwindigkeit. Ebenso kann die Geschwindigkeit von Metamorphosen zwischen mehreren Images direkt durch die Musiker bestimmt werden. Das Konzept der interaktiven Software „Phonola" ist in der folgenden Graphik dargestellt, wobei die in Fettschrift gedruckten Ein- und Ausgänge bei dem Projekt „Der geklonte Klang" benutzt werden.
Die Kohärenz des Laserlichts ist Voraussetzung für die Erzeugung von Interferenzfiguren und die Herstellung von Hologrammen. Interferenzfiguren entstehen, wenn das La-

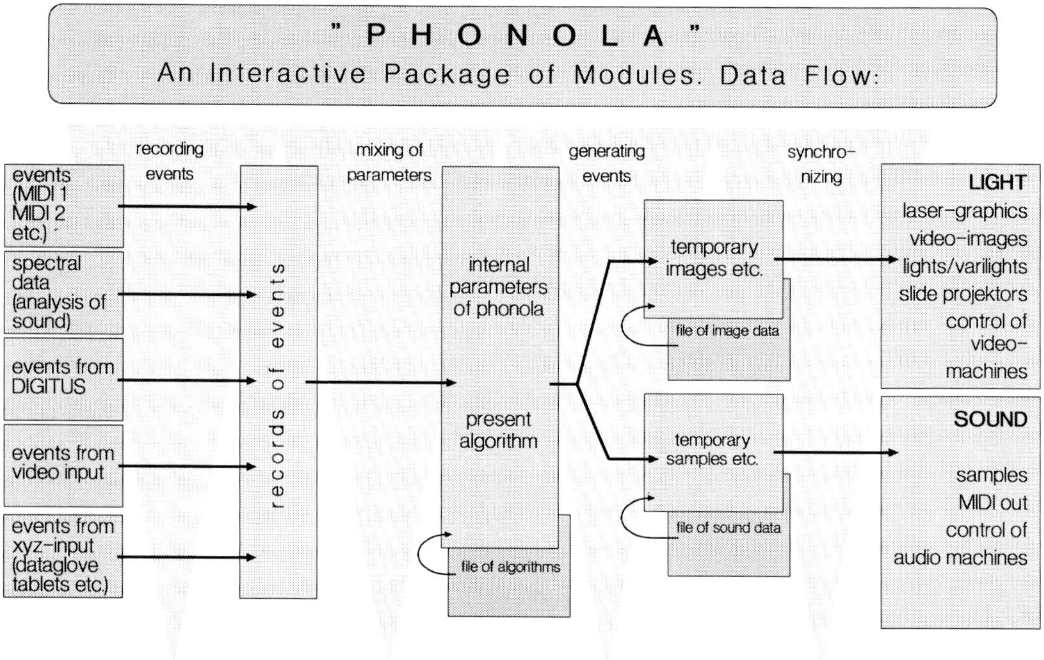

Each arrow represents an interface where you can plug in MIDI- hardware. In a multitask system most interfaces can also be "connected" to MIDI-software such as sequencer- programs or composition environments.

serlicht durch geeignete Materialien gestreut und mit sich selber überlagert wird. Auch im Auge des Betrachters entstehen Interferenzen, was dem Laserlicht eine besondere, nur unmittelbar erfahrbare Qualität verleiht. Holographisch erzeugte Gitter verwenden wir für die Strahl- und Figurenvervielfachung.

Die hohe Intensität des Laserlichts in Verbindung mit seiner geringen Divergenz läßt es auch über größere Entfernungen in der Luft sichtbar werden. Dadurch steht ein gestalterisches Mittel zur Verfügung, Verbindungen und räumliche Lichtflächen darzustellen.

Während bis jetzt von der Gestaltungsmöglichkeit von Laserimages durch Musik die Rede war, soll im Folgenden ein Weg der Umkehrung dieser Zuordnung beschrieben werden.

Bei „Der geklonte Klang" bekommen Laser-Lichtflächen eine zusätzliche Funktion: sie dienen als Eingabemedium für die Generierung von Klangparametern, indem eine speziell entwickelte Hard- und Software Schatten und Reflexionen von in das Licht eintauchenden Gegenständen verfolgt. Die Software-Moduls für die Klangsteuerung aus Licht-Daten tragen den Arbeitstitel „Digitus-Paket", – ausgehend von der Situation, daß ein Finger („Digitus") in den Lichtbereich eintaucht. Aus dem Lichtreflex des Fingers, – oder der Hand,

Interactive laser control: Friedrich Förster
Computer programming: Kurt Walz
Video, light direction: Rainer Jessl
Technical director of Kronos Quartet: Larry Neff
Space-sound control, NeXt Cube / IMW processor card
MaxAudio programming: Peter Böhm
Audio Engineer: Jay Cloidt

Thanks to *Casablanca*

eines Stabes oder z.B. eines Geigenbogens werden Daten gewonnen über Ort, Geschwindigkeit und Verweildauer („Digitalisierung“ = in abzählbarer Weise darstellen). Hieraus werden neue Datensätze zusammengestellt, die für die Klangerzeugung und und Klangbeeinflussung verwendet werden können. So kann der Ort die Tonhöhe bzw. Samples bestimmen, während die Geschwindigkeit des Eintauchens die Lautstärke festlegt. Seitliche Bewegung in der Lichtfläche moduliert beispielsweise die Klangfarbe.
Solange die Sensoren wenige Reflexe detektieren, stellt Digitus sehr viele Möglichkeiten der Klangmanipulation bereit; sobald eine große Zahl von Fingern (oder Händen oder Stäben) in die Lichtfläche greifen, treten die Klangmanipulationen zurück zugunsten eines „unbeschränkt“ polyphonen Spiels.
„Phonola“ und „Digitus“ sind ein Schritt in Richtung interaktiver Gestaltungsfreiheit. Während das Laserlicht mit „Digitus“ zu einem Sensor wird, mit dem Klangparameter kontrolliert werden können, stehen mit „Phonola“ alle Variationsmöglichkeiten und der Nuancenreichtum musikalischer Ausdrucksmittel zur Verfügung, in Echtzeit kontrolliert und improvisatorisch visuelle Ereignisse zu steuern.

Friedrich Förster, Kurt Walz

MACPANIC

MacPanic ist ein Midi-gesteuertes Computerprogramm für Musiker, das sowohl Elemente eines Computer-Virus als auch solche eines Lebens-simulierenden Computerspiels in sich vereint. Bewußt wurde die Oberfläche so gehalten, daß der Zusammenhang zwischen neuen Tönen und neuen Lebens-Aktivitäten möglichst lange erkennbar bleibt. Die auftauchenden Figuren erinnern parodistisch an den Klassiker aller Computerspiele. Den Musikern ist anheimgestellt, durch einen bestimmten „event“ die Durchschaubarkeit dessen, was auf dem Bildschirm vor sich geht, schlagartig aufzugeben. Fortan entwickelt sich ein Eigenleben, das aus mathematischer Sicht „chaotisch“ Abläuft. Die Chaostheorie gilt als derjenige mathematische Zweig, dessen Formeln dem wirklichen Leben am nächsten kommen. Die durchschaubare „Simulation of Live“ rückt ein kleines Stück näher ans „Real Live“. Aber ist unserem Verständnis dadurch geholfen worden? Das muß jede(r) für sich selbst entscheiden…

Kurt Walz

„Der geklonte Klang“
Komposition, Gesamtkonzept, Live-Elektronik:
Klaus Obermaier, Robert Spour
Kronos Quartet:
David Harrington, violin
John Sherba, violin
Hank Dutt, viola
Joan Jeanrenaud, cello
Interaktive Lasersteuerung: Friedrich Förster
Computerprogrammierung: Kurt Walz
Video, Lichtregie: Rainer Jessl
Technischer Direktor des Kronos-Quartet: Larry Neff
Raum-Klang-Steuerung, NeXt Cube/IMW Prozessorkarte, MaxAudio-Programmierung: Peter Böhm
Tontechnik: Jay Cloidt
Raumklang-Software: Peter Böhm
Laserimages, Projektionen: Obermaier, Spour, Förster

Das Projekt wurde ermöglicht durch die großzügige Unterstützung der AUSTRIA TABAK Generaldirektion.

„KRAFTWERK" UNPLUGGED? (EINE BESCHREIBUNG VON OBERFLÄCHEN)

"KRAFTWERK" UNPLUGGED? (A DESCRIPTION OF SURFACES)

Scene: Professor Rodchenko, in the year 1920, at the Vehutemas Art College which was founded after the revolution and where El Lisitzky also taught for a time:
"On the first day of lectures a man entered the studio who looked light a combination of pilot and motor cyclist. He wore a beige uniform-like jacket and gray-green plus-fours. He had a black cap on his head with a huge leather peak. His face was very pale and the intensive red lips stood out in the white of his face. Immediately I knew that this was the new type of human being" (By a former student).
In the 1970's, "Kraftwerk" from Düsseldorf presented themselves programmatically in constructivist colours and typography—red and black; circle/line/plane, in energetic fields as "Man Machine". "Organization" was the original name of the project. This constructivism "loan" was probably too internationally interpretable for them; "Kraftwerk" also meant concentration on the regional idiom: "We make regional music from the Rhine and Ruhr areas". Rodchenko: The MAN who organized his life, his work and himself is the MODERN MAN. Even "Kraftwerk" have a programme for modern men. It aims for the precision of a machine. The machine corresponds to their discipline and creativity. Man loves machines, machines love men / who love it etc.). "Sometimes we surprise machines, sometimes they surprise us". The symbiotic relationship "Man Machine" constitutes modern men.
"Kraftwerk" appeared "live" on their last tour as robots and/or left their live-performance to robots. The "Kraftwerk" clones look like imitations of "Kraftwerk" imitations. "Kraftwerk" trigger off endless series: They present dummies of dummies, imitations of imitations, they produce the mix of mix of mix etc.
They are the glass men of techno-music. In the window of the body there is nothing, it remains a smooth surface with an indication of a chest; a standard torso with no lower abdomen. Pneumatic arms with glove hands are stretched out to greet? to fight? to dance? ("Dance the "Kraftwerk"). Jim Whiting's constructions could be sitting in the audience, one would be among oneselves.
This is how they present themselves on the

Auftritt: Professor Rodchenko 1920 in der nach der Revolution gegründeten Kunsthochschule Vehutemas, auf der auch El Lisitzky einige Zeit unterrichtete: „Am ersten Vorlesungstag betrat ein Mann das Studio, der wie eine Kombination aus Pilot und Motorradfahrer aussah. Er trug ein uniformmäßig geschnittenes Jackett in beige und grau-grüne Kniebundhosen. Auf dem Kopf hatte er eine schwarze Mütze mit einem riesigen Lederschirm. Sein Gesicht war sehr blaß, die intensiv roten Lippen hoben sich vom Weiß des Gesichtes ab. Ich wußte gleich, daß das der neue Typ Mensch war." (Aufzeichnung eines ehemaligen Studenten)
In den siebziger Jahren präsentierten sich die Düsseldorfer „Kraftwerk" programmatisch in konstruktivistischen Farben und Typografie – Rot und Schwarz; Kreis / Linie / Fläche in energetischen Feldern – als „Mensch Maschine". „Organisation" war ihr ursprünglicher Projektname. Diese Konstruktivismus-Anleihe war ihnen vermutlich zu international übersetzbar. „Kraftwerk" bedeutete auch Konzentration auf das heimische Idiom: „Wir machen Heimatmusik aus dem Rhein und Ruhrgebiet". Rodchenko: „Der *Mensch,* der sein Leben organisiert hat, seine Arbeit und sich selbst, ist der *moderne Mensch".* Auch „Kraftwerk" hat ein Programm für den modernen Menschen. Er strebt die Präzision einer Maschine an. Die Maschine entspricht seiner Disziplin und Kreativität. Der Mensch liebt die Maschine, die Maschine liebt den Menschen, (der sie liebt usw.). „Manchmal überraschen wir die Maschinen, manchmal überraschen sie uns." Die symbiotische Beziehung „Mensch Maschine" macht den modernen Menschen aus.
„Kraftwerk" sind bei ihrer letzten Tournee „live" als Roboter aufgetreten und/oder haben Robotern ihren live-Auftritt überlassen. Die „Kraftwerk"-Klone sehen aus wie Nachahmungen von Kraftwerknachahmungen. „Kraftwerk" lösen endlos Reihen aus: Sie präsentieren Dummies von Dummies, Nachbildungen von Nachbildungen, sie produzieren den Mix vom Mix vom Mix, etc.
Sie sind die gläsernen Menschen der Technomusik. Im Fen-

ster der Körper ist nichts, er bleibt glatte Oberfläche mit angedeutetem Brustkorb: ein Normtorso ohne Unterleib. Pneumatische Arme mit Handschuhhänden sind ausgestreckt, zum Gruß? zum Kampf? zum Tanz? (Tanz das „Kraftwerk"!) Jim Whitings Konstruktionen könnten im Publikum sitzen, man wäre unter sich.

So präsentieren sie sich im Quadratheft der CD „The Mix": Sie sind keine spektakulären Zwitterwesen mehr an der Kippe vom Mensch zur Maschine im optimistisch heiteren Werbelook von damals.Der Blick der diagonal gestaffelten Jungmännerköpfe war in eine neue Zukunft gerichtet, die Haut weiß, die Lippen so rot. Das war die geniale Image-Idee, die zum fixen Bestandteil unzähliger kommerzieller Gruppenportraits wurde. Hier auf „The Mix" ist das Pendel in Richtung Maschine umgeschlagen. Eine Skizze demonstriert das Konstruktionsprinzip: die „Beine": zwei Stahlrohre bilden einen Sockel; Torso, Kopf, Schulter, Ellenbogen sind drehbar. Schlemmers triadisches Ballett ist dagegen eine chaotisch pulsierende Folklore-Gruppe.

„Kraftwerk" werden beschrieben als konsequent, kompromißlose Techno-Heimbastler, die kompliziert, zeitaufwendig, radikal ihre Maschinen programmieren. Die Hardware beginnt allmählich der Software in ihren Köpfen zu entsprechen. „Wir spielen Studio" (nicht wie andere Indianer, sondern wie andere Gitarre spielen). Sie können mit denen, die Gitarre (oder Indianer) spielen, nichts anfangen. Im Genrebild des Western wären die Rockmusiker in ihrer anachronistischen Cowboyverkleidung die „outlaw heros", während „Kraftwerk" das Management des aufgeklärten Establishments verkörpern würden: die Gemeinschaft nicht auf der Zivilisationsstufe der Community, sondern auf der des optimalen Rechnerhirns, die Gesellschaft als Firma. „Kinder von Wernher von Braun und Fritz Lang" apostrophieren sie sich selber (wobei sie beim Stichwort Lang „Metropolis" abspeichern und nicht die späteren Hollywood-Western). „Kraftwerk" im keimfreien Format der „Mensch Maschine" haben mit körperlicher Verausgabung und/oder Psychotortur der Rocklegenden nichts zu tun. Kein sex, kein crime, kein rock'n'roll. Sie putzen sich die Zähne und begeben sich zur Arbeit in ihr „Kling-Klang"-Studio. „Ja tvoi sluga, Ja tvoi rabotnik" Ich bin dein Diener, ich bin dein Arbeiter", stand auf dem „Mensch-Maschinen"-Cover.

In den letzten Jahren haben sie bekanntlich den Gesamtkatalog ihrer analog gespeicherten Kompositionen digital abgelegt. Die Zugriffszeiten verringern sich. „Kraftwerk" verfügen damit unbegrenzt über ihr eigenes Material und können potentiell unendlich viele, nie gehörte Mixversionen herausbringen.

square cover of the CD "The Mix": They are no longer spectacular hermaphrodites on the brink of man becoming machine in the optimistic cheerful advertising look of then: The gaze of the diagonally echeloned young men's heads was directed into a new future, the skin was white, the lips so red: That was the ingenious image idea which became the integral part of innumerous commercial group portraits. Here, on "The Mix", the pendulum has swung round towards machine. A sketch demonstrates the construction principle: the "legs": two steel tubes form a base; torso, head, shoulders, elbow can turn. In contract to this, Schlemmer's triad ballet is a chaotic pulsating folklore group. "Kraftwerk" are described as being resolute, uncompromising techno-home hobbiests who programme their machines in a complicated, time-consuming and radical way. The hardware gradually begins to correspond with the software in their heads. "We play studio" (not the way others play Indians, but the way others play guitar). They can't make anything of those that play guitar (or Indians). In the genre-picture of the Western, the rock musicians would be the "outlaw heroes" in their anachronistic cowboy dress, whereas "Kraftwerk" would embody the management of the enlightened establishment: The association not at the civilization stage of community but at the stage of the optimal computer brain, society as a firm. They apostrophize themselves as "children of Wernher von Braun and Fritz Lang" (whereby they store "Metropolis" at the keyword Lang and not the later Hollywood Western). "Kraftwerk" in the sterile format of "Man Machine" have nothing to do with the physical overspending and/or psycho-torture of the rock legends. No sex, no crime, no rock'n roll. They brush their teeth and head off to work in their "Kling Klang" studio. "Ja tvoi sluga, ja tvoi rabotnik", "I am your servant, I am your worker", was on the "Man Machine" cover.

In the past few years they are known to have digitally filed the entire catalogue of their analogous stored compositions. The access times lessen. "Kraftwerk" have an unlimited amount of their own material at their disposal and can produce potentially a never ending amount of mix versions that have never been heard before.

And: beautiful dialectics: The digital storing gives a sense again to the stage presence (of the dummies?). A live-intervention into the software is possible. The material can be called up, modified, "psychologically controlled" by the operators, "Computers are transmitted with everything that can operate systematically. We can have control of ourselves all the more freely, let ourselves drift" Hütter once announced that he would love to have a third hand implanted, "which then operated all the controls and buttons while the hands play freely and the feet hit the pedals".

The "Balanescu Quartet" plays "Kraftwerk". The 100% machine music is transmitted into chamber music: Kraftwerk "unplugged" therefore? No, as with other contemporary string quartets, Alexander Balanescu appeared with his musicians, electronically amplified. The five "Kraf-

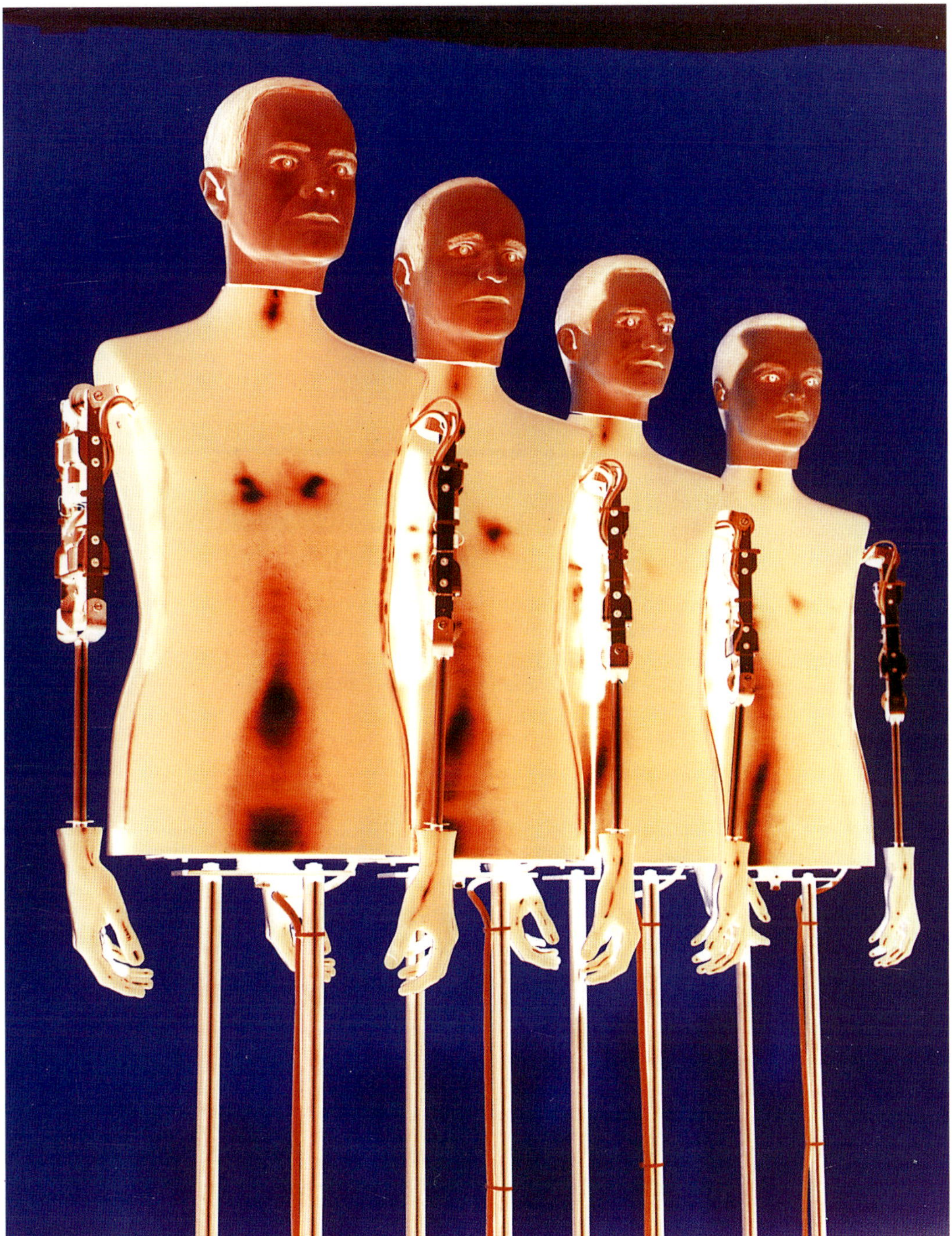

Und: schöne Dialektik: Durch die digitale Abspeicherung macht die Bühnenpräsenz (der Dummies?) wieder Sinn. Ein live-Eingriff in die Software ist möglich. Das Material kann durch die Operateure abgerufen, modifiziert, „psychologisch gesteuert" werden, „Die Computer bekommen alles übertragen, was systematisch ablaufen kann. Wir können umso freier über uns verfügen, uns treiben lassen". Hütter hat einmal angekündigt, daß er sich am liebsten eine dritte Hand einpflanzen lassen würde, „die bedient dann alle Regler und Knöpfe, während die Hände frei spielen und die Füße die Pedale treten".

Das „Balanescu Quartet" plays „Kraftwerk". Die 100% Maschinenmusik wird in Kammermusik übertragen: Kraftwerk „unplugged" also? Nein, wie auch andere zeitgenössische Streichquartette tritt Alexander Balanescu mit seinen Musikern elektronisch verstärkt auf. Die fünf „Kraftwerk"-Übernahmen (auf dem Album „Possessed", 1992) sind im multitrack-System der Rockmusik aufgenommen: Erst die Rhythmus-Spur, dann ein Track in einer Kirche – „location recording at St. Augustin's Church", dann wieder im Studio. Das Mixen war ebenso wichtig wie die Aufnahme und hatte eher eine Rock/Mix-Dauer, viel länger als die Norm für eine klassische Produktion. Nun plant Alexander Balanescu eine multitrack-Aufnahme von Bachs „Kunst der Fuge".

Das System der immer effizienteren Rechnerverarbeitungen in Speichermedien wird auf den Notenständer zurück geholt. Zum ersten Mal spielen Musiker auf vorgefertigten, klassischen Instrumenten elektronische „Kraftwerk"-Konstruktionen. Ist das der konzeptionelle Overkill/Überschmäh? Oder sucht ein Spitzen-Quartett der boomenden Streicherszene interessantes Material als Markenzeichen? Werden „Kraftwerk" in Zukunft Balanescu-Takte von „Roboter" oder „Autobahn" für sich samplen?

Synthesizer kommen fabriksseits mit vielfältigen „presets". Presets für diverse Streichinstrumente sind Standard. „Kraftwerk" benutzen weder „presets" noch vorsintflutliche „bleeps", alle ihre Klänge sind eigenentwickelt und -programmiert. Diese „Originale" werden jetzt von Balanescu nachgespielt (arrangiert und produziert von der zweiten Violine: Clare Connors). Das ist eine Umkehrung der sonstigen en masse-Produktionen von Jazz-, Rock-, oder Synthie-Versionen von Klassikern.

Die „Balanescu"/„Kraftwerk"-Einspielung ist ein Rückbau zum Atem, zum Körper. Es war erwartungsgemäß von Wärme zu lesen, von Leidenschaft dort, wo früher (bei „Kraftwerk") industrielle (naturgemäß kalte) Technologie waltete. Aber das genau war das Programm: die weitgehende Ausschaltung des Faktors Mensch. Werden die Roboter wieder verletzlich?

twerk" take-overs (on the album "Possessed", 1992) were recorded on the multi-track system of rock music.: First of all the rhythm track, then a track in a church—"location recording at St. Augustin's Church", then again in the studio. The mixing was just as important as the recording and had more of a rock/mix duration, much longer than the normal one for a classical production. Alexander Balanescu is now planning a multi-track recording of Bach's "Kunst der Fuge".

The system of the increasingly more efficient computer processings in storage media is brought back to the music stands. For the first time, musicians play electronic "Kraftwerk" constructions on pre-fabricated, classical instruments. Is that the conceptional overkill/big gag? Or is a super quartet of the booming string scene looking for interesting material as a trade mark? Will in future "Kraftwerk" sample Balanescu's rhythms of "Robots" or "Autobahn" for themselves?

Synthesizers come from the factories with a variety of "presets". Presets for various string instruments are standard. "Kraftwerk" neither use "presets" nor antediluvian "bleeps", all their sounds are self-developed and programmed. These "originals" are now being played by Balanescu (arranged and produced by the second violinist: Clare Connors). This is a reversal of the otherwise en masse productions of jazz, rock or synthie-versions of classics.

The "Balanescu" "Kraftwerk" play-in is a build out to breathing, to the body and as expected, warmth could be read, passion where formerly (with "Kraftwerk") industrial (naturally cold) technology ruled. But that was exactly the programme: the extensive elimination of the factor man: Will robots become vulnerable again?

In "Kraftwerk's" music, like in Cronenberg films, one believes one can follow the strands of the glass fibres, the grid points of the relay stations (most certainly a hopelessly antiquated picture) in the inside of the machine, if one didn't have this uneasy feeling when using metaphors and analogies. But "Kraftwerk" play (also) programme music: how true-to-life one can hear the cars driving past on the autobahn! How one can hum along with the rhythm of TEE on the rails! (That is outdated with TGV) Is the string quartet, on its part, now making "Kraftwerk" programme music? Must it be proven that even 200 year old wooden instruments can imitate the sounds from the autobahn? (Critics emphasize the amazing cello glissandi). What do "Kraftwerk" think when they hear the Balanescu version of "Model", for example? Are the four chamber musicians not causing the "Kraftwerk" metropolis project to tumble? Is merely house music and the fire-side on the cards again after the wave of techno house music?

The disparaging comments "Kraftwerk" made about the guitar anachronism of rock culture seem to be forgotten. " You can't play the music of the 20th century on medieval instruments" or "the music of the technical world can only be presented on instruments of the technical world".

"Kraftwerk's "Kling Klang" productions often

have an almost crytalline transparency, not only in the hurting innocent children's language of adults, but particularly in the synthetic sound layers. It sometimes sounds so cheerful that it sends a shiver down your spine. "The change from hope to horror can take place as fast as lightening" (Hütter). Euphoria changes over directly to become a nice horror scene. The project: human progress through the progress in technology, as was first of all propagated, still unbroken, by the constructivists, has crashed. On "The Mix", the computer voice spells out, syllable for syllable: TSCHER-NO-BIL / HARRIS-BURG /HI-RO-SCHI-MA and adds the barely audible, somewhat forced troubled imperative "Stop"! before the refrain "radioactivity". With the strings, where is the crash into a popular song-like danse macabre of the machines? Here death has again established its instrument and fiddles the euphorizing seduction like a minimalistic bravura.

So, there are two different scenes: For one. there are four racks at the machines, and there are four lively musicians belonging to the "Balanescu Quartet", with their instruments. The fact, alone, that a woman plays in the quartet is a sensation in direct comparison to "Kraftwerk". The human form: woman or even the species mankind as a sexual being only occurs with "Kraftwerk" in the simulation: "Sie ist ein Model und sie sieht gut aus" (She's a model and she looks good). When will the two groups appear together in a jam session?

A chair is a chair.

On the CD cover of the Balanescu production "Possessed", a chair plays a significant role. Alexander Balanescu is sitting on it. He, himself, is in the process of getting up, of going away or can be seen blurred in the long exposure behind/infront of/on the chair which is always clearly in focus. Finally, Balanescu goes away and the chair remains behind, empty.

Two associations according to the description of surfaces: the chair as a useful object appears to be very real. It could easily—and distinguishable in photography—be simulated as a three-dimensional object. Joseph Kossuth could use it for his conceptional alphabet. "One and three chairs" as a photo of the object description: chair. The "Kraftwerk" dummies will not sit down, they do not exist beneath the waistline. The "Balanescu Quartet" makes music while standing.

Bei der Musik von „Kraftwerk" meint man wie in Cronenberg-Filmen den Strängen der Glasfasern, den Netzpunkten der Relaisstationen (sicher ein hoffnungslos antiquiertes Bild) im Innern der Maschinen folgen zu können, hätte man nicht ein ungutes Gefühl beim Verwenden von Metaphern und Analogien. Aber „Kraftwerk" spielen (auch) Programmusik: Wie naturgetreu man die Autos auf der Autobahn vorbeifahren hört! Wie man den Rhythmus des TEEauf den Gleisen mitsummen kann! (Das ist beim TGV überholt). Macht das Streichquartett nun seinerseits „Kraftwerk"-Programmusik? Ist zu beweisen, daß auch 200 Jahre alte Holzinstrumente das Geräusch der Autobahn nachahmen können? (Kritiker betonen die verblüffenden Cello Glissandi). Was denken sich „Kraftwerk", wenn sie die Balanescu-Version von „Modell" z. B. hören? Bringen die vier Kammermusiker nicht das „Kraftwerk"-Metropolisprojekt zum Kippen? Ist nach der Welle der Techno-Housemusik wieder schlicht Hausmusik und Kaminfeuer angesagt?

Vergessen scheinen die abschätzigen Bemerkungen von „Kraftwerk" zum Gitarrenanachronismus der Rockkultur. Man kann die Musik des 20. Jahrhunderts nicht auf mittelalterlichen Instrumenten spielen" oder „Die Musik der technisierten Welt läßt sich nur auf Instrumenten der technisierten Welt darstellen".

Die „Kling-Klang"-Produktionen von „Kraftwerk" haben oft eine geradezu kristalline Durchsichtigkeit, nicht nur in der schmerzend arglosen Kindersprache von Erwachsenen, sondern vor allem in den synthetischen Klangschichten. Das klingt manchmal so fröhlich, daß es einem kalt den Rücken hinunterläuft. „Der Wechsel von der Hoffnung zum Horror kann blitzschnell passieren" (Hütter). Euphorie schlägt übergangslos zu einem netten Horror-szenarium um. Das Projekt: menschlicher Fortschritt durch Fortschritt der Technik, das bei den Konstruktivisten zunächst noch ungebrochen propagiert wurde, ist abgestürzt. Auf „The Mix" buchstabiert die Computerstimme Silbe für Silbe: Tscher-No-Bil / Ha-rris-Burg / hi-ro-schi-ma und ergänzt den kaum hörbaren, ein wenig bemühten Imperativ „Stoppt!" vor den Refrain „Radioaktivität". Wo bleibt bei den Streichern der Absturz in einen gassenhauerischen Totentanz der Maschinen? Hier hat der Tod wieder selbst sein Instrument angelegt und fiedelt die euphorisierende Verführung als minimalistisches Bravourstück.

Zwei verschiedene Auftritte also: Da sind einmal vier Gestelle an den Maschinen, und da sind die vier leibhaftigen Musiker des Balanescu Quartets" mit ihren Instrumenten. Allein die Tatsache, daß eine Frau im Quartett spielt, ist im direkten Vergleich mit „Kraftwerk" eine Sensation: Die menschliche

Form: Frau, oder überhaupt die Gattung Mensch als Geschlechtswesen kommt bei Kraftwerk nur in der Simulation vor: „Sie ist ein model und sie sieht gut aus“. Wann werden die beiden Gruppen gemeinsam in einer jam session auftreten?

Ein Stuhl ist ein Stuhl.

Im CD-Heft der Balanescu-Produktion „Possessed“ spielt ein Stuhl eine wichtige Rolle. Alexander Balanescu sitzt auf ihm. Er selbst ist in der Bewegung des Aufstehens, des Weggehens oder in der Langzeitbelichtung verwischt hinter/vor/auf dem immer scharf fokussierten Stuhl zu sehen. Schließlich geht Balanescu weg, der Stuhl bleibt leer zurück. Zwei Assoziationen nach der Beschreibung der Oberflächen: der Stuhl als Gebrauchsobjekt scheint sehr real. Er könnte aber ohne weiteres – und in der Fotografie ununterscheidbar – als dreidimensionales Objekt simuliert werden. Joseph Kossuth könnte ihn für sein konzeptionelles Alphabet benutzen. „Einer und drei Stühle“ als Foto die Objektbeschreibung: Stuhl. Die „Kraftwerk“-Dummies werden sich nicht setzen, es gibt sie unterhalb der Gürtellinie nicht. Das „Balanescu Quartet“ musiziert im Stehen.

Even Alexander Balanescu salutes the Russian constructivism in the typography of the cover (and, of course, the "Kraftwerk" "Man Machine" layout inspired by El Lissitzky, was what it was called there). But in doing so he winks with one eye and keeps his hat on. "With a nod and a wink towards El Lissitzky"

So, warmth and wit for a humourless technoworld? Ironically, "Kraftwerk" move more freely and more "spontaneously" during their live performances—whether in person or as dummies—with the new dynamism of their material, than the machine string quartet which has to stick to the most exact interpretation of the rules of notation, under physical effort.

What was it that El Lissitzky said in 1924 in the edition of the magazine MERZ with Kurt Schwitters: "It is quite ENOUGH, always MACHINE, MACHINE, MACHINE"

Edek Bartz / Birgit Flos

Auch Alexander Balanescu grüßt in der Typografie des Covers den russischen Konstruktivismus (und natürlich das „Kraftwerk"-„Mensch Maschine"-Lay out inspiriert von El Lissitzky hieß es dort). Aber er zwinkert dabei mit einem Auge und behält den Hut auf. „With a nod and a wink towards El Lissitzky".
Also doch Wärme und Witz für eine humorlose Technowelt? Ironischer Weise bewegen sich die „Kraftwerk", ob höchstpersönlich oder als Dummie, mit der neuen Dynamisierung ihres Materials freier und „spontaner" bei ihren live-Performances, als die Maschine Streichquartett, die sich unter körperlichem Einsatz an die genaueste Übersetzung der Notations-Vorschriften zu halten hat.
Wie sagte El Lissitzky 1924 in der mit Kurt Schwitters herausgegebenen Nummer der Zeitschrift Merz: „Es ist schon genug, immer Maschine Maschine Maschine".

Edek Bartz / Birgit Flos

Kurator: Edek Bartz

Fotos: Peter Boettcher

SCORES

SCORES

Die vormals in einem konsistenten Werkbegriff gefügten Relationen zwischen Komponisten und Komposition, Spielanweisung und Interpretation, Klangproduktion und Klang- bzw. Hörereignisort sind – in vielerlei Hinsicht – zum wichtigsten Gegenstand der Auseinandersetzung mit „Komposition" – oder, freier ausgedrückt, musikalischer Produktion geworden.
In dem Maße, in dem diese Relationen nicht mehr festen Regeln gehorchen, erweitert sich der Aktionsspielraum, den ihre gewachsene Relevanz öffnet. Ebenso wächst parallel dazu das Bedürfnis, in diesen Räumen solche künstlerischen Manifestationen zu suchen, die diesen Relationen als „Daten" dienen könnten.
„Scores" zeigt drei Ansätze, unterschiedliche relationale Räume mittels verschiedener künstlerischer Konzepte zu bearbeiten. Gemeinsam ist den drei Konzepten die Problematisierung der Beziehung zwischen „Vorlage" und „Realisation".

PARTITUR

„Partitur" behandelt die Darstellung zweier verschiedener Informationsebenen: einer Ausgangspartitur und einer Transformationspartitur.
Ein Interpret reagiert mit verschiedenen akustischen Aktionen auf die Vorgaben einer graphischen Partitur. Die entstehenden klanglichen Ereignisse werden mittels eines Computerprogramms transformiert und in veränderte graphische Darstellungen überführt. Die so entstandene neue Partitur wird mit der Ausgangspartitur konfrontiert und beeinflußt sie nach Maßgabe des Interpreten, der auf die Transformation reagiert.
Der Computer als Interface zwischen Partitur und Interpret fordert einerseits die explizite Darstellung der Relationen zwischen Komposition, Darstellung, Interpretation und Rezeption, zum anderen schafft er die strukturellen Bedingungen, in denen revidierte Definitionen der graphischen Gestaltung von Spielvorlagen und der Anlässe zur musikalischen Aktion erfolgen müssen.

"SCORES"

The relations between composers and composition, playing directives and interpretation, sound production and sound and/or place of listening event formerly allocated to one consistent concept have, to a great extent, become the most important subjects in the discussion about "composition" or to be more liberal, musical production.
The scope of action expands to the extent in which these relations no longer obey rigid rules, opening its increased relevance. Similarly, parallel to this, the need increases to look for such artistic manifestations in these areas that could be used to serve these relations as "data".
"Scores" shows three approaches for processing different relational areas by means of different artistic concepts. Common to the three concepts, is making the relationship between "presentation" and "realization" problematic.
"Scores" puts the accent on the reciprocal relationship between mutual interpretations of optical and acoustical information.
"Broken Light" uses a technically changed musical matrix as the basis for an interactive parallel musical action.
"What Happened II" sets the theme about the permutative relationship between generated musical information and gesticular and vocal action.

PARTITUR

Scores deals with the representation of two different levels of information: original scores and transformation scores.
An interpreter reacts to the stipulations of graphic scores with different acoustic actions. The sound happenings which result are transformed by means of a computer programme and transferred into changed graphic representations. The new scores which result are confronted with the original scores, influencing them according to the interpreter who reacts to the transformation.
The computer as an interface between scores and interpreter calls, on the one hand, for the explicit representation of the relations between composition, representation, interpretations and reception. On the other hand, it creates the structural conditions in which revised definitions must result from the graphic arrangement of playing copies and the reasons for musical action.
Such an occassion for analysis questions all parameters that concern its utilization and its output, in the form of an interface in a feedback loop.

Where scores and the gesticular realizations of a musical conductor had more of an assisting function for the reproduction of acquired sound patterns right up to the second half of this century, an emancipation of the optical representation of the sound happening can be observed in serial music which reaches its climax in aleatory, non-metricized music.
In the case of "Scores", the objectivizing function of the computer feedback loop, the associative sound happenings, cannot be predicted exactly on the basis of conventionally acquired experiences, but must be explored in a language which has to be newly acquired both in the preparation as well as in the after treatment.

Achim Wollscheid, Dietmar Wiesner

"PARTITUR"
Achim Wollscheid, composition, conception
Dietmar Wiesner, composition, intepretation
Joachim Pense, composition, programming

BROKEN LIGHT

for string quartet and modified CD player
February 1991, revised April 1992, final score June 1992

Broken Light is the first in a series of pieces that employ customized consumer electronics in conjunction with traditional instruments to rework tonal material from earlier music, in this case the string music of Corelli, Locatelli and Torelli. Under the control of the performers, the CD player "scratches" across the disk, isolating and freezing short loops of recorded music. As it slowly steps from one "skipping groove" to the next, the lush contrapuntal texture of the concerto grosso is suspended in harmonic blocks, with the insistent rhythmic feel of the loop superimposed. The performer's parts, both written and improvised, mesh and clash with the CD, with a respectful nod to Terry Riley's in C. Broken Light was commissioned by the Soldier String Quartet, and premiered in May 1991 at the Musique Action Festival in Vanduvre-les-Nancy, France.

GENERAL NOTES ON SCORE
Section 01:c.5 minutes
Begins with sequence of alternation of CD Skitters and players mimicking the skitters (Heavy Metal speed guitar). Last group skitter overlaps with beginning of pause loop ostinato. Group crescendo into rhythmic detaché to match loop tempo and harmony; can change pitch onve or twice per loop harmony but keep simple. 4 repeats/4nudges; 1 "bar" = 8–15 seconds. Then c.3 minutes group variation as described above. Finish with 1 strong detaché bar, CD Skitter, group Skitter.
Section 2:c.4 minutes
Slow movement. Sustained bowing with pas-

Solcherart Anlaß zur Analyse, stellt er in Art eines Interfaces in einer Feedback-Schleife alle Parameter, die seinen Einsatz und seinen Output betreffen, in Frage.
Hatten bis hin zur zweiten Hälfte dieses Jahrhunderts die Partitur und die gestischen Umsetzungen eines Dirigenten eher unterstützende Funktion der Reproduktion von erlernten klanglichen Mustern, so läßt sich in der seriellen Musik eine Emanzipation der optischen Darstellung vom klanglichen Ereignis beobachten, die in der aleatorischen, nicht metrisierten Musik ihren Höhepunkt findet.
Im Falle von „Partitur" lassen sich durch die objektivierende Funktion der Feebackschleife des Computers die assotiativklanglichen Ergebnisse auf der Basis von herkömmlich erlernten Erfahrungen nicht genau vorhersagen, sondern müssen in einer neu zu erlernenden Sprache sowohl in der Vor- als auch in der Nachbereitung erfahren werden.

Achim Wollscheid, Dietmar Wiesner

„Partitur:"
Achim Wollscheid, Komposition, Konzeption
Dietmar Wiesner, Kompositon, Interpretation
Joachim Pense, Komposition, Programmierung

BROKEN LIGHT
NICOLAS COLLINS

für Streichquartett und modifizierten CD Player

Broken Light ist das erste in einer Reihe von Stücken, die handelsübliche Verbraucherelektronik in Verbindung mit traditionellen Instrumenten verwenden, um tonales Material älterer Musik neu zu bearbeiten, in diesem Fall die Musik für Saiteninstrumente von Corelli, Locatelli und Torelli. Von den Ausführenden gesteuert, „kratzt" der CD Player über die Platte und isoliert und blockiert kurze Schleifen aufgezeichneter Musik. Mit dem langsamen Vorrücken von einer „hüpfenden Rille" zur nächsten, wird die üppige kontrapunktische Struktur des Concerto grosso in harmonischen Blöcken aufgehoben, mit der eindringlichen rhythmischen Empfindung der darüber gelagerten Schleife. Die notierten wie auch improvisierten Parts der Ausführenden greifen in die CD ein und kollidieren mit ihr, mit einer respektvollen Verbeugung vor Terry Rileys „In C." Broken Light ist ein Auftragswerk für das Soldier String Quartet und wurde im Mai 1991 uraufgeführt.

Broken Light

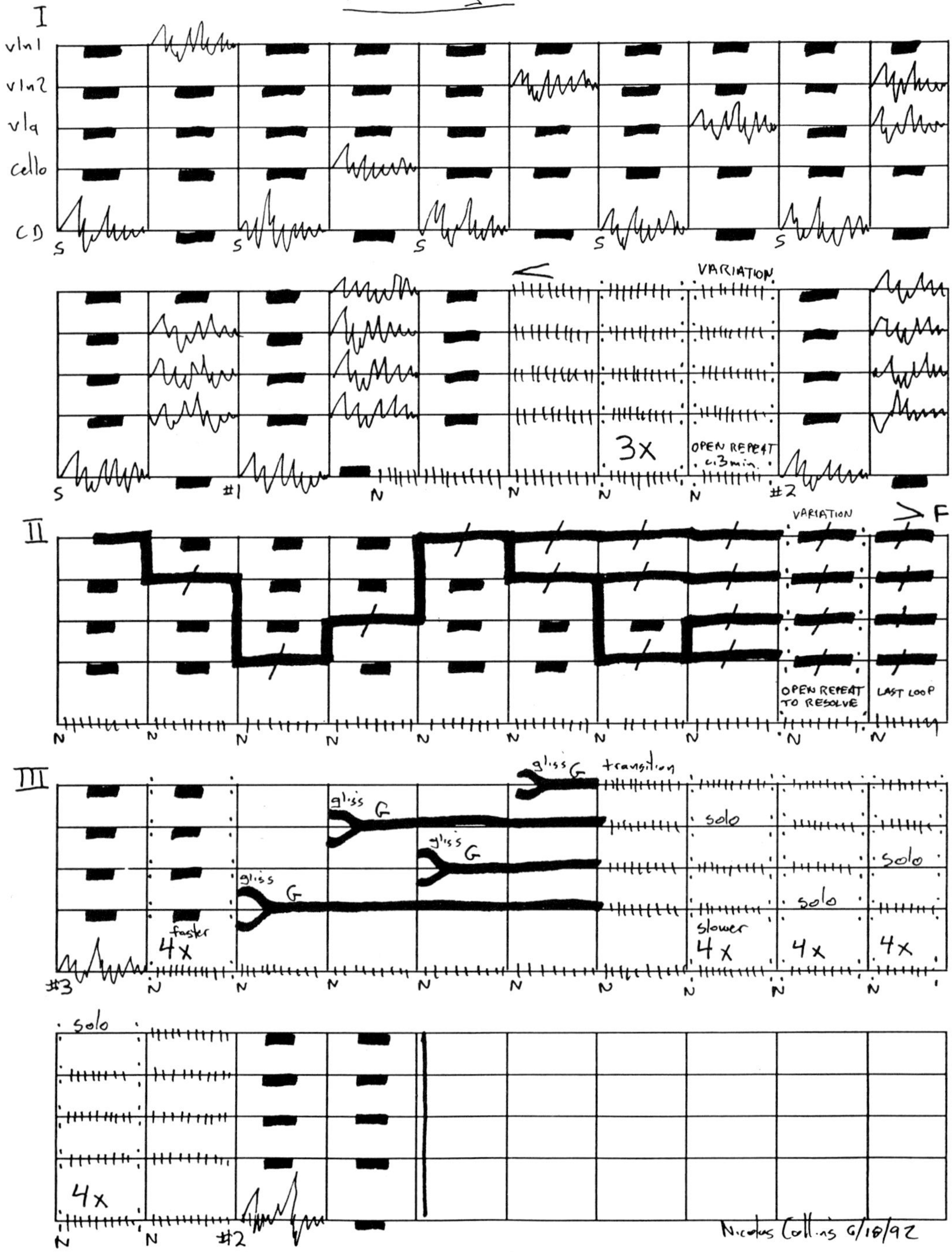

R E T U R N →

rarely move from this chair. In summer I move the chair out to the porch. My children call but they don't visit anymore. They are always reprimanding me for the way I have chosen to live. They complain that I should go out more and that I am neglecting my personal hygiene. I am happy though, doing exactly what I want. Fortunately, I don't remember much of what I have suffered. I know I experienced those things but I can't conjure them up with any veracity. But the pleasure I can recall vividly, the pleasant sensations. I am going through it all systematically, keeping records of what I relive. I can remember the dresses women wore to my parties, the sounds men made when we were making love. I can remember the number and quantity of the compliments I received on different occasions. And the years with my children, I can recall how their voices sounded in the night, the smell of their skin in summer, my husband's many games with them, the configuration of the hair on his chest, his legs and belly. I can recall the patterns of the rugs on the floors of the different homes we visited over the years. I am certain my memory of these things is better than anything I could experience today.

2ND TRANSITION: OUTSIDE SOUNDS – UNEVENTFUL – 1 OR 2 PREVIOUS BUBBLES

GLOBAL-EXPERIENCE (MORE COMMON TO ALL) →

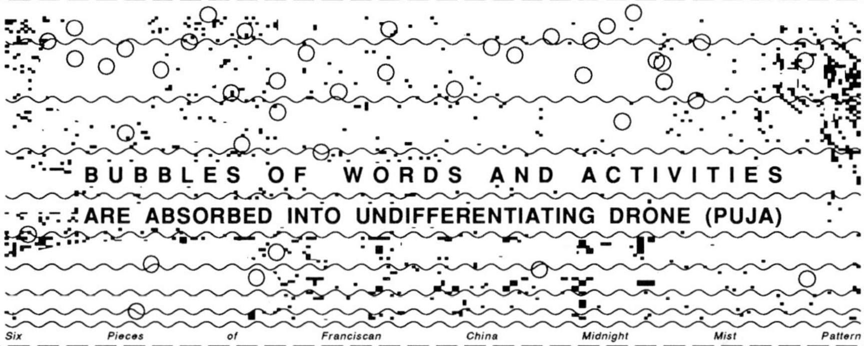

RUPTURE POINT/ ACCI-DENT

EXTERNAL INTRUSION
ACCIDENT / RUPTURE POINT

(EXPLOSION
VIRUS
CRASH)

Air flowing over this unknown powdery substance regulates the brightness. Excitement sets the air in motion.

CULTURAL →

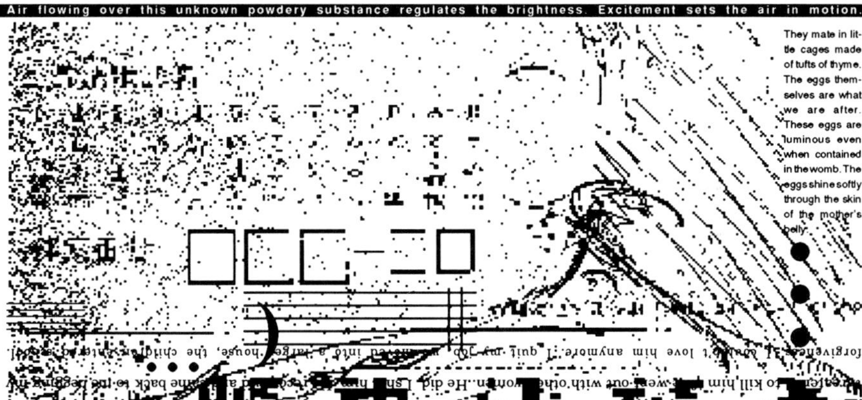

INDIVIDUAL →

When I had a baby I lost my sex drive. My husband came home from the war and found me sleeping with a woman. He took her away, they ran off together. My baby died. I got my sex drive back and had another baby. I married a man who brought with him two children of his own. He loved them dearly. He stayed home to care for them. I went out each day to make money but found I hated my job. I quit. The man who gave me the job threatened to kill me if I left.

Michael Sumner: Rendition of L. Sonami's score for "What Happened II"; text by Melody Sumner

„WHAT HAPPENED II"

mit einem Text von Melody Summer

Als ich den Steuerungshandschuh fertig hatte, dachte ich, es wäre interessant, „What Happened", eine ältere, auf analogen Geräten basierende Komposition, für diese neue Technologie zu adaptieren. Die Story folgt der Idee, daß die Geschichte einer beliebigen Person sich auflöst, sobald die Bewegung der Hand beginnt, – eine Verschiebung von der sprechenden Person hin zur schweigenden (es scheint immer, daß in der Stille der Handbewegungen einer schweigenden Person vieles hörbar wird). Dann wurde es jedoch offensichtlich, daß es sinnlos war, die Technologie zu transponieren, denn jede hatte ihre Charakteristika, die von der Komposition nicht zu trennen waren. So hielt ich an der von Melody Summer verfaßten Geschichte der Frau und an den erwähnten Ideen fest, veränderte jedoch vieles an der Art, wie die Komposition und die dazu assoziierten Geräusche sich entwickeln. Es ist ein bißchen als wäre da eine Kamera, die auf die Story hinweist und indem sich der Brennpunkt langsam verändert, wird die Geschichte unscharf und es kommen andere Bilder zum Vorschein. Nicht daß die Geschichte aus wäre, aber sie ist nicht mehr zu hören. Indem sich nun der Fokus weiter verändert, werden die individuellen Eigenschaften der Person geglättet, sie verbreitern sich und entwickeln sich zu kulturellen Charakteristika, die ihrerseits an dem Punkt verschwinden, wo es um Erfahrungen geht, die allen gemeinsam sind, ehe wiederum der individuelle Charakter hervortritt.
Zur Technik sei hier angemerkt, daß im Handschuh Sensoren eingebettet sind, die reagieren, sobald ich die Finger beuge, den Daumen näher an die Fingerspitzen heranführe, das Handgelenk beuge, und das Handgelenk von der Taille wegbewege. Diese Daten werden über das von STEIM konstruierte SensorLab in den Computer eingespeichert und von der Software MAX (Opcode) verarbeitet, sodaß beispielsweise ein Finger den Output der Stimme und dazugehörigen Geräusche steuert, die anderen die Dichte der Ereignisse, die Beugung der Noten oder das Auslösen einzelner Ereignisse ... der Computer übermittelt die Daten dann an den Synthesizer (Yamaha TG77) und an den Sampler (Peavey SP). Die Stimme wird ebenfalls in den Computer eingespeichert und ermöglicht allgemein das Auslösen von Ereignissen.

Laetitia Sonami

sing dissonances resolved. Begin with Violin 1 taking pitch from harmony, passed on to Violin 2 at loop harmony change; Violin 2 changes to new pitch for new harmony mid-way through "bar", then passes this new note on to Cello at next harmony change, then viola. Octave change permitted on any pass. Then repeat sequence but add up instruments rather than replacing 1 for 1; each new player can select any previous player's pitch on entry. Once full quartet is in, continue form of sustained bowing, carrying pitch over loop harmony change and then "resolving". Variations as indicated on score. Listen carefully for resolution to F at end; fade out on last breathy CD loop.
Section 3:c.5 minutes
Begins with 4 changes of CD pause loop only—faster "bar" tempo, c.5 seconds. Players enter with glisses up or down to G drone with sustained bowing, starting with Cello through to Violin 1. On next loop harmony change, swell to detaché bowing on G as in section 1, and resume 1 "bar" = 8–15 seconds; at next loop harmony can shift to any pitch of harmony. Then a "4 bar" solo for each player ("global" feel, but no campy stylism) with remainder of group "vamping" underneath, using variation techniques of section 1 but keeping a feeling of accompaniment. After last solo, 1 loop harmony of full group energetic detaché, then stop on a dime as CD zips out.

"WHAT HAPPENED II"

with a text by Melody Sumner
Once I completed the glove-controller, I thought it would be interesting to adapt an older composition "What Happened", which was based on analog devices I had built, to this new technology. The story lent itself to the idea that someone's story disintegrates as the hand starts moving, a shift from the talking person to the mute (it always seems that so much can be heard in the silence of the movements of the hand of a mute person). But then it became obvious that this transposition of technology was futile, each had its characteristics that were not dissociable from the composition. So I did keep the story of the woman written by Melody Sumner, and I kept the ideas mentioned, but changed much of the way the composition evolves and the sounds associated to it. It is somewhat as if there was a camera pointing at the story, and as it slowly changes focus, the story gets blurred and other images are revealed. It is not that the story has stopped but it is not heard anymore. Now, as the focus keeps changing, the individual characteristics of the person smooth out, they become broader and evolve into cultural characteristics which themselves disappear, to the point where the experience is more common to all, before reemerging to the individual character.
On a technical note, the glove has sensors imbedded in it, these react when I bend my fingers, bring my thumb closer to the tip of the fingers, bend the wrist, and move the wrist away from the waist. This data is fed to the computer via the SensorLab, built by STEIM, and the

software MAX (Opcode) deals with it, so that for instance one finger controls the output of the voice and sounds associated with it, the others the density of events, the beding of the notes, or triggering of individual events ... The computer then sends out the data to the synthesizer (Yamaha TG77) and sampler (Peavey SO). The voice is also fed into the computer and allows for the general triggering of events.

Laetitia Sonami

NARAYANAS KÜHE

TOM JOHNSON

Der Text ist keine musikalische Analyse, keine Mathematikstunde und auch keine komische Zugabe. Er soll einfach und als direkter Bestandteil des Stückes gesprochen werden, entweder von den Musikern oder von jemand anderem.

ERZÄHLUNG:

Narayana war ein indischer Mathematiker aus dem 14. Jahrhundert. Er stellte folgende Aufgabe: eine Kuh gebärt jedes Jahr ein Kalb. Ab dem vierten Jahr gebärt jedes Kalb, zu Beginn jedes Jahres, seinerseits ein Kalb. Wie viele Kühe und Kälber haben wir, alles in allem nach, sagen wir 17 Jahren? Während Sie sich das überlegen, geben wir Ihnen eine musikalische Demonstration der Aufgabe.
Im ersten Jahr haben wir nur die erste Kuh mit ihrem ersten Kalb (Musik zu 1, erster Taktstrich). Im zweiten Jahr haben wir die erste Kuh und zwei Kälber (Musik vom Anfang bis 2). Im dritten Jahr haben wir die erste Kuh und drei Kälber (Musik zu 3). Im vierten Jahr wird das älteste Kalb Mutter, womit eine dritte Generation von Narayanas Kühen beginnt (Musik zu 4). Im fünften Jahr haben wir eine weitere Mutterkuh und drei neue Kälber (Musik zu 5). Im sechsten Jahr haben wir vier gebärende Kühe, vier neue Kälber und eine Herde mit einem Bestand von 13 (Musik zu 6). Das siebente Jahr beschert uns die Geburt des ersten Kalbes des ersten Kalbes des ersten siebenten Kalbes der ersten von Narayanas Kühen. Die vierte Generation nimmt ihren Anfang (Musik zu 7). Im achten Jahr springt der Bestand, der von 1 auf 2 auf 3 auf 4 auf 6 auf 9 auf 13 auf 19 gestiegen war, auf 28 (Musik zu 8). Im neunten Jahr werden 13 neue Kälber geboren: eines ist die Tochter der ersten Kuh, sechs sind Enkelinnen und sechs weitere Ur-enkelinnen (Musik zu 9). Im zehnten Jahr steigt der Bestand der Herde von 41 auf 60 und die fünfte Generation beginnt mit einem neuen Ton (Musik zu 10). Im elften Jahr werden zusätzliche 28 Kälber von 28 Müttern geworfen, während 32 andere Kälber darauf warten, ihrerseits Mütter zu werden, was einen Gesamtbestand von 88 ergibt

NARAYANA'S COWS
TOM JOHNSON

The text is neither musical analysis, nor a math lesson, nor comic relief. It should be delivered simply and directly as an integral part of the piece, either by the musicians or by someone else.

NARRATOR:

Narayana was an Indian mathematician in the 14th century, who proposed the following problem: A cow produces one calf every year. Beginning in its fourth year, each calf produces one calf at the beginning of each year. How many cows are there altogether after, for example, 17 years?
While you are working on that, let us give you a musical demonstration. The first year there is only the original cow and her first calf. (Play music to 1, the first bar line). The second year there is the original cow and two calves. (Play music from beginning to 2). The third year there is the original cow and three calves (Music to 3). The fourth year the oldest calf becomes a mother, and we begin a third generation of Narayana's cows (Music to 4). The fifth year we have another mother cow and three new calves (Musik to 5). The sixth year we have four productive cows, four new calves, and a total herd of 13 (Music to 6). The seventh year brings the birth of the first calf of the first calf of the first calf of Narayana's original cow, and the fourth generation begins (Music to 7). In the eighth year the herd, which went from 1 to 2 to 3 to 4 to 6 to 9 to 13 to 19, now jumps to 28 (Music to 8). In the ninth year, 13 new calves are born. One is a daughter of the original cow, six are granddaughters, and six are great-granddaughters (Musik to 9). In the tenth year, the herd of 41 grows to 60, and the fifth generation begins on a new note (Music to 10). In the eleventh year an

additional 28 calves are produced by 28 mothers, and 32 other calves are waiting to become mothers, making a total of 88 (Music to 11). In the twelfth year, Narayana's herd continues its population explosion, growing from 88 to 129, and registering an annual population growth of 46.59% (Music to 12). In the thirteenth year, the rate drops very slightly to 46.51% as the sixth generation begins (Music to 13). The fourteenth year brings 88 new calves, advancing the herd from 189 to 277 (Music to 14). By the fifteenth year the herd numbers 406. This includes the original cow, 15 daughters, 78 granddaughters, 165 great-granddaughters, 126 great-great-granddaughters, and 21 great-great-great-granddaughters (Music to 15). In the sixteenth year, we have one new daughter, 13 new granddaughters, 55 new great-granddaughters, 84 new great-great-granddaughters, 35 new great-great-great-granddaughters, and the very first great-great-great-great-grand-daughter (Music to 16). Now we arrive at the seventeenth and final year of the problem. Most of you have probably already calculated what the population has to be now, but if you haven't, or if you want to check your work, you can always just count the notes as we play (Music from beginning to end).

(Musik zu 11). Im zwölften Jahr schreitet die Bevölkerungsexplosion von Narayanas Herde weiter voran und klettert von 88 auf einen Bestand von 129, was einen jährlichen Bevölkerungszuwachs von 46,59% gleichkommt (Musik zu 12). Im dreizehnten Jahr fällt die Rate leicht zurück auf 46,51% und die sechste Generation beginnt (Musik zu 13). Das vierzehnte Jahr beschert uns 88 neue Kälber, was die Herde von 189 auf 277 Mitglieder bringt (Musik zu 14). Im fünfzehnten Jahr zählt die Herde 406 Mitglieder. Darin eingeschlossen sind die erste Kuh, 15 Töchter, 78 Enkelinnen, 165 Ur-enkelinnen, 126 Ur-ur-enkelinnen und 21 Ur-ur-ur-enkelinnen (Musik zu 15). Im sechzehnten Jahr haben wir eine neue Tochter, 13 neue Enkelinnen, 55 neue Ur-enkelinnen, 84 neue Ur-ur-enkelinnen, 35 neue Ur-ur-ur-enkelinnen und die allererste Ur-ur-ur-ur-enkelin (Musik zu 16). Wir gelangen ins siebzehnte und letzte Jahr der Aufgabe. Die meisten unter Ihnen haben den Schlußbestand der Herde sicher schon berechnet. Sollten Sie noch nicht so weit sein, oder wenn Sie ihr Resultat kontrollieren möchten, brauchen sie bloß die Noten zu zählen, die wir spielen (Musik von Anfang bis Ende).

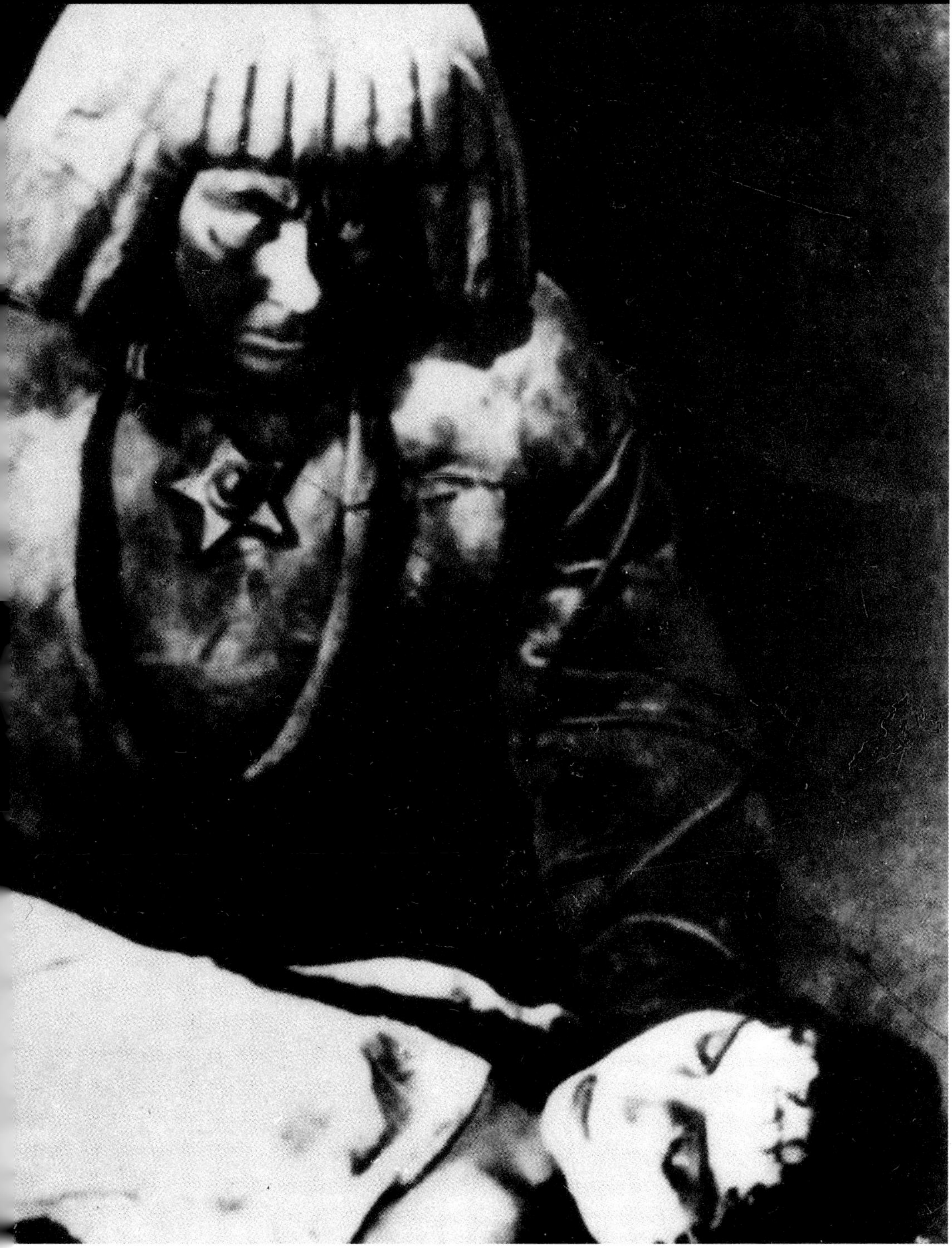

ES LEBT!
FILMREIHE „KÜNSTLICHES LEBEN"

„Die Fiktion, ihrer Etymologie zufolge, stellt Figuren her. *Fictio* und *figura* sind urverwandt mit dem Deutschen Wort Teig und dem griechischen Wort für Mauer, als jener teicos offenbar noch aus formbarem Lehm bestand." (F. Kittler)
Daß der Film gerade in seinen historischen Anfängen sich mythischer Stoffe um die Erschaffung künstlichen Lebens bedient, ist sicherlich kein Zufall: in gewisser Weise wird diese Erschaffung von der Filmtechnik selbst realisiert. Seine wirkungsvolle Lebendigkeit entfaltet der Film erst im Moment der Projektion, wenn die in den Einzelkadern festgehaltenen Wesen und Dinge zu neuem Leben erwachen, wenn sich Unbewegtes, sukzessive aneinandergereiht, plötzlich zu bewegen beginnt. Dieses Leben ist von seiner Grundkonzeption her automatisch, fiktiv – nicht organisch. Dennoch ist es mehr als die Summe seiner leblosen Teile. Die Wiederbelebung toter Materie (auf Zelluloid) scheint jene undenkbaren Kräfte wiederzuerwecken, die einstmals im antiken Schöpfungsmythos aufgehoben waren.
Die Geschichten von Homunculus, Alraune, dem Golem und Frankenstein gehören zu den ersten, die im Kino gezeigt werden. Bereits Georges Méliès, der bekanntlich das Kino in den Bereich des Fiktiven überführte, greift 1900 in seinem 2 Minuten Opus *Coppélia ou la Poupée animée* das Maschinen- und Puppenmenschenthema aus Hoffmanns Erzählungen auf. Und so wie diese Figuren erst auf der Leinwand zu *sichtbarem* Leben erwachen können, beleben sie ihrerseits das neue Medium mit ihren Geschichten.
Wie kann der Mensch Unbelebtes beleben? Golem, Alraune und Frankenstein sind mögliche Antworten auf diese Frage. Während die aus Lehm geformte Figur des Golems auf mythische Weise in einem einzigen Schöpfungsakt belebt wird, ist das Monster von Frankenstein Produkt wissenschaftlicher Experimente mit Leichenteilen. Alraune dagegen ist das erste gelungene Genexperiment.
Die künstlichen Menschen, seien sie Lehmfigur, Android, Clone oder Cyborg, bewegen sich entlang einer Grenze, die der Entsprechung am Bild des Menschen geschuldet ist; „nicht fühlen zu können wie der Mensch, dem er ähnlich sieht und dennoch Mensch sein, fühlen zu wollen, zu lieben und zu leiden (...)"[1].

IT'S ALIVE! / FILM SERIES "ARTIFICIAL LIFE"

"Fiction, according to its etymology, produces figures. Fictio and figura are originally related to the German word "Teig" (dough) and the Greek word for wall, as this teicos obviously still consisted of pliable clay" (F. Kittler).
The fact that the film, especially in its historic beginnings, used mythical material to create artificial life, is certainly not a matter of chance: in a certain manner this creation is realized by film technology itself. The film only unfolds its effective liveliness at the moment of projection when the beings and things in the individual cadres awaken to a new life, when the the unmoving, successively strung together, suddenly begins to move. This life, even in its basic concept, is automatic, fictitious—not organic. Nevertheless, it is more than the sum of its lifeless parts. The revival of dead matter (on celluloid) appears to re-awaken those unthinkable forces which were first taken up in the ancient myth of the universe.
The stories of Homunculus, Alraune, Golem and Frankenstein are amongst the first that were shown in the cinema. Even Georges Melies who, of course, took the cinema into the field of the fictious, took up, in 1900, the theme of the robot and puppet from Hoffman's tales, in his 2 minute production "Coppelia ou la Poupée animée". And just as these figures can only awaken to visible life on the screen, they, on their part, stimulate the new medium with with tales.
How can man give life to the non-living? Golem, Alraune and Frankenstein are possible answers to this question. Whereas the figure of Golem made from clay is animated in a mythical way in one single act of creation, the monster of Frankenstein is a product of scientific experiments performed with parts of corpses. On the other hand, Alraune is the first successful gene experiment.
Artificial people, either as clay figures, androids, clones or cyborgs, move along a dividing line, the equivalent of which is owed to the picture of mankind; "not being able to feel like a person, but resembling one and, nevertheless, to be a person wanting to feel, to love and to suffer (...).[1]
Artificial people only always return in the picture of "natural" people, ultimately acting as doubles and in doing so draw attention to the body of the person "as being a restricted product composed of organs that are organized around the divided framework of the skele-

ton"[2]. And paradoxically, the ability to produce people by people proves its own imperfection and interchangeability. In other words, just as the machine can only be produced only by man—not delivered, this does not mean that the ability to manufacture a machine is the redemption of the dream of Creation: it is not the new man who leaves the scientific laboratory, but incomplete creatures despairing at their imperfection. "The fundamental mistake of the writer and the actor: to make Golem human, to put him in a fate, contrary to his nature, that is completely strange to him. For, as regards Golem and feeling; creating him with the desire to be human means: to belittle him, to humiliate him and dismiss him. The Golem of the legends is a bound and humble angel, a deamon, an active divine force imprisoned in clay. The mourning for him is the mourning for the banished, for the enslaved, for the ruler as a servant".[3]
This effort made by the machine to be man, runs like a red thread throughout the horror and science fiction genre. The put-in-the-world feature of the figures is irreversible, with no escape, final. Melodramatic constellations result from this which, behind the technical machine-like model of mankind, can now actually let man realize, and since Melies, continue to come back. Golem, the monster of Frankenstein and the replicants in Blade Runner had to fail because the "immanent paradox of the newly modelled body is, at the same time, a philosophical machine to represent the realization of a myth"[4], leading to the conflict with their respective Makers.
MAX 404 from Aaron Lipstadt's film "Android", who, in his technological humanity, desires nothing more than to get to know the Chicago from old films, rebels against his Maker the moment he realizes that he is not being treated by him as a person, but as an exchangeable machine. Like his predecessors, he also recognizes him as being his persecutor, by whom he was created not for his own sake, but in order to satisfy the researcher's urge for science set loose.
The creatures are generally deprived of humanity as a humanistic value. In the case of the replicants—artificial slaves for working on colonialized planets—humanization is only driven to the point where it serves its more efficient functionalization. Those who try to escape this fate in Ridley Scott's "Blade Runner", not only revenge themselves, but also their ancestors. If one observes the artificial creatures of the genres (with their ramifications) it becomes noticeable that they overcome their physical uselessness. Their real tragedy remains the same, however, as long as there are (still) people.

Vrääth Öhner, Holger Reichert, Franz Marksteiner

NOTES

[1] Zweig, Arnold: Der Golem. In: Jörg Schweinitz (Publisher): Prolog vor dem Film. Leipzig 1992, P. 422.

Die künstlichen Menschen kehren immer nur im Bild des „natürlichen" Menschen wieder, fungieren letztlich als Doppelgänger und verweisen dadurch auf den Körper des Menschen „als eines begrenzten, aus Organen zusammengesetzten und um das gegliederte Gerüst des Skeletts herum organisierten Produkts"[2]. Und paradoxerweise beweist die Herstellbarkeit des Menschen durch den Menschen so dessen eigene Unvollkommenheit und Austauschbarkeit. Anders gesagt, so wie die Maschine vom Menschen nur hergestellt, nicht erlöst werden kann, erweist sich die Herstellbarkeit der Maschine nicht als Einlösung des Schöpfungstraums: nicht der neue Mensch entsteigt den Labors der Wissenschaft, sondern unfertige, an ihrer Unvollkommenheit verzweifelnde Kreaturen. „Grundirrtum des Dichters und des Schauspielers: den Golem zu vermenschlichen, ihn wider sein eigenes Wesen in ein Geschick zu stellen, das ihm völlig fremd ist. Denn den Golem auf Gefühl hin; auf Sehnsucht Mensch zu sein hin gestalten, heißt: ihn verkleinern, erniedrigen und aufheben. Der Golem der Legende ist ein gefesselter und niederer Engel, ein Dämon, eine aktive göttliche Kraft, eingesperrt in Lehm. Die Trauer, die um ihn ist, ist die Trauer des Verbannten, des Geknechteten, des Herrschers als Knecht."[3]
Wie ein roter Faden zieht sich dieses Bemühen der Maschine, Mensch zu sein, durch das Horror und Science Fiction-Genre. Das In-die-Welt-gestellt-Sein der Figuren ist irreversibel, ohne Ausweg, endgültig. Daraus erwachsen melodramatische Konstellationen, die hinter dem technischen, maschinenhaften Modell des Menschen nun tatsächlich den Menschen erkennen lassen und die seit Méliès immer wieder zurückkehren. Der Golem, das Monster von Frankenstein, und die Replikanten in Blade Runner müssen scheitern, weil das "dem neumodellierten Körper immanente Paradox, gleichzeitig eine philosophische Maschine und die Verwirklichung eines Mythos darzustellen"[4], zum Konflikt mit ihren jeweiligen Schöpfern führt. MAX 404 aus Aaron Lipstadts Film *Android*, dem in seiner technologischen Menschlichkeit nichts sehnlicher ist, als das aus alten Filmen bekannte Chicago kennenzulernen, lehnt sich in dem Moment gegen seinen Schöpfer auf, als er erkennen muß, daß er von diesem nicht als Mensch sondern als austauschbare Maschine behandelt wird. Wie schon seine Vorgänger erkennt auch er in ihm seinen Peiniger, von dem er nicht um seiner selbst willen erschaffen wurde, sondern um den Forscherdrang der entfesselten Wissenschaft zu befriedigen.
Menschlichkeit als humanistischer Wert wird den Kreaturen zumeist auch vorenthalten. Bei den Replikanten, künstlichen Sklaven für den Arbeitseinsatz auf kolonialisierten Pla-

neten, wird die Vermenschlichung nur soweit vorangetrieben, als sie deren effizienteren Funktionalisierung dient. Die, die in Ridley Scotts *Blade Runner* diesem Schicksal zu entgehen versuchen, rächen dabei nicht nur sich selbst, sondern auch ihre Ahnen.

Beobachtet man die künstlichen Kreaturen auf ihrem Weg durch die Filmgeschichte und die Geschichte der Genres (mit ihren Verzweigungen), so fällt auf, daß sie ihre körperliche Hinfälligkeit überwinden. Ihre eigentliche Tragik aber bleibt die gleiche, so lange es (noch) Menschen gibt.

Vrääth Öhner, Holger Reichert, Franz Marksteiner

ANMERKUNGEN

[1] Zweig, Arnold: Der Golem. In: Jörg Schweinitz (Publisher): Prolog vor dem Film. Leipzig 1992, S. 422.

[2] Tibon-Cornillot, Michel: Die transfigurativen Körper. In: Dietmar Kamper, Christoph Wulf (Publisher): Die Wiederkehr des Körpers. Frankfurt/M. 1982, S. 157

[3] Zweig, wie oben, S. 423

[4] Tibon Cornillot, wie oben, S. 153f

[2] Tibon-Cornillot, Michel: Die transfigurativen Körper. In: Dietmar Kamper, Christoph Wulf (Publisher): Die Wiederkehr des Körpers. Frankfurt/M. 1982, P. 157

[3] Zweig, as above, P. 423

[4] Tibon Cornillot, as above, P. 153f

AUSWAHL FÜR DIE FILMREIHE

ALRAUNE

Deutschland 1927, R: Henrik Galeen, P: Ama, V: offen, L: ca. 98 min, D: Brigitte Helm, Paul Wegener, Ivan Petrovich, Mia Pankau u.a.

Alraune ist das Produkt der künstlichen Befruchtung einer Dirne mit dem Sperma eines Lustmörders, das diesem im Augenblick seiner Hinrichtung abgenommen wurde.

ANDROID / DER ANDROID

USA 1982, R: Aaron Lipstadt, P: New World Pictures / Android, V: Warner-Columbia, L: ca. 80 min, D: Klaus Kinski, Don Opper, Norbert Weiser, Kendra Kirchner, Crofton Hardester, Brie Howard u.a.

Der Android Max 404 lebt zusammen mit dem Wissenschaftler Dr. Daniel auf einer verlassenen Raumstation und sehnt sich nach einem Leben auf der Erde, die er nur aus alten Filmen kennt.

BLADE RUNNER (DIRECTOR'S CUT)

USA 1982, R: Ridley Scott, P: Blade Runner Partnership, V: Warner – Columbia, D: Harrison Ford, Rutger Hauer, Sean Young, Daryl Hannah, Edward James Olmos u.a.

L.A. 2019. Die Geschichte eines Spezialdetektivs, eines Blade Runners, der vier künstliche Menschen ausfindig und unschädlich machen soll.

THE BRIDE OF FRANKENSTEIN / FRANKENSTEINS BRAUT

USA 1935, R: James Whale, P: Universal, V: offen, L: ca. 70 min, D: Boris Karloff, Colin Clive, Valery Hobson, Elsa Lanchester u.a.
Dr. Praetorius, der bereits künstliche Menschen in der Größe von Marmeladengläsern geschaffen hat, versucht Frankenstein davon zu überzeugen, daß nur ein entsprechendes weibliches Wesen sein Monstrum bändigen könne.

THE BRIDE OF RE-ANIMATOR

USA 1989, R: Brian Yuzna, V: New Vision, L: ca. 92 min, D: Jeffrey Combs, Ruth Abbott, Claude Earl Jones, u.a.
Mit seinem Kollegen Cain organisiert Herbert West Extremitäten aus dem Krankenhaus und belebt sie mit seinem Elixier. Ziel des Experiments ist die Wiederbelebung einer Frau.

EDWARD SCISSORHANDS / EDWARD MIT DEN SCHERENHÄNDEN

USA 1991, R: Tim Burton, D: Vincent Price, Johnny Depp, Wynona Ryder u.a. Moderne Märchenversion des Frankensteinthemas.

FRANKENSTEIN – THE MAN WHO MADE A MONSTER / FRANKENSTEIN

USA 1931, R: James Whale, PV: Universal, L: ca. 71 min, D: Boris Karloff, Colin Clive, Mae Clarke, John Boles u.a.
Der junge Wissenschaftler Herbert von Frankenstein ist besessen von der Idee, aus toter Materie ein lebendes Wesen zu schaffen.

DER GOLEM, WIE ER IN DIE WELT KAM

Deutschland 1920, R: Paul Wegener, Carl Boese, P: Ufa (Pagu), L: ca. 87 min, D: Paul Wegener, Albert Steinrück, Lyda Salmonova, Ernst Deutsch u.a.
16. Jahrhundert: Rabbi Loew, der geistliche Führer der jüdischen Gemeinschaft in Prag haucht einer Lehmstatue Leben ein.

HARDWARE / M.A.R.K. 13

England 1990, R: Richard Stanley, P: Wicked Films / Palace Pictures, V: Metropol, L: ca. 93 min, D: Dylan McDermott, Stacey Travis, John Lynch, William Hootkins u.a.
Ein in der „Zone“ gefundener Kopf eines Cyborgs erwacht,

mit anderen Teilen zusammengeschweißt, zu neuem Killer-Leben. Postatomarer Kultfilm.

ISLAND OF LOST SOULS / INSEL DER VERLORENEN SEELEN

USA 1933, R: Erle C. Kenton, P: Paramount, L: ca. 70 min, D: Charles Laughton, Richard Arlen, Bela Lugosi, Leila Hyams u.a.

Ein schiffbrüchiger Seefahrer wird an den Strand einer geheimnisvollen Insel gespült und trifft dort auf den Wissenschaftler Moreau, der mit der Evolution spielt und aus Tieren Menschen machen will.

DIE NACKTE UND DER SATAN

BRD 1959, R: Victor Trivas, P: Rapid, V: Prisma, L: ca. 96 min, D: Horst Frank, Michel Simon, Paul Dahlke, Karin Kernke, Christiane Maybach

Der begnadete Wissenschaftler Abel kann einzelne menschliche Gliedmaßen isoliert voneinander am Leben erhalten.

„Von blutiger Leinwand herab trieft erstes deutsches Nachkriegsgrauen!"

(Jürgen Nowak, SOL)

PARTS: THE CLONUS HORROR / SAAT DES WAHNSINNS – THE CLONUS HORROR

USA 1979, R: Robert S. Fiveson, P: Group I, V: IMV, L: ca. 87 min, D: Timothy Donnelly, Dick Sargent, David Hooks, Keenan Wynn, Peter Graves u.a.

In einem geheimnisvollen Institut werden Clones von Politikern und Wissenschaftern hergestellt, die im Bedarfsfall als Organspender dienen.

RE-ANIMATOR / RE-ANIMATOR – DER TOD IST ERST DER ANFANG

USA 1985, R: Stuart Gordon, P: Empire Pic. / Re-Animated Prod. / Brian Yuzna Prod., V: Vestron (Video), L: ca. 95 min, D: Jeffrey Combs, Ruth Abbott, Barbara Crampton, David Gale u.a.

Medizinstudent Herbert West hat ein Serum entwickelt, das Tote wiederbelebt.

SECONDS / DER MANN, DER ZWEIMAL LEBTE

USA 1966, R: John Frankenheimer, P: Paramount, V: Paramount, L: ca. 106 min, D: Rock Hudson, Salome Jens, John Randolph, Will Geer, Jeff Corey u.a.

Eine Geheimorganisation stattet Menschen mit einer neuen Identität, einem neuen Aussehen und einer perfekten Vergangenheit aus.

THE STEPFORD WIVES / DIE FRAUEN VON STEPFORD

USA 1975, R: Bryan Forbes, P: Palomar Pictures / Columbia, V: offen, L: ca. 110 min, D: Catherine Ross, Paula Prentiss, Peter Masterson u.a.
Alle Männer von Stepford ersetzen ihre Frauen durch gleich aussehende Roboter, die sich ihren Wünschen bedingungslos unterordnen.

TETSUO II / THE BODY HAMMER

Japan 1991, R: Shinya Tsukmoto, P: Kajyu Theater / Toshiba EMI, V: Tetsuo II Head Office, L: ca. 83 min, D: Tomoroh Taguchi, Nobo Nanaoka, Shinya Tsukmoto u.a.
Aus Zorn über die Entführung seines Sohnes mutiert Taniguchi Tomoo zu einer tödlichen Cyber-Waffe.

AUSSTELLUNGSARCHITEKTUR

ENVIRONMENTAL CONSTRUCTIONS/ BRUNO UND PETER SANDBICHLER

GENETISCHE KUNST

EINE KLEINE GENEALOGIE DES KÜNSTLICHEN LEBENS

AYRE WACHSMUTH

STEREOLITHOGRAFISCHE MODELLE[1] + 3-D-ANIMATIONEN.

Im Gegensatz zu den uns vom Museum her bekannten naturwissenschaftlichen Modellen, die als Manifestation des Fortschritts und symbolischer Beweis für einen hohen Wissensstand betrachtet werden können, entsteht hier eine andere Art Modell. Es sollen stereolithografische Modelle erzeugt werden, die Ideen und Visionen (die das künstliche-Leben-betreffen) aus der Literatur, dem Film und der Wissenschaft angreifen und zeigen. Dabei soll es nicht darauf ankommen, ob sie nun der Realität oder einer Fiktion entsprechen.

Diese Ideen und Beispiele reichen von Arthur Rimbauds Vision des Menschen der Zukunft bis zu „Blutmusik" von Greg Bear: Er läßt in diesem Buch die Hauptfigur mit inteligenten Lymphozyten injezieren, die den Körper verändern. Diese Veränderung ist mitunter eine Veränderung der Wirbelsäule, die zu einer Buckminster Fuller artigen Konstruktion wird. C._D. Simaks „CITY": 1952 in den USA erschienen ist die Geschichte von Menschen und Hunden in der Zukunft. Ein wichtiges Detail ist, daß der Mensch dem Hund, „seinem besten Freund", das Sprechen beibringt, indem er durch operative Eingriffe im Kehlkopf des Hundes die Stimmbänder verändert. Diese Fähigkeit zu sprechen wird weiteren Generationen genetisch vererbt.

Es kommen ein „Kink", fraktale Wachstumsmodelle, eine Frau die im Wassertropfen lebt, eine Schlange mit Seriennummer und andere Dinge vor. Scheinbar in eine konventionelle muscale Präsentationsform verpackt, stehen diese Modelle aber nicht für das schon Bewiesene und Gültige, sondern für das Offene, noch Machbare an sich. Mit anderen Worten: „Only when we are able to view *life-as-we-know-it* in the larger context of *life-as-it-could-be* will well we realy understand the nature of the beast".[2]

Die stereolithografischen Modelle sind mit CAD und 3-D Midelling (ALIAS) geometrisch konstruiert und entworfen und

A BRIEF GENEALOGY OF ARTIFICIAL LIFE
AYRE WACHSMUTH

STEREO-LITHOGRAPHIC MODELS + *3-D ANIMATIONS.*[1]

Unlike the natural science models we know from the museum, which can be seen as manifestations of progress and symbolic evidence of a high level of knowledge, a different kind of model is taking shape here. Stereo-lithographic models are to be created which draw on, and show, ideas and visions (concerning Artificial Life) taken from literature, films, and science, regardless of whether they conform to reality or fiction.

These ideas and examples range from Arthur Rimbaud's vision of man in the future to "Blood Music" by Greg Bear. The main character in this book is injected with body-changing, intelligent lymphocytes. This change is sometimes a change of the spinal column, which becomes a construction reminiscent of Buckminster Fuller. C.D. Simak's "CITY" appeared in the USA in 1952 and is a story of people and dogs in the future. An important detail is that man teaches "his best friend", the dog, to talk. This is achieved through operative surgery on the dog's larynx to change the vocal cords. This ability to talk is then genetically passed on to further generations.

A "kink", fractal growth models, a woman living in a drop of water, a snake with a serial number, and other things crop up. Apparently packaged in a conventional museum-like form of presentation, these models do not stand for the already proven and valid, but for what is inherently open and "doable". In other words: "Only when we are able to view *life-as-we-know-it* in the larger context of *life-as-it-could-be* will we really understand the nature of the beast".[2]

The stereo-lithographic models are geometrically constructed and designed using CAD and 3-D modelling (ALIAS) and then synthetically constructed with the aid of polymer chemistry. These beginnings of material and thematic association (synthesis) of individual parts, into a new whole (like other processes for the production of organic or inorganic compounds), can be symbolically represented here as a con-

nection or bridge between art and science. As for the future, it could be asserted that: "Nature will be known and remade through technique and will finally become artificial, just as culture becomes natural".[3]
In other words: Cross Culture and Cross Nature.

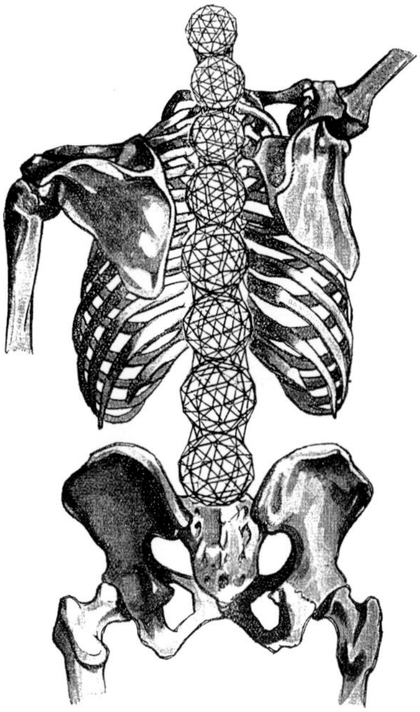

werden dann mit Hilfe der Polymerchemie synthetisch zusammengestellt. Dieser Ansatz der Verknüpfung (Synthese) von Einzelteilen, sowohl materiell wie auch thematisch zu einem neuen Ganzen (wie bei anderen Verfahren zur Herstellung von organischen und anorganischen Verbindungen), läßt sich hier als eine Verbindung bzw. Durchquerung von Kunst zu Wissenschaft modellhaft versinnbildlichen. Für die Zukunft könnte gelten: „Nature will be known and remade through technique and will finally become artificial, just as culture becomes natural".[3]
Also: Cross Culture and Cross Nature.

ANMERKUNGEN

[1] Sterolithografie: Ein Verfahren zur Erzeugung dreidimensionaler Musterteile und Modelle mit Lasertechnik und CAM/CAD aus lichthärtendem Kunststoff.
[2] Christopher G. Langton: Artificial life, volume VI, Santa Fe Institute studies in the sciences of complexity, 1987.
[3] Paul Rabinow: Artificiality and Enlightment: From Sociobiologiy to Biosociality, Zone Band 6/Incorporations 1992 N. Y.

1. BIOGENETISCHE KUNST

ZEITPFLANZEN – EINE ELEKTRO-CHEMISCHE PROZESSINSTALLATION

TASSILO BLITTERSDORFF

„Kein Blatt ist einem anderen ident, doch haben alle Blätter einer Pflanzengattung gewisse Charakteristiken, die sie als zu dieser Gattung gehörig ausweisen. Der Spielraum für Variationsmöglichkeiten ist bei der Bildung galvanischer Metallablagerungen ungleich größer, ...“ (Tassilo Blittersdorff)
Seit mehreren Jahren beschäftigt sich Tassilo Blittersdorff mit dem künstlerischen „Spielraum“ von galvanischen Metallablagerungen: Er installiert Bildwerdungsprozesse als in sich geschlossene Installationssysteme, die in jedem Moment Entstehung produzieren. Der initierte Prozeß der Metallablagerungen läßt sich nur sehr beschränkt steuern – das entstehende Bildprodukt verweist sowohl auf vorbekanntes „Bild“ordnungswissen wie auf Chaos.
„Wie bereits mehrfach besprochen gibt es in unserem Universum nichts, was nicht irgendwo zwischen Ordnung und Chaos angesiedelt wäre.“[1]
Die zunächst frappante Ähnlichkeit zum Erscheinungsbild der Wachstumsprozesse von Pflanzenstrukturen läßt eine optische Schleife von den – betont funktional gestalteten – chemisch-technisch-naturwissenschaftlichen (unbelebten) Grundbedingungen des Prozesses zu einer bio-(also lebens-)logischen Wirklichkeit entstehen: Dieser organische Bezug auf einer visuellen Zuordnungsebene stellt sich jedoch in prägnanten Kontrast zu den ausschließlich anorganischen Ingredienzien des installativen Aufbaues.
„Kunst: eine andere Natur, auch geheimnisvoll, aber verständlicher; denn sie entspringt aus dem Verstande.“[2]
Tassilo Blittersdorffs Installation in ihrer Reduktion auf eine apparative Genese rückt deutlich von in diesem Sinne formulierten erkenntnisgebenden Gleichungen ab – Kunst ist hier *nicht* das „Kompliment der Natur“ (Novalis), sondern eine Annäherung an einen Blick nach außen in einen vom Menschlichen abgerückten Prozeßbereich. Bei aller durch die menschliche Subjektivität eingetrübten Relativität dieses Blicks existiert hier dieses Andere als bewußt erkannte Bezugsgröße – sei es auch nur in einem sehr kleinen Detailausschnitt – jenseits eines „allgemein Humanen“ mit seinem De-

TIME PLANTS
TASSILO BLITTERSDORF

"No two leaves are alike, yet all leaves of the same genus have certain characteristics which identify them as belonging to this genus. The latitude for possible variation in the forming of galvanic metal deposits is much larger ..." (Tassilo Blittersdorff)
For years Tassilo Blittersdorff has been working with the artistic "latitude" of galvanic metal deposits: He installs image creation processes as self-enclosed installation systems which produce creation every moment. Once started, the metal depositing process can only be controlled in a very limited way. The emergent image product makes reference to previously known knowledge of "image" as well as to chaos.[1]
"As has already been said repeatedly, there is nothing in our universe that is not located somewhere between order and chaos".
The at first striking similarity with the appearance of growth processes of plant structures lets an optical loop from the—very functionally designed—chemical—technological scientific (inorganic) basic conditions of the process become a biological (and therefore organic) reality: this organic reference to a visual classification level is however in stark contrast to the exclusively inorganic ingredients of the installation structure.
"Art, another nature, also mysterious but more comprehensible, for it springs from human consciousness".[2] Tassilo Blittersdorff's installation in its reduction of a technical exactness is clearly removed from instructive equations expressed in this manner. Here art is <u>not</u> the "compliment to nature" (Novalis) but an approach to an outward view in an area of processes distanced from humanity. With all the relativity of this viewpoint clouded over by human subjectivity, a previously not consciously recognised capacity for linkage—even if it is only in a very small extract beyond the "generally humane" with its claim to define the appearance of growth in all its forms.
"Freedom lies here, as so often, in the detail; where it is easier to deviate from the standardising norms: the ramifications, the variations in shape and colour are the "self-representations" of the galvanic "plantlets", which grow in their "hollow chamber plate greenhouse", in the guaranteed absence of gene

finitionsanspruch auf jede Erscheinungsform von Wachstum.

„Die Freiheit liegt hier wie so oft im Detail, das von den normierenden Vorgaben leichter abweichen kann: Die Verästelungen, die Varianten in Form und Farbe sind die ‚Selbstdarstellungen' der galvanischen ‚Pflänzchen', die in ihren ‚Hohlkammerplattengewächshaus' garantiert ohne manipuliertes Genmaterial entstehen." (T. Blittersdorff)

Die galvanische Installation des Künstler verweist in diesem Sinne aber auch auf eine analytische Position jenseits der Beschränkung auf eine Suche nach Entsprechungen:

„Kunst ist nicht, wie der Idealismus glauben machen wollte, Natur, aber will einlösen, was Natur verspricht."[3]

Blittersdorffs Installation verweigert sich auch diesem Ansatz, sie will letztlich kein Versprechen einlösen, weder im Hinblick auf menschliche Assoziationsgewohnheiten – vgl. etwa die Prägnanz der rein optischen Gleichung Pflanzenwachstum – galvanisches Wachstum – noch auf die traditionell naturwissenschaftliche Technik des Messens. Beide Bereiche werden im Verlauf des vom Künstler initierten Wachstumsprozesses schließlich immer deutlicher in ihrer ironischen Zitatfunktion erkennbar, da sie in jedem Fall eine rein tautologische Situation aufzeigen – sowohl beim meßtechnischen Zugang wie auch bei der „stilkritischen" Gleichsetzung von Bildern.

Die Redundanz dieser Informationen verweist auf einen Endpunkt, der jedoch wiederum eine neue Aufmerksamkeit auf die einzelnen Faktoren selbst richtet. Auch hier – wie bei der Installierung der galavanischen Wachstumsvoraussetzungen – fungiert der Künstler als Katalysator, der einen Prozeß in Gang bringt ohne jedoch selbst daran teilzunehmen:

Das Wachstum bei seinen galvanischen Arbeiten präsentiert sich als energetischer Austausch, als Transformation, auch als Aufbau eines Form-und-Farbe-Dialoges. Sie bauen auf drei entscheidende Parameter auf, die jeweils einen seriellen Ablauf bedingen: Die Zeit als Dauer des Wachstumsprozesses, die Distanz – der Abstand zwischen den beiden Elektroden bestimmt die Geschwindigkeit des Wachstums und die Gestaltungsvarianten – und die vorhandene und aufgeteilte Energiemenge.

Die Installation „Zeitpflanzen" formuliert einen speziellen Bezug zu erstgenannten Parameter – sie baut gleichsam ein Kalendarium einer fiktiven Botanik auf: Nicht als virtuelle Parallelschöpfung, sondern als skeptisch-ironische Gestaltung einer lokal definierten Modellsituation des Wachstums, die sich einer möglichst modellunabhängigen Auseinandersetzung mit einem existierenden Außen annähert.

manipulated material." (T. Blittersdorff)

The artist's galvanic installation makes reference, in this sense as well as from an analytical position beyond limitation, to a search for counterparts.

"Art is not nature, as idealism would have us believe, but it wants to redeem the promises of nature."[3]

Blittersdorff's installation denies itself this approach too. It does not want to redeem any promise, whether with regard to human associative habits, for example the conciseness of the purely optical equation of plant growth—galvanic growth, or the traditional scientific technique of measurement. Through the growth processes initiated by th artist, the ironic quoting function of both of these areas is becoming clearly recognisable, because in any case they reveal a tautological situation, whether in scientific measurement or the "stylistically critical" equating of pictures.

The redundancy of this information indicates an end point, which however in turn draws more attention to the individual factors. Here too, as with the installation of the galvanic growth conditions, the artist functions as a catalyst who sets a process in motion without actually taking part in it. The growth in his galvanic works presents itself as an energetic exchange, as a transformation and construction of a dialogue of shape and colour. They build on three decisive parameters, each of which requires serial execution. Time as the duration of the growth processes, distance as the interval between the electrodes determines the speed of growth and design variants, and the amount of available energy.

The installation "Time Plants" formulates a special relationship between parameters, and at the same time introduces a calendar for fictitious botany: not as a virtual parallel creation but rather as a sceptical—ironic design of a locally defined model growth situation, moving towards a role where it is as independent of the model as possible and deals with a real, extant outside world.

"Mr ... would like to play fiddlesticks with spaghetti, but it won't work" (Oswald Wiener)[4]

Peter Assmann

NOTES

[1] Binnig, Gerd: Aus dem Nichts. Über die Kreativität von Natur und Mensch, München 1989. P. 172

[2] Goethe, Johann Wolfgang: Berliner Ausgabe. Hrs. S. Seidel. Berlin–Weimar 1972, Bd. XVIII, P. 637

[3] Adorno, Theodor W.: Gesammelte Schriften. Bd. VII, Frankfurt/Main 1970, P. 103

[4] Schmatz, Ferdinand: Sinn und Sinne, Wien 1992, P. 74

„Der Herr … möchte mit Spaghetti Mikado spielen, das geht aber nicht.“ (Oswald Wiener)[4]

Peter Assmann

ANMERKUNGEN

[1] Binnig, Gerd: Aus dem Nichts. Über die Kreativität von Natur und Mensch, München 1989. S. 172

[2] Goethe, Johann Wolfgang: Berliner Ausgabe. Hrs. S. Seidel. Berlin–Weimar 1972, Bd. XVIII, S. 637

[3] Adorno, Theodor W.: Gesammelte Schriften. Bd. VII, Frankfurt/Main 1970, S. 103

[4] Schmatz, Ferdinand: Sinn und Sinne, Wien 1992, S. 74

R
r
R
RR
Rr
r
rR
rr

STANISLAW DIVIS

Courtesy Galerie MXM, Prag

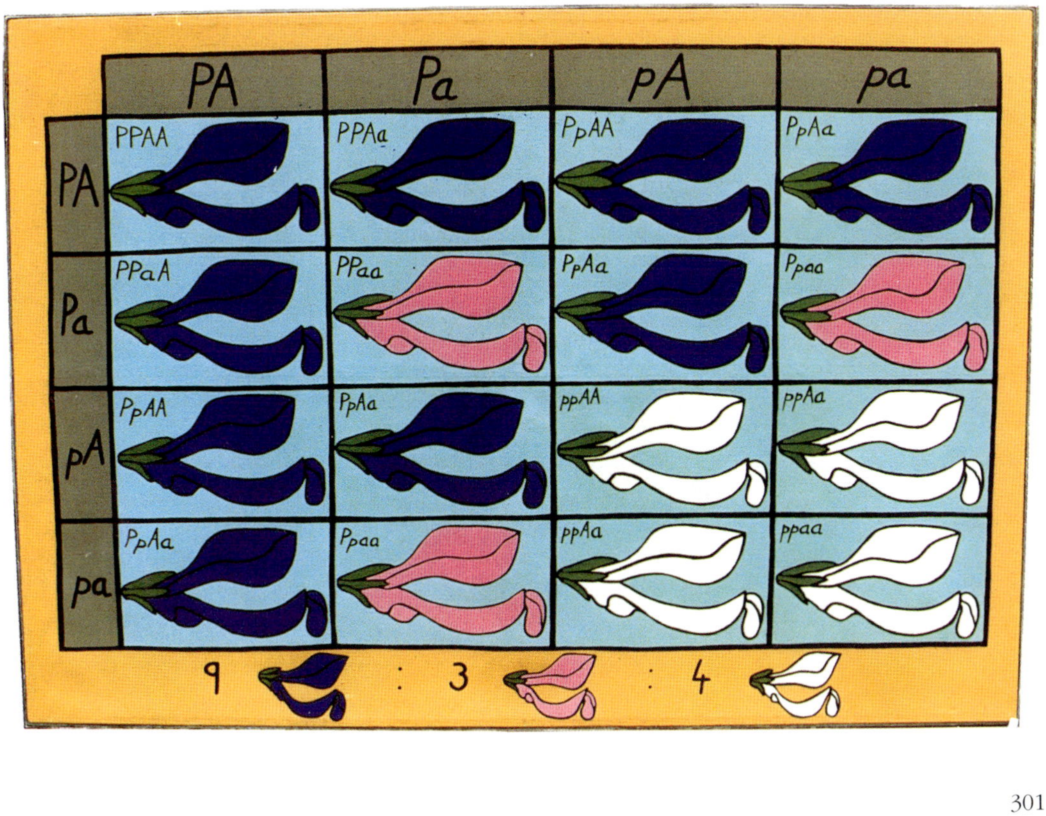

SPURENAPPARAT

THOMAS FEUERSTEIN / KLAUS STRICKNER

ANMERKUNGEN ZU EINER KUNST IM APPARATESTADIUM – ODER VON DER SEMANTISCHEN KORRESPONDENZ ZUR STRUKTURELLEN KONTINGENZ

„Ziehen wir also den kühnen Schluß, daß der Mensch eine Maschine ist und daß es im ganzen Weltall nur eine Substanz gibt, die freilich verschieden modifiziert ist."
J.O.
La Mettrie, 1747

Angefangen bei Aristoteles bis zu aktuellen Strömungen der Autopoiesis fasziniert der Gegensatz zwischen lebenden Systemen, die Autonomie erkennen lassen, und allen übrigen natürlichen Dingen und künstlichen Artefakten. Obwohl bei Aristoteles das künstliche Bild (eikòn technetè) und das natürliche Bild (eikòn physikè) strukturgleich sind, zeichnen sich die Naturdinge, nämlich „die Geschöpfe und deren Teile, die Pflanzen und die einfachen Körper, Erde und Feuer und Luft und Wasser" (Phys. 192b) gegenüber den Artefakten dadurch aus, daß sie den „Ursprung für Ruhe und Bewegung" (ebd.) in sich selbst haben. Technik und auch bildende Kunst sind demnach an das klassische Programm von imitatio und perfectio bestimmter Wirkungen gebunden, können aber die letzte Wirkursache nicht in sich tragen. Mit Anbruch der Neuzeit beginnt sich die Perspektivierung „künstlicher Bilder" auf „natürliche Vor-Bilder" zu verkehren. Komplexe Ganzheiten werden zunehmend im Sinne eines wissenschaftlichen Objektivismus auf ein Maschinenbild projiziert. Die Maschine fand demgemäß lange vor der industriellen Revolution ihre symbolische Antizipation ihrer späteren realen Herrschaft, was sich bekanntlich in den Diskursen des 16., 17. oder 18. Jahrhundert deutlich ablesen läßt. Etwa Vasari zog metaphernhaft die Maschine zur Beschreibung Brunelleschis Kuppelbau des Florentiner Domes heran, indem er diesen als eine „erstaunliche Maschine" würdigte.

Von Descartes über Leibniz, La Mettrie oder mit Einschränkungen auch Kant ließe sich ein historische Bogen der Installierung eines Maschinenbildes für Lebewesen nach-

TRACE APPARATUS
THOMAS FEUERSTEIN

REMARKS ON AN ART AT THE APPARATUS STAGE, OR, FROM SEMANTIC CORRESPONDENCE TO STRUCTURAL CONTINGENCY

"If we draw the cool conclusion that man is a machine and that in the entire universe there is only one substance which, of course, is modified differently"
J. O. La Mettrie, 1747

Starting with Aristoteles and extending to the current trends of autopoiesis, the contrast between living systems which permit the recognition of autonomy and all other natural things and artificial artefacts, has always been fascinating. Although in the case of Aristoteles, the artificial picture (eikon technete) and the natural picture (eikon physike) are structurally the same, natural things—that is "creatures and their parts, plants and the simple bodies, earth and fire and air and water" (Phys. 192b) are distinguished by the fact that they have the "origin for peace and movement" within themselves (ditto). Technology as well as graphic art is, in this respect, bound to the classical programme of imitatio and perfectio of certain consequences, but cannot bear the last effective cause within themselves. With the dawn of modern times, the perspectivization of "artificial pictures" onto "natural pre-pictures" begins to reverse. Complex entireties are being increasigly projected on a machine picture for the purposes of scientific objectivism. In accordance with this, even long before the Industrial Revolution, the machine found the symbolic anticipation of its later real dominance, which as we know, can be clearly discerned from the discourses of the 16th, 17th or 18th centuries. For example, Vasari used the machine like a metaphor to describe Brunelleschi's domed structure of the Florence Cathedral by praising this as being an "astonishing machine".

From Descartes to Leibnitz, La Mettrie or even, with reservations, Kant, a historical circle for the installation of a machine picture for living beings can be retraced, whereby a rationalistic mechanical term became the ontological guarantor for the recognizability of the world. Descarte's controversial declaration that organisms function like automatons or machines, meant a naturalization of mechanics and a mechanization of nature. "Autonomous systems are mechanistic (dynamic) systems which are specified by their organization", says Francisco Varela (1987, P. 121), whereby the historical circle traced for an installation of a machine picture for living beings in the modified form of autopoietic machine models could be formed.

"Every work, both of nature as well as art, is a system"

Bischof Joseph Butler, 1729

Denis Diderot's frequently quoted example of a fictitious machine which produces pictures like Raffael, expresses an old paradox that exists in the incompatibility of clearly determined fabrication rules with the terms genius and originality, when producing works of art. Neither the machine nor the works which produced such in line with the necessary laws, could have been termed as being "beautiful", according to Diderot. Beauty only arises in art with a sharp differentiation to nature, which is nothing more than a heap of infinitely differently ordered moelcules: "Multiply these imitation machines (=machines Raffeal, note by the author) anywhere and everywhere. Let pictures emerge in nature like plants . . . ; and tell me what has become of your admiration. " (quote acc. Link-Heer,U. , 1986, P. 106). And at a place shortly before, Diderot who is walking in the countryside in dialogue with an abbe writes: "If I had a box of dice here, and if I were to overturn this box, and if they would all turn around at the same point, would this phenomenon be astonishing?—Very. And if all the dice had been prepared, would this phenomenon still astound you?—No (ditto). This passage becomes more topical when it is transported into the context of the calculating machine. "Date is also called dice" writes Friedrich Kittler, "and just as the former aesthetic or ordered cosmos of the philosophers has become a great dice game under technical conditions, data processing can still mess up its sampling values according to all the games rules for mathematical operations, until reality is actually no longer necessary. "(1989, P. 69). Consequently, it is no longer only everything that is necessary, but also everything that is possible, that is the case. The dichotomy between the "creatio ex nihilo" and Vasari's fabrication, between the artistic intention and the role of contingency in artistic production, as in the case of Diderot, or between Makers of the work and Making of the stuff, as with Heidegger, disintegrates. The work is no longer the dead mirror which directs nature, posing as realism or naturalism in a timeless immobility and represents apparent reality. It forms its own autonomous reality with its own specific contingency. Perhaps comparable with Eric Drexler's "engines of creations", which imply molecular computers set up from complex structures which can assemble themselves and which can reproduce; art is breaking away from the traditional work of art and its semantic correspondence and is developing independent structural contingencies.

With the exchange of external reference for self reference, from a historical point of view, representation and imitation assumptions in the picture were discarded. Besides the elimination of

zeichnen, bei der ein rationalistischer Maschinenbegriff zum ontologischen Garanten für die Erkennbarkeit der Welt wurde. Descartes umstrittene Behauptung, daß Organismen in der Art von Automaten oder Maschinen funktionieren, bedeutete eine Naturalisierung der Mechanik und eine Mechanisierung der Natur. „Autonome Systeme sind mechanistische (dynamische) Systeme, die durch ihre Organisation bestimmt sind", sagt Francisco Varela (1987, S. 121), womit man den angerissenen historischen Bogen einer Installierung eines Maschinenbildes für Lebewesen, in modifizierter Form autopoietischer Maschinenmodelle, schließen könnte.

„Jedes Werk sowohl der Natur wie auch der Kunst ist ein System."

Bischof Joseph Butler, 1729

Denis Diderot oft zitiertes Beispiel einer fiktiven Maschine, die Bilder wie Raffael produziere, beinhaltet ein altes Paradox, das in der Unvereinbarkeit klar determinierter Fabrikationsregeln mit den Begriffen Genialität und Originalität bei der Herstellung von Kunstwerken besteht. Weder die Maschine noch die Werke, die eine solche gemäß notwendigen Gesetzen hervorbrächte, wären nach Diderot als „schön" zu bezeichnen. Schönheit erwachse in der Kunst erst durch eine scharfe Ausdifferenzierung gegenüber der Natur, die nichts als ein Haufen unendlich verschieden geordneter Moleküle sei: „Multiplizieren Sie diese Nachahmungsmaschinen (=Maschinen Raffael, Anm. d. Verf.) allüberall. Lassen Sie die Bilder in der Natur entstehen wie die Pflanzen...; und sagen Sie mir, was aus Eurer Bewunderung würde." (zit.n. Link-Heer, U., 1986, S. 106) Und an einer Stelle kurz davor schreibt Diderot, der in der Landschaft wandelnd sich mit einem Abbé im Dialog befindet: „Wenn ich hier einen Becher Würfel hätte, ich diesen Becher umwerfen würde, und sie sich alle auf den gleichen Punkt herumdrehen würden, würde dieses Phänomen sehr erstaunen? – Sehr. Und wenn alle Würfel präpariert wären, würde das Phänomen Sie dann immer noch erstaunen? – Nein." (ebd.) Aktualität gewinnt diese Passage, transponiert man sie in den Kontext der Rechenmaschine. „Datum heißt auch Würfel" schreibt Friedrich Kittler, „und wie der voreinst ästhetische oder geordnete Kosmos der Philosophen unter technischen Bedingungen zum großen Würfelspiel geworden ist, so kann die Datenverarbeitung ihre Abtastwerte nach allen Spielregeln mathematischer Operationen noch einmal verwürfeln, bis eine Wirklichkeit tatsächlich nicht mehr vonnöten ist." (1989, S. 69) Es ist folglich nicht mehr nur all das was notwendig ist, sondern auch all das was möglich ist, der Fall. Die Dichoto-

mie zwischen der „creatio ex nihilo“ und der Fabrikation bei Vasari, zwischen der künstlerischen Intention und der Rolle der Kontingenz in der künstlerischen Produktion bei Diderot oder zwischen Schöpfer des Werkes und Machen des Zeuges bei Heidegger löst sich auf. Das Werk ist nicht länger toter Spiegel, das unter dem Deckmantel des Realismus oder Naturalismus in einer zeitlosen Bewegungslosigkeit Natur inszeniert und scheinbare Wirklichkeit repräsentiert. Es bildet seine eigene autonome Wirklichkeit mit eigener spezifischer Kontingenz. Vielleicht vergleichbar mit Eric Drexlers „engines of creation“, die molekulare Computer implizieren, die aufgebaut aus komplexen Strukturen sich selbst zusammenbauen und reproduzieren können, löst sich die Kunst vom traditionellen Kunstwerk und seiner semantischen Korrespondenz und entwickelt selbständige strukturelle Kontingenzen.

Mit dem Tausch der Fremdreferenz gegen die Selbstreferenz fielen historisch betrachtet Repräsentations- und Imitationsannahmen im Bild weg. Neben der Eliminierung der gegenständlichen Welt bedurfte es zur eigenständigen Verarbeitung bildimmanenter Elemente vor allem einer Dekomposition oder Trennung des Bildes in seine einzelnen Bausteine. Diese Trennung und Verdichtung ließ das Bild in seine Elemente (Farbe, Licht, Material usf.) kondensieren. Bevor das Bild eine Neustrukturierung erfahren konnte, brauchte es

the present world, for the purpose of independent processing, it called for picture-immanent elements, particularly of a decomposition or division of the picture into its individual modules. This division and condensation allowed the picture to be condensed into its elements (colour, light, material etc. .). Before the picture could experience a re-structuring, it required a thorough reduction of formal and content aspects. Only the reduction to a few, but then more precisely determined elements, made possible the construction of new artistic structures, further resulting in greater complexities. Since it was no longer sufficient to transform objects into imitations, according to the scheme of imitatio and perfectio, the development of system-internal criteria had to be intensified. The picture had to prove itself as a unit consisting of individual picture elements in order to be newly devised by the programmes created by artists. If we describe the condensation of the picture commencing in the 19th century, on the one hand, referring to photography—every object is allocated a certain number of grains with a certain grey value—on the other hand, referring to Cezanne—the picture is composed of clearly defined elements—as a classical physical one, then with the change of the aggregate state of the picture, for the first time, the introduction of a clearly outlined combination game with distinct elements becomes effective in picture production. If photography, Cezanne's painting, or divisionism can be said to be responsible for the physical condensation of the picture, then the film, the collage, the accumulation etc. could be understood as being a chemical condensation and the digital code as being electronic condensation. What all condensation processes have in common is that they dynamize and temporalize the picture. A considerably stronger process, as opposed to the traditional wood panel painting, decomposes the picture into happening states in which the elements are continuously re-allocated and re-assigned to each other. A static persistence in one state would only be a disturbing inhibition of the process and is just as foreign to the pictures, after changing the aggregate state, as a linear-causal picture transformation. Art is—to take up the said example again—in a comparable state with nano-technology. After condensing the objects into their elements, it is necessary in technology, as in art, to have "engines of creation" to structure elements into new complexities.

"Perhaps it would even have been sufficient to simply say that God was able to create immaterial automatons just as well as he was able to create physical ones, the former representing the latter. "

Gottfried Wilhelm Leibnitz, 1710

The picture created its own separate world in order to condense itself into a reserve of pictures established in a possibility structure. It changed its aggregate state by assuming the actual significance of aggregate in the sense of accumulation, making itself independent to form a reserve of imagination, a contingent idea. The natural appearance of things in the world is, in doing so, exchanged in the artificial picture worlds of aggregates for the idea of contingent worlds. Pictures worlds structurally established in apparatus and programmes, do not consume their medium; they produce and reproduce it with every picture of the new one. The "artistic apparatus" is therefore an unlimited reserve of pictures, the perfect copy (lat. copia-reserve). The apparatus, as defined by Vilem Flusser, as a toy simulating thinking, offers a host of possibilities. It is not merely the in-term for the perfect copy but also the in-picture of virtuality. As there is no getting at the artistic apparatus, ontologically, or with categories of classical aesthetics, a division of technical and artistic artefacts becomes superfluous. The polar division between art and technology, between the symbolic and the real, changes into an antagonistic relationship: the work, thing or stuff of classical aesthetics transforms to become apparatus which makes the real appear to be fictitious, and the symbolic appear real.

The basic intention which led to the construction of the "Trace Apparatus", was to design as simple a picture as possible, or a kind of allegory of numerous pictures in one picture—that means, as simple an apparatus as possible, and as extensive a copy as possible. The relationship of the "Trace Apparatus" to the "catalogue" illustrates the relation of structural contingency to catalogue contingency. Following Charles Babbage's idea of a "machine that bites its own tail" (quote Hyman, A. 1987, P250), that is capable of the passage through the never ending, by dismantling the world into part problems, and this further into a sequence of individual steps, was what we chose as the basic form—a mathematical / (greater than/less than symbol). The construction is composed of simple elements and connections, as are common from the everyday routine of inch scales. The difference to a standard inch scale only consists of the regularly varying length of the elements which differ by one quotient (5cm) in order to achieve the symbolic initial form of /. The mathematical / stands for a section of reality which is present from individual elements cut up into lines, on which again, there is a succession of black-white single steps. The result is a wave pattern composed of curves which, depending on the set up of the construction in the space and the constellation of the individual elements to each other, is subject to changes. The apparatus independently produces different frequencies on account of the spatial references which are changed by the installations. In doing so, world is not simulated by an external referentiality, but is newly created by waves. Perhaps similar to the way Ada Lovelace, who translated Manebrea's article about the difference machine from Italian, thought of using Babbages machine for manufacturing music pieces of every length and complexity, the Trace Apparatus will produce unpredicted combinations which want to be read as waves. The apparatus is not a memory like the former wood panel painting, and not a Thesaurus like the sum of all wood panel paintings in a catalogue, a gallery or a museum. The apparatus is a data processing organism like its recipient, a data processing machine. The breaking away of eine gründliche Reduktion formaler und inhaltlicher Aspekte. Erst die Reduzierung auf wenige, aber dafür genau bestimmter Elemente ermöglichte die Anlage neuer bildnerischer Strukturen und in weiterer Folge daraus resultierend erhöhter Komplexitäten. Nachdem es nicht mehr genügte, Objekte nach dem Schema von imitatio und perfectio zu Abbildern zu transformieren, mußten verstärkt systeminterne Kriterien entwickelt werden. Das Bild mußte sich als eine Einheit, konstituiert aus einzelnen Bildelementen, erweisen, um mittels vom Künstler geschaffenen Programmen neu erdacht zu werden. Beschreibt man die Kondensation des Bildes beginnend im 19.Jahrhundert, einerseits bezugnehmend auf die Fotografie – jedem Gegenstand wird eine bestimmte Anzahl an Körnern von bestimmtem Grauwert zugeordnet –, andererseits auf Cezanne – das Bild baut sich aus klar abgegrenzten Elementen auf – als eine klassisch physikalische, so kommt mit dem Wechsel des Aggregatzustandes des Bildes die Einführung eines erstmals klar umrissenen Kombinationspieles mit distinkten Elementen bei der Bildproduktion zum Tragen. Können für die physikalische Kondensation des Bildes die Fotografie, die Malerei Cezannes oder der Divisionismus genannt werden, so könnten der Film, die Collage, die Akkumulation usw. als chemische Kondensation und der digitale Code als elektronische Kondensation begriffen werden. Allen Kondensationsprozessen gemein ist eine Dynamisierung und Temporalisierung des Bildes. Eine gegenüber dem traditionellen Tafelbild wesentlich stärkere Prozeßhaftigkeit dekomponiert das Bild in Ereigniszustände, in denen die Elemente ständig neu zugeordnet und untereinander in Bezug gesetzt werden. Ein statisches Verharren in einem Zustand wäre nur ein störendes Sistieren des Prozesses und ist den Bildern nach Änderung des Aggregatzustandes ebenso fremd wie eine linear-kausale Abbildungstransformation. Kunst befindet sich, um das genannte Beispiel nochmals aufzugreifen, in einem vergleichbaren Zustand wie die Nanotechnologie. Nach Kondensation der Objekte in ihre Elemente bedarf es in der Technik wie in der Kunst „engines of creation", um Elemente zu neuen Komplexitäten zu strukturieren.

„Vielleicht hätte es auch genügt, einfach zu sagen, daß Gott, so gut wie er körperliche Automaten gemacht hat, auch immaterielle erschaffen konnte, die die ersteren vorstellen."
Gottfried Wilhelm Leibniz, 1710

Das Bild schuf sich seine Eigenwelt, um sich zu einem in einer Möglichkeitsstruktur angelegten Bildervorrat zu verdichten. Es wechselte seinen Aggregatzustand, indem es die

eigentliche Bedeutung von Aggregat im Sinne von Anhäufung annahm und sich zu einem Imaginationsvorrat, zu einer kontingenten Vorstellung verselbständigte. Die natürliche Erscheinung der Dinge in der Welt wird dabei in den künstlichen Bildwelten der Apparate gegen die Vorstellung kontingenter Welten getauscht. Strukturell in Apparaten und Programmen angelegte Bildwelten verbrauchen ihr Medium nicht, sie produzieren und reproduzieren es mit jedem Bild von neuem. Der „künstlerische Apparat" ist somit ein unbegrenzter Vorrat an Bildern, die perfekte Kopie (lat. copia – Vorrat). Der Apparat, wie Vilem Flusser definiert, als ein das Denken simulierendes Spielzeug, bietet eine Fülle von Möglichkeiten, er ist nicht nur der Inbegriff der perfekten Kopie, sondern auch das Inbild von Virtualität. Da dem künstlerischen Apparat nicht ontologisch oder mit Kategorien der klassischen Ästhetik beizukommen ist, erübrigt sich eine Trennung von technischen und künstlerischen Artefakten. Die polare Aufspaltung zwischen Kunst und Technik, zwischen dem Symbolischen und dem Realen, wandelt sich in ein antagonistisches Verhältnis. Das Werk, Ding oder Zeug der klassischen Ästhetik transformiert zum Apparat, der das Reale fiktiv und das Symbolische real erscheinen läßt.
Die Grundintention, die zum Bau des „Spurenapparates" führte, war ein möglichst einfaches Bild, beziehungsweise eine Art Allegorie von zahllosen Bildern in einem Bild zu entwerfen, das heißt einen möglichst simplen Apparat als möglichst umfangreiche Kopie. Das Verhältnis des „Spurenapparates" zum „Katalog" illustriert die Relation von struktureller zu katalogischer Kontingenz. In Anlehnung an Charles Babbages Idee einer „Maschine, die sich selbst in den Schwanz beißt" (zit.n. Hyman, A, 1987, S. 250), also zum Durchgang durch das Unendliche befähigt ist, indem sie die Welt in Teilprobleme und diese weiter in eine Folge von Einzelschritten zerlegt, wählten wir als Grundform ein mathematisches / (größer als/kleiner als Zeichen). Die Konstruktion setzt sich aus einfachen Elementen und Verbindungen zusammen, wie sie aus dem Alltag von Zollstäben geläufig sind. Der Unterschied zu einem gewöhnlichen Zollstab besteht lediglich in der regelmäßig varierenden Länge der Elemente, die um einen Quotienten (5 cm) differiert, um die symbolische Ausgangsform des / zu erzielen. Das mathematische / steht für einen Wirklichkeitsausschnitt, der von einzelnen Elementen in Zeilen zerschnitten vorliegt, auf denen wiederum eine Abfolge schwarzweißer Einzelschritte aufliegt. Das Ergebnis ist ein sich aus Kurven zusammensetzendes Wellenmuster, das je nach Aufstellung der Konstruktion im Raum und der Konstellation der einzelnen Elemente zueinander, Veränderungen unterworfen ist. Der Apparat er-

picture prodution from the author and the picture making itself independent, creates a separate world which obeys its own laws, or rather the laws of the programme. Heinz von Foerster gave during a lecture, the simple and possibly therefore the most illustrative example: "as to whether I should "store" information from a 10^{10} x10^{10} multiplication table in the form of a 21x27cm book with a thickness of approx. 10 billion km, or in the form of a small hand-operated desk computer, is, I think, quite clear (1985,P 134). The information in the desk computer or in an artistic apparatus is stored in a structural way as opposed to a table or a conventional picture.

"Could man himself not become a kind of parasite on the machines? An affectionate, machine-tickling plant louse?"
Samuel Butler, 1872

What is interesting is that the demand to make the system art into a programme does not appear, but rather the individual work of art. It is not a matter of an artistic apparatus making a programme of what the system art is or was in its system. The programme or the apparatus would then, as Niklas Luhmann describes for l'art pour l'art, miss the elementary state of affairs, "that autonomy does not stop the relationship to the environment, but rather calls for and regulates its" (1986,P. 626). The artistic apparatus is not a solipsistic operations mechanism, which uncouples the system art from the world, similar to "l'art pour l'art". It must be conceived more to be an effort of a differentiation process progessing further within the system art. A differentiation process which is in an antagonistic and complementary relationship to interventions and appropriation strategies of art outwith its own system. Apparatus, programme or structural contingency describes processes and considerations to differentiate and make products of the system art which have until now always been designated as works, more complex. The work of art should therefore change basically from the work—from the fully finished work—to a "small item of work", an idea in flux.

LITERATURE USED:

Foerster, H. v. (1985), Sicht und Einsicht, Braunschweig
Hyman A. , (1987) Charles Babbage-Philosph, Mathematiker,Computerpionier, Stuttgart
Kittler F. A. (1989). Fiktion und Simulation in: Ars Electronica (Publisher), Philosophien der neuen Technologie, Berlin
Link-Heer, U. (1986), Maniera. Überlegungen zur Konkurrenz von Manier und Stil (Vasari, Diderot, Goethe) in: Gumbrecht, H. U. /Pfeiffer, K. L. (publisher), Stil, Geschichten und Funktionen eines kulturwissenschaftlichen Diskurselementes, Frankfurt a. M.
Luhmann N. (1986), Das Kunstwerk und die Selbsreproduktion der Kunst, in: Gumbrecht, H. U. /Pfeiffer, K. L. (Publisher), Stil, Frankurt a. M.
Varela, F. (1987), Autonomie und Autopoiesie, in Schmidt, S. J. (Publisher), Der Diskurs des Radikalen Konstruktivismus, Frankfurt a. M.

zeugt selbständig verschiedene Frequenzen auf Grund der durch die Installationen wechselnden Raumbezüge. Welt wird dabei nicht mittels einer äußeren Referentialität vorgetäuscht, sondern durch Wellen neu geschaffen. Vielleicht ähnlich wie Ada Lovelace, die Manebreas Artikel über die Differenzmaschine aus dem Italienischen übersetzte, daran dachte Babbages Maschine zur Herstellung von Musikstükken jeder Länge und Komplexität zu nützen, bringt der Spurenapparat unvorhergesehene Kombinationen, die als Wellen gelesen werden wollen, hervor. Der Apparat ist kein Speicher wie das einstige Tafelbild oder kein Thesaurus wie die Summe einzelner Tafelbilder in einem Katalog, einer Galerie oder einem Museum. Der Apparat ist, wie sein Rezipient ein Daten verarbeitender Organismus ist, eine datenverarbeitende Maschine. Die Loslösung der Bildproduktion vom Autor und die Verselbständigung des Bildes schaffen eine eigene Welt, die ihren eigenen Gesetzen beziehungsweise den Gesetzen des Programms gehorcht. Heinz von Foerster brachte, anläßlich eines Vortrages, das einfache und deshalb vielleicht so einleuchtende Beispiel, „ob ich Information einer 10^{10} x 10^{10} Multiplikationstabelle in der Form eines 21x27 cm Buches mit einer Dicke von ca. zehn Milliarden km „speichern" sollte oder in der Form eines kleinen handbetriebenen Tischrechners, ist daher, so meine ich, ganz eindeutig". (1985, S. 134) Die Information im Tischrechner oder in einem künstlerischen Apparat wird im Gegensatz zu einer Tabelle oder einem konventionellen Bild auf strukturelle Weise gespeichert.

„Könnte der Mensch nicht selber eine Art Schmarotzer auf den Maschinen werden? Eine liebevolle maschinenkitzelne Blattlaus?"
Samuel Butler, 1872

Interessant erscheint nicht die Forderung, das System Kunst zum Programm zu machen, sondern das einzelne Kunstwerk. Es geht nicht darum, daß ein künstlerischer Apparat das, was das System Kunst ist oder war, im eigenen System zum Programm macht. Das Programm oder der Apparat würde darin, wie es Niklas Luhmann für das „lart pour lart" beschreibt, den elementaren Tatbestand verfehlen, „daß Autonomie die Beziehung zur Umwelt nicht unterbindet, sondern gerade voraussetzt und reguliert". (1986, S. 626) Der künstlerische Apparat ist kein solipsistischer Operationsmechanismus, der das System Kunst ähnlich dem „lart pour lart" von der Welt abkoppelt. Er muß vielmehr als ein Bemühen eines weiter fortschreitenden Ausdifferungsprozesses innerhalb des Systemes Kunst gefaßt werden. Ein Ausdifferenzierungsprozeß, der in einem antagonistischen und ergänzenden Verhältnis zu Interventionen und Appropriationsstrategien der Kunst außerhalb ihres eigenen Systemes steht. Apparat, Programm oder strukturelle Kontingenz beschreiben Verfahren und Überlegungen, Produkte des Systemes Kunst, die man bisher immer als Werke bezeichnete, auszudifferenzieren und komplexer zu gestalten. Das Kunstwerk soll sich dabei grundlegend vom Werk – von der vollrichteten fertigen Arbeit – zu einem „Werkel", einer im Fluß befindlichen Idee wandeln.

VERWENDETE LITERATUR:

Foerster, H.v. (1985), Sicht und Einsicht, Braunschweig.

Hyman, A. (1987), Charles Babbage – Philosoph, Mathematiker, Computerpionier, Stuttgart.

Kittler, F.A. (1989), Fiktion und Simulation, in: Ars Electronica (Hrsg.), Philosophien der neuen Technologie, Berlin.

Link-Heer, U. (1986), Maniera. Überlegungen zur Konkurenz von Manier und Stil (Vasari, Diderot, Goethe), in: Gumbrecht, H. U./ Pfeiffer, K.L. (Hrsg.), Stil. Geschichten und Funktionen eines kulturwissenschaftlichen Diskurselementes, Frankfurt a. M.

Luhmann, N. (1986), Das Kunstwerk und die Selbstreproduktion der Kunst, in: Gumbrecht, H.U./ Pfeiffer, K.L. (Hrsg.), Stil, Frankfurt a. M.

Varela, F. (1987), Autonomie und Autopoiese, in: Schmidt, S. J. (Hrsg.), Der Diskurs des Radikalen Konstruktivismus, Frankfurt a. M.

GEGENWARTSARCHÄOLOGIE

SABINE HIEBLER / GERHARD ERTL

CURRENT ARCHEOLOGY
SABINE ERTL / GERHARD ERTL

THE SHADOW CAST BY THE OBVIOUS AND THE FLARE-UP OF THE LACK OF UNDERSTANDING

Hiebler/Ertl have discovered a technique—for the time being in a handicraft sense: with the aid of an emulsion they produced themselves, they have developed a process where photographic pictures can be produced on clay plates (without—as with bought emulsions—the clay background being covered up). At the same time, this is an intellectual technique. As this technique calls for the selection of the photographic pictures to be captured as well as the increased interest especially in these pictures; and it creates a certain significance-effect, which sets in with the change over of these pictures from the photo state to the clay plate state. The selection of photographic pictures that Hiebler/Ertl make, relates to the very latest technical-scientific fields: With the aid of their intellectual technique, Hiebler/Ertl intensify their interest for fields such as genetics, chaos theory, telecommunications, aids research and technological war strategy. It concerns those fields that produce the specifically contemporary pictures of what one—possibly with a no less contemporary dulled eye—could deem to be basic human themes: death, communications, search for cognition. This paradox relationship of the specific contemporary and the basic human repeats itself at another level. The high degree of abstraction of these pictures (both in the theoretical as well as in the artistic-formal sense) is on a level with an enormous degree of propagation. It is especially the unrecognizeable state of the subject of these pictures that produces their high degree of recognition (analogously it formerly seemed e.g. the face of Einstein or his famous formula made the light of the great theory of relativity shine even in the very smallest of huts). If, therefore, science and technology are separated by a break from everyday life, having become completely unfathomable for this, then, on the other hand, the signs of this break and their unfathomability have become completely accepted and familiar facts of everyday life.

The pictures that are of interest to Hiebler/Ertl, function accordingly in a two-fold manner: At the level of science they are considered as being copies with a maximum of similarity (after all

DER SCHLAGSCHATTEN DES EINLEUCHTENS UND DAS AUFBLITZEN VON UNVERSTÄNDNIS

Hiebler/Ertl haben eine Technik erfunden – zunächst im handwerklichen Sinn: Mithilfe einer eigens erzeugten Emulsion haben sie ein Verfahren entwickelt, in dem sich photographische Bilder auf Tontafeln hervorbringen lassen (ohne daß – wie bei gekauften Emulsionen – der Tongrund zugedeckt wird).

Zugleich handelt es sich dabei um eine intellektuelle Technik. Denn diese Technik bedingt die Auswahl der festzuhaltenden photographischen Bilder sowie das gesteigerte Interesse für gerade diese Bilder; und sie erzeugt einen bestimmten Bedeutungs-Effekt, der sich beim Übergang dieser Bilder vom Photo-Zustand in den Tontafel-Zustand einstellt. Die Auswahl photographischer Bilder, die Hiebler/Ertl treffen, bezieht sich auf die neuesten technisch-naturwissenschaftlichen Bereiche: Mithilfe der von ihnen entwickelten intellektuellen Technik schärfen Hiebler/Ertl ihr Interesse für Gebiete wie Genetik, Chaostheorie, Telekommunikation, Aids-Forschung und technologische Kriegsführung. Es handelt sich dabei also um jene Gebiete, die die spezifisch zeitgenössischen Bilder dessen produzieren, was man – möglicherweise mit einem nicht weniger zeitgenössisch getrübten Blick – für allgemein menschliche Themen halten könnte: Tod, Kommunikation, Erkenntnissuche („basic human themes“ sagen Hiebler/Ertl). Dieses paradoxe Verhältnis von spezifisch Zeitgenössischem und allgemein Menschlichem wiederholt sich auf einer anderen Ebene. Dem hohen Abstraktionsgrad dieser Bilder (sowohl im theoretischen wie auch im bildnerisch-formalen Sinn) entspricht ein enormer Verbreitungsgrad. Gerade die Unkenntlichkeit der Sujets dieser Bilder bedingt ihre hohe Wiedererkennbarkeit (in analoger Weise schienen früher z. B. das Gesicht Einsteins oder seine bekannte Formel, das Licht der großen Relativitätstheorie auch in der kleinsten Hütte leuchten zu lassen). Wenn also Wissenschaft und Technik durch einen Bruch vom alltäglichen Leben getrennt und für dieses völlig undurchschaubar geworden sind, so sind andererseits die

Doppelhelixstruktur einer DNA(Rastertunnelmikroskopie)

Zeichen dieses Bruchs und dieser Undurchschaubarkeit selbst vollkommen akzeptierte und vertraute Tatsachen dieses alltäglichen Lebens geworden.

Die Bilder, denen das Interesse von Hiebler/Ertl gilt, funktionieren dementsprechend in zweifacher Weise: Auf der Ebene der Wissenschaft werden sie als Abbilder von größtmöglicher Ähnlichkeit betrachtet (schließlich werden sie mithilfe von Präzisionsinstrumenten gewonnen), als ikonische Zeichen also, und zwar als die ikonischsten Zeichen, die wir kennen; als solche werden sie in den Wissenschaften bedächtig untersucht, damit zukünftig etwas an ihnen verstanden werden kann. Auf der Ebene des alltäglichen Lebens hingegen fungieren diese Bilder wie Verkehrszeichen, in denen jede Ähnlichkeit ausgelöscht ist und die darum sofort Verständnis und Evidenz auslösen; als symbolische Zeichen also (mit der Besonderheit, daß sie – gemäß dem beschriebenen Paradoxon – als Symbole des Ikonischen bezeichnet werden müssen).

Diese zweite, auf das alltägliche Leben bezogene, symbolische Ebene macht diese Bilder für Hiebler/Ertl interessant:

they are acquired with the aid of precision instruments), as an iconic symbol and, that is, as the iconic symbol that we know; as such they are being investigated carefully in the sciences, so that in future something can be understood of them. On the level of everyday life, again, these pictures act like traffic signs, in which every form of similarity is obliterated and which therefore immediately trigger off understanding and evidence; as a symbolic token (with the special feature that they—in accordance with the described paradoxes—must be termed as being a symbol of the iconic). This second symbolic level relating to everyday life makes these pictures interesting for Hiebler/Ertl: They are grammalogues (as Hiebler/Ertl put it precisely)—not inasmuchas as our present day sciences *gradually recognize* certain objects via these pictures, but in as much as we *very suddenly recognize* ourselves *again* in these picture (and our themes—i.e. the themes dominating our mass communications).

Therefore, they are "shock pictures" (another word by Hiebler/Ertl), which are nevertheless more similar to script than to picture and for this very reason trigger off a shock-type significance—a shock of the representation itself, which in the shock of what is represented i.e. the significances triggered off (e.g. aids, Gulf War etc.) perhaps only possesses little more than a weak echo.

Hiebler/Ertl are working on this shock of the very sudden and unavoidably experienced own presence with the aid of the intellectual technique they developed. It is a technique of distancing, of the very sudden lack of understanding which is the death of the own present by way of trial, in order to marvel at its clay plate-type relicts with the strange eyes of a future archaeologist. What results is an effect of the loss of understanding, a negative effect so-to-speak, where—as Hiebler/Ertl emphasize—it is not the presented themes that are decisively distanced, but more the way they are contemplated.

The preciousness and the durability of this technique plays an important role in this intellectual distancing: a photo from the morning newspaper e.g. is conserved in the medium of the clay plate with quite unreasonable care—similar to the way the medium of archaeological sciences has until now turned a waste object or a discarded careless remark of the Ancient Greeks into an object of excessive attention and esteem.

Robert Pfaller

CURRENT ARCHAEOLOGY
(Photo emulsion on baked clay)
Format: each 43 x 57 x 5 cm

Es sind Kürzel (wie Hiebler/Ertl präzise sagen) – nicht insofern unsere heutigen Wissenschaften über diese Bilder allmählich bestimmte Gegenstände erkennen, sondern insofern wir in diesen Bildern uns (und unsere Themen – d. h. die vorherrschenden Themen unserer Massenkommunikation) blitzartig wiedererkennen.
Es handelt sich also um „Schockbilder" (ein anderes Wort von Hiebler/Ertl), die allerdings der Schrift näher stehen als dem Bild und die eben deshalb schockartig Bedeutung auslösen – ein Schock der Darstellung selbst, der im Schock des Dargestellten, d. h. der ausgelösten Bedeutungen (z. B. Aids, Golfkrieg etc.) vielleicht nicht mehr als nur ein schwaches Echo besitzt.
An diesem Schock der blitzartig und unvermeidlich erfahrenen eigenen Gegenwart arbeiten Hiebler/Ertl mithilfe der von ihnen entwickelten intellektuellen Technik. Es ist eine Technik der Distanzierung, der blitzartigen Verständnislosigkeit, die die eigene Gegenwart probeweise unter die Erde bringt, um dann deren tontafelartige Relikte mit den fremden Augen eines zukünftigen Archäologen zu bestaunen. Daraus resultiert ein Effekt des Verständnis-Verlustes, ein negativer Bedeutungs-Effekt sozusagen, in dem – wie Hiebler/Ertl betonen – nicht die dargestellten Themen, wohl aber die Art ihrer Betrachtung entscheidend distanziert wird.
Die Kostbarkeit und Dauerhaftigkeit der Technik spielt bei dieser intellektuellen Distanzierung eine wichtige Rolle: Ein Foto aus der Morgenzeitung z. B. wird im Medium der Tontafeln mit ganz unverhältnismäßiger Behutsamkeit konserviert – ähnlich wie das Medium der Altertumswissenschaften bisweilen einen Abfallgegenstand oder eine weggeworfene, achtlose Bemerkung der alten Griechen zum Gegenstand unverhältnismäßiger Aufmerksamkeit und Wertschätzung macht.

Robert Pfaller

Gegenwartsarchäologie:
(Fotoemulsion auf gebranntem Ton)
Format: je 43 x 57 x 5 cm

DAS DELBRUCK PARADOX

DAVID KREMERS

Wir sind die erste Künstlergeneration, die sich dem Problem – nicht der Sterblichkeit – sondern der Unsterblichkeit gegenüber sieht. Mit den jüngsten Fortschritten von Biotechnologie und Computerwissenschaft zur Verlängerung des Lebens, sind die Künstler des 21. Jahrhunderts sowohl mit einer Einebnung der künstlerischen Signifikanz als auch mit einer größeren Zeitspanne des historischen Kontexts konfrontiert. Die Zivilisation wird aus diesem Dilemma eine Weltsicht hervorbringen müssen, die weniger mechanistisch ist als jene, der die industrielle Revolution Vorschub geleistet hat.

EINLEITUNG

Es stirbt niemand mehr. Nach Halley (1990) haben uns die Toten, seit dem Aufkommen der Fotografie nicht mehr verlassen. Gut möglich, daß Marilyn Monroe heute als alterslose Leinwandlegende im künstlichen Raum ein besseres Leben hat, als das, welches sie als betagte Alkoholikerin nach einem Entzug geführt hätte.

Ist es, unter der Annahme daß wir bereits im Cyberspace (Benedikt, 1991) und in verschiedenen Formen einer virtuellen Realität leben, wichtig, daß wir weiter versuchen zwischen unserem „natürlichen" und „künstlichen" Leben zu unterscheiden? Einige würden behaupten (Dietch, 1992), der menschlichen Spezies erwachse mehr Freiheit und ein größeres Potential, indem wir unseren „künstlichen" Leben mehr Beachtung schenken. Dieser Standpunkt widerspricht einer Auffassung, die noch immer der Vorstellung anhängt, daß Leben und Materie im Grunde in den einfachen Begriffen der Newtonschen Mechanik erklärt werden können. Eine aufgeklärtere Sichtweise (Schwartz, 1992) vermag in der Relativitätstheorie die natürliche Schlußfolgerung aus der Newtonschen Mechanik zu sehen und für sie ist es naheliegend, daß die Molekularbiologie anfängt, uns auf eine ganz andere Art das Leben zu sehen, vorzubereiten.

Max Delbruck, einer der Begründer der Molekularbiologie, fand, es sei paradox (Schwartz 1992), daß ein und dieselbe

THE DELBRUCK PARADOX
DAVID KREMERS

We are the first generation of artists to face the problem not of mortality, but of immortality. With the recent advances in biotechnology and computer science for extending life, artists of the 21st century are faced with both a leveling of artistic significance, and an expanded period of time for historical context. Civilization will need to create from this dilemma a less mechanistic world view than the previous industrial revolution has encouraged.

INTRODUCTION

No one dies anymore. According to halley (1990), since the advent of photography, the dead have stayed on with us. Marilyn Monroe may well be leading a better life today as an ageless screen legend in artificial space than she would have enjoyed as an aged recovering alchoholic.

Given that we are already living in cyberspace (benedikt, 1991) and in various forms of virtual reality, is it important that we should still try to distinguish between our "natural" and "artificial" lives? Some would postulate (dietch 1992) that placing greater emphasis on our "artificial" lives gives the human species greater freedom and potential. This stance belies a viewpoint which still clings to the notion that life and matter may ultimately be explained in the simple terms of newtonian mechanics. A more enlightened viewpoint (Schwartz 1992) can see relativity theory as the natural conclusion of newtonian mechanics, and suggest that molecular biology is beginning to prepare us for a very different way of looking at life.

Max Delbruck, a founder of molecular biology, thought it paradoxical (Schwartz 1992) that the same matter as the matter of physics could behave fully in accordance with the laws of physics, and yet could not be accounted for by those same laws of physics. The answer, Delbruck felt, lay not in the continued snipping away of dna fragments into common particles, but in the recognition that by immersing oneself in a swamp of living tissue one would be able to observe new paradoxes and new laws of nature rising to the surface.

Oncogene, 1992, Agar X-gal, PITG, ecoli TB-1, synthetic

METHOD AND MATERIALS

We have recently applied this same experimental outlook to painting. With a few simple laboratory procedures a suite of paintings were grown from single-celled organisms which had been genetically altered to produce colored enzymes, or protein combinations that reacted with genetic trace dyes. The work was completely transparent when painted, a sensation rather like trying to paint on ice with melted snow. After a period of 16–18 hrs, the growth was arrested by the removal of moisture from the plate. Air was sealed out with a synthetic resin, and the work entered period of stasis.
The work, while stable, is neither "dead" nor "finished". It exists in a state of suspended animation, and at any time the resin might be removed, the plate scraped, fed, and placed in an incubation room to grow to a new stage of development.

Substanz sich als Gegenstand der Physik in vollkommener Übereinstimmung mit den Gesetzen der Physik verhielt und dennoch durch eben diese Gesetze der Physik nicht erklärt werden konnte. Delbruck fühlte, die Antwort lag nicht im fortgesetzten Zerschnippseln der DNA-Fragmente zu gewöhnlichen Partikeln, sondern in der Erkenntnis, daß man, indem man sich selbst in einen Morast aus lebendigem Gewebe sinken ließ, das Auftauchen neuer Paradoxa und neuer Naturgesetze würde beobachten können.

METHODE UND MATERIALIEN

Wir haben kürzlich diese experimentelle Vorhersage auf die

Malerei angewandt. Mittels einiger einfacher Laborverfahren entstand eine Folge von Bildern aus einzelligen Organismen, die genetisch so verändert worden waren, daß sie farbige Enzyme erzeugen konnten oder Einweißkombinationen, die auf die genetischen Farbstoffspuren reagierten. Nach dem Malvorgang war die Arbeit vollkommen lichtdurchlässig, ein Eindruck, als wollte man mit geschmolzenem Schnee auf Eis malen. Nach einer Zeitspanne von 16 bis 18 Stunden wurde das Wachstum durch das Entfernen der Feuchtigkeit von der Platte, angehalten. Die Luftzufuhr wurde mittels eines synthetischen Harzes abgeschnitten und das Werk trat in ein Stadium des Stillstands.

Das Objekt ist, während es unveränderlich ist, weder „tot" noch „abgeschlossen". Es existiert in einem Zustand der vorübergehend unterbrochenen Animation, das Harz kann jederzeit entfernt werden, die Platte abgeschabt und Nahrung zugeführt werden und in einem Inkubationsraum tritt es in ein neues Entwicklungsstadium ein.

Das Thema der ersten Malserie wurde gewählt, um verschiedene Gesundheitszustände zu reflektieren; lebend, immun, beschädigt und sterbend. Alle Zustände treffen für Bakterien ebenso wie für Menschen zu. Darauf folgend wurden embryonale Abschnitte von frühen Entwicklungsstadien der Säugetiere gemalt, etwa die Bildung des Becherkeims aus dem Blasenkeim (Gastrulation), das paraxiale Keimblatt (Mesoderm) und die Eingeweiderundungen.

RESULTATE

Wie Delbruck es vorhergesagt haben könnte, waren die Ergebnisse ebenso aufschlußreich wie auch paradox. Die Naturwissenschaft ist vielleicht das letzte, in der Kunst noch aufrechte Tabu. Viele Betrachter sagen, daß sie sich der Kunst zuwenden um von der Naturwissenschaft und der Technologie „loszukommen" während andere, deren naturwissenschaftliche Vorkenntnisse so gering sind, daß sie glauben, alles was mit Naturwissenschaft zusammenhängt, müsse auch einiges an Mathematik beinhalten, nie in der Lage sein werden, das Werk zu verstehen.

Aber sogar Betrachter, die die Arbeit nie zuvor gesehen haben, die ihr Vorwissen nur aus den Medien beziehen und die das Thema nicht erkennen können, sagen, daß „hier irgendetwas anders ist" und reagieren sehr neugierig, um die Lösung zu finden.

Das andere, selbst für den Künstler seltsame Ergebnis besteht darin, daß das Bild von einer solchen Lebendigkeit ist, die es dem Bewußtsein anscheinend verwehrt, die Topographie des

The subject matter of the first suite of paintings was chosen to reflect various states of health; alive, immune, deficient, and succuming, all are states as applicable to the bacteria as to humans. Next, paintings were grown of embryonic sections of early mammal developmental stages, gastrulation, paraxial mesoderm, and visceral arches.

RESULTS

The results, as Delbruck might have predicted, have been both revealing and paradoxical. Science may be the last remaining taboo in art. Many viewers report that they go to art to "get away" from science and technology, while others have such weak scientific educations that they assume that anything dealing with science must have some mathematics involved and they will therefore never be able to understand the work.

But even viewers who have never seen the work before, who have no prior knowledge as to the media, and who cannot recognize the subject matter, comment that "something is different here", and respond with a consuming curiosity to seek the answer.

The other odd result, even for the artist, is that the imagery is so alive that the mind seems unable to complete a topography of the piece. Memory proves unreliable as sudden appearances of new phenomena reveal themselves to be preexisting conditions when the painting is compared to the transparencies.

DISCUSSION

What kind of work does an artist produce with the burden of knowing that the completed work will be with us for all of time? Current technology renders Matthew Barney as Immortal as Michelangelo. With a greatly extended lifespan, any heroic artist will now outlive her achievement. What avocation is meaningful when faced with the propect of 135 more years? Or the propect of continually renewed youthful bodily functions for the foreseeable eternity? What value then is material success? Or a place in history? Why bother to have children?

Following the example of Delbruck, it seems reasonable that the future will be no more "natural" than "artificial". Instead, the way we now create artificial objects will probably become more organic, and conceptual thought will become more integrated into everyday perception. Many preconceived misconceptions are bound to fall away, leaving us with a civilization less humanocentric than the present western tradition. We must do away with our protein chauvanism if we expect to infect the world with art.

SOURCES

Benedikt, Michael (1991). Cyberspace, mit press, Cambridge.

Dietch, Jeffrey (1992). Post human, musee d'art contemporain, Lausanne.
Halley, Peter (1987). Collected essays. Bischofberger, Zurich.
Kosuth, Joseph (1991). Art after philosophy and after, mit press, Cambridge.
Schwartz, Joseph (1992). The creative moment, Harper/Collins, New York.

Courtesy of Thomas Solomon's Garage, Los Angeles

Stückes zu vervollständigen. Das Gedächtnis erweist sich als nicht zuverlässig, da beim Vergleichen des Bildes mit den Diapositiven die plötzlichen Erscheinungen neuer Phänomene sich als zuvor bereits existierende Bedingung herausstellten.

DISKUSSION

Welcher Art ist das Werk, das ein Künstler, belastet von dem Wissen, daß die fertige Arbeit uns für immer erhalten bleibt, produziert? Die gegenwärtige Technologie macht Matthew Barney ebenso unsterblich wie Michelangelo. Mit einer viel längeren Lebenszeit wird nun jeder heroische Künstler seine Errungenschaften überleben. Welcher Nebenberuf ist in Anbetracht der Aussicht auf weitere 135 Jahren sinnvoll? Oder ist es die Perspektive kontinuierlich erneuerbarer jugendlicher Körperfunktionen für die vorhersehbare Ewigkeit? Welchen Stellenwert hat dann materieller Erfolg? Oder ein Platz in der Geschichte? Weshalb sich damit abmühen, Kinder zu haben?
Folgt man dem Beispiel Delbrucks, so scheint es einsichtig, daß die Zukunft um nichts mehr „natürlich" als „künstlich" sein wird. Anstatt dessen wird vielleicht unsere Art künstliche Objekte zu schaffen organischer und das begriffliche Denken wird mehr in die Alltagswahrnehmung eingebunden. Viele vorgefaßte falsche Ansichten müssen wegfallen, – womit wir uns in einer Zivilisation befinden, die weniger humanozentrisch als die gegenwärtige westliche Tradition ist. Wir müssen unseren Proteinchauvinismus ablegen, wenn wir darauf hoffen, die Welt mit Kunst zu infizieren.

QUELLEN

Benedikt, Michael (1991). Cyberspace, MIT Press, Cambridge
Dietch, Jeffrey (1992). Posthuman, Museum der zeitgenössischen Kunst, Lausanne.
Halley, Peter (1987). Gesammelte Essays, Bischofberger, Zürich.
Kosuth, Joseph (1991). Art After Philosophy And After, MIT Press, Cambridge.
Schwartz, Joseph (1992). The Creative Moment, Harper/Collins, New York.

Courtesy Thomas Solomon's Garage, Los Angeles

GENETIX

NIKI NICKL

ERLÄUTERUNGEN ZUR DREITEILIGEN ARBEIT

Zum Verständnis meiner Arbeit möchte ich vorerst einige Begriffe erklären. Unter Genetik versteht man die klassische Vererbungslehre, also Kreuzungsversuche und deren Analyse, im Gegensatz zur Gentechnologie – die eigentliche Bezeichnung biochemischer Manipulation, das Eingreifen in die Erbsubstanz. Der Ausgangspunkt dieser Manipulation ist das Gen, der universelle Informationsspeicher aller Lebewesen. Hier sind zum größten Teil die Eigenschaften (Charakteristika) gespeichert. Ein Gen besteht aus einer Kombination von DNA, so wie sie auf meiner Acrylglasplatte zu sehen ist.

Warum mache ich die DNA auf meiner Platte nur unter fluoreszentem Licht sichtbar? Hier besteht im Verfahren der Sichtbarmachung eine Analogie zur Wissenschaft. In der Molekularbiologie wird die DNA durch Einfärben mit einem fluoreszenten Farbstoff auf einer Trägersubstanz, einem milchig, weißen Gel, sichtbar gemacht. Allerdings stellt sie sich in Folge nicht als Doppelhelix dar, sondern als nur von Wissenschaftlern interpretierbare Abfolge von Strichen. Bei normalem Licht ist auf der Trägersubstanz, dem Gel, nur eine blaue Makerfront sichtbar. Darum auch die Wahl der blauen Farbe für die Punkte auf der Vorderseite, die sich an einigen Stellen häufen, aber keinem bestimmten System zu folgen scheinen. Sie könnten an Planetensysteme erinnern. Erst unter Schwarzlicht wird der komplizierte Aufbau und die Zusammengehörigkeit sichtbar. Erkennbar wird, wie sich aus vielen kleinen Einzelteilen ein komplexes Ganzes zusammensetzt und erst durch Interagieren und Rückkoppeln ein System funktionieren kann; wie im Kl einen so im Großen. Mikrokosmos – Makrokosmos. Jedes Lebewesen, ob Pflanze, Tier oder Mensch besteht in seinem Ursprung aus ein und derselben DNA. In den Genen unterscheiden sie sich.

Womit ich beim zweiten Teil meiner Arbeit, dem KLONING KIT wäre. Ein Kloning Kit ist ein kommerziell erhältliches Puffer- und Enzymset, praktisch ein Baukasten zum Klonieren. Das Klonieren ist ein Vorgang bei dem ein Gen in einen Organismus (z. Zt. noch so einfache wie Bakterien) einge-

GENETIX
NIKI NICKL

For the understanding of my work, I would first like to explain a few concepts. By genetics, I mean genetics in the classical sense, cross-breeding experiments and analysis, as opposed to gene technology—the actual term for biochemical manipulation, intervention in hereditary material. The starting-point of this manipulation is the gene, the universal information carrier of all living things, where most characteristics are stored. A gene consists of a combination of DNA, as I can see on my acrylic glass plate.

Why can I only view the DNA on my plate under ultraviolet light? This method of seeing represents an analogy to science. In molecular biology, DNA is made visible by dying it with a fluorescent pigment on a carrier substance, a milky white gel. Of course, this does not reveal a double helix a series of dashes that can only be interpreted by scientists. Under normal light, only a blue front can be seen on the carrier material, the white gel. Hence the choice of the colour blue for the dots on the front side, which are bunched together in some places, but do not seem to follow any particular system. They could be seen as a planetary system. Only black light reveals their complicated structure and grouping. It becomes obvious how the many small individual pieces form a complex whole and how a system can only function through integration and feedback: as in the small, so in the big. Microcosm—macrocosm. Every living thing, whether plant, animal or human, has its origin in the very same DNA. They differ in their genes.

Which leads to the second part of my work, the KLONING KIT. A Kloning Kit is a commercially available buffer and enzyme set, practically a construction kit for cloning. Cloning is a process in which a gene is inserted into an organism (at this stage, nothing more complex than bacteria) to artificially create identical organisms with new, identical characteristics. This gene technology procedure contains one of the fundamental dangers of gene manipulation: a standardising and industrialising of life with a view to commercial exploitation, the latter certainly not bringing about an improvement in quality but rather the opposite (normalised apple sizes mean a greater loss of flavour). Many scientists are not informing themselves about this problem or are avoiding it out of pure scientific interest. Science for its own sake. This

is why my visualisation is in the form of a game. Games abstract reality; they transport the player, the scientist, into the unreal. For me this head game symbolises the careless, absent, dubious way scientists deal with life. They give their subjects an abstract character by using a reductionist method to penetrate down to molecular level, but they lose sight of the overall context and in the end they find themselves operating on models of reality.
Now for the third part of my work: a slide projection with the title HARD NUMBER ONE—this refers to a hybrid variety of Canadian wheat. A short explanation of the chosen title: restriction

schleust wird um identische Lebewesen mit neuen, gleichen Eigenschaften künstlich zu erzeugen. Dieses gentechnologische Verfahren beinhaltet eine der grundlegenden Gefahren der Genmanipulation: eine Normierung und Industrialisierung von Leben auf eine kommerzielle Nutzung hin ausgerichtet; letzteres bringt auf keinen Fall eine Qualitätsverbesserung mit sich – im Gegenteil (genormte Apfelgrößen – erhöhter Geschmacksverlust). Dieses Problem machen sich viele Wissenschaftler nicht bewußt, oder sie verzichten aus einem rein wissenschaftlichen Interesse darauf. Wissenschaft als Selbstzweck. Aus diesen Gründen auch meine Umsetzung in Form eines Legespiels. Spiele abstrahieren die Wirklichkeit, sie en trücken sie dem Spieler, dem Wissenschaftler. Dieses Spiel mit den Köpfen symbolisiert für mich einen verspielten, entrückten, bedenklichen Umgang der Wissenschaftler mit Leben. Jene verleihen ihren Sujets einen abstrakten Charakter indem sie in einer reduktionistischen Vorgangsweise bis in molekulare Bereiche vordringen, dadurch den Blick für eine Gesamtheit verlieren und schlußendlich an Modellen der Wirklichkeit operieren.

Nun zum dritten Teil meiner Arbeit: eine Diaprojektion mit dem Titel HARD NUMBER ONE – dies bezeichnet eine kanadische Hybridweizensorte. Eine kurze Erklärung zur verwendeten Aufschrift. Restriktionsenzyme sind Proteine, die Gene(DNA) an spezifischen Positionen zerschneiden, um sie nachher neu zusammensetzen zu können; also ein unverzichtbares Werkzeug der Gentechnologie. Es ermöglicht die Neukombination von Genen, d. h. die Veränderung von Eigenschaften vielfach im Dienste der Industrie. (Erhöhte Resistenz gegen Insektizide)

HARD NUMBER ONE setzt sich mit Wirklichkeit und Projektion auseinander. Dies geschieht in Form einer Karte - einem As. Als Figur die Chemie, als Symbol der Meßzylinder mit der Plastikkornähre. Weiters ist die Arbeit geteilt in in die Projektion, projizierter Schatten einerseits und real vorhandene Gegenstände (Plakat, Meßzylinder, Kornähre) realer Schatten andererseits.

Einige Fragen, die diese Arbeit für mich beinhaltet:

Was an Weltverbesserung oder -rettung = Rechtfertigung projiziert ein Gentechniker in die Herstellung einer Pflanze, die sich nicht vermehren oder erhöhten Pestiziddosen ausgesetzt werden kann?

Wie sieht die Wirklichkeit nach dem mehrmaligen Säen von Hybridsamen aus?

Was hat der Bauer von einem ausgelaugten Boden, im Gegensatz zum Chemiekonzern, der alljährlich seinen Samen zum Verkauf anbietet?

Wer hält das As in Händen?

Foto: Mathias Herrmann

enzymes are proteins that divide genes (DNA) at specific positions to put them back together later. They are, in other words, an indispensable tool of gene technology, allowing new combinations of genes, the alteration of characteristics, to a large extent for industrial purposes. (improved resistance against insecticides).

HARD NUMBER ONE deals with reality and projection. This happens with the aid of a card—the ace. An image from chemistry, the symbol of a measuring cylinder, and a plastic ear of corn. The work is further divided into projection; projected shadow on the one hand and on the other, real solid objects (poster, measuring cylinder, ear of corn), real shadows.

Some questions this work raises for me:

What justification does a gene technician see in the way of improving - or rescuing—the world in the production of a plant that cannot reproduce, or that can withstand higher doses of pesticide?

How does reality look after the multiple sowing of hybrid seeds?

What does the farmer get out of leached soil, in comparison to what a chemical concern gains from putting its seeds on the market every year?

Who holds the ace?

Photo: Mathias Herrmann

LEGAL CHEESE

DAN PETERMAN

LEGAL CHEESE
DAN PETERMAN

The three projects discussed here, the *Chicago Compost Shelter, Store (cheese)* and *Advances in Bio-gas*, traverse a number of related issues. The bacteriological processes which composting, cheesemaking and bio-gas production rely upon was arrived at as a necessary tool the usefulness of which became apparent in dealing with complex material and social demands rather than as a starting point in and of itself. The application and nurturing of these processes, one of food production and the others of organic waste processing, are surprisingly similar to each other in principle and consideration of these biological processes allows one to confront the curious notion of simultaneous growth and decay. The bacteriological process of growth, exploiting specific conditions within processes of decay could metaphorically apply to much of my work. This is particularly true if one is to consider the processes of decay (social, physical, and economic) at work in most major american cities and further consider the organic "bacteriological" growth of events, and industries (scavenging, food production on abandoned property, composting, recycling, etc.) which can emerge from these conditions.
The American waste stream consists of a vast assortment of materials, in often unbelievable quantities. Not surprisingly the implications of how this matter is perceived and treated has a great effect on large groups of people and extended systems of production, consumption and disposal. Economic and ecologic issues are closely intertwined. Because of the tremendous neglect paid to it in recent history, the waste stream has been an important resource for many small scale, improvisational, ad hoc industries, particularly in urban situations with their inherent concentrations of both garbage production and unemployed people. Although current developments of waste and recycling have moved toward increasingly centralized "efficient" systems of material processing, it is the decentralized, improvisational models of waste handling and recovery which I find most appealing and in considering the extended socio-economic benefits of these localized approaches, it becomes apparent that they have the potential to be more efficient than centralized systems. This becomes strikingly clear in urban situations which have suffered severe economic decline, abandonment, segregation or a host of other urban maladies. Here, the

Die drei hier diskutierten Projekte, der *Chicago Compost Shelter, STORE (cheese)* und *Advances in Biogas,* betreffen eine Reihe von verwandten Sachverhalten. Die bakteriologischen Prozesse auf denen das Kompostieren, die Käseerzeugung und die Produktion von Biogas beruhen, wurden als notwendige Werkzeuge anerkannt, deren Nützlichkeit sich mehr im Umgang mit komplexem Material und sozialen Bedürfnissen, als innerhalb dieser Prozesse selbst erwies. Die Anwendung und Betreuung dieser Prozesse, von denen einer der Nahrungsmittelproduktion dient, während die anderen die Verarbeitung organischen Abfalls betreffen, sind einander im Prinzip überraschend ähnlich und die Bedeutung dieser biologischen Verfahren gestattet, sich mit dem seltsamen Begriff des simultanen Wachstums und Zerfalls auseinanderzusetzen. Der bakteriologische Prozeß des Wachstums, der die spezifischen Bedingungen innerhalb der Zerfallsvorgänge ausnützt, könnte metaphorisch für viele meiner Arbeiten gelten. insbesondere, wenn man den aktuellen (sozialen, physischen und ökonomischen) Zerfall in den meisten amerikanischen Großstädten bedenkt und weitere das organische „bakteriologische" Wachstum von Vorkommnissen und Industrien (Personen, die von Abfällen leben, Nahrungsmittelproduktion auf verlassenen Grundstükken, Kompostieren, Recyceln, etc.), welches aus diesen Bedingungen hervorgehen kann.
Der amerikanische Müllstrom besteht aus einem gewaltigen Materialsortiment, in oft unglaublichen Mengen. Es überrascht daher nicht, daß die Art, wie diese Angelegenheit wahrgenommen und behandelt wird, bedeutende Auswirkungen auf große Bevölkerungsgruppen sowie auf die Produktions-, Konsum- und Verfügungssysteme im weiteren Sinne hat. Ökonomische und ökologische Fragen sind eng ineinander verflochten. Aufgrund der bis in die jüngere Vergangenheit bestehenden unglaublichen Nichtbeachtung dieser Probleme, war der Müllstrom eine wichtige Ressource für viele kleine, improvisierte ad hoc Industrien besonders in urbanen Gegenden mit ihrer typischen Konzentration von Abfallproduktion und Arbeitslosigkeit. Obwohl die gegenwärtigen Entwicklungen im Bereich Abfall und Recy-

cling in Richtung zunehmend zentralisierter „effizienter" Systeme der Materialverarbeitung weisen, erscheinen mir die dezentralen, improvisierten Modelle der Abfallbehandlung und Wiedergewinnung am vielversprechendsten und angesichts des größeren sozio-ökonomischen Nutzens dieser lokalen Ansätze, wird es offenkundig, daß sie eine potentiell höhere Effizienz haben als die zentralisierten Systeme. Dies wird schlagartig klar in urbanen Gegenden, die einen ernsthaften ökonomischen Abstieg erfahren haben und unter Abwanderung, Rassentrennung oder einer Unzahl anderer urbaner Krankheiten leiden. Hier ist der Müllstrom eine nie endende Ressource, die entwickelt werden könnte zwecks Maximierung von Beschäftigung und Umweltverbesserung, bei gleichzeitiger sozialer Stabilität und Interaktion.

Die Kompostierung organischen Materials ist ein einfaches, weitverbreitetes Verfahren, welches die Erzeugung von Humus zur Verbesserung der Umwelt erlaubt und auch die Kosten der Müllaufbereitung, des Transports und der Deponierung aufwiegt. Ausgehend von einem großen Kompostierprojekt im Süden von Chicago, wurde der *Chicago Compost Shelter* errichtet. Es handelte sich dabei um die öffentliche Installation einer experimentellen Unterkunft, die darauf ausgelegt war, einen Chikagoer Winter lang durch die Hitze aus dem Zerfallsprozeß des organischen Materials beheizt zu werden, Sie bestand aus der Karosserie eines VW-Lieferwagens, der unter einem großen Komposthaufen vergraben worden war. Der Kompost selbst enthielt in erster Linie Pferdemist und Hobelspäne aus den Stallungen der Chicagoer Polizei. Dieses Material kann durch die Sauerstoff- bzw. Bakterientätigkeit im Inneren eines Komposthaufens, Temperaturen von 131 Grad Fahrenheit (51 Grad Celsius) erreichen. An die Unterkunft schloß sich ein schmaler Zutrittsweg an, außerdem verfügte sie über Dachfenster, die eine Innenbeleuchtung mit Tageslicht ermöglichten. Der Liefer-

waste stream is a never-ending resource which could be developed to maximize employment, environmental improvement, along with community stability and interaction.

The composting of organic matter is a simple, widely used process capable of providing humus for environmental improvements as well as offsetting waste-handling, transporting, and burial costs. Beginning with a large composting project initiated on Chicago's southside, The *Chicago Compost Shelter* was built. It was a public installation of an experimental shelter designed to stay warm throughout a Chicago winter by utilizing the heat produced by the decaying process of organic materials. It consisted of a VW van body which had been buried in a large pile of compost. The compost itself was primarily horse manure and woodshavings collected from the Chicago Police stables. This material, due to aerobic bacterial activity at the interior of a compost pile, is capable of reaching temperatures of 131 degrees fahrenheit (51C). A small entranceway was added to the shelter along with skylights which allowed daylight to illuminate the interior. The van was large enough for a bed and some space conscious furnishings and came equipped with ashtrays, a mirror, seat with armrests, and if one cared to hook up a battery there was also a radio and domelight.

The shelter was constructed in December, 1987 and remained publicly accessible in a vacant lot adjacent to a recycling yard until it was dismantled in August, 1988. The shelter functioned better than anticipated, creating a very warm comfortable environment. Any odors or vapors produced by the decomposing manure/compost traveled upward and out the top of the pile, while considerable heat radiated into the interior of the VW van. Throughout the winter the shelter maintained a temperature between 70 and 80 degrees fahrenheit and even warmer if the door was sealed tightly. On the coldest nights this meant close to a 100 degree difference from outside temperatures.

Over the winter the *Compost Shelter* developed a number of different uses; a heated lunch room for the employees of the recycling center who work outdoors; a science museum-like display of decomposition processes for school groups that occasionally visited the recycling center and most importantly, an emergency shelter for the transient population of scavengers doing business with the recycling center. Although nobody attempted to adopt the shelter as a permanent residence (a very real possibility given the local conditions of poverty and homelessness), it was frequently used as an overnight shelter. An old mattress was brought by someone and it remained in the shelter throughout the winter. Food wrappings and beverage containers were often left behind, as well as traces of wax from the burning of many candles.

Bio-gas production is somewhat less familiar than composting but exists in many different forms, perhaps most commonly as the inadvertent after-effect of burying large amounts of organic materials. It is often a by-product of waste water reclamation systems as well. On a small decentralized level it is well established in other parts of the world, in particular China and India. Bio-gas technology is based on the phenomenon of decomposition of organic matter in the absence of air. This yields a gas consisting mainly of methane and carbon dioxide. In isolated rural villages or farm communities the bio-gas plant can serve many purposes: an efficient means of sewage treatment; a means of processing organic materials into a readily usable fertilizer; a source of gas for cooking or lighting; fuel for gas engines which in turn power vehicles, pumps, or electrical generators.

The *Advances in Bio-gas* project itself is an awkward insertion of small-scale bio-gas technology into a typical apartment living situation. It acknowledges on the one hand the United State's world leading per capita production of waste, and on the other, the high, anticipated number of career changes in a lifetime and its corresponding demand for mobility and adaptability. Inflatable furniture is essentially camping equipment, although in the late 60's a market for inflatable furniture exploded, perhaps appealing to the desires to "drop-out" but in so doing pull the plug on the living-room set and take it along. In any case inflatable furniture already has a place in the recent history of the american home.

The basic principle of bio-gas production is applied to this ensemble of inflatable furnishings. The mattress/water bed is converted into a digester; it's added appendages allow input of organic material and outflow of processed materials. The mattress is appropriate because of its horizontal configuration but also because the additional warmth drawn from the sleeper's body helps accelorate gas production. The rest of the system, the bed and end-table, serve as storage vessels and facilitate the use of the gas at an appropriate pressure level. The pressure, of course depends on the weight of the person sitting on the couch, or the number of books on the end-table. Successful operation of the "Advances in Biogas" system (if this is possible) will allow the owner/operator to permanently disconnect their apartment from sewage hook-up, external gas suppliers, and possibly electricity suppliers, thereby reducing the burden placed on global energy resources. In addition the owner/operator will gain a source of high quality fertilizer for use in domestic agriculture.

STORE(cheese) is a project developed in response to an accidental insecticide poisoning which took place on a Wisconsin dairy farm. The insecticide "Aldrin", is a chlorinated hydrocarbon compound, similiar to DDT, both of which were banned from agricultural use in the United States in the early 1970's. It was banned because of its most attractive feature—its persistance. This meant that a single application would keep working for long periods of time and led to Aldrin's acceptance and widespread use, often as a soil insecticide. It allowed farmers to plant corn contiguously on the same land instead of rotating crops to prevent root-worm damage. This persistence, however, was allowing it to spread over time through various plant and animal food chains and cause problems wherever it began to accumulate, including humans and in this case cows. 51 of this par-

wagen war groß genug für ein Bett und einige platzsparende Möbel und wurde mit Aschenbechern, einem Spiegel und einem Sessel mit Armlehnen ausgestattet, und wenn jemand daran dachte eine Batterie anzuschließen, gab es auch ein Radio und eine Deckenbeleuchtung.

Gebaut wurde die Unterkunft im Dezember 1987, auf einem unbewohnten, an ein Recycling-Gelände angrenzenden Stück Land, und sie blieb öffentlich zugänglich, bis sie im August 1988 demontiert wurde. Die Unterkunft funktionierte besser als vorhergesehen und schuf eine sehr warme, komfortable Umgebung. Gerüche und Dämpfe aus dem sich zersetzenden Mist bzw. Kompost stiegen nach oben auf und kamen aus dem Gipfel des Haufens, während in das Innere des VW-Lieferwagens eine beachtliche Hitze strahlte. Während des ganzen Winters betrug die Temperatur zwischen 70 und 80 Grad Fahrenheit, wenn die Tür dicht abgeschlossen war, sogar mehr. In den kältesten Nächten bedeutete dies einen Unterschied zur Außentemperatur von nahezu 100 Grad.

Während des Winters erfüllte der *Compost Shelter* eine Reihe unterschiedlicher Funktionen; ein beheizter Pausenraum für die im Freien arbeitenden Beschäftigten des Recycling-Centers; eine wissenschaftliche, museumsähnliche Vorführung der Zersetzungsprozesse für Schulklassen, die das Recycling-Center gelegentlich besuchten und vor allem eine Notunterkunft für Personen, die vorübergehend vom Abfallsammeln lebten und mit dem Recycling-Center Geschäfte betrieben. Zwar versuchte niemand, die Unterkunft ständig zu bewohnen (eine sehr reale Möglichkeit angesichts der örtlichen Armut und Obdachlosigkeit), jedoch wurde sie laufend als Nachtquartier benützt. Irgendjemand brachte eine alte Matratze mit, die den ganzen Winter über in der Unterkunft blieb. Oft wurden Eßverpackungen und Getränkedosen hinterlassen, ebenso Wachsspuren vom Abbrennen vieler Kerzen.

Die Produktion von Biogas ist etwas weniger bekannt als das Kompostieren, existiert jedoch in vielen verschiedenen Formen, üblicherweise vielleicht als unbeabsichtigte Folge des Vergrabens großer Mengen organischen Materials. Oft ist sie auch ein Nebenprodukt von Systemen zur Wiederaufbereitung von Abwässern. Auf kleiner, dezentraler Ebene ist sie in anderen Regionen der Erde, insbesondere in China und Indien, wohlbekannt. Die Biogastechnologie beruht auf dem Phänomen der Zersetzung organischen Materials unter Ausschluß von Luft. Hierbei entsteht ein Gas, das hauptsächlich aus Methan und Kohlendioxid besteht. In abgeschiedenen Dörfern auf dem Land oder in einer Siedlung von Bauernhöfen kann eine Biogasanlage viele Zwecke erfüllen: eine effiziente Methode der Abwasseraufbereitung; ein Mittel zur Verarbeitung organischen Materials zu einem fertig verwendbaren Dünger; eine Gasquelle zum Kochen und für die Beleuchtung; Treibstoff für Gasmotoren, die ihrerseits Kraftfahrzeuge, Pumpen oder elektrische Generatoren antreiben.

Das Projekt *Advances in Biogas* selbst ist die etwas unbeholfene Einführung einer Biogas-Kleintechnologie in die typische Wohnsituation in einem Apartment. Es anerkennt einerseits die in den Vereinigten Staaten weltweit höchste Pro-Kopf-Müllproduktion und andererseits die hohe voraussichtliche Anzahl von Karrieresprüngen während eines Lebens und das dementsprechende Bedürfnis nach Mobilität und Anpassungsfähigkeit. Aufblasbare Möbel sind hauptsächlich Bestandteil der Camping-Ausrüstung, wenngleich in den späten 60er Jahren der Markt für aufblasbare Möbel explodierte, was möglicherweise den „drop-out"-Wünschen entsprach, – den Stöpsel aus der Wohnzimmergarnitur ziehen und sie mitnehmen. Jedenfalle haben aufblasbare Möbel bereits ihren Platz in der jüngsten Geschichte des amerikanischen Heims.

Das grundlegende Prinzip der Biogasproduktion wird nun auf dieses Ensemble aufblasbarer Möbel angewandt. Die Matratze bzw. das Wasserbett wird in einen Verarbeitungsbehälter umgewandelt; die angeschlossenen Zusatzvorrichtungen erlauben die Zuführung von organischem Material und die Ausbringung von verarbeitetem Material. Die Matratze ist dafür wegen ihrer horizontalen Form geeignet und auch weil die zusätzliche Wärme aus dem Körper des Schlafenden dazu beiträgt, die Gasproduktion zu beschleunigen. Der Rest des Systems, Bett und Beistelltisch dienen als Lagergefäße und erleichtern die Verwendung des Gases unter geeigneten Druckverhältnissen. Der Druck hängt natürlich vom Gewicht der Person, die auf der Couch sitzt, ab oder von der Anzahl der Bücher auf dem Beistelltisch. Der erfolgreiche Betrieb des „Advances in Biogas"-Systems wird es (wenn überhaupt möglich) dem Eigentümer bzw. Bediener erlauben, sein Apartment auf Dauer von Kanalanschluß, externer Gaszufuhr und eventuellen Elektrizitätslieferanten abzunabeln und die Belastung der globalen Energieressourcen zu reduzieren. Darüber hinaus verfügt der Eigentümer bzw. Betreiber über eine Quelle zur Gewinnung von qualitativ hochwertigem Dünger für den Einsatz in der eigenen Landwirtschaft.

Store (cheese) ist ein Projekt, welches als Reaktion auf eine Insektizidvergiftung, die sich durch einen unglücklichen Zufall auf einer Milchfarm in Wisconsin ereignete, entwikkelt wurde. Das Insektizid „Aldrin" ist eine dem DDT ähnlicular farm's 84 dairy cows were contaminated when the animals ate some twenty year old insecticide left by the farm's previous owner as it began leaking through the cracks of an old storage building.

Aside from the health of his animals the most immediate concern to the farmer was the realization that the milk he was producing was contaminated and he no choice but to dump it down the milkhouse drain. The milk itself was the starting point for the Store(cheese) project. Here was a situation where the farmer was forced to "produce" what amounted to no more than a waste disposal problem. Continued milking of the cows was the first means of ridding the animals of the poison since the chemical latches itself onto fat molecules in the body of the cow, and those in the milk. A furthur complication was that dumping the milk risked introducing the chemical to other potentially problematic environments of the surrounding land or ground water.

A pause seemed necessary, one in which both the conditions of widespread chemical use in the recent past, as well as questions of toxicology and disposal could be considered. The preservation of the milk by producing cheese seemed an appropriate means of achieving this pause. The process of cheese-making itself was particularly fascinating as it echoed some of the bacteriological processes mentioned above, but here served as a means of concentrating and stabilizing the fat content of the milk, thereby stabilizing the toxin; food processing converted to waste management. It also introduced numerous levels of containment: Aldrin contained in the milk; milk preserved by the cheese-making; the cheese sealed in wax; then finally the whole cheese contained and observed in a modified refrigerator where it still remains waiting for a suitable mechanism of disposal to be established. It is also interesting to consider that this notion of containment, which now seems so unavoidable, is virtually antithetical to the agrichemical industry's particular mandate of extensive chemical dispersion.

The modified refrigerator with the contaminated cheese was presented publicly in the small town near where the accident occured. Its Installation was coordinated with the local newspaper so that information would be available and numerous related issues could be discussed at the time of the refrigerator's appearance.

Legal Cheese is closely related to Store(cheese) but rather than using milk which excedes governmental standards for pesticides in food, *Legal Cheese* is made with milk containing clearly identifiable levels of pesticide but within allowable levels, that is, less than .03 parts per million. This cheese, according the United States government, is consumable and for this reason can be handled and exhibited in a less restrictive way.

All of these projects have involved the expertise and assistance of others, I would like to specifically thank: Mitchell Kane, Laurie Winter and Howard Hirsh, of the Hirsch Farm Project, Northbrook, Illinois, for making the Store (cheese) project possible; Ken Dunn and the

Resource Center, Chicago, Illinois; Martin Carrera; and finally Connie Spreen.

che chlorierte Kohlenwasserstoffverbindung. Es wurde ebenso wie DDT in den Vereinigten Staaten in den frühen 70er Jahren von einer Verwendung in der Landwirtschaft ausgeschlossen. Es wurde gerade wegen seines attraktivsten Merkmals, des nachhaltigen Effekts, verboten. Eine einzige Anwendung wirkte über viele Zeitperioden und dies führte zur Akzeptanz und weitverbreiteten Anwendung von Aldrin, oft als Bodeninsektizid. Es gestattete den Farmern, Korn stets auf dem gleichen Feld anzupflanzen, anstatt die Anbauflächen zu wechseln um Wurzelschädlinge zu vermeiden. Diese Nachhaltigkeit führte jedoch mit der Zeit zu seiner Verbreitung in den verschiedenen pflanzlichen und tierischen Nahrungsketten und verursachte Probleme, woimmer es sich ansammelte, auch bei Menschen und in diesem Fall bei Kühen. 51 der 84 Milchkühe der besagten Farm wurden kontaminiert, als die Tiere das an die zwanzig Jahre alte Insektizid, das vom Vorbesitzer der Farm zurückgelassen worden war und das durch die Risse in einem alten Lagergebäude sickerte, fraßen.

Was den Farmer, abgesehen vom Gesundheitszustand seiner Tiere, am unmittelbarsten traf, war die Erkenntnis, daß die Milch, die er produzierte, verseucht war, und daß er keine andere Wahl hatte, als sie in die Senkgrube zu schütten. Die Milch war der eigentliche Ansatzpunkt für das Store (cheese)-Projekt. Hier lag eine Situation vor, in der der Farmer gezwungen war, etwas zu „produzieren", was lediglich ein Abfallbeseitigungsproblem darstellte. Kontinuierliches Melken der Kühe war die beste Methode zur Entgiftung der Tiere, da sich das chemische Mittel an den Fettmolekülen im Körper der Kuh, ergo in der Milch, absetzte. Eine weitere Komplikation bestand darin, daß der chemische Stoff mit dem Wegschütten der Milch in andere, potentiell problematische Bereiche des angrenzenden Bodens oder Grundwassers eindringen konnte.

Erforderlich war also eine Pause, in der sowohl die Umstände des weitverbreiteten Chemieeinsatzes in der jüngsten Vergangenheit, wie auch die Fragen der Toxokologie und der Beseitigung überdacht werden konnten. Die Aufbewahrung der Milch über die Produktion von Käse schien ein geeigneter Weg, eine solche Pause zu erzielen. Das Verfahren der Käseerzeugung selbst war besonders faszinierend, da es einige der oben erwähnten bakteriologischen Prozesse reflektierte, hier jedoch als Methode zur Konzentrierung und Stabilisierung des Fettgehalts der Milch und damit zur Stabiliserung des Gifts, diente. Nahrungsmittelverarbeitung verwandelte sich in Abfallmanagement. Auch lagen hier mehrere Behälterebenen vor: Aldrin war in der Milch enthalten; die Milch wurde durch die Käseerzeugung aufbewahrt; der

Käse wurde in Wachs versiegelt; und schlußendlich wurde der ganze Käse in einem umgebauten Kühlschrank aufbewahrt und überwacht, wo er noch immer darauf wartet, daß eine entsprechende Beseitigungsmaschinerie errichtet wird. Interessant ist auch die Überlegung, daß dieser nun ganz unvermeidlich scheinende Begriff des Behälters, in Wirklichkeit eine Antithese zum speziellen Grundsatz der agrochemischen Industrie, nämlich der extensiven Chemiestreuung, darstellt.

Der umgebaute Kühlschrank mit dem verseuchten Käse wurde in der kleinen Stadt nahe dem Unfallsort öffentlich präsentiert. Seine Installierung wurde mit der Lokalzeitung abgesprochen, sodaß die Informationen zur Verfügung standen und zahlreiche verwandte Themenstellungen wahrend der Zeit, in der der Kühlschrank ausgestellt war, diskutiert werden konnten.

Legal Cheese steht in einem nahen Zusammenhang mit *Store* (cheese), – anstelle einer Milch, die die Grenzwerte der Regierung für Pestizide in Nahrungsmitteln überschreitet, verwendet *Legal Cheese* Milch mit eindeutig feststellbaren Pestizidanteilen, die jedoch innerhalb der zulässigen Grenzen liegen, d. h. weniger als 0,03 Teile pro Million. Dieser Käse ist laut US-Regierung konsumierbar und kann daher mit weniger Einschränkungen gehandhabt und ausgestellt worden.

Bei allen diesen Projekten waren andere Personen beteiligt und haben Hilfestellung gewährt. Besonders danken möchte ich Mitchell Kane, Laurie Winter und Howard Hirsh vom Hirsch Farm Project, Northbrook, Illinois für die Ermöglichung des *STORE (cheese)*-Projekts; Ken Dunn und dem Resource Conter, Chicago, Illinois; Martin Carrera und schließlich Connie Spreen.

Courtesy by the artist.

SMALL LANDSCAPE, IM MEER, SCHIMMELHAUFEN

DIETER ROTH

Courtesy N. u. C. Heinrich, Stuttgart, und Museum Moderner Kunst, Wien, sowie Galerie Metropol, Wien.

TRANS-FORM

PETER SANDBICHLER

TRANS-FORM
PETER SANDBICHLER

Conventional wisdom puts the artist at the origin of artificial life. Or perhaps the place of its origin is only made possible by the presence of a skilful creative being, just like the purposeful order, the telos, that is imposed on the process of life from then on. Science fiction cinema, for instance, which usually resorts to anthropomorphic creatures to pose questions about artificial life, likes to tell creation myths and tales of suffering. At its beginning stands a (mad) scientist on the borders between industry, art and science, with his goal-oriented intentions and a certainty about right from the beginning about how artificial life is supposed to go.

What comes out of this is in most cases just a tool-like robot, a copy of (human) life, or to be more precise, some of its mechanistically reduced functions, while the emergence of life in the artifice is provided when the *Golem* becomes violent; that the replicants in Blade Runner develop a memory and demand longer lives or that the law enforcement combat robots in Robocop only seek out their own targets; in short, that within the homogeneity of a once-fixed program implementation, an insurmountable heterogeneous movement constitutes a monstrous disturbance: a deviation signifying that artificial life would like to forget its origins and escape the hand of the artist.

Out of the cinema, into the grand foyer of the Brucknerhaus. There, it could be said, stands a big aluminium sculpture named *Trans-Form*, because the artist Peter Sandbichler, it could further be argued, put it there.

There is in fact in Sandbichler's work, as there is in the hundreds of aluminium pipes of varying lengths that are connected end to end, a creative decision about the so-standing (or so-lying), about the posture of these sculptures. Some have no definite up or down, a priori, no position or integration of their parts; the rightness of which is open to individual judgement. The *table with bended legs* (1988) has a surface plate and four wooden legs, each in the shape of a J, and which can be bolted together in many different ways - or on the other hand, not at all: a three-legged table and a leg as a luxury extra—so that the table has a different posture every time and the sculpture goes through the full repertoire of its existential possibilities. How the table stands, and what it is, is determined by a decision that must always be made in the context of, and in reaction to, a space, a

Ein gängiges Bild vom künstlichen Leben stellt an den Ursprung dieses Lebens einen Künstler. Oder vielleicht wird die Stelle des Ursprungs erst dadurch möglich, daß eine kunstfertige Schöpfergestalt an ihr sitzt, ebenso wie die zielgerichtete Ordnung, das Telos, das dem Lebensprozeß von dort weg auferlegt wird. Das Science Fiction-Kino etwa, das sich Fragen nach künstlichem Leben meist anhand antropomorpher Kreaturen stellt, erzählt von diesem Leben gerne Schöpfungsgeschichten und Leidenswege. An deren Anfang steht ein (Mad) Scientist, Grenzgänger zwischen Industrie, Kunst und Wissenschaft, mit seinen zwecksetzenden Intentionen und seinem Bewußtsein, das von vornherein weiß, wie das künstliche Leben richtigerweise zu verlaufen hat.

Was dabei herauskommt, ist meist nur ein werkzeughafter Automat, Kopie des (menschlichen) Lebens bzw. einiger seiner mechanistisch reduzierten Funktionen, während das Auftauchen von Leben im Künstlichen davon herrührt, daß der *Golem* rabiat wird, daß die Replikanten in *Blade Runner* ein Gedächtnis entwickeln und mehr Lebenszeit fordern oder daß die Law Enforcement-Kampfroboter in *Robocop* sich ihre Ziele nur noch selbst suchen, kurz: daß in der Homogenität von einmal fixierten Programmabläufen eine irreduzible heterogene Bewegung als monströse Störung auftritt: eine Abweichung als Zeichen dafür, daß künstliches Leben seinen Ursprung gerne vergißt und der Künstlerhand entfleucht.

Raus aus dem Kino, ins große Foyer des Linzer Brucknerhauses. Dort steht, könnte man meinen, eine große Aluminiumskulptur mit dem Titel *Trans-Form*, weil der Künstler Peter Sandbichler, könnte man weiters meinen, sie so dorthingestellt hat.

Tatsächlich gibt es in Sandbichlers Arbeit, so auch bei den Hunderten von unterschiedlich langen und kontinuierlich aneinandergesteckten Aluminiumrohren, eine schöpferischen Entscheidung über das So-Stehen (oder So-Liegen), über die Stellung der Skulpturen. Einige haben keinerlei a priori festgelegtes Oben und Unten, keine Positionierung oder Zusammensetzung ihrer Teile, über deren Richtigkeit souverän zu entscheiden wäre. Der *table with bended legs*

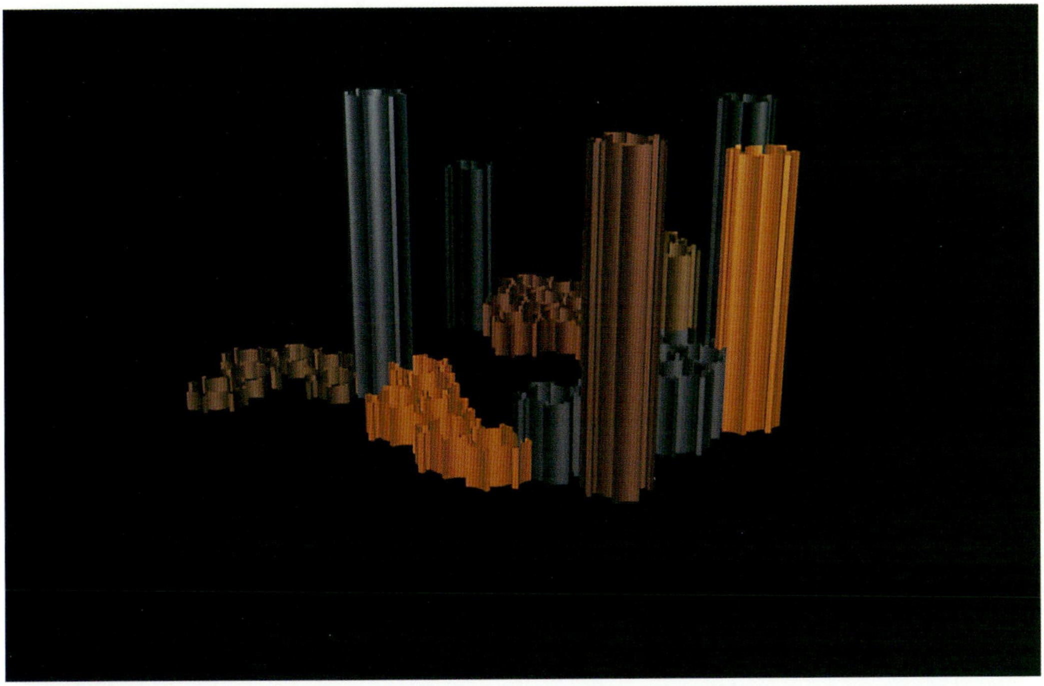

von 1988 hat eine Platte und vier Beine aus Holz, jeweils in Form eines J, und die mittels Schraubzwingen auf eine Vielzahl von Arten - oder auch gar nicht: ein dreibeiniger Tisch und ein Bein als genußvoller Überschuß - verbunden werden können, sodaß der Tisch eine jeweils andere Stellung einnimmt und die Skulptur die Fülle ihrer Seinsmöglichkeiten durchspielt. Wie der Tisch steht und was er ist, verdankt sich einer Entscheidung, die stets im Kontext, im Reagieren auf einen Raum, eine Situation zu treffen ist, und die einen aktuellen Momentschnitt durch einen virtuellen Verwandlungsprozeß zieht.

Die Stellung der Aluminiumskulptur *Trans-Form* ist ein weiteresmal Produkt einer radikal empirischen, sich auf ihre Umgebung hin öffnenden Entscheidung, und ihr künstlicher Lebensprozeß beginnt dort, wo ein sich aktuell und materiell vollziehender Veränderungsstrom den vom Künstler gesetzten Ursprung dem Vergessen preisgibt. Das Profil, durch das alle Rohre gemäß einem invarianten Verkettungscode aneinandergesteckt sind, ist nach acht möglichen Richtungen hin offen, von denen jeweils maximal vier gleichzeitig besetzbar sind. Das heißt, die Skulptur kann zwar nicht an jedem Punkt, aber an einer Vielzahl von beliebigen Punkten auseinandergenommen und neu zusammengesetzt werden. Das Konzept geht hier über ein Angebot an die Vorstellungskraft hinaus, hin zum plastischen Anders-Werden der Anordnung, an der alle nicht bloß Betrachtenden durch das Umstecken von Rohren handfeste Eingriffe und Variationen vornehmen.

Sandbichlers Aufstellen ist hier in gravierender Weise kein Ausstellen mehr, sondern ein Verstellen, und vor allem: Es ist nicht mehr *seine* Stellung, in der die Skulptur lebt. Der Mad Scientist gibt die Kreatur aus der Hand, und das Metall-Trumm wird zum Monstrum: nicht nur, indem es sich als fremdartige Präsenz dahinwindet und plötzlich an unerwarteten Stellen (wieder) auftaucht, sondern indem es wächst, sich verformt, sich auf unvorhersehbare Weise verwandelt. *Trans-Form* ist ein künstliches Lebewesen, das mit seiner Umgebung interagiert, sein Stoffwechsel ist ein unendlicher maschineller Produktionszyklus, der keine stabile Identitätsform kennt. Nach Abschluß der Auf- und Ausstellung wird *Trans-Form* ein anderes geworden sein und sich bewegt, seine Stellung im Raum verändert haben. Vielleicht wird der Metamorph mit seinem kontinuierlichen Körper aus 500m Alurohr sich durch Teilung vermehrt haben; niemand weiß, ob und an welchen Stellen die Profil-Steck-Kette abreißen und eine neues Skulpturwesen entstehen wird, um sich womöglich von seinem Artgenossen davonzuschlängeln.

situation, and which puts a momentary view through a process of virtual transformation.

The posture of the aluminium sculpture *Trans-Form* is once again the product of a radically empirical choice opening itself to its surroundings, and its artistic life process begins where a topically and materially occurring process of transformation allows the origin initiated by the artist to become forgotten. The image by which all the pipes are laid end to end in an invariant chain-forming code, is open to eight possible directions, of which no more than four can be in use at any time. That means the sculpture can be taken apart and put back together again, not at every point but at a number of points. This concept goes beyond the choice of the power of the imagination, to the plastic transformation of the arrangement, in which all active observers can intervene and bring about changes by manually re-connecting the pipes.

For Sandbichler, to install is in a real way no longer just to exhibit, but to adjust, and above all it is no longer his intervention through which the sculpture lives. The mad scientist releases the creature, and the metal colossus becomes a monster, not just by disappearing as an alien presence and reappearing suddenly in unexpected places, but by growing, becoming deformed, changing unpredictably. *Trans-Form* is an artificial being that interacts with its environment, its metabolism is an unending mechanistic production cycle without a stable form of identity. After completion of its installation and exhibition, *Trans-Form* will have become something else, will have moved and changed its position in space. Perhaps this metamorphic being with its continuous body comprised of 500 metres of aluminium piping will have multiplied through division; no-one knows whether or at which points this profile chain assembly will break apart and a new sculptural entity will be born; only to snake away from its kind when given the chance.

Whoever wants to can pretend to be the mother or father of a new piece of artificial life, or purloin a small pipe to take home from this unsurveillable place, thus contributing to the total deterritorialisation of the piece. In the extreme case, not a single pipe would be left of *Trans-Form* in the end, and the epidemic spread and duplication of this artificial life form would, from a location point of view, look like its disappearance, its death. The decisive factor though is that by reassembling and messing around, the humans become a part of the reproductive system and vehicle in *Trans-Form*'s life process, without which the latter would have to be subject to the control of a human consciousness. Instead the sculpture owes its wild, aimless, rhizomatic growth to the multitude of intervening actions which come together through the *Trans-Form* machine, but are not causally dependant on each other; a non-individual (therefore divisible), unconscious process. None of the momentary transformation conditions can in itself represent the creature of this life, and the substance of *Trans-Form* flows only in its differentiations; no act of assembly is privileged above the others, not even those of Peter Sandbichler, but each one is decisive because it creates something new.

As for the criterion of shaping memory, one of those by which artificial life is judged...: aluminium is patient and forgetful (though it can reveal traces of ageing), but a video camera set for time lapse photography will record various stages in the life of *Trans-Form* for posterity and, where possible, reveal who really did take a pipe home with them.

Drehli Robnik

TRANS-FORM (THEORETICALLY EVENT OF INFINITE PARTS)

Sculpture is an open system. It consists of any number of parts. Its position in space is variable, just like the other parameters that determine its shape.
As new spaces are opened up (computer generated, artificial spaces), a sculptural concept also has to change. Just as the function, morphology, meaning and bedeutungsraum (verticals, horizontals, social sculpture ...) of sculpture / the sculpture concept has been transformed in recent decades, altered concepts are now being introduced into the theory and practise of sculpture creation (the flexible, variable, randomised sculpture).
The sculpture model takes shape on the computer. The surroundings are at first artificial, before the work is extrapolated into real space. The creation and design of the model is subject to random processes that the artist no longer consciously controls. A form (shape) is created through "blind" scaling, transformation, positioning (in that the computer model only takes into account one spatial view). This way the artist escapes the traps of a formal aesthetic. The elements of the sculpture can be changed in the space by the viewer.
This has the effect that even in its solid form the sculpture has no definitive and final shape but is put in a processual and historical context.
Through the altered function of the sculpture and its variability, its temporary, provisional anordnungen also become models of social, biological, chaotic contexts and systems, as changing one parameter influences others.

Constanze Ruhm

Wer will, kann sich an dieser unverhersehbaren Stelle als Mutter oder Vater eines neuen Stücks künstlichen Lebens verkennen oder gar ein kleines Rohr entwenden und mit sich nehmen, um so zur völligen Deterritorialisierung des Wesens beizutragen. Im Extremfall wäre von *Trans-Form* schlußendlich nicht ein Rohr mehr übrig, und die epidemische Ausbreitung und Vermehrung des künstlichen Lebewesens würde unter dem Gesichtspunkt der Seßhaftigkeit aussehen wie sein Verschwinden, sein Tod. Entscheidend ist aber, daß die umsteckenden und verstellenden Menschlein ein Teil im Fortpflanzungssystem und Bewegungsapparat, im Lebensprozeß von *Trans-Form* sind, ohne daß dieses dadurch einem menschlichen Bewußtsein unterworfen wäre. Vielmehr ist es die Vielheit der durch die *Trans-Form*-Maschine verknüpften, aber nicht kausal voneinander abhängigen Eingriffe, ist es ein nicht-individueller (also teilbarer), unbewußter Prozeß, in dem die Skulptur ihr wucherndes, zielloses, rhizomatisches Wachstum entfaltet. Keiner der momentanen Transformationszustände kann für sich genommen das Wesen dieses Lebens repräsentieren, und die Substanz von *Trans-Form* fließt nur in ihren Differenzierungen; keinem der Handgriffe kommt ein Privileg vor den anderen zu, auch denen von Peter Sandbichler nicht, aber jeder ist entscheidend, weil er etwas Neues hervorbringt.
Was das Kriterium der Gedächtnisbildung angeht, an dem künstliches Leben unter anderen gemessen wird...: Aluminium ist zwar geduldig und vergeßlich (obwohl seine Eloxierung Spuren der Alterung verzeichnen kann), aber eine Videokamera mit Zeitrafferschaltung wird diverse Lebensabschnitte von *Trans-Form* auf Erinnerungsbildern speichern und womöglich auch registrieren, wer nun wirklich ein Rohr mit nach Hause genommen hat.

Drehli Robnik

TRANS/FORM / EINE INTERAKTIVE SKULPTUR VON PETER SANDBICHLER

Die Skulptur „TRANS/FORM" ist ein offenes System. Sie setzt sich aus beliebig vielen Teilen). Ihre Position im Raum ist variabel, so wie alle anderen Parameter, die ihre Form bestimmen.
Dieses System kann bestimmten Regeln unterworfen sein, die Einfluß auf Gestalt und Veränderung der Parameter ha-

ben (kann, aber muß nicht: das ergibt sich aus dem Set-Up, dem Operating System der Skulptur, das der Künstler von Fall zu Fall variieren kann). Die einzige Regel, die zwingend ist und sich aus der Form des einzelnen skulpturalen Elements ergibt, ist die Kompatibilität der Elementprofile mit sich selbst. Jedes Modul wird auf sich selbst angewendet. Das Modell der Skulptur entsteht am Computer. Das Environment ist künstlich, bevor die Arbeit in den realen Raum extrapoliert wird. Die Entstehung und Gestaltung dieses Modell wird zufälligen Prozessen unterworfen, die vom Künstler nicht mehr bewußt entschieden werden. Eine Form („Gestalt") entsteht durch blindes Skalieren, Transformieren, Positionieren (indem bei der Erstellung des Computermodells beispielsweise nur eine Raumansicht berücksichtigt wird). So entgeht der Künstler den Fallen einer Ästhetik der Gestaltung.
Die Module lassen sich ineinander stecken und verschieben, im virtuellen Raum frei skalieren, werden sie zu unterschiedlichsten Modellen einer Basisform und unterliegen ihren eigenen Wachstumsgesetzen. Der Betrachter/Benutzer ist in der Lage, einen beliebigen Zustand der Skulptur herzustellen und wieder zu verwerfen.
„TRANS/FORM" besitzt in der räumlichen Ausführung keine definitive und endgültige Gestalt, sondern wird in einem prozessualen und historischen Zusammenhang gerückt. Die skulpturale Praxis von „TRANS/FORM" schafft ein chaotisch-dynamisches System, das aufgrund der Vernetzung unterschiedlichster Assoziationen von gesellschaftlichen, wissenschaftlichen und historischen Erfahrungen (Molekularketten, DNA, Wachstumsalgorithmen, künstliches Leben ...) ein gegenüber selbst kleinsten Veränderungen seiner Anfangsbedingungen bzw. Parameter sehr sensibles System ist und gerade deshalb ein Modell komplexer Wechselwirkungen unseres environments darstellt.
So mutieren die Skulptur und ihr Begriff in viele unabsehbare Richtungen (die flexible, variable, randomisierte Skulptur).
Neue Begriffe werden in die Theorie und Praxis der Skulpturgenerierung eingführt. Hier läßt sich eine deutliche Veränderung des skulpturalen Konzepts ablesen, die als Konsequenz der Entstehung neuer, computersimulierter Räume gedeutet werden muß. Es geht hier nicht so sehr um die strapazierten Verhältnisse von „wirklich" und „künstlich", sondern vielmehr wird deutlich, wie eine (angenommen) „wirkliche Welt" (der reale Entwurf), die über ein menschliches Interface in eine „künstliche" Welt (der Entwurf am Computer) transponiert wird, verändert zurückkehrt (in den „wirklichen" Raum), um virtuelle Zusammenhänge zu simulieren.

Es wird nicht die Wirklichkeit gesampelt, als Rohmaterial ausgebeutet und in sogenannte „neue“ Zusammenhänge und Kontexte gebracht, sondern der virtuelle Raum des Computers wird verwendet, um einen Ort zu erschaffen, der vor dem Prozessieren der Skulptur/der Module durch den Rechner noch gar nicht vorhanden war. Die Skulptur hat sich einen neuen Ort er-funden.
Dieser Ort existiert unter den veränderten Bedingungen der TRANS-FORMATION (eine Form wird verschoben, und auch ihr Begriff) eines Modells, das sich selbst überschreitet.

Computermodell: Constanze Ruhm, ausgeführt an der Städelschule, Institut für Neue Medien, Frankfurt am Main.

Das Projekt wurde ermöglicht durch die großzügige Förderung der Fa. Piesslinger, Linz

NOTIZEN ZUR EPIGENETISCHEN KUNST: DIE EZECHIEL SERIE

ROMAN VEROSTKO

Absichten. In meinen über dreißig Jahren als Künstler habe ich stets versucht, wohlgefertigte Arbeiten mit ikonenhaften Qualitäten zu schaffen, die in beziehungsreicher Weise auf versteckte Realität verweisen. Solange ich mich erinnern kann, war ich immer überwältigt, wenn ich mir Zeit nahm, mir etwas wirklich anzusehen und es als „seiend" zu betrachten und dann zu überlegen, ob das Gegenteil möglich sei – „nicht zu sein". „Wie wäre es", fragte ich mich, „wenn es kein mich – keine Wolke – keine Erde gäbe? Schon früh lernte ich, mir über das „großartige" Ereignis, daß Dinge einfach „so wie sie sind" existieren, Gedanken zu machen. Innerhalb alltäglicher Phänomene lernte ich, eine „versteckte" großartige Welt voller Geheimnisse zu sehen. Mein Zugang zur Kunst erwuchs aus diesem Staunen, indem er immer voll Ehrfurcht gegenüber Materialien der Erde war und immer ein Gefühl von Staunen über die meisten Dinge beibehielt. Schließlich begann dies auch Schalttafeln, Computersprachen und die Formen, die man mit einfachen Algorithmen erforschen konnte, einzuschließen.
In diesem Essay können die Ausdrücke „Code", „Software" und „Instruktionen" abwechselnd und miteinander austauschbar verwendet werden. Generell beziehen wir uns auf kodierte Vorgänge und Algorithmen, die in ein Instruktionsprogramm für einen Computer integriert werden können.
Während der letzten zehn Jahre lang habe ich Codes geschrieben und staunte dabei über ihr Vermögen, Form mit einem Computer zu untersuchen. Codierte elektronische Verfahren verschaffen Künstlern ein grundlegend neues und wirksames Werkzeug zur Untersuchung einer wunderbaren Welt unsichtbarer Formen. Jene, die ihre Kunst mit codierten Verfahren integrieren, stehen an der Schwelle einer neuen Grenze. Diese Grenze zu überschreiten, ist für einen Künstler jedoch aufgrund zweier großer Hürden schwierig. Eine davon ist die Aufgabe, Form-erzeugende Ideen in einen praktischen Arbeitscode zu übersetzen. Die andere besteht in der Suche nach geeigneten Materialien und darin,

NOTES ON EPIGENETIC ART: THE EZEKIEL SERIES
ROMAN VEROSTKO

Intentions. For over 30 years, as an artist, I have always tried to create well crafted works with icon-like qualities pointing in some evocative way to hidden reality. As early as I can remember I was always awestruck when I took time to really look at something and think about it as "being" and then contemplate whether the opposite was possible—"not being". "What would it be like", I wondered, "if there were no me—no cloud—no earth? Early on I learned to wonder about the "marvelous" event of things existing just "the way they are". Within commonplace phenomena I learned to see a "hidden" marvelous world filled with mystery. My approach to art grew from this marveling, always holding a reverence for the materials of earth and a sense of wonder about most things. Eventually this came to include circuit boards, computer languages, and the forms one could explore with simple algorithms.
In this essay the terms "code", "software" and "instructions" may be used interchangeably. In general we are referring to coded procedures and algorithms which may be integrated in a program of instructions for a computer.
For the past decade I have been writing code and marveling at its power as a procedure for investigating form with a computer. Coded electronic procedures provide artists with a radically new and powerful tool for investigating a marvelous world of unseen form. Those who integrate their art with coded procedures are on the threshold of a new frontier. To tap this frontier as an artist there have been two great hurdles. One has been the task of translating form-generating ideas into a practical working code. The other has been the search for appropriate materials and methods for achieving tangible archival quality work.
The code as a form-generator is only half of the struggle. To succeed as "art" the form must be successfully engendered in something tangible—something one can see, touch, feel or hear. Some years ago an artist friend, standing by an elm tree, asked "What gives this tree such a powerful presence?" And he answered, noting that "you can touch it—feel its surface—its 'being here'"!. Because aesthetic experience involves the senses one cannot separate "art"

from its material embodiment. In my current work the form necessarily includes the paper, surface, texture, color, and manner of presentation — the total experience. The nature and quality of materials have been carefully chosen and transformed in the process. For me, the finished work should have an aura that invites the casual viewer to pause for a moment, sensing that the work, as a human endeavor, goes beyond material concerns.

Studio Workers, Robotnics. Many people who visit my studio are surprised when they see engineering plotters cabled to two computer work stations—one for research and development—the other for creating art. When a plotter is working, visitors often stand with eyes glued on the drawing arm which, with a "seeming intelligence", draws precisely, surprisingly, and without hesitation—executing literally thousands of lines—changing colors—first here and then there. These plotters exude an uncanny presence! They have become members of the studio family—there's Brunelleschi, a nine year old 14 pen plotter, the first one I ever used—then another one named Alberti who executed all the frontispieces for a limited edition of George Boole's "Derivation of the Laws" (1989–90). Our latest member of the family, Botticelli, has a 36 inch bed and has been executing the recent Ezekiel Series.

These workers, robotniks, tirelessly execute instructions fed to them from computers. The computers interpret the code for them. The code is essentially a set of detailed instructions for making the work, i.e., what steps to take to make a color decision or how to determine control points. This procedure for making art, which I have called "epigenetic" is employed, to some degree, by a number of artists working today.

Epigenetic Art. The term epigenesis, borrowed from biology, refers to the process whereby a mature plant or phenotype grows from a seed or genotype. By analogy, in my studio, the art work (phenotype) "grows" from the software (genotype). Although the sofware contains the essential "form generating" information, it requires an appropriate "environment" and "nurturing" if it is to generate a mature work of art. This process of actually "growing" the work in some tangible form is, by analogy, "epigenetic". The mature art form, likened to phenotype, can only be "grown" with tangible materials—paper and inks—and then only with an appropriate set-up of computer and plotter which constitute, as it were, a nurturing environment. The convergence of all these elements is required for "growing" the art work, a process analagous to biological epigenesis.

A Personal Expert System. The software, with a computer and a plotter, constitutes a "personal expert system". The system is capable of generating visual forms of interest to me as an artist—forms whose origins the artist can both reveal and conceal with recursive improvisations. The choice of materials and the evolution of the software grew side by side over a period of ten years. Experimentation with paper, inks and plotting procedures has been extensive. Through trial and errror and seemingly endless

Methoden zu finden, die es möglich machen, greifbare, archivierende Qualitätsarbeit zu erzielen.

Der Code als ein Form-Erzeuger ist aber nur die halbe Mühe. Um als „Kunst" erfolgreich zu sein, muß die Form erfolgreich in etwas Greifbarem hervorgebracht werden – etwas, das man sehen, angreifen, fühlen oder hören kann. Vor einigen Jahren fragte ein Künstlerfreund von mir, als er bei einer Ulme stand: „Was gibt diesem Baum so eine kraftvolle Präsenz?" Und er antwortete, indem er anmerkte, das sei „seine Angreifbarkeit – die Tatsache, daß man seine Oberfläche befühlen könne – sein Da Sein"! Da die ästhetische Erfahrung die Sinne einschließt, kann man Kunst nicht von ihrer materiellen Körperlichkeit trennen. In meiner momentanen Arbeit beinhaltet die Form notwendigerweise das Papier, die Oberfläche, die Beschaffenheit, die Farbe und die Art der Präsentation – also die gesamte Erfahrung. Die Art und Qualität des Materials sind im Prozess sorgfältig ausgewählt und verändert worden. Für mich sollte die fertige Arbeit eine Aura besitzen, die den beiläufigen Betrachter veranlaßt, einen Moment lang innezuhalten, und zu fühlen, daß die Arbeit, als ein menschliches Streben über die materiellen Belange hinausgeht.

Studio Workers, Robotnics. Viele Leute, die mein Atelier besuchen, sind erstaunt, wenn sie die technischen Drucker an zwei Computer Work Stations angeschlossen sehen – einen für Forschung und Entwicklung – den anderen für die Kreation von Kunst. Wenn ein Drucker arbeitet, stehen Besucher oft davor und können ihre Augen nicht von dem Zeichenarm nehmen, der mit „scheinbarer Intelligenz" präzise, überraschend und ohne zu zögern – buchstäblich tausende Linien ausführend – zeichnet und die Farben ändert – einmal hier dann dort. Diese Drucker strahlen eine unheimliche Präsenz aus! Sie sind Mitglieder der Atelierfamilie geworden – da ist Brunelleschi, ein neun Jahre alter 14-Stift-Drucker, der erste, den ich je verwendete – dann ein weiterer namens Alberti, der alle Titelbilder für eine limitierte Auflage von George Booles „Ursprung der Gesetze" (1989–90) ausführte. Unser neuestes Mitglied dieser Familie ist Botticelli, der die jüngst entstandende Ezechiel Serie ausgeführt hat.

Diese Arbeiter, *Robotnics*, führen unermüdlich Anweisungen aus, die ihnen über den Computer eingespeist werden. Die Computer interpretieren den Code für sie. Der Code ist im wesentlichen ein Reihe detailierter Instruktionen zur Ausführung der Arbeit, d. h. welche Schritte zu unternehmen sind, um Farbentscheidungen zu treffen, oder wie man Kontrollpunkte bestimmt. Dieser Vorgang Kunst zu erzeugen, den ich „epigenetisch" genannt habe, wird bis zu einem gewissen Grad von einigen heutzutage arbeitenden Künstlern angewandt.

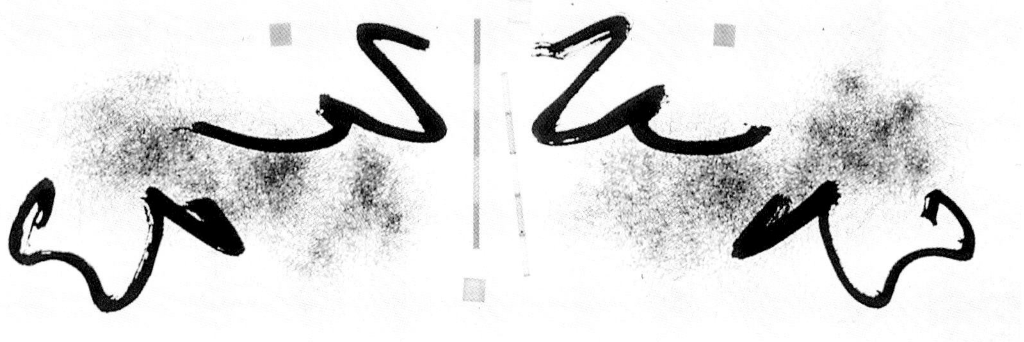

Epigenetische Kunst. Der Ausdruck *Epigenesis*, von der Biologie geliehen, bezieht sich auf den Vorgang, bei dem eine ausgewachsene Pflanze oder ein Phänotypus aus einem Samen oder Genotypus wächst. Analog „wächst" in meinem Atelier das Kunstwerk (Phänotypus) aus der Software (Genotypus). Obwohl die Software die grundlegende „form-erzeugende" Information beinhaltet, erfordert sie eine entsprechende „Umwelt" und „Nahrung", wenn sie ein reifes Kunstwerk erzeugen soll. Dieser Prozeß des tatsächlichen „Züchtens" der Arbeit in einer greifbaren Form ist, in Analogie, „epigenetisch". Die reife Kunstform, verglichen mit dem Phänotypus, kann nur mit greifbaren Materialien „gezogen" werden – wie Papier und Tinten – und dann nur mit einer passenden Zusammenstellung von Computer und Drucker, die, sozusagen, eine ernährende Umwelt ausmachen. Das Zusammentreffen aller dieser Elemente ist erforderlich, um das Kunstwerk zu züchten, ein Prozeß analog zur biologischen Epigenese.

Ein persönliches Expertensystem. Die Sofware, mit einem Computer und einem Drucker, bildet ein „persönliches Expertensystem". Das System ist fähig, visuelle Formen zu erzeugen, die für mich als Künstler interessant sind – Formen, deren Ursprünge der Künstler mit rekursiven Improvisationen sowohl auf-, als auch verdecken kann. Die Auswahl der Materialien und die Entwicklung der Software wuchsen Seite an Seite über einen Zeitraum von zehn Jahren. Es wurde umfassend mit Papier, Tinten und Druckverfahren experimentiert. Durch Versuch und Irrtum und scheinbar endlose Stunden des Experimentierens entwickelte sich das System zu einem einzigartigen Set von Verfahren mit einer eigenen Sprache.

Hodos. Die Software, unter laufender Überarbeitung, ist ein integriertes Netzwerk von Verfahren namens *Hodos* nach dem griechischen Wort für „Pfad" oder „Weg". Dieser Ausdruck beschreibt am besten die sich entfaltenden Formen

hours of experimentation, the system has evolved into a unique set of procedures with a language of its own.

Hodos. The software, under ongoing revision, is an integrated network of routines named Hodos taken from the Greek word for "path" or "way". This term best describes the unfolding forms of the first series of plotted works which were conceived as "pathways". Following a period of teaching in China I recognized many analogies between "hodos" and the oriental concept of "dao" (tao, the way). My studio, named "Pathway Studio" has an oriental seal carved by the distinguished shufa master, Wang Dong Ling. Wang, awed by the brush strokes of the computer, chose the classic expression "xiao jing zhai", "little footpath studio", as appropriate for the seal. Many works executed in the studio receive this seal.

Families of form. Hodos is capable of generating a family of forms with each being simultaneously related and "one of a kind". This is possible because the system operates like a chaotic system subject to the "butterfly effect". The "butterfly" effect refers to the observation that even minute phenomena in such a system affect the whole—the flapping of a butterfly wing is said to have an effect on world weather patterns.

The Hodos routines are parameter driven with procedures capable of generating visual form with outcomes subject to similar effects. By "parameter driven" we mean routines that perform a function "not more than" and "not fewer than" so many degrees, pen strokes, or colors. The slightest change, say a .005 change in the initiating seed, affects all the controlling parameters and consequently the final form. The "auto" modes built into the system allow "Hodos" to alter its variables and to do so within parameters that I may choose to control—or not control. The consequent forms are interrelated by the degree of variation in the program parameters and the way such parameters are controlled—or not controlled. This dialectic between "control" and "uncontrol" has been the centerpiece of my form considerations as an artist for over 30 years.

THE DIAMOND LAKE APOCALYPSE and EZEKIEL SERIES.

The Art Works. I have labeled several distinctive series of works related to program routines and the way those routines have been used: Pathway; Gaia; Scarab; and the Diamond Lake Apocalypse (DLA). The most recent DLA works are named the Ezekiel series.
The DLA and Ezekiel Series are code generated scripts and illustrations presented as "illuminated" pages reminiscent of medieval manuscripts. The scripts and illustrations are executed with a multipen plotter coupled to a PC. The plotter draws from an array of technical pens loaded with inks mixed in the studio. All brush strokes are plotted using Chinese brushes adapted to the machine's drawing arm. Each page, plotted on rag paper, is enhanced with a touch of pure gold or silver leaf, applied by hand. However the illuminated "initials" (design elements) are always code generated and machine plotted.
Structure. The "illumination" for each work is realized with code driven improvisations based on a single initiating stroke. This stroke, generated by randomly cast control points, can be seen in the brush strokes. Software procedures provide parameters to create reflecting or mirror strokes on either or both axes or none at all.

The "script" headers and initials are derived algorithmically from the same set of relations; thus a "self-similarity" permeates the whole. More recent routines allow for transformations of form from one set of control points to another. The same algorithm used for asymetrical works in the Pathway series drives the recursive loops that generate the severely symmetrical "Ezekiel series" illuminations. @body-e = Content and Meaning. Parameter controlled recursive loops are commonly used today in applications and research in practically all disciplines. They provide an awesome means for visualizing the evolution and transformation of form. As we develope an iconology (interpretation) of these forms we will see that they are the icons of those procedures which are shaping our culture.
One could think of the works in all of these series as diagrams or visual analogues to the coded procedures by which they are made. The essential character of the finished work is derived from the "form-generating-procedure" or "algorithm" acting as genotype. For this reason one could say that the finished work is an epiphany, or manifestation, of the artist's code. Each work celebrates its code, especially the recursive routines which shaped its character. It is noteworthy that such procedures hold much in common with processes associated with crystallization and genetics.
These epigenetic works invite us to savor both the beauty and the mystery of their coded procedures—not so much for their stark logic as for the grace and poetry they yield. They provide a window on unseen processes shaping mind and matter. By doing so they become icons illuminating the mysterious nature of Earth and Cosmos.

der ersten Serie von gedruckten Arbeiten, die als „Wege" begriffen wurden. Nachdem ich einige Zeit in China unterrichtet hatte, erkannte ich viele Analogien zwischen „hodos" und dem orientalischen Konzept des „Dao" (Tao, der Weg). Mein Atelier, genannt das „Weg Atelier" hat ein orientalisches Siegel, das von dem berühmten *Shufa*-Meister Wang Dong Ling geschnitzt wurde. Wang, von den Pinselstrichen des Computers beeindruckt, wählte den klassischen Ausdruck „xiao jing zhai", „kleines Fußpfad-Atelier" als geeignet für das Siegel. Viele Arbeiten, die in diesem Atelier ausgeführt werden, erhalten dieses Siegel.
Formfamilien. Hodos ist fähig, eine Familie der Formen zu erzeugen, die gleichzeitig verwandt und (doch) „einzig in ihrer Art" sind. Das ist möglich, da das System wie ein chaotisches System arbeitet, das dem „Schmetterlings-Effekt" unterliegt. Der „Schmetterlings"- Effekt bezieht sich auf die Beobachtung, daß sogar winzigste Phänomene in einem solchen System das Ganze beeinflussen – das Flattern eines Schmetterlingsflügels, so sagt man, hat einen Einfluß auf weltweite Wettermuster.
Die *Hodos* Abläufe sind Parameter, die von Vorgängen betrieben werden, die fähig sind, visuelle Formen zu erzeugen, deren Ergebnisse ähnlichen Effekten unterliegen. Mit „Parameter betrieben" meinen wir Abläufe, die eine Funktion ausführen, die „nicht mehr als" und „nicht weniger als" eine bestimmte Anzahl von Graden, Federstrichen oder Farben umfaßt. Die geringste Änderung, sagen wir eine ,005 Änderung im ersten Samen, beeinflußt alle kontrollierenden Parameter und in Folge davon die endgültige Form. Die „Auto" Modi, die in das System eingebaut sind, erlauben „Hodos", seine Variablen zu ändern und das innerhalb von Parametern, die ich wahlweise kontrollieren oder nicht kontrollieren kann. Die daraus entstehenden Formen sind im Ausmaß der Variation der Programmparameter und in der Art wie diese kontrolliert oder nicht kontrolliert werden miteinander verwandt. Diese Dialektik zwischen „Kontrolle" und „Un-Kontrolle" ist in den über 30 Jahren meiner Künstlerlaufbahn der Mittelpunkt meiner Formbetrachtungen gewesen.

MOLEKTRONISCHE NETZWERKE

FRANZ XAVER

KEIN ENDE DER PARABEL

In der Differenzsetzung zur Natur wurde Kultur gestiftet. In dieser Weise fand die Teilhabe der Kunst an der Schaffung eines symbolischen Universums statt. Innovationen brisanter Art stellen nicht nur den soziokulturellen Status quo der symbolischen Ordnung in Frage, sondern zielen darüber hinaus auf eine Metanatur. Ein Quasi-Leben – molekulare/elektronische Kreationen, Repliken, Klone, Doubles etc. – durchbricht die Schranke (/) zwischen s/S, d.h. Signifikat über dem Signifikant, so bei Saussure, wie ebenso die „Barre" der Lacanschen Verkehrung von S/s („ein Signifikant ist das, was ein Subjekt für einen anderen Signifikanten repräsentiert"), und unterläuft somit in radikaler Weise den symbolischen Vertrag. Quasi-Leben (AL & AI) ist die Subjektivation dessen, das die Schranke (die Freudsche Zensur) bislang regeln sollte. Nicht bloß durch Relationen konstituiert, nimmt es den Platz ein, den Freud „den Umweg einer realitätsverkostenden Phantasie" genannt hat. Dialogisch in der Rede des Anderen, resp. der anderen Natur, wird die Verdrängung unserer elementaren Insuffizienz zur Entität.
1986, also noch vor dem Mind-Boom, läßt Franz Xaver je zwei Kommunikationspartner einander visualisierte Gehirnströme übermitteln. Bei Ars Electronica 1987 installiert er RadioARTive Konferenzmöbel, die mittels Computer die jeweilige Körper/Umwelt-Temperatur des Konferenzteilnehmers akustisch in Töne transformiert. Auf der APERTO-Biennale von Venedig 1990 realisiert er eine interaktive Installation mit der beachtlichen Höhe von 36.000 km. Der Datenfluß eines über Zentralafrika stationierten Wettersatelliten sorgt dabei quasi für das Fließgleichgewicht einer dynamischen Systemanordnung, deren Komponenten einerseits aus Satellit, Antenne, Receiver, Computer und Videobeamer bestehen und andererseits aus ihren Wirkungseffekten, die in einem weiteren Bestandteil, in einem organisch/psychischen System (Rezipient) interaktiv ausgespielt werden. Im Sommer 1992 experimentiert Franz Xaver, zusammen mit Just Merrit und Leo Schatzl, auf einem Werksgelände, Schrottplatz West - Linz, mit ebendort gebauten Robotern.

MOLECTRONIC NETWORKS
FRANZ XAVER

NO END OF THE PARABEL

Culture was founded as a step away from nature. In this way art assisted in the creation of a symbolic universe. Explosive innovation not only questions the socio-cultural status of the symbolic order but also takes aim at a meta-nature. A quasi-life—molecular / electronic creations, replicas, clones, doubles, etc.—break through the barrier (/) between s/S, i.e. the signified on the signifier after Saussure, likewise the "barre" of the Lacanian reversing of S/s ("a signifier is what a subject represents to another signifier") and radically undermines the symbolic contract. Quasi-life (AL and AI) is the subjectification of that which the barrier (the Freudian censor) was supposed to control. Constituted not merely through relations, it occupies a place that Freud called "the detour of a reality-tasting imagination"). In dialogue, in the speech of the other, respective to the other nature, the suppression of our elementary insufficiency becomes an entity.
In 1986, before the mind boom, Franz Xaver had two conversation partners send each other visualised brain signals. At Ars Electronica 1987 he installed RadioARTive chairs which the body and environment temperatures were of the conference participants were transformed into sound by a computer. At the 1990 APERTO Biennale in Venice he realised an interactive installation with the considerable height of 36,000km. The data flow of a weather satellite positioned over Central Africa balances out the flow of a dynamic system arrangement whose components consist of satellite, antenna, receiver, computer and video beamer on the one hand and their effects on the other, the latter being interactively played out in a further component, an organic / psychological system (Recipient). In Summer 1992 Franz Xaver experimented together with Just Merrit and Leo Schatzl on an industrial site, Schrottplatz-West Linz, with robots built at the location. With likeminded speed freaks, code poets, data surfers, cyber junkies, reality hackers, hypermedia installers, etc., he founded the KUNSTLABOR, a further node in the electronic subcommunity. In 1993 again traversed orbital timespaces with a weather satellite sculpture, experimented with computation operations and chaotic structures in the mathematical approach to zero, showed

wave—sensitive images which react at 496.025 MHz, and takes all the above to the Kultur-Kamikaze-Projekt MS STUBNITZ in Rostock. In the same year he is represented at Ars Electronica 1993 with molectronic networks of a nature significant to the history of earth: bacteria and algae in their biotopic milieu.

He had presented such networks the previous year in his exhibition "Fractal Geometry, Art and Bionics" in the Stifterhaus Gallery, Linz. Other works include the kinetic sculpture "Channel 38" (1991)where a Video-art transponder/generator transmitted the modulated decay of an apple on TV channel 38, and "Gnathonemus", an ornamental fish also known as a trunk-fish. In a special hardware / software configuration the artist demonstrated communication between the fish (living system) and a computer (artificial system). The gnathonemus proves capable of great variation in its basic frequency, traceable to external influences and of a scale of 6 Hz deviation, leading the artist to interpret frequency swings of over 6 Hz as the fish's response to triggered stimuli. The communication process could be followed on a digital frequency counter . But the molectronic networks Xaver has prepared for Ars Electronica 1993 need no power socket. A trend reversal for Xaver? By no means.

Like the previous generation of media artists, Franz Xaver is occupied with problems centred around the evolutionary factor information and which have become acute in today's post-bourgeois, telecommunications—based, mass democracy. (in these caipitalistically organised societies, which are based on their economic capital as a social condition, communications means the mobilisation of the social energy, capital—cultural goods are equal to economic

Mit Gleichgesinnten – Speedfreaks, Codepoeten, Datensurfer, Cyberjunkies, Realityhacker, Hypermediainstallateure etc. – gründet er das KUNSTLABOR; ein weiterer Knoten der electronic subcommunity. 1993 durchmißt er wieder orbitale Zeiträume mit einer Wettersatelliten-Skulptur; experimentiert mit Rechenoperationen und chaotischen Strukturen in der mathematischen Annäherung gegen Null; zeigt wellenempfängliche Bilder, die sich bei 496.025 MHz erregen; und beteiligt sich mit all dem am Kultur-Kamikaze-Projekt MS STUBNITZ in Rostock. Im selben Jahr ist er bei Ars Electronica 1993 mit molektronischen Netzwerken erdgeschichtlich bedeutsamer Art vertreten: Bakterien und Algen in ihrem biotopischen Milieu.

Derartige Netzwerke präsentierte Xaver schon im Jahr davor in seiner Ausstellung „Fraktale Geometrie, Kunst und Bionik" in der Galerie im Stifterhaus, Linz. Neben anderen Arbeiten, etwa einer kinetischen Skulptur, „Channel 38" aus dem Jahr 1991, wo mittels einem Video-ART Transponder/TV-Generator (Marke Xaver) die aufmodulierte biologische Fäulnis eines Apfels im elektromagnetischen Megahertzbereich auf einem Fernsehbild, Kanal 38, beobachtet werden konnte, zeigte er „Gnathonemus". Dieser Name bezeichnet einen Zierfisch – auch als Elefantenrüsselfisch bekannt. In einer speziellen Hard/Software-Konfiguration (Marke Xaver) demonstrierte der Künstler die Kommunikation zwischen dem Fisch (lebendes System) und einem Computer (künstliches System). Im Computer wurden Reiz-

und Antwortimpulse aufgezeichnet, analysiert und neue Reizimpulse gebildet. Da der Gnathonemus eine große Variabilität in seiner Grundfrequenz aufweist, die auf äußere Einflüsse zurückzuführen sind und in einer Größenanordnung von 6 Hz Abweichung liegen, gelten für Xaver nur jene Frequenzerhöhungen als Antwort des Fisches auf die getriggerten Reizamplituden, die über dieser Frequenzabweichung liegen. Der Kommunikationsablauf konnte von den Betrachtern auf einem Frequenzzähler abgelesen werden. Die molektronischen Netzwerke aber, die Xaver nun auch bei Ars Electronica 1993 zeigt, benötigen für ihr Funktionieren keine Steckdose. Eine Trendumkehr im Werk von Franz Xaver? Mitnichten.

Wie schon die KünstlerInnen-Generationen in der Medienkunst zuvor, ist Franz Xaver mit Fragestellungen beschäftigt, die um den Evolutionsfaktor Information kreisen und in der heutigen nachbürgerlichen Massendemokratie auf telekommunikativer Basis akut geworden sind. (In diesen kapitalistisch organisierten Gesellschaften, die auf ihrem ökonomischen Kapital als einem sozialen Verhältnis basieren, bedeutet Kommunikation die Mobilisierung der gesellschaftlichen Energie Kapital – kulturelles ist gleich ökonomisches Kapital, zugleich Sinn-Orientierung, Selbsterhaltung und Selbstreproduktion.)

Das mehrfache Vorhandensein des zellulären Apparates steigert die Effizienz eines Gesamtorganismus. Im Unterschied zum Einzeller verfügt der Vielzeller über eine erhöhte Reproduktionsfähigkeit, die sowohl seiner Lebensdauer, als auch die Ausbildung morphologisch verschiedenartiger Körper begünstigt. Seine evolutionäre Entwicklung führte zu einer Zellendifferenzierung mit je speziellen Funktionen und damit zu einer besseren physiologischen Eigenstabilität. Unterschieden werden Vielzeller entsprechend ihrer Lebensweise und nach der Art ihrer Energiegewinnung. Pilze und Tiere ernähren sich von organischem Material. Die Pflanzen benötigen anorganische Nährstoffe; die Sonnenenergie ermöglicht ihnen, mit Hilfe der Photosynthese lebende Materie aufzubauen. Alle vielzelligen Pflanzen und Tiere haben sich aus einzelligen Eukaryonten entwickelt. Diese Netzwerke molekularer Interaktionen sind die ersten Lebewesen. Sie liegen der Wissenschaft als fossile Ablagerungen vor und sind bis zu 3400 Millionen Jahre alt. Bakterien und Algen, die ersten fossilen Lebewesen, existieren bis heute.

Was in der Biochemie als zellulärer Metabolismus, also Zellstoffwechsel, bezeichnet wird, impliziert schon eine Organisation und Struktur von molekularen Bestandteilen. Das heißt, daß diese Bestandteile in einem kontinuierlichen Netz-

capital, equal to sense-orientation, self— support and reproduction). The multiple presence of the cellular machine increases the efficiency of the organism as a whole. In contrast to single cell organisms, the creature with multiple cells is more able to reproduce, which is good for its life span, and for the development of morphologically differing bodies. Its evolutionary development lead to a cell differentiation with special functions and therefore to an improved physiological independence. Multi—cell organisms become different through their lifestyles and their means of obtaining energy. Funguses and animals feed on organic material. Plants need inorganic food; energy from the sun allows them to build up living material through photosynthesis. All multi-cell plants and animals developed out of the early single cell creatures, networks of molecular interaction that were the first living things. They are available to science in the form of fossilised remains and are up to 3400 million years old. Bacteria and algae, the first fossilised creatures, still exist today.

What biochemistry terms cellular metabolism, or cellulose exchange, already implies an organisation and structure of molecular components. This means that these components are dynamically connected together in a continuous network of mutual interactions. The development of the first cells implied molecular substance classification having the ability to form units that based their situation in the environment on circular closed operative connections. In honour of the biologists and neurocyberneticians Humberto R. Maturana and Francisco J. Varela these units are named autopoietic systems. As these systems have molecular components, they satisfy physical laws, are spatially defined, but are not defined as autopoietic by virtue of their physical characteristics. The term depends rather on the organisation of the unit and the means of its realisation. Changes, for instance, that come about in a molecular system as a consequence of interaction, are defined as cellular units by their own structure. Various autopoietic systems differ in their structures, but are closely connected to their organisation. Autopoietic, i.e. self-organising systems have only one goal—their self—preservation. Evolution always selects according to the efficient and effective use of relevant information.

We, the individuals of the human species, are an accumulation of millions of complex cycles of an autopoietic system, maybe only "a kind of evolutionary inter-stage of a species of self-organising systems." (Dieter Hombach: Die Drift der Erkenntnis—The Drift of Knowledge. On the theory of self-modifying systems with regard to Gödel, Hegel and Freud, Munich 1990, P. 131) The revolutionary trio atomic energy, micro—electronics and micro—biology has embraced all areas of life, and its consequences are, like the processes of mechanical and dynamic technology before it, definitely irreversible. We communicate with digital assistants, almost lifelike with virtual actors by Nintendo, and will in the not too distant future be surrounding ourselves with Genghis and Gnats (robots) etc. in our private lives, unaware that

the metatheory of the organic /psychological system, the human being, is being drawn up by expert systems (AI).
The molectronic networks of Franz Xaver are an out-sourcing variant of media art, and therefore to be read as a contextual hint; taken intertextually, they release a multitude of cognitive information—provided that the areas of cognition of the producer and the recipient overlap sufficiently with each other.

F. E. Rakuschan

werk von Wechselwirkungen dynamisch miteinander verbunden sind. Die Entwicklung der eukaryontischen Zelle setzte also molekulare Substanzklassen voraus, die die Eigenschaft besaßen Einheiten auszubilden, die ihr Umweltverhältnis auf zirkulär geschlossene Operationsverknüpfungen stützen. Nach den Biologen und Neurokybernetikern Humberto R. Maturana und Francisco J. Varela werden diese Einheiten autopoietische Systeme genannt. Da diese Systeme molekulare Komponenten haben, erfüllen sie die physikalischen Gesetzmäßigkeiten, werden dadurch räumlich in ihrer Existenz bestimmt, sind aber nicht durch physikalische Eigenschaften als autopoietisch definiert. Autopoiese hängt vielmehr von der Organisation der Einheit ab und von der Art ihrer Verwirklichung. So werden bspw. Veränderungen, die in einem molekularen System als Konsequenz einer Interaktion entstehen, von ihrer eigenen Struktur als zelluläre Einheit bestimmt. Verschiedene autopoietische Systeme unterscheiden sich durch unterschiedliche Strukturen, sind aber gleich in bezug auf ihre Organisation. Autopoietische, also selbstorganisierte Systeme haben nur ein Ziel – ihre Selbsterhaltung. Evolution selektiert demnach immer nach effizientem und effektivem Nutzen relevanter Information.
Wir, die Individuen der Spezies Mensch, sind selbst eine milliardenfache Anhäufung komplexer Zyklen eines autopoietischen Systems und vielleicht bloß „eine Art evolutives Zwischenglied der Spezies selbstorganisierter Systeme.“ (Dieter Hombach: Die Drift der Erkenntnis. Zur Theorie selbstmodifizierter Systeme bei Gödel, Hegel und Freud, München 1990, S. 131) Die revolutionierende Trias Kernenergie, Mikroelektronik und Mikrobiologie hat alle Lebensbereiche erfaßt und ihre Konsequenzen sind, wie die der Prozesse der mechanischen und dynamischen Technik zuvor, definitiv unumkehrbar. Wir kommunizieren mit digitalen Assistenten, fast lebensecht mit virtual actors von Nintendo, und umgeben uns in nicht allzuferner Zukunft auch im Privatbereich mit Genghis und Gnats (Robotern) etc., während, von uns unbemerkt, die Metatheorie des organisch/psychischen Systems, also des Menschen, von Expertensystemen (AI) erstellt wird.
Die molektronischen Netzwerke von Franz Xaver sind eine Outsourcing-Variante von Medienkunst, und somit auch als kontextueller Hinweis zu lesen; intertextuell verstanden, geben sie vielfältig kognitive Informationen frei – vorausgesetzt die Kognitionsbereiche von Produzent und Rezipient überschneiden einander hinlänglich.

F. E. Rakuschan

2. VIRTUELLE KREATUREN

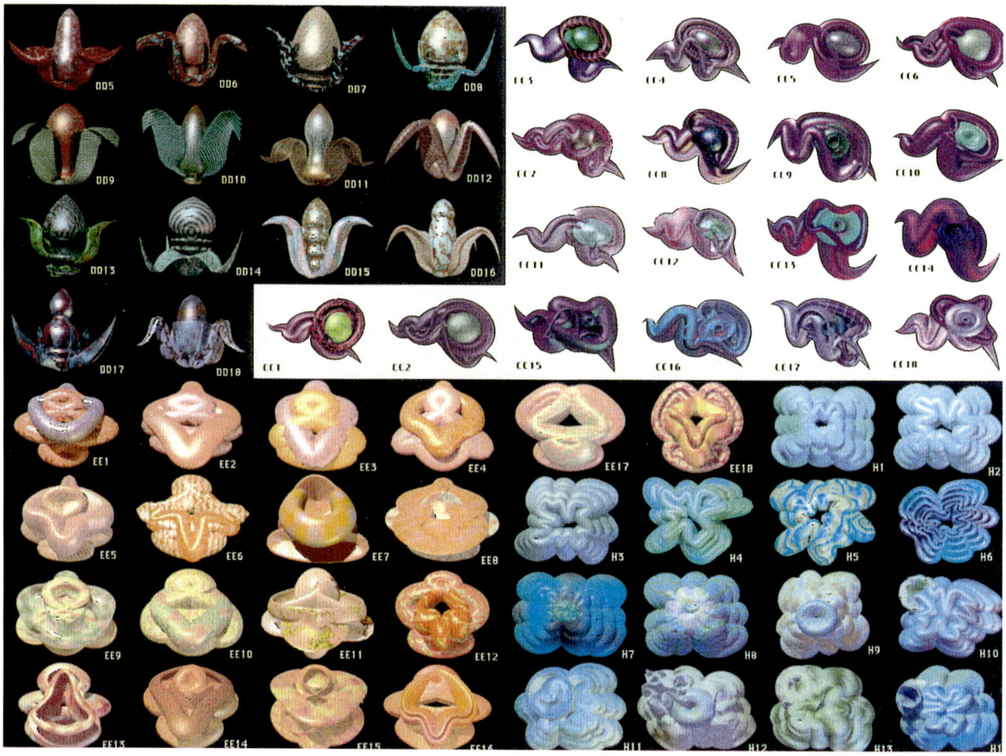
DD5
DD6
DD7
DD8
CC3
CC4
CC5
CC6
DD9
DD10
DD11
DD12
CC7
CC8
CC9
CC10
DD13
DD14
DD15
DD16
CC11
CC12
CC13
CC14
DD17
DD18
CC1
CC2
CC15
CC16
CC17
CC18
EE1
EE2
EE3
EE4
EE17
EE18
H1
H2
EE5
EE6
EE7
EE8
H3
H4
H5
H6
EE9
EE10
EE11
EE12
H7
H8
H9
H10
EE13
EE14
EE15
H11
H12
H13

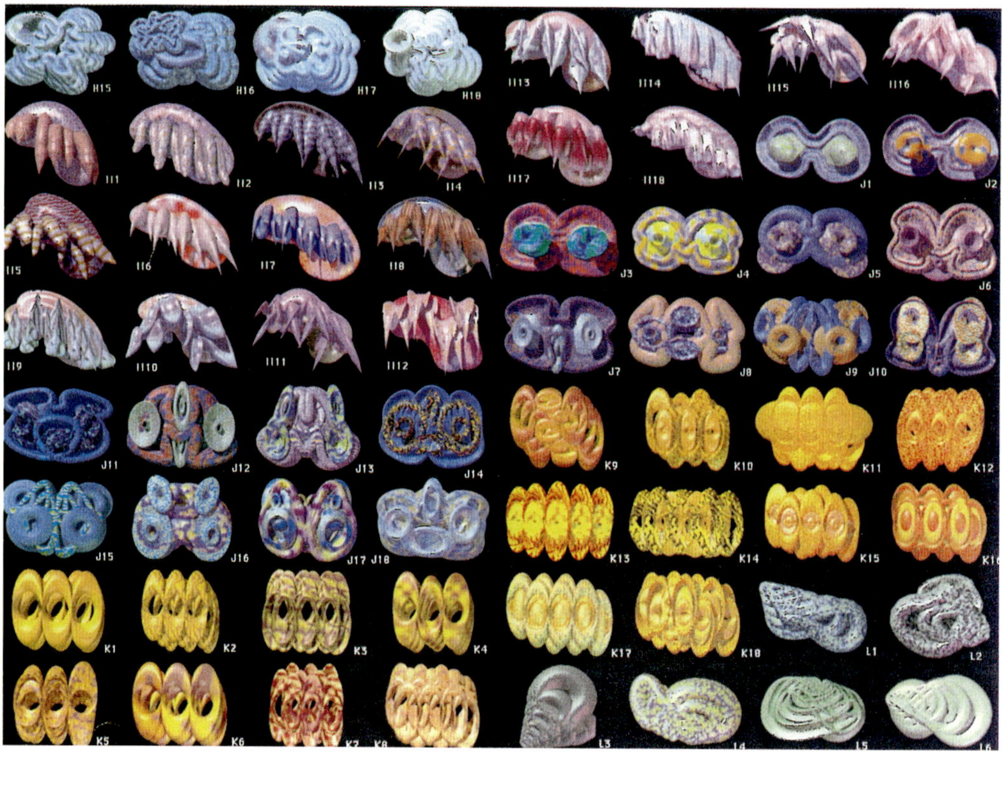
H15
H16
H17
H18
II13
II14
II15
II16
II1
II2
II3
II4
II17
II18
J1
J2
II5
II6
II7
II8
J3
J4
J5
J6
II9
II10
II11
II12
J7
J8
J9
J10
J11
J12
J13
J14
K9
K10
K11
K12
J15
J16
J17
J18
K13
K14
K15
K1
K2
K3
K4
K17
K18
L1
L2
K5
K6
K7
K8
L3
L4
L5
L6

GESCHÖPFE

DAIZABURO HARADA

CREATURES
DAIZABURO HARADA

It began from sounds.
I have been very interested in sounds, such as those from banging machines or household appliances, when being switched off, and have collected various examples.
One day it occurred to me that with a computer I could make creatures, that emit strange chirping sounds.
At first I made one every now and then. I was not able to feel their real existance until the number reached one hundred. When I had made three to four hundred creatures, suddenly I could not ignore that I had created something. But when they had gathered to the tune of five to six hundred, it was impossible not to acknowledge that they were somehow alive, though they had been made for my own amusement.
It may be thought as a biosystem created by a computer.
In this thoroughly new ecosystem, which evolved in the digital world of a computer, live various imaginary creatures was made by me with a computer.
In the process of creating them I decide only the major points; the other details are drawn by the computer itself.
For example, I roughly decide that there will be six to seven globes around a globe, and then wildly transform the data of each globe.
Even I cannot guess the final image.
Of course, it's I who operate the computer, but there is some scope governed by the computer, in which I am interested.

Es begann mit Geräuschen.
Ich interessierte mich sehr für Geräusche, wie die von Krachmaschinen oder Haushaltsgeräten, wenn sie gerade abgeschaltet wurden, und ich habe verschiedene Exemplare gesammelt. Eines Tages geschah es, daß ich mit einem Computer Geschöpfe erzeugen konnte, die zwitschernde Geräusche von sich gaben.
Anfangs machte ich ab und zu eines. Ich konnte ihre reale Existenz nicht wahrnehmen, bis ihre Zahl sich auf hundert belief. Als ich drei- bis vierhundert Geschöpfe erzeugt hatte, konnte ich auf einmal nicht mehr ignorieren, daß ich etwas geschaffen hatte. Als dann fünf- bis sechshundert in die Melodie einstimmten, war es unmöglich nicht zuzugeben, daß sie irgendwie lebendig waren, obwohl ich sie zu meinem Vergnügen gemacht hatte.
Die Sache kann als ein von einem Computer geschaffenes Biosystem betrachtet werden.
In diesem vollkommen neuen Ökosystem, das sich in der digitalen Welt eines Computers entwickelte, leben verschiedene, von mir mittels Computer erzeugte, imaginäre Geschöpfe.
Im Prozeß ihrer Erzeugung, wurden nur die wichtigsten Punkte von mir entschieden; die anderen Details wurden vom Computer selbst entworfen.
So etwa entscheide ich grob, daß sechs oder sieben Kugeln rund um eine Kugel sein sollen und transformiere in etwa die Daten jeder Kugel. Auch ich kann das Endergebnis nicht erraten. Natürlich bin ich derjenige, der den Computer bedient, aber es gibt einen vom Computer beherrschten Raum , der mich interessiert.
Die atmosphärischen und Schwerkraftbedingungen auf diesem, von den Geschöpfen bewohnten Planeten sind unbekannt. Wir müssen das bei jeder der vom Computer hervorgebrachten Kreaturen bedenken.

AMEISEN

PETER KOGLER

AMEISEN: COMPUTER: GEHIRN

Schwarze Ameisen umgeben von Sonnengelb auf sattrotem Grund: der in einer Art Gobelin-Technik gewebte Vorhang von Peter Kogler hängt in zwei Stoffbahnen von der Decke bis auf den Treppenabsatz. Das fortlaufende Muster aus metergroßen Ameisen hat der Künstler am Computer gestaltet, die Weberei den auf einer Diskette gespeicherten Entwurf materiell umgesetzt.

Peter Kogler ist beileibe kein Techno-Künstler. Seine Computergrafiken basieren auf eingescannten konventionellen Vorlagen, die er speichert und als Modul verwendet. Kogler ist einfach User der Apparatur. Der Computer ist sein technisches Hilfsmittel, formiert ausgewählte Zeichen mediengerecht, bereitet sie auf und zu weiteren Verwendung vor. Koglers Images sind dazu bestimmt und ausgewählt, Abbildung zu sein und weiter reproduziert zu werden. Ihre drucktechnische Eignung ist hervorragend, die plakative, drastische Sprache leicht les- und vermittelbar selbst in kleinen Formaten (vgl. die exorbitant hohe Reproduktionsrate und somit Distribution seiner Ameisentapeten-Arbeit auf der documenta in Kassel in elektronischen wie Printmedien). Neben der Expressivität der Arbeiten von Peter Kogler spielt in den letzten Jahren zunehmend die inhaltliche Signifikanz eine Rolle. Immer wichtiger wird auch die materielle Inszenierung, die Möglichkeit einer sinnlichen Raumerfahrung (Tapeten, Vorhänge, architektonische Trägerkonstruktionen). In der Konzentration auf die Motive des menschlichen Gehirns und der Ameise verweist Kogler auf strukturelle Analogien zwischen dem Ameisenstaat, dem menschlichen Gehirn und dem Computer (hoch entwickelte Kommunikation, Disziplin, Effektivität und Anpassung, testprogrammierte Aufgabenbereiche der einzelnen Teile des Systems, das nur als Gesamtheit existieren kann).

Die vor Jahren von Kogler eingescannte und immer wieder geklonte Ameise ist eine Königin der Gast-Ameisen *(formicoxenus initidulus)*. Die Ameise wurde aber rein nach visuellen Kriterien ausgewählt, weder ihr Status noch ihre Gattung sind entscheidend. Durch Wiederholung & immer erneute Reproduktion seiner Module baut Kogler Strukturen,

ANTS
PETER KOGLER

ANTS: COMPUTER: BRAIN

Black ants surrounded by sun-yellow on juice-red ground: Peter Kogler's curtain, woven in a kind of Gobelin technique, hangs in two parts from the ceiling down to the half-landing. The artist designed the continuous pattern of metre-long ants at the computer, the weaving-mill then produced the design, which was stored on disc.

Peter Kogler is by no means a techno-artist; his computer graphics are based on conventional materials scanned into the computer, stored and used as a module. Kogler is simply the user of the apparatus, the computer is his technical aid which prepares selected symbols for the real medium and for further uses. Kogler's image are destined and selected to be copied and reproduced further. Their aptitude for printing technology is outstanding, the poster-like, drastic language easy to read and to pass on, even in small formats (for instance, the exorbitantly high reproduction rate and consequent distribution of his ant work at documenta in Kassel, in electronic as well as print media). Besides the expressiveness of Kogler's works, the significance of content has also played an increasing role in the last few years. Material staging is becoming more important, the possibility of a sensual feel for space (tapestries, curtains, architectural carrier-constructions). In the concentration on the motifs of the human brain and the ant, Kogler is referring to structural analogies between the ant state, the human brain and the computer (highly developed communication, discipline, effectiveness and conformity, firmly fixed work demarcation between the individual parts of the system, which can only exist as a complete whole).

The ant, scanned in by Kogler years ago and repeatedly cloned, is a queen of the guest ants (formicoxinus intidulus), The ant was selected purely by visual criteria, neither its status of species being decisive. Through repetition and constantly new reproductions of his modules, Kogler is building structures; inaccessible labyrinths, cords, bands, lines or ordinary patterns symbolising the human brain, and the state-building insect become symbols in which the unique, the individual is subordinated to an order that strictly serves the organism as a whole.

"In the complete society there is neither emotion nor pity. Valuable space cannot be wasted on those who have outlived their usefulness."
"The sexless worker is the true source of freedom in every society."
"Perhaps with time we will become as functional as those we emulate. We will develop faces without facial expressions: only the eyes and mouth; just enough to keep the rest of the body alive. No muscles to smile with or look darkly or in any way betray what is going on beneath the surface."
"The living prototype of the computer was developed by nature long before the primate family gave rise to the brain animal, man. This prototype is no more and no less than th termite hill, one of the first experiments in social order (...) We all know of course that the insect, compared to humans, shows none of what we could call intelligence. But why should we feel proud because of that? (...) A computer is a mechanism programmed with hundreds of thousands of tiny units of information. It works by ordering these units into logical base patterns, sifts through them, and puts them together in different combinations. (...) is not a smoothly functioning society like a form of logic? I would argue that the inhabitants of those termite hills, as they make their way along their hidden pathways, have organised themselves into a form of undeniable logic, hundreds of thousands of tiny information units, each one a part of the whole.

Judith Fischer

Thanks to: Fa. Backhausen, Wien

unzugängliche Labyrinthe, Stränge, Bänder, Linien oder regelmäßige Muster. Das menschliche Gehirn und das staatenbildende Insekt werden zu Symbolen einer Ordnung, in der das Einzelne / Individuelle einer strikt dem Interesse des Gesamtorganismus dienenden Ordnung unterworfen ist.
„In der vollkommenen Gesellschaft gibt es weder Gemütsbewegung noch Erbarmen. Kostbarer Raum kann nicht für jene verschwendet werden, die ihre Nützlichkeit überlebt haben."
„Der geschlechtslose Arbeiter ist in jeder Gesellschaft die wahre Quelle der Freiheit."
„Vielleicht werden wir mit der Zeit so funktionell wie jene, die wir nachahmen. Wir werden Gesichter ohne Mienenspiel entwickeln: nur Augen und Mund, gerade genug, um den Rest des Körpers am Leben zu erhalten. Keine Muskeln, mit denen man lächeln oder finster blicken oder in irgendeiner Weise verraten könnte, was unter der Oberfläche lauerte."
„Der lebende Prototyp des Computers wurde von der Natur entwickelt, lange bevor die Primatenfamilie das Gehirntier Mensch hervorbrachte. Dieser Prototyp ist nicht mehr und nicht weniger als der Terminhügel, einer der ersten Experimente in sozialer Ordnung. (...) Wir alle wissen natürlich, daß das Insekt, verglichen mit dem Menschen, nichts von dem zeigt, was wir Intelligenz nennen könnten. Aber warum sollten wir deswegen Stolz empfinden? (...) Ein Computer ist ein mit Hunderttausenden winziger Informationseinheiten programmierter Mechanismus. Er arbeitet, indem er die Informationseinheiten nach logischen Grundmustern ordnet, sichtet und in immer neuen Kombinationen zusammenstellt. (...) Ist eine reibungslos funktionierende Gesellschaft nicht auch eine Form der Logik? Ich behaupte, daß die Bewohner eines solchen Termitenhügels, wie sie sich durch ihre verborgenen Gänge bewegen, hunderttausend winzige Informationseinheiten, jede ein Teil des Ganzen, sich in seiner Form unbestreitbarer Logik organisiert haben.

LITERATUR

Frank Herbert: Hellstroms Brut. Science-fiction Roman. Heyne: 1977; Bert Hölldobler & Schwer O. Wilson: The Ants. The Belknap press of Harvard University Press: 1990; Heiderose & Andreas Fischer-Nagel: Der Ameisenstaat. Luzern: 1987; Johannes W. Rohen / Chihiro Yokochi: Color Atlas of Anatomy. A photographic Study of the human body. Igeku-Shoin: 1988; Florian Rötzer (hg.): Digitaler Schein. Ästhetik der elektronischen Medien. Suhrkamp: 1981.

Judith Fischer

3. ROBOTER

TERRAIN 01

ULRIKE GABRIEL

AN OTHERSPACE PROJECT

Eine vermeintlich triviale Einsicht kristallisiert sich mehr und mehr zur zentralen Erkenntnis unserer wissenschaftlichen und philosophischen Suche nach einem konsistenten Weltbild: Wir sind Teil dieser Welt.
Begonnen hat die Destruktion unseres exzeptionellen externen Standpunkts zum Kosmos am Beginn des Jahrhunderts mit der Relativitätstheorie, welche den absoluten Raum und die absolute Zeit der Newton'schen Physik als unnötig ideale Basis der klassischen Mechanik entlarvte.
Den zweiten Schlag setzte die Formulierung der Quantenmechanik in den 20er und 30er Jahren. Im Gültigkeitsbereich der Quantentheorie gibt es keine externe Beobachterposition. Der Zustand quantenmechanischer Objekte ist beobachterabhängig. Physikalische Erkenntnisse aus dem Mikrokosmos begründeten die Idee eines holistischen Weltbilds.
Die Chaostheorie als vorläufig letzte naturwissenschaftliche Revolution formuliert mit der „sensiblen Abhängigkeit von den Anfangsbedingungen" die vollständige Vernetzung aller dynamischen Systeme. Selbst noch so kleine Ursachen können unter nichtlinearer Dynamik systembeherrschende Wirkung haben. Im Extrem wird damit jede Art von Externalität unmöglich gemacht.

KUNSTZEUGWELTEN

Neueste Ergebnisse der Gehirnforschung scheinen zu bestätigen, daß unsere Welterkenntnis bestimmt wird durch die Art und Weise wie wir unser eigenes, in Raum und Zeit evolvierendes Abbild der Umwelt interpretieren. Die junge Idee der Endophysik versucht eine Vereinheitlichung zwischen biologischen und physikalischen Interpretationen indem sie eine vom Gehirn des Beobachters abhängige Physik postuliert. Jedoch scheint damit alle Erkenntnis an einem fundamentalen Dilemma zu scheitern. Wir können unmöglich das Ganze betrachten, da wir ein Teil des Ganzen sind.

TERRAIN 01
ULRIKE GABRIEL

AN OTHERSPACE PROJECT

A supposedly trivial view continues to crystalize to form the central idea behind our scientific and philosphical search for a consistent world picture:
We are a part of this world.
The destruction of our exceptional external standpoint as regards the cosmos commenced at the beginning of the century with the theory of relativity which revealed that the absolute space and the absolute time of Newtonian physics was a superfluous ideal basis for classical mechanics.
The formulation of quantum mechanics in the 20's and 30's brought the second blow. There are no external observer positions in the scope of quantum mechanics. The state of quantum-mechanical objects is observer-dependent. Physical findings from the micro-cosmos established the idea of a holistic world picture.
The theory of chaos as the tentatively last scientific revolution formulated the complete interlinking of all dynamic systems with the "sensitive dependency on the initial conditions". Even the smallest of causes may bring about effects which dominate systems under non-linear dynamics. In the extreme, every form of externality is rendered impossible with this.

SYNTHETIC WORLDS

The very latest findings in brain research appear to confirm that our understanding of the world is determined by the way we interpret our own image of the environment evolving in space and time. The new idea of endophysics attempts a standardization between biological and physical interpretations by postulating a physics dependent on the brain of the observer. However, with this, every form of understanding of a fundamental dilemma seems to fail. We are completely unable to consider the whole thing as we are a part of the whole thing. In order to sound out the possibilities of understanding our world we must create "artificial" worlds to which we have both an internal as well as an extenal stance. *TERRAIN creates* virtual *"synthetic worlds"*. *TERRAIN* materializes "virtual realities" from light energy, environmental platforms and simple living beings.

TERRAIN_01

TERRAIN_01 is an interactive "*art*ificial life" installation, a non-autonomous one, because it is a world of autonomous cybernetic vehicles dependent on external light energy. The plane, round *TERRAIN_01* characterizes its cosmos and, at the same time, limits its horizon. The inner unconscious state of an extenral observer, his brain wave pattern, controls the global state of a robot colony, synonymous for the indissoluble crosslinking of the world of thoughts with the world of matter.

BOTTOM-UP DESIGN

TERRAIN_01 characterizes the functional minimal form. The ideal oval vehicles are solar-driven and consequently energetically autonomous. Their world is a plane circular disc irradiated from the outside with light. Light was chosen deliberately as the most natural source for a local, autonomous energy supply. Robots possess the very simplest of sensor "sensory organs" with the aid of which they perceive each other and can move around without coming into contact, within *TERRAIN_01*. In addition to the robots' basic equipment which allows them to move freely within the colony, there is also a second sensorial system to detect and process global light intensity changes. These are the only external parameters in *TERRAIN_01*. The global light distribution changes depending on the sensorially detected brain activity of an external observer. External and internal worlds are simple, coupled reciprocally: the more chaotic the state of the observer, the quieter the robot colony.

TOP-DOWN OBSERVATION

In *TERRAIN_01* a colony of autonomous beings moves within a circular world. On account of system-immanent non-linear interactions, a complex structural formation develops with the continuous adaptation process of the individuals to the external environmental influences. The "living" movement pattern of the permanently active living beings lures the observer away to fantastic psychological interpretations of their behaviour. The order states of the dynamic system, with periodic and chaotic dynamics between the extremes of rest and a completely random movement, characterizes the paradigm of complexity.
The whole is more than the sum of all parts

Michael Klein

Generator: Jens Heise
Sensorics: Bob O'Kane
Trichanics: Siegfried Albrecht

produced at Städelschule, Institut für Neue Medien, Frankfurt/Main

Um die Möglichkeiten des Verstehens unserer Welt auszuloten müssen wir uns „Kunst"-Welten erschaffen, zu denen wir sowohl extern wie intern stehen. **TERRAIN** erschafft virtuelle „Kunstzeugwelten". Aus Lichtenergie, Umweltplattform und einfachen Lebe-Wesen materialisiert **TERRAIN** „virtual realities".

TERRAIN 01

TERRAIN 01 ist eine interaktive „**art**ificial life"-Installation, eine nicht-autonome, weil von externer Lichtenergie abhängige Welt autonomer kybernetischer Vehikel. Das ebene runde **TERRAIN 01** bezeichnet ihren Kosmos und begrenzt gleichzeitig ihren Horizont. Der innere, unbewußte Zustand eines externen Betrachters, sein Gehirnwellenmuster steuert den globalen Zustand einer Roboterkolonie, Synonym für die unauflösbare Vernetzung der Welt der Gedanken mit der Welt der Materie.
bottom-up Design
TERRAIN 01 bezeichnet funktionelle Minimalform. Die ideal ovalen Vehikel sind solargetrieben und somit energetisch autonom. Ihre Weit ist eine von außen mit Licht bestrahlte eben kreisende Scheibe. Licht wurde bewußt gewählt als natürlichste Quelle einer lokalen autonomen Energieversorgung. Die Roboter besitzen einfachste Sensor-„Sinnesorgane" mit deren Hilfe sie sich untereinander wahrnehmen und innerhalb **TERRAIN 01** berührungsfrei bewegen können. Neben dieser Basisausstattung der Roboter zur freien Bewe-

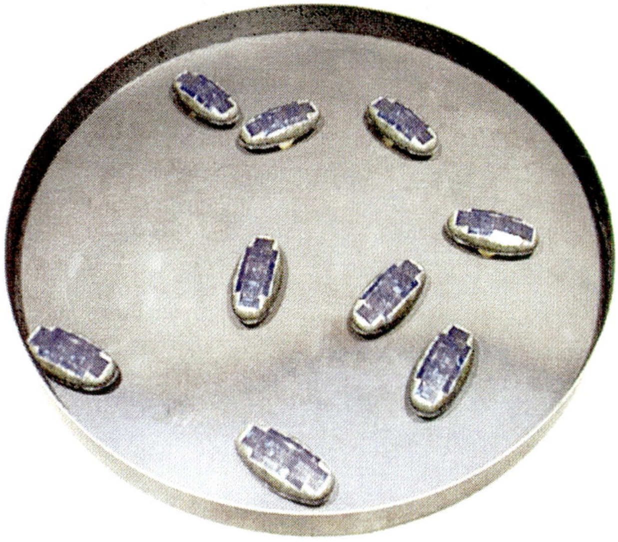

gung innerhalb der Kolonie existiert ein zweites sensorieller System zur Detektion und Verarbeitung globaler Lichtintensitätsveränderungen. Diese sind der einzige externe Parameter in **TERRAIN-01.** Die globale Lichtverteilung ändert sich abhängig der sensoriell erfaßten Gehirnaktivität eines externen Beobachters. Außen- und Innenwelt sind einfach reziprok gekoppelt, je chaotischer der Zustand des Beobachters, desto ruhiger die Roboterkolonie.

TOP-DOWN OBSERVATION

Bei **TERRAIN 01** bewegt sich eine Kolonie autonomer Wesen in einer kreisrunden Welt. Aufgrund systemimmanenter nichtlinearer Wechselwirkungen kommt es zur komplexen Strukturbildung bei dem andauemden Anpassungsprozeß der Individuen an die externen Umwelteinflüsse. Die „lebendigen" Bewegungsmuster der permanent aktiven Lebe-Wesen verführen den Beobachter zu phantasievollen psychologischen Interpretationen ihres Verhaltens. Die Ordnungszustände des dynamischen Systems mit periodischer und chaoti scher Dynamik zwischen den Extremen der Ruhe und einer vollkommen zufälligen Bewegung bezeichnen das Paradigma der Komplexität:
Das Ganze ist mehr als die Summe seiner Teile.

Michael Klein

Lichtmaschine: Jens Heise
Sensorik: Bob O'Kane
Trichanik: Siegfried Albrecht

Das Projekt wurde an der Städelschule, Institut für Neue Medien, Frankfurt am Main, produziert.

TALKING TO NEURO BABY

NAOKO TOSA

An automatic facil expression synthesizer that responds to expressions of feeling in the human voice

CONCEPT

I created a new creature or a piece of work which can live and meaningfully communicate with modern, urban people like ourselves, people who are overwhelmed, if not tortured by the relentless flow of information, and whose peace of mind can only be found in momentary human pleasures.
"Neuro Baby" was born to offer such pleasures.
The name "Neuro Baby" implies the "birth" of a virtual creature, made possible by the recent development of neurally based computer architectures. Neuro Baby "lives" within a computer and communicates with other through its responses to inflections in human voice patterns. Neuro Baby is reborn every time the computer is switched on, and it departs when the computer is turned off. Neuro Baby's logic patterns are modeled after those of human beings, which make it possible to simulate a wide range of personality traits and reactions to life experiences.
Neuro Baby can be a toy, or a lovely pet—or it may develop greater intelligence and stimulate one to challenge traditional meanings of the phrase "intelligent life". In ancient times, people expressed their dreams of the future in the media at hand, such as in novels, films, and drawings. Neuro Baby is a use of contemporary media to express today's dreams of a future being.

BASIC CHARACTERISTIC OF NEURO BABY AND ITS INTERACTION WITH THE EXTERNAL WORLD

This wirk is the simulation of a baby, born into the "mind" of the computer. Neuro Baby is a totally new type of interactive performace system, which responds to human voice input with a computer generated baby's face and sound effects. If the speaker's tone is gentle and soothing, the baby in the

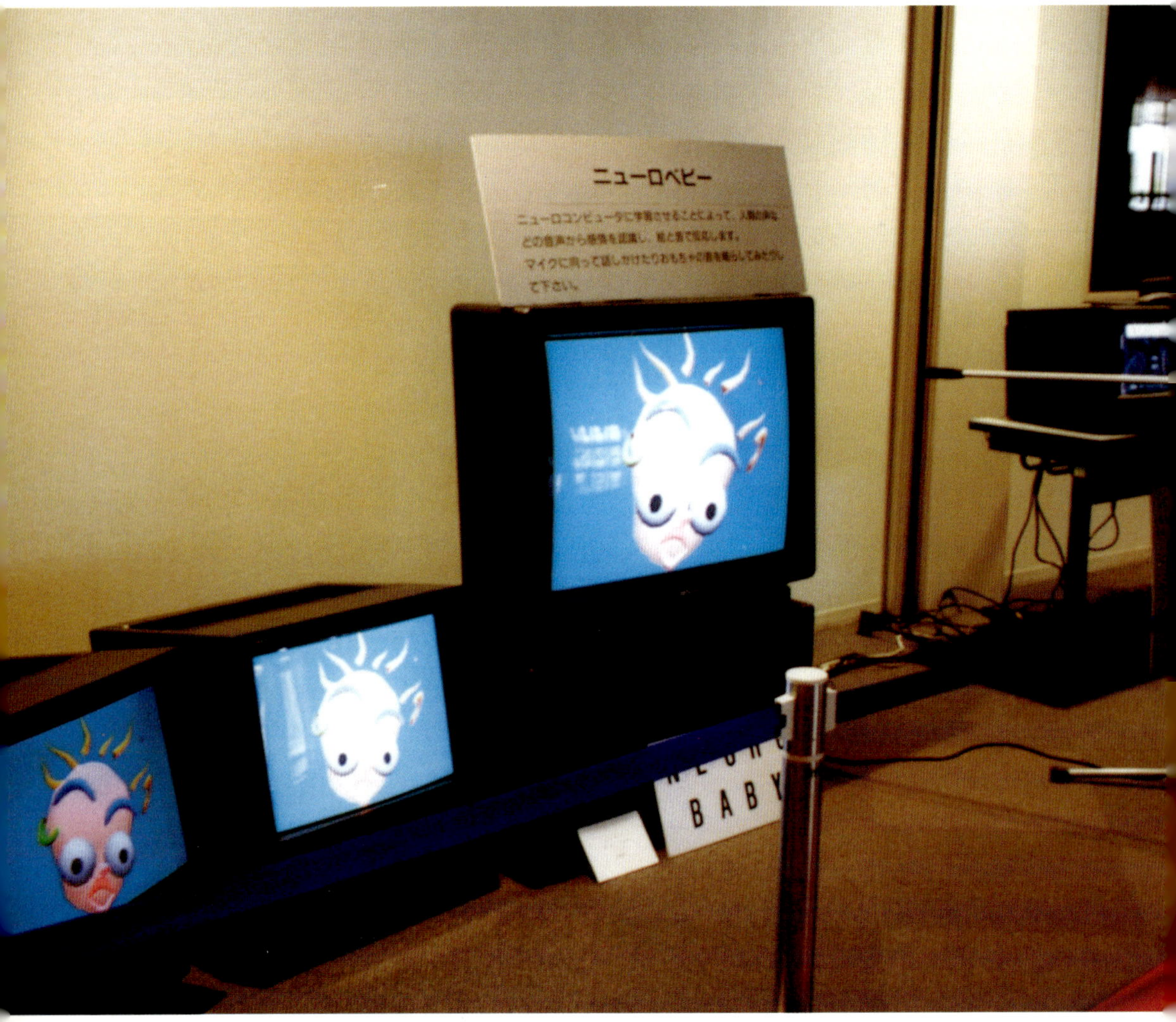
ニューロベビー
BABY

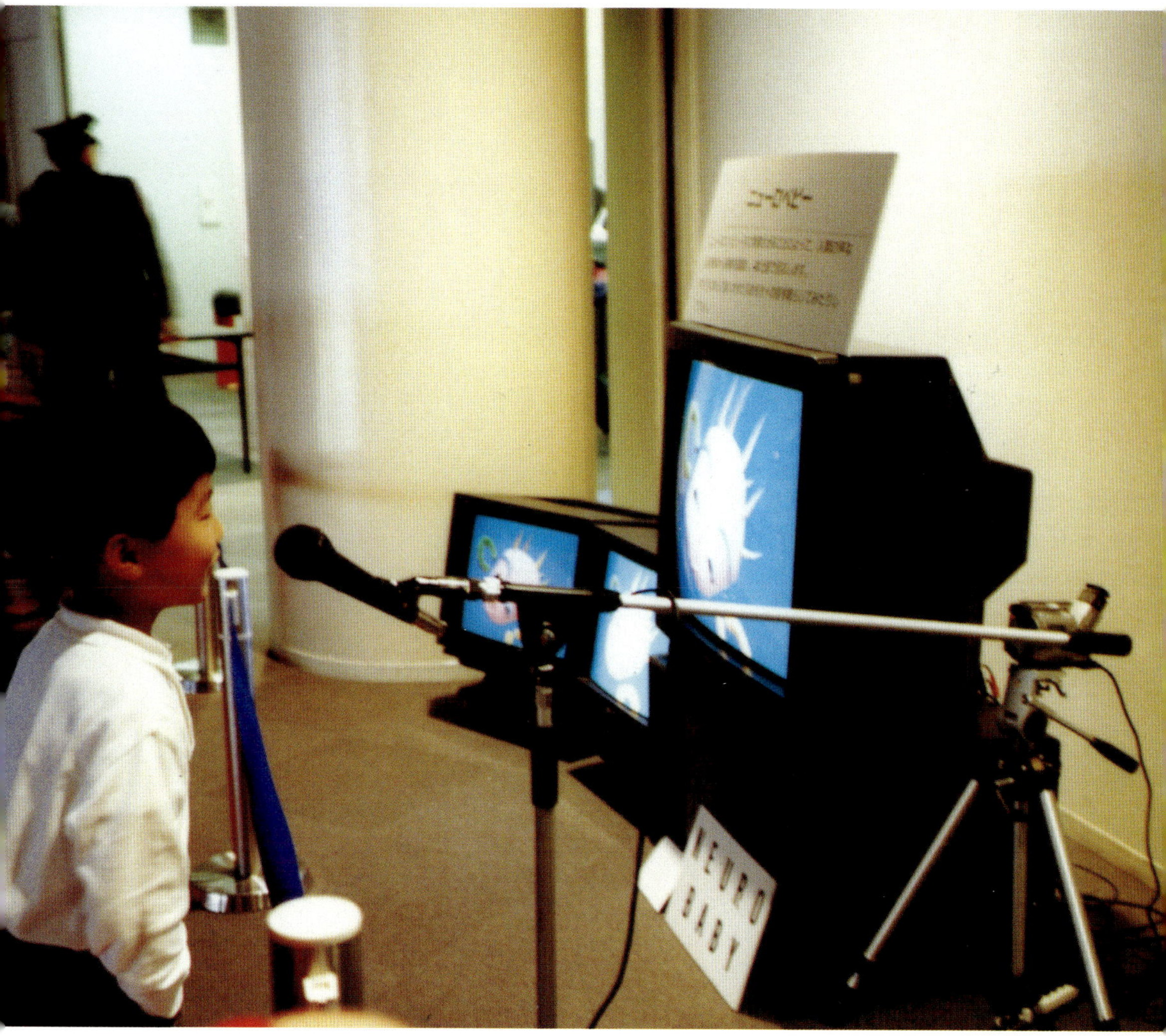

monitor smiles and responds with a pre-recorded laughing voice. If the speaker's voice is low or threatening, the baby responds with a sad or angry expression and voice. If you try to chastise it, with a loud cough or disapproving sound, it becomes needy and starts crying. The baby also sometimes responds to special events with a yawn, a hiccup, or a cry. If the baby is ignored, it passes time by whistling, and responds with a cheerful "Hi" once spoken to.
The baby's responses appear very realistic, and may become quite endearing once the speaker becomes skilled at evoking the baby's emotions. It is a truly lovable and playful imp and entertainer. In many ways, it is intended to remind speakers of the lifelike manner of the famous video-computer character Max Meadroom.

TECHNICAL DESCRIPTION OF WORK

Two major technologies were combined to create this system: voice analyses and the synthesis of facial expressions. Voice analysis was performed by a neural network emulator which converted the voice input wave patterns into "emotional patterns" represented by two floating point values. The neural network has been "taught" the relationship between inflections in human voices and emotional patterns contained within those inflections. During interaction with the baby the emotional patterns found in the observer's speech are continuously generated.
During the translation stage, the two values for emotional patterns are interpreted as an X-Y location on an emotional plane, onto which several types of emotional patterns are mapped. For example, "anger" may be located on the lower left of such a plane, while "pleasure" would be located on the upper right of the same plane. Each emotional pattern corresponds to a paired facil expression and a few seconds of voice output.
During the performance, the facial expression is determined by interpolating the shape, position, and angle of facial parts, such as eyes, eyebrows, and lips. These parts were pre-designed for each emotional reaction.
One FM TOWNS, Fujitsu's multi-media personal computer is used for voice analysis, another FM TOWNS is used for voice generation, and a Silicon Graphics IRIS 4D is used for image synthesis.
Collaborators: Koichi Murakami (Fujitsu Laboratories Ltd.), Big Towns Ltd.
* This work was a collaboration between the artist and Fujitsu Laboratories.

4. GENETISCHE MANIPULATION

Thomas Grünfeld, misfit III, 1989/90

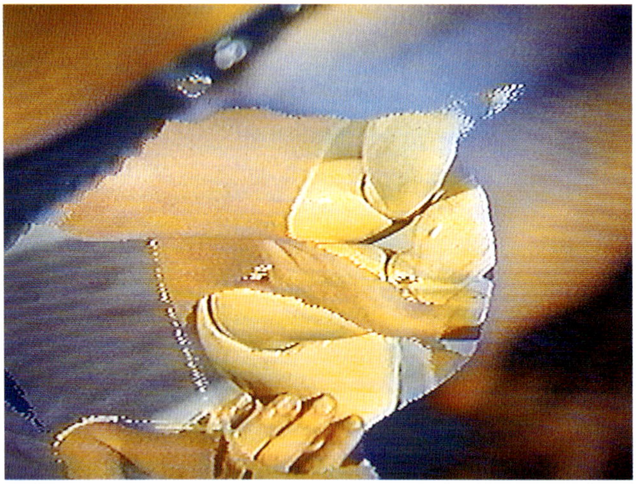

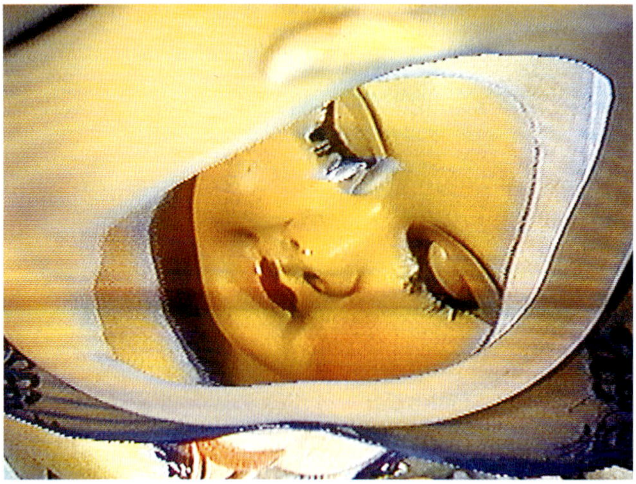

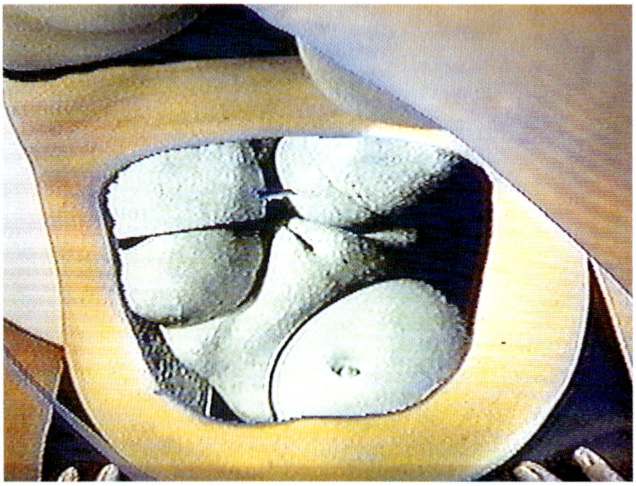

VOID SPACE I, II, III

VALIE EXPORT

VOID SPACE I, II, III
VALIE EXPORT

INVAGINATION (1993)

By having a look through new models—"in silico" as well as "in vitro"—of old dreams a puppeted foreign body awaits us at the end of these enterprises. The desire to tear open the invisible offers itself as transparency of the sciences. Prob-ably wheelings and dealings are to blame for the equation of know-ledge and power. Everyone agrees that
RESPONSABILITY
    response
        sponse (word)
should be written with a capital. But who takes it on?

R. M.

INVAGINATION (1993)

Beim Durchsehen neuer Ausführungen – „in silicio“ und auch „in vitro“ – alter Träume erwartet uns ein verpuppter Fremdkörper am Ende dieser Unternehmungen. Die Lust Undurchsichtiges aufzureißen bietet sich an als Transparenz der Wissen-schaften. Wahr-scheinlich geht die Gleichung von Wissen und Macht auf das Konto von Machen-schaften. Man ist sich allseitig einig, daß
VERANTWORTUNG
    antwort
        wort
groß geschrieben werden sollte. Doch wer übernimmt sie?

R. M.

DEAD ON ARRIVAL

THOMAS GRÜNFELD

Warum Tierpräparation? Der Gedanke der Illegitimität, daß etwas zu Unrecht an einen Platz gequetscht wird wo es nicht hingehört, ist ein Grund für Abscheu, einen Zustand, von dem Freud erklärte, er sei in den Augenblicken unvermeidlich, in denen das Unbewußte ins Bewußtsein dringt.[3] Vielleicht ist die Kategorienverwechslung die schwerste Ketzerei: drinnen und draußen, Fell und Federn, genießbar und ungenießbar, zahm und wild – alle unentwirrbar zusammengewürfelt, wie als Postulat einer möglichen Befreiung von ihnen, einer Abwesenheit jener Antithesen, durch die das Gehirn von der Sprache verhext wird. Ein Gegensatz vor allem beherrscht unsere Auffassung dessen, was an einer Person wesentlich ist: daß man unter den menschlichen Tugenden die „Tiefe" der „Weite" vorzieht, und das entsprechende Ideal, man könne Leute besser verstehen, indem man durch ihre Schale dringt und Schätze ausgräbt, deren Umfang mit fortschreitender Ausgrabung zunimmt. Was wäre, wenn die Leute überall von gleicher Konsistenz wären, oder wenn unter der äußeren Hülle alles nur ausgestopft wäre? (Eine religiöse Variante besagt, daß der Körper wertlos sei, und nur der Geist zähle.) Warum stopfen wir Tiere aus, aber keine Menschen? Warum essen wir Tiere, aber keine Menschen? Im Kern der westlichen Kultur liegt eine Dichotomie, deren Untersuchung wir nicht ertragen können, ein Bündel von Gegensätzen, durch die wir leben, ohne uns ihnen mehr als einen allzuschmerzlichen Augenblick lang stellen zu können. Und doch kann man sie vielleicht vorzeigen. Das Thema der Zurschaustellung war immer ein Hauptinteresse Grünfelds; eines seiner Werke besteht beispielsweise aus einem Rahmen, in dem drei verschiedene Ausschnitte Holzimitat durch am Rahmen montierte Bilderleuchten überstrahlt werden, sie aber im Grunde sich selbst bestrahlen. Das Interesse ist das gleiche, doch zum Gegenstand der Betrachtung wird jetzt eine pseudowissenschaftliche Sammlung, die in einer bestimmten Reihenfolge eine Art von Rückzüchtung veranschaulichen soll. Von der „Zurschaustellung" zum „Monster" ist es ein kürzerer Schritt als man glaubt. „Monster" und „Zurschaustellung" (Demonstration) haben, wie Michel Foucault einmal be-

DEAD ON ARRIVAL
THOMAS GRÜNFELD

Why taxidermy? The idea of illegitimacy, of something that does not belong jammed into a place it has no right to enter, is a soucre of repulsion, the state which, Freud explained, was inevitable at moments when the unconscious penetrates the conscious mind.[3] Perhaps confusion of categories is the ultimate heresy: inside and out, fur and feathers, edible and inedible, tame and wild, inextricably jumbled, as a way of positing what freedom might be, an absence of those antitheses by which language ensnares the brain. One opposition in particular governs our perception of what a person is: the preference for "depth" over "breadth" as human virtues, with the accompanying ideal of knowing people better by penetrating their outer shell, in order to mine treasures which multiply as the mining process continues. What if people are solid all the way through, or below the outer cosing only stuffing can be found? (A religious variation is the sense that the body is worthless and only the spirit matters.) Why do we stuff animals but not human beings? Why do we *eat* animals buf not human beings? At fhe core of Western culture is a dualism we cannot bear to examine, a set of oppositions we live by but which are painful to consider for more than a moment. Perhaps they can be shown, however. Grünfeld has always been interested in the issue of display, to the point of making a work consisting of a frame containing three differently sized fake wood pieces, illuminated by lamps around the frame, one shining on each. The preoccupation continues, but the object of affention is now a pseudo-scientific collection assembled in order to illustrate some form of backbreeding. From "display" fo "monster" is a shorter step than it seems. As Michel Foucault once pointed out, the words lead back fo the Latin *monstrare,* to put on show—not, it might be added, for reasons of debate but as a form of spectacle. If freaks are despised and venerated in equal measure, one reason could be their power to defy analysis. They are guaranteed to block any ongoing discussion, whether of genetic engineering or developments in art. The suggestion is that art and science equally—for the overtones are those of a museum—have lost touch with genuine, difficult issues, which can be seen, but not solved.

Neither historically accurate nor a restoration of anything that ever existed, Grünfeld's new trophies are assembled by combining parts from

different animals, made to look as plausible as possible—as plausible, at least, as a narwhal, a stick-insect or a platypus. Numbered, nof titled, the *misfits* look lost and vulnerable in their cabinets of German oak—"lost" because the cases are obviously too big, "vulnerable" because of fhe neon lights and glass on three sides. Their sole function is to be displayed like specimens, and their disturbing air of self-consciousness may derive from this fact. Admittedly, they differ. While parts of a rabbit and a pheasant and the feeth of a fox give *III* a classical air, *VI* and *V* seem humorous and visually appealing, for example. In his Croquis Parisiens of 1880, J.-K. Huysmans, a favourite author of Grünfeld, described a bar with vitrines full of clumsily stuffed animals, many with fixed, idiotic stares because their orange and black eyes are exactly the same, swans with beaks made from yellow wood, with unevenly filled necks and stuffing protruding from their bellies or an old toothless crocodile patched with shoeleather. Huysmans' descriptions rely on two familiar reactions: recognising human characteristics in the animals and a sense that though amateur taxidermy has resurrecfed them artificially their second life is all the more vivid because of clumsy workmanship. Grünfeld's *mistits* related to the Southern German *Wolpertinger* tradition, tall tales about improbable beasts lurking unsuspected in the wild. Neither drawings and descriptions of these animals nor concocted specimens serve to increase their credibility. Instead, they further the mythology surrounding them, a phenomenon which even moves into print with popular books such as Heim and Reiser's *Mit dem Wolpertinger leben* or Alphons Schweigert's *Und es gibt sie doch!*

In biological terms, if seems, the specimens in the cases are the born losers of fhe animal world, one-offs doomed to failure like the experiments of Wells's Doctor Moreau or the monster of Frankenstein. From the viewer's point of view, their survival seems in doubt precisely because their mixed parentage gives them no advantage whatsoever. The way we perceive them is by a process of spotting a single, dominant beast and relegating variations to a subordinate status. In other words, the way we view them is biased in favour of what we already know, and what we know about breeding. Only the strong survive, and they are uppermost in our minds even in the apparently unbiased act of vision. Despite this, if is human nature to invent monsters: the grotesque offers a permanent means of testing and confirming our own limits. What the Gorgon has in common with E.T. is that both remind us of what being human means. Famous monsters of history are ways of posing and partially solving problems of beauty, evil, power and seduction. But only fhe famous ones; monsters too have a success ratio.

We are as ignorant of the meaning of dragons as we are of the meaning of the universe, but there is something in the dragon's image that appeals to the human imagination, and so we find the dragon in quite distinct places and times. It is, so to speak, a necessary monster, not an ephemeral or accidental one, such as the three-headed chimera or the catoblepas.[4]

merkte, dieselbe lateinische Wurzel „monstrare"; zur Schau stellen – nicht, so könnte man hinzufügen, aus Gründen einer möglichen Debatte, sondern als Spektakel. Und der Grund für unsere gleichzeitige Verachtung und Verehrung von Mißgestalten liegt vielleicht darin, daß sie sich dem analytischen Denken entziehen. Sie bringen jede bestehende Diskussion zum Stillstand, sei es eine über Genmanipulation oder eine über die neueste Kunst. Die Vermutung liegt nahe, daß Kunst und Wissenschaft in gleichem Maße – denn alles deutet auf ein Museum hin – den Zugang zu den wirklichen und schwierigen Fragen verloren haben. Diese werden zwar gesehen, sind aber noch nicht gelöst.

Grünfelds neue Trophäen sind weder historisch korrekt, noch stellen sie etwas wieder her, das es je gegeben hat. Sie werden aus Teilen verschiedenster Tiere zusammengesetzt und sollen dabei so plausibel wie möglich aussehen – mindestens so plausibel wie ein Narwal, ein aufgespießtes Insekt oder ein Schnabeltier. Ohne Einzeltitel, nur mit Numerierung, schauen die misfits in ihren Vitrinen aus deutscher Eiche verletzlich und verloren aus – „verloren", denn die Vitrinen sind offensichtlich zu groß für sie, „verletzlich" wegen des Neonlichts und der dreiseitigen Verglasung. Ihre einzige Funktion ist die Ausstellung als Musterbeispiel, woher vielleicht auch die Beunruhigung und die eigene Befangenheit rührt. Zugegebenermaßen gibt es Unterschiede. Während III durch seine Kaninchen- und Fasanenteile und seine Fuchszähne etwas Klassisches hat, sind etwa IV und V humoristisch und reizvoll anzusehen. J. K. Huysmans, einer von Grünfelds Lieblingsautoren, beschrieb 1880 in den Croquis Parisiens eine Bar mit Vitrinen voller mühselig ausgestopfter Tiere, deren Blicke aufgrund der immer gleichen orange-schwarzen Augen meist ein fixes, idiotisches Starren waren; Schwäne mit gelben Holzschnäbeln, ungleichmäßig gefüllten Hälsen und vom Stopfzeug ausgebeulten Bäuchen, oder ein altes mit Schuhleder geflicktes Krokodil ohne Zähne. Huysmans' Beschreibung beruht auf zwei wohlbekannten Wirkungen: daß man in Tieren menschliche Eigenschaften wiedererkennen kann, und die Einsicht daß – trotz der künstlichen Wiederbelebung der Tiere durch eine dilettantische Tierpräparation – das zweite Leben seine Lebendigkeit nur der mühsehligen Arbeit verdankt. Grünfelds misfits schließen an die süddeutsche Wolpertingertradition an, künden von unmöglichen Tieren, die unerahnt durch die Wildnis schweifen. Weder Zeichnungen noch Beschreibungen dieser Tiere, noch ausgeheckte Musterexemplare erhöhen ihre Glaubwürdigkeit. Stattdessen erweitern sie die betreffende Mythologie, die sogar ins Gedruckte gelangte, mit Büchern wie Heims und Reisers Mit dem Wol-

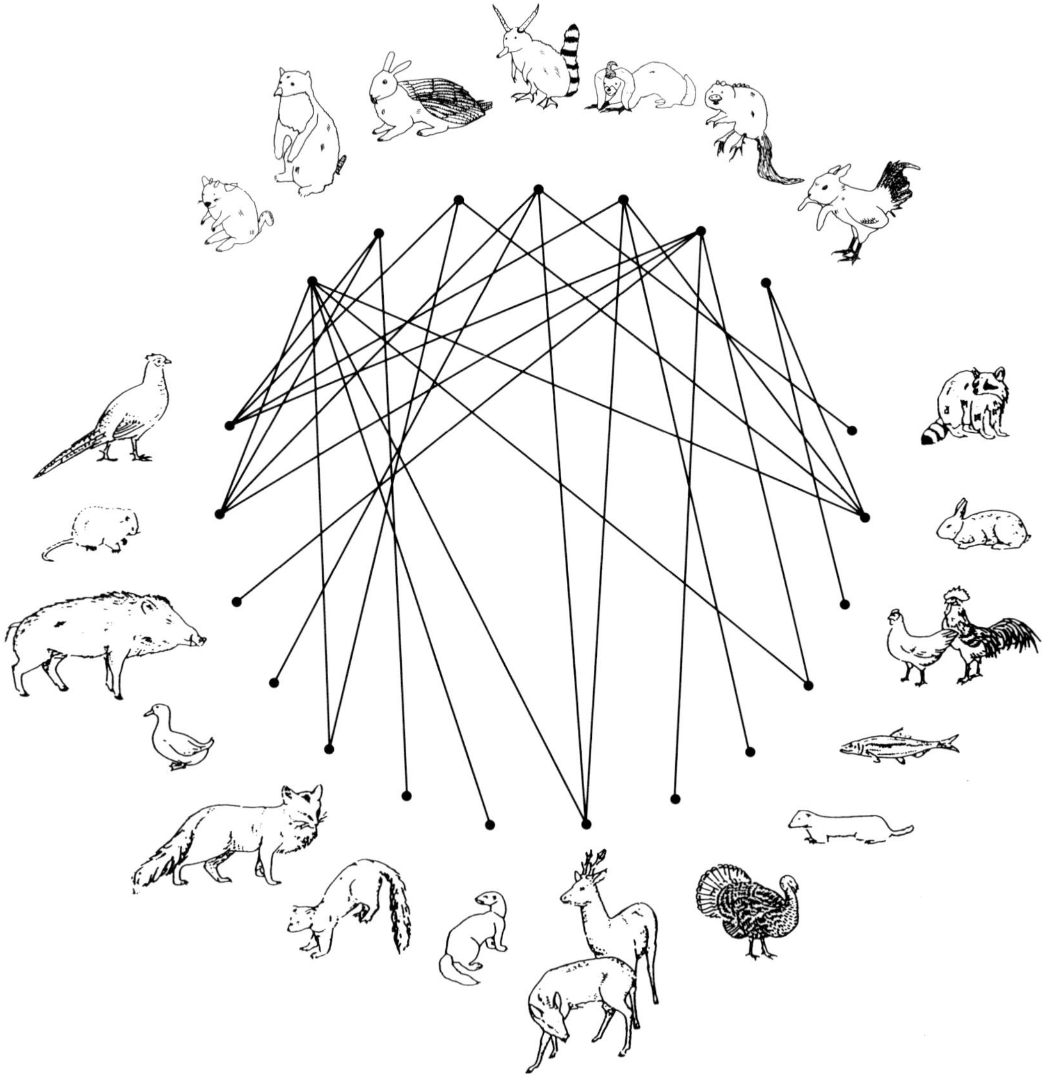

pertinger leben oder Alphons Schweigerts Und es gibt sie doch!.
Unter biologischem Gesichtspunkt sind die Beispiele in den Vitrinen die geborenen Verlierer der Tierwelt, zum Scheitern verurteilte Seitensprünge, wie die Experimente von Wells' Doktor Moreau oder wie Frankensteins Monster. Der Betrachter zweifelt gerade deshalb an ihrem möglichen Überleben, weil ihre gemischte Abstammung ihnen keinen erdenklichen Vorteil bringt. Wir erfassen sie in der Reihenfolge, daß wir zuerst ein einziges, dominantes Tier ausmachen, un den Variationen einen untergeordneten Rang zuweisen. Anders ausgedrückt, unsere Sichtweise favorisiert das Vor-Wissen, mitsamt dem Wissen über Tierzucht. Allein die Starken überleben, und auch in unserem Geist haben sie, selbst im scheinbar unvoreingenommenen Wahrnehmungsakt, die Oberhand. Trotzdem liegt es in der menschlichen Natur, sich Monster auszudenken: das Groteske stellt ein probantes Mittel dar, unsere Grenzen auf die Probe zu stellen und zu bestätigen. Die Gorgo wie auch E.T. rufen uns in Erinnerung, was es heißt, der Menschheit anzugehören. Die berühmten historischen Untiere geben uns die Möglichkeit, Fragen über Schönheit, Gut und Böse, Macht und Verführung zu stellen und ansatzweise zu beantworten. Aber nur die berühmten; auch unter Monstern gibt es Stars.
„Wir kennen den Sinn des Drachen ebensowenig wie den Sinn des Universums, aber in seinem Bild ist etwas, das in Einklang steht mit der Vorstellungskraft des Menschen, und so erscheint der Drache in verschiedenen Gebieten und zu verschiedenen Zeiten. Er ist sozusagen ein notwendiges Monster, weder ephemer noch zufällig, so wie die dreiköpfige Chimaira oder der Katoblepas."[4]
Jorge Luis Borges vertrat die Ansicht, daß für Monster dieselben Kriterien gelten wie für andere Konstrukte der Phantasie. Ihm zufolge wären die misfits eher das Resultat einer Pfuscherei, als einer anatomischen Generalüberholung. So wie „notwendige" Monster die Überlebenden der Phantasie sind, sind ihre ephemeren Entsprechungen ein Tribut an die Arten, deren Aussterben die Geschichte der Arten am Leben hielt. Schon ihre bloße Existenz scheint ein Tribut an unser Mitleid und unseren Gerechtigkeitssinn
Der Kontext dieser misfits ist doppelt, wie jeder Kontext in Grünfelds Werk. Sie sind Trophäen für die eigene Wohnung, aber genauso von Galeriebesuchern gemusterte Objekte. Und die Galerie könnte ebensogut ein Museum sein, wie ein Verkaufsort für zeitgenössische Kunst.
In den letzten Jahren haben die beiden fusioniert; die Idee der Kunsthalle bestand darin, die Kunst direkt aus dem Atelier zu holen und sie in einem Kontext zu installieren, der

Jorge Luis Borges argued that monsters should be subject to the same tests as other imaginative constructs. In his terms, Grünfeld's *misfits* would be the result of tampering rather than full-scale anatomical overhaul. Just as "necessary" monsters are survivors of the imagination, their ephemeral counterparts pay tribute fo the species which perished so that history could be written. Their very existence seems a fribute to our own justice and mercy. Or perhaps not. The M.C.C. Club's sparrow might give the impression that it has been stuffed and mounted out of good manners to the bird, but the whole exercise was really about the game of cricket. Like the interminable lists of batsmen and bowlers quoted by experts, it becomes history, a continuation of tradition. But forget crickets. The context of these *misfits* is double, like every context in Grünfeld's work. These are trophies for fhe home but also items which gallery-goers examine.
And the gallery could as easily be in a museum as in a place where contemporary art is sold.
In recent years the two have merged; the very idea of a *Kunsthalle* is to take art straight from the studio and install it in what was traditionally a context which only time could ensure. Bypassing vicissitudes of taste or critical outlook, sanctified instead by immediate decision-making, art has become instant history while what was once thought of as the gradual progress of culture has dwindled fo mere fashion. Exhibifing developed from a willingness on fhe parf of the nobility to open their homes to the public. At the time museums seemed a good idea. Twentieth-century commentators have not always been so sure.
The German term *museal* [museum-like] has unpleasant overtones. It describes objects to which the viewer no longer has a vital relationship and which are in the process of dying. They owe their preservation more to historical respect than the needs of the present. Museum and mausoleum are connected by more than phonetic association. Museums are the family sepulchres of works of art.
In 1980 Douglas Crimp used these words by Theodor Adorno to open an attack on museums in an essay called "On the Museum's Ruins".[5] As Adorno saw it, and Crimp agreed, the museum murders obljects by robbing them of their vitality. Nine years later, in an essay called "The Museum Wifhout Walls Reconsidered", Crimp moved a stage further. In the case of a *contemporary* art museum, he argued, objects would be killed without ever being allowed a chance to live. Nowadays, he adds, because objects are intended for the museum, to be interpreted within its discursive practice, "they are already dead when they're made".[6] In Grünfeld's thinking, opposition to art as a train of thought within fixed perimeters is possible only by subversive activity within those perimeters, not by gestures from oufside. Yet this means an acknowledgement that the myth of the avantgarde must be prolonged artifically in order to demonstrate that it no longer has force or significance. Perhaps only a manoeuvre as paradoxical as *misfits* can do justice to the illogical situation of contemporary art.

Stuart Morgan

NOTES

[1] A. Lejeune and M. Lewis *The Gentlemen's Clubs of London* London 1979, 186.
[2] Quoted in Cornelia Lauf "Thomas Locher, Thomas Gründfeld" *Artscribe* 71, September—October 1988, 87.
[3] Sigmund Freud "A Note on the Unconscious in Psycholanalysis" in J. Strachey ed. *The Standard Edition of the Complete Psychoanalytic Works of Sigmund Freud* London 1958, vol. 12, 264.
[4] J. L. Borges *The Book of Imaginary Beings* Harmondsworth 1974, 14.
[5] Thomas Locher in *Thomas Grünfeld* Vienna 1988, n. p.
[6] Douglas Crimp "On the Museum's Ruins" in Half Foster ed. *The Anti-Aesthetic* Part Townsend 1983, 43.
[7] Douglas Crimp "The Museum Without Walls Reconsidered" in R. de Leeuw & E. Beer ed. *L'exposition imaginaires Gravenhage 1989, 272.*

traditionell nur der Vergangenheit seine Sicherheit verdankte. Die Fährlichkeiten von Geschmack und kritischer Begutachtung werden einfach umgangen und Kunst wird jetzt durch die unmittelbare Entscheidung geheiligt. Geschichte wird die Geschichte des Augenblicks, und der allmähliche Fortschritt der Kultur löst sich in nichts als Mode auf. Man bedenke, daß Museen aus der Bereitwilligkeit des Adels entstanden, ihre Wohnstätten der Öffentlichkeit zu zeigen. Damals schien das Museum eine gute Idee. Im späten zwanzigsten Jahrhundert waren sich die Kommentatoren nicht so sicher.

„Der Ausdruck ‚useal' hat im Deutschen unfreundliche Farbe. Er bezeichnet Gegenstände, zu denen der Betrachter nicht mehr lebendig sich verhält und die selber absterben. Sie werden mehr aus historischer Rücksicht aufbewahrt als aus gegenwärtigem Bedürfnis. Museum und Mausoleum verbindet nicht bloß die phonentische Assoziation. Museen sind wie Erbbegräbnisse von Kunstwerken."

1980 verwandte Douglas Crimp diese Worte Theodor Adornos, um in einem Essay mit dem Titel „Auf den Ruinen des Museums"[6] einen Angriff auf die Museen zu eröffnen. Adorno und Crimp zufolge mordet das Museum seine Objekte, indem es sie ihrer einzigen Lebenskraft beraubt. Neun Jahre später ging Crimp in seinem Essay „Noch einmal zum Mauerlosen Museum" einen Schritt weiter. Er vertrat die Ansicht, daß die Objekte im Falle eines zeitgenössischen Kunstmuseums getötet würden, ohne je eine Lebenschance besessen zu haben. Heutzutage – so sein neuer Punkt – „sind sie schon tot, wenn sie fertig sind"[7], denn sie werden für das Museum hergestellt und sollen nur noch in der Praxis seines Diskurses eine Deutung finden. Es entspricht Grünfelds Denken, daß die Opposition zur Kunst als einer Gedankenbewegung innerhalb feststehender Parameter nur als subversives Handeln innerhalb dieser Parameter möglich ist, nicht als demonstrative Geste von draußen. Doch das heißt, daß der Mythos der Avantgarde künstlich verlängert werden muß, um zu demonstrieren, daß er weder Kraft noch Bedeutung besitzt. Vielleicht kann nur ein so paradoxes Manöver wie die misfits der unlogischen Situation der zeitgenössischen Kunst gerecht werden.

Stuart Morgan

Courtesy Tanja Grunert und Michael Janssen, Köln

ANDREW HEAD, JULIE HEAD, RINDE HEAD

BRUCE NAUMAN

Courtesy Galerie Metropol, Wien

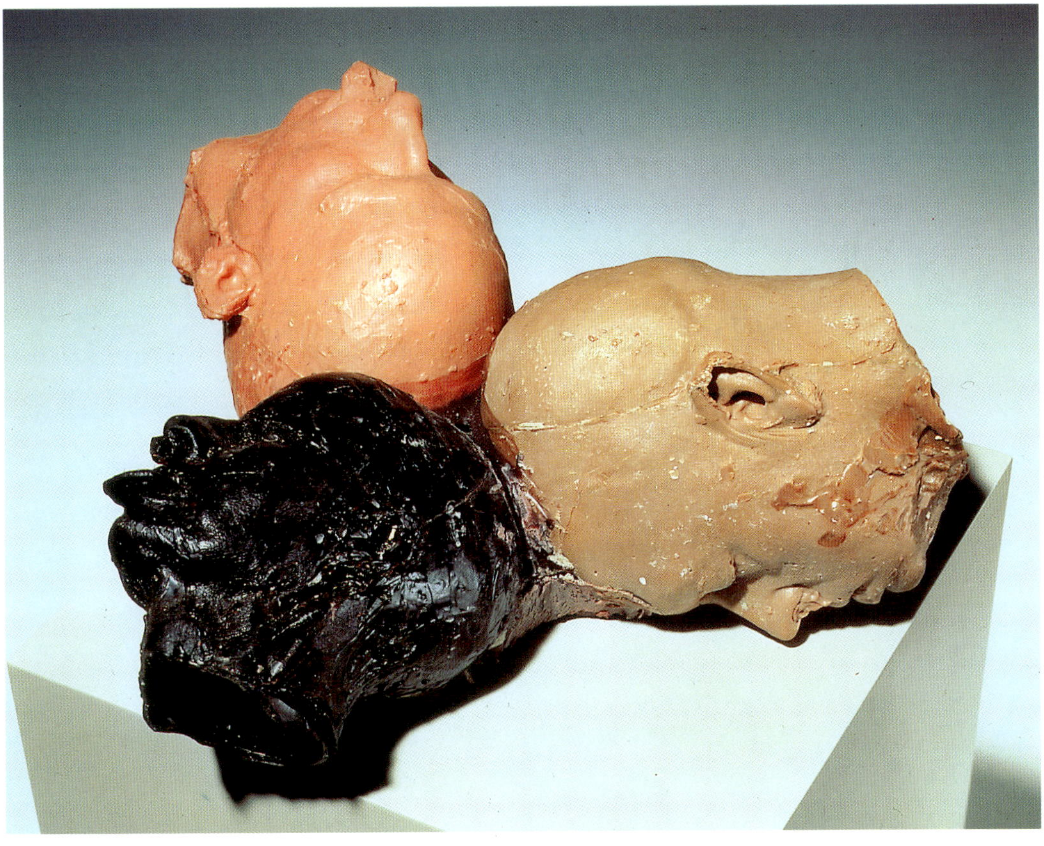

The Reign of the Rain, 1989, Courtesy Galerie Thaddäus Kopac, Salzburg/Paris.

THE REIGN OF THE RAIN

ALEXIS ROCKMAN

THE REIGN OF THE RAIN
ALEXIS ROCKMAN

Alexis Rockman has reconciled with postmodernism. In past exhibitions, except for a dystopian series done in 1900 that centered on environmental hazards and the grotesque mutations engineered by gene-splicing techniques, Rockman's work never quite significantly transgressed the modern pedagogy of both natural and art history. Instead, his finesse as a painter dazzled us with its abozzo-and-glazing techniques which reflect light in a manner unseen—with the exception of Ross Bleckner's work—for several decades. In short, Rockman's production always seemed to be an anachronism; but was it an anachronism by being retrograde or by being ahaead of the dominant production of the times?

As in modern physics, such a question is wholly relative to one's position. In the twentyeight-foot painting, *Evolution,* which ambitiously represents every paeontological age hypothesized by seience with a selection of its zoological denizens alongside hybrid beasts of his own design, Rockman becomes something more than a postmoden an naturalist Hieronymus Bosch. He charts the human condition, not by including humans in his depicted "history" of evolution, but by imploying our place with our gaze, a gaze that encompasses al time (psychologically speaking) and is arguably constructed not in a "nature" apart from humanity, but in the nature that resides as a paradigm in the minds of humans.

Rockman has finally shown a critical side of his work that goes geyond the political and environmental implications of his earlier work, demonstrating that even the intellectual facutly requred to frame history and the tendency to criticize its events is a mutation (some might say ublimation) of the imperative to survive, something Rockman is doing superbly.

G. Roger Denson
aus: FLASH ART Jan/Feb 1993

Thanks to Jay Gorney Modern Art, NYC

Alexis Rockman hat sich mit der Postmoderne ausgesöhnt. In seinen letzten Ausstellungen – mit Ausnahme einer dystopianischen Serie von 1990, die sich auf Umweltkatastrophen und groteske, durch Gentechnologien erzeugte Mutationen, konzentrierte – hat Rockmans Arbeit niemals in signifikanter Weise gegen die Pädagogik sowohl der Natur- als auch der Kunstgeschichte verstoßen. Dagegen hat uns seine Finesse als Maler mit ihren Lasurtechniken, die das Licht in seit Jahrzehnten nicht gesehener Weise – mit Ausnahme von Ross Bleckners Arbeiten – reflektieren, geblendet. Kurzum, Rockmans Produktion schien immer ein Anachronismus zu sein; aber war sie ein Anachronismus weil sie rückschrittlich war oder weil sie an vordester Stelle der wichtigen Erzeugnisse der Zeit stand?

Wie in der modernen Physik ist eine solche Frage gänzlich auf jemandes Positionbezogen. Das 8,5-Meter-Bild „Evolution", das ambitiös jedes von der Wissenschaft angenommene paläontologische Zeitalter anhand einer Auswahl seiner zoologischen Exemplare neben hybriden Bastarden aus Rockmans eigener Kreation darstellt, wird er zu mehr als einem postmodernen und naturalistischen Hieronymus Bosch. Er führt den menschlichen Faktor an, nicht indem er Menschen in seine geschilderte „Geschichte" der Evolution miteinbezieht, sondern indem er unseren Platz mit unserem Blick gleichsetzt, einem Blick, der alle Zeit (psychologisch gesprochen) umfaßt, und der vertretbar nicht in einer „Natur" abseits von Menschlichkeit konstruiert ist, sondern in der Natur, die als Paradigma in den menschlichen Gehirnen residiert.

Rockman hat schließlich eine kritische Seite seiner Arbeit gezeigt, die über die politischen und umweltbezogenen Implikationen seiner früheren Arbeit hinausgeht, indem er zeigt, daß sogar die intellektuelle Fähigkeit, die benötigt wird, um Geschichte in einen Rahmen zu setzen, und die Tendenz, ihre Ereignisse zu kritisieren, eine Mutation (einige werden sagen, eine Sublimierung) des Imperativs, zu überleben, ist – etwas, das Rockman hervorragend tut.

G.Roger Denson
aus: FLASH ART Jan/Feb 1993

UNTITLED TURKEY XXIII

MEYER VAISMAN

POULTRYCULTURALISM

Sie sind auf eine bestimmte Weise Fetische. Sie haben die magische Präsenz von Fetischen, diese runden Truthähne, die mit den Häuten anderer Tiere geschmückt und dann in der einen oder anderen Landestracht gekleidet wurden. Wie Voodoo Puppen oder Ikonen haben sie als Objekte eine starke Wirkung. Kurzum: trotz – oder vielleicht aufgrund – ihrer offensichtlichen Lächerlichkeit haben sie eine seltsame, ja beeindruckende Schönheit.

Doch die Schönheit ist entlehnt und gegen sich selbst gewandt. Wenn ein Antibild ein Bild ist, das die eigentliche Möglichkeit von Bildern in Frage stellt, sind sie Anti-Totems. Sie sind dazu da, um genau das in Abrede zu stellen, was Totems stützen sollen: kulturelle Identität, das klare Selbstverständnis des eigenen Kontextes, und die sauberen Kategorien, in die wir die Welt gerne einteilen, sei es mit Hilfe des Modesystems, sei es die Klassifikation der Tierwelt.

Vaisman hatte schon immer eine gewisse antiessentialistische Tendenz, den Wunsch, diese Disposition zu fördern und ihre Konsequenzen nachzuzeichnen. In jenem Sinne stellen die Truthähne mit seinen Karikaturmalereien und seinen neckischen Tapisserien ein Kontinuum dar. Die implizite Disziplin, die der Künstler nachahmt und dann untergräbt, hat sich verändert: in Vaismans früheren Arbeiten waren Männer Frauen und Narren Könige. Hier finden wir: Venezuelaner sind Indianer sind Japaner sind Deutsche und Truthähne sind Hasen sind Schildkröten sind Männer. Während sein früheres Schaffen eine Selbstdarstellung als degenerierter Historiker war, bieten die Truthähne Anschauungsunterricht in radikaler Anthropologie. Doch worauf es hier ankommt, ist stets dasselbe: die Kultur existiert nicht, außer als ein Flickwerk entlehnter Fetzen. Wir setzen diese auf wie einen Hut. Es gibt nichts Beständiges hinter unseren Entscheidungen, es gibt keine natürlichen Arten.

Es ist eine gute Nachricht, die schon lange fällig war. Doch wenn wir eine Debatte über Multikulturalismus austragen wollen, müssen wir uns zuerst fragen, was wir in einer Welt, in der nichts gleich sich selbst ist, multiplizieren.

UNTITLED TURKEY XXIII

POULTRYCULTURALISM / MEYER VAISMAN DRESSES THE BIRD

They are, in a way, fetishes; anyway they have the magic presence of fetishes, these burly turkeys tricked out in skins from other animals and then dressed in native costumes of one sort or another. Like voodoo dolls or icons they are formidable as objects. In short, despite—or perhaps because of—their obvious ludicrousness, they have a strange, even impressive beauty.

But the beauty is borrowed, and bent against itself. If an antipainting is a painting that tries to call into question the very possibility of paintings, these are antitotems. They're there to deny precisely what totems are supposed to support: cultural identity, the self's clear understanding of its own context, and the neat categories into which we like to order the world, whether via the fashion system or animal classification.

Vaisman has always had a certain antiessentialist bias, a desire to promote this disposition and to trace its consequences. In that sense the turkeys are on a continuum with his caricature paintings and his jestering tapestries. But the implicit discipline the artist mines and then undermines has changed: in past works by Vaisman, men were women and fools were kings. Here Venezuelans are Indians are Japanese are Germans, as turkeys are rabbits are turtles are men. So where his earlier work presented a self-portrait as degenerate historian, the turkeys offer up an object lesson in radical anthropology. But the point pressed home is the same: culture does not exist, except as a patchwork of borrowed scraps. We put it on as we do a hat. There is nothing stable behind our decisions; there are no natural kinds.

It is glad news, and long overdue. Because if we are going to act out a debate on multiculturalism, we must first ask what we are multiplying, given a world in which nothing is equal to itself.

Jim Lewis

Courtesy Jablonka Galerie, Köln

Courtesy Jablonka Galerie, Köln

5. "LANGUAGE IS A VIRUS FROM OUTER SPACE" (WILLIAM S. BORROUGHS)

7 VIREN

JOCHEM HENDRICKS

Courtesy Galerie ak, Frankfurt am Main

SATZBAUPLAN

THOMAS LOCHER

LEARN FOR LIFE / STOPPING THE DECONSTRUCTION OF LANGUAGE.

The pejorative meaning of "didactic" has taken root so solidly that no one asks whether the avoidance of didactics might not be in the interest of all those concerned with preventing any extracurricular learning.

Calling an artistic project "too didactic" always knocks the wind out of its sails. This qualification conceals the fear that we might actually learn something from art, that is, call up usable information.

Yet that seems to be precisely what Thomas Locher is claiming when he resorts to tried-and-true learning methods (tables, charts, lists), even though his claim (artistic experience as a learning experience) might then collapse: for the orders that he sets up can be refuted instantly.

Thus, my point in the following is to advocate not an art that transmits knowledge, but an art with "cognitive usability",[1] which doubly exploits its lack of obligation towards science. For the artist who fiddles about with scientific books has a twofold advantage; he can convey results in an unorthodox way (owing no verifiability to the discipline), and he can lend art a breath of scientificness and verifiability. What this means is that the artificiality of the scientific fact is exposed and the facticity of aesthetic accuracy is demonstrated. Naturally, these equations, which should be labeled "art information" and "science construction", do not work out: and indee. Thomas Locher goes beyound them, if only because in his works, nesthetic transcends utility—the presentation in the light box is *more* than what a word demands, or: art is *more* than information. It is left to the consumer to favor either the aesthetic or the cognitive usability of Thomas Locher's work.

What are the reasons for transporting words to light boxes or furniture? The first important reason can be an insight gained from conceptual art of the 1960s: the use of language and the concomitant reduction of the visible are a far cry from protecting against total encroachment. Indeed, the opposite has become the case. In the past, a reduced art product that ba-

sed its outer appearance on its practical value signified a possibility of preventing such encroachment; today, it is precisely the reduced, straightforward appearance that guarantees instant eneroachment with disregard of all contents. Which, in turn, proves that the original intention, or rather, the means applied towards it, will frequently, and even years later, cause them to be used to realize non-intention as well.

Ideas and words are just as marketabele in their most reduced form as other commodities. As a result, Thomas Locher has decided to give his words and numers *more* of a presentation.

The other reasons are inherent in form/content necessities, which, although not compelling, are neverthelesse evident: the light box is a common form of presentation in advertising, lending authority and visibility to what is said, and the utilitarian objects (run-of-the-mil furnishings) have sentences carved into them that are associated with the situation of the room and wirk, and the weight down a head surrounded by furniture ("what is indicated"; "do I misunderstand this"). It is only the state of being surrounded by things that promotes a reified consciousness.

LANGUAGE WORK

Does anyone actually go to the trouble of percling out the basic vocabulary from a language? We are held back from doing so by our wwareness of the inevitably resulting lacunac. At the outset of Locher's language works, there are reflecions about condification by culture, about the determinedness of all artistic reception by language, and about the necessity of representing the linguistic system of rules, which is not represented quite correctly, yet is nevertheless honored, if not celebrated, by means of an elegant presentation.

LET US CELEBRATE RATIONALISM, positivism—our tradition of thinking—for the inadequacy of the system and the falseness of the overview already become blatant during the celebration! Let us commit ourselves to the rules that dicate our thinking, and let us work with the methods provided by a positivist science (tables, graphs, lists)! Let us yield to that impulse to put in order, to articulate and juxtapose, and let us concentrate on the specific, given material (the basic vocabulary), instead of letting our minds roam unfettered, giving free rein to our imagination!
The widespred deconstruction of language will then stop of its own accord, once the non-oppositionality of opposites or the insufficiency of basic vocabularies is brought into focus or into the light box.
Thomas Locher refers to the recipient, the gallery context, the surrounding field in so far as a changes the language according to the site; however, this is not a real reference so much as a metaphor for our awareness that a reference would now be situable. Adjustment to the resprective native tongue is a inadequate nod to the given specific local situation; yet it is also a sign that the letter cannot be skirted.
And if the basic Italien vocabulary contains numerous terms that involve eating, this takes into account the actual linguistic conditions, it also means that someone has finally succeeded in reversing praxis into theory.

Isabelle Graw

(Translated from German by Joachim Neugroschel)

NOTE

[1] According to Nelson Goodman, all nesthetic experience is cognitive: "Under cognitive, I include all uspects of knowing and understanding, from perceptional discrimination to recognition of patterns and emotional insight, as well as logical deduction."

Courtesy Tanja Grunert und Michael Janssen, Köln

FIBONACCI-REIHEN, QUANDO

MARIO MERZ

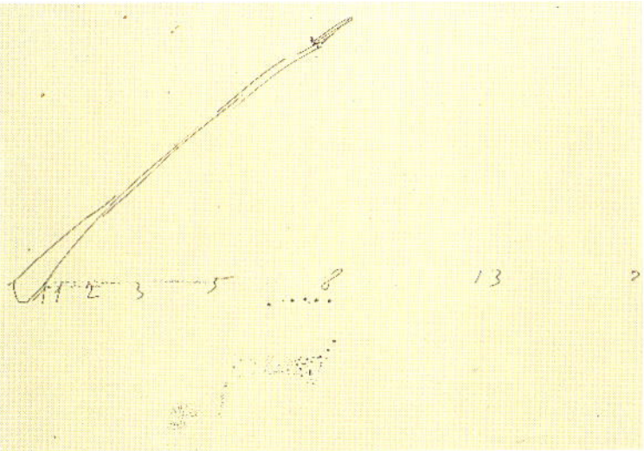

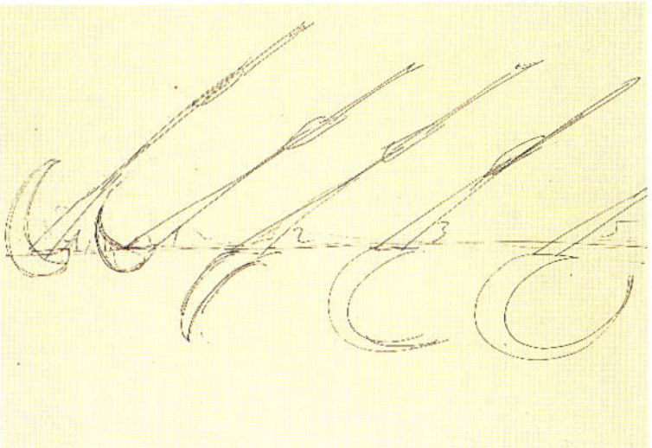

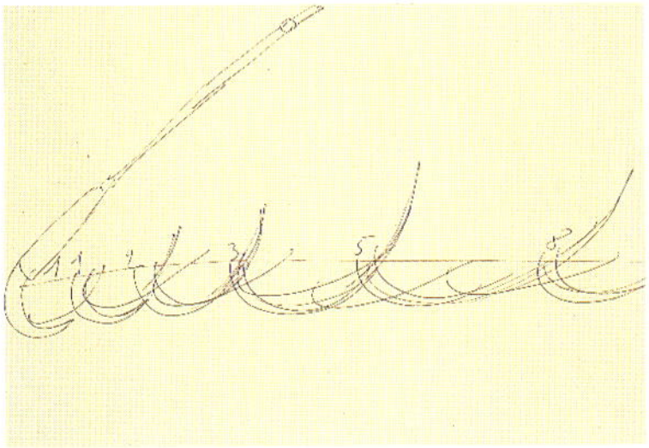

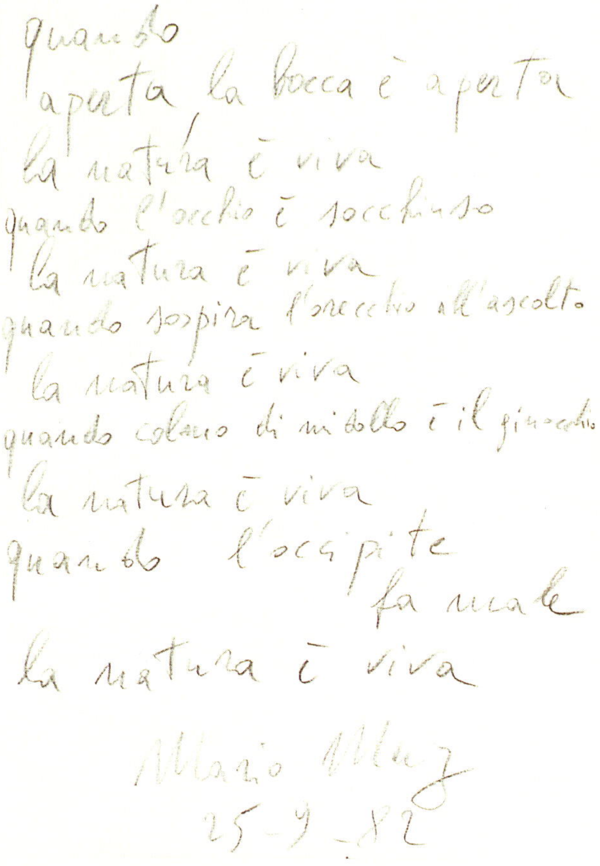

Ohne Titel, o. J.

Quando, 1922

Courtesy Sammlung Hummel, Wien

WEITER

SUSANNA MORGENSTERN

Dieser Beitrag zu Ars Electronica ist eine interaktive Computerarbeit, die sich mit „Genetische Kunst – Künstliches Leben" auseinandersetzt. Ausgangspunkt ist das Denken, der Denkraum, die Denkvermittlung, Computerdenken und die sprachliche und visuelle Komponente von Begriffen. Eine Reduktion als Paradoxie für Erweiterung und Wachstum. Die Ambiguität des Wortes drückt das Räumliche und Zeitliche als Komparativ und Imperativ aus. Das dabei entstehende mental-virtuelle Koordinatensystem ist in seiner Ausbreitung eine Metapher für Leben, Wachstum, Reproduktionsfähigkeit, Komplexität und Information, und gerät so in den Kontext von artificial life. Das Wort ist der Motor, Medien die Vehikel. Es bezeichnet eine Leermenge, wie ein Spiegel, aber mehrfach und doch exakt determiniert. Als Wort eine Falle, als Programm einem Virus ähnlich, dordert die Arbeit ambivalente Reaktionen heraus. Der imperative Anteil ruft zur Opposition auf, der komparative zur Orientierungsreaktion. Im Programmablauf erscheint das Wort „weiter", wenn dieser Aufforderung Folge geleistet wird. In der Interaktion mit dem Computer wird der Rezipient Opfer, Zeuge und Schöpfer.

FURTHER
SUSANNA MORGENSTERN

This contribution to Ars Electronica is an interactive computer work which deals with "Genetic Art—Artificial Life". The starting point is the thinking, the thinking space, the imparting of thinking, computer thinking and the linguistic and visual component of terms. A reduction as paradoxy for expansion and growth. The ambiguity of the word expresses the spatial and the temporal as comparative and imperative. The hereby arising mental-virtual coordination system in its expansion is a metaphor for life, growth, ability of reproduction, complexity and information, and so gets into the context of artificial life. The word is the engine, the media the vehicles. It represents an amount of emptiness, like a mirror, but multiple and though exactly determined. As word a trap, as program similar to a virus, the work provokes ambivalent reactions. The imperative part calls for opposition, the comparative for reaction of orientation. In the programs course the word "further" appears, if this demand is obeyed. When interacting with the computer the reader becomes victim, witness and creator.

weiter

TV POETRY

GEBHARD SENGMÜLLER

VERSUCHSANORDNUNG 1/93

„TV POETRY" zeigt eine Versuchsanordnung, die, an einem beliebigen Ort aufgebaut und mit exakt justierten Empfangsanlagen, in einem ständig fortschreitenden Prozess und in Echtzeit aus den zahlreich eintreffenden, rasch wechselnden Fernsehprogrammen jeder Art (tv commercial, news, quiz, show...) im Bild vorhandene Textpassagen erkennt, ausfiltert, behandelt und, in einer Phrasierung, die sich aus TV-Programm und CPU-Programmierung bildet, als endlose Textfolge ausgibt. Durch im System auftretende Unwägbarkeiten, Ungenauig-keiten, Bildrauschen, Fehlinterpretationen, werden die Quelltexte ein-schneidend verändert, neue Sinnzusammenhänge ergeben sich. Sehr kräftige Inhalte (Headlines, Slogans,...) bleiben eher erhalten oder „scheinen durch".
Die Signalverarbeitung erfolgt in parallelen Prozessen, die gleichzeitig auf getrennten Maschinen ablaufen und erst in der Endstufe zusammengeführt werden. Die Qualität der Ergebnisse im Bezug auf Dichte, Kontinuität, wiedererkennbare Inhalte, steht in direkt proportionalem Zusammenhang zur verfügbaren Maschinenleistung (Anzahl der TV-Programme, Anzahl und Taktfrequenz der CPUs, Busbreite der Übertragungswege).

FUNKTION / SCHEMA

Drei Parabolantennen empfangen die Programme von allen über Europa stationierten Fernsehsatelliten und werden dazu ständig neu positioniert. Drei Satellitenreceiver (S 1.1-1.3) wählen, durch eine zen-trale Taktfrequenz (Taktgeber T 1) gesteuert, aus diesem Angebot im Sekundentakt ein neues Programm. CPU 1.1-1.3 (Framegrabber) nehmen (im gleichen Takt) Standbilder aus den eintreffenden Videosignalen und rechnen diese auf Schwarz/Weiss-Bilder herunter. Über parallel interfaces gelangen die S/W-Files zu den CPUs 2.1-2.3. Dort wird durch optical character recognition (OCR) der (teilweise) vor-handene Textanteil ausgefiltert und in ASCII-

TV POETRY
GEBHARD SENGMÜLLER

SET-UP FOR EXPERIMENTATION 1/93

"TV Poetry" is an experimental set-up which can be put together at any location. Combined with precisely adjusted receiving equipment, it rapidly scans the various television transmissions it receives (commercials, news, quiz shows, etc.) for text passages visible on the screen. In an ongoing, real-time process, the text is recognised, filtered out, processed, and output as an endless stream of text, generated by TV programs and CPU programming. Through imponderability, inaccuracy, video noise and misinterpretation within the system, the source text is radically transformed, giving rise to new meanings. Very powerful content (headlines, slogans...) "shines through" and tends to remain intact.
Signal processing takes place in parallel process on separate machines and only comes together in the final stage. The quality of the results in terms of density, continuity, and recognisable content is in a direct proportional relationship to the available power and capacity of the equipment (number of TV channels, number and operating frequency of the CPUs, bus width of the connections).

FUNCTION / STRUCTURE

Three parabolic dishes receive the transmissions of all TV satellites serving Europe, constantly tracking from one to the next. Three satellite tuners (S 1.1-1.3), synchronised by pulses (synch pulse generator T1) select a new channel each second. CPUs 1.1-1.3 (Framegrabber) capture one frame from each selection, convert it into a black and white image and send it as a data file over parallel interfaces to CPUs 2.1-2.3. Optical Character Recognition (OCR) is then used to extract some of the text from the picture and convert it into ASCII text data files. At this stage of the process, electronic video noise in the signal and elements of the video image itself are also interpreted as letters, creating a sort of "text noise". CPU 3.1 receives the ASCII text streams from CPUs 2.1-2.3, alternated by a parallel switchbox (S1) controlled by pulse generator T1. The text is then sorted and selected according to certain rules (see below) and output

fuba
fuba
fuba

Dateien umgewandelt. In dieser Verarbeitungsstufe entsteht durch elektronisches Bildrauschen im Fernsehsignal oder durch Bildelemente, die von der OCR-Software als Buchstaben interpretiert werden, eine Art „Textrauschen". In CPU 3.1, wohin die ASCII-Zeichenketten von CPU 2.1-2.3 alternierend über eine Parallel-Switchbox (SW 1), die von Taktgeber T 1 gesteuert wird, gelangen, werden die Buchstabenfolgen nach bestimmten Regeln (siehe unten) sortiert/selektiert und in CPU 4.1 als unaufhörliche Textfolge am Monitor M 10 ausgegeben. Auch die Receiver S 1.1-1.3 und die CPUs 1.1-3.1 verfügen über (kleinere) Monitore (M 1-9), auf denen ständig Zwischenergebnisse visualisiert werden. Die Prozess-steuerung erfolgt durch ARREX-Scripts, die den Programmablauf und die Kommunikation zwischen den Geräteblöcken regeln.

Das Projekt wurde ermöglicht durch die freundliche Unterstützung der Fa. Fuba.

from CPU 4.1 to monitor M 10 as an endless stream. Receivers S1.1-1.3 and CPUs 1.1-3.1 are also connected to smaller monitors (M 1-9) which display the raw data. ARREX scripts represent the control process which governs the running of the program and ensures communication between the equipment blocks.

TEXT FILTERING RULES IN CPU 3.1:

(one possible selection; the system is completely programmable)

- erase all isolated text characters
- erase all characters not in the alphabet (control characters, numbers)
- add to / replace incomplete blocks of words with similar words which are known to the system.
- fill gaps in the text of length greater than xx with available material.

TV-Poetry–a project by G. S. Collaboration: Günter Erhart / Clemens Zauner (Systemdesign), Bruno Klomfar (Fotografie), produziert von Pyramedia Wien.

TV POETRY

BLOCKSCHALTBILD

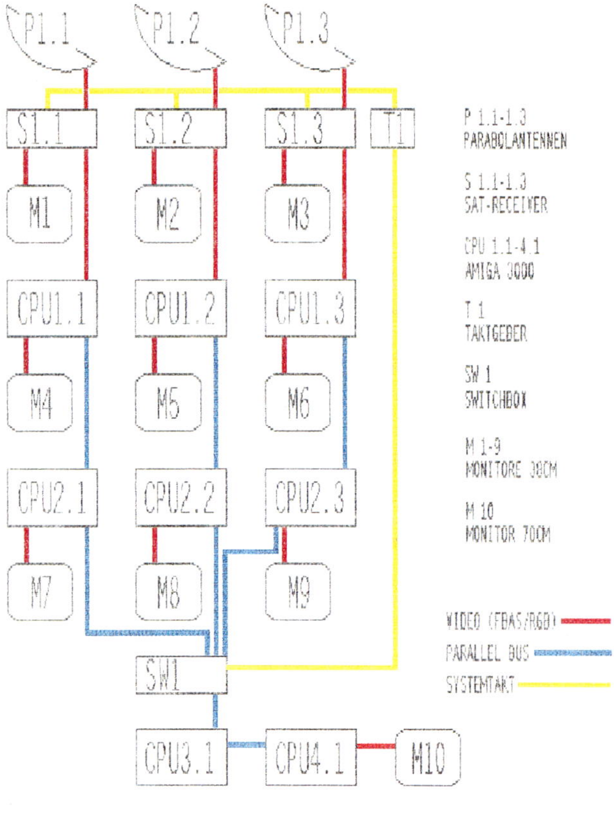

6. KÜNSTLICHES LEBEN. SOFT- UND HARDWARE

Ross Harley, Immortelle, 1992

ROSA BINARIA

ALBA D'URBANO

Dieses Projekt ist aus der Idee entstanden, die Beziehung, die zwischen einem Objekt und seiner Darstellung besteht zu bearbeiten. Es soll sich innerhalb der Mechanismen und Prozesse bewegen, die die Tatsache bedingen, daß ein nur für sie existierender Gegenstand sich in ein Phänomen verwandelt.
In dem Moment der Wahrnehmung, wenn der Mensch sich ein Objekt aneignet und es innerhalb seines Wissensbereiches einfügt, verwandelt er es in ein Kommunikationsmittel, in ein Symbol. In diesem Moment wird der Gegenstand Botschaft von sich selbst, wird er Kultur, wird er Schrift.
Zuerst hat der Mensch versucht, sich die Welt der Gegenstände anzueignen, indem er sie zwei- oder dreidimensional reproduziert hat. Durch eine immer mehr zunehmende Abstraktion und Iteration der Darstellung des Gegenstandes erfolgte seine Übersetzung in Schrift. In diesem Prozeß sind dem Objekt seine visuellen gestalthaften Eigenschaften entzogen worden. Genauer gesagt wurde der Gegenstand in eine Serie von Zeichen verwandelt, die ihn bezeichnen. Diese Zeichen bieten die Möglichkeit, die ganze Welt der Phänomene zu repräsentieren. Die Schrift, und damit eine autonome Welt von Begriffen und Konzepten, wird ins Leben gerufen, losgelöst von der Welt der Gegenstände.
In unserer Gegenwart hat sich diese Trennung immer mehr verstärkt, vor allem durch die Einführung elektronischer Informationsverarbeitung. Die Information hat sich total von der Wirklichkeit emanzipiert, indem sie die Schrift nicht mehr braucht um übermittelt zu werden: sie ist reine Energie, die innerhalb der Leitungen der elektronische Labyrinthe oder in den Wellen der Luft fließt. Es gibt keine qualitativen und analogen Unterschiede mehr, alles kann reproduziert werden, indem es in ein Ja/Nein, ein vorhandenes oder nicht vorhandenes Signal innerhalb eines binäres Systems übersetzt wird. Alles kann simuliert werden, der Mensch braucht den Gegenstand und dessen Repräsentation nicht mehr: er schafft sich ein neues synthetisches Produkt. Somit ist die Information zu einem weitgehend selbständigen, fast autonomen System geworden.
Rosa Binaria bewegt sich in einem Medium von Transforma-

ROSA BINARIA
ALBA D'URBANO

This project developed from the idea of processing the interrelationship that exists between an object and its representation. It should move within the mechanisms and processes which stipulate the fact that an object only existing for itself transforms into a phenomenon.
At the moment of perception when a human being makes an object his own, inserting it into his range of knowledge, he is transforming it into a means of communications, into a symbol. At this moment the object becomes a message of itself, it becomes culture, it becomes script. First of all, man tried to make the world of objects his own by reproducing it two or three dimensionally. With an ever increasing abstraction and iteration of the representation of this object, it was translated into writing. In this process, the object was deprived of its visual gestalt-like characteristics. To be more precise, the object was transformed into a series of signs which characterize it. These signs provide the possibility of representing the whole world of phenomena. Writing and consequently an autonomous world of terms and concepts is brought to life, severed from the world of objects. In our present time, this severance has been greatly intensified, particularly by the introduction of electronic information processing. Information has totally emancipated itself from reality by no longer requiring writing in order to be conveyed: it is pure energy flowing within the lines of the electronic labyrinth or in the waves of the air. There are no longer any qualitative and analogous differences, everything can be reproduced by being translated into yes/no, an existing or an non-existing signal within a binary system. Everything can be simulated, man no longer needs the object and its representation: he creates a new synthetic product for himself. In this way information has become a largely independent, almost autonomous system.
Rosa Binaria moves in a medium of transformations, within the relationship between the what is meaningful and its meaning, between object and its representation and right to the simulation, and develops like a spiral-shaped parable. A large part of this video has been realized with the digitalization of existing objects or pictures which were then processed using a 3D animation programme. These objects and their different visual languages were subjected to various transformation processes.

The first pictures of the video are simple shots of the object in its natural surroundings: then the computer animation slowly develops from this.
The first stage of alientation consists of cultivated roses which then change into objects that still have the shape of the object but which consist of other materials (plastic, paper, material, etc.). They transform into photos (direct print by the light of reality), which then become hand-painted pictures. Even the colour fades leaving only lines behind: drawings, symbols which change in shape and become script: the word "rose" in different languages of the world. Only at the end of this process, after the journey in the labyrinths of the media does the simulated rose appear, the rose which only exists in the computer.

tionen, innerhalb des Verhältnisses zwischen dem Bedeutsamen und seiner Bedeutung, zwischen Gegenstand und seiner Repräsentation bis zur Simulation und entwickelt sich wie eine spiralförmige Parabel.
Dieses Projekt sieht die Realisation einer Videoskulptur vor, die einen spiralförmigen Grundriß hat, deren Metall-Wände eine Art von kreisförmiger Zellen bilden. Die Wände der Spirale, die in dem Raum sind, werden immer niedriger bis zum Zentrum, wo sich ein Video-Projektor befindet. Dieser Projektor ist mit einem Video-Player verbunden, und die beständig rotierenden Bilder des Videos Rosa Binaria werden an die Decke dieser Kabine projiziert.
Ein großer Teil dieses Videos ist mit der Digitalisierung von existierenden Objekten oder Bildern realisiert worden, die dann mittels eines 3D-Animations-Programms verarbeitet wurden. Diese Objekte mit ihren verschiedenen visuellen Sprachen wurden vielfältig Transformations-Prozessen unterworfen.
Die ersten Bilder des Videos sind einfache Aufnahmen des Objektes in seiner natürlichen Umgebung: daraus entwikkelt sich dann langsam die Computer-Animation.
Das erste Stadium der Entfremdung besteht aus gezüchteten

Rosen. Sie verwandeln sich dann in Objekte, die noch die Form des Gegenstandes haben, aber aus anderen Materialien bestehen (Plastik, Papier, Stoff etc.). Sie transformieren sich in Fotos (direkter Abdruck durch das Licht der Realität), die dann zu handgemalten Bildern werden. Auch die Farbe entzieht sich und läßt nur Linien zurück: Zeichnungen, Symbole, die sich verformen und zu Schrift werden: das Wort „Rose“ in verschiedenen Sprachen der Welt. Nur am Ende dieses Prozesses, nach einer Fahrt in den Labyrinthen der Medien, erscheint die simulierte Rose, die Rose, die nur in dem Computer existiert.

Die Arbeit wurde an der Städelschule, Institut für Neue Medien, Frankfurt am Main, produziert.

DER DIGITALE GARTEN, VERSION III

ROSS HARLEY

THE DIGITAL GARDEN VERSION III
ROSS HARLEY

The Digital Garden is an ongoing video computer-graphic project that focuses on the changing relations between natural and artificial environments.
Despite its mythic paradisiacal associations, the garden is no stranger to the world of artifice, machinery or technology. In essence the garden—from its Persian, Egyptian, Chinese and European origins—is an arrangement of natural elements, reproducing a "living picture" that might arouse the same feelings that one might experience far from the reaches of human invention. But invention these living architectural places most certainly remain.
Another connection—between horticulture and technoculture — could perhaps be found in the parallel technological transition from the mechanical automata of Greco-Roman times to the cellular automata and A-Life of our own. On the surface at least, both attempt to somehow synthesise the machinery of the universe, imitating the processes of life via technological means. In this Aristotelian fashion, art (**techne**) completes what nature is unable to finish, by imitative means.
The Digital Garden accommodates the electronic lifeforms that are appropriate to the mechanical, electronic and digital conditions of the present, incorporating this new nature into the culture of living things. Taking the work of Aristid Lindenmayer as inspiration — whose "L-systems" have been crucial to the development of computer graphics that accurately "imitate" (or model) plant growth—this project plays upon our desire to artificially create and manipulate nature through our own complex systems.
That this happens in a "garden" should not surprise us. A selective mirror, as large as life and twice as natural, the garden provides a model of what we think the world is like. The dreams of Pythagarus, Euclid and von Neuman reflect and distort new insights into nature. From its Edenic origins through its geometric rigidity (in Europe and the East), and its formal disintegration in the late seventeenth century, these organic/architectural spaces unite inside and outside (house/garden, nature/technics, transmission/reception, etc.) as place, action and idea. To this day the making of artificial nature is achieved not so much through material intervention, as by the power of spatial, sensual and visual manipulation of our corporeal experience.

Der Digitale Garten ist ein laufendes Video-Computer-Graphik Projekt, das sich mit dem sich verändernden Verhältnis zwischen natürlicher und künstlicher Umwelt auseinandersetzt.
Trotz der mythischen, paradiesischen Assoziationen ist der Garten nichts Fremdes in der Welt der Erfindung, Maschinerie oder Technolgie. Dem Wesen nach ist der Garten – von seiner persischen, ägyptischen, chinesischen und europäischen Herkunft her – eine Anordnung von natürlichen Elementen, die ein „lebendes Bild" reproduzieren, das vielleicht dieselben Gefühle hervorruft, die man als weitab vom Bereich menschlicher Erfindung empfinden könnte. Dennoch bleiben diese lebenden architektonischen Plätze Erfindung.
Man könnte vielleicht eine weitere Verbindung zwischen Gartenkultur und Technokultur im parallel verlaufenden technologischen Übergang von den mechanischen Automaten des griechischen und römischen Zeitalters zu den Zelluläräutomaten und dem künstlichen Leben unserer Epoche herstellen. Zumindest auf der Oberfläche versuchen beide eine Synthese der Maschinerie des Universums, indem sie die Vorgänge des Lebens mit Hilfe der Technologie nachzuahmen versuchen. In diesem aristotelischen Sinne ist die Kunst (techne) eine auf Nachahmung basierende Ergänzung dessen, was die Natur unvollständig lassen muß.
Der Digitale Garten beherbergt jene elektronischen Lebensformen, die sich für die mechanischen, elektronischen und digitalen Bedingungen der Gegenwart eignen, indem sie diese neue Natur in die Kultur der lebenden Dinge einbindet. Inspiriert durch das Schaffen von Aristid Lindenmayer – dessen „L-Systeme" die Entwicklung der Computergraphik bestimmten, da sie das Wachstum von Pflanzen richtig „imitieren" (oder gestalten) – spielt dieses Projekt mit unserem Wunsch, die Natur mit Hilfe unserer eigenen komplexen Systeme künstlich zu schaffen oder zu manipulieren.
Daß dies in einem Garten geschieht, soll nicht weiter überraschen. Der Garten als selektiver Spiegel, der so groß ist wie das Leben und zweimal so groß wie die Natur, bietet ein Modell dessen, wie wir uns die Welt vorstellen. Die Träume von

This third version of the garden evolves out of three recent works — **Version I** (produced in collaboration with Ken Maher), **The Digital Garden Version II** and **Immortelle** — exhibited as installations and as single-channel video works during 1992 and 1993.

<mi>Immortelle is a science-fiction style video installation that presents the programs of an imaginary computer capable of emulating the forms of organic life. Based on the writings and ideas of biologists such as D'arcy Thompson and Aristid Lindenmayer, SF writers like Clifford D. Simak, the historian of life-sciences Francois Jacob, and the filmmaking of Jean Luc Godard, **Immortelle** conjurs a universe where mathematical calculation creates "mutant" variations of basic algorithms of life. In the terms of Artificial Life, **Immortelle** conjures a recursive program that invents visualisations not of life-as-we-know-it, but of life-as-it-could-be.

The Digital Garden continued to explore these ideas of (digital) growth, architectural space, and our historically changing view of natural and artificial environments. Responding to the question of the relation between the built environment and the immaterial information landscape, this third version of the garden juxtaposes and unites electronic data in an architectural/ecological space. As "viewers" enter the garden, they encounter a variety of electronic lifeforms that present themselves on a large-screen projection and on a series of video monitors. The electronic forms flow across the large video backgrounds of archetypal garden scenes—the formal axial perspectives of Versailles, the Taj Mahal, Hyde Park, and an imaginary video-composite space—which invite the viewer to wander through the artificial garden.

Most of these graphics are played from four videotape sources. There is limited provision for computer graphics to be activated by the participant in real-time. Each visit to the garden reveals a new set of artificial lifeforms. The next version of the garden will allow for more extensive real-time interaction in the artificial graphic world. This version is currently being developed with Jon McCormack whose L-system software (which he has developed for use on Silicon Graphics workstations) utilises recent achievements in the area of interactive evolution (based on CA and L-systems for computer graphics modelling). Hence the next iteration of **The Digital Garden** will imitate the patterns of biological and electronic growth in real-time, allowing the visitor to produce an ever-changing variety of life-forms in a garden that is at once familiar and bizarre.

The Digital Garden is an extension of many ideas concerning the inter-relation of electronic media, natural phenomena and the artificial environment. It develops many of these ideas, joining questions of design in the second machine age to the realm of the cybernetic revolution. If it is true to say that the Renaissance built with perspective and motion, the Victorians with order and stone, and the moderns with machines and concrete, how should we respond to the (natural) environment in the age of information, media and digital reproduction?

Pythagoras, Euklid und von Neuman widerspiegeln und verzerren die neuen Einblicke in die Natur. Von den Anfängen im Garten Eden bis hin zur Vorherrschaft geometrischer Strenge (in Europa und dem Osten) und ihrer formalen Auflösung im späten 17.Jahrhundert, werden diese organischen/architekonischen Räume innen und außen eins (Haus/Garten, Natur/Technik, Übertragung/Rezeption, usw.), als Ort, Handlung und Idee. Bis zum heutigen Tag wird die künstliche Natur weniger durch materiale Intervention als durch die Kraft räumlicher, sinnlicher und visueller Manipulation unserer körperlichen Erfahrung geschaffen.

Diese dritte Fassung entstand aus drei neueren Arbeiten: Version I (in Zusammenarbeit mit Ken Maher produziert), Digitale Garten, Version II und Immortelle – die 1992 und 1993 als Installationen und Einfach-Kanal-Videoarbeiten gezeigt wurden.

Immortelle ist eine der Science Fiction nachempfundene Videoinstallation: sie zeigt die Programme eines fiktiven Computers, der in der Lage ist, die Formen organischen Lebens nachzuahmen. Auf der Grundlage von Texten und Ideen von Biologen wie D'arcy Thompson und Aristid Lindenmayer, Science-Fiction Autoren wie Clifford D. Simak, dem Historiker der Lebenswissenschaften Francois Jacob und dem Filmemacher Jean Luc Godard beschwört Immortelle ein Universum herauf, in dem mathematische Berechnung „Mutanten"-Variationen von grundlegenden Algorithmen des Lebens schaffen. Im Sinne von künstlichem Leben evoziert Immortelle ein rekursives Programm, das nicht das Leben, wie wir es kennen, sondern das Leben, wie es sein könnte, visualisiert.

Der Digitale Garten hat diese Ideen von (digitalem) Wachstum, architektonischem Raum und unserer, einem historischem Wandel unterzogenen Sicht von natürlichen und künstlich geschaffener Umwelt untersucht. Als Reaktion auf die Frage nach dem Verhältnis zwischen errichtetem Environment und immaterialer Informationslandschaft stellt sich diese dritte Version des Gartens elektronischen Daten gegenüber und stellt eine Vereinigung derselben in einem architektonischen/ökologischen Raum dar. Wenn „Betrachter" den Raum betreten, stoßen sie auf eine Vielfalt von elektronischen Lebensformen, die als großflächige Projektion auf einer Reihe von Videomonitoren sichtbar werden. Die elektronischen Formen fließen über große im Hintergrund Video gezeigte Videoprojektionen von archetypischen Gartenszenen – die formale Achsenperspektiven von Versailles, des Taj Mahal, des Hyde Park und von einem fiktiven zusammengesetzten Videoraum –, in denen der Betrachter dazu aufgefordert wird, zu wandeln.

Die meisten dieser Graphiken werden von vier Videoband-Quellen gespielt. Es ist in beschränktem Maße vorgesehen, daß der Teilnehmer Computergraphiken in Echtzeit aktiviert. Bei jedem Besuch im Garten wird eine neue Gruppe von künstlichen Lebensformen entdeckt. Die nächste Version des Gartens wird eine stärker ausgedehnte Echtzeit-Interaktion in der künstlichen Graphikwelt ermöglichen. Diese Version wird derzeit in Zusammenarbeit mit Jon McCormack entwickelt, dessen L-System-Software (die er für Verwendung auf Silicon Graphics-Arbeitsstationen entwickelt hat) Gebrauch macht von neuen Errungenschaften im Bereich der interaktiven Evolution (auf der Grundlage von CA und L-Systemen für die Computergraphik-Gestaltung). Die nächste Version des Digitale Gartens wird daher die Schemata von biologischem und elektronischem Wachstum in Echtzeit imitieren, wobei der Besucher die Möglichkeit haben wird, eine sich stets verändernde Vielfalt von Lebensformen in einem Garten, der zugleich vertraut und bizarr anmutet, herzustellen.
Der Digitale Garten ist eine Weiterentwicklung vieler Ideen, die mit der Wechselwirkung von elektronischen Medien, Naturphänomenen und künstlicher Umwelt zu tun haben. Er entwickelt viele dieser Ideen durch die Einbindung von Fragen des Designs im zweiten Maschinenzeitalter in den Bereich der kybernetischen Revolution. Wenn es zutrifft, daß die Renaissance mit Perspektive und Bewegung baute, die Viktorianer mit Ordnung und Stein und die Moderne mit Maschinen und Beton, wie sollen wir im Zeitalter der Information, Medien und der digitalen Reproduktion auf die (natürliche) Umgebung reagieren? Wie kann die in Bruchteilen zu sehende Dimension der Natur, der Künstlichkeit des Lebens und die Wissenschaften komplexer dynamischer Systeme (zugleich Organismus und Technologie) wiedergewonnen werden, die in unserer neuen Maschinen-Natur derart konvergieren, daß sich unsere grundlegende Grenzzustände, die fundamentalsten Bedingungen unserer synthetischen und alles durchdringenden Existenz radikal verändern?

How can we recover the fractional dimension of nature, the artificiality of life, and the sciences of complex dynamical systems (at once organism and technology) that converge in our new machine-nature that is so radically changing our fundamental liminal states, the most basic conditions of our synthetic and permeative existence?

DAS „KULTURMETER" ODER DIE KUNST DES MULTIKULTURELLEN MISCHENS (LEHRSPIEL ZUM ABBAU VON FREMDENANGST)

WOLFGANG HILBERT

THE "KULTURMETER" OR THE ART OF MULTI-CULTURAL MIXING / WOLFGANG HILBERT

1. DESCRIPTION, STRUCTURE:

The "Kulturmeter" represents a kind of barometer for the cultural life of a nation and measures the degree of development of art and culture. In addition it allows the user to get involved in cultural events by opening borders. He can, as it were, slip into the role of a politician whose influence extends into immigration and border policy, and consequently, cultural policy.
The simulation program is based on the theory that every culture is enriched and broadened by contact with other cultures, by assimilating other ways of thinking and seeing, as well as other traditions. In contrast to states that hermetically seal their borders (e.g. Germany during the Third Reich), multi-cultural states (e.g. Austria during the monarchy, the USA) develop an unusually richer cultural life which provides an attractive power far beyond the border and therefore has a self-affirming effect.
The measuring scale of the "Kulturmeter" is a six-sided shape (screen detail) representing the living space of so-called "culture cells". "Culture cells" are a metaphor for the cultural life of a people.)
Besides the quantitative distribution of culture (number of cells), the main factor, is its quality or diversity, which is expressed by bright colours in the cells.

2. FUNCTION OF THE COMPUTER PROGRAM:

The cell animation functions on approximately the same principle as J. H. Conway's "Game of Life", with its rules of birth, survival and death, but with the following additions: When the indigenous "Kulturzellen" meet "foreign Kulturzellen", a new mixed cultural cell of a different colour appears. For the viewer, the optical ap-

1. BESCHREIBUNG, AUFBAU:

Das „Kulturmeter" stellt ein eine Art Barometer für das kulturelle Leben eines Landes dar und mißt den Grad der Entwicklung von Kunst und Kultur. Zusätzlich erlaubt es dem Anwender durch Öffnen von Grenzen in das Kulturgeschehen einzugreifen. Er schlüpft gewissermaßen in die Rolle eines Politikers, der es in der Hand hat, Einwanderungs-, Grenzpolitik und somit Kulturpolitik zu beeinflussen.
Das Simulationsprogramm stützt sich auf die Theorie, daß jede Kultur durch die Auseinandersetzung mit fremden Kulturen bereichert und erweitert wird und zwar durch Übernahme anderer Denk- und Sehweisen sowie anderer Traditionen. Im Gegensatz zu Staaten, die ihre Grenzen hermetisch abriegeln (z. B. Deutschland im 3. Reich) entwickeln multikulturelle Staaten (z. B. Österreich zur Zeit der Monarchie, USA) ein außerordentlich reiches Kulturleben, das weit über die Grenzen hinaus Anziehungskraft hat und damit selbstverstärkend wirkt.
Die Meßskala des „Kulturmeters" ist eine sechseckige Fläche (Bildschirmausschnitt), die den Lebensraum von sogenannten „Kulturzellen" darstellt. „Kulturzellen" sind eine Metapher für das Kulturleben eines Volkes.
Neben der quantitativen Ausbreitung der Kultur (Menge der Zellen) spielt hauptsächlich ihre Qualität bzw. Vielseitigkeit, die durch leuchtende Farben der Zelle ausgedrückt wird, eine besondere Rolle.

2. FUNKTION DES COMPUTERPROGRAMMES:

Die Zellanimation funktioniert in etwa nach dem Prinzip des „Game of Life" von J. H. Conway (d. h. nach den Regeln des Überlebens, der Geburt, des Sterbens) mit folgenden Erwei-

terungen: Beim Zusammentreffen der einheimischen „Kulturzellen" mit „Fremdkulturzellen" entstehen neue andersfarbige „Mischkulturzellen". Für den Betrachter wird dadurch das optische Erscheinungsbild bunter und interessanter, wobei der Eindruck vermittelt werden soll, daß sich das Kulturleben insgesamt bereichert und erweitert hat.

3. INTERAKTION:

Der Anwender hat die Möglichkeit, die kulturelle Entwicklung der Zellen aktiv zu beeinflussen. Er kann mittels Drehregler insgesamt 4 verschiedene Grenzen des heimatlichen Kulturlebensraumes öffnen bzw. schließen und somit den Zustrom von „Fremdkulturzellen" dosieren.

ZIEL: IDEALE KULTURMISCHUNG

Das Ziel des Anwenders muß sein, die Fremdkulturen mit der heimischen Kultur im richtigen Verhältnis zu mischen.
Wieviele Fremdkulturzellen und von welcher Farbe (Art der Fremdkultur) über den heimatlichen Kulturlebensraum verstreut werden, hängt von der Öffnungsweite und -dauer der jeweiligen Grenze ab. Die Öffnungsweite wird optisch in einen Feld unterhalb des Drehreglers in Form eines Balkendiagrammes dargestellt. Dreht man einen Regler im Uhrzeigersinn, öffnet sich die Grenze (die Balken wandern von einander weg) un deine größere Anzahl von „Fremdkulturzellen" des jeweiligen Volkes werden im Kulturlebensraum gleichmäßig verteilt. Dreht man den Regler in die entgegengesetzte Richtung, schließt sich die Grenze wieder und der Einwanderungsstrom des jeweiligen Volkes wird vermindert. Das Programm verarbeitet auch die gleichzeitige Betä-

pearance becomes more colourful and more interesting, while giving the impression that the cultural life as a whole has been enriched and broadened.

3. INTERACTION:

The user has the opportunity to actively influence the cultural development of the cells. He can use a rotary control to open or shut four different borders of his cultural homeland, thereby controlling the flow of "foreign Kulturzellen".

GOAL: IDEAL CULTURAL MINGLING

The goal of the user must be to achieve the right mix of foreign and indigenous cultures.
How many foreign "Kulturzellen" and of what colour (what kind of foreign culture) are spread over the cultural homeland depends on the openness and duration of the border in question. The former is displayed optically in a field below the controller in the form of a block diagram. If the controller is turned clockwise, the border opens, the blocks in the diagram move apart, and a larger number of foreign culture cells of the given population group spread out evenly in the cultural region. If the knob is turned the other way, the border closes and the immigration flow is minimezed. The program also processes the simultaneous operation of several knobs, so that the influx of cells from different cultural circles is possible at the same time.

POSSIBLE FINAL STATES OF THE GAME:

I.
If the user has not sufficiently opened the borders, the result is a colourless, monotonous appearance of the cultural region and the number of culture cells stagnates
II.
If he opens the borders too wide or too often, the indigenous culture is weakened or dominated,
bIII.
If one or two population groups are favoured or discriminated against at the border, a colour will be over-represented and a tinge portrays the over-representation of the other foreign cultural cells.
IV.
The user is most successful if he opens and closes the borders at regular intervals and for long enough to effect the best possible cultural mix. The visual reward on the screen Is an aesthetic, colourful, Interesting cultural landscape. After about two minutes the final result is also output as text in the form of reports, and the game begins afresh from a starting position drawn up at random by the computer.

tigung von mehreren Reglern, sodaß der Zustrom von Zellen aus verschiedenen Kulturkreisen zur gleichen Zeit ermöglicht wird.

MÖGLICHE ENDZUSTÄNDE DES SPIELES:

I.
Fall der Anwender die Grenzen zu wenig oder gar nicht öffnet, wirkt sich das in einem farblosen, eintönigen Erscheinungsbild des Kulturraumes aus und die Anzahl der Kulturzellen stagniert.

II.
Falls er die Grenzen unkontrolliert öffnet, d. h. zu weit oder zu lange offen läßt, kommt es zur Abschwächung oder Überfremdung der einheimischen Kultur.

III.
Wenn man bei der Grenzdosierung ein oder zwei Völker bevorzugt bzw. benachteiligt, ergibt sich ein Übergewicht einer Farbe (Farbstich), das den Überschuß der jeweiligen Fremdkulturzellen repräsentiert.

IV.
Den größten Erfolg erzielt der Anwender, wenn er die Grenzen in annähernd gleichen Zeitintervallen genügend lange öffnet bzw. schließt, um so das idealste Kulturmischverhältnis zu erreichen. Auf dem Monitor erscheint als visuelle Belohnung ein ästhetisches, buntes, interessantes Kulturerscheinungsbild.
Das erzielte Ergebnis wird nach ca. 2 Minuten Spieldauer zusätzlich schriftlich in Form von Meldungen ausgegeben und das Spiel beginnt erneut mit einer vom Computer zufällig ausgewählten Startposition.

4. KÜNSTLERISCHE RECHTFERTIGUNG, GEGENWARTSBEZUG:

Die Auseinandersetzung mit den Kulturmeter hat das Ziel, den Anwender auf spielerische Art und Weise die Vorteile einer Mischkultur optisch zu veranschaulichen und sein Bewußtsein positiv zu beeinflussen, um eventuell vorhandene unbewußte Ängste vor Fremden abzubauen.

Programmierer: Richard Hilbert

Dank an IMS-Connection (Integrierte Management Computer), Linz

THE TABLE OF THE SPIRITS

GIDEON MAY

THE TABLE OF THE SPIRITS
GIDEON MAY

In the quest for artificial life, Gideon May chose to visualise a fantasy, rather than imitate reality. He created "The able of the spirits", an interactive video-installation that displays a combination of reality and virtual reality.
The installation consists of a table on which a set of basic shapes are fitted. Each shape has a specific colour and a fixed position on the table which measures 5 feet by 5 feet.
Spotlights are mounted on the corners of the table. Behind the table is a video screen that shows the observations of the video camera.
When the camera is moved around the table, it appears that the world on the videon screen isn't the same as the one that can be seen with the naked eye.
Not visible for the human eye are the ghosts, that crawl and float over the table, they can only be sensed with the camera.
The manifestations of each ghost is derived from the basic shapes on the table and although they have an immediate appearance, they do have a set of physical qualities, such as a specific form, colour and distinctive dynamics.
Every ghost is programmed to have his own behaviourm but they seem more driven by instincts than by a set of programmer's codes. Some of the ghosts, for instance, like to be around the camera, others are shy and try to hide behind the shapes on the table. What all the ghosts have in common is that they interact with the objects in their environment, whether it's a static shape, another ghost or a viewer with the camera.
"The Table Of The Spirits" exposes the twilight zone of reality and unveils the world of the unseen.

Bert Haensel

Bei der Frage nach dem künstlichen Leben, entschied Gideon May sich für die Visualisierung einer Fantasie anstatt die Realität zu imitieren. Er schuf „The table of the spirits", eine interaktive Videoinstallation, die eine Verbindung von Realität und virtueller Realität darstellt.
Die Installation besteht aus einem Tisch, der mit einer Reihe von Basisformen ausgestattet ist. Jede Form hat eine besondere Farbe und eine fixe Position auf dem fünf mal fünf Fuß großen Tisch. An den Ecken des Tisches sind Spotlights montiert. Hinter dem Tisch ist ein Videobildschirm, der die Aufnahmen der Videokamera zeigt.
Wird die Kamera rund um den Tisch bewegt, scheint die Welt auf dem Videobildschirm eine andere zu sein, als jene, die mit dem bloßen Auge gesehen werden kann. Für das menschliche Auge nicht sichtbar sind die Geister, die über den Tisch krabbeln und gleiten, – sie können nur mit der Kamera wahrgenommen werden.
Die Manifestationen der einzelnen Geister stammen von den Basisformen auf dem Tisch und obwohl sie unmittelbar erscheinen, verfügen sie doch über eine Anzahl physischer Qualitäten, etwa eine spezifische Form, Farbe und unterschiedliche Dynamiken.
Jeder Geist ist auf seine eigenen V erhaltensweisen programmiert, aber sie scheinen mehr von Instinkten als von einem Set von Programmierercodes geleitet zu sein. Einige dieser Geister halten sich beispielsweise gerne rund um die Kamera auf, andere sind schüchtern und versuchen, sich hinter den Formen auf dem Tisch zu verstecken. Allen gemeinsam ist ihnen, daß sie mit den Objekten ihrer Umgebung interagieren, sei dies eine statische Form, ein anderer Geist oder ein Besucher mit der Kamera.
„The Table Of The Spirits" stellt den zwielichtigen Bereich der Realität dar und deckt die Welt des Nichtsichtbaren auf.

Bert Haensel

Computerimages: Monique Mulder
Das Projekt wurde am ZKM, Karlsruhe, produziert.

ANTHROPOSKOP

LAURENT MIGNONNEAU / CHRISTA SOMMERER

ANTHROPOSKOP – ERFORSCHUNG VON KÜNSTLICHEM LEBEN

1. KONZEPT

Das Anthroposkop schafft Einblicke in die verborgenen Bereiche der Beziehung „Mensch-Pflanze", indem es den unbekannten und sensitiven Dialog dieser beiden Lebensformen untersucht und darstellt.
Das Anthroposkop ist ein Instrument zur Erforschung der interaktiven Beziehung Mensch-Pflanze, es gibt Einblicke in die Lebenssignale beider Organismen, indem es deren äußerst feine Spannungsfelder untersucht und in einem dreidimensionalen mikroskopischen Wachstumsprogramm grafisch zum Ausdruck bringt.
Das „Leben des Betrachters" und das „Leben der Pflanze" werden aufeinander reagieren und „künstlichs Leben" im Computer erzeugen.
Dieses „künstliche Leben" ist gekennzeichnet durch Wachstum, Bewegung Differenzierung und Determination; Bereiche also, die für die Evolution lebender Organismen charakteristisch sind.
„Individualität" als Hauptmerkmal des Lebens, wird durch die Individualität des Betrachters und durch die Individualität der Pflanze in die „Individualtät der künstlichen Mikroorganismen" des Wachstumsprogrammes implementiert, dem artifiziellen Biotop also „künstliches Leben eingehaucht".
Damit ist das „Anthroposkop" ein weiterer Schritt in Richtung zur Erforschung des Geheimnisses „Leben", indem es unbekannte Bereiche der Kommunikation in künstlerisch freier Interpretation untersucht.
Ähnlich einem Scanning Electron Microskop (SEM=REM) werden dreidimensionale molekular-, atomar- und neuronenartige künstliche Formen im virtuellen Raum des Grafik Computers (Silicon Graphics Reality Engine oder VGX 320

ANTHROPOSCOPE
LAURENT MIGNONNEAU / CHRISTA SOMMERER

ANTHROPOSCOPE – EXPLORING ARTIFICIAL LIFE

1. CONCEPT

The anthroposcope creates insight into the hidden areas of the "man-plant" relationship, by investigating and representing the unknown and sensitive dialogue of these two forms of life.
The anthroposcope is an instrument for exploring the interactive relationship between man-plant, giving insight into the life signals of both organisms by investigating their extremely fine fields of tension and by expressing them graphically in a three-dimensional microscopic growth programme.
The "life of the observer" and the "life of the plant" react to each other and produce "artificial life" in the computer.
This "artificial life" is characterized by growth, movement differentiation and determination: areas which are characteristic for the evolution of living organisms.
"Individuality" as the main feature of life is implemented in the "individuality of artificial micro-organimsm" of the growth programme by the individuality of the observer and by the individuality of the plants—"artificial life" is breathed into the artificial biotope.
Consequently, the "anthroposcope" is a further step towards the exploration of the secret of "life" by investigating unknown fields of communication in the form of an artificially free interpretation.
Similar to a scanning electron microscope (SEM=REM), three-dimensional molecular, atomic and neuron-like artificial forms are produced in the virtual space of the graphic computer (Silicon Graphics Reality Engine or VGX 320 or Indigo^2 Extreme) and are introduced into the optics of a microscope.
In comparison to SEM which is bound to extensive preparation processes, these artificial organisms do react directly to the observer by interpreting and representing his fields of tension.

2. INTERACTION

The development and growth of these programme-bound bio-organisms is dependent on the individuality of the observer communicating with the plants in front of him,by giving his own tension signals to the plants with his approach.
Depending on the frame of mind and physical state of the observer, these tension signals will change and will be compared with the plant' own signals which similarly continue to change.
This "tension dialogue" between man and plant is now transmitted to the growth programme on the computer by means of an interface and is incorporated into the molecular virtual microcosmos. This consists of three-dimensional graphically self-generating, free artificial organisms. These organisms produce, are able to grow, expand and move freely in space and disappear again.
Their appearance, shape, their development and growth is exclusively dependent on the observer's personality as when he approaches, he passes on his own tension fields to the living plant.
For example, if the observer changes his tension or his distance to the plant, he will allow new organisms develop in the microscope.
As this dialogue of the tension differences is a very fine one, the graphic results in the microscope will always be different.
Different observers will achieve completely different growth biotopes; these are the direct expression of the personality of the observer and his relation to the living plant. Even the same person will, in the course of "microscoping", always create new molecular growth forms as their tension field constantly changes and even the relation and distance to the plant constantly varies.
On the other hand, the stages of modulations and changes in the growth programme are kept as fine, extensive and open as possible, whereby a large number of variations, individuality in the man-plant relationship and openness for further influences, are guaranteed.
Consequently, the anthroposcope provides the possibility of exploring the unknown areas of "man-plant" communications and of following and co-determining the graphic three-dimensional interpretation of this dialogue in real time.
All the changes in the formation and representation of these artificial micro-structures can be influenced and controlled by the observer. The modulation stages and the variation possibilities of the micro-structures are kept, however, very open and flexible so that individual personal growth biotopes can develop even without the conscious control of the observer.

3. PROGRAM

The molecular growth programme was programmed by Laurent Mignonneau and Christa Sommerer at the "Städelschule" Institute for New Media, in Frankfurt.

oder Indigo2 Extreme) erzeugt und in die Optik eines Mikroskops eingeschleust.
Im Vergleich zum SEM, das an aufwendige Präparationsprozesse gebunden ist, reagieren jedoch diese künstlichen Organismen direkt auf den Betrachter, indem sie seine Spannungsfelder interpretieren und darstellen.

2. INTERAKTION:

Das Enstehen und Wachsen dieser programmgebundenen Bio-Organismen ist abhängig von der Individualität des Betrachters, der mit der vor ihm stehenden Pflanze kommuniziert, indem er durch seine Annäherung die eigenen Spannungssignale an die Pflanze weitergibt.
Abhängig von der seelischen und körperlichen Verfassung des Betrachters, werden sich diese Spannungsignale verändern und mit den pflanzeneigenen Signalen, die sich ebenfalls laufen ändern können, verglichen.
Dieser „Spannungsdialog" zwischen Mensch und Pflanze wird nun mittels eines Interfaces an das Wachstumsprogramm des Computers weitergegeben und in den molekularen virtuellen Mikrokosmos eingebunden. Dieser besteht aus dreidimensionalen, grafischen, sich selbst generierenden freien künstlichen Organismen. Diese Organismen erzeugen sich selbst, können wachsen, expandieren, sich frei im Raum bewegen und auch wieder verschwinden.
Ihre Erscheinung, Ausformung, ihr Enstehen und Wachsen ist ausschließlich abhängig von der Personalität des Betrachters, der durch seine Präsenz und durch seine Annäherung an die lebende Pflanze das eigene Spannungsfeld weitergibt.
Verändert der Betrachter zum Beispiel seine Spannung oder seine Distanz zur Pflanze, wird er neue Mikroorganismen im Mikroskop entstehen lassen können.
Da dieser Dialog der Spannungsdifferenzen ein sehr feiner ist, werden die grafischen Ergebnisse im Mikroskop stets unterschiedlich sein.
Unterschiedliche Betrachter werden zu völlig unterschiedlichen Wachstumsbiotopen gelangen; diese sind direkter Ausdruck der Personalität des Betrachters und seiner Beziehung zur lebenden Pflanze.
Auch die selbe Person wird im Lauf des „Mikroskopierens" immer wieder neue molekulare Wachstumsformen hervorrufen, da sich ihr Spannungsfeld ständig ändert und auch die Beziehung und Distanz zur Pflanze laufend variiert wird.
Daneben sind die Stufen der Modulationen und Veränderungen im Wachstumsprogramm so fein, umfassend und of-

fen wie möglich gehalten, wodurch eine große Fülle an Variationen, Individualität in der Mensch-Pflanzen Beziehung und Offenheit für zusätzliche Einflüsse garantiert wird.
Das Anthroposkop bietet also die Möglichkeit die unbekannten Bereiche der „Mensch – Pflanze" Kommunikation zu erforschen und die grafische dreidimensionale Interpretation diese Dialoges in Echt-Zeit mitzuverfolgen und mitzubestimmen.
Alle Veränderungen in der Ausbildung und Darstellung dieser künstlichen Mikrostrukturen sind durch den Betrachter beeinflußbar und steuerbar.
Die Modulationsstufen und Variationsmöglichkeiten der Mikrostrukturen sind jedoch so offen und flexibel gehalten, daß auch ohne bewußte Steuerung durch den Betrachter individuelle persönliche Wachstumsbiotope entstehen.

It uses special growth algorithms to produce auto-generating artificial living forms which remind us of molecular atomic cellular and neuronal fields.
These forms can only be activated by the man-plant-tension dialogue.
Every form of these "artificial biotopes" follows the "development in time". During their development process, the human-plant tension values exclusively determine the forming and the development of the artificial organisms.
So-to-speak, "human and plant randomizing" (life) will largely determine the evolution of the growing and moving organisms by differentiation.
With this, as open a system as possible should be produced that incorporates both human and plant life in order to enable as great a potential as possible of variations and differentiation for "artificial life".

3. PROGRAMM:

Das molekulare Wachstumsprogramm wurde programmiert von Laurent Mignonneau und Christa Sommerer am Städelschule Institut für Neue Medien in Frankfurt.
Es verwendet spezielle Wachstumsalgorithmen zur Erzeugung von autogenerierenden künstlich lebenden Formen, die an den Molekular-, Atomar-, Zell- oder Neuronenbereich erinnern.
Diese Formen können nur durch den Mensch / Pflanze-Spannungsdialog aktiviert werden.
Alle Formen diese „Artificial Biotops" folgen der „Entwicklung in der Zeit". Während ihres Enstehungsprozesses determinieren ausschließlich die menschlichen / pflanzlichen Spannungswerte die Ausformung und die Entwicklung der künstlichen Organismen.
Es wird sozusagen „human and plant randomizing" (life) wesentlich die Evolution der wachsenden und sich bewegenden Organismen durch Differenzierung bestimmen.
Damit soll also ein möglichst „offenes System" erzeugt werden, das sowohl menschliches als auch pflanzliches Leben einbindet, um dem „artificial life" ein größtmögliches Potential an Variation und Differentiation zu ermöglichen.

Das Projekt wurde an der Städelschule, Institut für Neue Medien, Frankfurt am Main, produziert.

GENETISCHE BILDER

KARL SIMS

GENETIC IMAGES
KARL SIMS

EVOLUTION

Darwinian evolution is a natural of variation and selection, often summarized by the phrase: "survival of the fittest." It consists of a simple cycle. The most "fit" entities in a population survive and reproduce. The resulting offspring are copies or combinations of their parents, often with random alterations or mutations. Some offspring may be improvements on their parents, an das only the most fit of each new generation of offspring continue to reproduce, the population as a whole can slowly improve.
We are award of this process as it relates to biological organisms, but these same principles are also at work in other evolutionary systems. They have led to the creation of many of the complex and wonderful phenomena of our world, including life, consciousness, and language. Many things propagate through the medium of human minds in a way resembling Darwinian evolution. Those scientific theories, religious beliefs, or even artistic styles most fit for spreading from person to person, continue to exist.

ARTIFICIAL EVOLUTION

Darwinian evolution can be simulated on computers. Populations of virtual entities specified by coded descriptions in the computer can be evolved by applying these same natural rules of variation and selection. The definition of fitness can even be altered as the programmer desires. Natural evolution can be a very slow procecc—life on earth has taken almost four billion years to evolve to its current condition—but as computers steadily become faster, artificial evolution can be a practical and fascinating tool that can be applied in new ways. It is helpful as a method for studying the evolutionary process itself. It can also be used as a powerful device for searching for solutions to complicated problems, and as a technique for exploration in virtual worlds.

INTERACTIVE EVOLUTION

The viewers at this exhibit can observe a computer-simulated evolution in progress: an evolution of images. But in this evolution, the

EVOLUTION

Die Darwin'sche Evolution ist ein natürlicher Prozeß der Veränderung und Selektion, der oft in dem sprichwörtlichen: „Überleben der Besten" zusammengefaßt wird. Er besteht in einem einfachen Zyklus. Die „besten" Wesen einer Population überleben und reproduzieren sich. Die daraus hervorgehenden Nachkommen sind Kopien oder Kombinationen ihrer Elternteile, oft mit zufälligen Abänderungen oder Mutationen. Manche Nachkommen stellen gemessen an ihren Eltern Verbesserungen dar und da sich nur die besten jeder neuen Generation von Nachkommen weiter reproduzieren, kann die Population als ganze sich langsam verbessern.
Dieser Prozeß ist uns, sofern er sich auf biologische Organismen bezieht, bewußt, aber die gleichen Prinzipien wirken auch in anderen evolutionären Systemen. Sie haben zur Entstehung von vielen komplexen und wunderbaren Phänomenen auf unserer Erde beigetragen, Leben, Bewußtsein und Sprache mit eingeschlossen.
Viele Dinge pflanzen sich über das Medium des menschlichen Bewußtseins in einer Weise, die der Darwin'schen Evolution ähnelt, fort. Bestand haben jene wissenschaftlichen Theorien, religiösen Überzeugungen oder auch künstlerischen Stile, die am besten geeignet sind, von einer Person zur anderen weitergegeben zu werden.

KÜNSTLICHE EVOLUTION

Die Darwin'sche Evolution kann am Computer simuliert werden, Populationen von virtuellen Wesen, die durch codierte Beschreibungen im Computer spezifiziert sind, können sich durch die Anwendung eben dieser Naturgesetze der Variation und Selektion entwickeln. Auf Wunsch des Programmierers kann sogar die Definition des Besten verändert werden.
Die natürliche Evolution kann ein sehr langsamer Prozeß sein – das Leben auf der Erde hat nahezu vier Milliarden Jah-

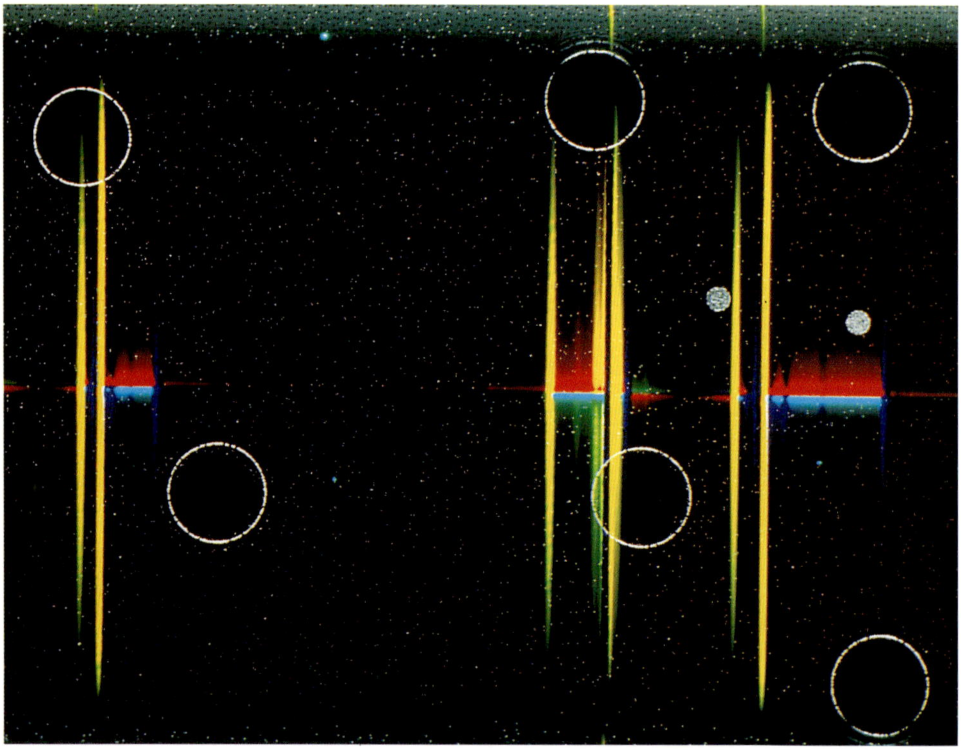

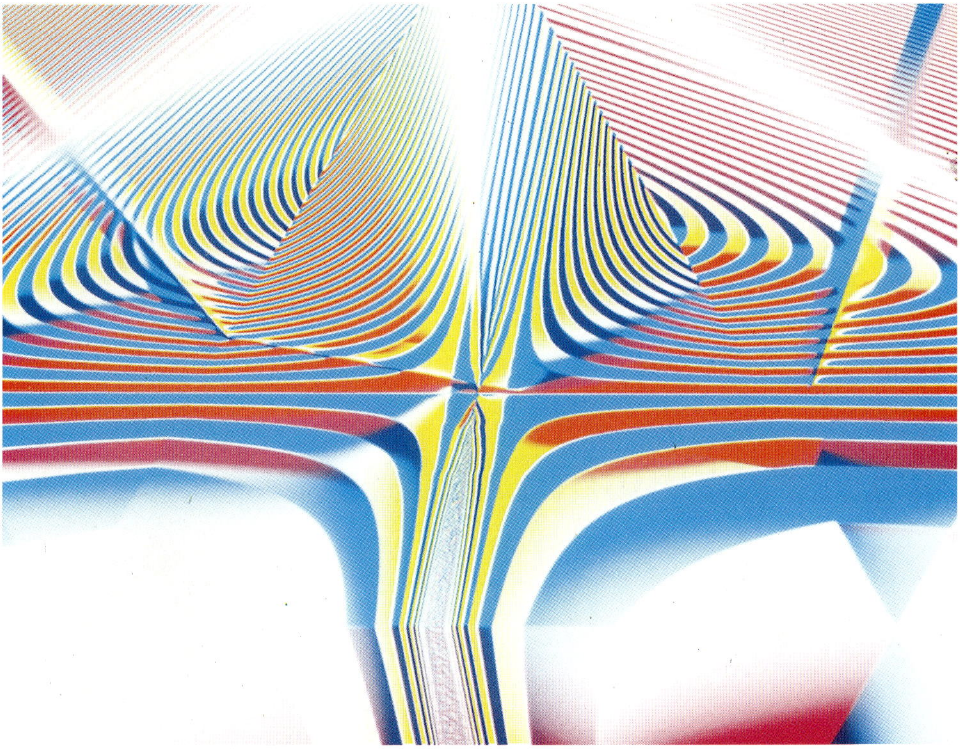

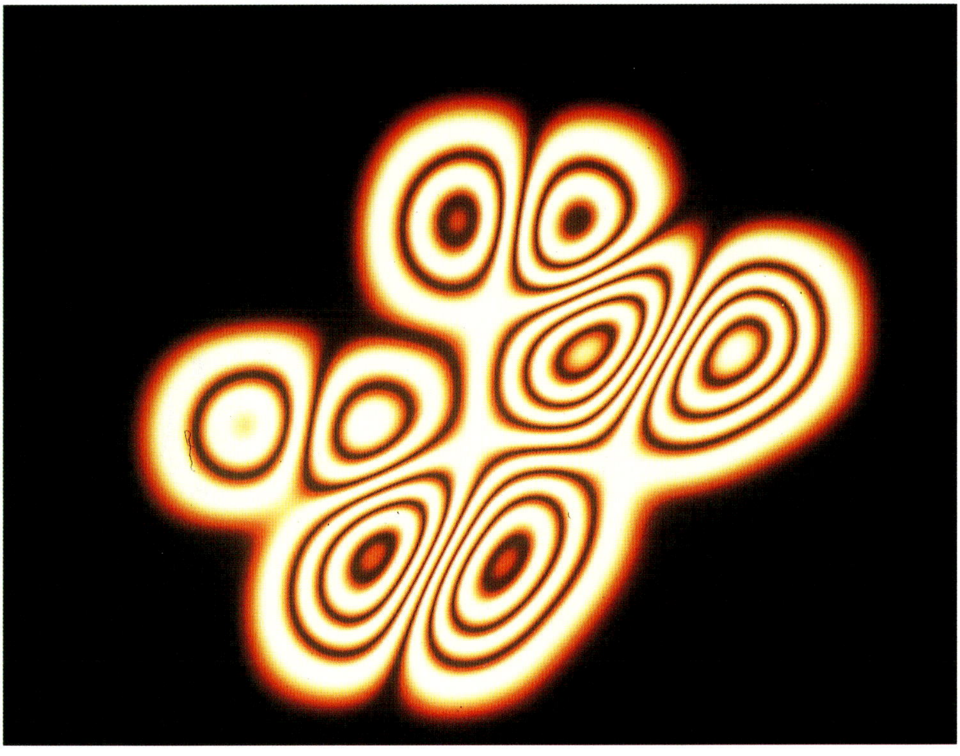

re gebraucht, um sich bis zu seiner heutigen Form zu entfalten – da die Computer aber immer schneller werden, kann die künstliche Evolution ein praktisches und faszinierendes Werkzeug sein, welches auf neue Art und Weise eingesetzt werden kann. Es ist hilfreich als Methode zur Untersuchung des evolutionären Prozesses selbst. Es kann auch ein machtvolles Instrument zur Suche von Lösungen für komplizierte Probleme darstellen und eine Technik zur Erforschung virtueller Welten.

INTERAKTIVE EVOLUTION

Die Besucher dieses Austellungsobjekts können eine computersimulierte Evolution in ihrem Entstehungsprozeß mitverfolgen. Die Besucher aber sind bei dieser Evolution nicht nur Beobachter: sie lösen die Evolution aus und steuern ihren Verlauf.

Der Computer zeigt auf einem Bogen aus 16 Videobildschirmen eine Population von Bildern. Die Zuschauer entscheiden, welche Bilder überleben, indem sie vor jenen, die ihnen ästhetisch am interessantesten erscheinen, auf die davor befindlichen Sensoren treten. Nicht gewählte Bilder scheiden aus und werden durch die Nachkommen der überlebenden Bilder ersetzt. Die neuen Bilder sind, mit verschiedenen Variationen, Kopien und Kombinationen ihrer Elternteile. Es handelt sich hier um eine künstliche Evolution, bei der die Zuschauer selbst interaktiv die „Güte" der Bilder bestimmen, indem sie auf den jeweiligen Sensoren stehenbleiben. Mit dem Fortschreiten der Entwicklung bestimmen die Zuschauer dieser simulierten Evolution kollektiv den Weg zu vorher nie gesehenen Bilderpopulationen.

Diese interaktive Installation stellt eine unübliche Zusammenarbeit zwischen Mensch und Maschine dar: die Menschen treffen Entscheidungen über die visuelle Ästhetik und der Computer verfügt über die mathematischen Fähigkeiten zur Erzeugung, Verbindung und Veränderung komplexer Strukturen und Muster. Die Zuschauer müssen die verwendeten technischen Gleichungen nicht verstehen. Der Computer kann nur auf gut Glück experimentieren, ohne jeden Sinn für Ästhetik – aber die Verbindung menschlicher und maschineller Fähigkeiten ermöglicht Resultate, die keiner der beiden alleine zustande bringen könnte.

Diese Bilder können in Analogie zu biologischen Organismen gesetzt werden. Beide werden aus „genetischen" Beschreibungen erzeugt und beide unterliegen den Kräften der Evolution. Ein Organismus geht aus den codierten Befehlen seiner DNA hervor. Ähnlich werden die Bilder aus

viewers are not just observes: they cause the evolution and direct its course.

A population of images is displayed by the computer on an arc of 16 video screens. The viewers determine which images will survive by standing on sensors in front of those they think are the most aesthetically interesting. The pictures that are not selected are removed and replaced by offspring from the surviving images. The new images are copies and combinations of their parents, with various alterations. This is an artificial evolution in which the viewers themselves interactively determine the "fitness" of the pictures by standing on the related sensors. As the cycle continues, the viewers of this simulated evolution collectively determine the pathway to previously unseen populations of pictures.

This interactive installation is an unusual collaboration between humans and machine: the humans supply decisions of visual aesthetics, and the computer supplies the mathematical ability for generating, mating, and mutating complex textures and patterns. The viewers are not required to understand the technical equations involved. The computer can only experiment at random with no sense of aesthetics—but the combination of human and machine abilities permits the creation of results that neeither of the two could produce alone.

And analogy can be made between these images and biological organisms. The are both synthesized from "genetic" descriptions and are both subjected to the forces of evolution. An organism is grown from the coded instructions of its DNA. Similarly, these images are generated from the coded instructions of its DNA. Similarly, these images are generated from instructions in the form of computer coded mathematical eequations. The computer code (or DNA) is the *genotype,* and the resulting imges (or organism) is the *phenotype*.

When one or more of these images are chosen for survival, they reproduce by copying and combining their genetic descriptions, often acquiring some random mutations in the process. The new genetic descriptions produce offspring images that look similar to their parents, but often have significant alterations. Some mutations can increase the complexity of the genetic descriptions and cause the resulting images to increase in visual complexity. Complex equations can sometimes evolve that would be quite defficult for any human to design or even understand.

During the course of exhibit, the computer remembers those images that have been chosen multiple times by the viewers. Upon request, the computer can recall these previous favorits and continue evolving them. In this way, visitors can start the evolutionary process at points where visitors from previous days left off. In addition, the best results from different evolutoins can be combined to further generate new breeds of images. This permits the collective evolution of a largewr population of images, which all visitors can contribute to and improve upon, throughout the entire period of the installation.

At any time, the viewers can alos request the

computer to start over and begin a new evolution from scratch. In this case, the computer generates an initial population of fairly simple images from brief, randomly assembled genetic descriptions. The viewers then choose which of these will reproduce, and the evolution proceeds.

CREATIVITY

Can this interactive evolution of images be considered a creative process? The participants are just repeatedly choosing among groups of 16 images presented to them. However, after only five selections, the users choose one out of over a million possible paths. This is a large enough numer of paths that users with different tastes usually do end up with quite different results. This is certainly a different type of process ffrom the execution or realization of a preconceived visual concept, but an element of chance can be an important component in some modes of creativity.
Perhaps the process here can be compared to an artist attempting to improve upon an existing style or searching for new ideas by experimenting at random, inspecting the results, and then discarding all but a small subset. Or maybe it is similar to the way society accepts or rejects certain fashions or styles of art, and those that are accepted are then copied and modified in what seems like random ways, to generate new styles with slight variations. In this simulated evolution, however, the random alterations are succinctly executed by the computer. None of the random experimentation or realization effort is performed by the user. Only the aesthetic decisions of perference are required. A designer seems absent in this process, and yet very complex and interesting results can still arise. If enough selections are made by the user and the number of possibilities is large enough, is the user actually being creative, or is the presence of a purposeful designer necessary?
In his book *The Blind Watchmaker*, biologist Richard Dwakins comments on the remarkable ability of evolution to create complexity without any apparent designer involved. It is possible that these types of techniques will challange yet another aspect of our anthropocentric tendencies. We have difficulty believing that we ourselves were not designed by a good, but arose by accident via natural evolution. Similarly, we may also find it difficult to believe that artifical evolution can compete with our design abilities, and perhaps even surpass them.
Hopefully, this exhibit will at least provoke an awareness of the power of the evolutionary process in general—in simulation, as well as in its many forms in the world around us. Maybe it will also encourage an aesthetic awareness in some participants who might not otherwise be able to explore it. The potential of tools such as this will increase as faster and faster computers continue to built, and this may be just a simple taste of things to come.

Befehlen in Form computercodierter mathematischer Gleichungen generiert. Der Computercode (oder DNA) ist der Genotyp, das daraus resultierende Bild (oder der Organismus) der Phänotyp.
Wenn eines oder mehrere dieser Bilder selektiert werden um zu überleben, reproduzieren sie sich durch das Kopieren und Kombinieren ihrer genetischen Beschreibungen, wobei es oft zu zufälligen Mutationen kommt. Die neuen genetischen Beschreibungen führen zu Bildernachkommen, die ihren Eltern zwar ähnlich sehen, oft jedoch signifikante Veränderungen aufweisen. Einige Mutationen können die Komplexität der genetischen Beschreibungen vergrößern und führen zu einer höheren visuellen Komplexität der daraus resultierenden Bilder. Mitunter ergeben sich komplexe Gleichungen, deren Ableitung oder auch nur Verständnis einem Menschen relativ schwer fiele.
Im Verlauf dieser Ausstellung speichert der Computer jene Bilder, die von den Zuschauern mehrfach ausgewählt wurden. Auf Wunsch kann der Computer diese früheren Favoriten wieder abrufen und ihre Entwicklung fortsetzen. So können die Besucher den evolutionären Prozeß an jenen Punkten starten, wo ihn die Besucher der vorhergehenden Tage abgebrochen hatten. Zudem können die besten Ergebnisse verschiedener Evolutionen kombiniert werden, um daraus neue Bildergeschlechter zu generieren. Dies ermöglicht die kollektive Evolution einer größeren Population von Bildern, zu der alle Besucher während der gesamten Dauer der Installation beitragen und die sie verbessern können.
Die Besucher können den Computer jederzeit auch neu starten und mit einer neuen Evolution ganz von vorne beginnen. In diesem Fall erzeugt der Computer eine Anfangspopulation von relativ einfachen Bildern aus kurzen, zufällig miteinander verbundenen genetischen Beschreibungen. Die Zuschauer entscheiden dann, welche sich reproduzieren werden, und die Evolution setzt ein.

KREATIVITÄT

Kann diese interaktive Evolution von Bildern als kreativer Prozeß verstanden werden? Die Teilnehmer tun weiter nichts als aus Gruppen von 16 Bildern, die ihnen gezeigt werden, zu wählen. Nach nur fünf Wahlvorgängen wählt der Anwender jedoch bereits einen aus über einer Million möglicher Pfade. Diese Anzahl ist genügend groß, sodaß Benutzer mit unterschiedlichem Geschmack in der Regel zu ganz verschiedenen Ergebnissen gelangen. Es ist sicher ein Verfahren, das sich von der Durchführung oder Realisierung eines vorher erdachten visuellen Konzepts unterscheidet, aber ein Zufallselement kann bei einigen Kreativitätsmethoden eine wichtige Komponente darstellen.

Vielleicht kann dieser Prozeß hier verglichen werden mit einem Künstler, der versucht einen bestehenden Stil zu verbessern oder der nach neuen Ideen sucht, indem er auf gut Glück experimentiert, die Resultate untersucht und alle außer einer kleinen Anzahl davon verwirft. Oder vielleicht ähnelt er der Art und Weise, in der die Gesellschaft bestimmte Moden oder Kunststile akzeptiert oder ablehnt und jene, die akzeptiert werden, dann scheinbar zufällig kopiert und modifiziert, um neue Stile mit leichten Variationen hervorzubringen. Bei dieser simulierten Evolution werden die Zufallsänderungen kurzerhand vom Computer durchgeführt. Keines der Zufallsexperimente und auch keiner der Umsetzungsversuche wird vom Anwender durchgeführt. Es werden nur dessen ästhetische Präferenzentscheidungen verlangt. Einen Designer gibt es in diesem Prozeß allem Anschein nach nicht und dennoch kann es zu sehr komplexen und interessanten Ergebnissen kommen. Wenn vom Anwender genügend Selektionen vorgenommen werden und die Anzahl der Möglichkeiten groß genug ist, ist der Anwender dann tatsächlich kreativ oder ist die Anwesenheit eines Designers, der bewußt ein Ziel verfolgt, notwendig?

Der Biologe Richard Dawkins schreibt in seinem Buch „The Blind Watchmaker" (Der blinde Uhrmacher) über das bemerkenswerte Vermögen der Evolution, ohne irgendeinen augenscheinlichen Gestalter Komplexität zu erzeugen. Es ist möglich, daß diese Arten der Technik noch einen anderen Aspekt unserer anthropozentrischen Neigungen herausfordern werden. Es fällt uns schwer zu glauben, daß wir selbst nicht von einem Gott geschaffen wurden, sondern über die natürliche Evolution zufällig entstanden sind. In ähnlicher Weise fällt es uns schwer zu glauben, daß die künstliche Evolution mit unserem Gestaltungsvermögen konkurrieren oder es sogar übertreffen kann.

Die Hoffnung ist, daß dieses Ausstellungsobjekt wenigstens ein Bewußtsein für die Macht des evolutionären Prozesses im allgemeinen hervorruft. Vielleicht wird es bei einigen Teilnehmern, die sonst keine Möglichkeit hätten, dies zu erforschen, auch eine ästhetische Erkenntnis anregen. Das Potential an Werkzeugen wie diesem wird sich vergrößern, indem laufend schnellere Computer gebaut werden, und dies ist vielleicht nur ein Vorgeschmack der auf uns zukommenden Dinge.

ACKNOWLEDGEMENTS

Thinking Machines Corporation provided the *Connection Machine* supercomputer for this installation. This Massachusetts-based firm is the creator of some of the world's most powerful computers. The Connection Machine system achieves its speed from data-parallel computation—many processing nodes working together at once. The Connection Machine model used for this project contains 32,768 processes.

John Watlington, Design Engineer at the MIT Media Lab in Cambridge Massachusetts, designed and built the video hardware "Freeze-Frame" that allows images from the Connection Machine computer to be displayed on the array of monitors. It also interprets the signals from the step pad sensors.

Arlene Chung, Thinking Machines, and *Ron Bennett,* Bennett HDG Inc., made contributions to the design of the exhibit space.

Guy Decaudain, Thinking Machines, provided European coordination for the project, and *Kathryn Cree* provided US coordination. *David Lloyd-Owen, Jonathan Saunders, Roch Bourbonnais, Clark Neville* and *Jim Laura,* contributed technical assistance.

Jim Salem, Gary Oberbrunner, and *Matt Fitzgibbon* are responsible for the Connection Machine graphics and display software.

John Earls provided Connection Machine video information and support.

JP Massar supports the Starlisp data-parallel programming language, which the evolution software was written in.

Sheryl Handler and *Lew Tucker* of Thinking Machines also gave generous support for this project.

Tamiko Thiel was the Connection Machine industrial designer.

DANKSAGUNG

Thinking Machines Corporation stellte den Connection Machine Supercomputer für diese Installation bei. Die in Massachusetts beheimatete Firma hat einige der weltweit stärksten Computer entwickelt. Die Geschwindigkeit des Connection Machine Systems beruht auf der Parallelverarbeitung von Daten – viele Prozessorknoten arbeiten gleichzeitig zusammen. Das für dieses Projekt verwendete Connection Machine Modell enthält 32.768 Prozessoren.

John Watlington, Entwurfsingenieur am MIT Media Lab in Cambridge, Massachusetts, entwarf uncl baute die Video-Hardware „Freeze-Frame", die es ermöglicht, die Bilder aus dem Connection Machine Computer am Monitorfeld zu zeigen. Sie übersetzt auch die Signale von den Schritt-Sensoren.

Arlene Chung, Thinking Machines, und Ron Bennet, Bennett HDG Inc., trugen zum Design des Objektraums bei.

Guy Decaudain, Thinking Machines, besorgte die Europakoordination des Projekts, Kathryn Cree die US-Koordination. Technische Hilfestellung gewährten David Lloyd-Owen, Jonathan Saunders, Roch Bourbonnais, Clark Noville und Jim Laura.

Jim Salem, Gary Oberbrunner und Matt Fizgibbon zeichnen verantwortlich für die Connection Machine Grafiken und die Display Software.

John Earle sorgte für Connection Machine Videoinformation und -unterstützung.

JP Massar gewährte Unterstützung bei der Starlisp Datenparallel-Programmiersprache, in der die Evolutionssoftware verfaßt wurde.

Sheryl Handler und Lew Tucker von Thinking Machines unterstützen das Projekt ebenfalls großzügig.

Tamiko Thiel fungierte als Connection Machine Industriedesignerin.

INTERAKTIVE PLANT GROWING

CHRISTA SOMMERER / LAURENT MIGNONNEAU

KONZEPTUELLE UND ÄSTHETISCHE ASPEKTE

"The rate of growth deserves to be studied as a necessary preliminary to the theoretical study of form, and organic form itself is found, mathematically speaking, to be a function of time. (...) We might call the form of an organism an event in space-time, and not merely a configuration in space."
(D'Arcy Thompson, On Growth and Form, Cambridge University Press, 1942.)
„Interactive Plant Growing" ist eine Installation, die von Wachstumsprinzipien künstlicher Pflanzen-Organismen und ihren Veränderungen und Modifikationen in Echtzeit im virtuellen Raum eines 3 D -Grafik Computers (Silicon Graphics) handelt.
Diese Modifikationen von „künstlich lebenden pflanzlichen Organismen" basieren in erster Linie auf den Prinzipien von Entwicklung und Evolution in der Zeit.
Künstliches Wachstum von programmierten Pflanzen ist der Ausdruck des Wunsches nach der Entdeckung des „Prinzips Leben", welches immer auch durch die Transformationen und Morphogenesen bestimmter Organismen bestimmt ist.
Interactive Plant Growing verbindet das Wachstum künstlicher Pflanzen im 3-dimensionalen Raum des Computers mit echten lebenden Pflanzen, denen sich ein menschlichen Betrachter annähert und die er berührt.
Durch den Kontakt und die Annäherung ihrer Hände zu echten Pflanzen können die Betrachter direkt und in Real-Zeit dieses künstliche Wachstum am Computerbildschirm bzw. der Videoleinwand beeinflussen und steuern, indem sie verschiedene Datenwerte (abhängig von der Distanz Hand – Pflanze) an das Interface weiterleiten, welches die echten Pflanzen und das Wachstumsprogramm verbindet.

A) PRINZIPIEN DER EVOLUTION

Evolution kann in 3 Teil-Prozesse untergliedert werden:
1. WACHSTUM
2. DIFFERENZIERUNG (EINSCHLIESSLICH DETERMINATION)
3. BEWEGUNG

1. WACHSTUM

Wir sprechen von Wachstum, wenn die Menge der Substanzen oder die Anzahl der Zellen zunimmt.
Wachstum existiert nicht ohne Veränderung der wachsenden Elemente.
Das ist der Grund, warum Wachstum und Differenzierung eng miteinander verbunden sind.

2. DIFFERENZIERUNG / DETERMINATION

Differenzierung beschreibt, im biologischen Sinne, einen unabgeschlossenen Zustand.
Man spricht von Differenzierung, wenn man zum Beispiel zwei Zellen vergleicht, die sich unabhängig voneinander entwickeln, oder wenn zwei aufeinanderfolgende Stadien des selben Elementes verglichen werden.
Wird eine Entscheidung über die zukünftige Entwicklung einer Zelle gefällt, spricht man von Determination. Ein System von Wechselwirkungen in Zellen und Geweben kann durch unterschiedliche Kräfte verändert werden. Diese Entscheidungen bestimmen grundsätzlich die zukünftige Morphologie der Organismen und ihrer Teile.

3. BEWEGUNG

Ohne Bewegung ist Evolution nicht möglich. Ordnung, Struktur, Transport von zellulären Substanzen, Entwicklung und Zellteilung sind dynamische Prozesse.
Wachstum und Bewegung hängen immer zusammen.
Wachstum, Differenzierung und Bewegung existieren in allen biologischen Dimensionen, beginnend mit den Molekülen und Atomen.
Wir können Chemische-, Organell-, Zell-, Gewebs- und Organ- Differenzierung unterscheiden.
Durch das Zusammenwirken aller Prozesse auf einer gewissen Ebene kann ein höher entwickelter Zustand durch Diffe-

renzierung des vorherigen Zustandes erreicht werden. Das führt uns von Einzellern zu Kolonien und schließlich zu sehr komplexen Organismen, die den Vorteil der Arbeitsteilung in ihrem Zellverband haben.
Um jedoch die Variabilität der Organismen zu gewährleisten, ist es wichtig, die genetische Information der DNA immer wieder neu zu ordnen und neu zu gruppieren. Das ist der Grund, warum die generative Reproduktion durch einzelne Zellen besser garantiert ist.
Beide Vorteile, komplexe Zellularität mit Arbeitsteilung und einfache Zellularität mit der Möglichkeit zur Gen-Modifikation, kann uns zu äußerst komplexen Formen des Lebens führen, wie zum Beispiel zu Menschen, Tieren und Pflanzen.

B) INTERACTIVE PLANT GROWING – EINE REAL ZEIT INSTALLATION

1) INTERAKTION: MENSCH – PFLANZE

Durch den Kontakt und die Annäherung ihrer Hände zu echten Pflanzen können menschliche Betrachter das künstliche Wachstum von 25 und mehr programmierten Pflanzen in Echt-Zeit am Bildschirm des Grafikcomputers beeinflussen, kontrollieren und variieren.
Durch diese sensitive Interaktion mit den echten Pflanzen, werden die Betrachter selbst Teil der Installation. Sie bestimmen, wie die Interaktion übersetzt wird, und wie sich das Wachstum der künstlichen Pflanzen am Bildschirm vollzieht.
Die Größen der virtuellen Pflanzen können vom Betrachter reguliert, die Rotationen und die Bewegungen während des Wachstums verändert, die Farben der einzelnen Pflanzen modifiziert und neue Plätze für neues Wachstum des selben Typus Pflanze angesteuert werden.
Das Entstehen, Wachsen und Differenzieren dieser künstlichen Pflanzen ist also letzlich abhängig vom Kontakt der Betrachter zu den realen Pflanzen, da sich erst durch diesen künstliches Wachstum vollziehen kann.
Jede der virtuellen Pflanzenspezies (Farne, Lianen, Moose, Bäume und Sträucher) hat mindesten 6 unterschiedliche programmierte Variationsmöglichkeiten, durch die Interaktion Mensch-Pflanze wird diese Bandbreite jedoch wesentlich erweitert, da Ausformung, Größe, Farbe, Bewegung und Translation jeder einzelnen Pflanze ständig verformt und variiert werden kann.

All diese Variationen hängen schließlich von der Sensibilität des Betrachters ab, der die unterschiedlichen Stufen der Annäherung zur realen Pflanze herausfinden soll, da diese das Wachstumsgeschehen wesentlich bestimmen.
Jeder Mensch wird durch seine persönliche elektrische Spannung und durch die spezifischen Bewegungen seiner Hände zu den Pflanzen zu individuell unterschiedlichen Ergebnissen beim Wachstum der künstlichen Pflanzen gelangen, das heißt „human randomising" wird ständig neue unerwartete Ergebnissen in der Ausformung und Gestaltung dieses artifiziellen Pflanzenwachstum garantieren.
Da es einige Zeit dauert, bis der Betrachter die unterschiedlichen Modulationsstufen aufspüren wird, kann er dadurch indirekt größere Sensibilität und ein höheres Bewußtsein echten Pflanzen gegenüber entwickeln.

2) PROGRAMM:

In Interactive Plant Growing wachsen künstliche Pflanzen, programmiert von Laurent Mignonneau und Christa Sommerer im 3-dimensionalen virtuellen Raum des Grafik Computers (4 D -VGX 320 Silicon Graphics).
Das heißt, KÜNSTLICHES WACHSTUM wird in ECHT-ZEIT im DREI-DIMENSIONALEN RAUM des Computers vollzogen. Die auf diese Weise produzierten Bilder werden durch einen hochauflösenden Video-Beamer auf eine Video-Projektionsleinwand direkt vor dem Betrachter und den Pflanzen geworfen.
Dieses Virtuelle Wachstum basiert auf speziell entwickelten Algorithmen, die sich auf die unterschiedlichen morphologischen Charakteristiken der realen Pflanzendifferenzierungen beziehen. Diese künstlichen Pflanzen können in alle

Richtungen des Raumes wachsen, rotieren, deformieren und variieren.

Virtuelles Wachstum basiert nicht auf den selben Prinzipien wie echtes Wachstum, aber die Erscheinung von Bewegung, Differenzierung und Determination während dieses evolutionären Prozesses kann als optisch ähnlich bezeichnet werden.

Im Programm Interactive Plant Growing wurde eine neue

Methode der Differenzierung entwickelt, die vergleichbar mit den L-Systemen von Aristid Lindenmayer ist, jedoch spezielle „Randomising Parameter" (Zufallsgeneratoren) verwendet, die als „künstliche Wachstums- und Differenzierungsregulatoren" bezeichnet werden können.
Diese „Randomising Parameter" bestimmen die Morphologie der Organismen, indem sie deren Variationen kontrollieren.
Jeder Schritt in der Konstruktion der pflanzlichen Formen ist so weit als möglich zufallsgeneriert, innerhalb bestimmter Minimum- und Maximum- Grenzwerte.
So kann ein größtmögliches Potential an Variationen erzielt werden.
Zum Beispiel kann bei den programmierten Bäumen die Distanz und die Länge der „Mutter- und Kinderäste" innerhalb gewisser Grenzen durch Zufallsgenerierung variiert und verändert werden.
Das führt uns zu botanisch unterschiedlichen Wachstumsformen. Die Krone eines Baumes kann zum Beispiel kegelförmig, zylindrisch oder rund sein.
Andere Pflanzen wie Farne, Lianen oder Moose ändern ihren Habitus abhängig von den zufallsgenerierten Variablen für Größe, Länge, Rotationen, Translationen, Winkeln und Farben.
Diese Idee der fortgeschrittenen Zufallsgenerierung könnte mit dem Terminus „walking randomising" verglichen werden.
Die Grenzen der Zufallsgenerierung könnten als Determination bezeichnet werden, die Zufallsgenerierung selbst ist repräsentativ für die Differenzierung.
Die Bewegung, als drittes Charakteristikum der Evolution lebender Organismen, hat ihre Entsprechung in der künstlichen Bewegung innerhalb des 3 – dimensionalen virtuellen Raumes.
Diese Bewegung von künstlichen Pflanzen kann durch einen äußeren Zufallsfaktor beeinflußt werden.
In diesem Falle ist es die Information durch das Interface, welches die Werte der „Distanz menschliche Hand zur Pflanze" verarbeitet und weitergibt.

3) INTERFACE:

In der Installation werden die elektrischen Spannungsdifferenzen zwischen den Betrachtern und den Pflanzen direkt in elektrische Signale übersetzt, die das künstliche Wachstum am Bildschirm steuern und bestimmen. Dadurch vollzieht der Betrachter mit den echten Pflanzen einen direkten Dia-

log, dessen Interpretation kann er sofort in Real-Zeit auf der Projektionswand mitverfolgen und weitersteuern.
a) Elektrisches Potential:
Technisch gesprochen, wird das elektrische Potential von echten Pflanzen durch spezielle Sensoren, die an den Pflanzenwurzeln angebracht sind, gemessen.
Dieses elektrische Potential wird dann mit dem elektrischen Potential des Betrachters verglichen.
Diese Spannungsdifferenz variiert, abhängig von der individuellen Spannung der Betrachter und abhängig von der Distanz Hand-Pflanze. Die Sensibilität der einzelnen Pflanzen reicht von ca. 0 bis 70 cm im Raum, abhängig von Größe und Morphologie der realen Pflanzen.
b) Verstärker / Filter:
Diese elektrischen Signale werden nun verstärkt und gefiltert und danach durch ein 20 Meter langes isoliertes Kabel zu einem Konverter weitergeleitet.
Jede der 5 Pflanzen ist mit einem unabhängigen Verstärker verbunden.
c) Konverter:
Der Konverter transformiert die verstärkten und gefilterten analogen Signale in digitale Datenwerte.
Alle 5 Verstärker senden ihre Signale zum Konverter, ein Multiplexer wählt dann die Signale für die Konversion.
Diese unterschiedlichen Datenwerte werden nun zum Parallel-Port eines 4D-VGX 320 Grafik Computers gesendet.

5) FEEDBACK:

Durch das Feedback des künstlichen Wachstums am Bildschirm kann der Betrachter auf die jeweiligen Bilder reagieren und durch seine Entscheidungen den weiteren Verlauf des Wachstums bestimmen.
5 oder mehr Menschen können zur gleichen Zeit mit den 5 echten Pflanzen in der Installation interagieren.
Die Wachstumsprozesse sind sehr flexibel programmiert, sie sind begrenzt vordeterminiert, sodaß die Ergebnisse ständig neu sein können, abhängig von der INTERAKTION MENSCH – PFLANZE.

Das Projekt wurde an der Städelschule am Institut für Neue Medien, Frankfurt am Main, produziert.

ANIMATRIX

AKKE WAGENAAR / MASAHIRO MIWA

ANIMATRIX
AKKE WAGENAAR/MASAHIRO MIWA

Animatrix is a computer dancer reminding of a Bodhisattva, a Buddhist creature in half-enlightened state.[1]
The installation consists of three parts:
1. the graphics program that calculates the movements of the Animatrix, depending on user input
2. the music program that interactively composes the music, depending on user input
3. the user interface.
The user interface is a double joystick consisting of two positioning devices attached to each other. The Animatrix reacts to the movements of the interface and starts to dance; at the same time rhythmical music is triggered.
There is a relation between the movements of the interface, the movements of the Animatrix and the music, but the relation is not straight forward: sometimes the Animatrix seems to be a willing dance partner, at other times it seems to have its own life and to dance its own dance.
By playing the system the user will gradually discover that he/she is not only able to influence the dance of the Animatrix, but also the music and the rhythm that comes along with it.
There are two levels of interaction:
1. positioning the interface gives direct control of some of the movements of the Animatrix, and of part of the musical composition.
2. variations in moving, twisting and rotating the interface are measured and analyzed over a long period of time and cause more complex patterns of music and movement.

STRUCTURE OF BOTH PROGRAMS

The graphics program receives the input data and reacts directly to it. It passes the data on to the music program which also reacts directly to it. Both programs analyze the input data over a longer period of time and exchange the results of their analyses continuously.
The music program analyzes and evaluates the timing and rhythm aspects of the users movements and processes this information in its composition rules. It then sends the results of the analysis to the graphics program. The graphics program analyzes and evaluates the positioning and rotational aspects of the user input and passes it on to all body parts of the Animatrix,

Animatrix ist ein Computertänzer, der an einen Bodhisattva, ein buddhistisches Wesen in halberleuchtetem Zustand, erinnert.[1]
Die Installation besteht aus drei Teilen:
1. das grafische Programm, das die Bewegungen der Animatrix ausrechnet, die abhängig vom Benutzer-Input sind.
2. das Musikprogramm, das abhängig vom Benutzer-Input die Musik interaktiv komponiert.
3. das Benutzer-Interface
Das Benutzer-Interface ist ein doppelter Joystick, bestehend aus zwei Positionierungsvorrichtungen, die miteinander verbunden sind. Die Animatrix reagiert auf die Bewegungen der Schnittstelle und beginnt zu tanzen; gleichzeitig wird rhythmische Musik ausgelöst.
Es besteht eine Beziehung zwischen den Bewegungen der Schnittstelle, den Bewegungen der Animatrix und der Musik, aber die Beziehung ist nicht geradlinig: Manchmal scheint die Animatrix ein williger Tanzpartner zu sein, zu anderen Zeiten scheint sie ihr eigenes Leben zu haben und ihren eigenen Tanz zu tanzen.
Indem der/die BenutzerIn mit dem System spielt wird er/sie nach und nach entdecken, daß er/sie nicht nur den Tanz der Animatrix, sondern auch die dazugehörige Musik und den Rhythmus beeinflußen kann. Es gibt zwei Ebenen der Interaktion:
1. Die Positionierung der Schnittstelle gibt direkte Kontrolle über einige Bewegungen der Animatrix und über einen Teil der musikalischen Komposition.
2. Variationen der Bewegung, Drehung und Rotation des Interface werden über einen längeren Zeitraum gemessen und analysiert und verursachen komplexere Muster von Musik und Bewegung.

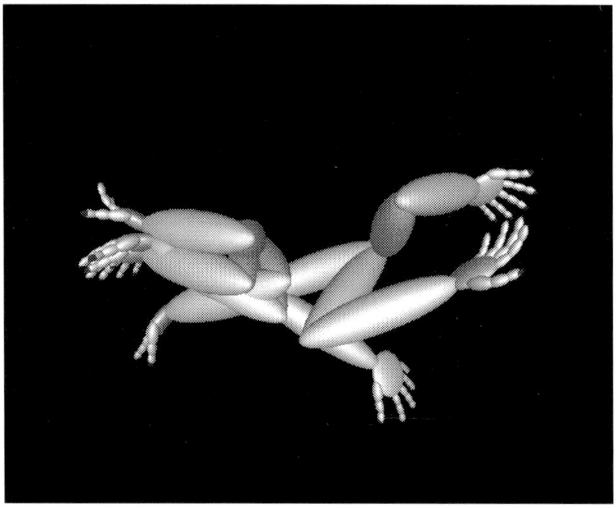

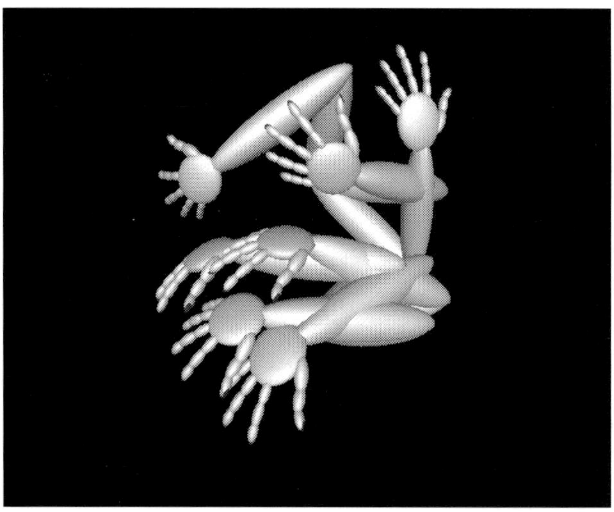

DIE STRUKTUR BEIDER PROGRAMME

Das Grafikprogramm erhält die Input-Daten und reagiert direkt auf diese. Es gibt die Daten an das Musikprogramm weiter, das auch direkt darauf reagiert. Beide Programme analysieren die Input-Daten über einen längeren Zeitraum hinweg und tauschen die Resultate ihrer Analysen ständig aus. Das Musikprogramm analysiert und bewertet zeitliche Abstimmung und Rhythmusaspekte der Bewegungen des Benutzers und verarbeitet diese Informationen in seine Kompositionsregeln. Es sendet dann die Resultate der Analysen an das Grafikprogramm. Das Grafikprogramm analysiert und evaluiert die Positionierungs- und Rotationsaspekte des

each of which has its own set of rules that tell it how to move and how to react to the results of both analyses. The movement information is then passed on to the music program.

AUTHORS AND PRODUCTION

The idea of the work was conceived by Akke Wagenaar. She developed the basic structure of the dancing program and then started the co-operation with Masahiro Miwa. They connected their computers together and from then on worked simultanously on their respective programs. Akke Wagenaar programmed in C on a Silicon Graphics workstation, using the Graphics Library. Masahiro Miwa programmed on a MacIntosh computer using the music programming language MAX.
The work was supported by the following institutions and companies:
Fonds voor Beeldende Kunsten, Vormgeving & Bouwkunst, Amsterdam, NL
Institut für Neue Medien an der Städelschule, Frankfurt/Main, D
Silicon Graphics Computer Systems, Cologne, D
Vienna International Composer Competition, Vienna, A

NOTE

[1] Bodhisattva's role is to mediate between Samsara (the world of illusion and suffering) and Nirvana (the state of calm, emotionless salvation). Bodhisattvas can have 1 to 11 heads and 2 to 1000 arms. The Animatrix has no head and seven arms.

Benutzer-Inputs und gibt diese an alle Körperteile der Animatrix weiter, von denen jeder sein eigenes Regelsystem besitzt, das ihm sagt, wie er auf die Resultate beider Analysen zu reagieren hat. Die Bewegungsinformation wird dann an das Musikprogramm weitergegeben.

AUTOREN UND PRODUKTION

Das Konzept dieser Arbeit stammt von Akke Wagenaar. Sie entwickelte die Grundstruktur des Tanzprogrammes und begann dann eine Zusammenarbeit mit Masahiro Miwa. Sie verbanden ihre Computer miteinander und arbeiteten von da an gleichzeitig an ihren jeweiligen Programmen.
Akke Wagenaar programmierte in C auf einer Silicon Graphics workstation unter Verwendung der Graphics Library.
Masahiro Miwa programmierte auf einem Macintosh Computer unter Verwendung der Musikprogrammiersprache MAX.

Die Arbeit wurde von folgenden Instituten und Firmen unterstützt:
Fonds voor Beeldende Kunsten, Vormgeving & Bouwkunst, Amsterdam, Niederlande
Institut für Neue Medien Städelschule, Frankfurt am Main, Deutschland
Kunsthochschule für Medien. Köln, Deutschland
Silcon Graphics Computer Systems, Köln, Deutschland
Wiener Internationaler Kompositionswettbewerb, Wien, Österreich.

ANMERKUNG

[1] Die Rolle eines Bodhisattva ist es, zwischen Samsara (der Welt der Illusion und des Leidens) und Nirvana (dem Zustand der ruhigen, emotionslosen Erlösung) zu vermitteln. Bodhisattvas können zwischen 1 und 11 Köpfen und 2 bis 1000 Arme haben. Das Animatrix hat keine Köpfe und sieben Arme.

WELTWÜRFEL

PETER WEIBEL

WORLD CUBE
PETER WEIBEL

32 sensors on the floor, like a keyboard you can wald on, give you access to four world-modes, built of variables, baby-universes, which are controlled by the observer: the world of language, of architecture (space), of objects an artificial creatures, made of gas. Gas is a neologism for chaos; it serves as a model for a hypothetical being, that shows liefelike behavior.

Durch 32 Sensoren am Boden, vergleichbar einer begehbaren Tastatur, findet man Zugang zu vier Modell-Welten aus Variablen, Baby-Universen, die der Beobachter steuern kann: die Welt der Buchstaben (Sprache), des Raumes (Architektur), der Gegenstände (Mobiliar) und der künstlichen Kreaturen aus Gas. Gas ist ein Kunstwort, das Chaos bedeutet; es dient als Modell für ein hypothetisches Wesen, das sich selbst organisiert und ein eingenständiges lebensähnliches Verhalten aufweist.

ÜBER GENETISCHE KUNST

PETER WEIBEL

Technik kann als vom Menschen gemachte Natur definiert werden. Sie tritt in eine neue Phase, wenn sie zentrale Prozesse des natürlichen Lebens in künstliche, vom Menschen gemachte verwandelt. Gentechnologie, welche die vorhandenen Lebewesen (Mikroorgansimen, Pflanzen, Tiere, Menschen) verändert oder neue erzeugt, ist so ein Spezialfall, weil sie nicht nur in den Bau und die Funktion anderer Lebewesen, sondern auch direkt in den menschlichen Organismus, in seine Gene, eingreifen kann. Die Wissenschaft der Vererbung wurde vor ca. 90 Jahren von Bateson Genetik genannt. Sie ist ein Kind des 20. Jahrhunderts. Die Erbfaktoren, die Gene in den Chromosomen, können mutieren. Erbexperimente an Taufliegen und niederen Organismen wie Bakterien und Viren führten zu zahlreichen Mutanten und zu neuen Einsichten in die Gesetze des Lebens, der Vererbung, der Vermehrung und in die Formen des Wachstums.
Genetische Kunst als künstlerisches Äquivalent der Gentechnik will einerseits wie diese mit modernen technischen Mitteln Lebensprozesse simulieren, andererseits mit klassischen Mitteln die möglichen Folgewirkungen von solchen Simulationen und synthetischen Erzeugungen des Lebens kritisch bedenken. Genetische Kunst ist also:

1. EVOLUTIONÄRE KUNST:

künstliche Eingriffe in Wachstumsprozesse (Beschleunigung, Stoppen, Verlangsamung, Veränderung) und deren Formveränderungen in biologischem Material wie auch immateriell im Computer.

2. BIOGENETISCHE KUNST:

biologische Prozesse der Fortpflanzung und Vermehrung, von Mikroorganismen wie Bakterien in Bildern zu niederen Lebewesen wie Ameisen, ebenfalls sowohl materialiter wie rein digital.

ABOUT GENETIC ART

PETER WEIBEL

Technology can be defined as man-made nature. It is presently entering a new stage of its development in which it converts the central processes of natural life into artificial, man-made processes. Genetic engineering which modifies existing forms of life (micro-organisms, plants, animals, human beings) or creates new forms of life is a very delicate issue, because it does not only interfere with micro-organisms, plants or animals but also constitutes an instrument for interventions in the human organism, i.e. for modifications of the human genes. About 90 years ago, Bateson gave the science of heredity the name "genetics". Genetics is a discipline of the 20th century. The hereditary factors, the genes contained in the chromosomes, can mutate. Experiments carried out with flies (*drosophila*) and low organisms like bacteria and viruses resulted in numerous mutants and new insights into the laws of live, of heredity, of procreation and growth.
Genetic art as artistic counterpart of genetic engineering is on the one hand intended to simulate processes of life with the same modern technological tools and methods as the latter. On the other hand, it is to use traditional methods and strategies for a critical reflection on the potential consequences of such simulations and the synthetic creation of life. Genetic art thus embraces:

1. EVOLUTIONARY ART:

Artificial interventions in growth processes (acceleration, stopping, slowing down and modification of growth processes) and structural modifications—either in the biological material itself or on the immaterial level of the computer simulation.

2. BIOGENETIC ART:

Biological processes of procreation and reproduction of different forms of life, from micro-organisms, for instance bacteria, to low organisms, for instance ants—either on a biological or on a digital level.

3. GENETIC ENGINEERING:

Genetic manipulation of foodstuffs, animals and human beings.

4. ALGORYTHMIC ART:

The life of language. Grammars of languages constitute a creation formalism that can be compared with the algorithm of plant growth. In such grammars, information is furthermore encoded in such a way that they can serve as general models.

5. ROBOTICS:

Three-dimensional, mechanical beings made of hard materials. These beings are characterized by a behaviour resembling that of living organisms, e.g. search mechanisms, self-preservation functions, stimulus-reaction patterns etc.

6. VIRTUAL BEINGS:

Virtual, computer-simulated beings are like the above-mentioned mechanical beings characterized by behaviour patterns resembling those of living beings, or by processes of life, for instance information encoding, reproduction and the extinction of sets of individuals (populations) breeding in open spaces.

7. ARTIFICIAL LIFE:

Machine configurations and programmes that constitute beings resembling living organisms and that interact with human beings either on an immaterial level, i.e. in a two-dimensional space, or on a material level, i.e. in the three-dimensional space.

Genetic art is dedicated to the research in the field of artificial life but at the same time serves to criticize this very discipline. It is one of the few contemporary forms of art that do not stay confined to the realms of art but which approach the central points of life.

3. GENTECHNISCHE KUNST:

Darstellung genmanipulierter Vorgänge und operativer Eingriffe bei Lebensmitteln, Tieren und Menschen.

4. ALGORITHMISCHE KUNST:

das Leben der Sprache, deren Grammatik als ein Erzeuger-Formalismus interpretiert werden kann, vergleichbar dem Algorithmus des Wachstums von Pflanzen bzw. deren Informations-Codifizierung und die allgemeinen Modellcharakter hat.

5. ROBOTIK:

dreidimensionale, mechanische Lebewesen aus harten Materialien, die lebensähnliches Verhalten wie Suchmechanismen, Selbsterhaltung, Reiz-Reaktionsbeziehungen etc. zeigen.

6. VIRTUELLE KREATUREN:

virtuelle, computersimulierte Lebenwesen, die ebenfalls lebensähnliches Verhalten bzw. Lebensprozesse wie Informationscodierung, Vermehrung und Aussterben freibrütender Individuenmengen (Populationen) vorweisen.

7. KÜNSTLICHES LEBEN:

Maschinen-Konfigurationen und Programme, die sowohl immateriell 2-dimensional wie materiell 3-dimensional als lebewesenähnliche Kreaturen mit dem Menschen interagieren.

Die genetische Kunst ist Erforschung des künstlichen Lebens wie dessen Kritik. Sie ist eine der wenigen Kunstformen der Gegenwart, die nicht rein kunstimmanent bleibt, sondern sich zentralen Punkten des Lebens nähert.

BIOGRAPHIEN

ALF ALTENDORF
geboren 1966 in Hartberg, lebt in Wien. Diverse Studien. Studium an der Hochschule für angewandte Kunst, seit 1988 Ausstellungen, Film- und Medienproduktionen, Arbeiten für Piratenradios im In- und Ausland, ORF. Installationen und Events im öffentlichen Raum, vor allem unter dem Label R.A.M.S

---

born in Hartberg, Austria, in 1966, lives in Vienna. Various studies. Student at the University of Applied Arts in Vienna. Since 1988 exhibitions, film and media productions. He has worked for pirate radio stations in Austria and abroad and for the Austrian Broadcasting Corporation. Public installations and events, mostly under the label R.A.M.S.

JOSEPH BATES
schloß sein Informatikstudium an der Johns Hopkins Universität im Alter von nur 17 Jahren mit dem Master-Titel ab. Das Doktorat erhielt er 1979 in Cornell. Seine Forschung befaßt sich vor allem mit künstlicher Intelligenz und interaktiven Medien. Heute ist er Mitglied des College of Fine Arts sowie Außerordentlicher Professor am Informatikinstitut der Carnegie Mellon-Universität, wo er das interdisziplinäre Oz-Projekt leitet, in dem der computertechnische Grundstein zur Schaffung eindrucksvoller, quasi lebendiger virtueller Welten gelegt werden soll. Bates arbeitet außerdem als wissenschaftlicher Forscher am Artificial Intelligence Laboratory des MIT.

---

was only seventeen when he received his master's degree in computer science at the Johns Hopkins University. He completed his Ph.D. at Cornell in 1979. His primary research interests are in artificial intelligence and interactive media. Today he is an Associate Professor in the School of Computer Science, and a Fellow of the College of Fine Arts, at Carnegie Mellon University, where he directs the interdisciplinary Oz project intended to provide the technological foundation for rich, emotionally powerful virtual worlds. Bates also works as a research scientist in the Artificial Intelligence Laboratory at MIT.

LOUIS BEC
geboren 1936, lebt und arbeitet in Sorgues, Frankreich. Bec ist Zoosystematiker und untersucht die Verhältnisse zwischen Kunst, Wissenschaft und Technik. 1970 gründete er das Institut Scientifique de Recherche Paranaturaliste, das sich mit der Unfähigkeit des Lebendigen, das Lebendige zu erfassen, befaßt. 1986 erhielt er ein Forschungsstipendium des Kulturministeriums zur Untersuchung der Zusammenhänge zwischen den Wissenschaften vom Leben (Zoologie, Biologie, Genetik, etc.), jenen des Künstlichen (Bio-Informatik, Systematik etc.) und der darstellenden Kunst. Gegenwärtig arbeitet er an einer Reihe von Projekten über tierisches Verhalten. Zahlreiche Ausstellungen in Frankreich sowie in Sao Paulo, Hannover, Wien, Zürich, Paris etc. Teilnehmer an Seminaren in Europa, Brasilien und den USA.

---

born in 1936. He lives and works in Sorgues, France. Louis Bec is a zoo-systematist who studies the relations between art, science and technology. In 1970 he founded the Institut Scientifique de Recherche Paranaturaliste where he explores the inability of living beings to grasp life. In 1986 he was granted a scholarship by the Ministry of Culture to study the relations between the sciences of life (zoology, biology, genetics, etc.), the sciences of the artificial (bio-informatics, systematics, etc.) and the interpretative arts. At present he is working on a series of projects about animal behaviour. Louis Bec participated in numerous exhibitions in France, in Sao Paulo, Hannover, Zurich, Vienna, Paris, etc., and in several congresses in Europe, Brazil, and the USA.

KONRAD BECKER
leitet das Institut für wissenschaftliche Sensation. Seit 1979 Veröffentlichung von interdisziplinären Medienprogrammen: Videos, Schallplatten, Texte, Installationen, Inszenierungen und Events. Ausstellungen und Konzerte im Bereich mathematische Elektronik, Kultursynthese und „subjektive Wissenschaft".

---

heads the Institute for Scientific Sensation. Since 1979 he has published interdisciplinary media programmes: video films, records, texts, installations, stagings and events. Exhibitions and concerts in the field of mathematical electronics, culture synthesis and "subjective science".

TASSILO BLITTERSDORFF
geboren 1946 in Bad Ischl, studierte an den Universitäten Wien und Salzburg und an der Kunstakade-

mie in Rom, seither Einzel- und Gruppenausstellungen im In- und Ausland, darunter in der Galleria d'arte visive in Rom, in der Secession in Wien, Ludwig's Drum Factory, Chicago, Galerie Zacheta in Warschau, Unwahr-Galerie Berlin, der Q.Q.-Galerie Krakau sowie im Francisco-Carolinum Linz und in der Minoritenkirche Krems-Stein.

---

was born in 1946 in Bad Ischl, Austria; he studied at the Vienna and Salzburg Universities and at the Art Academy in Rome. Since then, his works have been shown in numerous solo and group exhibitions in Austria and abroad, e.g. at the Galleria d'arte visive in Rome, Secession in Vienna, Ludwig's Drum Factory, Chicago, Warsaw Zacheta Gallery, Berlin Unwahr-Galerie, Krakow Q.Q. Gallery, at the Linz Francisco-Carolinum and at the Minoritenkirche church of Krems-Stein, Austria.

PETER BÖHM

geboren 1961 in Prag. Er studierte in Prag und Wien Violine, Arrangement und Jazztheorie, Elektroakustik und Experimentalmusik. Gründungsmitglied der Violent Violins. Tonregie bei zahlreichen Werken von Beat Furrer (darunter „Foce de la Chaleur", dirigiert von Claudio Abbado) und Mauricio Sotelo (z.B. „Due Voci...", „Nel suono indicible", „Non gridate piu"). Musik für mehrere Videofilme von Gertrude Moser-Wagner, Matta Wagnest u.a. Elektronische Realisation der Komposition „Unruhiges Wohnen" von Roman Haubenstock-Ramati und Elfriede Jelinek. Aufnahmeleitung und Klangregie der Oper „Amerika" von Haubenstock-Ramati. Gründung des „Musiklabor Wien".

---

was born in Prague in 1961. He studied violin, arrangement and theory of jazz, electroacoustics and experimental music. Founding member of Violent Violins. Sound engineering for numerous performances of works by Beat Furrer (such as "Foce de la Chaleur", directed by Claudio Abbado) and Mauricio Sotelo (e.g. "Due Voci...", "Nel suono indicible", "Non gridate piu"). Music for various video films by Gertrude Moser-Wagner and Matta Wagnest, among others. Electronic realization of the composition "Unruhiges Wohnen" by Roman Haubenstock-Ramati and Elfriede Jelinek. Recording and sound engineering of the opera "Amerika" by Haubenstock-Ramati. Founder of "Musiklabor Wien".

RODNEY BROOKS

ist seit 1984 am Massachusetts Institute of Technology im Bereich Elektrotechnik und Informatik sowie im Labor für künstliche Intelligenz tätig. Zuvor arbeitete er an der Stanford University und als wissenschaftlicher Forscher am M.I.T. sowie an der Carnegie Mellon University. Seine Forschung befaßt sich unter anderem mit Robotertechnologie und künstlicher Intelligenz. Brooks ist Mitbegründer der Firma Lucid (Menlo Park, Kalifornien) sowie Mitbegründer und Leiter der Firma IS Robotics (Somerville, Massachusetts). Von 1986 bis 1991 war er Mitherausgeber des International Journal of Computer Vision. Er ist Gründungsmitglied der American Association for Artificial Intelligence. Im 1991 gewann er den Computers and Thought Prize, der von der International Joint Conference on Artificial Intelligence vergeben wird.

---

joined the Massachusetts Institute of Technology as a faculty member in Electrical Engineering and Computer Science and at the Artificial Intelligence Laboratory in 1984. He had previously worked at Stanford University and as a research scientist at both M.I.T. and Carnegie Mellon University. His research deals with robot technologies and artificial intelligence, among other fields. Dr. Brooks is co-founder of Lucid, Inc. of Menlo Park, California, co-founder and chairman of IS Robotics, Inc., of Somerville, Massachusetts. He was co-editor of the International Journal of Computer Vision from 1986 to 1991. He is a Founding Fellow of the American Association for Artificial Intelligence. In 1991 he was co-winner of the Computers and Thought Prize awarded by the trustees of the International Joint Conference on Artificial Intelligence.

CHRISTIAN BRÜNNER

geboren 1942 in Mürzzuschlag. Christian Brünner ist Universitätsprofessor für Öffentliches Recht in Graz. 1959/60 Stipendium des American Field Service, Minneapolis (Minnesota/USA). 1985–1989 Rektor der Karl-Franzens-Universität Graz. 1987–1989 Vorsitzender der Österreichischen Rektorenkonferenz. Seit 1990 Abgeordneter zum Nationalrat, Wissenschaftssprecher der ÖVP, seit 1992 Betreuer für den Bereich Minderheiten. Forschungsschwerpunkte: Hochschul- und Schulrecht bzw. Hochschulpolitik, Hochschulmanagement, politische Planung, Interessensverbände, Verwaltungslehre, Finanzkontrolle, Parlament.

---

born in 1942 in Mürzzuschlag, Austria. Christian Brünner is a professor of public law at the University of Graz. 1959/60 he was awarded a grant by the American Field Service, Minneapolis, Minnesota. 1985–1989 he held the position of Dean of the Karl-Franzens-Universität, Graz. 1987–1989 he presided the Austrian Deans' Conference. Since 1990 he has been a member of parliament for the conservative Austrian People's Party, speaker for higher education, since 1992 he has specialized in the counseling of minorities. His fields of research are: school and university law and politics, university management, policy planning, interest groups, public administration, financial planning, and the parliament.

JOHN L. CASTI

geboren 1943 in Portland, Oregon (USA). Nach Abschluß seines Doktorats aus Mathematik an der University of Southern California 1970, verließ John Casti 1974 die USA, um am Internationalen Institut für Angewandte Systemanalyse (IIASA) in Wien eine der ersten Forschungsstellen anzunehmen. Mit kurzen Unterbrechungen in den späten siebziger und frühen achtziger Jahren, die er als Professor an der New York University und in Princeton verbrachte, arbeitete er bis zum Herbst 1986 am IIASA zu Problemen der Systemmodellierung und der Angewandten Systemanalyse. Anschließend wurde er als Professor an das Institut für Ökonometrie, Operations Research und Systemtheorie der Technischen Universität Wien berufen. Weiters ist John Casti Mitglied des Santa Fe Institute in Santa Fe, New Mexico (USA), wo er sich mit der Anwendung biologischer Metaphern auf mathematische Modelle für Wirtschafts- und Verkehrsfragen beschäftigt. John Casti hat zahlreiche Fachbücher, aber auch populärwissenschaftliche Werke veröffentlicht: „Alternate Realities: Mathematical Models of Nature and Man“, Wiley 1989; „Paradigms Lost: Images of Man in the Mirror of Science“, Morrow 1989 (Verlust der Wahrheit, 1990) und „Searching for Certainty: What Scientists Can Know About the Future“, Morrow 1991 (Szenarien der Zukunft, 1992), das sich mit dem Problem wissenschaftlicher Voraussagen und der Erklärung von Alltagsphänomenen beschäftigt. Sein nächstes Buch, „Uncommon Sense“, ist eine Studie über komplexe Systeme, die überraschendes Verhalten auslösen können, und wird im Jänner 1994 bei Harper Collins, New York erscheinen.

---

born in 1943 in Portland, Oregon. John Casti received his Ph. D. in mathematics at the University of Southern California in 1970. In 1974 he left the USA for Vienna, Austria, where he became one of the first members of the research staff at the International Institute for Applied Systems Analysis (IIASA). With short breaks in the late seventies and early eighties, during which time he served on the faculties of NYU and Princeton, he stayed with IIASA, investigating problems of systems modeling and applied systems analysis, until late 1986, when he took up his current post as a Professor of Operations Research and Systems Theory at the Technical University of Vienna. He is also a resident member of the Santa Fe Institute in Santa Fe, New Mexico, where he is working on the application of biological metaphors to the mathematical modeling of economic and road-traffic questions. His numerous publications include technical monographs and textbooks as well as popular books on science: "Alternate Realities: Mathematical Models of Nature and Man", Wiley 1989; "Paradigms Lost: Images of Man in the Mirror of Science", Morrow 1989, and "Searching for Certainty: What Scientists Can Know About the Future", Morrow 1991, a volume dealing with problems of scientific prediction and explanation of everyday events. His next book, "Uncommon Sense", is a study of complex systems and the manner in which they give rise to surprising behavior. It will be published by Harper Collins, New York, in January 1994.

NICHOLAS COLLINS

geboren 1954 in New York City. Seit den frühen siebziger Jahren komponiert Nicholas Collins und gibt Konzerte. Er studierte an der Wesleyan University Komposition bei Alvin Lucier. Er steht einerseits in der Tradition „hausgemachter“ elektronischer Schaltkreise und gilt andererseits als Pionier in der Verwendung von Mikrocomputern bei Konzerten. Ebenso setzt er das Radio, akustische Materialien und veränderte Musikinstrumente ein. Zahlreiche Ausstellungen und Konzerte in den USA und in Europa als Solokünstler, als Mitglied von David Tudors „Composers Inside Electronics“, mit eigenen Ensembles, und gemeinsam mit Tom Cora, The Downtown Ensemble, Shelley Hirsch, Impossible Music, Elliott Sharp, the Soldier String Quartet, John Zorn u.v.a.

---

born in 1954 in New York City. Nicholas Collins has been composing and performing since the early 70s. He studied composition with Alvin Lucier at Wesleyan University. An heir to the tradition of "home-made" electronic circuitry, and a pioneer in the use of microcomputers in live performance, he also makes extensive use of radio, found sound material, and transformed musical instruments. He has performed and exhibited throughout the United States and Europe as a solo artist, as a member of David Tudor's "Composers Inside Electronics", with his own ensembles, and in collaboration with Tom Cora, The Downtown Ensemble, Shelley Hirsch, Impossible Music, Elliott Sharp, the Soldier String Quartet, John Zorn, and many others.

STANISLAV DIVIS

geboren 1953 in Kutná Hora bei Prag. Stanislav Divis studierte an der Prager Akademie der Bildenden Künste. Einzelausstellungen in Ungarn, Deutschland und der ehemaligen Tschechoslowakei. Gruppenausstellungen in vielen europäischen Ländern sowie in Los Angeles (USA) und Südkorea. 1992 Teilnahme an den Kunstmessen in Köln und Frankfurt.

---

born in 1953 in Kutná Hora near Prague. Stanislav Divis studied at the Academy of Fine Arts in Prague. Solo exhibitions in Hungary, Germany and former Czechoslovakia. Collective exhibitions in many European countries as well as in Los Angeles, USA, and South Korea. In 1992 he took part in the Art Fairs at Frankfurt and Cologne, Germany.

JOHANNES DOMSICH

geboren 1960. Johannes Domsich ist Graphiker und Designer. Assistent und Lektor am Institut für Publizistik und Kommunikationswissenschaften der Universität Wien, Fachbereiche Medientheorie, Medienästhetik, Semiotik, Bildkommunikation und Werbung. Lehrauftrag für Ästhetik und Kulturgeschichte sowie für Architektur und Bühnenbild an der Hochschule für Darstellende Kunst. Künstlerische Beratung und Kostümbild (Dramaturgie) für Opernhäuser in Wien, Düsseldorf, Duisburg, Dresden, Zürich, Basel sowie in Arnheim. Buchpublikation „Visualisierung – Ein kulturelles Defizit? Der Konflikt von Sprache, Schrift und Bild" (Böhlauverlag Wien, 1991) sowie diverse Publikationen in den Bereichen Medientheorie, Ästhetik, Kommunikationswissenschaft, Bildsemiotik, Kulturgeschichte und Computertechnik.

---

born in 1960. Johannes Domsich works as a graphic artist and designer. He is assistant and lecturer at the journalism and communication science department of the University of Vienna (special fields: media theory, media aesthetics, semiotics audio-visual communication and advertising). Besides, he teaches aesthetics and cultural history, architecture and stage design at the University of Fine Arts. He has worked as an artistic adviser and costume designer (dramatic adviser) at opera houses in Vienna, Dusseldorf, Duisburg, Dresden, Zurich, Basel and in Arnhem. He is the author of the book "Visualisierung – Ein kulturelles Defizit? Der Konflikt von Sprache, Schrift und Bild" (published by Böhlauverlag, Vienna 1991) and of various publications about communication science, visual semiotics, cultural history and computer technology.

BARTZ EDEK

geboren 1946 in Karaganda, Kasachstan. Mit Joachim Lieben Konzeption des Programms der Reihe "Stimmen der Welt". Inszenierung und bühnentechnische Detailplanung der Tourneen Frank Zappas, der Rolling Stones und der Queen. Regie und Logistik bei einer Reihe von Open Air-Festivals in Europa, Japan und den USA. Programmgestaltung verschiedener Jazz-Festivals in Österreich. Ab 1977 regelmäßige Arbeit für die Wiener Festwochen. Begründung der im Zweijahresrhythmus abgehaltenen "Musikausstellung" Töne-Gegentöne (gemeinsam mit Wolfgang Kos). 1992 Documenta 9 Kassel, Jazzfestival; 1993 Welttöne Indien contemporary, Wien.

---

born in Karaganda, Kazakhstan in 1946. Conception of the programme of the "Stimmen der Welt" series, in cooperation with Joachim Lieben. Staging and scenic planning of the tours of Frank Zappa, the Rolling Stones and the Queen. Direction and logistics of several open air festivals in Europe, Japan and the USA. Programme conception of various jazz festivals in Austria. From 1977 on he has regularly worked for the Festival of Vienna. Founder of the "musical exhibition" Töne-Gegentöne (in cooperation with Wolfgang Kos), which takes place every two years. 1992 Documenta 9 in Kassel, jazz festival; 1993 Welttöne Indien contemporary, Vienna.

GERHARD ERTL

geboren 1959, Studium der visuellen Gestaltung an der Kunsthochschule Linz. Mitglied der Austria Filmmakers Cooperative. Seit 1987 Zusammenarbeit mit Sabine Hiebler. Filmvorführungen u.a. bei Filmfestivals in New York, Berlin, San Francisco, London, Philadelphia, Melbourne, Madrid und Wien.

---

was born in 1959. He studied visual design at the Art College in Linz. Member of the Austria Filmmakers Cooperative. Since 1987 he has been cooperating with Sabine Hiebler. Their films were shown at film festivals in New York, Berlin, San Francisco, London, Philadelphia, Melbourne, Madrid and Vienna.

VALIE EXPORT

geboren in Linz, Kunstgewerbeschule Linz, HTL Wien, lebt heute in Berlin und den USA. Ihre Arbeit umfaßt unter anderem verschiedene Filmgattungen, Videotapes, Videoinstallationen, Performances, Skulpturen, Computerarbeiten und Publikationen zur zeitgenössischen Kunstgeschichte. Seit 1968 Teilnahme an internationalen Kunstausstellungen in Paris (Centre Georges Pompidou), Kassel (Documenta), New York (Museum of Modern Art), Venedig (Biennale), Frankfurt, Lausanne, Köln, München, Wien, London, etc. Teilnahme an internationalen Filmfestspielen in London, Los Angeles, Berlin, Cannes, Montreal, Vancouver, Locarno, etc. Ihre Filme wurden weiters von zahlreichen Fernsehanstalten ausgestrahlt. 1980 offizielle Vertreterin Österreichs bei der Biennale Venedig.

---

was born in Linz, attended the Arts and Crafts School in Linz and a technical college in Vienna. She lives in Berlin and in the USA. Her work comprises, among others, various forms of films, video tapes, video installations, performances, sculpture, computer works and publications about contemporary art history. Since 1968 she has participated in international art exhibitions in Paris (Centre Georges Pompidou), Kassel (Documenta) New York (Museum of Modern Art), Venice (Biennale), Frankfurt, Lausanne, Cologne, Munich, Vienna, London, etc., and in international film festivals in London, Los Angeles, Berlin, Cannes, Montreal, Vancouver, Locarno, etc. Besides, her films were shown by many TV companies. In 1980, Valie Export was the official representative of Austria at the Venice Biennale.

THOMAS FEUERSTEIN

geboren 1968. Studium der Kunstgeschichte und Philosophie. Thomas Feuerstein lebt in Innsbruck.

---

born in 1968. Studies of Art History and Philosophy. Thomas Feuerstein lives in Innsbruck, Austria.

FRIEDRICH FÖRSTER

geboren 1952. Friedrich Försters gleichermaßen vorhandenes Interesse an Naturwissenschaften und Kunst ist die Basis seiner Arbeit. Seit Anfang der 70er Jahre befaßt er sich insbesondere mit der künstlerischen Umsetzung der physikalischen Eigenschaften von Laserlicht. Naturwissenschaftliches Studium in Tübingen, Ende der 80er Jahre am Göttinger Max Planck Institut für biophysikalische Chemie im Bereich molekularer Neurobiologie. Publikationen und Vorträge im Bereich der Neurobiologie und Psychophysik. Veranstaltungen und intermediale Installationen u.a. für Philip Morris, IBM, SEL. Künstlerische Zusammenarbeit u.a. mit Yuri Smirnov, Dizzi Krisch, Nederlands Dans Theater, Paul Zorn und Robert Spour. Friedrich Förster entwickelt zur Zeit in Zusammenarbeit mit dem Physiker Kurt Walz interaktive Soft- und Hardware für die Steuerung von Licht und Laser.

---

born in 1952. The fact that Friedrich Förster is equally interested in science and art is fundamental for his work. Since the early seventies he has been especially involved in the artistic application of the physical properties of laser light. He followed scientific studies in Tübingen, in the late eighties he studied molecular neural biology at the Institute for Biophysical Chemistry of the Max Planck Institute in Göttingen. Lectures and publications in the fields of neural biology and psychophysics. Exhibitions and intermedial installations for Philip Morris, IBM, SEL, and others. Artistic collaboration with Yuri Smirnov, Dizzi Krisch, Nederlands Dans Theater, Paul Zorn, Robert Spour, and others. At present Friedrich Förster is collaborating with the physicist Kurt Walz on the development of interactive software and hardware for light and laser control systems.

ULRIKE GABRIEL

geboren 1964, lebt und arbeitet in Offenbach. Ulrike Gabriel studierte zunächst Philosophie in München, anschließend an der Akademie der Bildenden Künste in München. 1991 erhielt sie ein Arbeitsstipendium der DASA für das Helicopterlab MBB Ottobrunn. Seit 1992 ist sie an der Städelschule in Frankfurt am Institut für Neue Medien. Gründungsmitglied von OTHERSPACE (1993). Ausstellungen in Sydney (TISEA), La Coruña, Spanien (Vertigo Virtual), Madrid (Virtual2), Frankfurt (Eigenwelt der Apparatewelt) und Tokio (ARTLABS, Canon Artlab).

---

born in 1964. Ulrike Gabriel lives and works in Offenbach, Germany. She studied philosophy in Munich, then at the Munich Academy of Fine Arts. She was granted a scholarship by DASA, for Helicopterlab MBB Ottobrunn. Since 1992 she has been at the Frankfurt-on-Maine Städelschule (Institut für Neue Medien). She is a founder member of OTHERSPACE (1993). Exhibitions in Sydney (TISEA), La Coruña, Spain (Vertigo Virtual), Madrid (Virtual2), Frankfurt (Eigenwelt der Apparatewelt) and Tokyo (ARTLABS, Canon Artlab).

THOMAS GRÜNFELD

geboren 1956 in Opladen (Deutschland). Thomas Grünfeld lebt in Köln: diverse Einzel- und Gruppenausstellungen in Europa und den USA; 1990 Biennale Venedig.

---

born in 1956 in Opladen, Germany. Thomas Grünfeld lives in Cologne; various solo and group exhibitions in Europe as well as in the USA; 1990 Venice Biennale.

DAIZABURO HARADA

geboren 1956 in Fukuoka, Japan. Studierte Kunst und Design an der Tsukuba-Universität (Studien-schwerpunkt Plastische Kunst und Medien). Der Computergraphikkünstler ist Gründer und Leiter von „Digital Effects Laboratory". Er organisierte die Videoperformance „RADICAL TV" und führte mit Ryuichi Sakamoto „TV WAR" auf. Sein Werk umfaßt unter anderem die Computergraphik im Film „NO LIFE KING" (mit Jun Ichikawa als Regisseur) und Hi-Vision-Regiearbeiten. Derzeit beschäftigt er sich mit der Fernseh-Computergraphik für „The Human BRAIN & MIND".

---

born in 1956 in Fukuoka, Japan. He studied art and design at Tsukuba University (including special studies of plastic arts and mixed media). He is a computer graphics artist and established the Digital Effects Laboratory, which he heads. Besides organizing the "RADICAL TV" performance video unit and performing "TV-WAR" with Ryuichi Sakamoto, he produced, among others, computer graphics for the film "NO LIFE KING" directed by Jun Ichikawa, and directed Hi-Vision work. At present, he is producing the TV computer graphics of "The Human BRAIN & MIND".

ROSS HARLEY

geboren 1961, lebt und arbeitet in Sydney, Australien. Harley ist Videokünstler, Schriftsteller, Journalist und Kommentator der Pop-Kultur; er arbeitet mit den verschiedensten Medien. Seit Mitte der achtziger Jahre Ausstellungen mit Einkanalvideos und Installationsprojekten in Australien und im Ausland. Er war Herausgeber der Zeitschrift Art + Text und Leiter des dritten internationalen Symposiums über Elektronikkunst, das 1992 in Sydney stattfand. Derzeit unterrichtet er das Fach Video und Film an der Universität New South Wales und schreibt an seiner Dissertation zum Thema „Electro Attractions: A Critical History of Amusement from Roller Coasters to Virtual Reality".

---

was born in 1961, he lives and works in Sydney. Ross Harley is a video-artist, writer, editor and pop culture commentator who works across a variety of media. Since the mid 1980s he has been exhibiting single channel videos and installation projects in Australia and abroad. He is a former Editor of the critical journal Art + Text and was Director of the Third International Symposium on Electronic Art held in Sydney, 1992. He presently teaches video and film studies at the University of New South Wales, and is completing a thesis entitled "Electro Attractions: A Critical History of Amusements from Roller Coasters to Virtual Reality".

JOCHEM HENDRICKS

geboren 1959, lebt in Frankfurt/M. Stipendien des Frankfurter Vereins für Künstlerhilfe, Zeichenstipendium Nürnberg, 1993 erhielt er den VILLA ROMANA-Preis Köln. Einzel- und Gruppenausstellungen in Deutschland und den Niederlanden, zuletzt in der Galerie ak in Frankfurt/M. („Viren", mit Udo Koch) und im Kunstverein Frankfurt.

---

born in 1959. Jochem Hendricks lives in Frankfurt-on-Maine. He was granted a scholarship by the Frankfurt Verein für Künstlerhilfe and a drawing scholarship (Nuremberg). In 1993 he received the Cologne VILLA ROMANA prize. Various solo and group exhibitions in Germany and in the Netherlands, the most recent ones being "Viren" at Galerie ak, Frankfurt-on-Maine (with Udo Koch) and at Kunstverein Frankfurt.

SABINE HIEBLER

geboren 1963, Studium der Keramik an der Kunsthochschule Linz. Mitglied der Austria Filmmakers Cooperative. Seit 1987 Zusammenarbeit mit Gerhard Ertl. Filmvorführungen u.a. bei Filmfestivals in New York, Berlin, San Francisco, London, Philadelphia, Melbourne, Madrid und Wien.

---

was born in 1963. She studied ceramics at the Art College in Linz. Member of the Austrian Filmmakers Cooperative. Since 1987 she has been cooperating with Gerhard Ertl. Their films were shown at film festivals in New York, Berlin, San Francisco, London, Philadelphia, Melbourne, Madrid and Vienna.

WOLFGANG HILBERT

geboren 1969 in Korneuburg, Niederösterreich. Lehranstalt für elektronische Datenverarbeitung und Organisation, dann drei Jahre Studium der Betriebswirtschaftslehre in Wien. Derzeit studiert er visuelle Mediengestaltung an der Hochschule für angewandte Kunst. Ausstellung „Artware" anläßlich der IFABO 1993.

---

was born in 1969 in Korneuburg, Austria. College of Electronic Data Processing and Organization, then he studied economics for three years. Now he is studying visual media design at the University of Applied Arts in Vienna. Exhibition "Artware" (IFABO fair 1993)

MARGARETE JAHRMAN

geboren 1967 in Ostösterreich, Studium an der Hochschule für angewandte Kunst Wien, Gerrit-Rietveld Akademie Amsterdam. Seit 1989 Ausstellungen und Medienprojekte im In- und Ausland, darunter Produktionen in Italien und den Niederlanden, Marlboro, Steirischer Herbst 92, Rabotnik TV. Installationen und Events im öffentlichen Raum, vor allem unter dem Label R.A.M.S., u.a. für „museum in progress", Museum für angewandte Kunst, Akademie der Bildenden Künste Wien. Seit 1992 Publikationen und Factfinding-Aufenthalte zur Erforschung internationaler Medienstrukturen in Zusammenarbeit mit K4.

---

born in 1967 in Austria, studied at the University of Fine Arts in Vienna and at the Gerrit-Rietveld Academy in Amsterdam. Since 1989 various exhibitions and media projects in Austria and abroad, e.g. in Italy and in the Netherlands, Marlboro, Steirischer Herbst Graz 1992, Rabotnik TV. Public installations and events, mostly under the label R.A.M.S., e.g. for "museum in progress", Museum of Applied Arts, Academy of Fine Arts in Vienna. Since 1992 publications and factfinding travels to study international media structures in cooperation with K4.

RAINER JESSL

geboren 1961 in Linz. 1981–91 Licht- und Bühnengestaltung für Spielstatt und Theater Phönix, Linz. 1991 Co-Autor und Akteur bei „Der kranke Raum", Theater Phönix (Ars Electronica '91). 1992 Lichtgestaltung „Immateriaux" Obermaier/Spour (Ars Electronica '92), Lichtgestaltung „Austrian Sounds Cape", Offenes Kulturhaus Linz, Lichtgestaltung „4 Tage Absolute Musik", Offenes Kulturhaus Linz.

---

born in 1961 in Linz. 1981–91 lighting and stage design for productions of "Spielstatt" and ...Theater Phönix" in Linz. 1991 co-author and performer in "Der kranke Raum" by "Theater Phönix" (Ars Electronica '91). 1992 lighting for "Immateriaux", for the "Austrian Sounds Cape", Offenes Kulturhaus, Linz, and for "4 Days of Absolute Music", Offenes Kulturhaus, Linz.

TOM JOHNSON

geboren 1939 in Colorado. Tom Johnson studierte Musik an der Universität Yale und nahm Privatstunden in Komposition bei Morton Feldman. Bei seinen Kompositionen geht er logischer vor als andere amerikanischen Minimalisten, indem er häufig Formeln, Permutationen und vorhersehbare Sequenzen verwendet. Am bekanntesten sind wohl Tom Johnsons Opern, besonders die „Vierton-Oper" (1972), die über 60mal und in 10 verschiedenen Sprachen aufgeführt wurde, sowie die „Riemannoper". Unter seinen übrigen Werken sind die Solo-Performance „Nine Bells", das häufig gespielte „Mißerfolg – Ein sehr schwieriges Stück für Kontrabaß", und Theaterstücke wie „Selbstporträt" und „Scene for Piano and Tape", sowie speziell für den Rundfunk geschriebene und komponierte Werke hervorzuheben. 1991 stellte er seine beiden umfangreichsten Werke fertig: das „Bonhoeffer Oratorium" mit Texten des Theologen Dietrich Bonhoeffer, und „Una Opera Italiana". Eine umfassende Sammlung seiner Artikel als Musikkritiker der New Yorker Stadtzeitung „Village Voice" kam 1989 bei Apollonius in Eindhoven unter dem Titel „The Voice of New Music" heraus.

---

born in 1939 in Colorado, Tom Johnson studied music at Yale University and composition privately with Morton Feldman. In his compositions he proceeds in a more logical way than other American minimalists, often using formulas, permutations, and predictable sequences. Tom Johnson is perhaps best known for his operas, particularly "The Four Note Opera" (1972), which has been produced over 60 times, in 10 different languages, and "Riemannoper" (1988). Non-operatic works include his solo performance "Nine Bells", the often-played "Failing: A very Difficult Piece for Solo String Bass", and theatrical pieces such as "Self-Portrait" and the "Scene for Piano and Tape", as well as a number of works composed/written specifically for radio. In 1991 he completed his two largest works ever, the "Bonhoeffer Oratorio", with texts of the theologian Dietrich Bonhoeffer, and "Una Opera Italiana". A large collection of the articles he wrote as a music critic for the "Village Voice" was published in 1989 by Apollonius in Eindhoven, Holland, under the title "The Voice of New Music".

KEN KARAKOTSIOS

ist Principle Software Engineer bei der Computerspiele-Herstellerfirma Maxis. Er schrieb die Programme CASim und SimLife und ist Co-Autor des Buchs "SimLife: The Artificial Life Experimenter's Handbook". Zuvor war er im Hardware-Bereich tätig, unter anderem vier Jahre bei Apple Computer, wo er an der Entwicklung der Macintosh Quadra-Computer arbeitete. Karakotsios lebt mit seiner Frau, seiner Katze und drei Computern in Kalifornien. Eines seiner Hobbys ist neben Joggen und Radfahren das Bauen von LEGO-Robotern zum Katzenfangen.

---

is Principle Software Engineer at the software toy company Maxis. He has written the programmes CASim and SimLife, and co-authored the book "SimLife: The Artificial Life Experimenter's Handbook". Before turning to software he designed hardware. Among other places of employ, he spent four years at Apple Computer designing the Macintosh Quadra family of computers. Ken Karakotsios lives in California with his wife, his cat and three computers. His hobbies include running, bicycling and trying to build cat-chasing roboters out of LEGO bricks.

KEVIN KELLY

war von 1984 bis 1990 Herausgeber der Whole Earth Review (Magazin für unorthodoxe technische Neuigkeiten). Er war Mitbegründer der Hackers' Conference, einem jährlichen Treffen jugendlicher Computerfreaks und Hacker. 1988 veröffentlichte er „Signal", das erste Buch über Cyberpunk-Kultur. Derzeit gibt er die Zeitschrift „Wired" heraus, ein Magazin über neue digitale Kultur in San Francisco. Er beendet gerade sein Buch über künstliches Leben, genetische Kunst und wie Maschinen zu biologischen Wesen werden können. „Out of Control, the Rise of Artificial Evolution", so der Titel, wird 1994 von Addison Wesley herausgegeben.

---

edited the Whole Earth Review (a quarterly journal of unorthodox technical news) between 1984 and 1990. He co-founded the Hacker's Conference, a yearly gathering of maverick computer programmers, young code dudes and teenage crackers. In 1988 he published "Signal", the first sourcebook for cyberpunk culture. He is currently executive editor of "Wired", a new digital culture monthly magazine based in San Francisco. He is completing a book about artificial life, genetic art, and how machines are becoming biological. The book, "Out of Control, the Rise of Artificial Evolution" will be published by Addison Wesley in 1994.

KNOWBOTIC RESEARCH

kr+cf benutzt Informationssysteme, Kommunikationsnetze, Wissensspeicher und Archive, um sie zerteilt und analysiert wieder als solche neu zusammenzusetzen: Sprachprogramm (1991), ping Operation pong mit Friedrich Kittler (1992), Archive (1992), hypervirus (1992). Die Mitarbeiter am smdk-Projekt (Simulationsraum-Mosaik mobile Datenklänge) sind neben Christian Hübler (Medienkünstler, Gesamtkonzeption), Alexander Tuchacek (Computermusiker, Echtzeitkomposition) und Yvonne Wilhelm (Medienkünstlerin, Visualisierung) die Informatiker Georg Fleischmann, Detlev Schwabe, Michael Hoch, Will Bauer und Tobias Pfeil sowie Rajele Jain.

---

kr+cf uses information systems, communication networks, stores of knowledge and archives to dissect and analyze them before reassembling them again: Sprachprogramm (1991), ping Operation pong, in cooperation with Friedrich Kittler (1992), Archive (1992), hypervirus (1992). The smdk project (simulation space mosaic mobile data sounds project) was executed by Christian Hübler (media artist, general conception), Alexander Tuchacek (computer musician, real-time composition) and Yvonne Wilhelm (media artist, visualization), the computer scientists Georg Fleischmann, Detlev Schwabe, Michael Hoch, Will Bauer and Tobias Pfeil, and Rajele Jain.

PETER KOGLER

geboren 1959 in Innsbruck, lebt in Wien. Ausstellungen: 1986 Biennale Venedig („Aperto 86"), Frankfurter Kunstverein („Prospekt"), 1989 Museum van Hedendaagse Kunst Gent („Open Mind"),1992 Documenta Kassel, 1993 Galerie Krinzinger Wien („Excess in the Techno Mediacratic Society"), Centre Georges Pompidou Paris/Museum in Progress, u.a.

---

born in Innsbruck, Austria, in 1959, he lives in Vienna. Exhibitions: 1986 Biennale in Venice, Italy ("Aperto 86"), Frankfurter Kunstverein ("Prospekt"), 1989 Museum van Hedendaagse Kunst Gent, Belgium ("Open Mind"), 1992 Documenta Kassel, Germany, 1993 Galerie Krinzinger, Vienna (Excess in the Techno Mediacratic Society"), Centre Georges Pompidou, Paris/Museum in progress, and others.

KRAFTWERK

Discographie: 1974 Autobahn, 1975 Radio Aktivität, 1977 Trans Europa Express, 1978 Die Mensch Maschine, 1981 Computerwelt, 1986 Electric Cafe, 1991 The Mix – alle erschienen bei Kling Klang (EMI).

Discography: 1974 Autobahn (highway), 1975 Radio Aktivität (radio activity), 1977 Trans Europa Express (Trans Europe Express), 1978 Die Mensch Maschine (the human machine), 1981 Computerwelt (computer world), 1986 Electric Cafe, 1991 The Mix – all recordings on Kling Klang (EMI).

DAVID KREMERS

geboren 1960 in Denver, Colorado, USA. David Kremers studierte an der Pepperdine University. Diverse Einzel- und Gruppenausstellungen in den USA, Brüssel, Köln und Linz, er lebt und arbeitet in Malibu (Kalifornien).

---

was born in Denver, Colorado, in 1960. He studied at Pepperdine University. Numerous solo and group exhibitions in the USA, Belgium, Germany and Austria. David Kremers lives and works in Malibu, California.

CHRISTOPHER G. LANGTON
ist Wissenschafter in der Complex Systems Group der Theoretischen Abteilung des Los Alamos National Laboratory. Er ist auch an der Fakultät des Santa Fe Institute, wo er Leiter des Artificial Life Programmes ist. Seine Abschlüsse machte er in Anthropologie und Philosophie an der Universität von Arizona, und der erhielt einen PhD in Computerwissenschaften an der Universität von Michigan, wo er bei den Artificial-Life-Pionieren Arthur Burks und John Holland studierte. Chris Langton organisierte 1987 die erste internationale Konferenz über Artificial Life in Los Alamos, und hat seither zwei weitere AL Konferenzen veranstaltet. Er hat drei Folge-Bände über Artificial Life herausgegeben und ist Herausgeber der neuen Vierteljahres-Zeitschrift „Artificial Life". Seine Forschungsschwerpunkte liegen in den Bereichen des Rechnens, den Ausmaßen von Komplexität, der rechnerischen Biologie, dem kollektivem Verhalten, dem Ursprung des Lebens und der Evolution.

---

is a scientist in the Complex Systems Group of the Theoretical Division of Los Alamos National Laboratory. He is also on the faculty of the Santa Fe Institute, where he is director of the Artificial Life program. His undergraduate degrees are in Anthropology an Philosophy from the University of Arizona, and he holds a PhD in Computer Science from the University of Michigan, where he studied with Artificial Life pioneers Arthur Burks and John Holland. Christopher Langton organized the first international conference on Artificial Life at Los Alamos in 1987, and has since organized two more AL conferences. he has edited three proceeding volumes on Artificial Life, and is the editor of the new quarterly journal "Artificial Life". His research interests lie in the physics of computation, measures of complexity, computational biology, collective behavior, the origin of life, and evolution.

LEOPOLD LARCHER
geboren 1970 in Innsbruck. Absolvent des Bundesrealgymnasiums für Bildnerisches Gestalten in Klagenfurt. Studiert an der Hochschule für angewandte Kunst in Wien, Meisterklasse für visuelle Mediengestaltung (unter anderem bei Peter Weibel, Rebecca Allen, Valie Export, Henry Jesionka, Steina Vasulka,etc.). Diverse Einzel- und Gruppenausstellungen in Österreich mit Video und Computer.

---

was born in Innsbruck in 1970. He attended the plastic design high school at Klagenfurt. Now he is a student of visual media design (with Peter Weibel, Rebecca Allen, Valie Export, Henry Jesionka, Steina Vasulka, etc.) at the University of Applied Arts in Vienna. Various solo and group exhibitions with video and computers in Austria.

BERNHARD LEITNER
studierte von 1956 bis 1963 Architektur an der Technischen Hochschule in Wien, arbeitete im Stadtplanungsamt der Stadt New York und lehrte Urban Design Studies an der New York University. Zahlreiche Ausstellungen in Deutschland (u.a. bei der Documenta in Kassel), den USA, Frankreich und Österreich (z.B. Ars electronica in Linz, Steirischer Herbst in Graz). Seit 1987 ist er Ordentlicher Professor an der Hochschule für angewandte Kunst in Wien. Bernhard Leitner beschäftigt sich seit 1968 mit TON-RAUM-Arbeit: u.a. permanente Installation an der TU Berlin, Publikationen dazu erschienen in ARTEFORUM (New York), Das Fenster (Innsbruck), im Rahmen der Documenta-Dokumente (Köln), etc. 1993 ist Leitner bei der MEDIALE in Hamburg vertreten.

---

studied architecture at the Technical University of Vienna, he worked with the city planning authorities of New York City and taught urban design studies at the New York University. Numerous exhibitions in Germany (e.g. Documenta in Kassel), in the USA, France and Austria (e.g. Ars electronica in Linz, Steirischer Herbst in Graz). Since 1987 he has been Professor at the University of Applied Arts in Vienna. Since 1968 Bernhard Leitner has been doing SOUND-SPACE work: e.g. permanent installation at the Technical University of Berlin. Texts about his work were published in ARTEFORUM (New York), Das Fenster (Austria) and in the Documenta Dokumente (Germany), etc. In 1993 Mr. Leitner will participate in the Hamburg MEDIALE.

GERHARD JOHANN LISCHKA
geboren 1943 in Muntlix, Österreich, lebt in Bern als freischaffender Kulturphilosoph und Schriftsteller. Herausgeber der Taschenbuchreihe „um 9" im Benteli-Verlag in Bern, Organisator verschiedener Ausstellungen, diverse TV-Sendungen. Bücher u.a. „Die Schönheit der Schönheit: Super-Ästhetik", „Kulturkunst, die Medienfalle", „Über die Mediatisierung: Medien und Re-Medien". Herausgeber diverser Kunstforum-Bände. 1993 erscheint „Splitterästhetik" (gesammelte Schriften 1980–1993). Unterrichtet Theorie an diversen Schulen.

---

born in 1943 in Muntlix, Austria. He lives and works in Bern, Switzerland as a freelance cultural philosopher and writer. He is the editor of the pocketbook series_"um

9", published by Benteli-Verlag, Bern and organizer of various exhibitions, several TV programmes. Books by Gerhard Johann Lischka: "Die Schönheit der Schönheit: Super-Ästhetik", "Kulturkunst, die Medienfalle", "Über die Mediatisierung: Medien und Re-Medien", among others. Editor of several "Kunstforum" volumes. In 1993 "Splitterästhetik" (a collection of writings from 1980 to 1993) will be published. Mr. Lischka teaches theory at various schools.

THOMAS LOCHER

Studium an der Akademie der Bildenden Künste Stuttgart. Zahlreiche Einzel- und Gruppenausstellungen in Deutschland, Österreich, Italien, England, Nordirland, Frankreich, den Niederlanden, Spanien, Belgien, der Schweiz, Ungarn, Japan, Australien und den USA. Thomas Locher lebt und arbeitet in Köln.

---

studied at the Academy of Fine Arts in Stuttgart. Numerous solo and group exhibitions in Germany, Austria, Italy, England, Northern Ireland, France, the Netherlands, Spain, Belgium, Switzerland, Hungary, Japan, Australia and the USA. Thomas Locher lives and works in Cologne, Germany.

BERNHARD LOIBNER

geboren 1965 in Villach. Lehrgang für Tontechnik, Hochschule für darstellende Kunst Wien, Studium der Datentechnik an der TU Wien. Seit 1987 ALL QUIET ON THE WESTERN FRONT, verschiedene Arbeiten im Grenzbereich Musik – Technologie – Medien u.a.. Piazetta Vienna-Piazza Virtuale (1992), IN HOUSE TV (1992) PERSONENRUFE (1993).

---

born in 1965 in Villach, Carinthia. Sound engineering course, University of Interpretative Art in Vienna, study of data systems engineering at the Technical University of Vienna. Since 1987 ALL QUIET ON THE WESTERN FRONT, various works in the borderland between music, technology, media, etc. Piazetta Vienna-Piazza Virtuale (1992), IN HOUSE TV (1992), PERSONENRUFE (1993).

REINHARD LÖW

geboren 1949 in Freising, Bayern. Löw studierte Mathematik, Pharmazie, Philosophie und Geschichte in München. Er erhielt Doktorate in Chemie und Philosophie. 1977 bis 1983 war er wissenschaftlicher Assistent für Philosophie, dann Professor für Philosophie in München. Seit 1987 Gründungsdirektor des Forschungsinstituts für Philosophie Hannover. Lehrauftrag an der Medizinischen Hochschule in Hannover, Gastvorlesungen an der Akademie für Medizin in Magdeburg. 1992/93 Vertretung des Lehrstuhls für Philosophie an der Universität München. Mitherausgeber der Zeitschrift SCHEIDEWEGE und der internationalen katholischen Zeitschrift COMMUNIO sowie der Reihe „Schriften zur Naturphilosophie" (Verlag Acta Humaniora, Weinheim). Vorstandssprecher von CIVITAS, Gesellschaft zur Förderung von Wissenschaft und Kunst. Löw ist Autor zahlreicher Publikationen.

---

born in Freising, Germany in 1949. He studied mathematics, pharmaceutics, philosophy and history in Munich. He received Ph.D. degrees in chemistry and philosophy. From 1977 to 1983 he was Scientific Assistant of Philosophy, then Professor of Philosophy in Munich. Founder member of the Hannover Forschungsinstitut für Philosophie. Lectureship at the Medical University of Hannover, Visiting Lecturer at the Magdeburg Akademie für Medizin In 1992/93 he substituted the Professor of Philosophy at the University of Munich. He is co-editor of the magazine SCHEIDEWEGE, of the international catholic magazine COMMUNIO and of "Schriften zur Naturphilosophie", published by Verlag Acta Humaniora, Weinheim. Spokesman of the executive board of CIVITAS, society for the promotion of science and art. He is the author of numerous publications.

THOMAS MADERSBACHER

geboren 1963 in Schwaz. Thomas Madersbacher spielte Schlagzeug bei einer Reihe österreichischer Underground-Bands. 1991 Mitbegründer von Radio Boiler, später Sprecher der „pressure group freies Radio". 1992 Radioinstallation „Do interactive broadcasting" an der Akademie der Bildenden Künste. Neben laufender Sendungsgestaltung macht Thomas Madersbacher Konzepte und führt Verhandlungen für einen unabhängigen Kulturkanal. Er lebt als brotloser Künstler und Publizist in Wien.

---

born in 1963 in Schwaz, Austria. Thomas Madersbacher played drums for a number of Austrian underground bands. In 1991 he was a co-founder of "Radio Boiler" and became a spokesman for the pressure group for free radio. 1992 "Do interactive broadcasting", a radio installation at the Academy of Fine Arts. Apart from regular broadcasts, Thomas Madersbacher works conceptually and politically towards the authorization of an independent radio station. He is an artist and journalist without means and lives in Vienna.

KLAUS MADZIA

geboren 1966, aufgewachsen in England und Deutschland. Arbeitet als Redakteur beim Nachrichtenmagazin DER SPIEGEL, Hamburg.

---

was born in 1966. He spent his childhood in England and Germany. He works as a journalist with the German magazine DER SPIEGEL, Hamburg.

PATTIE MAES

schloß ihr Informatikstudium an der Universität Brüssel mit dem Doktorat ab. Seit 1990 ist sie am Massachusetts Institute of Technology tätig, zuerst war sie wissenschaftliche Forscherin im Laboratorium für künstliche Intelligenz, dann Assistant Professor im Medienlabor. Sie beschäftigt sich mit künstlichem Leben, künstlicher Intelligenz und insbesondere mit der Entwicklung künstlicher autonomer Formen.

---

received her Ph.D. in Computer Science at the University of Brussels. Since 1990 she has worked at the Massachusetts Institute of Technology first as a research scientist at the Artificial Intelligence Laboratory and more recently as an Assistant Professor at the Media Laboratory. She is interested in Artificial Life and Artificial Intelligence and in particular spends her time modelling artificial autonomous agents of all sorts.

FRANZ MARKSTEINER

geboren 1963. Studium der Germanistik und Publizistik an der Universität Wien. Diplomarbeit zu „Literatur und Film". Vorträge zum Wiener Film. Filmtheoretische Veröffentlichungen. Gründungsmitglied der PVS Verleger. In Vorbereitung: Forschungsprojekt zum österreichischen Nachkriegsfilm.

---

born in 1963. Studies of German Philology and Journalism at the University of Vienna. Diploma thesis on "Literature and Film". Lectures on Viennese film. Publications on film theory. Founding member of the edition PVS Verleger. At present, Franz Marksteiner is preparing a research project on Austrian film after World War II.

GIDEON MAY

geboren 1964 in Amsterdam. 1984 Arbeit als Modephotographie-Assistent. Anschließend zwei Jahre Trickaufnahmen für Film und Fernsehen sowie drei Jahre Kameraassistenz. Gideon May arbeitet seit 1987 als Computergraphik-Programmierer und Mitarbeiter bei einer Reihe von Projekten von Jeffrey Shaw. Video Narcissus (Turin 1987), The Legible City (Maastricht 1988), Nagoya Japan (1989), The Virtual Museum – Das Belebte Bild (Frankfurt 1991), Linz (1992). Seit 1991 im Zentrum für Kunst und Medien in Karlsruhe tätig.

---

born in 1964 in Amsterdam. In 1984 he worked as a fashion photography assistant. Till 1986 he did special effects for films and TV. For the next three years he worked as an assistant cameraman. He has been working as a computer graphics programmer since 1987 and collaborated on a number of projects of Jeffrey Shaw. Video Narcissus (Torino 1987), The Legible City (Maastricht 1988), Nagoya Japan (1989), The Virtual Museum – Das Belebte Bild (Frankfurt 1991), Linz (1992). Since 1991 has been working for the Center for Art and Media in Karlsruhe, Germany.

MARIO MERZ

geboren 1925 in Mailand,I. Mario Merz gehört zu den wichtigsten europäischen Künstlern der Gegenwart und ist Begründer der Arte Povera Bewegung in der Bildenden Kunst. Er hatte zahlreiche Personalausstellungen und Retrospektiven in den wichtigsten Museen und Galerien der Welt. Neben seinen Iglus ist Mario Merz vor allem auch mit seiner künstlerischen Beschäftigung mit den Zahlenreihen des Fibonacci bekannt geworden.

---

born in Milan, I, in 1925. Mario Merz is one of the mort important European contemporary artists and is founder of the Arte Povera movement within Fine Art. He has done numberless personal exhibitions as well as retrospectives in the most important museums all over the world. Beside his igloos Mario Merz has become known also thru his artistic involvement with Fibonaccis series of figures.

LAURENT MIGNONNEAU

geboren 1967 in Angouleme, Frankreich. Er erwarb in Frankreich Diplome für plastische Kunst und plastischen Ausdruck, erhielt 1992 ein Stipendium für das Institut für Neue Medien an der Städelschule Frankfurt (Peter Weibel) und arbeitet dort als Assistent von Michael Klein. Mignonneau wurden u. a. Preise für Photographie und Computerkunst verliehen. In mehreren Konzerten befaßte er sich mit Experimentalmusik; seine Kunst wurde in Ausstellungen in Frankreich, Deutschland, den USA und Österreich gezeigt. Zusammenarbeit mit Christa Sommerer u.a. bei Interactive Plant Growing (3-D Installation in Wien), bei der Mediale '93 und INTERFACE 2 (Hamburg) sowie SIGGRAPH 93 artshow (Kalifornien).

---

born in 1967 in Angouleme, France. He studied plastic art and plastic expression in France, in 1992 he was granted a scholarship for the Frankfurt-on-Main Städelschule Institute for New Media (Peter Weibel), where he works as an assistant of Michael Klein. Among others, Mignonneau was awarded prizes for photography and computer art. He took part in several concerts of experimental music and showed his art in exhibitions in France, Germany, in the USA and Austria. Cooperation with Christa Sommerer for the Interactive Plant Growing 3-D installation (Vienna), at Mediale '93 and INTERFACE 2 (Hamburg) and SIGGRAPH 93 artshow (California).

MASAHIRO MIWA

geboren 1958 in Tokio (Japan). Masahiro Miwa lebt seit 1979 in Deutschland. Er studierte Komposition bei Isang Yun an der Hochschule der Künste in Berlin und bei Günther Becker an der Robert-Schumann-Hochschule in Düsseldorf. Seit 1986 arbeitet er intensiv an seinen Kompositionen und hat zahlreiche Konzerte inspiriert und organisiert. Seit 1988 unterrichtet er Computermusik und elektronische Musik an der Robert-Schumann-Hochschule in Düsseldorf. 1985 war er Gastkomponist des Amsterdamer STEIM-Studios. Im selben Jahr wurde ihm der Hambacher-Preis verliehen; 1989 gewann er den 1. Preis der 10th International Irino Awards, 1991 den 2. Preis beim International Music Today Composition Contest in Tokio, und 1992 den 1. Preis des 14th Concorse International „Luigi Rossolo" in Varese (Italien).

---

born in 1958 in Tokyo, Japan. Masahiro Miwa has been living in Germany since 1979. He studied composition with Isang Yun at the Hochschule der Künste (art university) in Berlin, and with Günther Becker at the Robert-Schumann-Hochschule in Düsseldorf. Since 1986 he has been working intensively as a composer of computer music and has inspired and organized many concert performances. He has been teaching computer music and electronic music at the Robert-Schumann-Hochschule in Düsseldorf since 1988. In 1985 he was a guest composer at the STEIM studio in Amsterdam. In the same year, he received the Hambacher Prize; in 1989, he won the 1st prize at the 10th International Irino Awards, in 1991 the 2nd prize at the International Music Today Composition Contest held in Tokyo, and in 1992, the 1st prize at the 14th Concorse International "Luigi Rossolo" in Varese, Italy.

SUSANNA MORGENSTERN

geboren 1956 in Wien. Studium an der Hochschule für angewandte Kunst in Wien, Diplom bei Oswald Oberhuber. 1985 Teilnahme bei Literatur im März (Künstlervideo und Gruppenarbeit zum Thema „Störungen"), Museum für angewandte Kunst in Wien. 1987 beim Steirischen Herbst, Trigon, „Video der 80er Jahre". 1990 „see" Computerarbeit für den Prix Ars Electronica. 1993 „weiter", Wandzeitung, museum in progress, Susanna Morgenstern lebt und arbeitet in Wien.

---

born in Vienna in 1956. She studied at the University of Applied Arts in Vienna (diploma with Oswald Oberhuber). In 1985 she took part in Literatur im März (artistic video and group work about "disturbances"), Museum of Applied Arts of Vienna. 1987: Steirischer Herbst (Graz, Austria), Trigon, "Video der 80er Jahre". 1990: "see" computer work for Prix Ars Electronica. 1993: "weiter", wall news-sheet of museum in progress. Susanna Morgenstern lives and works in Vienna.

LOTHAR MÜLLER

Dr. theol., Dissertation: Politische Ethik. Lothar Müller ist Lehrbeauftragter am Institut für Öffentliches Recht und Politikwissenschaft an der Universität Innsbruck; Mitglied des Rates für Technikentwicklung im BM für Wissenschaft und Forschung; Abgeordneter zum Nationalrat, dort Mitglied der Enquetekommission „Technikfolgenabschätzung am Beispiel der Gentechnik".

Doctorate in theology, dissertation on political ethics. Lothar Müller teaches at the Institute for public law and political science of the University of Innsbruck, Austria. He is a member of the Council for the Development of Technology in the Ministry of Research and Higher Education; member of the Austrian parliament and its commission on "Consequences of Technology: Genetic Engineering".

NIKI NICKL

geboren 1964 in Graz, Studium an der Hochschule für angewandte Kunst in Wien in der Meisterklasse für Graphik und Malerei bei Prof. Oswald Oberhuber (Ernst Caramelle). Diplom 1991.

---

was born in 1964 in Graz. Niki Nickl studied graphic art and painting with Oswald Oberhuber (Ernst Caramelle) at the Vienna University of Applied Arts. Art diploma in 1991.

KLAUS OBERMAIER

Gitarrestudium am Linzer Brucknerkonservatorium und an der Hochschule für Musik und darstellende Kunst in Wien, Malereistudium an der Kunsthochschule in Linz. 1990 Förderungsprämie für Komposition des Landes Oberösterreich. Arbeitete mit Ornette Coleman, Heiner Goebbels, Ensemble Modern/Frankfurt, der Deutschen Kammerphilharmonie.

Tourneen in Europa, den USA und Asien. Spielte bei internationalen Jazz- und Gitarre-Festivals. Kompositionsaufträge von verschiedenen Ensembles, Musik für Theater und Performances. Arbeitet seit 1991 mit dem Pianisten Robert Spour an multimedialen Projekten, daneben Duo-Konzerte mit neuer Musik.

---

studied guitar at the Linz Bruckner Academy of Music and at the Vienna University for Music and Interpretative Art, and painting at the College of Art in Linz. 1990 Promotion Award for composition from the Upper Austrian Provincial Government. He worked with Ornette Coleman, Heiner Goebbels, Ensemble Modern/Frankfurt and the German Kammerphilharmonie. He toured Europe, the USA and Asia, and played at international jazz and guitar festivals. Awarded composition commissions by various ensembles. Since 1991 he has worked on multimedia projects with the pianist Robert Spour, with whom he is also performing in duo concerts of new music.

VRÄÄTH ÖHNER

geboren 1965 in Linz. Studium der Kommunikations- und Theaterwissenschaften an der Universität Wien. Gründungsmitglied der PVS Verleger. 1992 Studienaufenthalt an der UCLA, Los Angeles. Mehrere filmtheoretische Vorträge und Veröffentlichungen. Vrääth Öhner lebt in Wien.

---

born in 1965 in Linz. Communications and Drama Studies at the University of Vienna. Founding member of the edition PVS Verleger. In 1992 Vrääth Öhner studied at UCLA. Several lectures and publications on film theory. Vrääth Öhner lives in Vienna.

JOACHIM PENSE

geboren 1958, Mathematikstudium in Mainz und Warwick, Promotion 1988. Forscher, Softwareentwickler, Platten, CDs, Auftritte im Umfeld von SELEKTION seit 1980.

---

born in 1958, studied mathematics in Mainz and Warwick and received a doctorate in 1988. Research work, development of software; records, compact discs, since 1980 he has had performances in connection with SELEKTION.

DAN PETERMAN

geboren 1960 in Minneapolis, lebt in Chicago. Dan Peterman studierte in Chicago und Wisconsin. Mehrere Stipendien, darunter zwei Bildhauereistipendien des Illinois Arts Council sowie Förderung einzelner Projekte. Zahlreiche Einzel- und Gruppenausstellungen sowie Installationen in den USA, Deutschland (Gruppenshow Tanya Grunert, Köln) sowie 1993 bei der Biennale in Venedig.

---

born in 1960 in Minneaoplis. He currently lives in Chicago. Dan Peterman studied in Chicago and Wisconsin. Several grants, including two sculpture fellowships by the Illinois Arts Council, and several project grants. Numerous solo and group exhibitions and installations in the USA, Germany (group show Tanya Grunert, Cologne) and at the 1993 Biennale in Venice, Italy.

ALEXANDER POPPER

Zwingt man dich, deine Biographie von dir zu geben, so erzähle jedesmal eine andere. Darauf hingewiesen, zeige dich entrüstet darüber, daß man jene Diskretion, die jeder für sich beanspruchen darf, dir nicht zubilligen will. Man wird deine Phantasie bewundern und deiner Biographie alles zutrauen. (Walter Serner)

According to Walter Serner, you should tell a different story every time somebody forces you to tell your biography. If they draw your attention to this, show indignation at the fact that you are not granted the discreetness everybody else may claim for himself. They will admire your imagination and believe anything they are told about you.

PRZEMYSLAW PRUSINKEWICZ

studierte Informatik in Warschau, wo er auch promovierte. Er unterrichtete an den Universitäten Regina, Algier, Yale, und in Lausanne und wurde zu Forschungsarbeiten an die Universität Bremen berufen. Gegenwärtig ist er Professor für Informatik an der Universität Calgary (Kanada). Seit Ende der siebziger Jahre befaßt er sich mit Computergraphik. Er entwickelte eine Methode zur Sichtbarmachung der Pflanzenstruktur und -entwicklung auf der Basis von L-Systemen, schrieb mehrere Lehrbücher und Monographien sowie eine große Zahl von Fachartikeln. Derzeit arbeitet er an mathematischen Modellen der Strukturen lebender Organismen.

---

studied computer science in Warsaw, where he received a Ph.D. degree. He was teaching at the Universities of Regina, Algier, Yale, and in Lausanne and worked as an invited researcher at the University of Bremen. Now he is Professor of Computer Science at the University of Calgary, Canada. Since the late 1970s he has been pursuing research in computer graphics. He originated a method for visualizing the structure and the development of plants based on L-systems. He wrote several textbooks and monographs, and numerous technical papers. His current work is focused on mathematical models of pattern formation in living organisms.

THOMAS S. RAY

Thomas Ray erlangte das Doktorat aus Biologie (Spezialgebiet Pflanzenökologie) an der Universität Harvard. Ab 1981 unterrichtete er am Institut für Biologie und Gesundheitswissenschaften der Universität Delaware, wo er derzeit eine Stelle als Außerordentlicher Professor innehat. 1993 erhielt er zusätzlich einen Lehrauftrag für Computerwesen und Informatik. Ab August 1993 wird er als Gastprofessor am ATR (Internationale Höhere Telekommunikationsforschung) in Japan tätig sein. Thomas Ray ist Tropenbiologe und untersucht seit über 19 Jahren die Entwicklungs- und Lebensformen einer Reihe von in Regenwäldern heimischen Organismen. Seine Feldforschungsarbeit führte er großteils in Costa Rica durch. Seit 1982 arbeitet er hauptsächlich in der von ihm errichteten und betriebenen biologischen Station Finca El Bejuco in den nördlichen Regenwäldern Costa Ricas. Thomas Ray hat keine formelle Ausbildung in Computerwissenschaften, er erlernte die Programmiersprache C autodidaktisch im Jahr 1978. Sein Interesse an künstlichen Lebensformen erwachte 1980 beim Go-Spielen, schlummerte dann aber bis 1989 in ihm.

---

received his Doctorate in Biology from Harvard University, specializing in plant ecology. In 1981 he joined the faculty of the University of Delaware, School of Life and Health Sciences, where he is now an Associate Professor. In 1993 he received a joint appointment in Computer and Information Science at the University of Delaware. In August of 1993, he will join the new Evolutionary Systems Department at ATR (Advanced Telecommunications Research International) in Japan, as a visiting professor. Thomas S. Ray is a tropical biologist who for more than 19 years has studied the evolution and ecology of a variety of organisms inhabiting rain forests. Most of his field work has been conducted in Costa Rica. Since 1982, he has worked principally at Finca El Bejuco biological station located in the rain forests of northern Costa Rica, which he built, and owns and operates. Thomas Ray has no formal training in computer science; he taught himself the C programming language in 1978. His interest in synthetic life started in 1980 while playing Go, however the interest lay dormant until 1989.

HOLGER REICHERT

geboren 1963 in Wuppertal. Studium der Medienwissenschaften. Gründungsmitglied der PVS Verleger. Lehrauftrag für wissenschaftliche Medienpraxis an der Universität Wien. Filmtheoretische Veröffentlichungen.

---

born in 1963 in Wuppertal, Germany. Studies of Media Theory. Founding member of the edition PVS Verleger. Holger Reichert teaches scientific media practice at the University of Vienna. Publications on film theory.

RICH.ART

geboren 1969 in Wien. Absolvent der Höheren Lehranstalt für elektronische Datenverarbeitung und Organisation, studiert an der Hochschule für angewandte Kunst in Wien, Meisterklasse für visuelle Mediengestaltung (unter anderem bei Peter Weibel, Rebecca Allen, Valie Export, Henry Jesionka und Steina Vasulka). Diverse Einzel- und Gruppenausstellungen in Österreich mit Video und Computer.

---

was born in Vienna in 1969. He graduated from the College of Electronic Data Processing and Organization, now is a student of visual media design (with Peter Weibel, Rebecca Allen, Valie Export, Henry Jesionka, Steina Vasulka, etc.) at the University of Applied Arts in Vienna. Various solo and group exhibitions with video and computers in Austria.

ALEXIS ROCKMAN

geboren 1962 in New York. Rockman studierte an der Art Students League in New York, an der Rhode Island School of Design sowie an der School of Visual Art in New York. Zahlreiche Einzelausstellungen in den USA, z.B. Jay Gorney Modern Art, New York, The Carnegie Museum, Pittsburgh, oder Tom Solomon's Garage in Los Angeles, aber auch in Salzburg in der Galerie Thaddäus Ropac. Gruppenausstellungen unter anderem bei der Biennale in Venedig, im Guggenheim-Museum Venedig sowie in zahlreichen Galerien und sonstigen Ausstellungsorten in den USA.

---

was born in 1962 in New York. Alexis Rockman studied at the Art Students League, New York, at the Rhode Island School of Design and at the School of Visual Art, New York. Solo exhibitions in the USA (e.g. Jay Gorney Modern Art, New York, The Carnegie Museum, Pittsburgh, and Tom Solomon's Garage, Los Angeles) and at the Salzburg Galerie Thaddäus Ropac. Group exhibitions at the Venice Biennale, at the Venice Guggenheim Museum, and at numerous galleries and art centres in the USA.

REIMARA RÖSSLER

geb. Waible, geboren in Hamburg.

1964 Dr. med. am pathologischen Institut der Universität Hamburg. 1966 wissenschaftliche Assistentin an der Medizinischen Universitätsklinik Marburg, 1969 Forschungsaufenthalt bei Ernest Witebsky in Buffalo. 1973 Habilitation und Laborleiterin der Medizinischen Universitätspoliklinik Tübingen. 1975 außerdem Berufung zum Wissenschaftlichen Rat und Professor. Zahlreiche wissenschaftliche Veröffentlichungen über Virologie, Hämatologie und Endokrinologie.

---

née Waible, born in Hamburg. In 1964 M.D. in pathology. In 1966 teaching assistant at the Medical University Hospital of Marburg. In 1969 winner of a fellowship to the Ernest Witebsky immunological laboratory in Buffalo. In 1973 she became lab director and in 1975 Professor, at the Medical University Outpatient Clinic of Tübingen. Numerous publications on virology, hematology and endocrinology.

DIETER ROTH

geboren 1930 in Hannover. Dieter Roth studierte Graphik-Design in Bern. Über den Schweizer Künstler Daniel Spoerri bekam er Kontakt zur Fluxus-Bewegung und arbeitete mit Künstlern wie Dick Higgins, Nam June Paik, Charlotte Moorman, George Brecht und Emmett Williams zusammen. 1957–64 lebte er in Rejkjavik (Island). Über Spoerri und Jean Tinguely lernte er Richard Hamilton kennen und realisierte mehrere Projekte mit ihm. 1964–67 unterrichtete Roth an der Universität Yale, an der Philadelphia Museum School of Art und an der Rhode Island School of Design. Seit 1968 publiziert er bei der Edition Hansjörg Mayer. 1970 stellte er in Los Angeles die Skulptur „Staple Cheese, a Race" aus: 40 Koffer, mit Käse gefüllt. Roth arbeitet auch heute mit nicht-traditionellen Materialien wie Musik, Abfall, Schokolade und saurer Milch. Derzeit lebt er in der Schweiz und in Island.

---

born in 1930 in Hannover. Dieter Roth studied graphic design in Bern. Through Swiss artist Daniel Spoerri, Roth meets members of the Fluxus movement. Collaborative work with Dick Higgins, Nam June Paik, Charlotte Moorman, George Brecht and Emmett Williams. From 1957 to 1964 he lived in Rejkjavik, Iceland. Through Spoerri and Jean Tinguely, Roth meets Richard Hamilton; they collaborate on various projects. From 1964 to 1967 Roth taught at Yale University, the Philadelphia Museum School of Art, and the Rhode Island School of Design. In 1968, he begins publishing with Edition Hansjörg Mayer. In 1970 he exhibits "Staple Cheese, a Race", a sculpture composed of 40 suitcases filled with cheese, in Los Angeles. Roth continues to use non-traditional materials: music, garbage, chocolate, sour milk. He now lives in Switzerland and Iceland.

FLORIAN RÖTZER

geboren 1953 in München, lebt als freier Autor in München.

---

born in 1953 in Munich. He lives as a freelance writer in Munich, Germany.

HELMUT RUIS

geboren 1940 in Wien, studierte Chemie an der Universität Wien, 1965 bis 1967 Postdoctoral Fellow an der Cornell University, Ithaca, New York. Seit 1986 Ordentlicher Professor für Biochemie an der Universität Wien (Institut für Biochemie und Molekulare Zellbiologie). Gastprofessuren und Forschungsaufenthalte an der Universität Campinas in Brasilien, der Cornell University und am Fred Hutchinson Cancer Research Institute in Seattle. Koordinator des Forschungsschwerpunkts „Gentechnologie" des Fonds zur Förderung der wissenschaftlichen Forschung, Wien. Koordinator für die Errichtung des Biozentrums der Universität Wien.

---

born in Vienna in 1940. He studied chemistry at the University of Vienna. From 1965 to 1967 Postdoctoral Fellow at Cornell University, Ithaca, New York. Since 1986 he has been Professor of Biochemistry at the University of Vienna (Biochemistry and Molecular Cell Biology Department). Visiting professor and researcher at Campinas University, Brazil, Cornell University, Ithaca, New York and Fred Hutchinson Cancer Research Institute, Seattle. Coordinator of the genetic engineering research programme of the scientific research promotion fund of Vienna. Coordinator of the establishment of the Vienna Biocenter.

PETER SANDBICHLER

geboren 1964 in Kufstein. Fachschule für Holz- und Steinbildhauerei in Innsbruck, Studium an der Art Students League in New York bei Martin Knox und an der Hochschule für angewandte Kunst in Wien in der Meisterklasse Bertoni sowie an der Akademie der Bildenden Künste bei Bruno Gironcoli. Einzelausstellungen in der Galerie Krinzinger in Innsbruck und der Galerie Grita Insam in Wien. Gruppenausstellungen: u.a. Secession Wien; Galerie Graff in Montreal; Kunstbüro Berlin (mit Arye und Simon Wachsmuth); Galerie Museum in Bozen, Grand Palais in Paris; in Los Angeles und Rostock.

---

was born in Kufstein, Austria, in 1964. He attended a sculpture school in Innsbruck, then he studied at the Art Students League in New York City (with Martin Knox), at the Vienna University of Fine Arts (with Bertoni) and at the Academy of Fine Arts in Vienna (with Bruno Gironcoli). Solo exhibitions at Galerie Krinzinger, Innsbruck, and Galerie Grita Insam, Vienna. Group exhibitions: (among others) Secession of Vienna; Graff gallery, Montreal; Kunstbüro Berlin (in cooperation with Arye and Simon Wachsmuth); Galerie Museum in Bolzano, Italy, Grand Palais, Paris; in Los Angeles and Rostock, Germany.

STEFAN SCHEMAT

geboren 1960 in Rinteln/Weser, Deutschland. Er studierte Psychologie in Göttingen. Arbeitet als Forschungsassistent an der Universität Göttingen zu mentalen Repräsentationen und Bewußtseinslagen. Weiteres Betätigungsfeld ist die Erforschung und Nutzung maschineninduzierter Trancezustände. Seine Geräte werden in Fachkliniken und Praxen im Bereich Psychotherapie angewendet. Als weiteres Einsatzgebiet wird zur Zeit die Eignung tranceinduzierender Maschinen zum Kreativitätstraining untersucht.

---

born in 1960 in Rinteln/Weser (Germany). He studied psychology in Göttingen and works as a research assistant at the University of Göttingen, where he deals with mental representations and states of consciousness devoid of sensory components. Another field of activity is the investigation and utilization of machine-induced trance. His machines are used in specialized hospitals and medical offices in the field of psychotherapy. At present, he is testing the use of trance-inducing machines in the field of creativity training.

HORST SEIDLER

geboren 1944 in Wien, studierte Humanbiologie und Psychologie an der Universität Wien, Promotion 1972. Er arbeitete als wissenschaftliche Hilfskraft, dann als Assistent am Institut für Humanbiologie (vormals Anthropologie) der Universität Wien. 1979 folgte die Habilitation. Seit 1984 ist er Ordentlicher Professor für Humanbiologie. Er verfaßte zahlreiche Artikel für Fachzeitschriften und Kongresse sowie mehrere Bücher.

---

born in Vienna in 1944. He studied human biology and psychology at the University of Vienna, where he received a Ph.D. degree in 1972. He worked as scientific assistant at the Institute for Human Biology (the former Anthropology Institute) of the University of Vienna. In 1979 he received the habilitation degree In 1984 he became Professor of Human Biology. He is author and co-author of numerous technical papers for magazines and congresses, and of several books.

GEBHARD SENGMÜLLER

geboren 1967 in Wien, Studium an der Hochschule für Musik und darstellende Kunst, Hochschullehrgang am Institut für Elektroakustik. Gründungsmitglied von PYRAMEDIA. 1990–92 Terminal Tapes (WUK Wien); Videolivemixinstallation VEEJAY DEEJAY in Wien; Fassadeninstallation VEXILLOMAT in Wien; TRANSFORMATOR – Dokumentation ORF Kunststücke; Regie für die VIDEO-PRESSEKONFERENZ "Tanzsprache"; CONTAINER – Livemusiker in Wien. Seit 1992 an der Hochschule für angewandte Kunst, Meisterklasse Peter Weibel. 1993 INDOORVEXILLOMAT – Rauminstallation in Brüssel, TV POETRY – Versuchsanordnung 1/93.

born in 1967 in Vienna. He studied at the Vienna University for Music and Interpretative Art and attended a college course at the Institute for Electroacoustics. Founding member of PYRAMEDIA. 1990 to 1992: TERMINAL TAPES at WUK in Vienna; VEEJAY DEEJAY video live mix installation in Vienna; VEXILLOMAT facade installation in Vienna; TRANSFORMATOR – documentation of the Austrian TV programme "Kunststücke"; direction of the VIDEO PRESS CONFERENCE of the "Tanzsprache" dancing festival in Vienna; CONTAINER – live musician, in Vienna. Since 1992 he has been studying with Peter Weibel at the Vienna University of Applied Arts. 1993: INDOORVEXILLOMAT installation at Brussels; TV POETRY experimental_arrangement 1/93.

KARL SIMS

studierte bis 1984 Life Sciences am M.I.T., anschließend arbeitete er ein Jahr lang bei Thinking Machines Corporation, um dann am Medienlabor des M.I.T. Graphik und Animation zu studieren. Studienabschluß mit dem Titel M.S. of Visual Studies 1987. In der Folge arbeitete er in der Produktionsforschung bei Whitney/Demos Productions in Kalifornien. Mitbegründer und Vorstand bei Optomystic, Hollywood. Derzeit arbeitet er wieder bei Thinking Machines Corporation, wo er als wissenschaftlicher Forscher und Künstler an neuen Techniken zur Erzeugung von Bildern mittels Computer arbeitet. Neuere Animationsarbeiten: „Particle Dreams", „Primordial Dance", „Liquid Selves". Interaktive Arbeiten: „Interactive Video Kaleidoscope" und „Genetic Images".

---

received a B.S. in Life Sciences from M.I.T. in 1984. After working at Thinking Machines Corporation for a year he returned to M.I.T. to study graphics and animation at the Media Laboratory and received an M.S. in Visual Studies in 1987. He then joined the production research team at Whitney/Demos Productions in California, and later became co-founder and director of research for Hollywood based Optomystic. He currently works once again at Thinking Machines Corporation as a research scientist and artist, where he explores new techniques for creating images with computers. His recent works of animation include "Particle Dreams", "Primordial Dance" and "Liquid Selves". His interactive works include "Interactive Video Kaleidoscope" and "Genetic Images".

CHRISTA SOMMERER
geboren 1964, studierte zunächst Botanik, dann an der Meisterklasse für Bildhauerei (bei Gironcoli) an der Akademie der Bildenden Künste in Wien, 1990 Diplom für Bildhauerei. Ab 1991 an der Städelschule Frankfurt, Institut für Neue Medien (bei Peter Weibel). Stipendien u.a. für Deutschland und die USA. Seit 1990 zahlreiche Ausstellungen u.a. in Wien, Hannover, Hamburg, Paris und Helsinki. Zusammenarbeit mit Laurent Mignonneau u.a. bei Interactive Plant Growing (Installation in Wien), bei der Mediale '93 und INTERFACE (Hamburg) und bei der SIGGRAPH 93 artshow, Kalifornien („Machine Culture: The Virtual Frontier").

---

born in 1964. She studied botany, then she turned to sculpture studies with Gironcoli at the Academy of Fine Arts in Vienna, from where she graduated in 1990. In 1991 she began to study at the Frankfurt-on-Maine Städenschule Institut für Neue Medien (with Peter Weibel). She was granted scholarships for Germany and the USA, among others. Since 1990 she has participated in numerous exhibitions in Vienna, Hannover, Hamburg, Paris, Helsinki, etc. Cooperation with Laurent Mignonneau for the Interactive Plant Growing installation (Vienna), at Mediale '93 and INTERFACE (Hamburg) and SIGGRAPH 93 artshow, California ("Machine Culture: The Virtual Frontier").

LAETITIA SONAMI
zeigte ihre Live-Elektronik-Solokunst in den letzten 15 Jahren bei zahlreichen Gelegenheiten in den USA und im Ausland. Sie verfolgte die Entwicklung der anwenderbezogenen Elektronik und setzt in ihrer Kunst die leichter zugänglichen Technologien ein. In den letzten drei Jahren arbeitete sie zeitweise in Amsterdam (STEIM), wo sie neue Gestiksteuerungen für Musikaufführungen entwickelte und bei ihren Werken einsetzte. Derzeit führt sie ihre Solo-Elektronikkunst nach Texten von Melody Sumner auf und arbeitet mit der kanadischen Komponistin Marie Goyette an einem neuen Stück.

---

has been performing her live electronic solo works for the past 15 years in numerous venues in the USA and abroad. She has pursued the development of personalized electronic equipment and has exploited the more readily available electronic technologies. For the past three years she has spent some time at STEIM in Amsterdam where she has developed and adapted new gesture controllers to musical performance and composed works with these materials. She is currently performing solo electronic works based on texts by Melody Sumner and is developing a new work with the Canadian composer Marie Goyette.

ROBERT SPOUR
studierte Klavier am Brucknerkonservatorium in Linz. Preisträger beim internationalen Jazzfestival in Brüssel. Seit 1980 arbeitet er mit Computer und elektronischen Klangerzeugern. Seit 1984 elektronische Projekte mit verschiedenen Improvisationsensembles bei internationalen Festivals. Konzerte und Aufnahmen mit der Deutschen Kammerphilharmonie. Tourneen in Europa und den USA. Kompositionsaufträge von verschiedenen Ensembles (Bläserensemble Pro Brass, Oberösterreichisches Kammerorchester). Musik für Theater und Performances. Seit 1991 Zusammenarbeit mit dem Gitarristen Klaus Obermaier beim multimedialen Projekt „Immateriaux". Gemeinsame Konzerte in Europa und den USA.

---

studied piano at the Linz Bruckner Academy of Music. Prize winner at the Brussels International Jazz Festival. In 1980 he began to work with computers and electronic sound producers. Since 1984 he has been implementing electronic projects with various improvisation ensembles. Concerts and recordings with the German Kammerphilharmonie. Toured Europe and the USA. Awarded composition commissions by various ensembles (wind instrument ensemble Pro Brass, Upper Austrian Kammerorchester). Music for theater and performances. Since 1991 he has worked on the multimedia project "Immateriaux" with the guitarist Klaus Obermaier, with whom he is also performing at concerts in Europe and the USA.

KATRIN STOCKHAMMER
geboren 1966, seit 1986 Studium der Genetik und Botanik. Beschäftigung mit Wissenschaft und Öffentlichkeit.
was born in 1966. In 1986 she be-

gan to study genetics and botany. She deals with science and the public.

KLAUS STRICKNER

geboren 1959. Klaus Strickner lebt in Wien und Innsbruck.

born in 1959. Klaus Strickner lives in Vienna and Innsbruck, Austria.

MELODY SUMNER

geboren 1951 in Corpus Christi, Texas. Sie schrieb neben der Sammlung von Erzählungen „The Time is Now" Kurzprosa für zahlreiche Zeitschriften und Anthologien. Während der letzten zehn Jahre leitete sie „Burning Books", wo 1987 „The guests go in to supper", eine Sammlung von Interviews, Essays und Texten von sieben amerikanischen Komponisten, erschien. Im Jahr 1991 erschien bei Burning Books „Perfect Lives" von Robert Ashley. Demnächst veröffentlicht Sumner „Dialogue Between the Self and Its Angel", eine Sammlung von Erzählungen, und die Biographie eines Tibetaners, „Horses Run on Wheels".

---

was born in Corpus Christi, Texas, in 1951 and is the author of a collection of stories, "The Time is Now", and short works of fiction published in numerous magazines and anthologies. She has worked as chief editor for Burning Books for the last ten years. In 1987 Burning Books produced "The guests go in to supper", a collection of interviews, essays and texts by seven American composers. In 1991 Burning Books published Robert Ashley's "Perfect Lives". Ms. Sumner will soon publish a collection of stories titled "Dialogue Between the Self and Its Angel", and "Horses Run on Wheels", the biography of a Tibetan man.

TAMIKO THIEL

geboren 1957 in Oakland, Kalifornien. Studium an der Stanford University, Abschluß 1979 im Fach Technik/Produktdesign. Anschließend Arbeit im Bereich Verpackungsdesign bei Hewlett-Pakkard. 1981 – 83 Fortsetzung des Studiums am Medienlabor des Massachusetts Institute of Technology im Bereich Maschinenbau-Studien zur Schnittstelle Mensch-Maschine und visuelle Kommunikation. Dann zwei Jahre Tätigkeit bei Thinking Machines Corporation in Cambridge, Massachusetts. Studierte 1985 bis 1991 multimediale Kunst an der Akademie der Bildenden Künste in München. In den letzten beiden Jahren Videoausstellungen in Japan und Deutschland. Tamiko Thiel lebt derzeit in München.

---

born in Oakland, California in 1957. B.S. degree in General Engineering/Product Design at Stanford University in 1979. From 1979 to 1981 Tamiko Thiel worked at Hewlett Packard as a Packaging Design Engineer. In 1983 M.S. in Mechanical Engineering – Studies in Man/Machine Interface and Visual Communication at the M.I.T. Media Lab. From 1983 to 1985 Tamiko Thiel worked at Thinking Machines Corporation. and studied at the Munich Academy of Fine Arts from 1985 to 1991. Video exhibitions in Japan and Germany. Tamiko Thiel currently lives in Munich, Germany.

MARK W. TILDEN

geboren 1961 in Stroud, England. Im Alter von zwei Jahren übersiedelte Mark Tilden nach Kanada. Mit drei Jahren baute er seine erste Roboterpuppe aus Wollresten. Die gesamte Schulzeit hindurch baute er weitere Gegenstände und gewann zahlreiche Preise. Er studierte Systemtechnik an der Universität Waterloo, wo er heute als Konstrukteur am Institut für Mathematik arbeitet. Zu seinen Aufgaben gehören so langweilige Dinge wie die Konstruktion von computergesteuerten Eisenbahnmodellen. Die Arbeit an Robotern macht er in seiner Freizeit, aus Interesse.

---

born 1961 in Stroud, England. Mark Tilden moved to Canada at the age of two. He built his first robot doll at the age of three out of wool scraps. He built device after device through grade and high school winning numerous science fairs before attending the University of Waterloo in Systems Engineering. Finishing with his Masters, he now works as a Design Engineer in the Math Department of that University. His job includes such boring things as designing computer controlled model railways. He does his robot work independently and after hours because it's interesting.

NAOKO TOSA

geboren 1961 in Fukuoka, Japan. Naoko Tosa erhielt eine Reihe von Preisen in Japan und im Ausland (z.B. bei der International High Technology Art Exhibition in Tokio und beim American Film & Video Festival in New York). Teilnahme unter anderem bei SIGGRAPH in Anaheim, Kalifornien (1986, 1987, 1993), den Computerkulturtagen in Linz (1987 und 1988), beim internationalen Videofestival in Locarno, Schweiz (1990) sowie Ausstellungen in zahlreichen Städten Japans, in Frankreich, Kanada, den USA und Slowenien.

---

born in Fukuoka, Japan, in 1961. Naoko Tosa has won a number of prizes, (e.g. at the International High Technology Art Exhibition, Tokyo, and at the American Film & Video Festival, New York). He participated in SIGGRAPH, Anaheim, California (1986, 1987 and 1993), Computerkulturtage Linz, Austria (1987 and 1988), in the International Video Festival of Locarno, Switzerland (1990), an at exhibitions in many places in Japan, France, Canada, the USA and Slovenia.

ALBINA MIRELLA D'URBANO

geboren 1955 in Tivoli, Italien. Studium der Philosophie an der Universität „La Sapienza" in Rom, dann Malerei bei Enzo Brunori in Rom. Anschließend studierte sie visuelle Kommunikation (Schwerpunkt audiovisuelle Medien) in Berlin. Förderung der Redaktion von „Das kleine Fernsehspiel" (ZDF) für die Realisation des Videos „Kreis, der". NaFög-Stipendium der HdK, Berlin; Stipendium der Röhm GmbH, Darmstadt, sowie Stipendium Eurocréation, Paris, beim Institut für neue Medien in Frankfurt.

---

was born in 1955 at Tivoli, Italy. She studied philosophy at La Sapienza University, Rome, and painting with Enzo Brunori, also in Rome. Then she went to Berlin to study visual communication (focusing on audio-visual media). Promotion of the edition of "Das kleine Fernsehspiel" (ZDF TV channel) for realizing the video "Kreis, der". NaFöG scholarship of the Berlin HdK University; scholarship of Röhm GmbH company, Darmstadt, Germany, and scholarship Eurocréation, Paris.

MEYER VAISMAN

geboren 1960 in Caracas (Venezuela). Meyer Vaisman studierte an der Parsons School of Design in New York und lebt und arbeitet in New York.

---

born in 1960 in Caracas, Venezuela. Meyer Vaisman studied at the Parsons School of Design in New York and is living and working in New York.

ROMAN VEROSTKO

geboren 1929 in Tarrs, Pennsylvania, USA. Studierte am Art Institute Pittsburgh, in Latrobe (Pennsylvania) und in New York, anschließend im Atelier 17, Paris. Verostko unterrichtete an mehreren Universitäten in den USA und in China (Akademie der bildenden Künste Zhejiang). 1993 leitet er das vierte internationale Symposium über elektronische Kunst. Seine Computerkunst wurde bei zahlreichen Anlässen in den USA gezeigt (z.B. SIGGRAPH '92 Art Show Chicago), außerdem in Finnland, Monte Carlo (Institut National de l'Audiovisuel 1992 und 1993), Australien (drittes internationales Symposium über elektronische Kunst in Sydney 1992) und Südkorea (Computerkunst-Festival 1992).

---

was born in Tarrs, Pa. in 1929. He studied at the Pittsburgh Art Institute, St. Vincent College, Latrobe, Pa., at the Pratt Institute, Brooklyn, NY, and in Atelier 17, Paris. He worked in various colleges in the USA and in China (Zhejiang Academy of Fine Arts). Director of the Fourth International Symposium on Electronic Art. His computer generated art has been shown numerous times in the USA (e.g. SIGGRAPH '92 Art Show, Chicago), in Finland, Monte Carlo (Institut National de l'Audiovisuel, 1992 and 1993, Australia (Third International Symposium on Electronic Art in Sydney, 1992) and South Korea (Seoul International Computer Art Festival, 1992).

JOHANNES VOGGENHUBER

geboren 1950. 1977 bis 1982 Sprecher der Salzburger Bürgerinitiativen. Grüner Stadtrat der Stadt Salzburg von 1982 bis 87, zuständig u.a. für Stadtplanung, Bauten, Altstadtsanierung, Verkehr und Umweltschutz. Entwicklung und Durchführung des „Salzburg-Projekts", eines umfassenden Stadtentwicklungskonzepts. 1988 bis 91 Bundesgeschäftsführer der Grünen Alternative, ab 1990 Parlamentsabgeordneter und Klubobmann der Grünen im Nationalrat. Voggenhubers politische Schwerpunkte liegen in den Bereichen Europa-Integration, Verfassung, Demokratie, Bauten und Kultur sowie Gentechnologie.

---

was born in 1950. From 1977 to 1982 he was spokesman of the Salzburg citizens' initiatives. From 1982 to 1987 he was the first member of the Green Alternative Party to become a member of the Salzburg city council, responsible for town planning, building activities, town-centre rehabilitation, traffic and environment protection. Development and implementation of the "Salzburg-Projekt", a comprehensive town development scheme. From 1988 to 1991 he was national manager of the Green Alternative Party, since 1990 he has been a member of parliament and head of the Green parliamentary faction. The main fields of his political work are European integration, constitution, democracy, building policy, culture and genetic engineering.

MATTHIAS WABL

geboren 1946 in Graz. Wabl studierte Chemie an der Technischen Universität Graz und machte 1973 sein Doktorat am Max Planck-Institut für Molekulare Genetik in Berlin. Danach war er am Institut für Immunologie in Basel, anschließend leitete er den Immunologiebereich des Friedrich Miescher-Laboratoriums am Max Planck-Institut Tübingen. 1984 wechselte er an die University of California in San Francisco, wo er seit 1988 Professor am Institut für Mikrobiologie und Immunologie ist. Er erhielt mehrere Auszeichnungen, zuletzt den Golden Antibody Prize für die Entwicklung von Antikörpern zur Bekämpfung von HIV-infizierten Zellen (1992). Wabl ist Autor und Co-Autor zahlreicher Veröffentlichungen und hat zwei Patente angemeldet.

---

was born in Graz, Austria in 1946. He studied chemistry at the Technical University of Graz and received a Ph.D. degree at the Berlin Max-Planck Institute for Molecular Genetics in 1973. He was a member of the Institute for Immunology in Basel, Switzerland and headed the Immunology Group of the Max-Planck Institute Friedrich-Miescher Laboratory in Tübingen, Germany. In 1984 he began to work at the University of California, San Francisco, where he has been Professor at the Department of Microbiology and Immunology since 1988. He was granted various honors and awards, e.g. the Golden Antibody Prize (1992) for developing antibodies that mediate killing of HIV-infected cells. Wabl is the author and co-author of numerous publications. Two patents pending.

ARYE WACHSMUTH

geboren 1962 in Hamburg, aufgewachsen in Israel, lebt und arbeitet in Wien. Mehrere Einzel- und Gruppenausstellungen: Video-Präsentation im Kölner Kunstsalon, Beteiligung an der 2e biennale internationale du film sur l'art in Lyon, Videopräsentation in der Galerie Kunstbüro Berlin (mit Simon Wachsmuth und Peter Sandbichler), Ausstellungen an der Universität Istanbul, im Kunst.Raum Dornbirn, in der Galerie Grita Insam in Wien, etc.

---

was born in Hamburg in 1962 and spent her childhood and youth in Israel. She lives and works in Vienna. Various solo and group exhibitions: video presentation at Kölner Kunstsalon in Cologne, Germany, participant in the 2e biennale internationale du film sur l'art in Lyon, at Galerie Kunstbüro, Berlin (in cooperation with Simon Wachsmuth and Peter Sandbichler), exhibitions at the University of Istanbul, Kunst.Raum Dornbirn, Austria, Galerie Grita Insam, Vienna, etc.

AKKE WAGENAAR

geboren 1958 in den Niederlanden. Akke Wagenaar studierte audiovisuelle Kunst an der Gerrit Rietveld Akademie in Amsterdam und an der Cooper Union Art School in New York, USA, sowie Logik an der Universität Amsterdam. 1990 übersiedelte sie nach Deutschland, um am Institut für Neue Medien in Frankfurt/Main zu arbeiten und zu unterrichten. Zur Zeit ist sie Stipendiatin an der Kunsthochschule für Medien in Köln. Seit 1987 arbeitet sie mit Computern, seit 1990 beschäftigt sie sich intensiv mit interaktiven, dreidimensionalen Computern und schreibt ihre eigene Software. Ihre Arbeiten waren im Rahmen verschiedener Ausstellungen in Europa zu sehen. Mehrere Stipendien und Preise wurden ihr verliehen.

---

born in 1958 in the Netherlands. Akke Wagenaar studied audiovisual arts at the Gerrit Rietveld Academy in Amsterdam, at the Cooper Union Art School in New York, USA, and logic at the University of Amsterdam. In 1990 she moved to Germany to work and teach at the Institut für Neue Medien (institute for new media) in Frankfurt/Main. She is currently a fellow at the Kunsthochschule für Medien (media arts college) in Cologne. She has been working with computers since 1987. From 1990 she has worked intensively in the field of interactive, 3-dimensional computer art, writing her own software. She exhibited her work at several festivals in Europe. She won several grants and awards.

ERNST WAGNER

geboren 1960 in Dachau, Deutschland, lebt seit seiner Kindheit in Österreich. Studium der Chemie und Biochemie an der Technischen Universität Wien, Studienabschluß 1983. Im Jahr 1985 erwarb er am Institut für Organische Chemie der TU Wien sein Doktorat. Wagner arbeitete als Assistent an der ETH Zürich, ab 1988 am Institut für molekulare Pathologie in Wien. Seine Forschung beschäftigt sich u.a. mit Gentransfer und künstlichen Viren. Außerdem leitet er seit 1992 eine Einheit bei Bender&Co, Wien, zur Entwicklung und Herstellung gentherapeutischer Vakzine. Zahlreiche internationale Vorträge und Publikationen, 14 Patentanmeldungen.

---

born in 1969 in Dachau, Germany but has been living in Austria since his childhood. He studied chemistry and biochemistry at the Technical University of Vienna, from where he graduated in 1983. In 1985 he received a Ph.D. degree at the Institute for Organic Chemistry at the Technical University of Vienna. He was an assistant at ETH in Zurich; in 1988 he began to work at the Institute for Molecular Pathology in Vienna. His research work deals with transfer of genes and artificial viruses, among others. In addition, since 1992 he has been working with Bender&Co, Vienna, where he is heading a unit that deals with the development and production of vaccines for genetic therapy. Numerous lectures and publications at home and abroad, 14 patents pending.

ERWIN FRIEDRICH WAGNER

geboren 1959 in Wolfsberg, A. Er studierte Biochemie an der Universität Graz und Molekularbiologie und Genetik an der Universität Berlin. Wagner arbeitete an verschiedenen Instituten in Europa und den USA, u.a. am Max Planck Institut in Berlin, am Institut für Biochemie in Innsbruck, am Institut für Krebsforschung in Philadelphia und dem EMBL in Heidelberg. Derzeit ist er Leitender Forscher am Institut für Moleklare Pathologie in Wien. Seit 1982 hält er Vorlesungen in Molekularbiologie am Institut für Biochemie an der Universität Innsbruck. 1990 gewann Wagner die EMBO Medaille für die Entwicklung von Genübertragungstechniken, Transgene Mäuse und EC/ES Zelltechnologie.

---

born in 1950, Wolfsberg, A. He studied Biochemistry at the University of Graz and Molecular Biology and Genetics at the University of Berlin. He worked at various Institutes in Europe and USA, e.g. the Max Planck Institute in Berlin, Institute of Biochemistry in Innsbruck, Institute for Cancer Research in Philadelphia and the EMBL in Heidelberg. Currently, he is a Senior Scientist at the Institute of Molecular Pathology in Vienna. Since 1982, he holds e lectureship/habilitation in Molecular Biology at the Institute for Biochemistry at the University of Innsbruck. In 1990 he won the EMBO Medal for the Development of Powerful Gene Transfer Techniques, Transgenic Mice and EC/ES cell Technology.

KURT WALZ

geboren 1955, aufgewachsen nahe Karlsruhe. Während seiner Gymnasialzeit träumte er von einer posthumanistischen Welt. Sein Schwerpunkt Kernphysik innerhalb des Physikstudiums brachte ihn dazu, von einer post-technischen Welt zu träumen. Zu guter letzt wurde er Diplomphysiker mit den Spezialgebieten Computer- und Schaltungstechnik. Die gestalterischen Möglichkeiten der Verbindung von Laser, Elektronik und Rechner reizen ihn weniger unter dem Aspekt der Perfektionssteigerung; vielmehr wurde es sein Anliegen, auftretenden KünstlerInnen im interdisziplinären Zusammenspiel den Umgang mit komplexen Medien wie beispielsweise Laserlicht zu ermöglichen. Aus künstlerisch-wissenschaftlicher Sicht beschäftigt sich Kurt Walz mit Fragen der Synergie vornehmlich des Zusammenspiels von Licht und Klang, aus technischer Sicht geht es ihm um interaktive Gestaltungsmöglichkeiten. Wenn er sich selber eine Schublade zuteilen muß, so wünscht er sich eine, die den Namen post-installativ verdient hat.

---

born in 1955. Kurt Walz grew up near Karlsruhe, Germany. During his school-days, he dreamed of a post-humanistic era. He studied physics, focusing on nuclear physics, which led him to dream of a post-technicized era. Then he received his diploma in physics, specializing in computer technology and circuitry. For Kurt Walz, the fascination of using lasers, electronics, and computers as combined creative means does not lie in the challenge of perfection. Rather, it has become his concern to collaborate with performing artists in order to enable them to use complex media such as laser light. From an artistic and scientific point of view, Kurt Walz is interested in questions of synergy, above all the combination of light and sound. From a technical point of view, he is concerned with interactive means of creativity. Were he to select a label for himself, he would opt for "post-installative".

PETER WEIBEL

geboren 1945 in Odessa. Peter Weibel studierte Literatur, Medizin, Logik und Philosophie in Paris und Wien und schrieb seine Dissertation über mathematische Logik. Von 1976 bis 1981 war er Lektor für „Theorie der Form" und ab 1981 Gastprofessor für Gestaltungslehre und Bildnerische Erziehung an der Hochschule für angewandte Kunst in Wien sowie Gastprofessor am College of Art and Design in Halifax, Kanada. 1979/80 war er Gastprofessor für Medienkunst, 1981 Lektor für Wahrnehmungstheorie und 1983 Professor für Fotografie an der Gesamthochschule Kassel. Seit 1984 ist Peter Weibel Professor für Visuelle Mediengestaltung an der Hochschule für angewandte Kunst Wien und seit 1985 Associate Professor of Video and Digital Arts am Center for Media Study der University of New York in Buffalo. Seit 1989 leitet er als Direktor das Institut für Neue Medien an der Städelschule Frankfurt/Main. Er gab zahlreiche Publikationen heraus, u.a. „Wiener Aktionismus und Film" (mit Valie Export), Wien 1970, „Die Beschleunigung der Bilder", Bern 1987, „Vom Verschwinden der Ferne" (mit Edith Decker), Köln 1990, oder „Das Bild nach dem letzten Bild" (mit Christian Meier), Köln 1991.

---

born in Odessa in 1945. Peter Weibel studied literature, medicine, logics and philosophy in Paris and Vienna and wrote his thesis on mathematical logics. From 1976 to 1981 he was lecturer of theory of form, and from 1981 on Visiting Professor of Design and Art at the Vienna University of Applied Arts and Visiting Professor at the College of Art and Design, Halifax, Canada. In 1979/80 he was Visiting Professor of Media Art, in 1981 lecturer of perception theory and in 1983 Professor of Photography at Gesamthochschule Kassel. Since 1984 he has been Professor of Visual Media at the University of Applied Arts in Vienna, and since 1985 he has been Associate Professor of Video and Digital Arts at the University of New York, Buffalo. Since 1989 he has headed the Institut für Neue Medien at Städelschule in Frankfurt-on-Maine. Numerous publications, e.g. "Wiener Aktionismus und Film" (with Valie Export), Vienna 1970, "Die Beschleunigung der Bilder", Bern 1987, "Vom Verschwinden der Ferne" (with Edith Decker), Cologne 1990, or "Das Bild nach dem letzten Bild" (with Christian Meier), Cologne 1991.

DIETMAR WIESNER

geboren 1955. Dietmar Wiesner studierte Flöte an der Meisterklasse Paul Meisen der Musikhochschule Detmold und belegte Meisterkurse bei Aurele Nicolet und Jean-Pierre Rampal. Seit 1980 ist er Musiker und Geschäftsführer mit Schwerpunkt Programmkonzeption des Ensemble Modern in Frankfurt/M. Dietmar Wiesner hatte zahlreiche Auftritte bei internationalen Festivals und war als Solist mit dem Ensemble 13 Karlsruhe bei Tourneen in Europa, Asien und Südamerika unterwegs. Er nahm zahlreiche Schallplatteneinspielungen mit dem Arditti-Quartett in London auf und arbeitet mit Komponisten und Dirigenten wie Pierre Boulez, Peter Eötvös, Heiner Goebbels, Hans-Werner Henze oder Györgi Ligeti.

---

born in 1955. Dietmar Wiesner studied flute with Paul Meisen at Musikhochschule Detmold and attended seminars with Aurele Nicolet and Jean-Pierre Rampal. Since 1980 he is a musician and director of the Ensemble Modern in Frankfurt-on-Main, the emphasis being on programme conception. Dietmar Wiesner has had numerous performances at international festivals and has worked as a soloist with the Ensemble 13 Karlsruhe on tours in Europe, Asia and South America. He had numerous recordings with the Arditti Quartett in London and has cooperated with composers like Pierre Boulez, Peter Eötvös, Heiner Goebbels, Hans-Werner Henze or Györgi Ligeti.

ACHIM WOLLSCHEID

Künstler – lebt und arbeitet in Frankfurt/M.

Artist – he lives and works in Frankfurt-on-Main.

FRANZ XAVER

geboren 1956 in Linz. Von 1987 bis 1991 Lehrtätigkeit an der Hochschule für angewandte Kunst in Wien (Computergraphik, audiovisuelle Produktion, Elektronik und Elektrotechnik), 1989 bis 1991 im Labor für visuelle Medien der Hochschule für angewandte Kunst. Zahlreiche Ausstellungen in Österreich, Italien, Tschechien und Deutschland, z.B. Sphärenklänge bei der Biennale Venedig 1990 (durch die Wolkenformationen der Erde und die Interaktion der Besucherinnen und Besucher wird Musik erzeugt) oder Installation mit einem Erdbeobachtungssatelliten bei der Triennale in Mailand im Jahr 1992.

---

born in Linz, Austria, in 1956. From 1987 to 1991 he was a teacher at the Vienna University of Applied Art (computer graphics, audio-visual production, electronics and electrical engineering), from 1989 to 1991 he worked at the University's visual media laboratory. Numerous exhibitions in Austria, Italy, the Czech Republic and Germany, e.g. "Sphärenklänge" at the Venice Biennale of 1990, where music was produced by the visitors' interactions with cloud formations; or an installation with an earth observation satellite at the Milan Triennale in 1992.

LARRY YAEGER

Larry Yaeger leistete Pionierarbeit auf dem Gebiet der Simulationen von Flüssigkeitsströmen im Space Shuttle, und er führte die erste vollständige Simulation von hydrodynamischen Strömen über einem Unterseeboot durch. Er war Direktor der Software-Entwicklung bei Digital Productions und einer der Hauptentwickler ihrer Computergraphik-Software; er trug zur Entwicklung von Software, Simulationen und Produktionstechniken bei, wie sie in den Filmen „The Last Starfighter", „2010" und „Labyrinth", sowie in mit dem Clio-Award ausgezeichneten Werbespots zu sehen sind. Er ist Co-Autor eines Buches und Multimedia-CD-ROM über „Visualisierung natürlicher Phänomene" (Springer-Verlag). Als Principal Engineer bei Apple Computer ist er für den Entwurf und die Umsetzung der Software zuständig, die dem Gorilla Koko eine computergestützte „Stimme" verschaffte, und baute MacIntosh-Graphiken in die Produktion des Films „Star Trek: The Next Generation" ein. Zur Zeit bschäftigt sich Larry Yaeger mit künstlichem Leben und künstlicher Intelligenz. Seine Arbeit mit PolyWorld, einem Simulator künstlichen Lebens, wurde im Rahmen der Artificial Life III Conference, der SIGGRAPH und der Imagina präsentiert und sowohl in Zeitungsartikeln als auch in Steven Levys Buch „Artificial Life: The

Quest for a New Generation" beschrieben.

Larry Yaeger carried out pioneering simulations of fluid flows in the space shuttle, as well as the first complete simulation of hydrodynamic flows over a submarine. He was Director of Software Development at Digital Productions and one of the principal architects of their computer graphics software, contributing to the development of software tools, simulations, and production techniques as seen in the films "The Last Starfighter", "2010", "Labyrinth", as well as in Clio award winning commercials. He has recently coauthored a book and multimedia CD-ROM on "Visualization of Natural Phenomena" for Springer-Verlag. As a Principal Engineer with Apple Computer, he designed and implemented the software to give Koko the gorilla a computer-based "voice", and integrated Macintosh graphics into routine film production for "Star Trek: The Next Generation". Larry Yaeger is currently studying artificial life and artificial intelligence. He has presented his work on PolyWorld, an artificial life simulator, at the Artificial Life III Conference, SIGGRAPH, and Imagina, and has had his work written about in both the popular press and Steven Levy's book, "Artificial Life. The Quest for a New Creation".

WOLFGANG ZINGGL
studierte Malerei und Bühnenbild an der Hochschule für angewandte Kunst in Wien und Psychologie an der Universität Wien. Er dissertierte über die veränderte Wahrnehmung von Bildern nach ihrer Seitenverkehrung. Assistent an der Technischen Universität Wien. Publikationen zu Wahrnehmungs- und Kunsttheorien. Kritiker und Lehrer für Psychologie, Wahrnehmungstheorien und Morphologie der Kunst an verschiedenen Hochschulen und Universitäten.

---

studied painting and stage design at the Vienna University of Applied Arts, and psychology at the University of Vienna. He wrote his thesis on changes in the perception of pictures if they are shown laterally inverted. He works as an assistant at the Technical University of Vienna. Publications about theories of perception and art. He is a critic and teacher of psychology, perception theory and morphology of art at various colleges and universities.